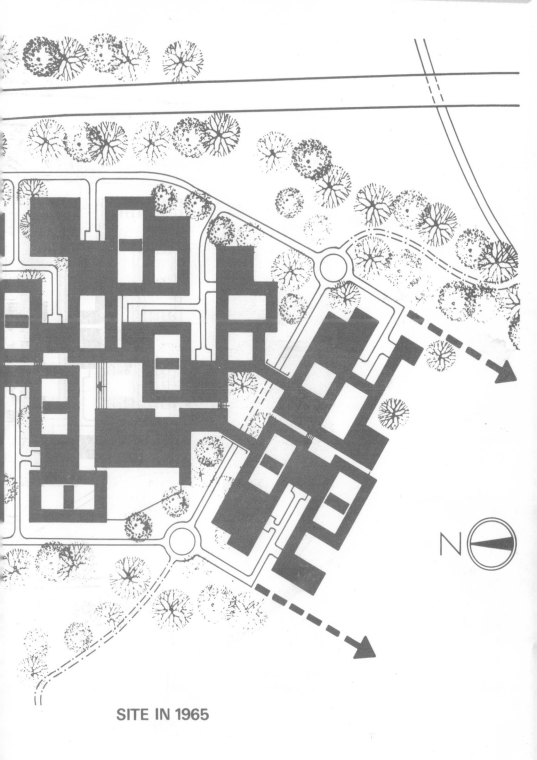

SITE IN 1965

University of Lancaster: Quest for Innovation

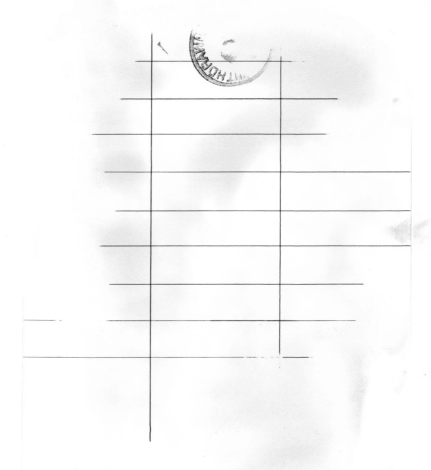

The Chancellor presiding at a degree congregation in the Great Hall, July 1973. (The principal of Cartmel College, Mr. G. M. Cockburn, is standing at the microphone.)

John Donat

University of Lancaster: Quest for Innovation

(a history of the first ten years, 1964-1974)

Marion E. McClintock

The University of Lancaster 1974

Published by The University of Lancaster in cooperation
with MTP Medical and Technical Publishing Co. Ltd.,
and The Construction Press Ltd., Lancaster

© 1974 Marion E. McClintock

Printed in Great Britain by Clarke, Doble and Brendon,
Plymouth
First published 1974

ISBN 0 904406 02 4

Message from the Chancellor

I have such vivid memories of the first time I came up to Lancaster in 1964 and waded through muddy fields. Since then, I have witnessed over the last ten years astonishing progress. I feel that Lancaster University is very much a pioneer among new universities and, because of this fact, I am particularly proud to be Chancellor.

July 1974

Alexandra

Contents

List of Illustrations

Foreword

Given the money, founding a new university is actually rather easy. There is the excitement of a new beginning: a sense of community is easily created when numbers are small: the strong drink of new experiment can be tasted, undiluted by the efforts of vested interests to keep influence and money to themselves. The real test comes when numbers grow, habits are set, pioneers grow old. "From far below you", wrote Cornford, "will mount the roar of a ruthless multitude of young men in a hurry. You may perhaps grow to be aware what they are in a hurry to do. They are in a hurry to get you out of the way."

What Mrs. McClintock has achieved, with a high standard of historical scholarship, is a portrait of a university at this time of testing. Even those who came to the University of Lancaster at its first beginnings will be surprised to see how much discussion and experiment and change there has been in ten short years. There is sadness here, of early hopes disappointed and brave ideas emasculated: but also, I believe, evidence of sensible adjustment to reality and of a continuing willingness to seek fresh enlightenment. I hope that those who write our history in five hundred or a thousand years will find encouragement in this tale of our infancy.

CHARLES F. CARTER
Vice-Chancellor

1974

Introduction

I well remember seeing in November 1961 a map of England, published in a national Sunday newspaper, which showed for the first time the locations of all seven of the proposed new universities which were to be established (or, in the case of Sussex, were already admitting students), but I little guessed that I would later be writing a book about one of them. Now in its tenth year, Lancaster, the seventh of these new institutions to be announced, has 3,195 full-time students, 517 teaching and research staff and an annual turn-over, for 1972-3, of £3,854,773: it offers over eighty first degree courses, over thirty master's degrees, and has a wide-ranging programme of doctoral and post-doctoral research. Already it has granted 3,409 first degrees, 1,175 M.A. and M.Sc. and 222 M.Litt. and Ph.D. degrees.

A mere catalogue of statistics, however, tells the onlooker very little about any kind of institution and what follows is an account of the university's first decade of development. Rather than merely narrate the events of each academic year, I have divided the subject matter into themes so that the reader interested in, for example, the evolution of the disciplinary system, the development of assessment techniques, or the growth of various kinds of extra-mural activities, can turn at once to the relevant section. Only the first chapter, which describes the coming of the university to Lancaster and the early organizational machinery involved in setting it up, is conventionally chronological. The second chapter describes the building programme, and the third the academic structure (including the advent of individual subjects, the function of boards of studies, the composition of the Lancaster first degree and the examination system). The fourth chapter looks at the constitution of the university, and from there leads on to certain aspects of the administration, as well as to a discussion of student representation. The fifth chapter deals with the interaction, at many levels, between the university and the community, and the sixth describes student life (including the role of the colleges, discipline and welfare).

All the new universities of the 1960's set out with the highest hopes and ideals. It was felt that there was an opportunity to innovate within the British University system, to discard what had become obsolete or unnecessary elsewhere, and at one and the same time to re-think old ideas and to implement the new. Staff, and later students, would become more involved in the decision-making processes, new subjects could be introduced into the curriculum and existing subjects could be approached in a fresh and challenging way, there would be more feeling of community than at some of the longer-established universities, discipline would be humane and minimal rather than imposed by obsolete statute and out-moded convention, buildings would be more skilfully planned both to meet immediate purposes and for future flexibility—in a word, there were seven clean slates waiting for the first marks to be made upon them. It seemed to be an opportunity unique in higher education at the time anywhere in the world; it is one, furthermore, which perhaps will never be repeated, because although there has been talk of further large-scale expansion of higher education in the 1980's no one really knows what form it will take or, writing as I am in the pessimism at the end of 1973, whether it will take place at all.

This book, therefore, is a study in depth of how one of these seven new universities—Sussex, Essex, East Anglia, Kent, Warwick, and York being the other six (since Stirling and Coleraine came somewhat later and under slightly different circumstances)—took advantage of its opportunities and how first ideas were modified in practice. The reader is enabled, by close reference to the documents of the period, to see what the objectives of the people concerned were at any particular time, and to follow the reasons why this experiment succeeded, a second faltered and a third fell away.

The account is intended also to show the kind of pressures which blunt the edge of idealism and innovation, whether they be of finance, the career aspirations of students, the inherent conservatism of some university teachers or the woolly radicalism of others, the conflicting demands upon members of a new university which mean that crucial decisions must be made hastily or with incomplete consultation, or the implications, sometimes unforeseen, that one kind of decision will have for a whole series of others, as well as the pressures from other universities or from society in general that certain expectations be fulfilled. Thus, although the reader can follow through such themes as particularly interest him or her, to obtain the full flavour of life in a new university, it is necessary to read the work as a whole, since (as the footnotes frequently indicate) one area of activity so often interacts upon others that it is difficult to isolate any particular event and treat of it without reference to other concurrent events. Moreover, a topic will frequently recur in several different contexts.

In looking for material for the book I have made heavy use of the minutes of the main governing bodies of the university. I have had unrestricted access to the minutes of and supporting documents of the Council, the Senate and the Court, and have attended at least one of each of their meetings. I have, in addition, read substantial proportions of the minutes and documents of many of the sub-committees of these bodies, an exception being, naturally, those papers which relate to the personal affairs of individuals. I have also read the early papers relating to the setting-up of the university which have been generously deposited in the university by the officers of the County Council, and have had access to the minutes of the Federation of Junior Common Rooms and the Student Representative Council, as well as to student and staff journals and ephemera of various kinds.

I have drawn upon these documents in the way which seemed to me to illuminate most clearly the nature of any issue and have, where it seemed relevant to show the nature of the decision-making process or an event of particular interest, gone into considerable detail so that the reader can follow the steps of the argument and see for himself why a particular conclusion was reached. In addition I have talked to a number of people who have been involved from the beginning of the university. Besides members of the university, I have benefited from meetings with, amongst others, Sir Noel Hall (Chairman of the Academic Planning Board), Mr. Charles Flatt (of the Lancashire County Council), Mr. J. D. Waddell (the Town Clerk of Lancaster), the former Bishop of Blackburn (Dr. C. R. Claxton), the late Alderman Douglas Clift, and Dr. Gabriel Epstein (site development architect). Of course, the interaction of personalities is crucially important in any institution and I have naturally stopped short of including details of events which could be in any way hurtful or offensive to individuals, most of whom are still in mid-career. However, while the application of the rule may have meant the exclusion of some amusing or painful anecdotes, it has not affected the main thread of the discussion of any particular theme.

A very important reason for writing a book of this kind at this time is to present a kind of case-book, not often drawing general inferences, but allowing the documents and reported views of individuals to speak for themselves while the documents are still extant and while the reasons for particular actions and decisions can still be recalled. There is no doubt that the actions taken in the first year or two of a new institution's existence mould it in many respects for the future; in Lancaster's case I think I would select the period from late 1961, when the Academic Planning Board and the Executive Council began their work, to 1966 when the first departments moved up to Bailrigg, as being the most important years for setting the tone of what has followed. One *caveat* should be entered, however. This book has been two years in the writing, from January 1972 to December 1973, and already some of the sections written in the earlier months of this period could be modified, and additional material added, to bring them up to date. In certain cases, where particularly important changes have taken place, footnotes have been added to update particular activities. A more general point arises, however, which is that a work of this kind must be seen as a kind of portrait, true for the time at which it is drawn. Recognition should be given to the fact that a university is constantly in a process of evolution; and an institution in a state of continuing change cannot be pinned down, like a butterfly on a pin, by a portrait of one particular period of its existence. With the hindsight of another decade, many of the positions being taken up in the academic year 1973–4 may seem as anomalous as some of those of 1963–4 now do.

Each section, as I have explained, can be read independently of the others. Technical terms, however, are explained in detail once only; where they seem particularly crucial to a later section, a footnote to an explanation of them is included as a signpost. Failing this, reference should be made to the index. Furthermore, following the example of Sir James Mountford in his book on Keele, I have forborne to include references to minutes, which are merely tedious without being very informative to anyone except initiates; I have, however, made frequent reference to the month and the year of particular documents or reports of discussions so that they can be seen in context, both of the rest of the book and the general climate of the time. Where possible I have made comparative references to the experience of other British universities, especially the new ones, although lack of space has precluded the insertion of as much of this material as I had intended.

Constraints of time and space have also meant that certain topics which I originally intended to include have been curtailed or omitted. Amongst these are such matters as conditions of service of members of staff, consideration of a six-term year, student wastage, teaching methods or training of university teachers; such matters, as well as others, are sometimes touched upon tangentially but not comprehensively discussed.

No work of this kind can be written without the invaluable assistance of many other people. I am particularly grateful to the Vice-Chancellor for launching me on this project and for his very helpful critical comments. I should like to thank the University Secretary, under whose aegis this work has been carried out, for his encouragement and support; and his personal secretary, Mrs. Sheila Braithwaite, who has given me valuable help with access to archives. I should like to express my particular gratitude to the following people and their staff: Mr. Merton Atkins, Mr. John Creed, Mr. Michael Forster, Mr. Wacek Koc, Professor Tom Lawrenson, Mr. John R.

Martindale, Mr. James Nicholson, and Mr. Donald Smith and members of the Building Development Office (especially Mr. Wilfred Chadwick). The occupants of the General Office during 1972 and 1973 have patiently interpreted my handwritten manuscript, and my husband, Dr. Peter McClintock, has been indefatigable both in listening to me expound on what was about to be written and in giving me valuable advice as it appeared. To these people, and to many others who have contributed in different ways and at different stages to this book, I am especially glad to have this opportunity of acknowledging my indebtedness.

University House,
Bailrigg

MARION E. McCLINTOCK

1974

B

CHAPTER I

Origins

In the history of Lonsdale South of the Sands, the town of Lancaster is entitled to peculiar distinction for its antiquity, local advantages, and the circumstance of having from time immemorial given its name to the County, of which it has consequently been called the metropolis.

Several political events in this island contributed to the local pre-eminence of Lancaster; particularly the establishment of a Roman camp on its elevated site, in the first century; the subsequent settlement of the Saxons on the spot, as is evident from the very name of the place; and the distinction to which it was exalted as the seat of limited sovereignty soon after the Conquest, when Roger Pictavensis founded the castle which was afterwards enlarged by successive Princes of the Blood Royal, especially the celebrated John of Gaunt, who held his court there, and raised the County of which it was the capital to the dignity of a Palatinate.

Thus wrote John Corry in 1822, when Lancaster, at a time of prosperity,

presents to the pleased observer, all the interesting varieties of an increasing and intelligent population of upwards of ten thousand persons, inhabiting 1900 houses, all built of beautiful freestone, and several of them lofty and commodious.

He saw coming into Lancaster from the West Indies "sugar, rum, coffee, cotton, mahogany,[1.1] logwood and fustic", and exports going out of British manufactured goods:

[1.1] Robert Gillow's famous cabinet and furniture-making firm, which made particular use of mahogany from the West Indies, is usually dated from 1729. The late eighteenth and early nineteenth centuries saw the upsurge of the cotton-producing

To a stranger accustomed to the throng in the crowded thoroughfares of London, Lancaster appears dull; but a slight acquaintance with the inhabitants will convince him that they are equally intelligent and urbane; and if he delights in good air and extensive views, a walk on the terrace at the southern and western sides of Lancaster Castle, and on the northern side, through St. Mary's Churchyard, will afford him all the gratification obtainable from a diversified and vast prospect of cultivated fields on the south, including part of the Hundreds of Lonsdale and Amounderness; extensive marshes, and a winding river spreading into a broad estuary as it approaches the distant sea on the west; and Morecambe bay, the cultivated plains, and hilly regions of Furness on the north; behind which appear the dim bluish mountains of Westmoreland.[1.2]

Bailrigg,[1.3] which lies two miles south of Lancaster, was a hamlet within the township of Scotforth[1.4]; in some early deeds it is described as a manor. Although its 2,880 acres were owned by Count Roger and his successors, its titles went not to the alien Church of the Blessed Mary of Lancaster (the Priory, which had been granted to the Benedictine Abbey of St. Martin of Seez in Normandy) but to the Premonstratensian abbey of Cockersand. It gave a name to a local family, Roger de Bailrigg and his descendants. In 1469 the land was granted to John Gardiner, who endowed the Royal Lancaster Grammar School, and after numerous owners it was in 1887 purchased by Sir Thomas Storey, who presented the Storey Institute to the town of Lancaster. He died in 1898, the year in which Bailrigg Mansion was completed, and the estate passed to his son, Mr. Herbert Lushington Storey. This area was to be the site of the new university of Lancaster, but before looking at what was to happen locally, it is necessary to look at the national background of university education.

After the Second World War the future development of further and higher education in Britain became an increasingly important concern of the Government and the U.G.C. as the gradual recognition emerged that it would need considerable expansion to meet the needs of an increased population that came with peace-time conditions, and which had a rising expectation of and interest in tertiary education, and supposedly to provide the necessary skills for the increasingly urban and technological age in which Western Europe

---

industry of Lancashire. In Lancaster there were also two small ship-building yards, and oilcloth and linoleum were produced from the middle of the century in businesses founded by James Williamson and Sir Thomas Storey.

[1.2] John Corry, *The History of Lancashire*, Vol. I (London, 1825), pages 552–3, 574 and 593.

[1.3] *Victoria County History of the County of Lancaster*, Vol. 8 (London, 1914) page 57.

[1.4] In 1900 the urban portion of Scotforth was taken into the borough of Lancaster, and the remainder, which was mostly open agricultural land, into Lancaster R.D.C.

now found itself. People questioned whether this expansion should necessarily be in the university sector: and even when that decision had been taken there was debate about whether the increase should all be in existing institutions, or whether some new foundations should be established. The university population grew by a quarter in the fifties, and doubled in the sixties, but it was not until the announcement of the seven new universities between 1958 and 1961 that the public became aware of this increase, and it was even later before all the implications became clear. One significant feature of the increase in student population was the greater percentage who had access to public financial assistance. Before the war 40 per cent of students had grants of one kind or another; by 1961 this figure had risen to 87·1 per cent and local education authority grants were automatic for those students who were accepted, having obtained two passes at Advanced Level G.C.E. (subject to a means test of their parents' income).

There is an extensive literature documenting the evolution of attitudes and decisions of the period,[1.5] and a particularly useful account in the report of the University Grants Committee for the 1957-62 quinquennium.[1.6] They identified three distinct phases, the first being from 1946 to 1953 which saw the return of those whose university education had been interrupted or postponed by the war. As the wave of ex-service students diminished, there was a decline in the total university population[1.7] which gave rise to a false impression that there was a period of relative stability of numbers ahead in the universities:

> The question of founding completely new university institutions had arisen, as might be expected, in connection with the prospective increase in student numbers after the war. But, as shown earlier, the response of the existing institutions to the demand for increased university places made it unnecessary to establish any new universities or colleges. At that time there were nine universities with less than 1,000 full-time students.[1.8]

One university college, Southampton, was granted its charter as a fully autonomous institution in this period, and one new institution, the University College of North Staffordshire, was founded, the justification for it being

---

1.5 See, for example: W. R. Niblett, *The Expanding University* (1962); and H. J. Perkin, *Innovation in the New Universities of the United Kingdom* (1969).

1.6 H.M.S.O., *University Development 1957-62*, Cmnd. 2267 (1964), pp. 3-4, (paras 8 to 12), 20-22 (paras 55-63) and 65-113 (paras 184-326).

1.7 University student (undergraduate and advanced) numbers were:

1938-39:	50,002
1949-50:	85,421
1953-54:	80,602
1961-62:	113,143

1.8 H.M.S.O. Cmnd 2267, *op. cit.*, para 257.

"the need for educational experiment".[1.9] In addition, a number of places were suggested as suitable locations for new universities and although

> In many cases the approaches to the Committee were too tentative to reach the stage of consideration in detail . . . the claims of Brighton, York and Norwich were strongly supported and deputations were, in fact, received from these three places in January, April and May 1947 respectively. Committees too, had been set up in Kent and Lancaster to investigate the possibility of establishing universities in these two areas. . . . While the Committee were unable to recommend financial support for any new institutions at that time, they did encourage Brighton, Norwich, and York to maintain their interest and to develop in detail proposals for the establishment of a university in case conditions should materially change in the future.[1.10]

In the second phase, from 1953 to 1961, it was clear that any planning based on stability of student numbers would be unrealistic. Serious discussion of future expansion and its cost took place between the universities and the U.G.C. on the one side, and the Committee and the Government on the other. Amongst existing institutions, three university colleges, Hull, Exeter and Leicester received their charters as fully autonomous institutions, and nine technical colleges and institutions were upgraded to the status either of colleges of advanced technology, or special colleges of science and technology. In addition, Dundee was given semi-autonomy as the Queen's College, University of St. Andrews.

In 1956, at the time of the first discussions with the universities, the Financial Secretary of H.M. Treasury had stated:

> It is the Government's desire that all those boys and girls who have the mental and general abilities to profit by a university education shall get that opportunity,[1.11]

and in 1957 the U.G.C. was enabled to assure the Government that the universities could provide 123,500 places by 1965. On 20 February 1958 the Chancellor of the Exchequer announced that he had authorized university building programmes up to the value of £15 million in each of the four years 1960 to 1963, since

> The universities are, in fact, expanding faster than had been expected, and though the future rate of increase cannot be assessed with any confidence the increase beyond 124,000 foreseen for the late 1960's may well prove to be permanent. . . . Meanwhile, in deciding on a provisional total

---

[1.9] *Ibid.*, para 260.　　　　　　　　[1.10] *Ibid.*, paras 258 and 259.
[1.11] *Ibid.*, para 219.

programme of £60,000,000 for new university building in the four years in question, they have taken account of the possibility of larger ultimate expansion.[1.12]

Part of the reason for this very high capital investment was the past under-provision and growing obsolescence of buildings, which had become increasingly evident since the war. The £60,000,000 included, however, £1·5 million for the new University of Sussex, which the Chancellor announced in the same speech of February 1958.

In 1959 the U.G.C. advised the Chancellor of the Exchequer that, having regard to all the various reasons for university expansion, a maximum of 200,000 places would be needed by the end of the 1960's. The Chancellor agreed that the Committee could discuss with the universities a minimum provision of between 170,000 and 175,000 places by the late 1960's. Further discussions with the existing universities took place, from which it became clear that they could provide for up to 155,500. Sussex would take in its first students in 1961 and have 2,500 students by the early 1970's, and the two new universities of York and East Anglia would by then have at least 1,500 students each. This left 9,000 places outstanding and the Committee therefore recommended the immediate provision of a further four new universities to absorb this number.

1961 was a crucial year in the history of British university education. In February the announcement was made of the appointment of the Robbins Committee, whose report was to appear two years later but whose findings and reflections were to be of great importance both to Government and universities for at least the next decade. In May the new Universities of Essex, Kent and Warwick were authorized, "leaving the question of the other new institution to be considered later in the summer". To assist them in their choice of locations the Committee had in April 1959 established a sub-committee to "examine and report on proposals received by the University Grants Committee for new university institutions". This sub-committee held eight meetings in the ensuing two years, and they or their officers received sixteen deputations and visited ten of the most promising sites. Following on the announcement of Sussex, enquiries were received concerning twenty-eight different localities in England and Scotland.

A policy on the choice of sites can be said to have evolved over a period of years. Keele had been based in North Staffordshire because of the evangelical zeal of Lord Lindsay and his local supporters, especially the Rev. Thomas Harwood, who were determined that it should be in the Potteries.[1.13]

[1.12] *Ibid.*, para 205. In fact, £85 million was eventually spent during the four years (excluding £18·5 million for the Imperial College of Science and Technology).

[1.13] An account of this initiative is to be found in W. B. Gallie, *A New University* (1960), 46ff. See also H. J. Perkin, *op. cit.*, pp. 70–82.

Brighton was selected by the U.G.C. for special reasons:

> There is now no university in the densely populated area south of the Thames east of a line from Reading to Southampton. A new institution at Brighton would thus help to serve the population of an area which is now largely dependent on London University. Moreover, lodgings are available in Brighton in large numbers, and the demand for them there is a seasonal one, of which the peak comes in the university vacation. For this reason it will not be essential to provide living accommodation during the first stages of development so that the initial cost of a university college at Brighton should be lower than it might be elsewhere.[1.14]

By the time that the choice of the other six new institutions was being made, the U.G.C.'s policy had become more deliberate. The Committee assumed: (i) that the proportion of students in university residence would rise; (ii) that a university, "if it is to be fully effective, should be part of the community in which it lives"; (iii) that the situation in England and Wales was more urgent than in Scotland; (iv) that great weight should be given to the local interest and enthusiasm shown by the sponsors from the various areas, as well as "material evidence of interest and support in the form of financial contributions to either capital or recurrent expenditure"; (v) that "the presence of industries in an area could provide a useful association", while at the same time the universities should be placed not in large industrial conurbations but in "the midst of well-established civic communities in which the university could play an important part"; (vi) that, since the new institutions were to accommodate not less than 3,000 students (which might rise to seven or eight thousand), an initial site of not less than 200 acres was desirable, within two or three miles of the centre of the city, thereby avoiding the heavy cost of a more central area while still having access to the requisite city services; (vii) that there should be a supply of suitable lodgings at reasonable prices; and (viii) that the area should be attractive to academic staff, both as far as local amenities and ready communication with other centres of learning were concerned.[1.15]

Meanwhile, the Lancashire County Council were taking the keenest interest in the possibility of there being a university of the north-west. When a letter from Mr. R. E. Hodd, the chief education officer of the County Borough of Blackpool, was received just before Christmas 1960, by Mr. Percy Lord,[1.16] asking for a meeting between members and officers of the County Council

---

[1.14] H.M.S.O., *University Development 1952–1957*, Cmnd. 534, para. 20.
[1.15] H.M.S.O. Cmnd. 2267, *op. cit.*, paras. 278 to 286.
[1.16] Sir Percy Lord, Chief Education Officer of Lancashire, was knighted in the New Year's Honours List of 1968 and died in December of the same year.

and the Blackpool authority, Mr. Lord wrote to Mr. Patrick McCall[1.17] to ask for "a meeting of the special sub-committee that was set up to deal with this question". At the meeting, which took place at the Imperial Hotel, Blackpool, on 10 January 1961, the borough's representatives offered two hundred acres of land, on its Stanley Park site, as well as the product of a threepenny rate each year, as its contributions towards the proposed foundation, and asked the County Council to sponsor their proposal. After discussion, in which the officers of the County made clear their support in principle for a university of the north-west, a note of the meeting reads:

> It was eventually agreed that Blackpool would keep their proposals and offer silent for the time being to enable the County Council to receive a report as soon as possible on the general principle so that from that the County Council could make progress towards meeting the University Grants Committee and sponsoring the idea of a University as soon as possible. At that stage it would be quite free for other authorities to make any suggestions they had for places or any other help that they might be prepared to give and Blackpool could come in with their offer.

An application from Lancaster followed hard on the heels of the one from Blackpool. After reference to the Education Committee of the County Council, the proposals were presented to the policy-making Parliamentary Committee on 18 January, and from there adopted by Lancashire County Council. Mr. McCall was then in a position to write on 6 March 1961 to Sir Cecil Syers, the secretary of the U.G.C.:

> I think it would be right to say that there has from time to time been talk of a new University in various parts of Lancashire, but no doubt little progress was made in the past because it may have been felt that there was not much prospect of success at that time. More recently I think that the indications given by the starting of new Universities in other parts of England that in fact funds may now be available have given considerable impetus to the move in Lancashire . . . I think we would like to make the case that at present there is no University lying further North than the Universities of Manchester and Liverpool and that the establishment of one in [north] Lancashire would spread University facilities geographically so as to take advantage of the interest and enthusiasm of the large population which such a University would serve.

However, not only Blackpool and Lancaster were presenting themselves as candidates for the new university. During the first three months of 1961

[1.17] Sir Patrick McCall, who was the Clerk of the County Council, was knighted in 1971 and retired in December 1972. However, at the time negotiations about the university were proceeding, he was Mr. McCall, and will therefore be referred to as such in this narrative.

Mr. McCall received applications from Lytham St. Anne's, Burtonwood, the Fylde area, Southport, Ulverston and Morecambe. Lancaster and Blackpool were the strongest contenders not only because each had a significant area of land to offer, but because they could provide backing for the other points to which the University Grants Committee paid particular attention:

> cultural background; proximity to learned institutions, libraries, etc.; good communications, both internal and external; housing, facilities and amenities for staff, including good schools for their children; lodgings for students . . . local interest and financial support (both public and private, including industry); a good site of two hundred acres or so. These are the main points, but I have not put them in any order of priority. I might add that the Committee do not nowadays attach the same importance to the "student catchment area" as used to be attached to it, since Universities nowadays are national, not local institutions.[1.18]

However, although the County Council aided by Mr. McCall and his assistant, Mr. Charles Flatt, were prepared to make every effort towards setting up a university, including an offer of financial support to the extent of £50,000 per annum for ten years (as well as possible capital endowment), the main proponents of the scheme were anxious that "the real problem of the new University of Lancashire, namely how an impetus is to be given to it without that impetus virtually being purely a County Council one"[1.19] should be solved. The Secretary of the U.G.C. on 10 March had referred to the setting up of a Promotion Committee, as had been done at Sussex and elsewhere, for as a report to the County Council's Parliamentary Committee commented:

> experience emphasizes the importance of the case being as broadly based as possible so as to be truly representative of the community as a whole with as much influential backing (financial and otherwise) as possible from all sections of it. . . . It is intended that for the purpose of coming to a decision on the location to be proposed for the University and launching the Promotion Committee, the County Council should assume responsibility for convening very soon a meeting representative of as many as possible of the bodies and interests named above. The immediate role of the Promotion Committee would then be to assess the order of local interest and financial support which might be expected, and submitting a case to the U.G.C. for the establishment of a University for North Lancashire.[1.20]

[1.18] Letter of Sir Cecil Syers to Mr. Patrick McCall of 10 March 1961.
[1.19] Letter of Mr. McCall to Sir Andrew Smith of 6 March 1961.
[1.20] Supplementary agenda for the County Council's Parliamentary Committee, 27 March 1961.

There was a pressing need to take rapid action, for it was now the end of March and the U.G.C. had emphasized that any submission would have to reach the U.G.C. by mid-May. (It is a matter of interesting conjecture to look at the reasons why the body of people who were to take such particularly prompt and decisive action during the next three months had not acted until nudged by the County Borough of Blackpool: no doubt the continual pressure of other business in one of the largest local authorities meant simply that there was no spare capacity at the time for officers to think of any business other than that which reached their desks and required immediate action.)

Letters were accordingly sent out at once to interested persons who represented particular community interests, as well as to those who might be able to suggest other such people. These explained the action taken so far by the County Council, outlined the criteria upon which the U.G.C. would probably base their decision; and announced a meeting to be held on 14 April, to bring together those people who were interested in supporting a venture to form the Council for the Promotion of a New University in North-West Lancashire[1.21] and from within the larger body to appoint an Executive Committee to select a site and prepare a case for submission to the U.G.C.

Copies of the letter were sent to local bishops and other church leaders, the vice-chancellors of Liverpool and Manchester, the national headquarters of the T.U.C. and the F.B.I. (now the C.B.I.), the headmasters of local independent schools, the national headquarters of the N.U.T., the training colleges, and the Joint Four, as well as the County Secretary of the N.F.U., and the secretaries of the Conservative and Labour groups of Lancashire members of Parliament. The response in all cases was immediate and favourable. Particularly warm support came from the Bishop of Blackburn, Dr. Claxton: "I am indebted to you for your letter and the project has my wholehearted personal support." In addition, the Lord Lieutenant of the County, the Earl of Derby, was approached to see whether he would allow his name to go forward as president of a promotion committee. He agreed, saying: "I had heard talk of this, and would be very pleased to support it in any way I can."

As mentioned above various local authorities had submitted written applications for the honour of becoming the home of the new university, but by 14 April only Blackpool and Lancaster remained as serious contenders. Mr. Percy Lord had noted in January that Lancaster had been making tentative suggestions about a university there for a number of years and Mr. Coates, the County Planning officer, had mentioned that he understood there to be "in Lancaster an Advisory Development Committee which has given some thought to the matter".

[1.21] The term "North-West Lancashire" was used only in this context, and has no specific local government meaning.

In fact, a suggestion for a university for the Fylde Coast had been made by the late Alderman John Grime, the editor of a local newspaper, in 1898; and a serious attempt to found a university in Lancaster had been made soon after World War II. In 1947 a young Lancaster solicitor, Mr. (later Alderman) Douglas Clift,[1.22] had written to the *Lancaster Guardian*, commenting that "the whole trend of events in recent years has been to take away the former position of Lancaster as the County town and to give to Preston or Manchester the pride of place which should rightly be ours."[1.23] In particular he noted that Preston was now one of the towns in which divorce cases could be heard, whereas Lancaster was not,[1.24] and that Carlisle was going ahead with plans for a university there while "we appear to sleep yet again". Local pride was stirred and a public meeting held in February, from which emerged Lancaster University College Committee, with the headmaster of the Lancaster Royal Grammar School in the chair and Mr. Clift as secretary. Other members included the Earl of Derby, Sir James Aitken (chairman of the County Council), a representative of Manchester University and two local members of Parliament. The idea at that time was to link Lancaster with some existing university as a university college. Lancaster already had connections with Liverpool's extra-mural department, making that seem the most appropriate sponsor: members of the committee therefore went down to see the Registrar. The planners' thoughts were directed very much to departments of applied or vocational interest, such as agriculture, veterinary science, industrial chemistry, engineering, medicine and law. Sites were discussed, and two in particular found favour—Quernmore Hall, and the site of the present cattle market; and local industrialists were approached for promises of financial support. Representatives of the committee also went to London to see the secretary of the U.G.C., but were told that "capital expenditure was being greatly discouraged, and no help would be forthcoming at present. He did not negative the possibility in the future, and considered it an ideal to be kept before the public of the district."[1.25] For the time being, however, the Committee was disbanded, and when Mr. Don Waddell, the Town Clerk of Lancaster, began work on the idea in 1958, he did so in direct conjunction with the City Council.[1.26] He visited the Vice-Chancellor of Manchester University, Professor (later Sir William) Mansfield Cooper, who made private enquiries and reported that there was apparently some chance of Lancaster being selected; at about the same time the U.G.C.'s

---

[1.22] Alderman Clift who served on both the city council and the county council, was mayor of Lancaster from 1969–70, as well as taking a leading role in many aspects of the life of the city, including theatre and sport. He died on 20 May 1973.

[1.23] *Lancaster Guardian*, 10 January 1947.

[1.24] Redressed in 1972, when Lancaster acquired its own divorce court.

[1.25] *Morecambe Visitor*, 19 November 1947.

[1.26] The borough of Lancaster was raised to the status of a city by George VI in 1937.

report for 1952–7, with its comments on expansion, gave impetus to the city's hopes.

An article by Professor Balchin of the University College of Swansea, discussing possible sites of new regional university colleges, isolated Lancaster as a potential site, sharing with places such as Brighton, Canterbury, Carlisle, Lincoln, Plymouth and York the advantages that

> these localities are well removed from existing university facilities, all have good accessibility to their region, most have substantial population hinterlands comparable with many established university centres, some have good accommodation possibilities and some have good cultural backgrounds.[1.27]

As had been done in 1947, various local industrialists and other representatives of the community were approached, at the end of the 1950's, both for funds and in order to spread as widely as possible the enthusiasm for this venture. One practical step which Mr. Waddell also took, in relation to finding a site, was to discuss with the management board of the Royal Albert Hospital the possible deployment of this building as the core of a new university. This large edifice, built in a style reminiscent of the Ruskin-inspired University Museum in Oxford, had been a private hospital for mental defectives until 1948 when it came under the National Health Service. However, the extensive grounds (264 acres), its imposing and already existing buildings, and a situation at once on the edge of Lancaster but also reasonably close to the centre, seemed to a number of people to argue it as a very promising site.

Other, informal meetings, unrecorded in official correspondence, helped to create an atmosphere of informed interest. Dr. Claxton recalls one such, which took place in the early days of 1961, when at a party in the Town Hall organized by the Priory he fell into conversation with Lord Peel. The outcome of their conversation was a lunch in the Mayor's Parlour at which the Mayor, Lord Peel and various other local people decided that they would make every effort to bring a university to the district, and to Lancaster in particular.

Thus by the beginning of 1961, when the officers of the County Council were desirous of taking an active interest in such a development, Lancaster was able to be immediately receptive to their approaches; and on 2 March Mr. Waddell wrote:

> I am now asked by the Council to place before the County Authority the relevant facts and to seek the assistance of the County Council in sponsor-

---

[1.27] W. G. V. Balchin, "University Expansion in Great Britain" in *The New Scientist*, 12 March 1959.

ing the establishment of a new University in this City. I could write at length on the City's tradition and history, its ideal geographical situation, its ease of access both by road and rail, and undoubted excellent record as an Education Authority for many years up to the time when its educational powers were transferred to the County Council, its standing as a local authority and similar matters, but I think these are all well known and need not be enlarged upon at this stage.

He then gave an estimate of local financial support, stating that Lancaster city council had indicated they would make an annual contribution of £15,000, while Morecambe and Heysham had also accepted the principle of an annual contribution of £5,000.[1.28] He also thought £15,000 each year a realistic sum to expect from local industrialists.

The meeting of those interested duly took place on 14 April at County Hall, with Sir Andrew Smith[1.29] in the chair and

> because of the urgency to get a case before the University Grants Committee, the meeting set themselves up as a Promotion Council and appointed an Executive Committee to select the location and then to proceed with the submission to the U.G.C. It was decided to invite Lord Derby to be President of the Promoting Council.[1.30]

Invitations were accordingly issued to the remaining serious contenders to meet the Executive Committee on the afternoon of 21 April, after the Committee had enjoyed the first of a series of university planning lunches at County Hall. In the event, only the Town Clerk of Lancaster and the Deputy Town Clerk of Blackpool (Mr. Jim Swaffield) were seen and questioned—all the others having either withdrawn or been dissuaded from continuing—and the eloquence of both men is still well remembered by those who heard them. Both Lancaster and Blackpool had already submitted extensive documentation in support of their bids, covering particularly their historic and cultural backgrounds; geographical advantages and industrial developments; availability of housing, lodging and education; general amenities; a site description; and the expected level of local commitment and financial support. At the meeting Mr. Waddell pushed strongly the idea of the Royal Albert site, having negotiated with the hospital authorities to release the whole site provided that a replacement could be established. However, he has told the

---

[1.28] £15,000 from Lancaster was to be the product of a 6d. rate, and £5,000 from Morecambe of a 2d. rate (pre-decimal coinage). These contributions, however, did not prove to be permanent.

[1.29] County Alderman Sir Andrew Smith, C.B.E., J.P., was Labour chairman of the County Council from 1952 to 1955, and from 1958 to 1961. He was knighted in 1960, and died in 1967.

[1.30] Extract from letter sent by Mr. McCall to interested persons unable to be present on 16 April.

writer that, while travelling back from Preston later in the day, he realized that insistence on the Royal Albert might jeopardize Lancaster's chances, especially since Blackpool was offering a virgin site. The City Surveyor had previously suggested that the city might look outside its boundaries and Mr. Waddell, having consulted the chairman of the city's finance committee, Mr. Preston,[1.31] took the personal initiative of approaching Mr. and Mrs. Barton Townley, the owners in 1961 of Bailrigg Mansion, the surrounding parkland and the adjoining Bigforth Farm. Within a few hours he was able to telephone Mr. Preston to tell him that, provided they were not deprived of a neighbouring house in which to live, the Townleys were prepared definitely to sell the mansion and their land for £50,000.

As Mr. Waddell wrote on 26 April,

> It was emphasized at the last meeting of the Executive Committee that the City Council wished to base their case on the immediate availability of the Bailrigg site, but at the same time requesting the Executive Committee to look at the Royal Albert Hospital. . . . It was further indicated . . . that the owner had indicated his willingness to sell the house and the land for University development. Since the last meeting this has been confirmed with the owner, who is most enthusiastic . . . [and] agreement has been reached whereby if the Executive Committee were minded to choose the Bailrigg site, that site would be made available by the City Council to the appropriate authority as a free site.

The City was fortunate in having a capital sum, set aside at the time of the change from a local water authority to the Lune Valley Water Board, available for this purpose.

Thus, when the Executive Committee on 26 April visited Lancaster they looked at Bailrigg and also at the Royal Albert. The omens seemed unfavourable, for the Ribble bus in which the members travelled, having a very wide wheelbase which took up the whole width of the Bailrigg drive, stuck firmly in the mud. Blackpool later in the day, however, was no more fortunate, for Stanley Park was thickly shrouded in mist.

The final choice between the two places was not, however, to be made until 2 May. Additional information about local laboratory and research facilities, called for by Dr. Burkhardt of Manchester University (as a member of the Executive Committee), was supplied by both parties, and in addition Mr. Waddell went into detail over the matter of students' lodgings:

> I think the Executive Committee should be made aware that on Friday evening last a sample survey of approximately 3,000 houses was undertaken

---

[1.31] Alderman Preston owns a family business, founded in Lancaster in 1832, of fellmongering. He was chairman of the city's Finance Committee in 1961 and Mayor in 1964. He has subsequently been a devoted supporter of the Town and Gown Club.

and in that number there was not only the ability, but also the willingness, to accommodate 330 students. Every house surveyed was less than $1\frac{1}{4}$ miles distant from Bailrigg, although in taking this radius it was known that there were other areas of the City which might reasonably have been expected to produce a higher figure.

The Town Clerk of Blackpool similarly supplied details of lodgings available, as well as road proposals for the Stanley Park site, and drainage and services there.

Lunch was taken at County Hall and the meeting opened with Sir Andrew Smith in the chair.[1.32] Discussion was lengthy and vehement, but in the end centred around the fact that, of the 680 acres at Stanley Park, 480 were under negotiation with a developer who proposed "the creation of pleasure gardens and an entertainment attraction which would be unique in Great Britain".[1.33] As far as lodgings, provision of educational facilities, libraries and communications were concerned, there was not a great deal to choose between the two authorities, but the ramifications of the "unique attraction" and the impact it might have on a contiguous enterprise greatly troubled the committee. The Bailrigg site, on the other hand, was part of a green belt which was felt to be a safeguard against undesirable development. At last a vote was taken, and by the figure of 22 to 1 the Executive Committee decided

> That the case to be submitted to the University Grants Committee should be on the basis that the proposed new University should be located at Lancaster and the Bailrigg site was selected for that purpose.[1.34]

The Committee had exactly ten days[1.35] in which to prepare a formal document for submission to the U.G.C.: bound in maroon covers with silver lettering, forty copies of it were driven to London on 12 May, and a formal letter of submission followed three days later. The kernal of the submission was the dual strength of Lancaster as being strongly supported within the region but also, while at a reasonable distance from other northern universities, being an appropriate site for a national foundation, and one which would

---

[1.32] Although the Conservatives had won the County Council elections held on 10 April, the custom is that the existing chairman carries on until the annual meeting, which in 1961 was held two days later, on 4 May.

[1.33] Submission by Blackpool to the Executive Committee of April 1961. The area suggested for the university is now the site of a zoo.

[1.34] Letter from Mr. McCall to Mr. Waddell of 2 May 1961.

[1.35] A draft of the submission was sent out to members of the Executive Committee on 3 May (with a complete list of the Promotion Council following on 4 May), amendments were in by 6 May, and the document, with map and photographs, was with the printer by 8 May.

with its cultural heritage and background, its peace for study, its communications, and all the necessary amenities and facilities for staff and students, fulfil all the requirements of a University town.

The members of the Promotion Council were listed; a conclusion added by Sir Alfred Bates,[1.36] summarizing the grounds of Lancaster's case; followed by an appendix listing science-based industries and research establishments, as well as photographs of the site and the surrounding terrain, and a map of the area. Lord Derby put his name to a foreword, which concluded:

> Lancashire is well-known as a strong, virile and imaginative County and the Promoting Council believe that the educational and cultural life of that great part of it which exists beyond the Cities of Liverpool and Manchester and their urban hinterlands, would be vastly stimulated and enriched by a University at Lancaster. Lancaster would undoubtedly provide an ideal home for such an Institution; but what is even more important, a new University there would be able to contribute in no small way towards the solution of the growing national need for more university places.[1.37]

The local sponsors could do no more for the time being. The Lancaster case, along with those from other parts of England, was laid before the U.G.C.'s Sub-Committee on New Universities on 24 May and a decision notified to Mr. McCall the next day that representatives of the U.G.C. would like to visit Lancaster during June, both to see the site and to meet the promoters. The submission was released to the local and national press: a considerable volume of interest had now developed, increased by the Chancellor of the Exchequer's answer to a question in the House of Commons on 14 May, when he announced the establishment of new universities at Canterbury, Colchester and Coventry and said the location of the fourth choice was being considered by the U.G.C., who "hope to report on this in the next two or three months". On 14 June Sir Keith Murray (chairman of the U.G.C.) together with Professor Asa Briggs (of Leeds University, and Vice-Chancellor elect of Sussex University), Lord Heyworth (former chairman of Unilever), and Professor T. E. Wright (of St. Andrew's University), together with the U.G.C.'s deputy secretary and their superintending architect, came to look at the Bailrigg site. This time there were no mishaps; not only no mud, but a marked itinerary and stiles put through hedges at

---

[1.36] Sir Alfred Bates entered on his third term of office as Conservative Chairman of Lancashire County Council on 4 May 1961, continuing until the elections in 1964, when Labour returned to power. He was chairman of the Executive Council for the Establishment of a University of Lancaster, has been a deputy pro-chancellor from 1964 onwards, and a member of the university's Council from 1964 to 1967 and from 1971 onwards.

[1.37] This submission was to become a model for a number of other aspirants to university institutions, including Stirling.

appropriate places. The U.G.C. representatives, accompanied by a selection of Executive Committee members, walked over the site, viewing it from every angle and asking detailed questions about whether, for example, there was a sufficient tract of land which would be flat enough to make adequate playing fields.

Afterwards they had lunch[1.38] at the Town Hall with the complete Executive Committee, followed by a discussion, at which the Town Clerks of both Lancaster and Morecambe were interviewed. A letter from Mr. McCall to Lord Derby the next day sums up the feelings of those present:

> We had we think a very encouraging meeting with the University Grants Committee at Lancaster yesterday. . . . We were perhaps blessed more than anything with a most wonderful day and the Grants Committee saw all we had to show them under the very best conditions. They are very keen on the aspect of getting the University within the 200 acre or so perimeter, including the playing fields, and this perhaps weighs more heavily with them than any other consideration, and, therefore, the site is vitally important.
>
> We had the feeling that they were very considerably impressed with the case and the site and the background of Lancaster for a University and that we do stand a very strong chance of succeeding, but, as you know, there are one or two others in the field, such as, for example, we believe Chester,[1.39] Cheltenham and Gloucester, and the Grants Committee have a very difficult decision to make later this summer. . . .
>
> I would only add one thing . . . that the Grants Committee said that if they had had to make a case themselves for a University of Lancaster, then they found it difficult to say in what way they could have bettered the case we had put up to them, which was very kind indeed of them and certainly most encouraging.

Now came another period of waiting when the U.G.C. had reported to the Chancellor of the Exchequer and the only local activity was to begin to seek preliminary planning permission for the revised use of land, which hitherto had been solely agricultural. One objection which caused some difficulty came from the tenant of Bigforth Farm. However, after discussion between the farmer (Mr. R. Townley), representatives of the National Farmers' Union, Mr. McCall and the Town Clerk of Lancaster, it was decided that Whinney Carr Farm, which lies within the grounds of the Royal Albert Hospital, and is a dairy farm as Bigforth had been, should be purchased by the city and the tenancy transferred there, the buildings having first been brought up to the same standard as those at Bigforth. This was accomplished in principle in

---

[1.38] Their host was the Mayor, Councillor Mrs. Margery J. Lovett-Horn.

[1.39] Chester was the closest rival to Lancaster, with a superb site by the river Dee (now a golf course) to offer.

July 1961, and the objection formally placed by the N.F.U. on behalf of Mr.
Townley withdrawn before the meeting of the County Planning and Development Committee (which had the duty of deciding, having regard to the Town
and Country Planning Act of 1947, whether to recommend to the Minister
of Housing and Local Government that the land be made available for a
university). The regional Land Commissioner of the Ministry of Agriculture,
because of objections from the Ministry, had at first demurred at the proposed
use of the site, but after a discussion at County Hall, gave his assent to the
scheme.[1.40]

As the months went by and the Chancellor of the Exchequer declined,
despite being pressed in the House of Commons during August, to make any
statement about the location of the fourth new university, tension in the city
and county grew. At last, however, on 23 November 1961, the Chief Secretary
to the Treasury, Mr. Henry Brooke, stated in the House of Commons that
"The Government has accepted the advice of the University Grants Committee, that the fourth new university should be established at Lancaster".[1.41]
The U.G.C. report for 1957–62 has this comment:

> It had been suggested to us that there was a need for a further university
> in the north on the grounds that, once students moved southwards, they
> tended to stay in the south. This was creating difficulties for industries and
> some of the professions in the north. We sympathized with this argument
> and therefore decided to recommend that the seventh new university
> should be located at Lancaster. This advice was accepted by the Govern-
> ment and the foundation of this new university was announced in
> November 1961.[1.42]

Congratulations came in from all sides. A brief meeting of the Promotion
Council was held in December, followed by another in January 1962, at which
the Executive Committee of the Promotion Council was dissolved, to be
reincarnated later in the same month as the Executive Council for the
Establishment of a University at Lancaster. This new body, which had most
of its members in common with the former Executive Committee, was

---

[1.40] The university's supporters were fortunate in receiving such ready assent. It is
interesting to compare Lancaster's experience with that of the University of East
Anglia, which went to a public enquiry and a personal decision by the Minister of
Housing and Local Government. (See R. G. Jobling, "The location and siting of a new
University", in *Universities Quarterly*, Vol. 24, No. 2 (Spring 1970), pp. 123–36.)
[1.41] *Lancaster Guardian*, 24 November 1961. Christopher Driver has drawn atten-
tion to the lack of Parliamentary debate about whether any new universities should be
created and, if so, where:
  The decision in principle to build new universities was taken in Britain not by a
  Minister, but by the Civil Service on the advice of a non-governmental body. (*The
  Exploding University* (London, 1971), page 177.)
[1.42] H.M.S.O., *University Development 1957–1962*, Cmnd. 2267, para 290.

for the purpose of taking all necessary action towards the foundation and provision of the University (other than that appropriate to the Academic Planning Board) until such time as a Royal Charter of Incorporation for the University has been obtained and, pursuant to that, the Governing Body of the University has been set up and is able to take over. For this purpose, it was accepted that the Executive Council should become a corporate legal entity by incorporation under the Companies Act, 1948.[1.43]

This Executive Council had a threefold task. First, it was to "petition Her Majesty in Council for the grant of a Royal Charter of Incorporation for the University and to promote in Parliament any local or private Bill which the Company may deem desirable." Secondly, it had the responsibility for setting up, on the advice of the University Grants Committee, an Academic Planning Board which would work in close consultation both with the sponsors and the U.G.C.; and, thirdly, it had to be able to accept financial contributions, make payments, hold land and other property and finance, and carry out other necessary monetary transactions.

There was a need for immediate finance since, as a document of January 1962 explained, the U.G.C. was prepared to recommend the provision of

---

[1.43] The constitution of the Executive Council was set up as a limited company on an analogy with the University of Sussex (rather than, for example, as a trust, which was the solution adopted by the University of East Anglia at the same stage of development). Because the Ministry of Education had ruled that they could not approve of local education authorities making grants under section 84 of the Education Act, 1944, to a university or university college not yet in existence, it was necessary to set up some interim machinery to allow the authority to pay the necessary contributions to the nascent university.

Because of the special educational nature of its business, the company had no share capital but was limited by guarantee; that is, the liability of members was limited to a nominal sum of £1 each. Further, a licence was obtained from the Board of Trade to enable the word "limited" to be omitted from the name of the company, which implied a degree of Government recognition of the licensed body as formed for promoting a useful object, and that its activities were of substantial public importance.

The Council was registered as a limited company on 7 June 1962 with a Memorandum and Articles of Association approved and signed by seven original subscribers (the minimum number permitted), and subsequently registered as a charity by the Ministry of Education. At the first meeting of the Council on 20 June 1962 the first directors (there had to be a minimum of two), who were in practice the same as the subscribers, admitted to membership of the company the other members of the unincorporated Executive Council, as well as all the members of the Academic Planning Board. Sir Alfred Bates was made chairman of the directors, and alternate directors were appointed. The Vice-Chancellor Elect, Mr. Charles Carter, also became a director from December 1962. At the time of the Council's first annual general meeting, in October 1963, the membership comprised forty-three persons.

Mr. McCall, who had been honorary secretary of the Promotion Council, and its Executive Committee, became the first honorary secretary of the Executive Council, and his parallel appointment as honorary secretary of the Academic Planning Board provided a particularly useful link between the two bodies (with Mr. Flatt acting for him when necessary).

financial assistance from the Exchequer both for capital development and recurrent grant only after satisfactory agreement was reached between themselves and the Academic Planning Board. In the meanwhile there was a hiatus when Exchequer finance was not available, and since the Executive Committee of the Promotion Council

> have taken the view that it would be improper for any moneys donated from private sources to be used to meet preliminary administrative expenses . . . the local education authorities represented upon the Promoting Council have been asked to consider making their respective contributions available as from and as early as possible in the financial year 1962/63 so that a fund will be available.[1.44]

The question of soliciting financial support had been a delicate matter, for it was necessary to provide the U.G.C. with as concrete evidence as possible of money available, while not going any further than obtaining promises of support. (At one stage the U.G.C. had gained the impression, from over-enthusiastic press reports, that actual sums of money were being collected and some explanatory correspondence was necessary between County Hall and the U.G.C. to put the record straight.) By January 1962, however, the Honorary Financial Adviser[1.45] had received promises of annual contributions not under covenant to the value of £80,000 p.a., including amounts promised by local authorities as contributions towards the immediate running costs of the University.

The unincorporated Council was to meet twice (in January and May 1962), one of these meetings being together with the Academic Planning Board; and the directors of the incorporated Council met on twelve occasions, at four of which the Board were also present. However, of these twelve meetings, the last two (in November 1964 and May 1965) were purely for the formal business of winding up the company, leaving ten meetings spanning the period from July 1962 to October 1964 when the university emerged from being a theoretical concept in the minds of a small group of local sponsors and the U.G.C., to the status of an operating institution. All the members of the Council whom the author has met have stressed how very rewarding they found this period. To quote Mr. Flatt, however hectic it was, they were all constantly involved in helping to make decisions which they could watch

---

[1.44] Appendix by the Chairman of the Promotion Council to the agenda of 10 January 1962. The money thus made available was to cover, amongst other items, the expenses of the Academic Planning Board and the salaries of the initial University appointments. The first of the ten grants of £50,000 from the Lancashire County Council, for example, was paid in August 1962 to cover the university's financial year 1 August 1962 to 31 July 1963.

[1.45] The late Mr. N. Doodson, the County Treasurer, was Honorary Financial Adviser to the Promotion Council, and Honorary Treasurer and Accountant to the later Executive Council.

turning at once into substantial form, whether it was the appointment of the staff of the university, the selection of architects, or the leasing of the Waring and Gillow factory for the initial operation of the university. Sir Alfred, as chairman, was to become irritated from time to time at delays on the part of various bodies which he felt could have been avoided, but in fact Lancaster moved smartly ahead in comparison with the other new universities.

We have seen above that it was necessary to seek planning permission for the revised use of the land. At the request of the Ministry of Housing and Local Government, and because the proposed usage of the Bailrigg site was so far from the provisions of the approved County Development Plan, the formal application for the change was advertised in the local press immediately the Government decided that a University should be located at Lancaster. Since no objections were received, the Ministry agreed, in January 1962, that the County's Planning and Development Committee should authorize development of the site. The Notice of Planning Consent, issued in April 1961, had carried a clause to the effect that:

> This consent relates only to the development of this site for the purpose of a University, with its ancillary development, and does not purport to grant approval to its use for any form of educational or other purpose not directly related to such a University. . . . This consent has only been granted because of the special requirements of the development forming the subject of this application. The injury to agricultural and other interests would not be warranted for other development.

Safeguards concerning the detailed layout, the retention of trees, access to the A.6 and separation of the site from the motorway and the main road were also included, some of the clauses being the subject of tough negotiation between the County Council and the Ministry of Transport, both in 1961 and again in 1964 when the site was being developed.

There was, however, another necessary procedure to be carried out. Bailrigg and the land around it was in Lancaster Rural District and it was necessary to extend the city boundary sufficiently so as to take in this area; it would then come under the jurisdiction of the city for the provision of services, rating and local government generally, and would meet the undertaking made by the city to the U.G.C. that such a transfer would be made. Accordingly, under the County of Lancaster (City of Lancaster) Confirmation Order, 1962, it was determined that certain "parts of the rural district of Lancaster and of the parishes of Ellel and Scotforth . . . shall be transferred to the city and parish of Lancaster, and shall form part of the Scotforth ward of the city and of the Lancaster South electoral division of the county". The county and the university had reason to be grateful for the generous attitude of the Rural District Council over this arrangement.

The land, however, was not able to be an outright gift to the University, but has been leased by the City Council to the university for a term of 999 years at a peppercorn rent of £1 a year. The Executive Council was informed on 25 April 1963 that the chairman had approved the lease and the company's seal was accordingly affixed. At a ceremony the same day in the Town Hall the Mayor, Alderman Gardner, handed the lease over to Lord Derby, the Pro-Chancellor Elect, and congratulatory speeches were made.

In May 1962 there was the first of the meetings between the Executive Council and the Academic Planning Board, which gave the one side the opportunity to find out from the Board what their thinking on academic structure was so far, and the other to find out what were the main areas of concern amongst the local sponsors. By June the first three officers of the university had been selected, Her Majesty the Queen (the Duke of Lancaster) had accepted the invitation of the Council to be the Visitor,[1.46] and, because of the special relationship of the Duchy to the Crown, is so in her personal royal form instead of through the Privy Council as at other universities. Her Royal Highness, Princess Alexandra of Kent, the Hon. Mrs. Angus Ogilvy, had similarly accepted the office of Chancellor; and the Lord Lieutenant of County, the Right Honourable the Earl of Derby, M.C., agreed to be the first Pro-Chancellor.[1.47]

The meetings of the Council soon fell into a regular pattern, of decisions about investment policy, temporary accommodation, superannuation, the appointment of staff, the selection of an architect and the development of the site, and formal business. At several meetings there was a report from the Academic Planning Board; at each meeting after his appointment the Vice-Chancellor had some matters to bring to members' attention; and they had the responsibility, with the Board, of considering the constitutional arrangements. The Academic Planning Board had as its terms of reference:

(1) To consider the arrangements by which the Universities may be assured of the maintenance of satisfactory academic standards at the

---

[1.46] Robert O. Berdahl, in *British Universities and the State* (1959), pp. 113–4, comments that universities may have Visitors. Their powers are theoretically broad, and include interpretation of the corporation's statutes, settling disputes between its members, and acting as a court of appeal on general questions of administration. The Visitor has no power to revoke gifts, change usages, divest of rights, or examine books.
The University of Lancaster's Charter has this definition:
We, our Heirs and Successors, Kings and Queens of the Kingdom, Realms and Territories aforesaid shall be in person and remain the Visitor and Visitors of the University and in exercise of the Visitorial Authority We and Our Heirs and Successors shall have the right from time to time and in such manner as We or They shall think fit to direct an inspection of the University, its buildings and equipment, and also an enquiry into the teaching, research, examinations and other work done by the University.

[1.47] The Earl of Derby resigned from the Pro-Chancellorship in April 1971 and his place was taken in January 1972 by the Rt. Hon. the Lord Greenwood of Rossendale.

University, on the assumption that it will award its own first and
higher degrees.

(2) To consider the range of subjects to be studied at the University
during the first years of its existence and the length and general
character of the undergraduate courses.

(3) To prepare a petition for a Royal Charter for the University and a
draft of such a Charter, and to select, in consultation with the local
sponsors, the persons to be named in those documents as the first
governing body of the University.

(4) To select and nominate, in consultation with the local sponsors, the
first Vice-Chancellor of the University, and, with his advice, Professors of the principal subjects.[1.48]

The stated duties of the Board represented a dramatic evolution in the
status of a new university in comparison with the foundations of the late
nineteenth and early twentieth centuries.[1.49] Such universities as Liverpool,
Leeds, Sheffield and others of that vintage had passed through early stages
of development as university colleges, often having attained that status from
simple and local beginnings. Some prepared their students for external
degrees of London University, and some of them served a probationary period
of over fifty years before being given autonomy and full degree-granting
powers. A significant change came with the University College of North
Staffordshire (later Keele) which, although it went through a period of
thirteen years of sponsorship before achieving full degree-granting powers,

> was given the power from the outset to confer the degree of Bachelor of
> Arts under certain conditions, one of which was the establishment of an
> academic council of eleven of whom six—the majority—represented the
> Universities of Oxford, Manchester and Birmingham. . . . While this form
> of organization enabled the new University College to introduce courses
> of a novel kind, freed from the prescription imposed by the London
> external degree, it involved disadvantages in relation to advanced work
> since the college had no power to grant its own higher degrees, and the
> higher degrees of London University were not open to its advanced students;
> nor did the arrangements to take higher degrees of the three sponsoring
> universities appear to us to have provided a satisfactory solution.[1.50]

[1.48] Taken from the agenda of the Promotion Council for 10 January 1962. The
wording in the H.M.S.O. report, *University Development 1957–1962* (Cmnd. 2267,
para. 291), is identical.

[1.49] For more detailed information about the evolution of the independence of the
new university institutions, see H.M.S.O., *University Development 1957–62*, Cmnd.
2267, paras. 253–6, 265–272, 291–295.

[1.50] *Ibid.*, para 256. See also Sir J. Mountford, *Keele: An Historical Critique* (1972),
chapters 3 and 4.

By the time that Sussex was being planned, the U.G.C. had had an opportunity to watch the pattern of development of new university foundation, and so for the first time the device of an Academic Planning Board, to act as a liaison between the local sponsors and the U.G.C., was used. The terms of reference of membership of the Sussex board had been discussed with the Committee of Vice-Chancellors and Principals and with the U.G.C., whose report continues:

> It will be noted that the assumption in the first term of reference was confined to the awarding of degrees of Bachelor of Arts and Bachelor of Science, but we told the Board that this did not preclude their advising the sponsors that the institution should be allowed to grant higher degrees. It will also be noted that the terms of reference applied to the founding of a university college and to the selection and nomination of a Principal. Before application was made for a Charter, we had, however, come to the conclusion that such new institutions should be, from the outset, full universities and consequently that their heads should be Vice-Chancellors.[1.51]

An important precedent had been set and when the time came to plan the six later universities, there was no question that they would not have academic planning boards with the terms of reference quoted above on pages 21 and 22; and that they would be allowed to grant their own first and higher degrees, and achieve full university status from the outset. The planning boards, in conjunction with the local sponsor, had, therefore, a mandate to plan for the long-term future and to effect their innovations with individual integrated schemes, rather than to make piece-meal reform of existing curricula. Sussex acknowledged a debt to the radical approach of Keele; Lancaster and her sister institutions were able to start from the Sussex experience and proceed from there.[1.52]

Each board customarily had something in the region of seven members, a pattern which Lancaster followed. The Chairman for Lancaster was Sir Noel Hall, Principal of Brasenose College, Oxford, a political economist who had previously been principal of the Administrative Staff College at Henley, and who was having parallel experience as a member of the academic planning board for Kent.[1.53] Professor F. S. Dainton, F.R.S. of Leeds University was, as a chemist, one of those representing the natural science interest on the

---

[1.51] *Ibid.*, para 272.

[1.52] Sussex took its first intake of students in October 1961, six months before the Lancaster A.P.B. was set up and had before it opened its doors been the recipient of a great deal of publicity and analysis.

[1.53] Sir Noel Hall subsequently became a member of the Council of the University, retiring from this office in 1973, the same year as that in which he retired as Principal of Brasenose College, Oxford.

Board.[1.54] Sir Malcolm Knox, Vice-Chancellor and Principal of St. Andrews University, was a philosopher; Professor Kathleen Major, Principal of St. Hilda's College, Oxford, was a modern historian. Professor R. J. Pumphrey, F.R.S., who was a zoologist at Liverpool University, died in August 1967. Mr. J. A. Ratcliffe, C.B.E., F.R.S., who had been reader in physics at Cambridge University and was in 1962 the Director of the Radio Research Station at Slough, represented the lay interest on the Board. Finally, Professor B. R. Williams, a political economist who had been one of the founding professors at Keele, was in 1962 at Manchester University and subsequently became Vice-Chancellor and Principal of the University of Sydney. Of these seven, four had received their first degree from Oxford and two from Cambridge (the seventh member being an Australian with a first degree from Sydney). The Lancaster Board held fourteen formal meetings, some extending over two days, between March 1962 and May 1964, in which the Vice-Chancellor took part after his appointment in December 1962. One of these was held jointly with the Executive Council, and the final one with the Shadow Senate.

The University's first students came up in October 1964; and in July 1965 the Academic Advisory Committee met for the first time. This body was to assume the duties of the Academic Planning Board from the date of the Charter and its membership, including the Vice-Chancellor, was identical to that of its parent body. The original statutes declared that the Committee

> shall keep under review and shall certify annually to the Council that it has satisfied itself about the standard of education and research in the University, the procedure for the appointment of members of the Academic Staff, the organization and conduct of the University examinations, and the standard of the Degrees awarded.[1.55]

Because of the intendedly transitory nature of this body, crucial for the safeguarding of standards and for the establishment of a national academic reputation on a par with all other British universities, the Charter made provision that

> On the motion of the Court, with the concurrence of the Council and after receiving comment on the motion from the Academic Advisory Committee, the Lords of Our Most Honourable Privy Council may determine

---

[1.54] Professor Sir Frederick Dainton (he was knighted in 1971) was Vice-Chancellor of Nottingham University from 1965 to 1970 and has been Dr. Lee's Professor of Chemistry at the University of Oxford since that time. From October 1973 he has been appointed chairman of the University Grants Committee.

[1.55] *Statutes of the University of Lancaster*, 13(3), July 1964. When the Statutes were revised in 1971, the need for an Academic Advisory Committee was past, and it is not mentioned, although the section referring to it in the Charter has remained.

a date with effect from which the Academic Advisory Committee shall be dissolved.[1.56]

The Advisory Committee met five times, in the summers of 1965 to 1967, and the autumns of 1968 and 1969 respectively, often combining a meeting with the university's Development Committee alongside their own discussions. The formal dissolution by the Privy Council, however, signifying the end of the University's academic probation, did not take effect until 11 October 1970.[1.57] At this time it was hoped that meetings between the former members of the Board and the University might be arranged informally on an annual basis, and two such have taken place in March 1971 and July 1973, when the members of the former Committee were shown around the site and met the college officers, chairmen of the boards of studies, and other key members of the University.

The brief of the Advisory Committee was very wide, and the topics with which they concerned themselves ranged from a survey of new building to be put up, to a discussion of Enterprise Lancaster.[1.58] Future development was obviously of particular interest, and as well as discussing and agreeing to the creation of new departments or facilities, such as the School of Education, the engineering department or remedial mathematics, a member of the Committee sat on each of the appointing committees for chairs. They kept a continuing watch on the qualifications and experience of staff, both at professorial and other levels, and a recurring note was a concern as to whether the exigencies of life in a new university meant that the research time of staff was being too much curtailed. Naturally they were consulted about student numbers as well as the inauguration of new masters' degree courses, and saw the results of all examinations. They approved the appointment of the external examiners, and scrutinized the reports which these same examiners made on standards achieved and methods of assessment. Finally, they were able to take a broad view: to look at the college system, or the boards of studies, or the growth of business studies, and at the relationship of each of these to the rest of the university from a viewpoint that was both fully informed but also detached. It is possible that the generality of the university gradually became less aware of the committee's existence, but nevertheless it remained a point of external reference which could only be of value to a new institution.

However, let us return to 1962. The first task to which the Academic Planning Board turned their minds was the appointment of a Vice-Chancellor.

[1.56] *Charter of Incorporation for the University of Lancaster*, 14(3), July 1964.

[1.57] At the time of the last meeting in October 1969 the membership was: Sir Noel Hall, Chairman; Dr. G. N. Burkhardt, of the University of Manchester; Professor F. S. Dainton; Professor Kathleen Major; Lord Morris of Grasmere, K.C.M.G.; Regius Professor David R. Newth, of the University of Glasgow; and the Vice-Chancellor.

[1.58] See Chapter 5, pages 304 to 306.

Although in January 1965 the Academic Planning Board for the University of Stirling took the unprecedented step of advertising the post of vice-chancellor, and in June 1972 the University of York was to advertise for "those who may wish to be considered [as a successor to Lord James of Rusholme] or who wish to suggest names", such posts were being filled in the early 1960's (as they commonly are today) rather in the way of bishoprics in the Church of England. In 1961 not only were the six newest universities seeking their queen bees, but also two of the longer-established civic universities. The Executive Council in this matter could only wait for the Board to make nominations for, whilst it retained the right of veto, it could not itself make suggestions. This situation made for an inherently delicate balance between the Board and the local sponsors, and one frustrating for the latter since, as Sir Noel Hall said,

> The difficulty is that the Promotion Committees came into being in order to raise heads of steam and naturally want to get on quickly; whereas the Academic Planning Boards have to deliberate carefully and even slowly about the basic intellectual pattern.[1.59]

In a new university the Vice-Chancellor is, of course, a key figure in shaping that pattern. What kind of person is a Vice-Chancellor, and what role does he play? Lord Robbins' Committee in 1963 saw him as

> at once a member of the governing body and the chairman of the main academic councils. He must, therefore, be at the centre of all discussions involving broad questions of internal policy or relations with the outside world. He must represent his institution in all formal or informal relations with the University Grants' Committee; he must be present at meetings of the Committee of Vice-Chancellors and Principals.[1.60]

The discussion continued in the Franks' Report, where a discussion of the possible need for a Vice-Chancellor with a longer term of office, or even a permanent appointment to retirement, leads to a delineation of the delicate relationship between this officer of the University of Oxford and the other decision-making and sovereignty-holding bodies within it.[1.61] Dr. D. G. Christopherson, himself both a Vice-Chancellor and chairman of another academic planning board (at Kent), commented wryly that

> I heard it said the other day that to be a successful Vice-Chancellor there are six qualities you have got to have, but none of them in fact have more

---

[1.59] Professor Boris Ford, "Creating the New Universities" in *The Sunday Times* for the 17th and 24 June 1962.

[1.60] H.M.S.O., *Higher Education: Report of the Committee*, Cmnd. 2154 (1963), para. 676.

[1.61] See *Report of Commission of Inquiry*, Volume I (University of Oxford, 1966), paras. 492–503, 509–512, 538–550.

than two. The most important quality, which is never mentioned in public, is that you must be a peacemaker,

while Sir Noel Hall saw him as

a person who has achieved something in his own right and in doing this he will probably have experienced both success and failure. But in this way he will have been able to establish his own self-respect. Then, will the better academics feel they can work with him? He must obviously be a unifier, and also he must have humility. Incidentally, I am sceptical about people having "administrative ability", as these words are sometimes used.[1.62]

Mr. Charles Frederick Carter, on whom the choice of the Academic Planning Board alighted, and whom they presented to the Executive Council at the latter's meeting of 4 December 1962, is the son of Dr. F. W. Carter, F.R.S., an electrical engineer, and the brother of Professor G. W. Carter of the University of Leeds. He was born on 15 August 1919, and after going to school at Rugby he read mathematics and economics at St. John's College, Cambridge, and was later given a Hon.D.Econ.Sc. from the National University of Ireland. He became a lecturer in statistics at the University of Cambridge, as well as being appointed a Fellow of Emmanuel College. In 1952 he moved to The Queen's University, Belfast, to take up a chair of applied economics, and in 1959 was appointed as Stanley Jevons Professor of Political Economy and Cobden Lecturer at the University of Manchester, where he stayed until he took up his new post in Lancaster on 1 April 1963. He has written, sometimes jointly, several books on aspects of economics, as well as venturing into other areas, as with his *The Northern Ireland Problem,* with D. P. Barritt, the more recent *Patterns and Policies in Higher Education* (with George Brosan *et al.*), and the Swarthmore Lecture for 1971, *On Having a Sense of All Conditions* (reflecting his family's and his own Quaker interests). Amongst his other appointments, we may particularly note that he has been chairman of the North West Economic Planning Council (1965–8), and of the School Broadcasting Council for the United Kingdom (1964–70), and is currently Secretary-General of the Royal Economic Society, Chairman of the Centre for Studies in Social Policy, a trustee of the Joseph Rowntree Memorial Trust and of the Sir Halley Stewart Trust, and a director of the Friends' Provident and Century Insurance Company.

He in his turn, with the joint assistance of the Academic Planning Board and the Executive Council, selected the first members of staff. When the university took in its first students in October 1964 there were thirteen

---

[1.62] These quotations come from the articles by Professor Boris Ford, *loc. cit.*

professors[1.63] and thirty-two other members of the teaching and research staff, as well as a librarian and his seven members of staff, and fourteen administrators on academic grades.

The Librarian appointed was Mr. A. Graham Mackenzie, who was born in 1928, and who, after reading for an M.A. in Classics at Glasgow University, spent eight years in the University Library at Durham as assistant librarian, and later Keeper of Science Books, and was in 1963 coming from the Brotherton Library at the University of Leeds, where he had been Deputy Librarian. The University Secretary, Mr. A. Stephen Jeffreys, born in 1923, had obtained a first class B.A. at Bangor and a B.Litt on the philosophy of art from the University of Oxford, followed by appointments as tutor and academic secretary at Bangor, and later as deputy registrar at the University College of Swansea, where he had worked closely with John Fulton (later the first Vice-Chancellor of Sussex), during an important period of Swansea's development and expansion.

The Academic Registrar and Deputy Secretary, Mr. Michael Forster, born in 1931, obtained a first class degree in economics at The Queen's University of Belfast and was later awarded an M.A. for the work published in his monograph, "An Audit of Academic Performance". After working as personal research assistant and administrative assistant to Sir Eric Ashby, Mr. Forster became senior administrative assistant with the Association of Commonwealth Universities from 1958 to 1964.

The next important task for the Academic Planning Board, the preparation of the draft Charter and Statutes, was begun in the summer of 1962. The form of government adopted at Lancaster is discussed in Chapter 4, and need not detain us here. What should be realized, however, is the length of time which the drafting of such instruments of government takes. The Academic Planning Board approved a form of words and consulted the Executive Council about the draft. Officers of the local authorities and other bodies were consulted over certain matters relating to the Court, and because of the special relationship of Lancashire with the Crown, the advice and help of the Duchy of Lancaster's Office was also sought.[1.64] By June 1963 the time was approaching when the Executive Council would wish "to petition Her Majesty in Council for the grant of a Charter of Incorporation", and it was necessary

---

[1.63] For those who have a taste for such statistics, of the thirteen professors, ten were aged between forty and forty-six: most of them had given active service in the Second World War.

[1.64] In February 1964 Sir Robert Somerville, of the Duchy of Lancaster Office, wrote to Mr. McCall saying

I think you will like to know that the Duchy is going to endow a scholarship or studentship, preferably in history, which is to be known by The Queen's name. The Queen has directed that this endowment should come out of Duchy revenues and be associated with her position as Visitor.

to make out a case for material divergences from the Privy Council model in conjunction with the Parliamentary Agents;[1.65] although since the Lancaster draft had been copied in large part from the charter already granted to Sussex, it was hoped that such innovations as the subordination of the Court[1.66] to the other governing bodies and the binary division of responsibility between the Council and the Senate would not cause difficulties about acceptance of the structure proposed.

In October 1963 the draft Petition, Charter and Statutes, having been seen by the U.G.C. (who act as principal advisers to the Privy Council on such documents) were formally accepted by the Executive Council and the seal of the company attached. The Parliamentary Agents had raised one point with the chairman of the Executive Council, querying the phrase about there being "no test related to moral belief", but although such a clause had not previously been proposed to the Privy Council, no objection was raised to it. The one substantial amendment that the Executive Council requested should be made, at the insistence of Sir Alfred Bates, was to alter the membership of the Council so that the Court was enabled to appoint six members to it instead of the previously suggested number of three. The U.G.C. gave approval to such an increase early in November, and the printed document was lodged with the Privy Council. Then followed a highly technical debate about the position of the university in relation to the investment of trust funds between the Parliamentary Agents and the university's sponsors arising out of a suggested amendment by the Privy Council.[1.67] Meanwhile, Mr. Jeffreys was in correspondence with those who were either being invited to accept *ex officio* membership of the Court, or who were invited to make appointments to it.

When the Privy Council had agreed to the Charter and Statutes with the university's sponsors they were passed to the Law Officers of the Crown, and a certain amount of rewording in the section concerning removal from office took place. When this had been completed the Humble Petition,[1.68] Charter

---

[1.65] Parliamentary Agents (in Lancaster's case Sherwood & Co.) are specialist firms of lawyers who draft and present private Bills for Parliament, and incidentally advise on submissions to the Privy Council.

[1.66] There was even some discussion about whether the Court should be abolished altogether, but this was not pursued.

[1.67] The same problem arose at Essex, Warwick and Kent universities and in April 1964 the Privy Council Office explained to the Parliamentary Agents for Lancaster that the wording used in some earlier charters (including the recent one for East Anglia) had not been entirely clear, and that "I am to confirm that the new provision is not intended to be more restrictive than the powers granted in earlier cases and, therefore, there is no question of discrimination as between new universities".

[1.68] The Humble Petition rehearsed the steps that had been taken so far to set up the university and concluded:

Having regard to the circumstances mentioned herein your Petitioners humbly submit that the time has come for a University to be established in Lancaster.

YOUR PETITIONERS, therefore, most humbly pray that Your Majesty may

and Statutes were at last ready to lay before H.M. the Queen, who "was pleased at the Council held by her Majesty yesterday [27 July 1964] to approve the Grant of a Charter constituting and founding The University of Lancaster".[1.69] The Charter, however, did not come into effect until the Great Seal had been affixed to it and there was anxiety lest this should not be completed in time for the installation of the Chancellor, due to take place in November. At last the Letters Patent under the Great Seal, dated 14 September 1964, were received from the Home Office by the Parliamentary Agents, and thereafter the university had a legal and corporate identity.

Although Lancaster was the last of the new universities to be announced, it preceded both Kent and Warwick in its date of opening. Mr. Carter had been quoted in the *Daily Telegraph* as early as 5 December 1962 as having said that he did not expect Lancaster to take in its first students *before* October 1964. The feasibility of such a rapid opening depended not only on finding suitable staff but on being able to provide accommodation for them and the students. The Town Clerk of Lancaster, Mr. Waddell, entered into correspondence with the Ministry of Housing and Local Government in April 1963 about the possibility—since the Finance and Parliamentary Committee of the City Council had decided to purchase for £90,000 certain warehouse premises formerly occupied by Waring & Gillow Ltd., the City having in view its ultimate use for flatted factory development—[1.70] of a lease "of part of the accommodation which would be suitable for adaptation to meet the needs of the University until such time as permanent buildings are erected on the University site". At the beginning of July 1963 the Vice-Chancellor told the Executive Council that the possibilities were reduced to two only; either to lease and convert the Waring & Gillow property, which the County Architect recommended, or to erect temporary buildings (as was done at East Anglia) and retain them for fifteen years. The Vice-Chancellor reported that

> the County Architect's report had been sent informally to the University Grants Committee, who had indicated that provided a six-year lease of the premises with an option to renew was obtained, a capital grant of the order of £75,000 to cover the cost of the necessary adaptations would be forthcoming.

---

be graciously pleased in the exercise of Your Royal Prerogative to grant a Charter in terms of the draft herewith submitted or in such other terms as may to Your Majesty seem proper.

[1.69] Letter of 28 July 1964 from the Parliamentary Agents to Mr. McCall.

[1.70] Certain members of the City Council were critical of the decision not to reserve these buildings for immediate industrial use, but in fact the City stood to benefit by the lease in the long run because of the capital finance made available for the conversion.

The Executive Council therefore agreed that authority be given for the conversion. Time was of the essence, however, both to secure the Waring and Gillow premises so that work could begin there and to obtain additional loan sanction for the lease of Whinney Carr Farm. The Ministry of Housing and Local Government had declined to give any views on the loan sanction for the Waring and Gillow premises in advance of a formal application from the City. There was some anxiety that this would mean the Ministry would have objections when the formal application was submitted. To expedite the proceeding, therefore, Mr. McCall wrote to Dame Evelyn Sharp on 15 July 1963

> to make sure that you do know how firmly the County Council stand behind Lancaster Corporation, and indeed appreciate all they are doing, in their efforts to assist in the establishment of the new University in the City generally and in the effort which the University is making to get organised with staff and temporary accommodation with the object of accepting students from October 1964 onwards. You will appreciate that the County Council are themselves doing everything possible to encourage and support the University which makes them all the more ready to stand behind and, if necessary, to consider assisting Lancaster in relation to the financial commitments which the City will be taking on to help the University to get on its way. . . . We shall be most grateful for your special interest and help.

A formal application, along with the District Valuer's report, was submitted and on 12 September Sir David Walsh wrote to Mr. McCall about

> two purchases of property the City of Lancaster intend to make to help the new University—one concerned a furniture factory, and the other, land for a replacement farm.
> You will be glad to hear that loan sanction is being issued to the City Council for both these projects.

Although the loan sanction for the farm arrived at once, another six weeks elapsed before the City received it for the Waring & Gillow premises; the lease was then quickly signed[1.71] and work began on the site before Christmas, leaving nine months to complete the conversion and to furnish and equip the building.[1.72]

1.71 The rent was agreed at £7,800 p.a., the City being responsible for external and structural repairs.
1.72 Harold Armstrong, writing in the *Lancaster Guardian* in October 1964 described how

> As yet, however, there is only Gillow's old building, with its various floor levels that need "watch the steps" signs.
> Everything is bright and new, without being too bright; everything that can be

D

Additional accommodation was needed. At the beginning of October the City's Estates Committee was asked for approval to take in some further property in St. Leonardgate as well as a lease of 20 Castle Hill, a former stained glass factory, at a rent of £375 for nine months, which was to be used for the reception, unpacking and cataloguing of library books.[1.73] Approval had already been given in April by the Executive Council for estimates "amounting to £15,000 prepared by the Lancaster City Architect for the repair, adaptation and decoration of Bailrigg House". Finally, lodgings were needed for the students and the lodgings officer, Mr. Malcolm Ellacott, set to work to find the necessary places; amongst other techniques a public meeting was held in the College of Further Education in April 1964 at which the Vice-Chancellor spoke and "details of requirements and conditions of acceptance" were discussed.

It will be remembered that offers of financial help came into the nascent university at an early stage. At the time of the submission to the U.G.C. in May 1961 offers in principle of some £90,000 per annum for between seven and ten years had already been made, enabling the Promotion Council to declare, in their submission to the U.G.C., that

> We have recognized that Universities are invariably founded through the authorisation of their local sponsors notwithstanding the fact that by far the greatest part of the cost is met from Government funds. It is, nevertheless, appreciated that such enthusiasm may, to some extent, be measured in terms of local financial support and this is therefore a matter which we feel it right to mention in this submission.

After listing the "spontaneous offers" already received, the document went on:

> We regard this as a very encouraging beginning and a real indication of the scale and generosity of the local financial support which may confidently be expected. Apart from the County Council, the other local education authorities represented on the Promoting Council who do, of course, support the project, will be considering the extent to which they will contribute financially. In addition, we would anticipate a widespread appeal being made, at the appropriate stage, not only locally but to Lancastrians and other supporters from all over the country and perhaps wider afield.

Further serious consideration was next given to the Appeal in February 1963 when Sir Alfred Bates, Sir Frank Bower and the Vice-Chancellor Elect were

---

portable is made that way, so that when the time comes, it can be moved to the new premises. Even the laboratory benches have adjustable feet, so that the unevenness of the old floors can be allowed for.

[1.73] The City agreed to find the necessary £1,000 for the necessary structural repairs to this building. These premises now house the Portofino Restaurant.

constituted as a committee of the directors to deal with the appeal. Sir Frank was active in visiting other universities to obtain the benefit of their experience, and began to draft brochure material and plan the campaign. He was, however, living in Essex and therefore could not manage a campaign which was principally to be mounted in the north-west.

By the end of the summer of 1963 the Vice-Chancellor was actively engaged in obtaining promises of financial support in advance of the public appeal and on 28 October Lord Derby held a reception at Knowsley for the chairmen of some fifty leading commercial and industrial firms. Serious thought was by now being given to bringing in a firm of fund raising consultants, and in a report of March 1964 to the Executive Council the Vice-Chancellor reported that Colonel Shine of the firm of Hooker, Craigmyle and Company had been appointed as the Appeal Director from 2 March. Miss Jean Owtram joined him as an administrative assistant later in the year and an office was established in Bailrigg Lodge. Lord Derby agreed to become President of the Appeal and he, the Vice-Chancellor and Colonel Shine decided on the strategy, which was to work by territorial groupings, covering Lancashire and areas to the north (twenty-seven in all, ranging from the very localized—Nelson and Colne, or Morecambe and Lonsdale, to the very wide—Cumberland or Westmorland). Each region was to have a chairman, who would be responsible for recruiting stewards. By June 1964 a short list of possible chairmen had been submitted to Lord Derby who, when he had made his selection, invited them to attend a reception at Knowsley in September: this was followed a couple of months later by a reception at St. Leonard's House which included all the stewards. There everyone was addressed by the Vice-Chancellor, met staff and students, and were shown the development plan and the St. Leonard's House conversion. Two days later, on 23 November, the appeal was publicly launched at a press conference at the Midland Hotel, Manchester, when it was announced that £1 million was already in sight: such a statement was made possible because in October Mr. McCall had made a definite announcement about the gift of County College.[1.74] Ten thousand copies of a brochure were printed, asking for a total of £2 million[1.75] because

> The establishment of a new university in the North involves special responsibilities and special difficulties. Wealth flows more easily to the Midlands and the South; proximity to London confers special advantages; the South carries less weight of obsolete buildings and industrial devastation, and has for long attracted a favoured share of cultural and educational facilities. We think it to be part of our function to alter the balance.

[1.74] See Chapter 2, page 75.
[1.75] Raised in November to a target of £2½ million.

Special emphasis was laid on aid to the building programme for 1964 to 1974, and in particular for colleges, a central hall and the first stage of the recreational facilities, as well as a theatre and a centre for music and the arts. Progress in the different regions was very uneven, but by the time the third subscription list was compiled in August 1965, £1,910,747 had been received or promised,[1.76] with expenses over the period 1 March 1964 to 31 August

Type of subscriber	Number of type	Percentage of total	Average sum
Industry and commerce	430	61·6%	£1,612
Local authorities	56	19·0%	£3,788
Trusts and associations	46	12·2%	£2,954
Individuals and Partnerships	168	7·2%	£ 490

Colonel Shine withdrew at the end of August 1965 and Miss Owtram continued as Appeal Secretary until August 1966.

1965 amounting to £14,437. Three events had provided useful, if somewhat unconventional publicity: the first was the Lancastrian Ball at Hoghton Tower in April 1965, organized by the chairmen and committee of the Chorley region; the next was the Drury Lane Spectacular on 30 May 1965, organized in London by a committee under Lord Derby to commemorate Jack Hylton,[1.77] and the third was the university stand at the Royal Lancashire Agricultural Society Show at Blackpool in July 1965. By January 1966 the first £2,000,000 had been received and thereafter the amounts received slowed down: by February 1969 the amount totalled a handsome £2,352,700.

At last all the preparations were complete: the students who had accepted the first places at Lancaster could be taught, accommodated and fed. There was a library, a bookshop, and common rooms, all in the centre of Lancaster while, three miles away, the site at Bailrigg was about to be developed. A report by the Vice-Chancellor to the Executive Council of 27 October 1964, summarizing progress made in the period of just under two years since he had first met the Executive Council concluded by saying that this was

> no more than an abbreviated and formal record of a great number of events, decisions and plans. It needs to have added to it the human content of gratitude to the Executive Council, and especially to its officers,

---

[1.76] A breakdown of the first seven hundred subscriptions credited to the Appeal shows the following:

[1.77] Jack Hylton, a Lancashire man and a leading impresario, died in January 1965 and his friends in show business decided to create a permanent memorial to him by the donation of £50,000, raised mainly by the spectacular which was introduced by Sir Malcolm Sargent and televised live under the title "The Stars Shine for Jack".

for helping us in so many ways. We have not had time to consult the Council about all the decisions which lie in its area of authority, and we have greatly appreciated your willingness to give wise advice, to administer the occasional check, without fussing about detail. You have left to your Vice-Chancellor in particular an astonishing degree of discretion. Perhaps a more sedate and correct procedure would have avoided errors; but unfortunately it would also have deprived 330 young people of the chance to enter the University in 1964.

The students to which he referred came up to Lancaster on 6 October; the *Morecambe Visitor* described it as a "momentous day for us all" and assured them "that Lancaster is proud to have them. They are very welcome". Three days later H.R.H. Princess Alexandra attended a special service at the Priory in Lancaster at which Dr. Donald Coggan, Archbishop of York, gave an address, while the act of dedication was led by the Bishop of Blackburn, Dr. Charles Claxton.

Walking beside the Vice-Chancellor in the procession entering the Priory was Dr. Hugh Pollard, principal of S. Martin's College, which was dedicated and blessed by the Archbishop of York later the same day. The coming of this new college of education, which opened its doors at the same time as the university, had to a certain extent been contingent on there being a university at Lancaster.[1.78]

After the Education Act of 1902 the country was divided into local education areas which set up their own teacher training colleges and no new church colleges were founded. In the late 1950's, however, the Ministry of Education had decided to embark on an expansion programme and offered a 75 per cent grant: the Church of England responded by deciding to build a new college at Canterbury, and then began to think of establishing a second one, in an area without an existing church college, close to a university, with an adequate supply of schools for teaching practice (especially church schools) and with a welcoming local authority. Lancaster seemed to meet all the requirements and the Bishop of Blackburn, already a member of the Executive Council, was very enthusiastic about the idea. The proposal ran into opposition in the Church Assembly when large education estimates were presented. However, it was eventually let through on a small majority, and the Church undertook to pay £150,000 which, with £25,000 donated by the city of Lancaster, covered the required 25 per cent of the £700,000 which was the estimate in 1962–3. In actual fact costs escalated to £1,200,000, making a shortfall from the Church of £125,000. The Principal displayed his very considerable gifts of coaxing donations from various benefactors: William

---

[1.78] See Graham Brown, "S. Martin's College" in University of Lancaster *Regional Bulletin*, Vol. 2, No. 7 (Summer, 1973), pages 4 to 5.

Thompson of Burnley, for example, gave £50,000 towards the men's residences, and his sister, Sarah Witham Thompson, £15,000 towards residences for women students. Other donations were received to a total of £135,000, and the balance was lent to the College by the Church.

At first Dr. Pollard and his staff were accommodated in the Town Hall—he in the Mayor's dressing-room and some other members of his staff under the stage of the Ashton Hall. By September 1964 they were able to move, in company with the first eighty-eight students, to their permanent and very central and striking site of thirty-four acres in Lancaster itself, at Bowerham Barracks, the former depot of the King's Own Royal Regiment, which had been closed in 1959. The building programme, which was partially a conversion of the existing stone buildings, was designed for a college of 450 students, but the Department of Education and Science steadily increased the target figure, and only in 1969 was it fixed at a final figure of 730 students. Not only was S. Martin's to become an associated college of the university in 1967 but its close geographical proximity to the university and the fact that both institutions were new at the same time has inevitably meant that they had a good deal in common, which has led to a considerable degree of interaction (not least because so many of the university's graduates have taken their one-year graduate diploma at S. Martin's).

The university was not to lack in outward trappings of a university. A memorial was sent to the Earl Marshal in the autumn of 1964, supplicating for a Grant of Arms, and the Vice-Chancellor was able to tell the Executive Council, in his report of October 1964, that the design of Arms by Lancaster Herald was approaching finality.[1.79] Equally the students were able to appear at the Priory service in their new undergraduate gowns made up in the university colours of light Quaker grey with a Lancaster red yoke.[1.80] Already the university had a motto—*Patet omnibus veritas* (Truth lies open to all)[1.81] —which had been thought of by Professor William Murray as the Shadow

---

[1.79] The arms were finally granted in October 1966. Mr. Robert Boumphrey, the university's first finance officer, had worked with Lancaster Herald on the arms for over two years: see Appendix (iv) for a description and explanation of them.

[1.80] The Robemakers to the university are J. Whippell and Company of Exeter. A pamphlet, published in 1966, gives details of the academic dress for the masters' and doctors' degrees of the university. For the Chancellor, Pro-Chancellor and Deputy Pro-Chancellors, and the Vice-Chancellor and Secretary, special robes were made up from a hand woven silk brocade, with the red rose of Lancaster woven into the design, and ornamented with gold oak leaf lace.

[1.81] The words are from Seneca's *Epistolae Morales*, and were quoted by the seventeenth-century medical writer Theodor Turquet de Mayerne in his *Famose Apologia*.

In 1967, Mr. John Creed composed a short, neutral Latin grace which was accepted by the Senate for use on formal occasions:

"Gratias iis agamus quorum opera ac labore haec bona sunt suppeditata" (Let us give thanks to those by whose agency and work these good things have been supplied). To her regret the writer has never heard it used on any university occasion.

Senate at its meeting of May 1964 sat considering the various suggestions which had so far been made.

One important event, however, took place well into the term, and that was the installation of H.R.H. Princess Alexandra as first Chancellor of the university. A special congregation for this purpose was held in the Ashton Hall on the morning of 18 November 1964. The previous afternoon the Chancellor had made a tour of the Bailrigg site, suitably equipped with gumboots and headscarf, and in the evening had attended a dinner party given by the Vice-Chancellor at the Town Hall. The following morning a long procession could have been seen making its way from St. Leonard's House to the Town Hall; first the students in their red and grey, and then the university's senior staff, together with visiting principals of colleges of advanced technology and university colleges, vice-chancellors and representatives of other universities, and local civic dignitaries. The Vice-Chancellor opened the congregation and called upon the University Secretary "to read those sections of the Royal Charter which relate to the establishment of the University and the appointment of the Chancellor". The Pro-Chancellor then requested the Vice-Chancellor and the University Secretary "to wait upon Her Royal Highness the Chancellor and to invite her to enter the Congregation". The Chancellor's procession entered the hall, the Vice-Chancellor welcomed her and, after she had made a "declaration to maintain and uphold the privileges and rights of the University", installed her. The Chancellor in her turn conferred honorary degrees on Mr. Harold Wilson (who had just become Prime Minister, though he had been invited before this event), Sir Noel Hall, Sir Alfred Bates, County Alderman Mrs. Fletcher,[1.82] and Field Marshal Lord Slim. After visiting St. Leonard's House and meeting some of the students, the Chancellor then attended a special lunch, to which more than five hundred guests were invited, at the Winter Gardens, Morecambe.

The Chancellor has visited the university on many occasions since 1964, sometimes for formal degree ceremonies and at other times for more informal gatherings, such as the Garden Party held at Bailrigg House in June 1965 when all the students' landladies were invited to be present, or for a blend of the two, as when she came up to confer degrees and at the same time opened the new Assistant Staff House. The university has cause to be deeply grateful to her for the charm and grace with which she has illuminated every visit she has paid to the university, giving lasting pleasure to students, their families and the local townspeople.

[1.82] Mrs. Fletcher had been chairman of the Lancashire Education Committee when the question of submitting the case for a university was first mooted, and had served on the Executive Committee of the Promotion Council and on the Executive Council. She was also well known for her interest in the proper care of young children. She died on New Year's Day, 1966.

What we should look at in conclusion, perhaps, is the people for whom all this effort was expended—the students. The writer, in early 1972, sent out questionnaires to all those admitted in 1964 and 1965[1.83] asking them various questions about their expectations and how they were realized in practice. It is difficult to do justice to their replies, which deserve to be quoted at length. For present purposes, however, we must restrict ourselves to looking at a small selection of the comments.

The first two questions were concerned with the students' reasons for coming to Lancaster and in enquiring (particularly with regard to 1964, when the university was not using the U.C.C.A. scheme), how they had come to hear of its existence. Of the respondents, 16 in 1964 came as the only place offered, while only 11 of the larger 1965 group of replies gave that as their reply. On the other hand, 50 of the 1965 group came because of Lancaster's course structure, as against 16 in 1964, suggesting perhaps, that word got around about what Lancaster had to offer. 29 in 1964 and 47 in 1965 came because of the challenge and feel of adventure about a new university, and 19 in 1964 and 41 in 1965 mentioned the liberal entrance requirements, such as omitting the kind of language or mathematics prerequisite customary elsewhere. A small number each year came either because it was near home and they had prior knowledge of the area—or, alternatively, because Lancaster was far away from home and they liked the sound of it. One or two replies mentioned pleasant introductory letters and helpful and interesting interviews. In both years a significant proportion had heard of Lancaster through their school-teachers or headmasters and mistresses, some through friends and family, others by means of the university prospectus, and others through articles in newspapers (of which a Sunday colour supplement was particularly remembered). By 1965 the largest number were, naturally enough, coming through U.C.C.A., but such comments as a student having heard of its being planned since he was fifteen, or another student's father having been involved in some capacity in its establishment, or that it was "impossible to open a newspaper without reading of *some* new university at that time", also appear.

Later questions were concerned with what students were expecting to find in a new university in the way "of experiments, academic and social and other innovations", and how these expectations were either realized, or disappointed. While one can sympathize with the respondent, who said that "I knew nothing about universities, new or old, so would not have recognized

---

[1.83] 274 questionnaires were sent to students who entered in 1964, of which 53 were returned completed; and 422 to those who entered in 1965, to which there were 89 completed replies. I have omitted quotations from responses about topics current in 1972, and also the (few) replies which were an expression of general disillusionment with universities. Responses received did not show marked tendencies towards particular types of reply from students reading for a particular degree.

an innovation if it had hit me in the face!", it is nevertheless interesting to discover how many were hoping for quite tangible benefits to come from being at a new university. Course structure was expected to be more flexible and individual courses more interesting and, in 1965, there is also some evidence that people anticipated attempted integration of arts and science subjects. Better staff-student ratios and relationships were frequently mentioned, as characterized by the reply: "A better personal relationship with staff. I liked the idea of being a 'guinea pig' with regard to courses etc. I felt one's opinions and experiences would be listened to by staff". More intangibly, several in 1964 and a large number (41) in 1965 looked for a small, friendly university and a more informal atmosphere and a few in 1965 even spoke of "A less formal, class-ridden atmosphere than that encountered at Oxbridge". Others felt there would be good opportunities (rather than excellent facilities) for creating social life, and a few hoped for greater freedom, while a handful in 1964 mentioned the creation of links with Lancaster. A small number from each year mentioned examination methods, and the Lancaster emphasis on continuous assessment. Some reported reactions to Lancaster were based on detailed comments about the context or teaching methods of certain courses, while others are essentially a record of the normal adjustment from school to university ("it did come as a shock to find myself making personal decisions about small points, i.e. whether to go to such-and-such a lecture or what time to go home at night"), while there can also be detected a certain dissillusionment about other students; "I think I had an image of the average University student as a more witty, cultured individual". Nevertheless over twenty from each year commented on the good staff-student ratio or staff-student relationship, ("in particular relations with staff seemed considerably better than those experienced by my contemporaries in Redbrick universities"). 26 in 1964 and 46 in 1965 found courses wider, more interesting and more flexible, and 14 in 1964 and 11 in 1965 enjoyed the prevailing atmosphere of starting a new venture together; 14 in 1965 also commented on the sense of belonging to a small, close-knit community. There was a much smaller response, and a mixed reaction, to the distant minor and teaching methods, and fairly consistent disagreement with the custom of wearing gowns "which incidentally was dropped because of its incongruity with the surroundings". A large number each year noticed how easy it had been to make friends, although inevitably, perhaps, answers such as "Socially, the first year was to me a failure. Dances in the J.C.R. followed a dull pattern and if you were going out with somebody, entertainment in Lancaster was nearly zero" were in conflict with those who made statements like: "I was never bored for a minute in the whole of the three years and made more and better friends than I ever had made previously, most of whom I am still in contact with" (the same person also noting "I had not expected it to rain absolutely non-stop for my first three weeks at university"). Many of the first year's students appear to have had a sense of spacious freedom, shown in replies like the following:

> The fact that *everything* had to be done oneself in the way of social and recreational facilities gave the place a tremendous unity of purpose among the personnel. It was nothing like one's conventional ideas of what a University was like—it was small, in most unlikely premises; exceptionally unified and full of very "untypical students",

or this:

> One had a completely free hand in designing entertainment and forming groups with similar interests. University staff were more than helpful in this respect.

The fact of the university being in temporary accommodation at first meant that there was a big discontinuity for staff and students in 1966 when many departments moved up to Bailrigg, leaving the natural sciences at St. Leonard-gate. Another item on the questionnaire invited students to react to this change. There can be no doubt that the move was deeply felt. Figures for the 1964 students (proportionally similar to those for 1965) show that only 4 noticed no change ("we simply returned to our old Lancaster haunts each evening") and 3 a slight one, while 9 did not move. All the rest were affected by the change, the reasons given including a dislike of the new buildings (3 mentions), pleasure in having new facilities (12), loss of pioneer spirit (4), and loss of contact with the town and people in it—some being glad about this but a majority seeing it as a privation (19). Other disadvantages perceived were the split of arts and science students (6 mentions), and the frustration of an increase in distance from flats and digs (5), and an atmosphere variously described as more remote, or impersonal, or intro-verted (28). Some of those left behind felt "a complete break-up of team spirit, I suppose you would call it. We who were left at Waring and Gillow sometimes feeling completely out of it"; or "Never went there. Environ-mental Sciences still at Lancaster. Felt lost at Bailrigg. Hundreds of people, I didn't know in a rather synthetic environment." The sense of loss was strong, for the removal from "the church etc. and the cramped facilities led to a loss of atmosphere, less communication between students and I think less between staff and students. The pioneer spirit was lost, and the University was taken away from Lancaster where we used to mix considerably, in the shops and pubs, with the local community", or again "No more essay writ-ing on damp beer mats in the 'Shake'. The first and second year intakes hated University expansion and hence their consequent decline in status/ power".

Or this:

> At St. Leonard's House there had existed a close knit friendly community,
> at Bailrigg the atmosphere was not at all friendly and it was very cliquish.
> This was probably because at St. Leonards, the close proximity of teaching
> departments promoted intermingling. However, at night, since there were
> no residences everybody went their separate ways, and so were able to
> leave the University environment. People had to work for their organiza-
> tions and entertainment. At Bailrigg, however, the teaching departments
> are separated preventing intermingling of discipline. Study rooms and
> residences encourage aimless timewasting and talking. Often people only
> emerge from these to work. People see each other too often, so nodding
> acquaintances do not develop, instead a sort of nodding exhaustion sets in.

The loss of the 1964 students in 1967 was regretted: one reply spoke of
their departure as having "left a huge vacuum of personality", while another
felt they "were characters and when they left their place was hard to fill".
But, although several commented on Bailrigg in the same terms as the one
who spoke of "the oppressive newness of good taste", there were others who
recalled that students had "disliked St. Leonard's House because it was
congested and extremely stuffy, particularly in the library. Not very satisfactory for working in—almost like a liberation when the University moved
to Bailrigg".

The final question invited respondents to make any further comments
about their time at Lancaster that they felt to be of interest. Digs in
Morecambe inevitably came in for criticism—they are mentioned as grim and
lonely, of landladies having, in this first year, little idea "of what was needed
to help us study", or "one bath a week on a Saturday afternoon and if you
missed that you waited until the next week. No fire in the bedroom—'The
fire risk was too great'. Nappies drying in the sitting room where we were
supposed to study!" while others speak of being "readily accepted by the
people of Lancaster and Morecambe", or of the first students being "welcomed by the town. There was no difficulty in finding flats etc. During my
three years we kept this happy atmosphere. Many of us formed friendships
with 'locals'—I feel I have become one", of finding a good place and remaining "friendly with my former landlady ever since".

Nor were the positive feelings towards Lancaster confined only to those
who made a great success of their time at Lancaster, as can be seen from this
comment which comes from a student who left at the end of his first year:

> Two points: after the initial shock of finding that Lancaster was just a
> mill-town with a castle (I had expected something like York!), I found the
> town and its inhabitants charming. Secondly, I made such a large number
> of friends—inevitably in such a small community—and spent so much time

with them that I neglected my studies to an appalling extent. It was a year which I wasted dreadfully, but one which I shall always remember with nostalgia.

One student had come up at Easter when a series of one-day talks were being given to would-be entrants at the Storey Institute and the university was merely a shell:

> I didn't think it would be ready for the following October. In fact the building had suffered a couple of fires around that time. The story was that a blow-torch had set alight inflammable glue, left in the fabric of the building, that had been used for sticking together gliders during the war—how much truth there was in that we never found out. By the time we arrived in October the building was amazingly ready, though without a lecture theatre—we used the Grand Theatre for the first year—dismally lit as I recall, hardly inspiring. We also used the church at the bottom of St. Leonardgate, though this may have been in the second year. There were no science graduates in the first year. I think the 300 of us knew one another pretty well by the end of the year, during which time most of the clubs and societies were started, plus the Beat Group (Flowerpot Men) who used to play at the numerous dances at the Alexandra Hotel. We were almost all living in Morecambe at the time, packing the buses from Euston Road every day. I suppose it was quite a few weeks before we got to looking very much at Lancaster City, though quite a number preferred the attractions of the Windmill Cafe in China Street, the Coop, and other eating places to the refectory. It was even longer, except for a guided tour by Prof. Manley shortly after we arrived, before we started to travel around the surrounding countryside.

Wild stories also circulated about the Bailrigg site, "for instance that a bulldozer was built into one of the new buildings at Bailrigg by mistake, with the result that a wall had to be knocked out to get the machine out", and affection was felt for other temporary accommodation, "When we had lectures sitting in pews in the old church".[1.84]

One theme stands out particularly—the high level of involvement of all students in the first year or so, for regarding

> Student politics and social activity: The first S.R.C.—when no one knew anyone else—were disastrous. The second elections—when everyone knew everyone else—produced an S.R.C. in the second year that probably hasn't been rivalled since. In a small community half the students would

---

[1.84] The Congregational Centenary Church.

attend debates, 70–80 per cent attend J.C.R. meetings—100 societies[1.85] were maintained by 300 students, (and) two newspapers. Small integrated communities clearly work best—are more secure, more satisfying.

Another reply makes similar points:

> The "newness" of Lancaster showed itself in the proliferation of societies. It became a joke that anyone could form a society for the furtherance of anything they wished. I remember belonging to a Marxist society, and a joke being made among the teachers that not one of us knew what Marx had said. It was true. The newspaper, *Carolynne*, was called after the girlfriend of the boy who started it. It seemed rather ridiculous that there was Carolynne in our midst, and there was a real printed magazine which bore her name. Because everything was coming from us, and because we all knew each other so well the things we did and made seemed rather funny and not important.

Or this:

> We were new to Morecambe, to the town, to the freedoms of being at a University and in addition we had a curious and quite unexpected importance in the eyes of the University itself. As students we were all very young. There were an extraordinary number of engagements between students which aroused curiosity amongst the staff. . . . We loved the town. It was pretty, the fish and chips were good, and it was delightful to walk around and meet friends everywhere. We enjoyed the countryside too. After this one ebullient year, I went on to Bedford College and realized from the contrast between it and Lancaster how unique the year at Lancaster was. At Lancaster the impression which remains is of someone saying "You don't like it? Then we'll change it", though I know I exaggerate.

Someone else mentioned having been joint editor of

> John O'Gauntlet, Chairman of Art Society, Swimming Club, Secretary of Socialist Union etc. I started these—how many other nineteen year olds had these opportunities?,

while yet another was grateful for having been able to work on a student newspaper, since he was sure he would not have had the self-confidence to push himself "into such positions in a larger place. I acquired a degree of maturity at Lancaster which I probably wouldn't have acquired elsewhere". The first students were special in another way, for they constituted the

---

[1.85] Another reply mentioned fifty societies; the actual figure, as far as the writer can determine, seems to have stabilized at thirty-eight. The current student guide lists forty-eight.

senior year for the whole of their time as undergraduates. One reply described this experience:

> First year students like myself stayed younger longer as we were "oldest" all the way through. When we were third years then the second year were more sophisticated in many respects than we were, i.e. we loved our gowns and they abolished them.

Returning for the first time in five years as a school-teacher with a pupil himself intending to go to university, a first-generation Lancaster graduate remarked:

> I was lost of course. When I graduated, only Bowland, Lonsdale and Admin. were up. Alexandra Square was only a pit. I was very impressed— as was my pupil, and hope to return to some kind of reunion gathering some day. We will be strangers on our own Campus now but I still felt as if I were part of it. Being a "first student" was something I would not have missed.

CHAPTER 2

The Building Programme

Letter by Jefferson to Littleton Tazewell dated 5 January 1805:

> The greatest danger for new colleges will be their overbuilding, by attempting a large house in the beginning, sufficient to contain the whole institution. Large houses are always ugly, inconvenient, exposed to accident of fire, and bad in cases of infection. A plain small house for the school and lodging of each professor is best, these connected by covered ways out of which the rooms of students should open. These may then be built only as they shall be wanting. In fact an university should not be an house but a village.
>
> The whole of these arranged around an open square of grass and trees would make it, what it should be in fact, an academical village.

★   ★   ★   ★   ★

By the end of the academic year 1973–4, the university will have a stock of buildings constructed at a cost of some £12 million, put up over a period of ten years. In addition to these the university leased and converted various properties in the city of Lancaster, to meet the requirements of the university from 1964 to 1966 and, for some departments, as late as 1971. The main building so converted was the previous Waring and Gillow furniture factory (which during the Second World War had been used for making parts of gliders). It was named St. Leonard's House, after the part of the city, St. Leonardgate, in which it is situated, but in fact is three linked, stone-faced buildings with a frontage of some 360 feet and a floor area of about 69,000 sq. ft. A local architect, Mr. C. E. Pearson, was employed for the conversion of this building, as well as a local builder, William Eaves of Blackpool. The Executive Council had decided in July 1963 that temporary accommodation should be created in this building and by the following February all the necessary architectural and consultant work and the internal demolition were finished.

The basement and part of the first floor were used as a library, with a stack and shelving for 70,000 books, staff rooms, and work and reading rooms to seat about two hundred people. The rest of the ground floor and part of the second provided rooms for teaching and administration. The second and third floors were made into teaching and research laboratories for science subjects and above that were more arts teaching and research areas. A common room for the students and a refectory and adjoining kitchen capable of feeding two hundred people were also accommodated.

For the year 1965-6 the university required more accommodation, as its rate of expansion was somewhat faster than had at first been expected. In addition to St. Leonard's House, therefore, three houses, numbers 108, 112 and 114 St. Leonardgate, were leased from the city; as well as Centenary House (the former Centenary Congregational Church with its associated halls and rooms); Skein House in Queen Square; and a room for quiet study in Great John Street. At Bailrigg the mansion was converted for use as the administrative headquarters and temporary Vice-Chancellor's residence[2.1] and Bailrigg Lodge which stood at the entrance to the university from the A.6 became the headquarters for the University Appeal. There was also, by the second year of the university's existence, a Biology Field Station, which still stands.

By leasing and renting these properties the university avoided the need to put up temporary premises, and it was therefore possible to begin planning, the permanent buildings at Bailrigg. The whole programme was coordinated by the University Secretary, together with the Building Development Office. The head of this office is Mr. Donald Smith, who began his career with his father (who was a builder) and after war service qualified and practised as an architect. His assistants are Mr. Wilfred Chadwick, who had experience as a quantity surveyor before coming to Lancaster and who has particular responsibility for negotiations with the U.G.C. and the statistical and financial aspects of the programme; and Mr. William Harwood, also an architect by training, who deals mainly with the physical aspects of development. Mr. James Cansfield, the Engineer and Maintenance Officer, has also played a large part in the design and supervision of the installation of site and building services, as well as the operation and maintenance of these services; he is

---

[2.1] Bailrigg House was subsequently re-converted as the Medical Centre, while a property in the city (Emmanuel House) was purchased for the Vice-Chancellor's residence.

St. Leonard's House, St. Leonardgate

By courtesy of the Lancaster Guardian

Bailrigg Mansion before 1961

By courtesy of the Lancaster Guardian

Building work in progress, 1967

By courtesy of The Visitor

The underpass and Bowland College at an early stage of construction

Anthony Price

assisted by Mr. J. A. Corless (for the mechanical services) and Mr. A. S. Hartland (on the electrical side), besides a team of three qualified engineers.

The new universities of the 1960's were all developed in a similar manner, usefully documented in Tony Birks' *Building the New Universities*[2.2] and, in common with the others, Lancaster employed a site development architect. The site chosen for the new University of Lancaster was a parcel of farm land called Bigforth, two hundred acres in extent.[2.3] Later the university purchased at auction a further hundred and fifty acres at Hazlerigg Farm, on the western side of the M.6 motorway,[2.4] and in 1967 the U.G.C. made a capital grant to facilitate the private purchase of a further ninety acres at Barker's Farm, to the immediate south of Bigforth. The university therefore possesses a total holding of slightly over four hundred and forty acres. A fairly level plateau of about seventy-three acres is being developed as the building area, twenty-five are used as playing fields and another hundred and forty for general recreation, while two hundred are leased out to tenant farmers.[2.5]

The area is a medley of spinneys, copses, small patches of water, and grassland used mainly for small-scale dairy farming, with a number of the stone farmhouses and adjacent shippons characteristic of North Lancashire and the Lake District. The site of the university—universally known as Bailrigg in spite of being separate from the hamlet of that name—is bounded to the west by the trunk road (the A.6) from Preston to Lancaster and the main London–Glasgow railway line, and to the east by the M.6 motorway; and is part of a flat coastal strip lying between the Lune estuary and the foothills of the Pennines. The western part of the site is low-lying and traversed by a stream, and the contours then rise steeply to a flat plateau on the eastern side, bounded by the edge of the cutting for the M.6 motorway. It is on this plateau that the university buildings are situated. To the south-east is the River Conder, which has been extremely valuable for draining a site that is liable to be seriously water-logged due to underlying impermeable clay. The prevailing wind is from the south-south-west, and for this reason the development was planned on a north-south axis.

A list of architects was considered by the Executive Council as early as April 1963, when a number of suitable names were submitted to the Ministry of Education. A letter from the Ministry dated 16 April 1963 enclosed comments about particular architects and noted that

[2.2] David & Charles, 1972, with photographs by Michael Holford. See especially chapters 1 to 6, and 13.
[2.3] See chapter 1, pages 12 to 21 for an account of the purchase of this land and the donation of its leasehold to the new university.
[2.4] Purchased for £36,400 on 4 May 1965.
[2.5] See University of Lancaster Accounts, 1972–3 for usage figures and other general statistics.

E

In planning a development of the type and magnitude of Lancaster University you will be considering not only the facilities required for 3,000 students but also the provision to be made inside and outside the University for the academic and other staff and their families and for the community amenities which they will share with the general public. Indeed, this inevitably develops into something akin to a town-planning operation, which makes it very advisable to begin by drawing up a plan for a phased development over a number of years. This is best done by appointing a firm of architects with the necessary breadth of vision who can consider, in close consultation with the University authorities, the broad picture of development. The appointment of architects for individual buildings in the phased plan comes later: often more than one firm of architects may then be involved.

In compiling the notes we have mainly had in mind the choice of an architect for a strategic plan. The architects of the University Grants Committee have had a good deal of experience of this kind of development and I suggest that you consult them before long.

On 17 and 18 June the short-listed architects were interviewed by Lord Derby, Sir Alfred Bates, the Vice-Chancellor and Sir Frank Bower, on behalf of the Executive Council, at Lord Derby's London offices, who "decided unanimously to recommend the appointment of Messrs. Bridgwater, Shepheard and Epstein[2.6] of London".

Mr. Gabriel Epstein had previously seen the site with Mr. Peter Shepheard. Some of his previous experience had been concerned with the design of teacher training colleges and universities and he was keenly interested in organization and growth patterns, particularly as they affected the inter-relationships of people in an urban or institutional setting. He and Mr. Shepheard duly appeared at the appointed hour in Lord Derby's Sloane Street office, and were asked whether they had yet formed any ideas about how to develop the site. Mr. Shepheard was about to give a polite demurral when Mr. Epstein asked for a sheet of paper. There and then he sketched out a diagram of a long pedestrian spine with buildings on either side, and perimeter roads, parallel to the central spine, on the outside of the building area with smaller roads at right angles to them leading into cul-de-sacs whence people could reach the central spine on foot. These and other fundamental principles of the final design he was able to show in outline form on the spot, demonstrating that he had a definite scheme in mind; and, as an incidental benefit, being accepted in association with this particular design, thus saving months of discussion afterwards which might have been spent on debating

---

[2.6] Later changed to "Messrs. Shepheard and Epstein".

and discarding various alternatives. As it was, the sketch on the single piece of paper grew into the buildings as they can now be seen on the ground.

On 2 July 1963 the Executive Council issued a press release announcing the appointment of Messrs. Bridgwater, Shepheard and Epstein as consultant architects and a letter to Mr. Shepheard from the Vice-Chancellor of the same date noted that

> While we would hope that you would also accept a later commission to design individual buildings, or to act in a consultant capacity to co-ordinate the designs of other architects with the general plan, there would be no commitment either on your side or on ours to proceed to these further steps. At this stage it is the outline development plan alone which is the subject of our commission.

Planning started at once, with an aerial survey and exploratory boreholes. Very quickly several possibilities were discarded. For example, the architects were asked at the interview whether they would wish to use stone, the predominant material in the Lancaster area, as their main building material. The idea was considered, and discussed with the county architect, but rejected, principally on grounds of expense, even for an outer cladding.

One possibility was that the buildings be positioned Capri style, in steps up the contours of the hill, with under-crofts to the buildings for use as basements or storage space. At an early stage Mr. Epstein came up to look at the site in the most unfavourable conditions, in the rain and wind of a cold autumn day. Walking around the site, he discarded the low lying area to the west as the "rheumatism belt", as it is windswept and boggy. Further up the hill the wind was broken by the ring of woods encircling the plateau. Up there was the natural defensive position, the view was excellent and the drainage much better. He therefore abandoned any idea of building up the line of the slope, which would in any case have been more expensive; furthermore, series of terraces and steps would segregate people too much and prevent their easy and unforced communication with each other. If, as Mr. Epstein imagined, pairs of people were strolling about, deep in conversation, any barrier which caused them to break their step would be deleterious to easy discourse.[2.7]

But there was an even more compelling reason in Mr. Epstein's mind for wishing to use the flatter platform to the east, and that was the inter-relationships that he was hoping to create, both between the different

---

[2.7] Some steps, at one side of Alexandra Square, and in the south spine, were necessary because of the contours of the site. When flights of stairs have been made thus necessary, however, they have been designed to be as wide as possible, and are half the height of a single storey. At a later stage consideration was given to the needs of handicapped students and some provision has been made for them.

buildings, and between them and the people moving between them. For the past century, he feels, towns and smaller settlements have suffered from a fragmentation which, amongst other things, has had the effect of removing large numbers of people from the central areas in the old towns which had been the focus of the community, and which included the church, the town hall, or the shops. He believes that the degeneration and anaemia of present town life are not simply a function of its size but because people feel themselves to be physically remote from the centre. Human beings experience this feeling of being cut off from the centre of activity and decision when they have to use a vehicle to reach that centre rather than go on foot. Therefore Mr. Epstein has attempted to evolve patterns of town organization that are arranged so that everyone living in the town is near the centre and can reach it on foot, and, having arrived, can use the centre to stroll or eat, read or shop, meet friends or push prams around. This centre, in Mr. Epstein's philosophy, should be exclusively for pedestrians and should be reasonably comfortable in terms of protection from the elements. The scale should always be human, and there should be a constant interplay between what is happening in the buildings and events outside. In terms of Bailrigg, therefore, Alexandra Square, at the geographical centre of the university, was intended also to be the focal point of life in the university, with people moving to and fro or sitting outside. This flurry of activity was then to be continued along the two halves of the spine, as people walked into snack bars, or looked in at exhibition cases, or used a launderette or a billiard table. There was to be careful landscaping, to soften the concrete and brick, and every now and again the spine, as it grew longer, would open out into squares lined with trees and provided with chairs for people to sit and talk. The site was windy, and he therefore wished to make it sheltered and compact to protect the people walking about inside it. Since the main traffic was to be of pedestrians moving about then the walk must be pleasant and not aggravating, and protected against the rain; consequently there should be covered walkways all round the university. At night the whole site was to be well illuminated, so that the bustle and business could be continued into the evening hours.

Meanwhile the loop perimeter road was designed to bring the traffic as closely as possible to where the driver needed to be. He could bring his vehicle into one of the cul-de-sacs leading off the loop road and leave it in one of the car parks which were to line each side. He could then penetrate through to the spine by means of one of the small ginnels connecting car park and pedestrian areas—unless, as would often happen, he was in any case entering one of the buildings adjoining the car parks. In this way drivers would have a minimum of walking, there would not be sprawling, unsightly car parks scattered around the site and, since U.G.C. money for car parks is invariably scanty, the small amount available could be used for the spaces on which the cars actually stood, since their turning area would be part of the access roads. The one exception to all traffic being diverted around the outside edge of the building area would be an underpass lying underneath Alexandra Square, which would carry traffic on the east-west axis through the centre of the university without intruding on the pedestrian areas. The underpass was to be high enough to allow double-decker buses to pass through, which meant that students could be let off in the dry and climb up by means of two staircases into Alexandra Square.

We have seen that it was intended that members of the university would have cause to move up and down the length of the university as they went about their various tasks. This principle was taken even further in that buildings were not segregated into types—such as colleges, or science buildings, or recreational facilities—but were to be mixed together in what Mr. Epstein refers to as a fruit salad of functions. This juxtaposition of dissimilar pursuits accorded well with his scheme, both as regards the contrast of heights and as encouraging the readier intermingling of people. There was no danger that the colleges would be silent and empty during the day, or the arts teaching accommodation morgue-like all evening. The sequence in which money was given to the university for particular types of building would importantly determine what was neighbour to what, because it was a condition of the plan that new buildings should always be erected next to those already existing. Thus the central administration building, the library, two colleges (incorporating some arts teaching accommodation) and some science blocks were the *sine qua non* for the infant institution and also obvious candidates for central positions in the total plan. The whole scheme was therefore self-regulating, and both architect and client were prepared to allow this element of the haphazard to operate.

Lest the reader by now assume that the whole plan was a short-cut to anarchy, a glance at the plan of the university should make clear at once that this fluidity of function was to be contained within and controlled by a strict formula. Although the finished scheme was not to be nearly as rigid as at first envisaged, early sketches show a grid of unrelieved rectangles; the first exception to this was the curve of the science lecture theatre fan shape, first introduced in drawings of early 1965. The grid, in theory, was to be so arranged that a high building would alternate with a low (or with one of the cul-de-sacs), in both the lateral and the opposite directions. Furthermore, the width of the building would be about 35 feet, and its internal courtyard was in each case to be 100 feet; the width of each cul-de-sac was also to be 100 feet. In this way, assuming that the width of the walls in each case would always be the same, the grid could be continued indefinitely without falling out of alignment or spoiling the patterning of high and low—itself a device to ensure that sufficient light came into the various ground-floor windows and court-yards. Furthermore, the two ends of the site, to the north and south-west, were open-ended and therefore there was always allowance for expansion on a reasonably broad front in either direction—with the development para-meters being slightly more favourable to the south-west.[2.8] The growth would always be outwards from the developed area, so that the people already working in the university would not be living in a constant sea of mud and contractors' lorries. Nor would buildings that needed to increase their size at a later stage of development, such as the library or the science buildings, be put at a disadvantage by this system, because provision was made for them to be able to expand outwards from the centre, increasing the width of the built-up area but not disturbing what was already there. Thus the main administration building, which is L-shaped, or the chemistry/physics building, which is rectangular, can expand by elongating one end at right angles to the main north-south axis, while a college, whose final size is known from the outset, can be fitted in the spaces which will later be constricted by the growth of neighbouring buildings. The one exception to this linear growth was the Indoor Recreation Centre, which Mr. Epstein permitted to start in a space by itself because he knew that Biological and Environmental Sciences would shortly be coming. He feels that the expanse of mud that surrounded the building for so long was an excellent illustration of why his usual *modus operandi* was the best for the university.

The vertical proportions were also to be carefully controlled. Essentially Mr. Epstein looked for buildings that were in a proportion of one height to three widths. Originally there were to be no tall buildings in the university, but, after designing the buildings around Alexandra Square to match in height the rest of the university, Mr. Epstein was faced with the problem of the boilerhouse chimney, which would stand up prominently above the other buildings. Additional funds were available from the U.G.C. for this chimney, which had to be a minimum height of 125 feet to satisfy the requirements of the Clean Air Act. He therefore conceived of the idea of creating a tower around it, thus lending it structural strength, and reducing its insulation costs, and creating a tower. After considering different possible uses for this tower, it was agreed to use it as a residential annexe for Bowland College. As only limited funds were available, many of the rooms were designed as double rooms to an extent not found elsewhere at Bailrigg and, because Mr. Epstein wanted

---

[2.8] The site, without using Hazlerigg, was originally estimated to be capable of providing for the needs of six thousand students. This figure has been constantly revised upwards, however, especially since the purchase of Barker's House Farm, and a number of over ten thousand is now spoken of before using the land on the other side of the motorway.

a slim profile for the tower, the residence spread also into the adjoining low-rise wings.[2.9]

While the chimney and tower were being discussed the U.G.C. offered an additional and unexpected quarter of a million pounds for residence and this meant that the fourth (eastern) side of Alexandra Square, which had previously been left open, could be filled in and the tower incorporated into the corner. In practice the tower has given a focus to the centre of the university and lifts the eye upwards in a not unpleasing way. It also gives balance to the large expanse of Alexandra Square, which was originally to have been even wider—153 feet instead of the final 126—until considerations of finance and aesthetics made Mr. Epstein narrow it. The Square, of course, forms a natural amphitheatre, whether for student meetings, with the student officers upon the raised platform under the verandah of Bowland College's south front, haranguing the assembled multitude in the Square, or for activities, such as dramatic performances, which take place in the Square with the spectators sitting above on the steps.[2.10]

This proportion of one height to three widths does not take into account the penthouses on the roofs of the colleges, which were designed to present a broken skyline and which have become perhaps the most conspicuous design feature of the site. Mr. Epstein, having once decided that flat roofs would suit the Bailrigg site, decided that they could serve as positions for flats, rather than have blocks of flats or maisonettes on the ground, forming a kind of suburbia. If positioned on top of the colleges, he hoped, the flats' occupants would be undisturbed by the activities of the rest of the college, but at the same time could be readily available to participate in college life or to take whatever action was necessary if they had a custodial or disciplinary function. There were to be difficulties of finance in the later colleges, which has limited the opportunity of continuing to provide residence in this way, but at least the first six colleges were able to afford this amenity.

Another advantage of a compact site was the opportunity of providing very

---

[2.9] Double rooms have become increasingly unpopular and, after some months of use for undergraduates, much of the tower accommodation has been converted for use by married students, while other double rooms have been converted to singles.

[2.10] An explanation of the boulder placed at the corner of Alexandra Square closest to University House, was contributed by the late Professor P. W. S. Andrews in the *Staff Newsletter*, Vol. I, No. 1, June 1968:

The site at Bailrigg, as is obvious whenever we excavate, is notable for the large numbers of boulders in the clay, ranging in size and substance and frequently interesting in shape. In Michaelmas term 1967 excavations for the Library extension exposed a large pinkish-grey boulder, apparently some sort of sandstone conglomerate. This is an amateur description; no geological examination has been made. Indeed, it was the shape and size of the boulder, rather than its interest as a geological specimen, that attracted attention. Ovoid, measuring approximately 60″ at its widest circumference, and 30″ in length, the boulder was thought to be sufficiently attractive in form to be preserved as a piece of tectonic "sculpture".

economical services. There is, under the spine, a six-and-a-half foot square duct of waterproof concrete, tall enough for people to walk about in, dry and well illuminated. In this single duct are laid telephone and electricity cables, water and gas pipes, and drains (foul drainage going north into the city's system at Burrowbeck Bridge and surface water after passing through a break tank and filter, eventually running south into the River Conder). Maintenance under these conditions is easy, there is no necessity to take up parts of the spine when servicing is being carried out, and there is built-in flexibility for the future, as more cables and drains can be installed in the same duct. When the duct reaches Alexandra Square, it becomes a single pipe carried on the underside of the square, in the roof of the underpass. The boilerhouse was to be sited very centrally, the boiler fired by natural gas[2.11] and the high pressure hot water distributed through the spine duct to a calorifier in a plant room for each building from which water at a lower temperature could be pumped round pipes and radiators for space heating, and as hot water, or steam could be supplied to catering outlets.

Mr. Epstein planned that all deliveries should come only as far as the outer perimeter of the site and then be channelled into particular areas with direct access to shops or refectories. He was, however, rather concerned about fire regulations, and had ready all kinds of concessions that he was prepared to make provided that he did not have to provide for fire engines driving up and down the spine. The fire officers, however, pronounced themselves satisfied with the access that they could obtain from the cul-de-sacs and the fire hydrants, although close to the buildings they serve, have not encroached on the pedestrian areas.

From a distance, therefore, the buildings were to be seen as a grouping on the crown of the hill; as Tony Birks has said "uncannily like a Mediterranean hilltop town".[2.12] The top edge of each building, and any excrescences on its roof, were to be painted white, and this uniformity of colour amidst a variety of shapes lightens the whole exterior and gives relief from the austerely horizontal lines. This white motif is carried over onto the exterior of the Senate Chamber, on the west side of Alexandra Square, and into the balconies and superstructure of the tower. Tony Birks[2.13] comments that clad in this colour, "the tower has a nautical air, like the funnel of a newly painted ship", and this is a not inexact image for the whole set of buildings; particularly those that look out westwards, to the Lune estuary, with the sun sparkling on the paintwork, or the strong westerly winds buffeting their sides, give to

---

[2.11] In the early days of the university the fuel used was oil, but the university changed when North Sea gas came to Lancaster. Dual fuel burners have, however, been installed and the university holds a limited oil supply as a stand-by fuel.

[2.12] T. Birks, *op. cit.*, p. 114.

[2.13] *Ibid.*, p. 120.

anyone at the top of the library or the main administration building a sensation similar to that of standing on one of the upper decks of an ocean-going liner.

Inside all was to be compact and highly organized, but with the tightness of the organization softened by the presence of trees and shrubs, and grass and creepers, as well as benches: in short, a marriage of the functional with the elegant. The planting scheme was the particular responsibility and interest of Mr. Peter Shepheard, and elaborate plans were drawn up to make provision for even the most outlying corner of the site. The architects had in any case a moral obligation about trees at Bailrigg, for in the earliest days of discussion Mr. Epstein had had a long discussion with the County Planning Officer, Mr. Aylmer Coates, who declared himself to be very pleased with the design so far propounded, except for the loss of trees, since he was afraid there would be a public outcry if Mr. Epstein cut down as many as he had proposed. Mr. Epstein recalls his dismay, because he could not use the whole width of the plateau, especially on the northern and western sides, without cutting down a fair number. He therefore at once promised Mr. Coates that for every tree he cut down, there would be two planted instead, and on this note agreement was reached: he estimates that in fact something like 35,000 trees have been planted so far.[2.14]

Unfortunately for the success of this ambitious planting programme—which excluded flowers because of the high maintenance and labour costs that would be involved—many trees and shrubs died in their first year. It will be remembered that perennial problems of the site have been poor drainage and high winds, so that conditions, particularly in the north spine, were adverse. Furthermore, the problem of the sodden ground needed the most attention just at the time when there was already something of a current crisis (in 1967) about whether certain portions of the first phase of buildings could be completed in time, with the result that the proper agricultural drains were not put down along the north spine. The soil there is clay, with a few natural springs, and because of ducts and foundations of buildings, the water table rose to just below the paving of the spine. Anything planted there, or (to a lesser extent) in the courtyards of the first two colleges, therefore had its roots standing in water, and rotted away. By the time that buildings north of Cartmel College had been reached, more appropriate drains were being laid, and the trees and plants had a much better start. It may well be asked how it is possible to have trees in Alexandra Square, since this is in effect a suspended floor; and the answer is to be found in the fact of all the trees being at one side of the square, where well-drained, nine-foot cubical pits of soil were prepared to give sufficient depth for tree roots.

As site development architect, Mr. Epstein agreed from the beginning that

---

[2.14] See the special brochure, "A Note on the Landscape at the University of Lancaster" (Peter Shepheard, 1969) for more complete information.

he would be happy to work in conjunction with other architects on particular
buildings. He was, he has said, committed utterly over the underpass, and
there were several other features of the design that he strongly advocated his
fellow architects to follow—although there are some exceptions to almost all
his principles. He had, for example, decided that brick, to be used sometimes
structurally and sometimes just as cladding, was the only material of a reasonable cost that would weather gracefully. He wanted a type with a distinctive
character, and mentioned that he had used, for a preparatory school attached
to New College, Oxford, a brick called Stamford Stone. Sir Noel Hall agreed
to look at it, reported back that he liked it very much and so it was adopted.[2.15]
When County College came to be designed, however, the County Architect
was insistent on concrete; and Cartmel College, although brick, is of a
different type and character, due to unusually heavy demands on the brick
supplier at that time. Again, Mr. Epstein has a very individual style of
fenestration, with the emphasis on the horizontal, random openings, altera-
nation of recessed and non-recessed panels, and his customary white paintwork: County is again an exception. As we have already seen, the relative
height and mass, the spacing and siting, and the rectangular form of the buildings were basic tenets, but a major exception to some of these was made in the
case of the Chaplaincy Centre and the Learning Aids Building, especially as
regards shape and styling. Yet all the buildings bear a family relationship to
each other and it may be felt—as it is by the writer—that the variations in
style have been welcome innovations rather than obtrusive interruptions of
the plan. Very often a compromise was possible, as for example when Mr.
Haydn Smith was planning Cartmel and Mr. Roger Booth County, and they
both asked whether they could bring their respective buildings west
towards the spine. Although the central spine had always been shown as a
straight line for the whole of its northern length, Mr. Epstein now agreed to
turn it westwards by twelve degrees, putting Cartmel, County, the
Learning Aids Building and the Great Hall complex at a slightly different

---

[2.15] In a letter of April 1964 to the University Secretary, Sir Noel Hall said:
The bricks I think are really attractive, and I don't think their use in mass would
tend to make the University buildings like dismal 19th Century penitentiaries. This
view, however, is subject to two qualifications. . . .
First of all, the pointing in the New College Preparatory School Building is
extremely happy; to my taste, precisely right for the bricks. It is sometimes difficult
to reproduce with different water and different basic materials, exactly the colour
effect which has been achieved in the New College School building. If there is any
risk of this not being achieved, it might be wise to reconsider the brick question.
Secondly, the area of uninterrupted brickwork is not too large; the windows as a
percentage of the wall area are certainly on a more generous scale than in your
19th Century penitentiaries. Moreover, they have relatively large areas of uninterrupted glass sheet, and the frames and mouldings into which they are set, while
very clearly defined, are neither obtrusive nor extravagant in the area which they
cover.

alignment to neighbouring buildings and modifying the severe regularity of the spine.

Finance was to be a problem, as the Government cut back on funds available for the new universities' capital building programmes. Mr. Epstein has consistently emphasized the need to spend what money was available on the highest quality of structure, particularly as regards the permanent exterior elements. Most of the interiors are plain and unfurbished—increasingly so in later buildings—but missing items can be supplied later if more money becomes available. Mr. Epstein saw Lancaster as a marriage of the austere and the beautiful: the severe discipline[2.16] of a grid system, but the severity to be softened by trees, fountains, ornamental lamps and decorative arcades. Buildings and courtyards were intended to be adorned with noble materials which would have enriched the brick texture, by the addition of stone or marble or the more attractive types of wood. His vision could not be fully realised not only because of lack of money but also because of climatic difficulties, as an environment suited to southern Europe was translated into the harsher north-west of England; because of the great speed with which the programme, particularly in its initial stages, had to be carried out; and because of bad behaviour within the community. The tower of Bowland College was to have been illuminated from below, for instance, but students dropped stones down from the balconies and smashed the lights; and trees and shrubs are often damaged. There are, nevertheless, certain embellishments around the site, such as the copy of Barbara Hepworth's Dual Form outside the Great Hall, and Anna Hirsch-Henecka's Daphne sculpture in Cartmel College. Wooden benches are appearing at various places in the university, such as along the edges of Lake Carter, and hanging baskets of flowers are sometimes placed in Alexandra Square and certain courtyard interiors. A sculpture is also planned for an external wall of the physics building, and recently the greyness and gloom of the underpass were much diminished by the painting of vertical stripes of different colours on both walls to a design prepared by Mr. David Atkinson.

No two people ever agree in their subjective reaction to an architectural environment. It may be said without fear of contradiction that Mr. Epstein has created an environment which to visitors is strikingly distinctive, compact and well-ordered. Some student members perhaps regret that their environment is so totally urban and speak of a feeling of claustrophobia at walking around a concrete world. When the trees and shrubs come nearer to maturity,

---

[2.16] There is a trace of severity also in the nomenclature of the internal road system which, based wholly on points of the compass (thought up by Mr. Epstein and the Vice-Chancellor on a train journey between London and Lancaster and subsequently ratified by the Buildings Committee), can be very confusing to newcomers standing in an internal courtyard on an overcast day.

no doubt the rigid contrast between the urban interior of spine, courtyards and buildings and the open farmland outside will lessen and, although the parkland atmosphere of Stirling or York or Sussex has deliberately not been emulated at Lancaster, there will be less feeling of containment than is sometimes experienced by the present generation of students. Already the lawn-like grass and shrubs by Lake Carter and what is left of Bigforth Farm[2.17] has brought people out of the centre of the site and down the hillside. Perhaps another inhibiting feature has been the lack of a grand entrance. Apart from the later, and almost incidental, approach to the Great Hall there is no ceremonial entrance, for the area outside University House and the first two colleges is severely utilitarian. Mr. Epstein, of course, envisaged people as coming in equally from all access points, leaving their cars and infiltrating into the courtyards: he agrees, however, that there is a need for a different kind of entrance for special visitors to the university and may in time modify the area in front of University House to take account of this.

Nor have the central areas of the university been as thriving centres of activity, perhaps, as Mr. Epstein had hoped. Partly this is a function of there being so far less than half the number of students on the Bailrigg site than he designed it to contain—three thousand instead of seven or more. Partly it is because students have tended to congregate more in their warrens of communal kitchens and bars: at night there are no bars or concert halls in use close to Alexandra Square and it often seems almost deserted. Each academic year, however, brings a new modification of staff and student habits and no finally determined or irrevocable pattern of behaviour can yet be said to have established itself.

Noise has, not unexpectedly, been a continuing problem. Modern structures are not soundproof and the kind of insulation that would make them more so is very costly. Many of the disciplinary problems[2.18] have been connected with noise, both within buildings and between them, [2.19] and the compactness of the site and the thin materials exacerbate the problem. So bad is it that students are permitted to have noisy functions on only one night a week, and at the Court meeting in December 1970, the Dean of Lonsdale College, Dr. M. A. Stewart, commented

> that many members of staff were concerned about the means by which economies had been achieved in building costs. He referred particularly to

---

[2.17] The farmhouse of Bigforth has been demolished but the farm buildings are used by the university's groundstaff. The only other alteration to the existing site, apart from the demolition of the gate lodge, was the closure of Murder Lane.

[2.18] See Chapter 6, pages 344 to 346 and 377 to 379.

[2.19] The Great Hall activities can be heard in the Nuffield Theatre Studio and the Lonsdale College residences; and traffic noise from the underpass sometimes brings conversations to a stop in rooms overlooking the approach to it, to give but two examples.

the close proximity of buildings and inadequate soundproofing (e.g. of residential areas), to poor accoustics in lecture rooms and to disturbance from building work during vacations. In his view most of the academic and other student problems which arose at the university were attributable to the physical planning of the University rather than to delinquency.

The Vice-Chancellor, in reply, said

> that there was no evidence that Dr. Stewart's views were shared by a majority of staff or students and he pointed out that the buildings had been designed within the standards permitted by the University Grants Committee, and that the cost of the college buildings had also been substantially subsidized from the University Appeal funds.

Although Dr. Stewart's statement was unusually strong, the friction that noise problems brings should not be overlooked in any modern university.

The reader will not have overlooked the absence of any mention of the university's academic staff being involved in the planning. Consultation had perforce to be carried on between the architects on the one side, and the Vice-Chancellor, University Secretary and the Building Development Officer on the other, with the Executive Council and the Academic Planning Board remaining in the background and being kept informed, as was the Shadow Senate. By the time the first sod was cut in November 1964, therefore, and the excavation for the underpass begun, the university had obviously committed itself to the Shepheard and Epstein plan. Such staff as were already about were consulted: Mr. Wacek Koc, the Research Fellow in Teaching Methods, for instance, made proposals to Mr. Epstein over the arts teaching accommodation. This kind of discussion was the exception, however, for although there was a Buildings Committee which held regular meetings from November 1963 (chaired until October 1968 by Sir Stanley Bell, and since then by Sir Percy Stephenson), no regular member of the academic staff other than Mr. Koc sat on it until October 1964. The Vice-Chancellor, listing the work in progress late in 1965, was to comment on his first annual report to the Court that

> All this work, totalling in value over £5 million, is controlled by a single small Buildings Committee; so far there has never been time for the gentler processes of democratic consultation, and it has been left to the Building Development Officer and his staff to keep in touch with academic needs, instruct the teams of architects, and satisfy the University Grants Committee's officers on innumerable points of principle and of detail.

Sometimes of course, the informal processes of consultation have not worked, and proposals have been made for the reference of the planning of each building to a special project committee. I think that we have been right to resist such demands. Any formal committee structure would have slowed down planning to a serious degree, and I do not believe that the advantages to be gained would have offset the disappointment caused by a slowing of the University's growth rate.

Thus we find, in October 1963, a report from the Vice-Chancellor to the Executive Committee, informing them that various consultants had been appointed: Messrs. F. J. Samuely of London to advise on the bearing capacity of the ground and to give general advice on systems and types of construction; Foundation Engineering Limited of London to do seven bore holes; and Gleeds of Regent Street as quantity surveyors.[2.20] By November Messrs. Shepheard and Epstein had completed their preliminary sketches and were able to give the Council "an illustrated preliminary report."

Bridgewater, Shepheard and Epstein are a relatively small architectural partnership in terms of numbers of personnel and had in any case agreed from the beginning to work alongside other architects. In November 1963, however, Mr. Epstein wrote to the University Secretary indicating that their office would like to design the buildings scheduled for 1966 "in order to start giving the university the kind of character we feel it should have." While being anxious to avoid "office-elephantosis", he felt his firm "could probably handle the colleges, arts, library and administrative buildings, but would need assistance with the science buildings from firms with experience of these projects." It was a difficult time. The implication of the Robbins Report, which had come out a month before, was that there was a need

for roughly 30,000 more university places by 1967–8, but only a further 10,000 by 1973–4. As the higher education plans called for extensive development of schools as opposed to universities during the period 1967–73, it was clear that low priority would be given to university development schemes after 1966, but greater priority before that date. In view of this, the tentative Lancaster scheme with the bulk of the development scheduled for 1967–73 would have to be radically altered so that as many buildings as possible were completed by 1966.[2.21]

[2.20] Gleeds have remained as the quantity surveyors to the university throughout the total building programme. As the one consultant who has been in a position to watch over the progress of all the jobs on the site, they have given valuable continuity to the programme. G. N. Haydn & Sons of London have been responsible for the design and installation of most of the heating, electrical and other services in the early buildings, and the main contractors have been Simms Sons and Cooke (of Nottingham), Brown and Jackson (of Fleetwood), F. Parkinson (of Blackpool), William Eaves (of Blackpool), and J. Turner (of Preston).

[2.21] Quotation from the notes of an informal meeting with the architects, 7 November 1963.

The university therefore set to work to speed up its building programme as much as possible, and the Vice-Chancellor wrote to the U.G.C. at the end of November 1963 saying that

> My Executive Council authorizes me to say that we shall do all in our power to contribute to the national need for student places during the next four years. We have now approved the broad plan of development proposed by our architects, and we have completed, or nearly completed, statements of requirements for our site works and first buildings, which will enable us to submit the Schedules 1 to your Committee early in 1964. We are ready to appoint architects for these buildings.
>
> This represents an increase ... of 36 per cent, on our original plans for 1967–8. It would provide a base from which we could expand to 4,000 students, instead of 3,000, by 1973–4.

Therefore, in November 1963 and even more strongly in February 1964, the university was urging its development architects in the strongest terms to make sure that they had the resources commensurate with the magnitude of the task which they had undertaken, and particular comparison was drawn with the new University of York, which had a very large design team.[2.22] The Vice-Chancellor said he felt the programme needed

> a design team of 10 immediately, rising to 25 for at least a year from this May. Furthermore, it seems to us essential that some part of this design team should be based in Lancaster; rapid and effective liaison on details over a distance of 240 miles is impossible.

Shepheard and Epstein declined, however, to have a local office in Lancaster; and declined again in 1966, when building progress on site was temporarily falling behind schedule and the next increase of staff and students was hard upon their heels. At that time, however, Mr. Epstein agreed that someone should come up from the London office to Lancaster twice a week, and very regular visits, as well as what he looks back on as a very ulcer-creating pace of work, saw these stages of the programme through.[2.23]

This, however, is to anticipate. In March 1964 a different note from the accent of haste was struck both to the Council and to the Shadow Senate as the Vice-Chancellor wrote that

---

[2.22] See, for the approach to their building programme, *University of York, Development Plan 1962–1972* (1962).

[2.23] During the early days of the building programme, Mr. Victor Berry of Bridgewater, Shepheard & Epstein was closely associated with the Lancaster work but had to resign because of ill health; latterly Mr. Peter Hunter of the same partnership has been closely involved.

I regret to say that I must report a serious setback to our plans. You will know that, immediately after the publication of the Robbins report, all universities were asked by the University Grants Committee to indicate what help they could give with the proposed rapid expansion of the number of university places.

After consulting this Council, we replied in a letter dated 29 November 1963. In that letter we proposed to alter our plans, which had originally implied student numbers in the coming four years of 250, 480, 700 and 1,100, so as to provide for 300, 600, 1,000 and 1,500. . . .

Early in January it became known that the total of the universities' proposals for expansion exceeded the requirements, and that each university would be invited to discussions with the Chairman of the U.G.C. to consider what reductions would have to be made. Mr. Jeffreys and I accordingly met the Chairman, Mr. Parnis and Mr. Coppleston on January 13, bearing with us some alternative ideas for the scaling-down of our programme. To our surprise and pleasure, however, we were informed that since our proposals, excluding residence, involved expenditure of about £1·25m per year in place of the £1m previously authorized, they would involve no difficulty; and we were invited to submit by the end of January detailed proposals for the 1964 and 1965 programmes. This was the first official reference to a previous authorization of £1m per year, and no record of such an authorization had ever been sent to us. Early in February, however, we were informed of a "pre-Robbins allocation" of £1m for capital starts in 1964 and the same sum in 1965, *inclusive of site works*; whereas our discussion on January 13 was on the basis of a clear reference to expenditure *exclusive* of site works.

A letter of 28 February from the U.G.C. noted that

"The Committee have been impressed by the willingness of the University of Lancaster to expand as far and as fast as is practicable. But they have felt bound, in planning the present emergency operation and in scaling down the overall proposals which were submitted to them, to have regard to the relative costs of expansion between the various Universities. Moreover, it has seemed to them that the proposals of certain Universities would be more appropriately considered in the context of the ten-year programme of expansion to 1973–4 than in that of the present operation. In the light of these considerations, they came regretfully to the conclusion that they would not be justified in making an additional allocation to your University. . . ."

The implication of the U.G.C. decision . . . is that we must return, not only to our original programme of student numbers, but probably to something considerably *smaller*. This is because we now have a firmer

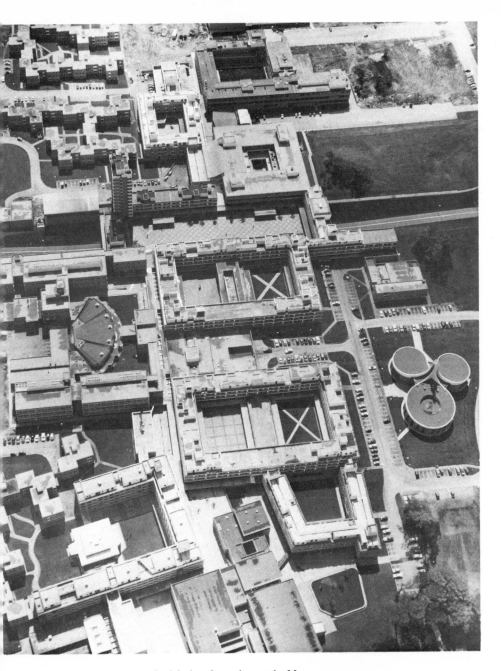

Aerial view from the north, May 1971

By courtesy of Peter Joslin

Aerial view of the site from the north in 1971

estimate of the very heavy cost of the site works which must be undertaken right at the beginning of the site development.[2.24]

The site works referred to included any necessary alterations at the entrance from the A.6 that the university had to make;[2.25] a new approach road from Bigforth Farm, along the contours of the hill to the first roundabout, and the construction of two roundabouts; the perimeter roads, cul-de-sacs and parking spaces; road lighting and signposting; the paving to the spine and the main concrete duct; two sewers, one for foul sewage and one for surface water; eighteen acres of tree planting and felling; the demolition of the lodge and some of the Bigforth Farm buildings; the formation of a proper lake and tow path (in practice diverted to a later part of the programme); the formation of a two-sided, four-staircased underpass over four hundred feet long;[2.26] and provision for incoming services (such as gas, electricity and water). All these items were estimated by Mr. Epstein in December 1963 to come to a cost of £1·1 million—but, of course, most of them were jobs of a type that would not recur later.

In the end the U.G.C. agreed to a building programme of £1,202,000 for the 1964–5 programme, which, besides conversions in the city to house the first two intakes of students, was for site works, the administration building and the first social/study/teaching building (i.e. Bowland College), with a special allowance added for the covered walkways. The university used £58,000 from its appeal fund, of which £47,000 was to be spent on staff flats on the roofs of the colleges. The U.G.C. gave a further million pounds for the 1965–6 programme, which was to cover the first stages of the library, the chemistry and physics buildings, the second social/study/teaching building (Lonsdale College), and the first stage of the central boiler house; telephones; further site works; a biology field station; and recreation facilities. A further quarter of a million pounds was to come out of the appeal fund for various special facilities—including for revenue-producing outlets such as shops and banks. The third year would see the second stages of the chemistry and physics buildings, and of Lonsdale College; the first phase of the third college (Cartmel), the computer building, and central catering (later abandoned); the theatre workshop (i.e. the Nuffield Theatre Studio, to be paid for by an ear-

---

[2.24] Costs of the new universities' buildings inevitably appeared high at first because site works applicable to a ten- or twenty-year development were charged against the student numbers for the third or fourth year.

[2.25] After many different alternatives had been considered, it was agreed to construct a section of dual carriageway at the entrance to the university, with two sets of traffic lights, operated by the vehicles coming down the university drive or along the main road.

[2.26] Two staircases were later deleted when the underpass was made narrower to reduce costs.

F

marked donation); and further shops, site works, and conversions at St. Leonard's House: for this period the U.G.C. was prepared to contribute £1¼ million and the university appeal fund would support the remaining £180,000.

A word of explanation should be given about the playing fields.[2.27] The U.G.C. had been most anxious to obtain, as sites for the new universities, pieces of land which would be of sufficient area to provide both for the necessary buildings and the requisite playing fields. The original Bailrigg site, however, although close to the required acreage, is long and narrow in shape, and most of the original area, before the Barker's Farm land was added in 1967, was too constricted and too steep for use as playing fields. The university looked around for some additional land but near the university it was likely to be required for future development, and therefore expensive; and land further away, and less convenient, was likely to be of both high agricultural value and also to meet with opposition from the Ministry of Agriculture. The suggestion was therefore made to the university by the County Planning Officer that some land in Oxcliffe Marsh and Salt Ayre should be used. The City of Lancaster and the Borough of Morecambe agreed in principle, early in 1965, to sell to the university this marsh land, which had been used as a tipping area since 1952: twenty acres would be available immediately and there could be as much as an eventual hundred and twenty acres for the university's use. The U.G.C., also, were prepared in principle to approve the acquisition of the first twenty acres. Although the purchase price was relatively low at £100 per acre, however, the cost of reclamation was very high, being estimated at over £1,000 an acre. Furthermore, the land had been used as a free tip for domestic and other refuse; the rubbish had not been put down in layers, nor had it been treated. The final settlement of the land would therefore take a long time and saucer depressions were likely to occur for some years, creating a high annual reinstatement and maintenance cost. Again, the top surface was salt marsh soil and special topsoil would therefore have to be brought to the site, to make a settled depth of six inches. Therefore, in spite of the attractiveness of the scheme as a joint town-gown venture, it was decided to make the best use of what land could be made available at Bailrigg for recreational purposes, and the only outpost in Lancaster is the university's boathouse (which had previously been a railway station at Halton) near the aqueduct on the River Lune. With the addition of Barker's Farm, a more adequate supply of land was available and there is outdoor provision for football, rugger, hockey, tennis and cricket. A pavilion, clad in cedarwood, stands on higher ground above the pitches, and a play-

---

[2.27] The grounds superintendent, Mr. Frank Smith, has had published a book, *Hard, porous and all-weather surfaces*, on the care and maintenance of playing fields like those at Bailrigg.

group centre for the young offspring of staff and students, has been built in the same area.[2.28]

It would be both too lengthy and too complex to go through a chronological account of the total building programme; a complete list of architects and their buildings can be found in Appendix vii, and the Vice-Chancellor's annual reports to the Court are a valuable source for anyone who wishes to obtain a panoramic view of the work in progress. We will therefore go for an imaginary walk around the site; starting as most visitors do, in Alexandra Square, by University House.

A letter from the U.G.C. of November 1963 went into considerable detail about the kind of accommodation which would customarily be found in an administration building; including an office for the Vice-Chancellor in association with a Senate Room, other accommodation for the university secretary, the academic registrar, and the bursar (with their staffs), and a building development office. Also mentioned were a telephone exchange and a general typing pool and duplicating office. All these were indeed fitted into University House, as well as, at the outset, accommodation for medical staff and a limited number of beds, and laboratory and office space for the department of Environmental Sciences. The Senate Room was placed on the top floor, with windows looking east to the hills and west to the sea: at the beginning, some teaching even went on there; the adjoining Senate Dining Room is also made to double up as an additional committee room.

Although Lonsdale College was begun a full year after Bowland, the two colleges were designed in tandem from the beginning. To some extent their facilities were to be shared in common, or "twinned", for although their junior and senior common rooms and their bars, for example, were to be quite separate, their kitchen accommodation was to be common to both and their refectories were to present a single front to the spine. Each was to have a double courtyard, paved on the one side where the public rooms were to be, and grassed on the other where the quieter seminar rooms were to be found, with a lecture theatre in the middle dividing the rectangle. Arts teaching accommodation, including both staff rooms and seminar rooms, was to be on the ground and first floors. A memorandum written by the Vice-Chancellor in January 1964 expounded on the principles of the scheme:

Although we propose to use very diverse teaching methods, it is evident that small-group teaching (groups of up to 12) will be common. We find that this can best be provided for by having no normal staff rooms, but instead having combined tutorial and staff rooms allocated to particular

2.28 More recently the university has leased an attractive house known as Clapdale Farm, near Clapham, which is to be the headquarters of an outdoor activities centre for hiking, climbing, potholing, canoeing and other activities.

members of the teaching staff. The addition to a standard size of staff room needed to accommodate 12 students is much smaller than a separate seminar room for these students, and this compensates for the lower utilization by students which would be expected. Greater flexibility of the time-table can also be achieved, if seminars with different members of staff are no longer competing for the same seminar room: and this will be a considerable advantage in a university which is experimenting with numerous combinations of subject.

Our basic unit for non-laboratory teaching consists of 6 tutorial and staff rooms of 240 square feet, an unallocated "special purpose room" (e.g. language laboratory) of the same size, a large seminar room for groups of 20 or for small lecture classes, two "mixing bays" off the corridor where people can meet and hold informal discussions, a room for a secretary and records, and a small research assistants' room.

He saw further advantages of such integration as bringing a closer relationship between staff and students, teaching facilities could also serve student social needs, and the integration of two types of building would mean greater standardization. Later there was to be a great debate[2.29] concerning the location of future arts teaching; but in the early days integration of collegiate with teaching accommodation accorded with the views both of client and architect. Study places for non-resident students were planned as a feature of the first phase of both colleges, because the Vice-Chancellor was anxious that every student should have at least a *pied à terre* at Bailrigg—although again, later, the levelling downwards of U.G.C. norms hastened the reduction of such space. In 1965 additional money was made available for extra residence[2.30] which was located, together with more study rooms, above the shops and banks in Alexandra Square, and designated as belonging to Bowland College. The finance was skilfully adjusted to the exigencies of the situation, for the ground floor of the Bowland annexe, consisting of shops and banks, was built from appeal money as were the staff flats on the roof, whereas the two floors in between, of study bedrooms and study workrooms, were financed by the U.G.C. Additional residence was also provided for Lonsdale

[2.29] See Chapter 6, pages 333 to 337 and 351 to 352.

[2.30] A letter of January 1965 from the Vice-Chancellor to Sir John Wolfenden had asked for additional help with residence on the grounds
   (a) It is now evident that the amount of *suitable* lodging accommodation in the area has been over-estimated. . . .
   (b) The main areas available to us for lodgings are some seven or more miles away. We think that there are very strong educational grounds for having a large nucleus of students resident on the site, acting as a centre for student life and preserving a sense of community . . .
   (c) We have one large benefaction to provide help with residence, but this will yield 250 places in *1969*. This is too late, and the number is in any case only a small part of the total residential places needed by that year.

College and, in 1966, application was made to the U.G.C. for this to be integrated with special accommodation at ground floor level which was to be designated for use by assistant staff. By 1969 there were expected to be about four hundred technicians, clerks, secretaries, maintenance and catering staff, cleaners and porters and, on a site three miles from the centre of Lancaster, it was felt appropriate to make provision for them over and above the facilities already provided for the students within the colleges. This would perhaps help to

> foster a strong corporate spirit amongst the ranks of the assistant staff. It is becoming increasingly difficult to recruit in these parts assistant staff of the right calibre and the University will be at a distinct disadvantage if it cannot offer a range of communal and recreational facilities at least equal to the splendid facilities available to such categories of employees in local industrial, commercial and business organizations.[2.31]

After some initial hesitation by the U.G.C. about the apparently lavish scale of the provision—a total area of almost 5,000 sq. ft. was being suggested—they acceded to the university's request and agreed to a schedule of accommodation which included a dining room with a capacity for a hundred people to sit and eat, or a hundred and fifty to dance, with suitable food servery areas adjacent to it. There was to be a bar, a lounge, games rooms which would include billiards, snooker, and table tennis, and office and committee room space which could be put on the first floor. There would not be sufficient space to cook full meals there, but Cartmel refectory would be close enough to make it possible to bring food over from there: in practice, it has been practicable to provide meals only at lunchtime, but snacks are usually available in the bar. The Assistant Staff House, as it was named, is under the control of an association of its own members, who also organize social and recreational activities—its success may be measured by the fact that many other categories of people within the university are eager to share in its facilities.

Alexandra Square, therefore, is bounded by University House to the west; Bowland College to the north, east and south-east with shops and banks on the ground floor on two sides; and the library, with the generously proportioned bookshop on the ground floor and an adjacent coffee and snack bar to the south-west.

The Librarian, Mr. Graham Mackenzie, was fortunate in having been a particularly early appointment and therefore able to plan his building in the way he saw as best suited to its specialized purposes, in conjunction with the architect, Mr. Tom Mellor. By January 1964 he had produced a final and

---

2.31 Letter from the Building Development Officer to the U.G.C., December 1966.

very detailed policy document with a careful exposition of the desired spatial relationships between the various parts of the library, and flow diagrams of such processes as book purchases and binding, to ensure that the physical layout echoed the theoretical requirements[2.32] as closely as possible. The library, he said, should eventually be able to accommodate two thousand readers and one million volumes, with all the necessary ancillary services; in a building which must be self-contained and yet capable of expansion, in whole or in part, even beyond this final figure of 1,000,000, without vitiating the principle on which the present design is based. He went on to define the functions of the library as: the acquisition, organization and storage of books and other research material; the provision of facilities for members of the university to make use of these materials, or remove them for use elsewhere; the provision of space for readers to use their own materials; the organization of bibliographical and bibliothecal training, and the provision of cultural amenities. We are, he said,

> anxious to get away from the classic conception of a library as a large reading room, with a small number of books around its walls, and a separate vast stack for storage of all but the most-used materials; this carries with it the disadvantage that the undergraduate tends not to explore the full resources of the library. In a "diffused" library, on the other hand, even if he is at first bewildered by the size of the collection, he will quickly learn, with skilled help, to find his way about, and the experience thus gained is a vital part of the educative process. . . .
>
> We therefore wish the reading and book storage areas to be intermingled, either on a chequer-board pattern, where small areas of books and tables alternate, or in some modification of this principle. The most satisfactory building for this purpose is a completely modular one, with all floors capable of bearing book stacks at 4' 6" centres, for their full width, and self-contained in respect of lighting, power, and ventilation. . . .
>
> Such a design is made even more desirable by the fact that we cannot forecast what the patterns of library use and service will be in 50, or even 20 years from now; current technological developments in telecommunications and micro-storage of information, to name only two fields of research, might well force us to recast the shape of the Library in the not too distant future.

The Library will be organized on a subject divisional basis, whereby

---

[2.32] Graham Mackenzie, "Bailrigg Library: Building Programme, 1966–1973" (January 1964) from which the quotation below is taken: since the library as it now stands adheres very closely to Mr. Mackenzie's stated principles, reference should be made to the complete document by the interested reader. See also "The Library Building: University of Lancaster" (Univ. of Lanc. Library Miscellaneous Publications Series, 1972), especially for diagrams, technical information, and photographs.

each Assistant Librarian . . . will be responsible for book selection, classification, and bibliographical teaching and services in one subject or a cognate group of subjects. . . .

The principle of diffusion of books and readers does not rule out the need for some concentrated book storage; in every library, no matter how expert and careful is the selection of incoming material, there remains a proportion of books which have only archival significance, which are outdated, or which for any other reason should not be placed on the open shelves. This type of material may be as much as 20 per cent of the whole collection, and we propose to supply, in a basement, compact storage shelving for an appropriate number of volumes, with direct access limited to senior research workers.

A third sequence of books should be formed, consisting of multiple copies of much-used texts, to be kept under strict control by the library staff; these will normally be available for use within the building, or for short term loan.

A most pleasant environment has been created, especially since the opening of Phase III in January 1971, with the addition of the fountain courtyard, open-air seating on terraces opening out from the upper floors, a special exhibition room and a graduate student study area. The building is carpeted throughout, which greatly reduces noise, and acoustic treatment of the special areas in which people are allowed to talk means that elsewhere it is possible to work undisturbed. The necessity to install a Diver Detection Device has meant the creation of a perhaps rather forbidding turnstile, but once past that, the catalogue and service desk area are spacious and welcoming, and the signposting to other parts of the library is made easily intelligible to the greenest novitiate.

Leaving Alexandra Square and proceeding along the north spine, the pedestrian is protected by the covered walkway between Bowland College on his left and science buildings on the right; although, to let in some light, portions of the walkway are open to the sky on alternate sides of this portion of the sky, making those underneath on rainy days zigzag to and fro in order to keep dry.[2.33] Physics and chemistry, on the right, were amongst the original subjects which it was decided should be offered from the outset, and it was therefore possible for Mr. Tom Mellor to design these buildings, with their associated lecture theatres and service areas, as a single complex. The three lecture theatres lie side by side, like spokes of a fan, and have no natural light; the middle one, called the Faraday Lecture Theatre, is able to seat two hun-

---

[2.33] Despite the care taken with the covered walkways they reduce the natural light to many ground-floor rooms and also act as wind tunnels in the weather conditions of north Lancashire.

dred and eighty people, while the physics and chemistry lecture theatres can hold a hundred and forty-five each. All three have a versatile system of interior fittings, and the physics lecture theatre can receive, by closed circuit television, the proceedings from laboratories and the Faraday (which itself has a full range of projection facilities). The curved outer edge of the fan is a single continuous passage, and forms a concourse shared by the three lecture theatres as well as a link between the two departments: there is also a generously sized lobby abutting onto the spine. Although the physical layout of the two buildings is very similar, in the physics department each floor is devoted to one speciality—physical electronics, nuclear physics, or solid-state physics—and includes complete provision for the particular subject area, including a workshop, undergraduate teaching rooms, and post-graduate and staff research laboratories and offices. A member of staff is, therefore, able to look after several concerns at once because physically they are so closely associated. The building is wider than most, with staff offices and undergraduate teaching areas on the outer sides of the building and the windowless advanced research laboratories on the inside: this necessitates the use of artificial light and mechanical ventilation in these rooms, but permits the maximum amount of wall space to be made available for complicated apparatus and also simplifies the provision of specialized laboratory services. Behind the physics/chemistry complex is one of the familiar cul-de-sacs and a generous service yard, so that vehicles can come and deliver, for example, liquid nitrogen direct into the storage vessel, helium gas in cylinders, or bulk metal straight into the loading bay. Two phases of the chemistry laboratory, and three of physics, have already been built, and there is land available for the third phase of chemistry when it is required.

Immediately beyond the chemistry building lies Cartmel College, which was originally to have been twinned, in the same way that Bowland and Lonsdale are, with the fourth college. When, however, The County College was selected as the fourth college to be built, it became evident that the County and Cartmel styles would be too divergent for any twinning to be practicable: the earlier idea, however, accounts for the positioning of the Cartmel refectory and snack bar at the northern end of the college. Policy on catering in the early days was that it should be under collegiate control,[2.34] and when university policy on this matter changed, the effect on the college of having the dining areas put under the jurisdiction of the controller of catering meant that there was a wedge of university-controlled premises interjected into the area under collegiate control, which has interrupted the fusion of activities intended by the architect.

Cartmel College is the first of Mr. Haydn Smith's buildings at Bailrigg, the

---

[2.34] See Chapter 4, pages 254ff.

others being Fylde College, the Furness College residences, the Engineering building, the central workshops, and the conversion of Bailrigg House for use as a medical centre. He comes from a Mancunian architectural partnership which has included in its activities educational, religious and medical buildings. The Vice-Chancellor wrote to Mr. Smith and others, inviting them to put their names forward and, after interview with members of the Building Committee and various university officers, he was commissioned to design Cartmel. Later he had detailed discussions with several people, including Mr. Epstein and Mr. Roger Booth. Mr. Smith's regret is that he was not given a more identifiable customer client with whom to negotiate: by the time the Cartmel planning committee was set up and a college planning officer (Miss Jacqueline Marrian) selected, several of the major decisions had already been made; for example, he had already drawn in provision for a senior common room in a college that was later to repudiate such provision as a matter of principle. He was glad to find, when working on other colleges, that planning committees were set up earlier while they were still able to make decisions about the distribution and relationships of different parts of the buildings.

He was very willing to adopt the Epstein principles: to make his buildings depend on the horizontal rather than the vertical; to alternate higher with lower to allow as much penetration of sunlight as possible; and to have the public rooms overlooking the spine and the study bedrooms facing away to the quieter, eastern side. The accent on the interior was on grass, rather than the paved courtyards of Bowland and Lonsdale, and in the middle of the rectangle there was to be a large multi-purpose hall. This was designed to be versatile inside, equally capable of accommodating an examination, a formal dinner (with the kitchen areas almost en suite), a committee meeting, or an undergraduate lecture.

The rectangle was not destined to be completed, however. Money was made available and schedules approved, in 1965 and 1966, by the U.G.C., for the first two phases of the college, covering the teaching, dining and studyroom accommodation, but not for the third phase of crucial residential accommodation. The uncommitted residue of the appeal fund, leaving aside the special earmarked donation for the County College, stood by this time at about £250,000; and there were many calls on this fund besides costly capital building ventures. The university, realizing that Government funds for residence were becoming scarcer, had been pondering on new types of building and, during 1966, explored tentatively the possibility of constructing, with commercial capital, a number of self-contained flats for students, at rents no higher than those in the area, which would be leased by the university and sub-let to students. The original scheme, although approved in principle by the Senate and the Council, proved to be abortive, but a special working party of the Council nevertheless continued to explore the possibility of providing student residence by borrowed funds from private enterprise, and between the autumn of 1966 and the summer of 1967 the Vice-Chancellor and the University Secretary worked very hard to secure the necessary help from the Friends' Provident and Century Life Office and the Barclays Bank Pension Fund, as well as agreement from the U.G.C. and Lancaster city, for a scheme that would be financially viable and attractive to the students and staff of the university. The matter was of considerable urgency, because by now not only was Cartmel needing money for residence, but so also were Furness and Fylde colleges; and the scheme, as described below, must be seen as applying to 160 student places for Cartmel, and 448 for Furness and Fylde.

The legal position of such an enterprise was carefully investigated, and the university was advised that it should not undertake the formation of a limited company to undertake responsibility for mortgage payments, but should handle such repayments as a loan direct from the company lending the money. A difficulty arose, however, over security for a mortgage, because the university is not in a position to give a lender the normal recourse if the university were to be wound up, i.e. the possession of the property, it being a condition of the lease of the land from the city that the buildings on it must be used for university purposes.[2.35]

The next question was the style of building that could be put up, and here Mr. Haydn Smith, with a background that included work for local education authorities, was well able to help. He was asked in January 1967 for a feasibility study, based on the requirements: that the cost yardstick would be £700 per student (instead of the £1,200 that each student place was costing at that time in conventional halls and residence); that the rental should not be more than they were customarily paying in the area already; that full self-catering facilities would be provided, with kitchens to serve groups of ten to twelve students in a mixture of single and double rooms; and that the space heating of the study-bedroom should be capable of control by the student. At the same time the building proposed had to accord in material and general appearance with the overall site development and be compatible with the developing environment of the main university buildings. Student opinion was extensively canvassed—even to the extent of inviting students from the universities of Sheffield, Manchester, Liverpool and Leeds to contribute their views in addition to those of the Lancaster students. It was generally agreed that students were increasingly attracted to living in flats where they could

---

[2.35] This lack of the usual kind of security caused severe difficulties and although the city was concerned purely with the (unlikely!) eventuality that the university would cease to exist, in the end the Friends' Provident and Century Life Office who were lending the initial £500,000 generously agreed to waive any obligation on the part of the city.

cater for themselves and live in a small, informal group, and where they could sleep, work, relax, entertain visitors, keep their books and personal belongings and yet still have the advantages of being on site. A questionnaire was sent round the student body in June 1967 and well over half of the eight hundred and more who replied were prepared to pay £3 a week for a single room, and half of them £2.10.0 for a double room. A distinct preference for single rooms, however, manifested itself, and the number of double rooms provided for in the scheme was reduced accordingly. If the occupancy of the rooms could be extended beyond the thirty weeks of term, by conferences, by graduate students whose work proceeds all through the year, or by undergraduates staying up during the vacation, then a rental of £3 for a single room was feasible.[2.36]

What Mr. Haydn Smith came up with was a system of building, based on load-bearing brick walls, that would be in style with neighbouring buildings but so designed that they could be built by relatively small firms which were engaged in house-building. The cost of the buildings was estimated, early in 1967, as costing between sixty-five and seventy-two shillings per square foot and would be based on the fitting together of two basic types of unit, one comprising single (or double) study bedrooms and the staircase, and the other comprising study/bedrooms, the cooking and dining facilities and the sanitary accommodation (including showers but no baths), the two units being complementary, similar in plan form and built to satisfy building, fire and health regulations. Different shapes could be made by combining two or three of these basic units, in the form of a three-storey block, with a staircase common to the whole. The single rooms would have a usable area of 108 sq. ft. or slightly more, and the double rooms of 180 sq. ft.[2.37] These individual blocks could in turn be placed in a variety of patterns so that there was no possibility of monotony, or tedious, neat rows of little boxes: it was intended that the natural features of the ground, including rising contours, could be used, and the irregularity of the enclosed space would provide interest to the eye. While the standards of the rooms would be as good as in other types of student accommodation—although problems of noise were again to prove troublesome[2.38]—and the kitchens much better equipped than in the conventional halls of residence, every effort was made to pare costs to the minimum. Professional fees were lower than usual because no special consultants other than an architect and a quantity surveyor were needed, and the

[2.36] For fuller details of finance and specifications, see "The University of Lancaster: Loan financed student residences" (W. Hadyn Smith, 1969).

[2.37] Originally only the double rooms had their own washhand basins, but now all rooms in the commercially sponsored residences are equipped with them.

[2.38] The finishes are "generally vinyl floor tiles to the rooms with a sound absorbing tile in the corridors, all set on a screed which is insulated from the main structure by glass wool on top of the precast concrete structural floors. This provides a minimum of 48 decibels sound reduction between floors" (ibid, p. 10).

university engineer took responsibility for the service installations. There was a minimum use of site plant so that the work would be within the scope of a number of local contractors, and as far as was feasible the separate trades carried out their work without waiting on others. Details were so designed that there was little waste from cutting and as many standard components and dimensions were used as possible.

After much delicate negotiation, the university managed to secure a loan of £500,000 from the Friends' Provident and Century Life Office and the Barclays Bank Pension Fund at the very favourable rate of 8 per cent interest, to be paid back in yearly amounts of £44,000 over a period of thirty years. Word was still awaited from the U.G.C. about what contribution they would be able to make, although its officers had received the idea with approbation in the first instance and its deputy chairman had come up to Lancaster in February 1967 in order to discuss it in more detail with the university. Although the scheme was still just viable without U.G.C. help, the university nevertheless hoped very much for a subvention for furniture and fittings, rates, and professional fees. In the end, after a delay of eight months while the matter of principle was discussed with the Department of Education and Science, the university was told that it had been granted the first two, but not the third; but that this grant was related strictly to the particular proposal from Lancaster.[2.39]

The difficulties having therefore been overcome, the university was enabled to go ahead with the scheme, and Cartmel's first eight blocks were duly erected and completed in a very tight time schedule, by October 1968. This was not quite the end of building in Cartmel, however, for in June 1969 the Vice-Chancellor noted that

> A shortage of space in the colleges at Bailrigg has been causing us some trouble. The main reason for this is the growth of research units attached to non-science departments—a growth which is of course to be welcomed, but now uses up some 48 teaching rooms. . . . As a consequence, a substantial number (up to 200) of non-resident students cannot be provided with a place in a study at Bailrigg during 1969–70, and (despite the completion of Furness College) the situation will be much the same in 1970–71 and 1971–72. . . . We levy a special fee of £20 per student on local authorities, one of the main justifications for which is that in the shared study-rooms we provide exceptionally good study facilities. We therefore have a strong moral responsibility to provide these facilities for *all* students, and it will cause discontent if some are excluded.

[2.39] The initiative shown by Lancaster was vindicated in April 1968 when, in a circular sent by the U.G.C. to all universities, Sir John Wolfenden announced that £900,000 in grant-aid over the years 1968–72 had been set aside to help with rates and furnishings for loan-financed residences of the Lancaster type.

After considering all possibilities, he therefore suggested that a further two blocks of commercially-sponsored residence be added to Cartmel, and that forty-eight students be moved into these from the main college building (thus releasing teaching and study room space), as well as providing accommodation for an additional sixteen. The university was able to secure a further £55,000 from the same company as before—although this time at an interest rate of 10½ per cent—and the two extra blocks were duly added.

The County College, of course, had no financial problems of this kind, because of the generous benefaction by Lancashire. A minute of the Executive Council, 27 October 1964, records that

> Mr. McCall reported, in confidence, that the Lancashire County Council, in pursuance of their earlier promise to consider at a later stage, the making of a capital grant to the University, were being recommended by their Finance Committee to contribute to the University the equivalent of the capital cost of building a Hall of Residence for 250 students, up to a cost not exceeding £500,000.

The Executive Council expressed their "great pleasure" at this news; and planning went forward almost at once. At a meeting of December 1964, between officers of the County Council and the University, the Vice-Chancellor suggested a site to the north of the science complex, with a frontage on the spine. There was discussion about whether the building should include teaching accommodation, at the university's expense, as well as study spaces for non-residential students along the lines planned for the other colleges. The Vice-Chancellor

> hoped that it might be possible to exploit the County's project as an opportunity to experiment to see how the cost of student residence might be reduced and how provision could be made to fit more closely with what students really want. He thought it would be right to guard against the sort of building which might confine students to an institutional sort of life and that there was a case for breaking the space up into smaller units (groups of 10 or 20) who could prepare light meals for themselves and to mix socially. Apart from this, however, it was hoped that the college would be in a self-contained unit which might cater for conferences and out of term activities and it was thought that this would be particularly attractive to the County Council who might wish to use it for these purposes. The County's officers were sure that this would be greatly welcomed by the County Council who were at present often in difficulties through not having accommodation of this sort available to them.

It was clear from the outset that the County Architect, Mr. Roger Booth, would be the project architect for this building, although acting in this instance as a private architect; and a provisional completion date of July 1969 was fixed. Mr. Booth, although greatly admiring the overall development plan for the university as being cohesive and exceedingly well integrated, did not wish to follow the material or colour used elsewhere at Bailrigg, but did want to incorporate a particularly handsome oak tree which stood to the north-east corner of the site into his scheme. These two facts together suggested the site which was eventually chosen. It was also recognized that, although the gift of money meant that the university would not be as closely tied to the wishes of the U.G.C. as when grant-in-aid finance for a whole project was being provided, if they would agree to give a grant to the university for the professional fees, and the furniture and equipment associated with the building, then the whole of the donation from the county could be devoted to the building itself. Care was therefore taken to set the plan within the limits normally laid down by the U.G.C.,[2.40] who in March 1965 agreed in principle to help with fees and furnishing, as well as with fixed kitchen equipment.

Mr. Roger Booth contributed an article in December 1969 to the first issue of the *County College Gazette* explaining the principles on which he worked. He comments that the forerunner of the college was in fact the Castle School in that part of Lancaster known as the Ridge for, in 1962, the County Architect and his staff had

decided to depart for their major buildings from normal methods of building in the traditional vein, using the traditional crafts and materials. This is the first basic difference between County College and any other building at Lancaster University. Such a departure was seen by the County Architect at that time to be the necessary resultant of the social, economic, and industrial forces which are at work within the community, and which will, before too long, supersede timber, brick-work, and masonry. . . .

Thus, the first decision to be made at the County College was automatic. It should be panel-built in reinforced concrete, of a pre-cast method of production, manufactured off-site. It should not pay any regard to previous methods involving brick-work and carpentry in its general form. Such a basic decision can, of course, only derive from the top, but from this point on, as the idea grew, the expansion of it lay between three people—the County Architect, the Project Architect, and the Chief Structural Engineer. . . . Understandably there were other disciplines which had to be observed, the College being an integral part of a larger nucleus of Architecture, whose Architects had already decided to design in a continuous theme, using more traditional methods. . . .

The next concept in the question of form was a recognizable horizonta-

---

[2.40] The same principle was adopted with all the buildings financed primarily by appeal funds.

lity throughout the University. . . . Thus, an expression of horizontality (as opposed to verticality) became the second basic concept of sympathy in which County College could keep faith with the rest.

A third basic thought which affected the Architects was the cardinal fact of the University system itself, which can only be described as traditional in the sense that Lancaster is a Collegiate and not a Departmental University. All its units are Collegiate in the mediaeval sense that each is self-contained and, in order to express such an individual community value, nothing has ever been invented yet which can supplant what happened in Oxford in the 13th century when the first College, Merton, was built around a squarish quadrangle. Such courtyards had one entry only—a hole or archway in one side of the square; in essence a terribly simple idea and, furthermore, one which still actually works. . . .

Given a general idea of location there was, of course, only one possible way of siting such a square and that was around the oak tree—whose ultimate destiny could not possibly have occurred to the agricultural labourer who had spared it as a sapling a hundred and fifty years ago.

He then explains that two schemes were toyed with: the first was a tower unit for student rooms, with some independent and loosely related two- or three-storey blocks for communal and teaching activities; and the second was a double courtyard, with a free-standing lecture theatre linking the two. At this stage, however, the County Council decided that they did not want their gift confused with U.G.C. teaching accommodation but that the county's building must be seen as a separate entity of its own. The architect therefore took out one courtyard square from the second scheme, while making it four storeys instead of three. He continues:

If the discipline of regularity in the detailed design of 300 students' rooms . . . could be achieved, this would give the opportunity to standardize components, meaning mass manufacture from the same concrete moulds, meaning the economy of structure which could afford the required quality —and even a bit more communal accommodation than had been requested, for, to be honest, we needed a bit more to make the ground floor fit decently under the three students' floors. . . .

The final work-out showed an overall rate of £5.11.0. per square foot of floor area—exactly commensurate with any other College, and this included the white stone-facings, the best kind of aluminium windows, a wash-basin in each room, a lot of good tough mahogany on the internal fittings, and an external surface which is virtually maintenance free—this latter being very important for the University funds. Selective Employment Tax and the addition of two lifts put the half-million pounds up to the £540,000 mark.

That ruthlessness previously mentioned had been applied, and the pre-cast concrete method was refined down to the barest minimum—at the end only ten concrete parts, the hard-core nucleus being, at the ground floor, a repetitive series of pre-cast concrete "portal" arches, or, in other words, a cloister based on a modern cantilever instead of on an ancient vaulting system. . . .

The cloister-posts continued concentrically right up through the corridors, tier on tier, and in the transverse direction from inner to outer walls they were met by concrete cross walls, each wall cast in one piece. The floors went from rib to rib over the ground floor and from wall to wall on the upper floors, each room floor again being cast in one.

This left only the oriel window panels and the outside corners to be dealt with. The oriels really give the College its surface geometry and their design also aimed at a smaller window area per room than a lot of modern architecture is prepared to allow. It seemed to us that the exposure of the University site in a northern coastal climate should put a distinct limit to the size of windows on upper floors. Privacy for the individual student was another consideration. . . .

Coupled with the design of the oriels is the white stone banding between each floor and over the complete facade of the ground floor arches. This is the carboniferous limestone of the North Country, a magnificent stone of Palaeozoic age which can be sawn into a thin facing slab, having the endearing quality of keeping its silvery white colour on the faces exposed to rain.

He then goes on to explain that the partition walls between rooms were to be of heavy concrete which, with a thickness of only six inches, would nevertheless give sound insulation against 45 decibels, while the staff penthouses on the roof were to be of lightweight insulated timber with claddings of tiles, copper and lead.[2.41] He sees it, he concludes, as

a proud building—severe and incapable of compromise. It may yet show a fault or two in this respect, but although it is ancient in its basic form it is truly twentieth century in its technique and expression of that form; and all the men in the Lancashire Architects' Department like to think that because of these qualities it may conceivably have some chance of remaining timeless.

Certainly Mr. Booth has achieved a building distinctive in appearance—and helped to create a college which probably has more of an individual ethos than any other at Lancaster; partly, perhaps, because there is no teaching

---

[2.41] Mention should also be made of the floor of the courtyard, which is paved with a handsome limestone of a colour like dark slate, brought from Moher, Co. Clare, which was rough riven and sand-blasted to give it its uneven texture.

accommodation within the college and fewer non-residential students (since there has not been the same provision of study spaces as elsewhere). In its particularity the County College perhaps gives one of the clearest examples at Bailrigg of how closely physical provision and social interaction are bound up together. The building was completed, at the cost of some last-minute panics, by the beginning of the Michaelmas Term 1969 and was officially opened by H.M. The Queen during her visit on 17 October.

Retracing our footsteps, we come to the Great Hall complex, which includes the Great and Minor Halls, the Jack Hylton Music Rooms, the Nuffield Theatre Studio and adjoining workshop, and the Fine Arts Studios, as well as the necessary administrative and circulation areas.[2.42] Originally Professors Tom Lawrenson and W. A. Murray, who were responsible for much of the initial planning of the Nuffield Theatre Studio, wished it to be a separate building standing by itself, but there were possibilities of reductions in costs, in areas such as cloakrooms, if facilities could be shared with a larger complex.

A memorandum of February 1965 over their names and the Vice-Chancellor's states that the purpose of the proposed studio would be "to allow practical scholarly investigation of the history of world theatre, by the reconstitution of the physical conditions of the theatre at any moment of its past (stages, decors and, to a limited extent, auditoria)". For example, the document went on, one of the great difficulties "in the understanding of early seventeenth century French staging conventions has always been our ignorance of the dimensions of the stage of the one Parisian public theatre of the time—the Hotel de Bourgogne. . . . With our experimental 'stage' we would be in a position to solve the problem *by building it to lifesize proportions*, and working out the practical staging difficulties from the authentic text". Another function would be "to serve as an area in which new ideas for decor, for relations between stage and auditorium, and for staging conventions, can be evolved in their preliminary stages, and in which drama groups can construct, paint and try out their decor, and (subject to availability) conduct their rehearsals".

[2.42] Despite the very full range of facilities for the performing arts and special occasions described below, problems of conflict of usage, and of noise, caused some of the student body, in 1969, to dream up what became known as the Umbrella Project; that is, a domed building which would have been built of glass reinforced plastic and capable of seating up to 450 people. Originally sponsored by the Theatre Group, the building would also have been a general recreational and noisy area, especially as it was to be sited well away from other buildings on the top of the hill beyond the pavilion. Unfortunately the cost of the scheme was seen to be increasing greatly as investigation of it developed; a further stumbling block would have been that the square footage it represented would have been used by the U.G.C. in calculation of student communal areas, thereby reducing the space available for general student use in the colleges at a time when it was already being cut back by the reduction of U.G.C. norms (which have fallen from about 10 to 7 sq. ft. per student since the university began its building programme).

G

However, the studio

> would *not* be a theatre, though it would be convenient to provide it with
> simple and movable seating for small audiences, since the relationship of
> audience to actor would be one of the subjects to be studied. . . . The
> Studio is conceived as an open space on which movable stages can be
> built, with a roof capable of carrying scenery in many different positions,
> and electrical services at a great number of different points on floor, ceiling
> and walls so that various schemes of lighting can be tried. The basic
> internal requirement is flexibility; there must be no permanent structure
> on the floor; stages and auditoria would be simulated by dry-building or
> the assembly in different forms of simple units. . . .
>
> The basic requirement is a large heated shed, whose walls support a
> strong grid-type ceiling at a height of about 36 feet. Natural lighting is
> unnecessary. Consideration of various possible types of stage suggests to
> us basic dimensions of 75 feet by 150 feet, but the form need not be
> rectangular: for instance, it would be convenient to have an increase of
> width at one point to enable us to simulate the European Renaissance
> stage, which had flat wings sliding to the sides of the stage on grooves.

There were also to be associated cloakrooms, office space and generous
workshop provision.

The Nuffield Foundation, in March 1965, having been re-assured that the
building would be "more than a helpful adjunct to teaching used now and
then", offered to make a grant of £70,000 towards building such a drama
studio and workshops (a sum later increased to £80,000), and the university
appointed a special consultant, Mr. Stephen Joseph, of the University of
Manchester and secretary to the Society of Theatre Consultants, to assist with
the design. Unfortunately, although no one knew it, he was already a very ill
man, and he died, in his thirties, before he was able to see the enterprise
come to fruition. Shepheard and Epstein were appointed as the project
architects for the whole of the Great Hall complex, including the Nuffield
Theatre Studio, and worked with Stephen Joseph on outline ideas for the
theatre workshop; although, because of shortage of funds and problems of
illness, this was one of the less smooth planning and building operations.
One of Professor Lawrenson's concepts which was lost, for example, was that
of having the studio built in a T-shape, so that the top bar of the T would be
100 ft. wide and the long leg 150 ft. long, to give the necessary distance for the
viewer, for instance, to stand back from even the most extreme form of
perspective set. This long leg of the T could also be used as the area for
constructing stage-sets and painting scenery. In order to fit in the accommodation for Fine Arts, however, Mr. Epstein had to move the long leg to
one side, thus forming a rectangle with a section taken out of one corner. The

dimensions were also altered, so that the studio is 75 ft. square in plan and 24 ft. high, and the workshop, which leads off it, is 80 ft. by 35 ft. After much debate it was agreed that there should be a central well in the studio (which was originally to have had two levels, but finally only had one): this pit is 5 ft. deep and 50 ft. square. Above the pit is a rigid but easily removable floor, mainly in units of 8 by 4 ft., which also contains a revolving stage unit 25 ft. in diameter. Overhead there is a gridded ceiling, from which to hang curtains or projection screens, together with a system of catwalks spanned by eight moving gantries. There is a generously sized and fully sound-proofed projection box and the studio can be used for film, television, sound recording or broadcasting, as well as live performances ranging from an opera to a single guitar player. There is also scope for mounting exhibitions of various kinds, and ample space for dances or special functions.[2.43]

The Fine Arts Studios, in the north-west corner of the rectangle housing the theatre studio, were financed from the appeal fund, and include space for painting, sculpture (in stone, wood or metal), and pottery (including a kiln). The Great Hall, on the other hand, was financed by the U.G.C. and is a rectangular box, two storeys high, with a gallery on three sides at first floor level. As Professor Murray noted in 1966, the design had to be a compromise because of the variety of functions it has to fulfil, which include concerts, dances, examinations, exhibitions and degree congregations. The project architect, Mr. Epstein, found this a difficult building to organize since, unlike some of the others, there was no particular client or user committee. Furthermore, although he saw the need for a great part of the floor to be flat, he wished to raise part of it because he believes that people will always want to view from a vantage point above the main proceedings: after much discussion it was therefore agreed to raise the margin of the hall by one foot in height, with a width equal to that of the balconies above it. Mr. Epstein hoped also by this means to encourage the use of the long sides of the hall, so that, for example, a string quartet might perform on a raised area abutting the raised margin, and have an audience grouped in a semi-circle around it. This suggestion echoes ideas he has had at different stages for an open-air amphitheatre: in the early days he sketched one in on the hillside in the area where the pavilion

---

[2.43] The logistics of the Nuffield Theatre Studio have proved to be complicated, because of conflicting claims on space, and equipment which demands a fairly high level of technical skill: a good many hours need to be expended to arrange the studio's facilities in the various configurations that are required. There is no doubt that a multi-functional building will always have a variety of claims made on it, and very skilful timetabling is necessary to dovetail undergraduate teaching, graduate research, student projections and existing shows. In 1969, in order to permit the introduction of live audiences, who would pay for their admission, the Nuffield Theatre Club was created; but the cardinal principles of the studio, such as having no fixed seating, proscenium arch or particular playing area, have been adhered to.

now stands, and in the first plans of the Great Hall complex there is a smaller amphitheatre behind the hall itself. This idea disappeared, however, in later plans, the most unconventional shape he achieved being the open courtyard which lies between the Great Hall and the Jack Hylton Music Rooms, and the main Jack Hylton Music Room itself, both of them being stepped down towards the centre on all four sides, with a gallery above. Thus music can be performed in the centre space with people clustered round on the steps and in the gallery above, or a platform stage can be formed along one side, with the audience, facing the musicians, being seated in the central well and on the rest of the steps. The university was extremely fortunate in attracting funds for such a comprehensive range of music rooms, which include teaching and practice rooms, recording and artists' rooms and accommodation for the director of music and his staff: £50,000 was donated in memory of Jack Hylton[2.44] and on 7 July 1967 the Rt. Hon. Jennie Lee (at that time Minister with Special Responsibility for the Arts) came to lay the foundation stone, assisted by Mr. Bernard Delfont. Having such a generous area set aside as custom-built accommodation for music, especially when the 2,500 sq. ft. of the Minor Hall is included, has helped substantially to give the university its strong and early start in music.

Some of the early documents for the Great Hall complex make mention of a specialized applied linguistics building, and because of his special interest in both the technology and the application of linguistics, Professor W. A. Murray was involved in the planning of what has been known at different periods as the language laboratory, the audio-visual aids centre, and the learning aids building. Originally it was intended that this building should be sited between Chemistry and Cartmel College, but Professor Bevington was not in favour of this positioning and instead the Buildings Committee agreed to place it between the Great Hall complex and County College. The preamble to the Schedule II, sent to the U.G.C. in February 1967, noted that

> This building is intended to provide language laboratory, audio-visual and teaching machines services for the University of Lancaster up to a capacity of 3,500 students in the university as a whole. This accommodation is based on the following assumption:
>
> That approximately half the students will be Arts and Social science students, and that approximately half these students will be directly concerned with language study as part of their final degree. It is thought that another substantial fraction of the student numbers, possibly one-fifth, might be concerned with a language at some stage in their university career and require some language laboratory facilities.
>
> The amount of language laboratory capacity which seems necessary on

---

[2.44] See Chapter 1, page 34.

these assumptions might be of the order of 2,800 student hours per week (excluding vacation term uses and library uses). . . . The third laboratory we regard as essential for the Library uses which have developed since our phase I began to work. The laboratory in phase I is now used quite extensively for the reproduction of lectures for students whose subject choices are eccentric, and difficult to reconcile with the timetable in a manner economical in the use of teaching staff. . . . The remaining laboratory is intended to meet the language requirements of Science and Technology, in which there is certainly going to be a demand for the provision of elementary language training. Since the accommodation is of a flexible nature and can be used either for language laboratory or for audiovisual or teaching machines work, it is thought probable that internal adjustments of equipment from time to time will look after any disparity between the estimates now made and their eventual realization in practice. Each laboratory, on the assumption that it is used for a full working day of 8 hours minimum, 6 days per week, ought to produce 1,200 student hours per working week. . . .

It will be seen from the attached plan that this building now contains a small television studio and associated control facilities. This is intended to act as the central control for all the uses of C.C.T.V. in the arts and social science departments of the university.

The U.G.C., however, were not entirely happy about the building, and queried the cantilevered overhang of the first floor, the circular shape (on grounds of cost), and the siting and shape (which they felt would make it difficult to extend or alter). The university pointed out that a circular shape reduced the amount of non-usable floor space, and in any case, when the quantity surveyor had costed both the rectangular and the circular schemes, they came out to within £300 of each other. A further building to the north was expected to take care of the next 3,500 students. The U.G.C. acceded to the plan, but, in designating it as an arts rather than as a science building, cut back on the gross area allowed for it; and substituted mechanical ventilation for the planned air-conditioning. These delays naturally held back the building and although planning of it was proceeding from the early days of the university it was not completed until the summer of 1969.

If we leave the north spine and turn west and southwards we come to the Chaplaincy Centre, standing prominently in front of Lonsdale College and a main feature to which the eyes of everyone coming up the approach road are drawn. At the outset Mr. Epstein had suggested a site to the north-west of Alexandra Square for a chapel, and at first it was to have been linked to University House. However, a letter of June 1964 from Mr. Gerald Cassidy to Mr. Epstein noted that

The Roman Catholic Diocesan Authorities are most anxious that agreement should be reached at an early stage on the precise placing and size of site, together with a precise schedule of accommodation and massing of their building. The Bishop of Lancaster, who has instructed me, has asked for a separate building which will be used purely for the purpose of Catholics attending the University and which will incorporate a small hall, library, games room, several meeting or study rooms, together with accommodation for a resident Chaplain. The main feature will be a Chapel, probably to seat 200 or 300.

Mr. Epstein saw this new proposal as being intrinsically different, because the area would be larger, necessitating a removal to a site further north, and its use would be both more social and more frequent than he had envisaged. He wondered whether an outlying site would now be so appropriate:

> If I were a Roman Catholic I would feel that social rooms such as these should be on the spine to have a chance of becoming popular. The site previously suggested would I think be large enough for what they want but people would not pass there by chance as it were. Another problem is of the resident chaplain. I am sure that our principle of not having individual houses must be adhered to through thick and thin, unless we plan the formation of a suburb, which would in my opinion be a terrible thing. Maybe we could put the chaplain on the upper floor of the meeting rooms, etc.

In the meantime, however, other denominations were becoming interested in sharing in the centre; as contributors of finance a committee consisting of the (Anglican) Bishop of Blackburn, the (Roman Catholic) Bishop of Lancaster, and the Rev. G. A. Maland (representing the Free Churches), held discussions together, while agreeing to retain Cassidy and Ashton (a firm specializing in religious buildings, especially for the Roman Catholic church) as architects. Later on the Jewish community joined in the venture and helped to contribute the necessary finance; and the U.G.C. agreed to help with the cost of fees and fittings for the social areas of the centre (as opposed to areas reserved strictly for religious observance). Talk, early in 1966, of a centre which would "consist of three structures so designed as to form an architectural unity" gradually became the unified clover-leaf building that we see today. In Mr. Cassidy's own words:

> Initially there were to be separate chaplaincies and then as the Christian denominations became increasingly united in intent, it was decided that the building should comprise two linked Chapels, one for joint Anglican and Free Church use and the other for Roman Catholics. The rest of the accommodation would be shared and would generally be used to

encourage joint activities common to all churches and exploratory meetings with those of other faiths or of no faith at all.

Within the shared section, but not originally envisaged, is a suite reserved for Jewish meeting and worship, and on the first floor are flats for the resident Chaplains with guest space, further small discussion rooms and library/reading space.

As soon as the brief began to clarify, it was felt that, anxious though the churches were to preserve individuality of worship, there must be no thought of two quite distinct chapels linked (and separated) by accommodation for communal activities. The individual elements of two chapels and other accommodation were seen to be of equal importance, but subservient to the whole theme, and the process of design forced the conclusion that by far the most important feature was the link which quite literally held the pieces together.

The shape follows naturally from this philosophy. While the identity of each element is preserved, each develops into and is swept upwards towards a tripartite spire surmounting and giving majesty to the central link area and enabling it to dominate the whole. The difficult visual task has been not only to retain the individual identity of each part while making it subordinate to the general mass, but also to provide facilities for joint use without an undue feeling of separation. To this end the whole glazed screen to the rear of each chapel glides back to open very fully to the central area which will be the hub of joint services.

Although the design interior of the building was rapidly agreed, however, there was some difficulty about the external appearance. At first the Buildings Committee were very hesitant about the shamrock layout, for the three segments were flat, like three drums laid together. Mr. Epstein therefore insisted that the drums must sweep upwards towards the centre of the building, and also that the top should be white, to match the rest of the buildings. Although greatly at variance in style with the rest of the buildings the Centre was nevertheless agreed to by the Buildings Committee, and by the rest of the members of the university when the design was explained in a talk given by Mr. Cassidy.[2.45] It has become a building, which although still controversial, is exciting in its visual impact and has been one of the most acclaimed single buildings on the site by many visitors to Bailrigg. The prominent position, however, served to heighten a later controversy, in the summer of 1968, about what should be placed on the top of the three spires of the building. Some Jewish and other students found the three crosses on the tops

[2.45] Talks on architectural plans for the university were a fairly regular feature of the early days of the university, whether by Mr. Epstein or the other architects; the last of these was given in June 1970, when members of the university were invited to contribute their views for onward transmission to Mr. Epstein.

of the spires, as originally planned, offensive on theological grounds—although the Chief Rabbi had no strong feelings against them—and wanted a Star of David on one of them instead. The matter was taken up by Federation who, in May 1968, passed a motion to the effect that

> if the Chaplaincy Centre is to fulfil its functions as an inter-religious centre then it should not be dominated by symbols representing any particular religion.
>
> The three crosses above the Centre, at present, exclude all but Christians from worshipping there, this is unjustified in the light of the financial contributions made by the minority groups. The meeting urges the Chaplaincy Committee to urgently reconsider the matter.

This view was endorsed by some members of the university's staff, as well as interested and informed people in Lancaster and it was felt that (to quote from a minute of a Chaplaincy Centre meeting of the time), "since the Centre is appreciably larger than anticipated and enjoys an extremely commanding position on the Bailrigg site . . . to add to it three rather conspicuous and specifically Christian symbols might cause the Centre to be regarded as obtruding itself to an unwarrantable and discourteous extent on the University scene at large and might also be interpreted as a declaration by the University to the outside world that the University of Lancaster is a specifically Christian foundation". The new Michaelmas Term was about to start, however, and the three crosses were still in position when the compromise suggestion for the removal of the cross bar and top section of the highest cross was carried out. That is why, in spite of an alternative suggestion by the Bishop of Blackburn that there should be mounted on the top spire a weathervane with the symbol of the fish, there still remain one spike and two crosses.

The Centre was completed early in 1969 and dedicated on 2 May by representatives of the main churches involved; the Rev. J. A. Figures (Moderator of the North West Province of the Congregational Church in England and Wales), the Rev. M. Weisman (chaplain and counsellor to Jewish students), the Bishop of Blackburn (the Right Rev. Dr. C. R. Claxton), and the Roman Catholic Bishop of Lancaster (the Right Rev. B. C. Foley). The building has more than justified itself, both as a purely religious centre, and as neutral ground on which staff and students can meet freely together; and it has already been used, in February 1971, for a B.B.C. television recording of a "Songs of Praise" programme and a live broadcast of a Sunday service.

Walking back towards Alexandra Square, we pass the Computer Building on our right, which adjoins University House: essentially this is a custom-designed building, of one and two storeys high, to house one highly specialized piece of equipment, and its architecture is strictly functional. From there we retrace our footsteps through Alexandra Square to the south spine which begins, rather forbiddingly perhaps, with more shops to the left and the blank east wall of the Library to the right. Overhead is a plastic (Oroglass) canopy, secured by weights hanging from the underside, which serves to keep out the elements but let in the light. The contours fall away at this point and there is more than one flight of steps to negotiate before we reach Furness College on the left and a building housing the departments of Biological and Environmental Sciences to the right. Furness—and later Fylde—were planned from the outset as having a main college building, of which the social and community activities were to be financed by the U.G.C. and, separated physically but forming part of the same collegiate entity, blocks of commercially sponsored residences with, on their roofs, a certain limited number of staff flats. The configuration of the residence blocks of these two colleges, in contrast to the filling up of sides of a rectangle that had taken place in Cartmel, show the greater freedom that Mr. Haydn Smith now enjoyed. The principles on which they were built were identical to those of Cartmel, and need no further elucidation, but a word should be said about the additional residences which it was agreed in 1969 should be built for Fylde. The university was fortunate in being able to raise another loan, this time from the Co-operative Permanent (Nationwide) Building Society, for up to a further six blocks at a cost of £23,000 per block, at an interest rate of 9½ per cent per annum, with the condition that all the blocks were grouped together under one college and not scattered between several.[2.46]

One further point of interest concerning Furness College is that it marks the end of separate and full-scale catering facilities for each college. At the time when the college was being planned, in 1969, the new Controller of Catering had just been appointed and consultations were being held with the U.G.C. about future catering needs.[2.47] The upshot of these discussions was that the university decided to have four small, separate outlets in Furness, consisting of a take-away fish and chip shop, a grill room, a salad bowl, and a private dining room for specific orders on particular occasions. So far, only the fish and chip shop has been equipped and the salad bowl used as a coffee and snack bar. By the time that Fylde was being planned, only a drinks bar and associated snacks were included;[2.48] and Pendle and Grizedale, the seventh and eighth colleges, will be equipped in the same scant way.

Completing our tour of the college accommodation in the south spine, therefore, we come to the building operations associated with Pendle and Grizedale colleges, which will be twinned in an even greater intimacy than Bowland and Lonsdale were, to the extent of sharing the same reception and

[2.46] In the event, only an additional four blocks are being built.
[2.47] See Chapter 4, pages 265 to 267.
[2.48] Furness College, of course, has its own bar.

porters' are, and with the respective colleges opening off the two sides of the same entrance hall. The financing of these colleges proved to be something of a cliff-hanging operation and demonstrates very well the increasing difficulties obstructing the way of university building schemes. In January 1972 the Vice-Chancellor consulted the student body over "whether to proceed with the residential parts of Pendle and Grizedale Colleges, which are to be loan-financed. The matter is rather urgent: the non-residential parts of Pendle and Grizedale are in the 1973–74 approved building programme, just announced, and there is not much time for planning if a start is to be made on April 1st, 1973". He then discussed student rent levels and the extent to which they would be affected if further loan finance was procured, in view of the general principle that "adding new units should not increase the burdens on other students". Taking into account possible increases in student grants and a rise in conference income, he predicted that the weekly rent increase for a single room anywhere on the site, with washbasin but no heating, would be 15 to 20 new pence higher than it otherwise would be. He wanted to know whether the students wished the university to go ahead with the building of residences for Pendle and Grizedale—bearing in mind that if they were deferred, more students would be seeking flats, with a consequent rise in rents. The answer came back in the affirmative as to the building of the colleges, and the next problem was to seek the necessary finance. By early summer they were fortunate in having secured the offer of £750,000 from the university's own bankers, the National Westminster Bank Limited (helped by the Area Manager, Mr. A. V. Nelson), at an interest rate (after completion) of 2 per cent over the bank's base rate, to be paid back over a period of twenty-four years. Inflation interest rates were increasing rapidly, however, and in January 1973 the Vice-Chancellor was forced to write to the chairman of the Student Representative Council, Mr. Jerry Drew, to say that not only were the tenders likely to come in at higher figures than had originally been estimated, but that the

> annual payments of principal and interest, which were estimated at between 7 and 9 per cent, have risen to at least $11\frac{1}{2}$ per cent, and other costs have also increased more than expected since the estimates were made. The consequence is that the weekly rent for a single room with central heating and wash basin, which is £4·25 this year and £4·45 next year, would have to rise in 1974/5 to not less than £5·00 in order to cover the costs of the additional building. This is 35p more than we were originally estimating, and it would still leave us with a deficit over the whole of the residence accounts. . . .

A rent of £5 in 1974/5 will still be below the U.G.C.'s permitted maximum. It does, however, represent a higher figure than was in mind when

S.R.C. encouraged us to go ahead with the residence scheme and agreed that a small consequent increase in the rents of all accommodation would be acceptable. I should be most grateful if you would find out from S.R.C., if possible within a week, whether you think that we should still go ahead with the scheme on the assumptions about rent which now have to be made, or whether you think that it should be halted.

The S.R.C. still considered that the risk ought to be taken but the tenders, when they came in, were even higher than had been feared, leaving a shortfall of about 15 per cent over the whole contract. Much frenetic negotiation took place both with the U.G.C. and within the university (and it was decided, at the same time, to conduct an immediate internal inquiry into the apparently high administrative and general running costs of all the colleges). The upshot of all this activity was that, as the Vice-Chancellor noted in a memorandum of March 1973, the U.G.C.-financed main college building (including rooms for the Centre for Visual Arts) would be built within the cost limits, but that the proposed staff flats would have to go. He said:

> The main problem has been with the student residence. At the present level of U.G.C. subsidy, there is no way of making the scheme viable. However, there is believed to be a chance that this week the U.G.C. will announce a higher level of subsidy; and, *if this is done*, we are satisfied that it is just possible to take the risk of allowing the whole of the residence to proceed, and that the alternative of building only *part* of the residence is less attractive. . . . Care is being taken not to make savings by an unacceptable reduction of building standards.
>
> In assessing the situation, we have assumed that rents will continue to increase in proportion to, but not significantly faster than, student grants. Looking at the situation in detail, we find that the difficulty of building at a reasonable rent arises much more from the cost of *maintenance and administration* of the colleges (which take two-thirds of the rent) than from interest charges. The U.G.C. has noted that these costs are high, and they will expect us to do all in our power to reduce them.
>
> If no reduction of costs is achieved, there will be in 1974–75 a loss at a rate of about £30,000, probably diminishing in later years, but falling on general funds. This would be equivalent (e.g.) to doing without eight or ten lecturers. This sum is almost certainly in excess of what the U.G.C. would consider reasonable.

Fortunately for the university the U.G.C., within a day or two of its own deadline for acceptance of a tender, announced an increase in its subvention for loan-financed residence of up to 25 per cent of the cost. Nevertheless, the cuts in standard of accommodation, furnishings and fittings had to be cut back with a severity that impelled the planning officer for Grizedale College, Dr. Alan Wellburn, to resign and a certain degree of student discontent was observable.[2.49] Innovations in these colleges are the units for occupation by six students each, which will be more akin to sharing a flat, and a certain number of units for two people, intended for married students.

We have now reached the most southern point of the site and, as we turn back on our route, we should observe the building operations for Gillow House, which is being built to house the departments that comprise the School of Management and Organizational Sciences, thus being the closest that the university has come to having a special building for non-science subjects. The existence, location and name of Gillow House have all been the subject of vigorous controversy within the university, but for reasons that have little or nothing to do with the building programme.

Opposite Gillow House is the Engineering Building, which also houses the Department of Systems Engineering. The university was particularly anxious to keep costs to a minimum on this building because of national stringency. £10 million of approved university building had been deferred from the 1969–70 programme, and the only encouragement that the university had received was a letter of February 1969 from the U.G.C., which commented that it was possible funds might be found for additional work in 1971–2. The architect for the project, Mr. Haydn Smith, saw his brief as designing a building that the economic climate could afford, i.e. more cheaply than is customary for a building of this type, while coming up with a solution which would give the occupants the space they needed (including a very large workshop) and leaving the greatest amount of flexibility that could be achieved for subsequent change of use. He envisaged the building as a great envelope, which would stabilize the internal and external conditions, and a Building Committee minute of May 1969 mentions a standard industrial Portal-type frame in which to fit all the necessary accommodation. The minute continues:

> Offices could be at a mezzanine level within the main laboratories and workshop accommodation at ground floor level. Circulation would be provided by using aisles between the various project spaces rather than corridors. . . . It was considered that a basic cost of £5.5.0 per square foot gross [as against £8 to £10 per square foot, which was the usual figure at that time for Engineering buildings] could be achieved provided there were no excessive site costs and external works. . . . [The meeting noted that] these buildings were usually purpose built for the specific needs of a particular head of department. Any rigidity of design in this particular instance would be offset by providing more accommodation

---

[2.49] See Chapter 6, pages 356 to 357.

for a given sum of money whilst still retaining a measure of internal flexibility.

Fortunately, the physical needs for the type of engineering studied at Lancaster are not as onerous as in engineering curricula elsewhere and Professor French, the head of the department, accepted some limitations in order to reduce capital expenditure. The university, in order to do all it could to secure finance for the building, suggested building the first phase in two separate sections but, because the university was ready with its plans at a time late in 1970 when other universities were unable to start their projects by the end of the U.G.C. financial year, both phases were able to be started together. The final costing for which tenders were invited came to £470,000, a figure which was the cause of warm congratulation from the U.G.C.

Proceeding back along the south spine we reach the Indoor Recreation Centre. Recreational facilities were being considered by the Shadow Senate as early as March 1964, but very much in terms of joint ventures with local Lancaster facilities. In January 1965, however, in the course of a general discussion about the building programme which included some nominal figures for recreational facilities towards the end of the 1964-8 building programme, the Senate, while expressing general approval, "agreed to recommend to the Buildings Committee and the Council that greater financial provision should be made in the 1966-7 programme for recreational facilities." This was followed up in March by a memorandum from Dr. R. W. H. Small commenting that

> The acceptance by Senate of the building programme for 1964-8 which included provision for physical recreation facilities is assumed to imply that the principle of providing these facilities within the University is an acceptable one. It will be unnecessary therefore to stress the contribution such amenities make to University life except to say that physical activities do have an educational value and it is hoped that we shall treat such pursuits as having more than mere amusement value. Physical education could well fit into the broad concept of educational experience which we have recently considered to have creative and cultural elements.
>
> The material provisions proposed in the building programme are in conformity with some estimates of a general nature discussed at a recent colloquium on "Universities and Physical Education" held in the University of Sussex. These were, roughly, that the cost of creation of a reasonable range of physical activities is £100 per student place and that a playing field area at the rate of 1 acre per 50 students is acceptable. The proposals already made in the building programme compare favourably with those of other new Universities.
>
> The actual form of amenities was discussed at the Sussex colloquium,

several useful ideas were provided; two of these, which might be mentioned in relation to the plans for Bailrigg, were (1) Multipurpose halls which combines use for examinations and indoor sports such as badminton; these were said to receive sympathetic consideration by the U.G.C.; (2) An out-of-doors hard porous surface capable of all the year round, all-weather use e.g. hockey and soccer in winter and tennis in summer.

A Joint Athletics Committee was set up, with Dr. Small as chairman. No decisive moves, however, were taken until 1966 when, at a meeting of the Buildings Committee in March, the Vice-Chancellor said that

at the last meeting of Council, Lord Derby had commented on the serious shortage of recreational facilities and suggested that priority should be given to the provision of a swimming bath. However, the Joint Athletics Committee considered that the first priority should be the provision of a general purpose sports hall and it was intended to allocate up to £50,000 from Appeal Funds for this purpose.

The scheme duly went ahead and the first phase of the building was opened in 1967. It was not long, however, before there was a clearly demonstrable need for an extension of indoor recreational facilities, including judo, trampoline, gymnastics and fencing, as well as additional areas for squash and table tennis, and the provision of sauna baths and additional changing rooms and office space. Further expenditure of £70,000 from the Appeal was approved in 1969, although the subsequent application for Treasury funds for furniture and equipment was cut back fairly radically. So successful, however, is the director of physical education, Mr. Joe Medhurst, in involving students and staff, as well as the local community, in what he has to offer, that the facilities under his control are always very fully booked; so much so that, at the time of writing, further squash courts are in the process of being built.

Finally we come to the combined building for Biological Sciences and Environmental Sciences. Both these subjects were part of the Lancaster curriculum from the outset and were from the beginning included in the provisional 1967–8 building programme. The building, whose planning went ahead vigorously during 1966, was to be in three phases but, for a number of reasons, including the Government's decisions concerning the number of science students there should be in the country's universities, only two phases have so far been built. There is much need in a building of this kind for specialist equipment, including, for example, tanks for different kinds of fish under controlled conditions, a suite for radioactive work and another for animals, an electron microscope, and a special room on the roof for growing specimen plants for use in practical experiments, as well as the full range of undergraduate practical laboratories, and postgraduate and staff research facilities.

Thus we return to Alexandra Square and the plaque that commemorates the 1968 Civic Trust Award for the first stage of developments on the Bailrigg site. Given for "contributing to the environment by the creation of good, simple buildings and pleasant spaces", the official citation continued:

The sensitive handling of surfaces and plant material contributes to that end and helps to unfold the changing spaces between and within the buildings, thus providing a fitting setting for university life. The design successfully constitutes a finished entity at all stages of growth and has a flexibility which will allow freedom of choice of development and size for the university. The low rise buildings fit into the landscape, and first indication of the extensive landscape scheme with large forest trees is good.

CHAPTER 3

Academic Development

(i) The first degree structure and boards of studies

We saw in Chapter 1 how a new University came to be at Lancaster: we shall now look at the academic fabric and how it has been modified in certain respects since 1964.

It may be helpful first to describe some of the more unusual categories of student at Lancaster: most are here for the customary three-year honours degree course, but some attend for shorter periods. First of all there are each year a small number of "occasional" students, most of whom come from Western European universities to study for a brief period of anything between an academic term and one academic year. Subject to courses not having been over-subscribed, they have enormous freedom to choose courses which suit the requirements of their home universities and their own personal levels of attainment. They are not registered for a qualification of the university, but can be given documents showing which courses they have audited and what marks they have received for their written work.[3.1]

Recognized students, according to the official definition issued by the Senate in April 1968, are

> Students with standing at another university who undertake a period of full-time study at the University of Lancaster and who, although they are not registered for a qualification of this University, might in appropriate

---

[3.1] There is a problem about numbers: a Senate minute of December 1973 noted that the number to be admitted in 1974 could not be raised above the 1973 level because so many students were converging on a single department (English) and because "the question of student accommodation was problematic".

cases be provided with some form of certification of their work which gave them "credit" at their home university.

The understanding is that such students, who again are a small number and who may come from any part of the world, stay at Lancaster for two or three terms, and undertake particular courses with a view to completing them in full. They are assessed in exactly the same manner as other students, except that they usually have the option of whether or not to take the formal Part I and Part II written examinations.

There had been a few of both the two categories of student described above from the early days of the university. In December 1967, however, Professor Smart put a paper to the Senate in which he mentioned that

> Some people I met in the States were very interested in the possibility of sending students from colleges, etc., for a year abroad, at Lancaster.

After calculating that even if more than the overseas student fee were to be charged, the university could still offer a year in England, including fares, for the price of a year in a private college or university in the U.S.A., he continued

> The surplus fees could, if there were a predictable number per annum of students from this source, pay for extra people to teach in the University as a whole (it would be undesirable to segregate such students, presume). In return, Lancaster could offer a sensible system of credit applicable to the conditions prevailing in the students' home colleges.

The Senate, after discussion, agreed that Professor Smart's suggestion should be explored further, and students have been admitted under the scheme since 1969.

There have been a few difficulties, of course, of expectations not wholly met; in general, however, the scheme has been a great success and the small numbers admitted are because of the operation of a severe quota system and not for lack of applicants. Indeed, Mr. Martindale reports that not only are applications greatly in excess of places offered, but additional American students apply independently in the hope of entering as recognized students, and other universities in the United States have made overtures to Lancaster to see if they can be admitted under the scheme.[3.2]

The junior year of an American degree is, of course, the third in the four-year first degree that is usual in the U.S.A. This means that the visiting students are able to take courses from those offered in Part II, both from the second and third year offerings (with some bias towards the former) and, if

---

3.2 A significant proportion of the American students each year seek permission to stay on at Lancaster and complete the full degree course; a small number have been permitted to do so, and have achieved good results.

H

they still have not accumulated all the credits appropriate to their degree, they can make them up during their senior (fourth) year at their home institutions. So far the university has been able to guarantee them places in residence which has enabled them to play a full part in all aspects of university life: the university will, for example, particularly remember their contribution to drama. Usually one mentor from an American university participating in the scheme comes with them and stays at Bailrigg for the year, and additionally two or three of Lancaster's staff take responsibility as academic advisers. Two pleasant outcomes of the programme are that, each year, Lancaster has been presented with £1,000 by the Pennsylvania Colleges, a sum which is at the disposal of the Vice-Chancellor, and which he has normally given to a cause proposed by the Student Representative Council after a ballot of all students;[3.3] and that the University of Colorado has provided the funds for one graduating Lancaster student to go there each year to take a master's degree course.

One other special category of students should be mentioned: the mature undergraduates, who at Lancaster are defined as anyone of twenty-three or older, whether married and with children or not, who may seek admission with a lack of the conventional qualifications (a minimum of two subjects at Advanced Level) or whose previous formal education ended some years previously. From the beginning the university had a policy of admitting some such students each year, and of taking particular pains over applications from them: a document written by Professor S. G. Sturmey in 1964 speaks of looking for some older students to provide "sager counsel", who would enable the students to be more independent in their decision-making because of their wider experience. Statistics from the 1967 intake onwards which show that on average 8·6 per cent of the admissions has been of mature students,[3.4] but although such a figure may not be much in excess of the national average, the university's policy is that it is "in general favourably disposed towards applications from mature candidates" an attitude noted by the Advisory Centre for Education who reported finding Lancaster "particularly sympathetic" to mature students.[3.5]

Nevertheless, by 1971 there was growing evidence that local education

---

[3.3] Projects so far supported are the university's playgroup and crèche, University Radio Bailrigg, Clapdale Farm, and New Planet City (a playground project for the children of Lancaster with which a number of students have been associated).

[3.4] The complete figures are:

1967–68	7·9 per cent
1968–69	8·5
1969–70	9·4
1970–71	11·1
1971–72	6·4
1972–73	6·4
1973–74	10·3

[3.5] A.C.E. magazine *Where?*, May 1973 edition.

authorities were becoming worried about the number of such candidates admitted to universities with minimal qualifications, and were increasingly unwilling to make discretionary grants to them. The Undergraduate Admissions Committee discussed whether Lancaster should enter a scheme similar to the special mature matriculation examination organized by the J.M.B., or set an entrance examination which would strengthen the students' case when applying for a local education authority grant. The Lancaster admissions officer, Mr. Stephen Lamley, therefore wrote round to find out the practices of a sample of other universities in England and, predictably, found a wide divergence of attitude. Some universities used the Joint Matriculation Board examination or some form of written test devised by themselves; all the universities expected to interview mature applicants (a practice already well in train at Lancaster). Mr. Lamley found that while "about half the universities I have consulted have detailed and effective means of scrutinizing applications from mature candidates", the rest relied either on departmental decisions or on matriculation requirements (a process which Lancaster students, in common with students of some other newer universities, do not undergo). After further discussion, and consultation with the Chief Education Officer for Lancashire, the Undergraduate Admissions Committee agreed that applications from mature students would be sorted separately. In the case of those who had qualifications which would satisfy the Awards Regulations, departments would be encouraged to interview, with members from two departments present, where possible; and in cases of doubt the Admissions Officer would look for evidence that at least two Part I departments had been involved in the selection process. For those not so qualified the university would look for evidence of having recently undertaken some course of formal study, and would ask for a sample of recent written work before the interview. Difficult cases would be referred to the Undergraduate Admissions Committee; and the situation would be kept under review. As the prospectus comments, "the University *must* have satisfactory evidence of ability to pursue and profit from a degree course", for however willing the university is to admit such students, any failure represents frustration and disappointment for the student, and a waste of resources by the university.[3.6]

This is perhaps a convenient point at which to consider undergraduate admissions in general. In the first year of the university's existence Lancaster

---

[3.6] The particular problems of mature and married students should neither be exaggerated nor overlooked. In a paper to the Committee of Colleges of November 1972, a survey on these students mentioned problems of accommodation (particularly price, and proximity to Bailrigg), availability of employment for spouses and child-minding facilities for offspring, the reconciliation of a university life for one marriage partner while the other is not involved, adjustment back to being a student (including study problems), and the creation of a satisfactory relationship with a group many of whom will be significantly younger than the mature student.

operated outside the U.C.C.A. scheme, writing to schools inviting invitations, as well as advertising in relevant newspapers and journals. In spite of this unorthodox approach, forced upon the university by the lateness of the decision to take students in October 1964, the university had received by February 1964 no fewer than 1,381 applications, and was able to admit 287 undergraduates in October with not unduly unconventional qualifications.

There was a great deal of debate about which bodies in the university should be responsible for admissions. The possibility of the colleges taking part in this procedure disappeared at an early stage, but the boards of studies only gradually took a second place to the departments. Indeed, Mr. Lamley commented to the Undergraduate Admissions Committee in April 1971 that the university prospectus pretended

> that candidates for admission are considered by boards of studies: though Boards B & D do admit that the process is carried out by their constituent departments.

Despite the growing importance of the departments in the selection process of candidates for individual degree schemes—a shift reflected in the wording of the current prospectus—the boards of studies nevertheless have to consider what numbers of students they wish to admit. Proposals are then put by the Undergraduate Admissions Committee to the Development Committee,[3.7] who fix the quotas. When these come back to the Boards, they each have the duty of apportioning the numbers of students between the degree schemes of the board.

Undergraduate admissions is, of course, a key activity and very far from being the necessary chore that some members of staff regard it. The balance of subjects, the quotas for additional academic staff, the recurrent grant and the next quinquennial settlement, and many other aspects of university planning are profoundly affected by whether or not the admissions meet with reasonable precision the quotas or targets set, neither exceeding them nor falling short. In order to accomplish this very careful estimates have to be made, for example, of how many candidates will accept and take up places on the basis of particular kinds of offer made to them under the U.C.C.A. scheme; and to enable these estimates to be based on a foundation more solid than guesswork, detailed statistics are presented to the Senate each autumn by Mr. Lamley.[3.8] In 1973, for example, he drew attention, as he had pre-

---

[3.7] The Development Committee may sometimes fix a target, as it did for 1973, without consulting anyone else.

[3.8] Some of the information is of a more general nature. The 1973 report, for example, includes the geographical distribution of candidates and entrants (39·9 per cent of entrants, for example, come from Northern England but only 3·7 per cent from Eastern England), the candidates' parental occupations (30 per cent had parents in manual occupations, 29 per cent in the professional and technical groups—figures very close indeed to those for 1972).

viously, to the importance of attracting candidates who will make Lancaster
their first choice for, as

> has been apparent in the last few years, a first choice is still six times as
> likely as a fifth choice eventually to appear. This should perhaps be borne
> in mind in compiling lists of candidates for interview: there is so far no
> evidence that substantial numbers of fourth- or fifth-choice candidates can
> be induced to change their preference.

He was also able to comment on national trends, such as the increased
popularity of vocational courses, the unlikelihood of being able to preserve
what had previously been considered a desirable balance between arts and
science subjects, and the increase of the desire to have a year's break between
school and university. He is able to discern differences in offer between
Lancaster and other universities in particular subjects at the different stages
of the admissions process, and to compare gains or losses in numbers of
applications to each department with the national average. The applications
received come to his office and are then transmitted to the departments, who
make a decision about which candidates should be rejected, which given an
offer and which interviewed (between about a fifth and a quarter of the total).
The offers are sent out by the central office, who monitor, through the regular
U.C.C.A. reports, what the current situation is and deal, in consultation with
the department concerned where necessary, with any correspondence
involving individual candidates. In August the Advanced Level results come
through: these are recorded on each application form, a few days later
consultation takes place between departments and the Admissions Office on
what decisions might be made on borderline candidates, and running totals
are kept during the hectic few weeks when the remaining candidates are
finding themselves a place somewhere in the university system. The intimate
relationship between the work of the admissions office and the strategic policy
of the university is illustrated by the following comment of Mr. Lamley's:

> Proposals on staff numbers in departments in 1973–74 were put forward
> before admissions targets were agreed or there had been much indication
> of the trends of applications. The Undergraduate Admissions Committee
> in fact said to the Development Committee and to departments last
> November that it did not regard the target of 1,018 as practicable and that
> it considered a final total of 900–950 more probable. We cannot look back
> on this prediction with much complacency since although it was, in the
> end, accurate, on all past experience admissions seemed much more likely
> to be in the 830–850 range. . . .
>
> 1973 was never intended to be a crucial year in the expansion of the
> University. Admissions had been between 750 and 850 in each of the five

years 1968 to 1972, and the object was simply to try to break clear of this
rather static pattern, and head for the large intakes that will be required
in 1974, 1975 and 1976 in order to fulfil the target settled by the U.G.C.
and accepted by the University. This target is 4,463 undergraduates in
1976–77; to reach it, allowing for "wastage", requires admissions of about
1,400, 1,600 and 1,700 in the last three years of the quinquennium.

He then goes on to describe the means by which the university sets out to
attract applications, including the provision of a prospectus "modified so that
it is now much more apt to its primary purpose of informing prospective
applicants about the University's facilities and (in particular) courses and
admissions policy", as well as circulating to schools a less formal document
giving a summary of crucial information. Conferences of head teachers have
been held at the university in the last year or two, which have proved useful
in attracting candidates, and increasingly there are open days in certain
departments, as well as various types of sixth-form conferences which build
up a body of information about universities: visits by the admissions officer
himself to schools also aid the important flow of information to school-leavers
and their teachers. It is an interesting reflection that there has been a relatively
rapid change in universities from a situation where applications far out-
stripped places available to one in which candidates and places for them are
far more even numerically. As the Vice-Chancellor noted at the meeting of
Court in December 1973, we simply do not know and cannot predict what
will happen in the future to numbers of applications, or whether what we
are observing is a short-term fluctuation in demand or a long-term and
international movement away from higher education.

The first degree course at Lancaster is of three years'[3.9] duration and
always leads to an honours degree which is awarded as a B.A. In their first
year students read three subjects of equal academic standing, including
subjects they will not necessarily have studied, or had available to them at
school. At the end of the first year they take a Part I qualifying examination
and, having reached a satisfactory standard in that, are required to make a
personal decision about which area of their studies they wish to specialize in.
Most students concentrate on a major subject, supplemented by a minor of
a half to a third of the major's weight (in terms of time expended), and
cognate to it, normally continuing two of the subjects they have taken in their
first year. Other students give equal emphasis to two of the three subjects,
taking what is known as a combined major, and a few carry on particular
integrated schemes of three subjects, known as triple majors.

This system is analogous to the American first degree in that a student does

---

[3.9] Certain degree courses in Russian, Engineering and French extend over a period
of four years and other four-year courses may be set up in the future.

not proceed through a predetermined honours course in which the relationship of the parts of a subject are invariably mapped out for him in advance but, within the major and minor (or combined or triple major degree scheme), must make for himself, with some guidance from the academic staff, his own selection of course units which will have coherence and which satisfy his interests and aspirations. The student is thereby put in a situation which challenges him to create his own relationships between the parts of his subject area. This is a process which can be daunting for those not previously accustomed, or who are temperamentally unsuited, to shaping their own intellectual development. In addition, a student in his second year takes what is termed a free ninth unit which he is at liberty to pick out from any discipline in the university, subject to certain specified pre-requisites.[3.10] By the time he graduates, therefore, a student will usually have read four subjects, two for all three years (although probably in different proportions to each other), and two more for one year apiece.

To particularize, let us suppose that a student has taken the fairly usual Advanced Level combination of history, French and English. When he comes to Lancaster, he might choose for his first year history, French, and philosophy, declaring that his intended major is history. By the end of his first year, however, he could opt for major philosophy with minor French and a free ninth unit in Czech. Or again, another may have taken physics, chemistry and mathematics at Advanced Level, and in his first year read mathematics, physics and environmental sciences, declaring an intended major in physics. This could lead instead to a Part II combined major in physics of the environment (an integrated course in the physics of the earth and its surroundings).

These two examples are fairly commonplace shifts of emphasis, and more radical changes of direction have been successfully completed by students. If reference is made to the university prospectus, the reader will notice that the examples given above may not only involve the individual student in shifts of subject, but also in movement between the boards of studies who have responsibility for him; and demonstrate how the structure lying behind the individual degree schemes gives support to students making such cross-disciplinary connections. This had been the intention of the Academic Planning Board, who had seen the boards of studies as being entities,

> in which teachers in different subjects will be grouped as the balancing of subjects for teaching, examinations and other academic purposes requires. We do not recommend at this stage the setting up of orthodox Faculties with the tendency to rigidity which had been associated with them in the past. The Chairman of each such Board, not already being a member of

---

[3.10] See pp. 127–128 below.

the Senate, will become a member of the Senate during the tenure of his chairmanship.[3.11]

Sir Noel Hall has explained to the author that the Board had in mind as many as twenty or more boards of studies eventually being set up, each emerging from the formulation of a cluster of ideas, rather than the structure first being set up and the subjects being poured into them as though into a mould. He saw an infinite degree of flexibility being made possible, with the separate subject areas appearing in different conjunctions and groupings. It will be noticed that the Board spells out to the U.G.C. provision for a non-professorial chairman of each board, with his own *ex officio* access to a seat on the Senate. This cuts away at the familiar civic university pattern of a senior professor becoming dean of a faculty, which can become a self-enclosed domain, exclusively teaching some students and as exclusively ignoring others. Jurisdiction under the Lancaster structure was to be diffused: the system was to be sufficiently complex in its workings for heads of departments to be forced to share tasks around their staff, thus enabling even junior and relatively inexperienced members of staff to play a full part on boards of studies and their sub-committees, and to participate in the formulation and implementation of policy. Staff were to have their interest actively sought, not just in a single board where their department was formally represented, but rather in all boards where pertinent areas of the subject were under discussion.

Thus, in a paper to the Shadow Senate of September 1964 the Vice-Chancellor defined the functions of the boards as including,

1. For each major subject or combination of subjects assigned to them by Senate, to recommend a scheme of studies . . .
2. To keep under review the inter-relationship between the separate courses contained in a scheme of studies.
3. To keep under review the teaching methods employed and to consider schemes for the training of university teachers.
4. To nominate internal and external examiners, and to keep under review methods of examination.
5. To receive from the examiners the results of the examinations and to authorize their publication . . .
6. To inform the candidate's College Tutor when, in their view, that candidate should be discouraged from entering on or continuing a scheme of studies under the Board which is his first preference. . . . Where possible, the Board will propose an alternative scheme of studies suitable for the candidate.

[3.11] *Interim Report of the Academic Planning Board to the Chairman of the University Grants Committee* (March 1963), paras 7 and 16.

7. To make recommendations to Senate for special or shortened schemes of study for students where required and justified by special circumstances.

In practice only the first two and the seventh remain unaltered to the present time, while the third and fourth continue in essence, although the review of teaching methods has not played an important part in the boards' deliberations and methods of examination have become the province of a special committee by that name. An important variation occurs in the case of (5), since the practice has been that each year the departments regroup themselves into boards of examiners who report direct to the Senate. As for care of students in academic difficulties, as we shall see below[3.12] much elaborate machinery has evolved to take care of them, most of it by-passing the boards of studies. Only when the other bodies concerned have made their decisions do cases which could set academic precedents, or which present difficulties between departments, come to the boards for discussion and resolution.

Four boards were established at once: Board A contained all members of the departments of Biology, Chemistry, Mathematics and Physics (plus representatives from Economics, Environmental Studies and Operational Research); Board B the members of Biology, Economics, Environmental Studies, and Operational Research (with representatives of History and Mathematics); Board C the members of Economics, History, Philosophy and Politics (plus representatives of English, French Studies and Mathematics), and Board D the members of Classics, English, French Studies and History (with a representative of Philosophy).[3.13]

There was, of course, an enormous amount of wasteful duplication in this arrangement for, as the Vice-Chancellor pointed out in June 1965,

every subject is available "in" each Board of Studies: in the sense that at least some of the students under that Board can do a course in that subject.

He therefore suggested a more economical distribution whereby everyone would be a member of the board looking after the single majors of that board, there would be two members from closely related departments, and one from each other department. He went on:

I suggest that Professors should serve on only one Board, and that no-one should serve on more than two Boards. . . . It is assumed that junior members of staff who represent departments on Boards will be supported by a knowledge of departmental policy obtained in regular staff meetings.

[3.12] See Chapters 4 and 6.
[3.13] In the case of each there were, in addition, representatives of other boards, a library representative and certain named individuals.

Gradually the position was rationalized, and there is now both a more reasonable grouping of subjects within boards and much less duplication—while retaining still the principle that all teaching staff (together with other appropriate persons who have been nominated by their head of department and approved by the board concerned) have as a right and a duty the membership of a board.[3.14] In 1967 a special board (Board E) for the School of Education was established; in 1971 Board F was set up for departments concerned with business studies; and in 1973 Board H (also for School of Education work) was founded. This gives an existing total of seven boards, and although in 1970 there was pressure for a board specifically concerned with the social sciences, the proposal came to nothing.[3.15]

Although each of these boards is responsible for the setting up and the syllabus of any master's degrees or other advanced courses of their constituent departments, a Board of Graduate Studies was also created in 1964 which has the responsibility of admitting all graduate students and looking after the regulation of all research studies, including examination supervision, and care of special cases.[3.16] The course-orientated M.A. and M.Sc. degrees are, in spite of not being the capstone of the first degree as was intended, nevertheless very popular: in June 1973, for example, there were 283 such students out of a total of 777 full and part-time graduate students of the university.

All teaching members of staff, therefore, are compulsorily members of at least one board, and the original system of having a good deal of cross-representation of individual members of a department or a board on other boards persists, the cross-representation tapering away as subjects are perceived to be more distant. Since departments have no statutory right to make their own decisions the outcome of most departmental decisions necessarily comes to the relevant parent board for ratification and subsequent report

---

[3.14] To relieve individual board members of the necessity to attend all board meetings, some boards have courses committees which do a lot of initial sifting, whilst others have nominated representatives who are morally obliged to be present.

[3.15] See the university's prospectus for the present membership of boards.

[3.16] The Board was originally to be given the title of Research Studies. In 1964 the Vice-Chancellor suggested having a fresh look at the nomenclature of higher degrees because "otherwise we shall give up all chance of clearing up some confusions which are very apparent in other universities", particularly in the usage of the Ph.D. He suggested an M.A. for an advanced course training of one academic year or more, a Certificate of Research Training "where there has been some identifiable act of training", a Ph.B. for a piece of work slighter than for a doctorate, a Ph.D. for doctoral work submitted within seven years of the first degree, and a D.U. (Doctor of the University) for work of the same standard after a longer period, a Higher Diploma in Arts for the "failed but meritorious Ph.D.", and one honorary degree only, Dr. Univ. The Senate, however, did not accept this particular invitation to innovation, and after considerable discussion and some modification as time went by, the university's higher degrees are very similar to those elsewhere.

to the Senate. In theory this means that all academic decisions are made jointly by the members of a board consisting of members from cognate departments, but the practice is variable. Unless there is some special and idiosyncratic reason why a particular suggestion stirs the attention of a member of a board from another department, quite fundamental changes of curriculum or teaching method may go by on the nod, on the assumption that the matter has been fully debated by the experts in the field within the department. On the other hand, if a proposal arouses some specialized interest or latent antagonism of another department, or superficial questioning reveals a fundamental area of disagreement within the initiating department, a vigorous debate can ensue in which the proposal may undergo very radical alteration. Yet again, a board may decide that the subject under discussion is too specialized and may refer it back to one of its own sub-committees for further definition of detail, or on to another university committee (such as the one for examinations).

The one substantial theoretical discussion about the boards of studies in recent years was at the Senate conference of 1970, when the Vice-Chancellor contended that most of the boards' functions were being carried out elsewhere: for example, he said, initiation and investigation of proposals for future academic development were being done by individuals, *ad hoc* groups, departments and the boards in consultation with the Development Committee, and other matters which the boards handled were not dealt with systematically, implications had not been explored or the details were left untidy. He argued that the functions he described required bodies of differing size and composition, and suggested that there should be a general board of studies, which would be "an open forum for the discussion of general educational matters, teaching and examining methods, proposals for future development, and ideas for new schemes of study and significant new courses". All members of the academic staff and some students would be members of this large body. The Development Committee, as he envisaged the scheme, would have added to its functions that of recommending new schemes of study and taking account of the views of a Sectional Board: this in its turn would consist of supervisors (in charge of, for example, new schemes of study or making examination arrangements) of major or advanced courses assigned to the board and some additional members appointed by the Senate.

The idea of a general board did not find favour, except perhaps as a venue for the occasional open discussion (along the lines of the forum at Warwick) of general academic policy for the future. This is probably because people felt it would be as being too large and would lack the power to implement the decisions it made; they were also reluctant to relinquish the right, which marked Lancaster out from so many other universities, of everyone having an automatic place on one statutory and decision-making body of the university. By inference, therefore, they were lacking in enthusiasm for the sectional boards and neither were created.

Let us return to a consideration of the course structure. A pessimistic article in the *New Statesman* late in 1972 questioned the value of the broad courses of new universities. Mr. Irwin commented:

> In common with several new universities Kent set out to achieve something very bold; to establish a complex of courses as coherent, as educational, as intellectually valid as the traditional specialized courses, but in a new mode. In terms of this scale of ambition Kent has beyond question failed. I can say "beyond question" because the development of the university is almost all in the direction of returning to orthodoxy, of cutting down the inter-disciplinary work.
>
> Partly this has been because we have taken on too many teachers unable or unwilling to tackle this kind of syllabus; but the chief reason has been a growing realization that such courses can only succeed at the desired intellectual level by dint of extraordinary effort from all concerned. Potentially they are not merely as rigorous as the conventional course, but far more so. By definition the student is working in an area where there are few books or articles to fall back on: he must break new ground. The supervisor himself is no longer self evidently an authority. The traditional training he received is of limited help in this new territory, and he, too, has to be speculative.[3.17]

Kent took in its first undergraduates only a year after Lancaster, so that it is not surprising that the writer has heard similar arguments at Lancaster about the kind of degree the students are receiving and doubts expressed about its worth in terms of depth or concentration of knowledge. This is a self-conscious and self-critical era, and there are no easy, or final, answers lying to hand about what constitutes an academic discipline, what are all the essential elements of a subject area or where the subject boundaries are.[3.18] Nor do we yet know very much about the learning process and, because we argue still about that, teaching methods are constantly being re-examined. Lancaster has striven honestly to reach the best *modus operandi* it can, balancing on the one side the desire to introduce new subjects in new ways, and on the other to have an organization which is simple to operate, capable of being understood by newcomers (staff as well as students) without prolonged explanation, and acceptable to the rest of the university world as a soundly-based first degree.

The Academic Planning Board's report to the U.G.C. of March 1963, in

---

[3.17] Michael Irwin, "A Framework for Contraction" in *New Statesman*, Vol. 84, No. 2178, 15 December 1972, pp. 892 and 894.
[3.18] See also below, pages 126 and 160.

explaining what eventually became the course structure described above at the beginning of this section, had been optimistic about new structures. They described how they wished

> to avoid excessive specialization in a single subject or, indeed, in facets of a single subject. We equally seek to avoid undisciplined spread over several subjects more or less at the option of the individual undergraduate.

The boards of studies were to be the mechanism to fulfil the role of overseeing the best conjunctions of courses. In March 1964, for example, there was a discussion at the Shadow Senate about a student's first year in the light of memoranda received from seven of the founding professors. It is interesting to compare their approach to degree schemes at this stage: Professor Dobbs, for example, saw physics as providing joint courses with chemistry or biology, but felt that such experiments should be postponed until there were more staff; for the first year he wished the students to take physics, pure mathematics and either another experimental science or a social study, while the second and third years should be devoted wholly to different branches of physics. Professor Sibley, on the other hand, saw possible joint degrees with social studies, the natural sciences, or languages; he wished first-year students to take one natural science, one arts, and one social science subject and to be able to continue all three subjects they by now had a grounding in during the remaining two years.

The Vice-Chancellor proposed that the second year consist of one major subject, alongside two minors, one of which would be related to the major and "place it in a wider perspective" and the other a more distant subject "included primarily for its general educational value", with the major and the related minor continuing in the third year. When the Academic Planning Board met the Shadow Senate in May, Professor Dainton expressed concern lest the course structure proposed for the natural science subjects "would result, in practice, in many students restricting their selection of university subjects to more science subjects", and Dr. Ratcliffe and Professor Pumphrey "both stated their view that it would be difficult to achieve a broadening of the courses without exerting strong pressure on students". In spite of these expressed concerns, however, it was decided neither to have a four-subject first year, nor to make compulsory the taking of a non-school subject. Later in the same meeting the natural science professors explained that the reason for opposing a three-subject pattern in the second year (as the Vice-Chancellor had proposed) "was the difficulty of reconciling a broadening of the education of scientists with the production of professionally qualified scientists".[3.19]

[3.19] A similar concern had been expressed at Keele: both there and at Lancaster, however, the professional bodies involved were prepared to give their stamp of approval to the degree schemes set up.

What emerged was a degree structure that varied somewhat between different subject areas of the university, with the arts and social sciences in general making more unusual interdisciplinary cross-connections than the science subjects, and also being more prepared to leave space in their allocation of time to the distant minor subject. Once the pattern had been established, no far-reaching discussion of it took place until the Senate conference of September 1969. The discussion was prolonged (the summary of it takes eighteen closely-argued pages of the conference report) and highly technical, but essentially the idea was that there should be more flexibility (a) in the apportionment of the ninety weeks that each first degree student spends at Lancaster, (b) in developing inter-connections between subjects, especially having regard to the unreality of some divisions so far created between them, and (c) in the final degree assessment, whether it be of the existing nine units or under a duo-decimal system suggested by the Vice-Chancellor. Some people felt with Professor Perkin that the existing system had strong merits:

> namely, the opportunity it gave students to find out what different subjects mean and to delay their final choice of major and minor courses until they were able to make an informed choice. The Lancaster system was unusual in that, not only was Part I broadly based, but (at least in the humanities) the degree of specialization was limited throughout Part II.

Others complained of lack of strong relationships where these ought to occur between subject areas, the difficulty caused by the lack of the fourth year written into the original plans of the university and the need for more flexibility in the apportionment of the existing nine units within particular degree schemes.[3.20] What they might also have added, although they did not do so, was that under a system where a student's time is shared so precisely between different departments and different parts of a degree scheme there inevitably arises an element of quantification about the allocation of his time that may be inimical to learning in the broadest sense. If a student knows, for example, that someone is expecting him to put in between thirty-five and forty hours a week, of which between six and ten are contact hours (lectures, seminars and tutorials), that he has to prepare two seminar papers (four hours each), do the reading for two essays (five hours each), go into town to interview immigrant children as part of a project (four hours), and prepare for a test (three hours), it is easy to see that background reading, exploring topics which have arisen out of casual conversation or seminar debate, and looking at aspects of cognate subjects which would be illuminating to the student's main

---

3.20 Professor Woolrych, in a paper for Board C of 1964, suggested a final classification based on nine units and his suggestion was adopted by inference during the Shadow Senate meetings without debate.

subject will inevitably be relegated beyond the immediate tasks and may be omitted altogether.

A working party was set up to look at the breadth subject[3.21] and at the whole course structure. The Vice-Chancellor in a paper to the working party of December 1969 commented that

> if the alternatives available to students run into many hundreds, let alone 100,000, it seems to me to follow (a) that the units will not be related to each other: for it is too complicated to bother about relations with scores or hundreds of other courses: (b) that the final classification must be reached by an arithmetic rule. . . . Personally, I think that it is worth while giving up a lot of freedom of choice in order to keep alive the idea that the parts of a degree course should be planned in association, and examined by a group of people who can meet round a table. But there are different sorts of "association": for instance, the relationship of units *within* a history department (which is easily arranged): the relationship of a European History course to a French course: the relationship of a mathematics "tool" course to a Physics course. . . .
>
> I suggest therefore
>
> —that departments shall be grouped in Schools, some departments belonging to more than one School.
>
> —that each School should be responsible for certain named degree schemes, for each of which it would claim 4, 5, 6 or 7 units: these units being used for a major course or for a joint major, but in every case being planned as a related set by the School responsible.
>
> —that the responsible School should be able to nominate Minors of 2 or 3 units. This means, in the case of a 7+2 or 6+3 scheme, that the whole degree course would be determinate; and, in the professional subjects, this may well be necessary. But schemes such as 6+2, 5+2, 5+3 would have units unused: these would be at the free choice of the student outside the units available for his major course. . . . In my view, the "enrichment" subjects should be an extra, not compulsory, but with the inducement that good course work performance in them is counted favourably in the degree classification. I would prefer 50 per cent of students to take them of choice, than 100 per cent under compulsion.

His ideas were taken up and expanded in the statement from the report of the working party to the Senate in January 1970 that

> Because of the great differences in the range of subjects taught by departments in the University, the Working Party wishes to pass beyond the idea that the course structures should rest on the principle of a certain number

---

[3.21] See pages 118 ff.

of subjects or course units being taken from the range of course units offered by departments.

Instead the Working Party attaches great importance to the principle discussed at the Grange Conference [in September 1969] that a course structure should depend upon the interrelationship of the units studied, without any formal requirement to observe at the same time defined departmental boundaries.

The Working Party supports . . . (i) Undergraduates being allowed to take as part of their major course two or even three courses from another department; (ii) "Consortial" courses arranged jointly by two or more departments; and (iii) Joint departmental staff appointments and the appointment of members of staff who are not attached to a department or departments. The Working Party believes that Boards of Studies must assume a more definite and active role in planning and initiating desirable degree schemes.

This new attitude showed again when the Working Party reported a second time to the Senate in May 1970, after consulting various bodies around the university, and were glad to be able to say

that the aim of allowing Boards of Studies the opportunity to put forward for consideration degree schemes of more flexible design than some of the schemes at present available has, in general, been favourably received. . . .

Members of the Working Party were a little surprised that some of the comments received on the proposals had interpreted them as a suggestion that undergraduates should have total freedom to choose the "package" of course units which they would read in Part II. This is certainly not the intention of the Working Party. Rather it is proposed that following detailed consideration and approval by the relevant academic authorities degree schemes of educationally related course units, arranged in a more numerous system of combinations than there are at present, will be available to undergraduates. The Working Party believes that the justification for the introduction of a particular collection of course units must be that it is believed to be educationally desirable and relevant. . . .

In the formal proposal set out below it is recommended that each Part II degree scheme should contain a total of nine course units, each of equal weight. In some schemes all nine units will be specified and will be taught by one or perhaps by two cognate departments. All the others will contain eight units, undergraduates being left a genuinely free choice of the ninth unit.

The Working Party believes that amongst the eight courses there should be a central core of at least three course units which either come from one department or section, or form part of a closely co-ordinated plan. It recognizes that certain combinations of units will necessarily contain, and will state, some pre-requisites. . . .

The aim of the Working Party is to allow departments, Boards of Studies, inter Board Committees, individual members of staff and groups of members of staff the opportunity to put forward for consideration degree schemes of a variety of combination of course units which are believed to have a real educational relationship. It is a move to allow an additional element of freedom into the structure of our courses, not an attempt to remove the status quo.

Since 1970 there has been more readiness to think in terms of new groupings of courses which together make up a coherent degree scheme, but which are far from being the usual kind of single honours degree. The university's prospectus for 1974–5 lists no fewer than eighty-one different schemes of study, and other groupings are likely to appear, as for example, under the new European Studies or Mediaeval Studies umbrellas, in the future. Not that the old debate about what is appropriate to be included in a first degree is by any means over at Lancaster. On the one hand there are those who will always be striving for more range, balance and flexibility; while others, feeling that only a single honours degree of the traditional kind is at all useful, will argue, as one member of an arts teaching department has within recent months (in asking that all a student's Part II units could be within one department), that the university should acknowledge and legitimize what he described as a "significant number of students who use the present scheme adroitly to engineer for themselves what amounts to (and would be recognized in any other university as) a single honours Part II . . . when the University already offers to those who want to take advantage of it what amounts to a single honours degree, it seems illogical to bar the way to other combinations simply because they happen to occur in the same department. In doing so we are in fact reducing flexibility, not ensuring it".

This is possibly an unreal debate for two reasons. First, Sir Noel Hall has told the writer that the present system at Lancaster, whereby there is a complete spectrum all the way from the very variously selected degree course to what might be thought of at other institutions as a single honours degree, does not represent to him a distortion of his original intentions. He had always intended that the different types of student could grow up alongside each other, provided that the examinations at the end were sufficiently rigorous and were related to what the students had been studying.[3.22]

The second reason follows on from the first, which is that arguments of this

---

[3.22] Nevertheless, Sir Noel also argues that for the scholar a fourth undergraduate year in which a student could specialize in a single subject and learn something of research techniques, is still badly needed.

kind underestimate the great adaptability of the Lancaster system. While it is true that at present no degree can be taken with all nine units coming from under the one departmental umbrella, this is only to say that parts of a discipline, for reasons as arbitrary as staffing, become distributed between the different departments; a student is at liberty to choose courses in his minor subject which are extremely close to his major, and to take his free ninth unit in either his major or his minor subject, making nine units with very intimate connections. At the opposite extreme the logical culmination of the Lancaster system is the bold experiment of Independent Studies. Mr. Wacek Koc had been one of the prime movers in the original informal discussions that had gone on for some months before the Senate conference of April 1972, when a document was presented setting out some of the objectives of the proposed development:

> The students, who enter the School after completing Part I of their degree, propose their own schemes of study, which after acceptance by the School would become the basis for the award of a B.A. degree after two years. Each scheme would be monitored closely and could be adjusted in its scope and/or direction with the developing interests and competence of the student concerned. Methods of assessment would be chosen which were considered most appropriate for each scheme of study and external assessors would supervise the conduct of assessment and ensure the maintenance of standards. . . .
>
> The School would not pursue educational aims which differ in any radical way from those originally conceived by the founders of this University. It would be concerned to achieve the same targets of flexibility, balance and depth in academic studies. Like the University it would aim to steer a safe course between over-specialization and over-generality, and to give the student the opportunity to acquire what Sir Noel Hall has called a "harmonious intellectual discipline".
>
> It would, however, seek to pursue these ends through means which *are* radically different from those so far employed at Lancaster. It would set out to dispense with the apparatus of an agreed and uniform course structure, and to make the individual student a producer of his own curriculum rather than a consumer of one designed for students in general. The School is planned so as to be free from constraints on the use of its academic resources such as are imposed by timetabling schedules or by the course structure in which teaching and lecturing is precisely planned in advance, and is organized in equally weighted units. At the same time, it is in no way the intention of this project to *oppose* itself to the current educational practices of the University. It should be regarded as an alternative *within* the University structure, not as an antithesis to it. . . .

The most controversial principle implicit in the project for a School of Independent Studies is likely to be that of allowing students to participate in determining their own schemes of study. It should be stated at once, therefore, that the School does not intend to produce a generation of Chekhovian grasshoppers moving from one fragment of knowledge to another without any clear sense of purpose of acceptance of intellectual discipline. This is certainly not a camouflaged proposal for the introduction of a "general" degree. Furthermore, although students in Independent Studies may often be expected to combine elements from a number of "disciplines" in the course of their work, they will be expected to achieve and demonstrate a mastery of their associated intellectual concepts, techniques and methodologies, just as would other undergraduates in the University.

Its proponents believed that under this scheme students would be encouraged to think about what they wanted to study, learning would have very specific aims, interdisciplinary studies would be facilitated, students could regulate the pattern and intensity of their own activity, and staff would be able to teach on an individual basis. At the same time, as the initial document recognized, the level of psychological stress on an individual student to assume responsibility for his own work, both in its planning and execution, would be increased, and he would be "deprived of some of the sense of psychological security conferred by a more highly organized academic system". Assessment was envisaged as a continuous process, with periodic appraisals of a student's work as a whole, even to the extent of a substantial redirection of his energies; and a wide range of assessment procedures was to be used.

Sufficient interest was shown at the Conference for the scheme to be taken further, including discussions between the planning committee and the Steering Committee of the Senate. By October 1972, when the proposal came to a regular meeting of the Senate, more specific suggestions had been formulated. Nevertheless, a document by Professor Potts also accompanied the proposals to the Senate meeting (attended by three members of the planning committee), which described the scheme as designed to undermine degree examinations, the honours degree, the position of the Senate and of heads of departments, and as having little appeal to anyone outside the social sciences and the humanities. Substantial discussion took place and the Senate, on a vote, decided that it agreed "with the educational value of a programme of independent studies" but wished the planning committee to provide answers to various specific questions. Painstaking negotiations continued with relevant individuals and committees through the following months, as the supporters of the scheme tried to fit it sufficiently closely into the existing degree structure of the university and safeguard the standard of the university's first degree without doing violence to the underlying principles of the original idea. Finally, at the Senate meeting of March 1973 a further document was presented and the scheme agreed, with only small modifications, for an initial period of five years; although a significant degree of dissent, particularly from the science boards, was noticeable.

The scheme, as accepted and finally agreed, differed in certain important aspects from its original form. Students were to proceed through their first year, and the first two terms of Part II, before transferring to "supervised independent study of an approved subject". There was to be a small pilot group of less than a dozen students in 1973–74 and a quota of up to thirty-five for the following year. The school would have a director, and while it would not (as under the Lancaster constitution, it quite properly could have) form a board of its own, neither would it be absorbed into any other. Staff would come into three categories: those who assisted on a part-time basis and who would not have their normal duties diminished; those whose Independent Studies load would require, in consultation with the heads of their departments, a cutting back of their usual teaching commitments; and those who would be seconded to the School on a full-time basis for a specified period. Students would be expected to approach the School's director towards the end of their first year to indicate an interest in such a scheme, and would be given a director of studies. The student would then register for Independent Studies and for an existing Part II degree scheme, and would undertake to study for them both.[3.23] A detailed scheme of study would be submitted to the Committee for Independent Studies who would tell each student by 15 March of his second year whether it had first stage acceptance, and he in turn would have to make a final decision about whether or not to remain registered with the school. For those who do remain the School "shall approve the teaching arrangements needed to implement the schemes of study, propose external examiners to the Committee of the Senate and agree the schemes of study with these examiners. A scheme of study approved by an external examiner has 'final acceptance' and may only be altered with the approval of the Committee and the examiner".

It is, of course, much too soon to judge the success of the scheme, with the pilot group only part-way through their second year at Lancaster and the first full group still to emerge from Part I; but it is an interesting and worthwhile experiment.

Nor should we, when considering how much flexibility there is in the Lancaster system, overlook the extent to which changes of major subject are

---

[3.23] This is not as unendurable as it at first sounds, as a student will probably choose a degree scheme which contains at least some elements in common with his Independent Studies area of interest.

made at the end of Part I, demonstrating that students take seriously the opportunity offered them of shifting subject area. Mr. Stephen Lamley has told the writer that between 1967 and 1970 he estimates that about 33 to 35 per cent exercised the option of changing their major, and that this went up to 40 per cent in the summer of 1971. Appendix xvi shows detailed figures for such changes in two particular years, 1972 and 1973, and even if a certain proportion of these are merely an alteration of major subjects into minor, the number of changes is still very high. Indeed, it will be noticed that, within some particular major degree schemes, the gains and losses, if added together, exceed the total of either the stated number of intended majors at Part I, or of fully-fledged majors at Part II. Sociology, for example, in 1973, had had 29 intended major students and lost 14 of them; the department gained, however, 18 from the other students reading the subject as a second or third Part I choice, making a total of 33 for the Part II major. Other departments show a similar pattern.

What these figures also reveal is the very large movement away from combined and triple major subjects at the end of the first year, a feature of the Lancaster situation which has been fairly constant since the early days of the university. A paper to the working party on course structure of November 1969, for instance, shows that only 40 per cent in 1966, 28 per cent in 1967 and 20 per cent in 1968 were taking the same combined major for which they were admitted,[3.24] and in a memorandum of November 1971 Mr. Lamley pointed out that

> Only 18·9 per cent of those admitted for combined major courses are now reading for those same courses, a dropout rate of over 80 per cent. . . . Almost 71 per cent of those first registered for single major courses are still reading those major courses.

Discussions that the writer has had at other new universities suggest that this problem is by no means confined to Lancaster, but the reasons for it are not so obvious. It has been suggested that, in certain subjects at least, schools advise their pupils to apply for combined major courses because, being less popular, they would not carry such a high entry qualification. The number of departments in which there is such a pressure of applications, however, is diminishing, but there is not a corresponding fall in the number of transfers out of combined majors. Others feel that too much is expected of students in combined and triple majors and that the finals results indicate that only a few, particularly gifted, students should be allowed to read for combined major degrees. Still others feel that not enough is done to integrate

---

[3.24] The figures for those taking the same single major are 69 per cent for 1966, 76 per cent for 1967 and 67 per cent for 1968.

the parts of the combined majors by use of bridging courses or joint teaching. If university staff are interested in making these inter-disciplinary connections, it seems that further investigation is necessary into what the elements of such degree schemes should be and how they may best be welded together to make a corporate whole which is more than the sum of the component parts.

One further point should be mentioned. It will be remembered that the Senate conference of 1969 was hoping that the boards of studies would take over the role of the Development Committee in certain matters. This committee is very interesting in the context of Lancaster. A parallel to its main functions is perhaps to be found in the Hebdomadal Council at Oxford, a committee whose characteristics are that it is small in number, its members are senior, experienced and respected members of the university who will take a broader view than merely their own collegiate or departmental affiliation, and, although it has the responsibility only to make recommendations to other decision-making bodies in the university, its actual powers far transcend those laid down for it in principle, coming as they do with all the authority of supremely well-informed and fully-developed discussions. The Development Committee's brief includes the following:

> To advise the Senate on the allocation of the sum set aside by the Finance Committee for academic purposes between the various possible uses in view of the university's development, following the previously determined policy for the quinquennium and any directions from the University Grants Committee and the secretary of state for education and science and including the number of academic staff to be recruited and the overall intake of undergraduates and graduate students;
>
> To oversee generally academic policy, e.g. by scrutinizing, from the point of view of the general interests of the university and before their submission to the Senate, proposals for new courses . . . etc. by evaluating implications of such proposals for the allocation of resources;
>
> To be responsible for the overall view of the development of research in the university.

It is difficult to imagine a brief much wider than this definition and, although its terms of reference were not stated so fully in the earliest days of the university, documents from any period show that its influence and position in the university has been constant. Even in a university of over 3,000 students, its membership is limited to six people; the Vice-Chancellor as chairman, the senior pro-vice-chancellor, a natural scientist, a social scientist, a student of the humanities, and a technologist or member of staff concerned with business studies (all four being appointed by the Senate). From time to time the Committee will discuss certain major proposals with the chairmen of the boards of studies and representatives of the student body, and it is expected to publish "as full a report as possible of the decisions of the committee" in the *Reporter*. From time to time, however, people in the university become concerned about so much power being concentrated in the hands of this single small committee. Professor Ninian Smart for example, in a document of February 1972, made it clear that while he did not intend to criticize the "heroic work undertaken by members of the Development Committee", he nevertheless wondered whether examination of course proposals to see if they fitted general policy could not be dealt with by a scrutineer working with the Vice-Chancellor and problems being referred to the Development Committee or the Senate, and whether the formulation of general plans and policies for the future could not be more open to general discussion so that good ideas could get through the machinery of the committee structure.

Yet, although in certain respects the boards have increasingly become stronger and more involved in, for example, quinquennial planning, the Development Committee has retained its pre-eminence. It was in the light of this that, at the Senate conference of April 1972, Mr. Michael Kirkwood suggested that there be an Academic Planning Board, whose members would be derived in large part from the boards of studies, who would have the "responsibility for deciding education policy and examining schemes of study", and who would produce a blueprint for the construction of degree schemes, look again at existing degree combinations, scrutinize new free ninth unit courses, advise boards and departments on new aids to teaching, and "be responsible for the organic development of the University as a whole in terms of the balance of departments, and areas of future expansion, and for advising the University of operational, financial and administrative constraints operating against development". This idea was taken up by the Senate early in 1973, and in October the Senate agreed that there should be an Academic Planning Group which would report to the Senate through the Development Committee, whose purpose would be

> To consider the academic state of the university and to examine and assess from the point of view of academic desirability, proposals for major new academic developments, which are either referred to the group by the Development Committee (or the chairman of that committee) or are submitted by boards of studies, departments or individuals (*ab initio* or in response to an invitation from the group) or are generated within the group itself.

Such a body, with members appointed by the Senate but who are not necessarily members of it, has now been set up, and it remains to be seen whether it alters the way long-term planning is carried out at Lancaster.

(ii)   The inception and reincarnations of the distant minor subject

In the Interim Report of the Academic Planning Board to the U.G.C. of March 1963, the hope was expressed that

> the early science appointments will include people prepared to make experiments in the teaching of science including the provision of courses for those who wish to study it as a part of a general education without necessarily intending to enter the scientific professions. An attempt might well be made to present science, at Honours level, as an educational subject rather than as a tool for use in research, and to present it in such a way that it could be studied by those who in their later years at school had concentrated on other subjects.

These were brave words, and were to take the university community on a lengthy and time-consuming search for a broader education; a bold idea by the Academic Planning Board was altered into a necessarily more neat, accessible and amenable pattern; and the reaction of individuals, both staff and students, ranging from a rugged determination to experiment at any cost, to a caution, almost a timidity, about the standards or the academic purity of a degree which might be threatened are of considerable interest. This venture, one of the biggest paper-creators in the history of the university, serves as a paradigm of the kind of decision-making that can occur in a new institution.

The U.G.C. had drawn attention as early as 1953 to the problem of overloaded undergraduate syllabuses, making students become unduly pre-occupied with examinations and preventing them from using their time at university to broaden their minds.[3.25] As C. P. Snow pointed out in his famous Rede Lecture of 1959, and its postscript of 1963, there were not a few intellectuals and leading academics who were concerned by this developing narrowness, but it was not until he had given his Two Cultures lecture that the popular imagination was appraised of this danger. Keele had attempted, by the use of the Foundation Year, to compel both arts and science students to look at disciplines other than those they had specifically come up to read, to

> emerge as a latter-day Renaissance man, versed in all aspects of knowledge —at home if he is on the arts side, with the nature and method of the sciences, and, if he is a scientist, able to pen a respectable, grammatical and well-spelt essay on literary and historical topics.[3.26]

[3.25] H.M.S.O., *University Development 1947–1952*, Cmd. 8875, paras 82 and 83. See also H. Butterfield, *The Universities and Education Today* (Keele, 1962).

[3.26] *Times Educational Supplement*, 21 April 1972 .See also Chapter 5, "Lindsey and Keele in Context", in Sir James Mountford, *Keele* (London, 1972).

It had been found necessary, however, to make use of an extra year to accomplish this aim. The other new universities were also attempting to broaden their curricula.

Lancaster had on its Board a particularly keen enthusiast for the teaching of science to arts students, Mr. J. A. Ratcliffe, who had made efforts to introduce the idea into the Cambridge first degree system during the 1950's. He had started from a definition of general education as "that part of a university education which is of value to a student who afterwards makes no use of the detailed knowledge he has acquired".[3.27] He stated that he thought it a duty of a university to provide a general education in this sense, which could be made "even better if half of it were provided through science and half through an arts course". At present those reading science, he said, were not using it as a general education from which to become the country's administrators and managers, because the present science courses were not amenable to this kind of application. Out of 630 M.P.s in 1957, 335 had had a university education "but fewer than 40 had any sort of scientific training or experience". He therefore wished to propose a new kind of honours degree in which a valuable general university education would be provided by a combination of arts and science courses. An example in physics might be the study of radioactivity and nuclear energy, where at the end of the course the student would have

> a fairly good knowledge of one important branch of physics, and how it has developed. He would have learnt, in considerable detail, how a completely objective argument can be built up on firmly established facts, and can lead to conclusions which can be tested by experiment. He would appreciate something of scientific method by seeing its application to one particular field of knowledge. . . . It would need to be taken along with an arts course, and the two together would, I believe, be an improvement on the arts course alone.

His proposals had the strong backing of both Professor Dainton and Sir Noel Hall, as can be seen from the account of the discussions with the Shadow Senate in the early part of 1964. The Academic Planning Board's report of March 1963 to the U.G.C., however, shows that although it is science teaching for arts students which is spelt out most explicitly, the members also had in mind the broadening of courses for scientists to include some arts teaching. For example, in the list given for illustrative purposes of possible combinations of subjects, they listed not only history, with language and

---

[3.27] J. A. Ratcliffe, "Can Science Courses Educate?" in the British Association's *Advancement of Science*, No. 53, June 1957, pp. 421–426, from which this and the next three quotations are taken.

literature, and principles of science; but also science with mathematics, operational research, economics and philosophy.

The University's first prospectus idealistically proclaimed:

> An educated man should have some idea of the habits of thought both of science and of the humanities; to this end particular attention is to be given to studies that cross traditional faculty boundaries, and a course in Principles of Science is to be devised, to be taught from the literature by a case-study method, and accessible to students who do not intend to become professional scientists.[3.28]

Furthermore, at the first assembly of the Shadow Senate in January 1964 the Vice-Chancellor suggested that when heads of departments were considering possible combinations of subjects,

> they should bear in mind the need to provide courses or groupings of subjects which cross the traditional Arts-Science boundaries. Many of the proposals will inevitably bring together the obvious cognate subjects; but it is hoped that the various proposals . . . will make an immediate and worthwhile contribution towards narrowing the gap between the Arts and Science subjects.

Thus so far the spirit of the Academic Planning Board's intentions was being observed. By March, however, two implicit assumptions seem to have appeared. The first was that the arts and science elements of an honours degree which gave the more general education envisaged by J. A. Ratcliffe should not have equal weight, i.e. that it should not be a degree made up of equal components of arts and science courses, but be primarily, for example, an arts degree with a contrastive science element, which would be placed within one year of it. The second was that *all* students' degrees should contain this contrastive element uniformly through all departments and all degree schemes, and not with variations of type.

In summing up the Academic Planning Board's report of the year before for the Shadow Senate at the March 1964 meeting, the Vice-Chancellor commented:

> It will be seen that the A.P.B. had in mind (a) a spread over *related* subjects, to avoid dangers of excessive specialization: (b) the inclusion of *more distant* subjects (e.g. science for arts students) as an important element in general education. . . .
>
> A "more distant" subject could be placed in the *first* year, on the Keele principle of getting culture out of the way before one gets down to business: in that case, it would be simpler to plan on the basis of *four*

[3.28] *University of Lancaster Prospectus, 1963–64*, p. 11.

first-year subjects. It can be argued, however, that the first year is *not* the point at which relief from specialization is needed nor is it the point at which a student is most likely to make thoughtful use of an unusual subject. There are disadvantages in placing it in the *third* year, for there it would be liable to suffer from the examination pressures of the main subject. On educational grounds, the *second* year has much to commend it as a place for the "more distant" subject.

After much discussion it was agreed that a student should only take three subjects in the first year, which had the effect that the more distant subject would not be taken then but, as the Vice-Chancellor suggested, a student would study, along with a major subject,[3.29] two minor subjects in the second year,

> one of which would be related to the major subject, and place it in a wider perspective, and the other which would be a more distant subject included primarily for its general educational value.

The major and the related minor were then to be continued in the third year.

By May the divergences between the boards of studies were becoming clearer. The Vice-Chancellor summarized the differences succinctly for the Shadow Senate:

> Board "A" [i.e. the natural scientists] proposes to achieve "breadth" by requiring Economics, Environmental Studies or Philosophy in the first year. . . . The other Boards have minor and/or "distant" subjects in the second year.
> Does this difference matter?
> Is Board "A" satisfied to confine its broadening activities to the three subjects—of which one (E.S.) is virtually another science? What about English, History, Classics, French? . . .
> Similarly, Board "B" in general obtains breadth by taking in subjects of Board "A". . . . What about English as a subject of study for Economists? As an editor, I can confirm that few of them know this language.
> . . . Boards "B", "C" and "D" are prepared to use Principles of Science. We must decide who is to work out the details of this course.

Furthermore, Board A had by now decided that a student should be majoring in only one subject by the third year, without continuing a minor subject.

Discussion at the May 1964 meeting of the Shadow Senate, held jointly

---

[3.29] This is the first appearance of American terminology at Lancaster, usages which have become commonplace at British universities in the past decade. Other examples are: campus, major in (rather than "read"), course units, transcript, and chairman (of a department).

with the Academic Planning Board at Leamington Spa, tackled at last the central question of whether students should be required or encouraged to achieve breadth. The science professors

> expressed the view that breadth should be achieved by encouragement . . . rather than by prescription; they foresaw embarrassment if good science students were held up through failure in a distant subject which they had been forced to take against their will.

The Academic Planning Board members pressed Board A on the proposed composition of a student's second year. They were told that Board A was concerned about the production of professionally qualified scientists, and the difficulty of reconciling this with the broadening of their education, especially since the scheme of studies at Lancaster was already more broadly based than elsewhere: for example, students majoring in Chemistry could take courses with a bias towards physics or biology. Eventually Board A were requested to go away and think again over their proposed course structure, and the professor of physics, Professor E. Roland Dobbs, was asked to prepare detailed plans for the principles of physics course. Other cross-connecting courses which were being thought of at this stage included the history and philosophy of science, a course in English based on appropriate scientific texts, another in French with an emphasis on early French writings on evolutionary theory—all these being for scientists—as well as a course in mathematics for non-scientists. This last course, accepted by the Shadow Senate meeting at the end of May, was intended to give, according to Professor Emlyn Lloyd,

> some account of mathematical concepts, aims and methods to students who have a negligible mathematical background . . . it will be impossible to avoid manipulation entirely, but the emphasis will be on ideas. . . . I wish on the one hand to show the creative and imaginative aspects of mathematics, and, on the other hand, to bring the students to a degree of understanding of specific topics comparable with, shall we say, an educated mathematician's understanding of music or architecture.

Professor Dobbs was now thinking of a course in basic principles of physics; while Professor John Bevington suggested that a course for non-scientists should also include some chemistry. The formulation of special arts courses for scientists was not an urgent matter because no natural science undergraduates were to be admitted until 1965, a year after their arts colleagues. Perhaps with hindsight we can see that some valuable impetus was lost as a result of this delay?

The schemes of study for the arts students, however, were being drawn up in outline for all three years, and whilst the courses in Principles of Physics and Principles of Chemistry would not be taught until 1965, it was felt to be important for undergraduates to have some appreciation of the total three-year span of their studies at the time of their first entry to the university in October 1964. A year later they first encountered the contrastive element in their degrees and were given a choice of ten such courses. The mark derived from this course was to become one of the range of nine marks which would determine their final degree class; although the mode of examining would vary between the subjects, and from year to year.

But whilst students in the arts and social science fields had such courses as a compulsory part of their first degree, the natural scientists, a year later, were merely to be "strongly encouraged to read in Part I a subject which they have not studied to Advanced level".[3.30]

One specially designed distant minor course, Principles of Physics, was fortunate in that staff of the departments of higher education and physics took a keen interest in evaluating the course as it was taught. While the detail of their reports lies beyond the scope of an institutional history, they form a valuable documentation[3.31] of a particularly interesting educational experiment, giving a full account of objectives, content, types of learning environment, examples of tests, detailed syllabuses, and an overall evaluation. Registration figures and examination results for students on the course were:

Year	Number Taking Course	Credit	Pass	Fail
1965–66	24	5	17	2
1966–67	11	5	4	2
1967–68	13	5	4	4
1968–69	26	14	9	3
1969–70	13	6	7	–
1970–71	8	3	4	1

In May 1966, when the distant minor courses for arts students were still in their first trial year and science students were registering for the first time for second-year courses—which for some included a contrastive (but Part I level) arts course, and for others only their major discipline and a cognate subject—the Senate held a special distant minor conference, open to all members of the academic staff. The Vice-Chancellor had invited them to send him memoranda on the subject, although the ones he received,

(if I may say so), illustrate to a striking extent that lack of sympathy and understanding between scientists and non-scientists, which was one of the

---

3.30 *University of Lancaster Prospectus, 1965–66 and 1966–67*, p. 40.
3.31 See "A Report to the Leverhulme Foundation on Research into Higher Education" (September 1966) by J. Heywood (University of Lancaster Library); particularly Part B, "A Group Study of Staff and Student Attitudes to the Distant Minor", and Part C, "An Exploratory Study in Teaching and Examining of a Section of a Principles of Physics Course for Arts Students". See also "The Teaching of the Principles of Physics to Arts Students: An experiment in Curriculum Development" by J. Heywood and H. Montagu-Pollock (September 1969)—in mimeograph.

reasons why the Academic Planning Board proposed courses which cross Faculty lines.

Having commented that arguments about courses being professional or not were unhelpful, that the structure of a sound education is not uniform for all subjects, and that intrinsic differences between subjects needed to be investigated rather than assumed to be self-evident, the Vice-Chancellor gave his own justification for more distant courses. He pointed out that there are differences of structure of thought and method of enquiry which vary between subjects and are frequently unperceived: in their working life people will need to understand what is said by practitioners of subjects very different from their own, and that in such circumstances, the man who does not perceive his own limitations is dangerous. He continued:

> Those most in need of greater humility are the least likely to perceive that need. Consequently there is no strong case for a voluntary scheme. If Senate decides that the study of a different way of thought should not be compulsory, we may as well opt for the alternative advantage of more time for specialization. . . . A satisfactory "distant" course must effectively represent its discipline. This must surely imply that it is limited in scope and has depth and rigour. . . . There is no reason why courses should not be devised which attach themselves to the student's main motivation, while still fully representing a different discipline: for instance, courses in the English of Science, the Economics of Engineering Projects. . . . Within a three-year degree, we can only hope to give understanding of some *one* other area. There is a presumption in favour of arts and social science students doing a course in science or technology (and vice versa). . . . Logically, however, economics is "distant" to classics, and might well be a proper choice for a student who has had a broad education up to A-level. The danger is, of course, that it would be chosen by the wrong students, as a soft option.

On this basis he propounded the idea of a Different Discipline Subject.

The exigencies of the academic year seem to have prevented discussion of the documents circulated. It was not until October 1966 that they were debated and a study group set up, with a representative from each department, to consider views and suggestions, and make recommendations for the future. From this a working party was organized, which came back to Senate in April 1967 with a new suggestion of a large number of short supplementary courses, each consisting of only twenty hours' teaching, which would be taken either in the second or the third year. Students could satisfy the need to study a different intellectual approach either through one of these, or by taking in their first year one contrastive subject or, for Board A students, by offering History of Science as a minor subject in Part II.

This proposal, however, did not find favour either with the Senate or the Academic Advisory Committee. For example, it was asked, should the contrastive element be contained in a student's Part I course, or should the principle be adhered to that all his three first-year courses should be capable of leading to a major subject? There was a difficulty of definition of objective: was the distant minor to be specifically a science subject for an arts student (and vice versa) or could it be, more generally, a different type of intellectual discipline? Uniformity was another vexed matter—for instance, whether or not it was important that Board A should come into line with the other boards—and, related to this, the continuing question of the degree to which distant minor courses should be voluntary or compulsory. The level at which such teaching should begin, what its minimum aims should be (particularly in regard to the assimilation of a new language), and how many formal teaching hours constituted an adequately weighted course, also exercised the Senators. Above all, the extent to which such a course should affect the final degree classification was becoming increasingly problematic.

Special meetings as well as prolonged discussions during statutory Senate meetings, continued. By October 1967 the term most frequently being used to describe the distant minor was "breadth subject" and a committee was set up under that name to exercise general supervision over the system of breadth courses, to propose to the boards the development of new ones, to suggest methods of study, and to consider recommendations for individual students' exemption from this requirement. There followed a kind of uneasy truce, in which a number of intricate regulations were applied less and less rigidly, and a case law emerged from consideration of individual cases. Efforts were made to produce an approximate uniformity of weighting and level, although the continuing difficulty of comparing unlike with unlike meant that the compromise of a description of the *status quo* was as much as could in practice be achieved. Board D (language subjects) was not well represented in the breadth offerings available, and although new ideas were bandied about, this continued to be an area of weakness; romanticism, and the twentieth-century European novel, were two ideas that did not get beyond the stage of preliminary planning, and English for scientists was never made a realistic possibility (although efforts continued as late as 1971 to alter this situation).

Two regulations in particular were too complicated for hard-pressed departments to operate effectively. The first, later abandoned, was that the breadth subject should be taken from a board of studies other than that of a student's major subject: having regard to some of the artificialities of the board structure and the continuing review of this method of distributing departments, this provision did not necessarily safeguard the objective of a different intellectual approach. The second was a desire to consider a student's total educational experience to date, both in the sixth form and in the first year at university, and form a judgment on an appropriate breadth course which had regard to a student's overall development. Thus the prospectus for 1969–70 wistfully stated that the course structure at Lancaster provided flexibility, depth, balance and breadth:

> Importance is attached to breadth for the following reason: if a student concentrates his attention at school on a related group of subjects and if he continues to work wholly within the same group on arrival at the University, there is some danger of a lack of intellectual contact and sympathy with those educated in another specialism. The University thus feels a responsibility to encourage the development of cross-links.[3.32]

This period of relative calm (or exhaustion) came to an end, however, when members of the university began seeking yet again for what they regarded as first principles. The whole topic underwent its most fundamental discussion at the Senate conference of September 1969. Dr. Stanley Hussey described the existing tortuous situation, showing that there were different types of breadth courses with divergent aims, that breadth could be satisfied in different ways, and that the distribution by student choice was very uneven. From the kinds of selection they were making he concluded that, with the exception of Biology and Man, they wanted not breadth but enrichment, which he would personally support and wish to see included in the first year. This suggestion led to a discussion of the structure of the first degree, to see how the distribution of nine terms and two long vacations could be manipulated to bring the maximum benefit to students. At the conclusion of the debate, however, the deployment of the time available remained as it had been, and the one fresh suggestion of the meeting came from Professor Ninian Smart. He examined the variety of patterns in what counted as a subject at Lancaster and, having established that it was unwise to equate subjects with departments, the members of the conference moved on to a consideration of the number of final units of assessment which made up a degree: this still stood at the original nine.

A working party on course structure was therefore set up, to consider amongst other matters

> the decision that the present breadth requirement should be abolished but that a pattern of course structure should be evolved which will if possible incorporate the virtues of existing and projected breadth courses. In this connection, the Committee was asked to consider the proper place (if any) of the proposed new concept of enrichment in the degree structure.

By the following spring the discussion had moved back to the Senate and its sub-committees and, during the ensuing debate, Professor Ninian Smart, in

---

[3.32] *University of Lancaster Prospectus,* 1969–70, p. 41.

a well-remembered memorandum headed "Course Structure: no Change for Tradition; New Possibilities for All" described variations of the degree scheme and coined the phrase "free ninth unit". Another eighteen months of detailed negotiation took place, but in October 1971 the prospectus declared that

> Part II of Schemes of Study provide for a "free ninth unit" with the exception of a few Schemes which omit it on educational grounds: this free unit carries equal weight with each of the other eight units of assessment which enter into the final degree classification.[3.33] The undergraduate selects the free unit from a wide-ranging list of courses covering almost every discipline in the University: some of these courses have been specially designed for undergraduates with little or no previous experience of the particular subject,[3.34] whilst many others are offered from the range of specialist options which are also available to those taking a major or minor course in the subject. The free unit can, at the student's choice, be any course on the Free Unit List which (i) he is qualified to take; (ii) he can fit into his timetable.[3.35]

Many people, on the adoption of this scheme, gloomily prophesied the extinction of any sort of contrast, but figures so far available seem to belie this fear. In 1971–2, for example, only seven out of over eighty major historians were taking a free ninth unit in the history department, and other subjects being taken by them included biology, classics, German, philosophy, politics, Russian, music, law, and History of Western Architecture. Looking at the natural scientists, we find the chemists, for example, taking free ninth units in biology, economics, history and history of science, operational research, religious studies, and sociology.

This is not to say, of course, that discussion is now concluded. At the Senate conference of April 1972 Mr. J. M. Kirkwood saw the Lancaster system as "eclectic in the worst sense" for

> the flexibility is peculiarly rigid. As the numbers and size of departments grow, so does the number of special subjects, major course options, minor options and free ninth units. It becomes increasingly difficult to timetable all the options, so restrictions have to be introduced for *non-educational* reasons. On the other hand departments determine largely what are

[3.33] Previously the distant minor and breadth subject had been assessed internally' but this ninth unit, which can come from a student's major or minor area of study, or any other (subject to certain conditions) is assessed externally.

[3.34] Special free ninth unit courses available for 1972–73 included: the oil industry, exploration of the environment, history of science, history of western architecture, Czech language, Roman art and archaeology, German studies, music, and introduction to English Law.

[3.35] *University of Lancaster Prospectus 1973–74*, p. 29, where slightly more detailed stipulations for selection of courses are given.

K

permissible combinations and what are not, hence restrictions operate from that direction. As the number of courses grows so does the number of caveats and pre-conditions. In effect the University is strangling itself with a rope of its own manufacture.

The restless search for an educationally balanced but academically sound degree is not yet ended.

(iii)   Selection of subjects

The several prospectuses that the university produces give a lucid and detailed account of the subject areas being covered in both undergraduate and graduate work as the university nears the end of its first decade. There is no need for the writer to amplify these statements, backed up as they are by a statement of the philosophy behind each scheme of study and by the research interests of all the teaching members of staff; and, for many of the holders of chairs, reference may be made to the inaugural lectures they have given as an indication of the scope of their interests, as well as to the articles some of them wrote for a special supplement to the *Lancaster Guardian* in April 1964.[3.36] What is of interest, however, is the growth of the academic structure since the Academic Planning Board first sat down in March 1962 to discuss the matter.

A. E. Sloman, at Essex, has commented on the critical nature of a university's decision on its choice of what to study, for

> When it has chosen to pursue a particular subject it must appoint staff, build up a library, perhaps erect a building and install equipment. And all this will probably commit it to the subject irrevocably. Appoint a professor and establish a department, for whatever reason, and you have probably accepted the subject for all time. The professor will die but his department may well live on for ever.[3.37]

Whether or not the present holders of chairs in British universities are comforted by these intimations of immortality, it is certainly true that an enormous momentum is set up with the creation of any new academic development and there are very few instances in British academic history of departments being closed down. On the other hand, as Lord James of Rusholme at York has pointed out, plans must be made, and fairly quickly, by the new university's academic planning board, for

> If inadequate plans are made, either the university becomes far too much the expression of the ideas of one man, the first vice-chancellor, or there is too long a delay while senior academic staff are recruited in sufficient number to make discussion profitable.

[3.36] See Appendix vi for a list of inaugural lectures.
[3.37] A. E. Sloman, *A University in the Making* (1964), p. 23.

He also points out, however, that

> if the academic planning board plans in very great detail, the vice-chancellor and staff will feel themselves circumscribed. In the case of York, the Academic Planning Board avoided these dangers by appointing a vice-chancellor who was clearly in sympathy with the plan which they had prepared, by leaving the final drafting of the plan until after the vice-chancellor was appointed, so that modifications were still possible in the light of discussions with him . . . and, above all, by putting forward a scheme both of organization and of curriculum which, although firm enough to indicate what *kind* of university York was to be, was yet sufficiently flexible for modifications as time went on and as staff were appointed.[3.38]

The Lancaster Board acted in a not dissimilar way as regards procedure, and Charles Carter was involved in its discussions from the beginning of 1963, in time for the preparation of the document of March 1963 to the U.G.C. outlining the Board's intentions.

We are told that at Essex only a narrow range of subjects was chosen, the criteria for selection being national need, the special features of the region, and the need for a balance of subjects within the university. In the first years, therefore, the Essex planners decided to restrict themselves "to only three fields of study: the physical sciences, social studies, and comparative studies. There [were to] be serious omissions: the biological sciences, for example, important branches of the humanities, and all the professional schools."[3.39] Similarly, at York, it was decided that

> only a fairly limited range of subjects should be studied. Nothing is more wasteful of staff, the scarcity of which is the most critical element in the whole university scene, than for every university to attempt to offer every subject, and in particular those subjects for which only a very few students will apply, or for which there are already sufficient places at other universities.[3.40]

Sussex, on the other hand, was particularly concerned to "depart from the usual pattern of departmental organization in favour of degree courses associated with schools of study". A decision was therefore taken to have a system of core and contextual subjects on the arts side (with something similar on the science side), so that two aims were covered,

---

[3.38] Lord James of Rusholme, in Murray G. Ross, *New Universities in the Modern World* (1966), chapter 3, p. 33.

[3.39] A. E. Sloman, *op. cit.*, p. 23.

[3.40] Lord James of Rusholme, *op. cit.*, p. 42.

first to ensure that the core subject is set within a wider content of scholar-ship and reaches out to kindred fields: second, that the whole is made up of parts (core and contextual subjects) that speak significantly to one another and both illuminate and are illuminated by one another.[3.41]

The Lancaster approach was something akin to that of Sussex: the main emphasis of the recorded discussion centres around the approach to subjects rather than the elimination of some and the inclusion of others. Thus as we have seen, the first discussion of the Lancaster Board concerned itself very deeply with experimentation in the teaching of science, and whether "there were aspects of science of which any well educated person ought to have some knowledge", and when it came to the point of discussing the arts subjects, Miss Major at once introduced the concept of joint degree courses in, for example, English and history, or modern languages and history. This was taken up by Sir Malcolm Knox who expressed a wish to see

> a central discipline around which a faculty of Arts is built. He said that in Scotland faculties of Arts were based on philosophy but he thought it preferable for a new faculty to be built on history as the main discipline. . . . To his mind the important thing was that the theoretical discipline would have to be geared to the period or the country whose history was being studied, so that the student would understand the inter-connection between the economics, philosophy and culture of the period being studied.[3.42]

Thus the first year for someone who was to concentrate on history would be spent on language study and the student would then proceed to ancient, mediaeval or modern history, with an appropriate supporting subject. For example, a student might wish to concentrate on the contemporary period, and therefore combine history with economics and modern political theory.

When the discussion turned to more specific subject areas, the tenor of debate was concentrated on fields of study rather than individual subjects; on whether, for example, there might be a move towards biochemistry and bio-physics rather than towards nuclear physics, or whether there should not be

---

[3.41] Sir John S. Fulton (now Lord Fulton) in Murray G. Ross, *ibid.*, p. 28.

[3.42] At a subsequent meeting, Sir Malcolm amplified these comments by explaining that he "believed strongly in people taking subjects which are cognate with each other. . . . He was opposed to a wide choice of unconnected subjects and was aiming at a degree in two subjects. This he felt would make for less specialization than existed in most Faculties of Arts at the present time." Professor Bruce Williams, writing from Australia in May 1962 was "not convinced that history should be the central discipline of the Faculty" because "the success of Sir Malcolm's scheme would depend in some measure on getting (in my experience the rather rare) historians who really understand what a civilization is. I suspect too that requiring each student to have two languages would have a rather serious effect on the recruitment of students. I feel sure that Sir Malcolm's main objectives could be achieved by creating more than two parts to the Arts course, and by allowing more choice within the first year studies."

applied as well as pure science.[3.43] When, at a meeting at the end of April, however, Sir Frank Bower asked whether research in applied science might be a speciality of Lancaster,

> It was recalled that the U.G.C. had expressed doubts as to the need for industrial research to be expanded in the university field beyond the existing level which they considered to be adequate to meet existing needs. Apart from this, the Board inclined to the view that it was wise for a university to establish itself and its standards academically before entering into relationships with industry on research, and that, in any event, it was undesirable to give undue weight to technology.[3.44]

Meanwhile, the "desirability of every Arts student having to devote some time to the study of science and conversely of Science students having to acquaint themselves with the Arts" was raised.[3.45] There was even discussion about whether the arts student, after what would in effect have been a remedial year, would be capable of taking an honours degree in a science subject. Thought was also given to subjects or departments which would bridge the arts and science subject groupings, and a proposal made that history of science be established. This was a development subsequently undertaken in October 1966 with a not inconsiderable degree of success, as a section within the Department of History: it has enabled scientists to acquire an extra dimension to and understanding of their own background which is nevertheless not as unrelated to the rest of their work as a study of some purely aesthetic set book would be, and it gives the students of the humanities a glimpse of scientific methodology and techniques at times when the natural sciences were groping their way through first principles.

By the time, therefore, that the Academic Planning Board had a joint meeting with the Executive Council, the members of the former were able to be fairly concrete in their proposals, while explaining that the Board members wished to place emphasis "upon the educational values for the general run of undergraduates which can be secured from a careful grouping of subjects to be studied and from their method of treatment," whether in the arts, or the natural and social sciences. The Board showed an early awareness (a year before the Robbins Report appeared) of what the nature of post-Robbins university education was likely to imply when they declared that

> After a central treatment of suitably inter-related subjects in the first one or two years, opportunities for specialization in a final year or years will be provided. It is hoped by this method to give to senior members of the Faculty opportunities to teach their specialities at the highest level and at

---

[3.43] Minutes of the Academic Planning Board, 20 March 1962.
[3.44] Minutes of the Academic Planning Board, 26 April 1962.
[3.45] See the discussion on breadth, pages 118 to 128, above.

the same time to arrange the central teaching of the University in ways that will give maximum benefits to those who desire to have a balanced education.[3.46]

At that stage the Board were thinking of a complicated system, which was later rejected, of awarding an honours degree on that part of a student's course which had been taken for two years. It was even suggested that some students might take two years over Part I, reach an honours degree standard on that, and proceed to general degree work in Part II: this arrangement would have made it "possible to extend the typical undergraduate course from three years to four (a probable contemporary trend) without disturbing the organization or basic work of the University". Teachers could thus wait until they had seen one, or even two years' work before advising a student on the courses which would suit him best. The essential point was that there would be opportunities within the Lancaster system for students to make a choice depending on their capabilities and their choice of likely future career: they could either choose courses from cognate but varying subject areas and fuse them together to a degree which would nevertheless be of an honours standard, or concentrate their studies and select one of the more specialist degree courses which would be made available. Sir Noel Hall has told the writer that his experience at Princeton, in contrast with his time both at Oxford and at University College, London, had convinced him of the value of avoiding both premature specialization and specialization for people to whom it is not appropriate. Nevertheless, the Board members saw the success of the scheme as dependent to some extent on the existence of a fourth year, at least for some students. For example, if an undergraduate wished to read for a degree composed of disparate elements but nevertheless wished to go on to higher degree work, the Board felt he would need the experience of absorption in a single subject in order to give him the necessary confidence and expertise with which to go on to research. Or again, if he were to make a drastic change of direction during his degree course, he might need an extra year to reach an honours degree standard within his newly chosen field. Although the U.G.C. were sympathetic to the idea of four-year degrees for certain students, and although certain universities, notably in Scotland (including Stirling) customarily have such a length of degree course, the Board was advised that it was unlikely that such a proposal would be accepted by the Treasury. The report of the Board to the U.G.C. nevertheless argued that

> the trend in the future may be to lengthen the period of some under-graduate courses from three years to four. We think it desirable that the possibility of such extensions should be borne in mind from the early

[3.46] Paper by Sir Noel Hall for the Executive Council meeting of 15 May 1962.

stages of the University, and, where appropriate, undergraduates should be encouraged to embark on a longer rather than a shorter period.[3.47]

However, in realistic terms they were beginning to follow a line argued by Professor Bruce Williams who contended that

Most of the valid objections of the specialists to general degrees can be met by introducing the appropriate forms of post-graduate training. It is therefore important not to think of first degrees except in relation to forms of post-graduate instruction. Post-graduate courses have two functions—to train specialists and to protect undergraduates from trained specialists[3.48]

—that is, to give university teachers somewhere to air their current research obsessions other than to undergraduates who need less specific teaching! The Board thought the fourth year might

suitably be spent in instruction of a kind that provides either advanced knowledge or systematic training for research. This supplementary year might in these cases lead to a Master's degree or some suitable alternative.[3.49]

Already some subjects were set aside, at least for the time being. Geography was not regarded as a front-runner at this stage,[3.50] agriculture was spoken of as being dependent on what the Ministry of Agriculture had to say, medicine and dentistry were held to be expensive and existing facilities possibly adequate,[3.51] and law was deferred until later, especially since its need for a good library was emphasized,[3.52] as were music and art.

[3.47] Interim Report of the Academic Planning Board to the U.G.C., March 1963, para. 14.

[3.48] Letter of May 1962 from Prof. Bruce Williams to Mr. Patrick McCall.

[3.49] Interim Report, *op. cit.*, para. 14.

[3.50] A chair in geography is again under active discussion as of late 1973; but see also below, pages 136 and 180 to 181.

[3.51] The struggle of Keele to have a school of medicine should be noted: see Sir James Mountford, *Keele* (1972), pages 96–7, and 202–6. Lancaster made strenuous efforts to attract a medical school. Late in 1965 an extended memorandum, arguing Lancaster's case, was submitted to the Royal Commission on Medical Education. In May 1968, however, the Vice-Chancellor was obliged to report to the Council that new medical schools were proposed for Southampton, Leicester and Swansea, and possibly for Keele or Hull, Norwich and Coventry but "No request for oral or for further written evidence was addressed to this University". The small size of the Royal Lancaster Infirmary, the (apparently) long distance from Preston, and the desire to have a university of 4,000 students before allowing a medical school, were considered as overriding arguments. No further serious attempts were made after 1968, and in March 1973 the U.G.C. noted that the university should reconcile themselves to the fact that "there was no prospect of their being allowed to develop a medical school or work in pre-clinical medicine".

[3.52] Law is currently (in late 1973) under serious discussion in the university: the proposal is to set up a chair and a small professional department in the present

The Academic Planning Board had other matters pressing for attention, however, such as the appointment of a vice-chancellor, the constitutional and governmental structure of the university, and the drafting of the Charter and first Statutes of the university. Theoretical discussion of degree courses therefore did not figure so large in meetings after the late spring of 1962 and, in any case, the Board had agreed with Professor Dainton when he observed that they "would no doubt wish to guard against attempting to lay down too much detail in the early stages which might provide difficulties for the academic staff of the University who ought to be free to work within and develop the broad framework which it was for the Board to determine at the outset". By March 1963 the Board, having by now had the benefit of discussions with the incoming Vice-Chancellor, were able to provide the U.G.C. with the following list of candidates for founding subjects: biology (including biochemistry and biophysics); chemistry;[3.53] classics; economics; English; European studies; history; mathematics, pure or applied, including statistics; operational research; philosophy; physics;[3.54] and politics. These were regarded as suitable basic disciplines, and it will be noticed that there was intended to be a solid base of natural science subjects. The Board was at pains to explain that "in the science group of subjects the intention is to have, quickly established, a really effective senior staff in at least one major area of study; and to recognize from the outset the importance of developing cross-connections between different scientific subjects."[3.55] Something of wishful thinking seems to have crept into their deliberations at this stage, for the document also speaks of "an early appointment [who] will be a leader in a suitable field of research [and] who may be able to bring the nucleus of a research team with him" but "preferably in a field where effective work can be carried on *without the prior provision of costly apparatus and buildings*" (author's italics). The level of appointment was to be left open, "the consensus of opinion being that Chairs should be established at the outset in cases where outstanding men are available to fill them,[3.56] and that fairly stringent standards should be set for bright young men at the more junior levels".

---

quinquennium, so that it can move ahead rapidly in the next. The external assessors who have been approached described it as "feasible, not impossibly expensive, and timely".

[3.53] The early interests of the Department of Chemistry included polymer science, spectroscopy, molecular structure and reaction mechanisms.

[3.54] The earliest research in the physics department was in experimental and theoretical solid state physics, to which were subsequently added elementary particle physics and physical electronics.

[3.55] Interim Report, *op. cit.*, paras 17 and 18.

[3.56] Of the teaching departments established in 1964 and 1965, only Russian had a non-professorial head of department.

The groundwork of the social sciences was therefore prepared, and an augury of the later business school revealed by the inception of economics, politics (with sociology already mentioned as a further development), and applied mathematics and operational research. With regard to the last group, the Board took the view that, although a senior post in Operational Research was included,

> This does not indicate an intention to provide undergraduate courses in Business Management. We think that the study and teaching of Operational Research at all levels in a university is well worth experiment as providing a form of intellectual discipline, and of training in techniques of analysis, which has a direct bearing on undergraduate and graduate instruction in a number of different subjects.
> With regard to Business Studies generally, our view is that detailed work in this field at the research and graduate levels can most effectively be carried out in metroplitan centres. . . .
> We have also given some thought to the place of the Mathematics Department and to the teaching of Mathematics. We conceive of this department as providing a service for both experimental sciences and social sciences.[3.57]

European studies were to be established in the literature and language of at least French, German and Russian, and would be part of the cluster around a subject like history as well as subjects in their own right.[3.58] A chair in English was to be instituted and emphasis would, the Board hoped, "be placed upon the encouragement of creative work and the need generally to broaden the discipline beyond the critical and highly specialized fields":[3.59] from the beginning it was intended to contain a linguistic element which was to prove valuable in linking it with the theoretical study of the European languages. Classics was not a favourite choice of the new universities,[3.60] but Lancaster was intended to have a strong interest in languages *per se*, outside bodies such as the Classical Association and The Society for the Promotion of Roman Studies in May 1962 pleaded the cause of classical studies, and it was an obvious and logical companion for the other humanities subjects so far chosen. The Board decided it should be accepted "in order to ensure that the classical interest is represented in the

[3.57] Interim Report, *op. cit.*, paras. 20–22.
[3.58] See below, page 178.
[3.59] Minutes of the Academic Planning Board, 21 February 1963.
[3.60] Apart from Lancaster, only Kent (as at 1973–4) has a fully established, although small, classics department; additionally Sussex has a department of classics and mediaeval studies.

University in terms of the history, philosophy, language and literature of Greece and Rome".[3.61]

The grouping of the subjects for undergraduate courses was to be decided by the Senate—emphasis was given to the hope that degrees would be developed that would cross the normal arts/science boundaries—and such combinations as, to quote just two examples from several described, a science subject with one of mathematics, operational research, economics and philosophy, or classics with philosophy and principles of science, were envisaged.

The university adhered remarkably closely to these initial plans,[3.62] although the department of classics did not begin until 1965, nor the natural science departments take in any undergraduates until their second year of operation. Nor was German introduced until rather later, in 1971, although an effort was made to fill the chair in the early days of 1964. No subjects were dropped, but one was added; Environmental Studies.[3.63] A post had originally been advertised in Geography, the Board having altered its collective mind about not having the subject established in the first instance. Professor Gordon Manley was invited to apply, and he came back with proposals for Environmental Studies, for he saw Lancaster as affording an opportunity,

> beyond almost any of its rivals, of bringing to the mind of students every aspect of environmental change on every time-scale; of training them in the art of measuring those changes; and of discussing their consequences, for industry, for human achievement and happiness for future planning . . . environmental studies combined with physics may well make a meteorologist.[3.64]

Additionally, F. H. Lawson, Professor of Comparative Law at Oxford, who was about to retire from Oxford, was invited to come and give courses on the legal systems of France and Central Europe (as well as, later on, a breadth course in English law, and courses to certain students studying finance).

The Board also readily agreed "to the suggestion of the Vice-Chancellor Elect that he should be assisted as soon as possible by a well-qualified research worker into the methods of university teaching". The Leverhulme Trust agreed to provide money for such a purpose and the Board expressed the

---

[3.61] Minutes of the Academic Planning Board, 21 February 1963. The stress of classics at Lancaster is to make the subject interesting and relevant, and to try to reach a wide audience, while at the same time not losing the rigorous grammatical knowledge of the languages.

[3.62] See Appendix (xi) for the dates at which each of the university's departments came into being.

[3.63] This later became Environmental Sciences.

[3.64] *Lancaster Guardian*, Special Supplement (April 1964), p. 7.

hope that "as a result of this investigator's experiences in helping with the development of a new university, a centre for the continuous and systematic study of the methodology of higher education may develop".[3.65]

Meanwhile, in order to secure the necessary calibre of staff in the first appointments, the Board decided to approach two or three advisers from outside who might also act as assessors to the individual appointing committees when they were set up. An advertisement was placed in the national newspapers asking for letters from people who might be interested in academic posts at Lancaster. Over six hundred replies were received and, in a circular letter of summer 1963 from the Vice-Chancellor which was sent out to all of them, emphasis was laid on the necessity of the university being created

> by its staff, junior as well as senior. The Academic Planning Board naturally has to have some sort of idea of the shape of the future university, to guide it in making the first appointments; but our greatest concern is to find lively people and to give them freedom to experiment—and if these experiments lead in directions which we have not so far imagined, we shall not be at all alarmed. . . .
>
> On particular subjects we have formed preliminary ideas—for instance, on the desirability of encouraging creative work in English: on the need for mathematics courses relevant to the training of school teachers: on the possibility, at a later stage, of having a joint arrangement with other universities to develop management studies. But on these and similar matters we hope for guidance from the assessors whose help we are now seeking for each subject.

Interviews were duly held, and regular bulletins on the progress of the appointments came back to both the Academic Planning Board (on teaching staff) and the Executive Council (for administrative and library staff). Another task carried out in the autumn by the Vice-Chancellor was the drawing up of the first prospectus. In 1964–65 the following subjects were to be on offer to undergraduates: Mathematics, English, Modern History, Philosophy, Economics, Politics and Environmental Studies. He drew up a list of subject combinations for Part I (with postulated study for the following two years). The complexity inherent in the Lancaster degree system was perhaps beginning to reveal itself, for in a footnote the Vice-Chancellor asked the Board, "Please do not think of more alternatives—there are too many here already". It was fortunate that so many of the new staff, although not necessarily taking up their posts, were available to come to planning meetings: on Saturday and Sunday, 11 and 12 January 1964, the Shadow Senate met for

---

[3.65] Interim Report, *op. cit.*, para. 23.

the first time[3.66] at Bailrigg House, and were greeted by a telegram from Sir Noel Hall hoping that they would "have as much pleasure and satisfaction in working out and developing your own ideas for the University of Lancaster as we have had in preparing a little raw material for you". Readers will not be surprised to learn that the Senators sat down to an impossible agenda covering not only the academic structure, the constitution, staffing, student numbers and admissions, the establishment of boards of studies, the library, extra-mural and graduate work, colleges and lodgings, and the building programme, but also relationships with colleges of education, academic dress, scholarships, road research, a coat of arms and a motto and, last but not least, the selection of a representative for the City of Lancaster Regatta! Later meetings and agendas were equally over-loaded, and frequently, under one item alone there is recorded "general discussion", "some discussion", and "further discussion", so that those early members of the university who have told the writer of almost continuous meetings, at all hours, seem to speak with some veracity. At January 1964, however, the first students were due to arrive in nine months' time and it is a testimony to everyone's endurance that so many substantial—and lasting—decisions were made in that brief span of time.

At this first meeting there was a discussion on whether there should be a department of higher education,[3.67] and also on whether theology and related studies should be introduced. It was further reported that the Joseph Rowntree Charitable Trust had "offered to provide £4,000 a year for six years to support a Senior Research Fellowship to study the fundamental nature and causes of conflicts and the means of avoiding their dangers",[3.68] that it was proposed there be an Institute of Industrial Economics, and that certain outside persons and bodies were interested in the possibility of creating a chair of accountancy.

Nor were the Shadow Senate's deliberations confined only to under-graduates, for a considerable debate went on about graduate studies, which were to be "as soundly established as staff, amenities, resources and students allow from the very beginning"; although to the Academic Planning Board the Vice-Chancellor had entered the *caveat* that graduate students should not at first be admitted in subjects which drew heavily on library resources.

[3.66] Present on this occasion were the Vice-Chancellor, Professors Bevington, Dobbs, Lawrenson, Manley, Reynolds, Rivett, Sturmey and Woolrych, the University Librarian and the University Secretary, and in attendance Mr. Koc and Drs. Mercer and Small. This represented half of the teaching staff already appointed. The Senate remained a 'shadow' body until the granting of the Charter in September 1964.

[3.67] The work that this department, when established, undertook was later subsumed in the Department of Educational Research.

[3.68] There is now a flourishing section for Peace and Conflict Research within the Department of Politics.

One-year master's degrees and two-year doctoral degrees were there and then established. Already higher degrees in a subject like Operational Research were seen as suitable for sandwich courses, with spells at the university interleaved with periods in industry or commerce.[3.69]

Thus the university was enabled to open in October 1964 with a strong base in the humanities and social sciences and with the groundwork laid for the natural sciences. Planning of new departments is, however, one activity that, judging by the minutes of the Lancaster Senate, never slackens in a new university. We shall therefore now look at the other new academic ventures of the university since 1964, with particular reference to the quinquennial submissions and settlements for 1967–72 and 1972–77. Already in October 1964 the Vice-Chancellor was pondering about future developments, and in a letter to staff of that month he drew together points culled from deliberations of the Academic Planning Board and the Shadow Senate:

Having established a strong base in Operational Research, Industrial Economics and Statistics, it will be sensible to move into other subjects which relate to the organization of industrial, commercial or government operations: first, Marketing . . . and then Financial Control and Systems Analysis.

There is much interest in the possibility of a course which would be a common foundation for those intending to specialize in architecture, town planning or building technology. . . .

Engineering developments are somewhat conjectural, because of the present surplus of engineering places. But it might be possible to found an engineering school in close relationship to a group of large firms, who would provide facilities for training and a means of keeping staff in touch with the latest engineering practices and problems. . . . The engineering departments would touch, at one side, Materials Science (developing from Solid-State Physics and Chemistry), and at the other Systems Analysis. . . .

Among the non-science subjects, the need for an Education department depends on Government policy in relation to Training Colleges, which is still not clear. Pressure is building up for the early opening of a Sociology department, and there is also interest in the further development of Russian studies and the establishment of Chinese or Far Eastern studies. Developments in Music, Art, Theology and Law have all been examined, but it is too soon to put forward any definite plans.

At least part of his foreshadowings were put into immediate effect, for in October 1965 the departments of marketing and systems engineering came

---

[3.69] The Department of Operational Research were not only the first to press for higher degrees, but the first to mount a course at the university; on Simulation, from 13 to 17 April 1964, for people from industry, commerce and the public services.

into being. The first discussion of marketing had taken place at a Shadow Senate meeting of March 1964 when the Vice-Chancellor noted that, although it was a major subject of study in the United States, it had not been introduced into this country until the recent establishment of a chair at the London School of Economics. The Vice-Chancellor and Sir Noel Hall had been in touch with the Director of the Institute of Marketing, who was reported to be anxious that Lancaster should develop the subject. The Senate minute notes that

> some doubts were expressed about the establishment of the subject as an independent department; it would be better as part of the department of Economics. It was agreed, on the Vice-Chancellor's suggestion, that if Marketing were to be established, there should be considerable emphasis on research in the early days.

There was particular concern, both in the mind of Sir Noel Hall and expressed by the Senate, that such a department should examine the general principles underlying the subject, such as the operation of a free market, or the satisfaction of needs, rather than that it have too great a slant towards advertising or salesmanship. By May the Vice-Chancellor was able to report that the Institute of Marketing were looking at the possibility of raising some money from its members to enable the university to develop the subject, and in July that it had set up an educational trust which was to launch a special appeal for funds. In the case of systems analysis, the Vice-Chancellor reported to the Senate of May 1965 that Imperial Chemical Industries had offered the university £7,000 a year for three years, with a strong prospect of continued support thereafter. The offer was accepted by the university and the U.G.C. commented favourably on the proposal, so that moves went ahead to fill the chair.[3.70]

Quinquennial planning by early 1965 became the main preoccupation of the Senate and the Academic Advisory Committee. In May 1964 the Vice-Chancellor had put before the Shadow Senate a document postulating growth of staff and student numbers, as well as new subjects (categorized under arts and social science, science, and technology), over periods of the next seven, and the next ten, years. Assuming that the university would reach 3,800 students by 1973, then four to six professors could be added each year from 1967 to 1973, either in existing or in new subject areas, reaching a total of fifty-one by 1973. The Senate meeting notes that the "broad outlines" of the development programme "appeared to command general approval", and planning about particular subjects commenced. It was decided, for example, that German should be deferred, in favour of establishing a chair in education,

---

[3.70] Both these subjects were taken over by the U.G.C. after the end of their initial grant period.

certainly by 1967 but perhaps as early as 1965. Professor Lloyd strongly advocated a chair in hydrology, which he saw as both inter-disciplinary and as having particular reference to the north-west region, but although discussion of it as a separate development was still proceeding as late as 1970, it finally came as part of Environmental Sciences. Links were sought between the pure and applied sciences by means of such subjects as materials science, and hopeful looks were cast towards accountancy; about which the Vice-Chancellor is reported to have said "that if the accountancy profession wanted such a development it would have to be prepared to finance it", and no offers had so far been received.

Certain professorial members of the staff were also alert to the question of future development, and at the Senate of March 1965 Professors Sibley and Dobbs had a number of suggestions to make. Professor Sibley wished the arts subjects to be as radically re-thought as certain science subjects had recently been, especially since the suggestions he was making were commonplace at American universities, and he saw "nothing in principle quixotic or utopian about them". He proposed "that we should include, not as hit-or-miss extra-curricular activities but as an organized and vigorous part of the university programme, courses devoted to the creative arts and designed to encourage and develop creative work by students. There are at first count, four areas in which such work might be developed: 'creative writing', the plastic arts, music, dramatic arts". The emphasis was to be practical; in music, for example, the emphasis was to "be primarily on composing, secondarily on performing and only incidentally on musicology or history. In drama, it should be on writing, acting, direction and production." He saw such courses as fulfilling breadth or minor requirements, and he himself saw

> no objection ultimately to having even major courses in these subjects for the few students who prove outstandingly gifted, but in the beginning the creative arts courses could be secondary to the more academic major courses. These departments might also provide facilities and a focus for extra-curricular activities in the Universities and for artistic activities in the community and region. They could both strengthen and draw upon the various existing but struggling groups and organizations in the North West, for instance, by bringing in local chamber, orchestral and choral groups for joint town and gown concerts, even perhaps for an arts or music festival.

He wished to see such departments because he believed that there was a very strong case, in the modern world, for universities being not only "centres of learning but also centres for the arts, functioning as patrons, purveyors and leaders in their own regions". Further, within "a university there is an extraordinarily different atmosphere when a considerable proportion of the students (and staff) not only think it not amiss to be regularly writing, painting or composing, but can regard such activities and official discussion of them as a serious part of their programme". If it were objected that

> the university is not the place for this and that it would absorb time and effort needed for more academic pursuits, the reply surely is that education should involve not just learning and scholarship but should be practical and artistic as well. . . .

Like other citadels which have fallen, one always wonders whether the walls were ever as thick as people supposed but, in any event, Lancaster in time has accepted the main purport of what Professor Sibley wrote in November 1964. He also advocated further developments in languages as well as more of the social sciences. Professor Dobbs proposed that the university consider possible new fields in pure and applied science and in technology, such as experimental psychology, materials science, agricultural chemistry, building design, or transport. Other new suggestions which were thrown up in the course of discussion included financial control, architecture, human geography or ecology, developments in computer-based sciences, Asian, African and Latin American studies, information science, Dutch studies, the history and philosophy of science, meteorology, demography, and actuarial studies. The importance was stressed, however, of "maintaining a correct balance between the development of undergraduate and graduate studies, and of keeping in mind the need for 'interlocking' with existing subjects when considering the establishment of new subjects".[3.71]

A document by the Development Committee of June 1965 attempted to make projections of staff and student numbers, based on optimistic and pessimistic forecasts of what Government finance would be available. The interdependence of that factor with the building programme, the growth of student numbers and the introduction of new subjects was made clear. If the limited funds available were to be applied to science and technology buildings, there would be a shift towards science and a slowing down of total student growth. If instead the arts and collegiate buildings were given preference, then there would be a shift towards arts subjects and a faster growth in student numbers. If, however, the whole building programme were advanced more slowly, there would be waste and inconvenience. By December the Senate was asked to consider a draft of the submission to the U.G.C. which began:

[3.71] That the control of new courses was a constantly growing problem can be seen from a minute of a Senate conference in March 1966 when it was agreed to "raise with the Boards of Studies the problem of the difficulties which might arise in attempting the premature proliferation of courses, and to invite the Boards to set up appropriate machinery to look into this matter and to consider the possible need for limiting the number of combinations offered to ensure that proper integration of courses was being achieved".

No discussion on future student numbers has ever (so far as we can trace) taken place with this university; and we are therefore uncertain about the thinking of your Committee on the question.

The following points were given special emphasis:

(i) If we are to retain good staff, we must bring our present activities to a viable size quickly. . . .

(ii) Certain new departments must be added to give a satisfactory balance to existing courses. . . .

(iii) Shortly after the next quinquennium a further considerable expansion of student numbers is expected. We shall be well placed to offer a contribution to this expansion, easily and at relatively low cost. If we are to play a proper part in the 1970's, we ought by 1970 to establish a number of new activities, so that they are "on their feet" before the large increase in demand occurs.

(iv) There is ample evidence among the students we ourselves have accepted of the widening circle from which entrants are taken; for instance, from the secondary modern school–technical college stream. We think it probable that the official estimates of demand during the coming quinquennium, already higher than those in the Robbins report, will prove to be too low.

After discussion of the full use of the Bailrigg site, of postgraduate courses (by now Lancaster had seventy-one full-time and seventeen part-time postgraduate students, drawn from twenty-four universities or colleges of advanced technology), and of student residence, the document moved on to a discussion on the balance between teaching and research:

From the beginning Lancaster has, of course, recruited academic staff (senior and junior) on the understanding that they are expected to advance their subject by advanced studies or research (in addition to their other duties). . . .

It has been argued in some quarters . . . that the emphasis on research in the universities is excessive, and that university teachers devote too much time and energy to their personal research to the detriment of their teaching. The situation in Lancaster (and probably in all the new universities) is markedly different because the weight of teaching (and other obligations) in the early years is such as to prove seriously detrimental to research. This suggests that the new universities, for the first few years of their existence, should enjoy a staff/student ratio more favourable than the national average if the accepted balance between teaching and research is to be maintained.

L

Amongst the items listed as making great demands on the time and energy of staff were: the necessity for members of staff to become acquainted with the academic interests of their colleagues in order to explore and exploit to the full inter-disciplinary co-operation; the devising of new syllabuses; the desirability of fresh thought on teaching and examining methods; the hammering out of details of constitutional and administrative machinery; the organization of the social life of the university; and the planning of new buildings and adaptation of existing temporary accommodation. However idealistic some of these proved to be in practice, there is no doubt that early members of the university staff had to push themselves to their limits; although, to compensate, there seems to have been a pioneering spirit and sense of achievement at the beginning which unfortunately was partly lost, perhaps as early as by the middle of the first decade.

The problem about drawing up ambitious plans for further development, as the Vice-Chancellor had realized in June 1966, is that people expect them to be fulfilled, and are inevitably disappointed when not all of them can be realized at once. The recurrent grant allocated to Lancaster for 1967–8 was set at £910,000, some £200,000 less than had been asked for, and mid-way between the most pessimistic and most optimistic projections: the sums for the rest of the quinquennium rose by gradual stages to £1,583,400[3.72] for 1971–2.

A Senate meeting of December 1966 discussed the allocation for the first year of the quinquennium, and that of November 1967 for the rest of the five-year period to July 1972, but since it was in effect two parts of the same discussion and no change of basic principle took place in the year's interim, what follows below is an amalgamation of both stages.

The U.G.C., in its visitation of March 1966, had made it clear that the 1967–72 quinquennium was to be something of a plateau.[3.73] They were also looking for a balance of developments between "What might appear to be attractive peripheral activities and the essential hard-core activities". However, the new universities were acknowledged as having two special problems:

[3.72] These figures were later revised upwards, so that the range of finance received was from £993,422 for 1967–8 to £2,072,528 for 1971–2. These figures exclude provision for rates, and from 1968–9 onwards also "exclude expenditure on (capital) equipment for teaching and research in existing buildings, which will be covered by the new system of equipment grants" (letter of 13 November 1967 from Sir John Wolfenden to the Vice-Chancellor).

[3.73] The U.G.C. looked for a total of between 220,000 and 225,000 university places by 1971–72, superseding the previous Government commitment of 218,000 places by 1973–74. They stated that they were "very anxious to ensure a due flow from the schools and therefore have consciously taken the view that the undergraduate numbers are a genuine priority. They have moreover taken the view that in the light of present A level trends the major increase must be in the numbers of arts-based, rather than science-based, students."

first, that there had not been discussions with them, as there had been with the older foundations, over student numbers. Secondly, at a time when universities were being encouraged to make, wherever possible, more intensive use of their buildings and capital equipment, Lancaster was faced with a temporary situation of excess capacity in buildings, to such an extent that the Vice-Chancellor was concerned that the demand for approved lodgings would largely disappear and that even the proposed privately financed residences might not be fully used. In addition, although the chairman of the U.G.C., Sir John Wolfenden, recognized "that a University's deployment of its block grant is a matter for its own responsible budgetary autonomy; and that a University has a right to frame its own priorities", he nevertheless added that he knew universities "are increasingly sensitive to national needs and anxious to play their part in meeting them". The U.G.C. had therefore "felt (and the visitations provided evidence that many universities felt the same) that it would be right for them to give the clearest possible guidance" on "certain areas or themes to which the Committee, and their subject sub-committees, have given special attention".[3.74] Thus, when the Vice-Chancellor was preparing the Senate for a worsening of the staff-student ratio, he spelt it out as

> inevitable, and I have no doubt that it is the Government's intention to enforce it. This does not necessarily imply a decline in the quality of education, or harder work for all staff; but it does imply a limitation of choice and a lessening of complexity in degree schemes. I believe that there is much to be said for accepting now (in moderation) what will in any case be inevitable within five years. There is no basis of public or Parliamentary sympathy for universities which would enable us to succeed in an attempt to maintain our present standards; on the contrary, we are widely regarded as the pampered darlings of the educational system.

In fact, the university had been complimented at the time of the U.G.C. visitation on its staff/student ratio which was usually "very favourable in the early stages of a new University; here the ratio was about average and the University had been very economical, not taking on staff until there were students for them to teach". The weighted staff-student ratio in December 1966 was 1 to 11·3, and the Vice-Chancellor proposed that it be allowed to rise to 1 to 12 (instead of 1 to 10·5, the national average at the time).

The main difficulty was that the U.G.C. had made grant allocations which were substantially less than had been expected and which, although they were nominally related to student numbers smaller than those proposed by the

---

[3.74] Letters of 21 December 1966 and 13 November 1967 from Sir John Wolfenden to the Vice-Chancellor.

university, did not take account of the substantial fixed costs at this time.[3.75]
Nor was it practicable to meet this difficulty by further reductions in planned
student numbers, since total expenditure was relatively insensitive to student
numbers.[3.76] The Development Committee, the Vice-Chancellor explained,
had therefore concluded that the university might as well take advantage of
this insensitivity and aim at larger student numbers than those on which the
U.G.C.'s grants were based. As far as the balance between arts and science
was concerned, nationally the U.G.C. was

> providing for a reduction in the proportion of scientists and technologists
> only from 56 per cent to 54 per cent, and for an increase in the absolute
> numbers by about 15,000. The severe cuts made in the plans of the new
> universities are thus the consequence of previously planned expansions of
> science elsewhere, perhaps especially in the former C.A.T.'s. It will not be
> easy to obtain 15,000 more science students, especially as the numbers
> entering specialized Science sixth forms have been falling since 1964, and
> are not expected to recover this fall during the quinquennium. The
> competition of the Polytechnics must also be allowed for. . . .
>
> We have therefore considered whether to recommend that no attempt
> should be made to exceed the U.G.C. figures for science students at
> Lancaster. This, however, would sharply disappoint some expectations in
> the science departments, while putting a heavy load on a still limited range
> of arts departments. . . .
>
> We therefore suggest that departments in Board A should be allowed to
> accept students without precise adherence to any quota . . . provided that
> the difference in A-level performance between entrants to science and
> non-science courses is not seriously increased: and provided that it is
> understood that increases in staff, beyond the minimum allowed for by an
> expansion to reach the U.G.C. figures, will carry only minimal increases
> in departmental allocations. . . . This method would provide considerable
> problems of estimating, each year, how much expansion the science
> departments would in fact achieve, and it is almost certain that as a result
> they would be over-staffed relative to other departments (if, indeed, it is
> assumed that equal staff-student ratios are desirable); but Senate may

---

[3.75] The cost of maintaining buildings at this early stage of development as a percentage of expenditure was 23·5 per cent, against a national average of 13·5 per cent. Administrative costs also contained a number of inflexible items and were (temporarily) unusually high.

[3.76] For instance, to reduce a deficit in 1971–2 by as little as 1 per cent of expenditure in 1971–2 would have required (with a weighted staff-student ratio of 1 to 12) a reduction of some 80 non-science students, and this reduction would have raised the cost per head, for those that remained, by 2½ per cent. At this time the net marginal cost of admitting one additional arts student was only about £180 p.a.

think that the harm which would be done to the University by an un-balanced expansion is a more important consideration. We do not think that our case for the next quinquennium will be seriously weakened by a moderate success in exceeding the assumed number of science students; we cannot of course propose a return to the 50 per cent ratio of the quinquennial plans.[3.77]

Various economies were suggested, amongst them being that for at least one year, in 1967–8, all posts should be filled at the (still then extant) assistant lecturer grade, or in the lowest part of the lecturer scale.

As far as specific subjects were concerned, the U.G.C.'s Memorandum had specifically discouraged agriculture, architecture, or "undue proliferation of small departments" on the arts side. They had noted that there was already over-provision in, for example, Russian, and linguistics was to be encouraged to grow at particular centres, which included Essex and York.[3.78] The U.G.C. also noted that many universities had proposed considerable expansion in fine arts, and made the comment that an impediment to such a development was the recruitment of suitable staff. On the other hand, the U.G.C. wished to encourage one-year postgraduate education courses, taken as a professional qualification, as well as welcoming experiments that combined education "with other specialist subjects in a first-degree course", and were also pleased "to note the ready response that Universities have shown to the need for improving the teaching of Management Studies. They hope for a further substantial expansion of student numbers in the new quinquennium. . . . Further undergraduate courses in Management Studies are not encouraged."

In Lancaster's particular case, therefore, the U.G.C. gave warm support to the establishment of a school of education and the strengthening of work in physics and chemistry. They did not feel able to make provision for a Centre for the Study of Central and South Eastern Europe, or the introduction of either chemical technology or architecture and planning studies. These guidelines were transmuted, after discussion at the Senate meeting of November 1967, into decisions to look for outside funding for Central and South Eastern European studies, to hold discussion with the Science Research Council on a particular development in chemical technology, and not to proceed with building science, architecture or planning, nor other subjects tentatively suggested. However, sociology and financial control were still left as new developments which would be undertaken, both of which were

---

[3.77] See the U.G.C. document "Allocation of Quinquennial Grant 1962–72: Memorandum of General Guidance" (November 1967), from which the quotations attributed to the U.G.C. in this section are taken.

[3.78] The development of linguistics was related to universities at which audio-visual aids were to be particularly encouraged. These were Essex, York, Leeds, Liverpool, Manchester, UMIST, Newcastle, Sussex, Glasgow and Strathclyde.

"valuably [to] diversify the range of offerings, and relieve pressure on certain Arts departments".

The one remaining problem was engineering which, as we have seen, was a development which had been on the cards since the beginning of the university. In September 1965 a special meeting had been held in Kirkby Lonsdale at which members of the Senate and industrialists had exchanged ideas. Following on from that the Vice-Chancellor had drafted a document for the Senate, suggesting that the university should commence the teaching of engineering, because Lancaster could offer a degree course which would cooperate with industry and could bring into it, by careful management of its content, students who at other universities would miss the opportunity. The introduction of the subject would give better balance to the subjects on offer from the university, and Lancaster could probably mount such a course substantially cheaper than departments elsewhere. He underlined the point that to attract funds from industry or to enjoy the support of the U.G.C. there must be an integration of the university course with industrial training. The integration could either be by means of a complete year away from the university, or by selected single terms.

The Senate, uncertain what to do, set up a special committee on engineering which met industrialists and representatives of the U.G.C.'s technological sub-committee, who gave the university considerable help and backed the new development. In May 1967 Professor Gwilym Jenkins prepared a document for the Senate, which that body endorsed, dilating on objectives and teaching techniques. The course he envisaged would last four years, of which the first would try to capture the imagination of students, describe to them the nature of engineering in all its ramifications, and provide an introduction to systems engineering. One period in the second year and one in the third would be spent in industry and the remaining time would be spent on study of different branches of engineering science. The degree would be capped by a specialization year, in which the student would study one branch of engineering in depth, take part in an industrial design project (under the direction of both industrial and university supervisors), look at the structure of industry, and examine in greater detail the systems engineering side of the subject. Throughout there would be projects, progressively more ambitious and individually tailored to the students' own interests, which would encourage the development of a creative approach to engineering and demonstrate that, for engineers, principles must always be illustrated by uses.[3.79]

These proposals found favour in the eyes of the Senate and were included in the submission to the U.G.C., but when they were not specifically

[3.79] The imaginative practical work and the projects are, it seems, a particularly successful part of the Lancaster engineering degree.

mentioned in the quinquennial settlement, the chairman of Board A in November 1967 "drew attention to the fact that staff could only be provided for this new department at the expense of those already in existence". Thus, while the development was supported in principle by the board, the members were reluctant to recommend that any increase in resources should be devoted to it. The debate continued at Senate and in January 1968 Professor Jenkins submitted another paper, drawing attention to this continuing postponement and inferring from the size of the equipment grant the U.G.C. had given the university, and by the lack of positive discouragement, that the U.G.C. was giving tacit approval to the establishment of engineering at Lancaster. He continued:

> It has been stated at a previous Senate meeting that Lancaster should not waste its resources on what is normally regarded as expensive training. This misses the point made in our proposals to the U.G.C. that much of the training of engineers involving the use of machines will be carried out in industry. This means that it will be *at least as cheap* to train an engineer at Lancaster as it is to train a pure scientist, and possibly cheaper.
>
> We are well placed to attract a very substantial endowment from industry to support these proposals. A sum of about £12,000 has already been earmarked for this purpose from the General University Appeal. There is every reason to suppose that this can be augmented to £100,000–£500,000.
>
> Therefore, I propose that plans for engineering should be allowed to proceed on a reduced basis, but that an appeal should be launched to cover the bulk of the running expenses of the department in this quinquennium.

The Senate agreed in principle to set up the department and at its next meeting in March agreed that the first chair should be advertised, with the specification that candidates should "be interested in developing new methods of teaching engineering in co-operation with industry, and should already have strong and recent industrial links and experience". Mr. Michael French's appointment as professor in engineering was announced in July, and the first students were admitted to the department in October 1969. The formula adopted for the first three intakes of students was that they spent their first year at Lancaster, one term in the second year and one in their third year in industry, and the remaining four terms of their second and third years, and the whole of their fourth year, at Lancaster. Worthwhile and interesting periods spent in industry, particularly on a part-time basis, however, are not always easy to find. For this reason the pattern has since been modified so that the first and second years are spent at Lancaster, and the student then has a choice of taking a complete year away in industry and coming back to Lancaster for a fourth year, or of proceeding immediately to his final year.

This is, however, to run ahead of our chronological sequence. We have seen how the departments of Classics, Marketing and Systems Engineering came into being in 1965, and in 1966 History of Science, as a section with the department of History, took its first students. 1967 saw the emergence of two new departments, Religious Studies and Educational Research. It will be remembered that theology was one of the subjects being canvassed at the original meetings of the Academic Planning Board, and, following on from a joint meeting of the Board with the Executive Council, the Bishop of Black-burn and the Rev. G. A. Maland addressed a memorandum to the Board, asking that theology be included in the planned developments, for "There is little doubt that the world's knowledge is rapidly outgrowing its wisdom; that people trained in the assessment of facts are often incapable of thinking in terms of values. Theology in its widest sense is concerned with values which constitute the ultimate realities."

Theology was not given a place in the list of founding subjects sent to the U.G.C. in March 1963. However, at the first meeting of the Shadow Senate in January 1964 the Vice-Chancellor noted that proposals of three different kinds had been mentioned: a complete school, capable of providing a pro-fessional training; studies intended especially for school-teachers; or studies in moral philosophy or Christian ethics, designed to help students think clearly about future problems of choice.

The Vice-Chancellor felt that the first would be difficult to justify in terms of professional need, the second might be accomplished by the appointment of an independent lecturer in biblical studies, and the third might be provided within a department of philosophy if the head of that were sympathetic. In March, however, the Vice-Chancellor is recorded as taking the view that the university could not afford such a development within the resources provided by the U.G.C.; if the promoters of the idea wished the university to take action they would have to find a benefactor.

Undaunted by this discouragement, however, a memorandum by Canon Browning, Canon Theologian of Blackburn, was presented to the October 1964 meeting of the Senate, and discussed in December. Canon Browning noted that

> There are at present twelve faculties of theology and nine departments of theology in the universities of Great Britain, in which 216 professors and lecturers (some part-time) are employed. Of the universities which have come into being since the war, only Keele offers a course in theology. . . . The scheme of these theological courses was determined when Oxford and Cambridge Anglicans initiated theological schools in the 1870's, explicitly

intended as vocational courses for ordinands and which pre-supposed a thorough education in Latin and Greek. Faculties of theology founded afterwards, as at Manchester and London, were designed to be more acceptable to Free Churchmen by a choice of subjects, such as biblical languages, where the denominational commitments of the teachers would not need to be evident.

He went on to say that, in modern Oxford, eight of ten compulsory papers were on the Bible, although Hebrew was now optional. New Testament Greek was compulsory at every theological honours course in the country, and at most places there were compulsory papers on church history, or the history of Christian doctrine. Theology, however, was not being read simply by intending ordinands, but also by future teachers, probation officers and personnel managers. He quoted Dr. Alec Vidler, who had advocated attention being turned to questions "of general human interest in the contemporary world", the questions which should be pressed to include

"What is the purpose of human existence? How important are persons and personal relationships? Is there a moral law by which human beings should seek to direct their lives? If so, what is its ground and its content? Can such ultimate questions be significantly asked? How far do traditional answers to these questions hold good today? Where have the traditional answers broken down, and why? In what ways does new scientific knowledge—biological, psychological, sociological—demand that new answers be given to the basic human questions?

"It is not for a pluralist university to impose a single set of answers, whether Christian or otherwise, to these questions, but it ought to make sure that their importance is acknowledged and recognized and that students are stimulated to think about them as honestly and openly and deeply as possible. Ought not a divinity faculty to be one of the agencies from which this kind of stimulus proceeds? If it is to be so, it will manifestly have to extend its horizons."

A new university, Canon Browning suggested, might provide open lectures for the whole university as well as extra-mural lectures; and offer an honours course in theology, without requiring knowledge of Hebrew or even New Testament Greek but including contemporary philosophy and literature, the comparative study of religion, religious sociology and Christian doctrine and ethics.

Professor Frank Sibley, however, at once threw down a challenge in the paper which accompanied Canon Browning's; the university, he said, would need to make a fundamental choice between a department of theology whose teaching members would normally, perhaps necessarily, be active Christians, and a department of religious studies whose staff need not, and often would not, be committed to a particular religious standpoint but whose aim would be "to provide instruction concerning religion as such, its nature, varieties, history, and place in human life, together with its influence upon cultures and civilization". He saw a further distinction between subjects which, if they were not being taught from a specifically Christian point of view, could properly fit into a department of philosophy, particularly moral and social philosophy, and the philosophy of religion. On the other hand he could see at least four subjects which, while falling outside the scope and competence of a philosophy department, would constitute a valuable addition to the university curriculum and have close ties with other subjects; comparative religion, history of religion, developments in modern theological thought, and developments in Christian ethics.

The Senate, after a "lengthy discussion", decided not to give any support to the setting up of a professional school of theology, touching only a small number of students, and there was little support for the establishment of a department concerned exclusively with the Christian religion. The minute of 3 December continues:

> A substantial number of members did however favour the creation of a Department of Religious Studies, the scope of whose studies would not be limited to the Christian religion. The function of such a department would not be to convince students of a revealed truth . . . but rather to examine in a rigorous and scholarly manner the variety of human religious belief and experience, and the impact of religions upon culture and civilization. Whilst, no doubt, members of staff of a Department of Religious Studies would often be convinced Christians, this would not be a condition of their employment, and the Department could well include members who were not committed to a particular religious standpoint.

The matter was thus referred to the Development Committee. Soon afterwards, however, the Bishop of Blackburn, at a meeting of the Council, expressed his disappointment that no practical steps had so far been taken to establish a department of Religious Studies. The Vice-Chancellor explained the position, and went on to say that first priority had to be given to strengthening existing departments until they reached a viable size: there was now no possibility of new developments in 1965–6. The Council urged the importance of making an early start with this development, and of providing it from the outset with an adequate range of senior staff. The Development Committee and the Senate remained firm, however: they were not prepared to allow the department to start on a scale which they considered too small in 1966, but strongly recommended that a chair in the subject be established in 1967, subject to finance being available. At the same time, the Senate was still not prepared to give it the highest priority until other competitors for resources had been considered alongside it. Nevertheless, sufficient pressure had by now been created that at a meeting of the Senate in March 1966 it was announced that the Development Committee recommended, along with a wave of second chairs for various departments, the establishment of a new chair in Religious Studies,[3.80] the outside assessor for which would be Professor Ninian Smart of the University of Birmingham. A rather embarrassed minute of September 1966, explaining that the Vice-Chancellor, acting under his emergency powers over the long vacation, had replaced Professor Smart with Professor H. D. Lewis of the University of London conceals a story, told in a lively way by Christopher Driver,[3.81] of how the assessor himself became the chief candidate for the post, how the advertisement for the chair included the phrase "of any religion, or none", which at first shook the Bishop of Blackburn (and others) to a not inconsiderable extent, and how Professor Smart came to Lancaster and has built up a very thriving and unusual department which examines, amongst other items, Christianity and Western Atheism, Buddhism, Hinduism, Islam, Chinese and Japanese religions, as well as providing such courses as 'Religion in Edwardian England', 'Freud and Jung', and 'Catholic Modernism'.

With regard to the other development of 1967, in Educational Research, a clear distinction needs to be drawn between the department and the School of Education. We have already seen that the university appointed, as one of its very earliest posts, a research fellow in teaching methods (Mr. Wacek Koc), and he was joined shortly afterwards by a Research Fellow in University Examining Methods (Mr. John Heywood), who together made up the nucleus of a department of Higher Education. In the first year of the university's existence Mr. Koc and Mr. Heywood looked at admission and selection procedures, and Mr. Koc carried out an investigation of the first-term workload problems of the first undergraduate intake. What seems to have happened is that some departments overlooked the implications of a student carrying three subjects during his first year, and serious overloading took place. Mr. Koc discovered what he later described as "widespread anxiety among students about their inability to meet university demands for reading and written work", which increased as the first term went on. He distributed a two-part questionnaire to all students and from the 90 per cent response received, he found, as background to their work problems, that study conditions in lodgings were often unsatisfactory, and physical conditions in the temporary library and the (inevitable) scarcity of books made work difficult. There were only a very limited number of Part I subjects to choose from at such an early stage in the university's development, and a majority of students felt they had insufficient information about the content of courses, while even more stated that they had no information about methods of study or the exact nature of the demands that university work would make on them. Yet, Mr. Koc went on,

> within a day or two, before much teaching could have been possible, they were writing their first essays. Practically none of them had done any prescribed reading before coming up, and there was from the first week a scramble for necessary books, some of which existed in the Library only in single copies and could not be bought in town. . . . [The Library was closing early and] In the meantime there grew up a pattern of weekend exodus from Lancaster, thus effectively shortening the working week.
>
> The survey showed further that in the first term the students were expected to produce three or four essays, etc., of various lengths for each of their three subjects so that the total demand could not have been less than one written piece every week.

Learning of some subjects was being done at the expense of others, students of some subjects were spending practically all their time on preparation of written work, and a majority felt they did not know enough to contribute sufficiently to discussions in small group teaching, could not keep up with the required reading, or lacked time for general reading. Mr. Koc concluded that further thought should be given to the "preliminary preparation the students should get; what, in view of the nature of the intake, conditions of study and available time, should be the appropriate pace of assimilation of material; and what demands could properly be made and when, in order to achieve lasting learning of genuine quality, without the students' will to honest endeavour being destroyed in the process".

Meanwhile, the Senate was beginning to think about broadening the scope of the department, and there was debate at the Senate conference of March 1965 about having a new department of education which might contribute towards undergraduate courses, and set up one-year master's degree courses. In September 1965 the Senate set up a committee to look at the research programme of the department of Higher Education, and in July 1967 it was agreed to merge the existing department into a new department of Educational Research, which would continue to carry out internal research projects as before, but would also teach postgraduate students and keep a guiding eye on external research projects on higher education independently funded by outside bodies. Professor Alec Ross, the director of the new School of Education, would also be head of the department of Educational Research. At first the new department concentrated on external research projects, together with the teaching of graduate students, but more recently the department has moved into undergraduate work and in 1974 is to mount its own major degree course; already there are combined majors with chemistry, religious studies, sociology and linguistics, and applications for these courses are strong. One project under the department, financed by the Department of Education and Science, was to investigate

> the possibility of the accelerated teaching of higher level mathematics (using all appropriate aids to learning) to students who have fallen behind or missed opportunities of doing mathematics at school. The fact that in British schools it is possible to stop learning mathematics at an elementary level is an increasing embarrassment in higher and further education, since mathematical knowledge is increasingly essential, not only in science and technology but also in the social sciences.[3.82]

Such a programme was duly set up in 1967.

We have already seen how Professor Sibley had pleaded the cause of creative subjects in the university's development, and at a meeting of the Senate in October 1966 his views were endorsed by both Boards C and D, who proposed "that courses of a creative kind be introduced into the curriculum at the earliest opportunity, initially as one-year 'more distant' minor courses to be taken in the second year", and that the allocation of staff should accordingly be reconsidered. Boards A and B were not unsympathetic to such a development and so a special committee for music and the fine arts was set up, which in a report to the Senate of July 1967 recommended that directors for music and visual arts should be appointed from 1 January 1968. The director of music would

> In co-operation with musical groups in the region and jointly with S. Martin's College . . . help to create and direct a university orchestra, stimulate the formation of amateur choral, operatic and instrumental groups within the university and the performance of appropriate works: encourage students to learn instruments . . . and take over the responsibility of advising . . . on the organization of professional concerts at the University,

while the director of visual arts would have a responsibility "to stimulate creative art and the appreciation of the Visual Arts throughout the University. He will be in charge of the three studios assigned to Fine Arts". Although Professor Sibley expressed regret at the lack of emphasis on the integration of creative work into the undergraduate curriculum, the Senate "approved and warmly endorsed" these proposals. Meanwhile, on the completion of the Nuffield Theatre Studio, a director, Mr. Kenneth Parrott, was appointed, and

---

[3.82] University of Lancaster, *Third Annual Report presented by the Vice-Chancellor to the Meeting of the University Court* (December 1967), page 10. Such a programme was duly set up in 1967.

teaching began in drama; at first in a tentative way, emerging out of the interests of existing members of staff, but later with a lecturer specifically for drama.

The quinquennial settlement, however, did not make provision for music and the fine arts to become part of the curriculum during the 1967–72 quinquennium. Although money had been set aside for the two directors already suggested, the Vice-Chancellor came back to the Senate of December 1967 to ask whether it might not be desirable to appoint instead a director of music on a higher level than had previously been envisaged, who would move ahead on the organization of first-rate musical and artistic events; interim help in the fine arts, he pointed out, might be available from the Granada Fellows. Some regret was expressed that both posts could not be filled at a high level forthwith, but after discussion the Vice-Chancellor's suggestion was acceded to, and it was also decided that a practitioner in the arts, such as a practising sculptor, should be appointed for a period.[3.83] The directorship of music was advertised and Mr. John Manduell took up his post in December 1968.[3.84] At first the department did not have a teaching role within the regular curriculum but, particularly since the appointment of the second director, Dr. Dennis McCaldin, the department has built up its academic courses with an emphasis, not always found in university degree courses, placed on the attainment either of practical musical skills or of the ability to compose.

The other department which came into being in 1968 was the long-promised department of Financial Control,[3.85] made possible because of funds donated by the Wolfson Foundation, whose interests were to extend to "all aspects of the financial and accounting activities of the business enterprises: forecasting, planning, measurement, appraisal, and control; as well as to relationships with shareholders, creditors, tax collectors and employees". In 1969 this was followed by another subject, Behaviour in Organizations, which was related to the area of business studies. In fact, the setting up of this particular department also marked the growing recognition by the U.G.C. of the importance of business studies at Lancaster. The Vice-Chancellor was able to report in March 1968 that they had offered the university grants of £5,000, £9,000 and £10,000 for the three academic years 1969 to 1972 to support new developments in management studies, and he discussed with the heads of existing departments what the next development might be. In June 1968 he reported back that

---

[3.83] A sculptor, Mr. John Hoskins, was consequently appointed for three years.

[3.84] See Chapter 5, pages 308 to 309, for an account of the university's wider musical interests.

[3.85] Now the Department of Accounting and Finance. In 1971 an International Centre for Research in Accounting, funded by the J. Arthur Rank Organization, was also set up.

The policy of the University of Lancaster in the field of Business Studies has been to develop a series of specialist departments, with a strong interest in post-experience courses and in project work in industry, commerce and public authorities; but to avoid the creation of a "Management School" for general management studies, on the grounds that this would be an unreasonable degree of overlapping with the Manchester and London Business Schools. There are signs, however, that our present exposition of this policy leads people to underrate the scale of our work. For instance, the University of Warwick has given considerable publicity to its programme of industrial and business studies: but the 1968–9 Prospectus (published in 1967) shows a staff of 4, whereas we show in the Prospectus for the same year a staff of 27. Furthermore, the interrelations between our departments have become more evident and important as time goes on, and there are signs of the emergence of further joint courses of special relevance to business at the undergraduate as well as the post-experience level.

The proposal was therefore made that, "to encourage joint planning and for purposes of joint publicity", there should be a Lancaster Centre for Business Studies, which would comprise the work of Financial Control, Marketing, Operational Research and Systems Engineering, together with the relevant aspects of Economics, the computer science aspect of Mathematics, and Politics: later a separate board of studies for business subjects was envisaged.[3.86] It was at this stage that the existing business departments began to talk of setting up the new department of Behaviour in Organizations, whose area of study would relate to the behaviour of human beings in organizations, including questions of industrial relations and industrial sociology, but one which would not be limited to the formal theory of the behaviour of organizations. Such a subject was felt to be useful as an adjunct to other business studies, and as a support course for engineers and others who were likely to go into industry. The Senate approved the proposal for the new department without further ado, and accepted the idea of the Centre in principle. In February 1969, however, it was finally agreed that the centre be named the School of Business and Organizational Studies,[3.87] to cover the subjects already mentioned, except for Politics.

Anxiety has from time to time been expressed by members of the university about its involvement with business studies, particularly in 1970 and 1971, when the student body were anxious that Lancaster should not become a "business" university, and that any profits obtained should be for the benefit

---

[3.86] Board of Studies F, for business studies, was established in 1971.

[3.87] Subsequently changed again in 1973 to the School of Management and Organizational Sciences. The School has its own administrator, Mr. J. O. Halstead, who is also secretary of Board F.

of the institution as a whole. In fact, in order to set up an orderly system, and to meet particular needs or research interests, a number of associated companies and units have been established. It is also of interest to recall what Professor Alan Mercer had to say about research and consultancy within the framework of a university at the Senate conference of September 1970:

> The operational research department through its associated company Lancord, which is a University owned limited company, undertakes research and consultancy for outside organizations. This is done because it is the view of all members of the department that operational research cannot be taught within the confines of the University, since the outside world is the operational research laboratory. Whilst fees are obtained for much of the work carried out by members of staff, this is not invariably true. Even where fees are charged, the projects would not be undertaken unless it was judged that they further the academic objectives of the University, in providing either a realistic training for students or a basis for the research of the staff. Whilst the Managing Director of Lancord now signs the contracts, the detailed negotiations with possible client organizations are usually undertaken by the member of staff who is likely to conduct the study. In this way it is hoped to ensure that the staff's research interests are considered adequately. Equally, feedback is obtained from Masters students towards the end of their course to give guidance on the selection of projects for their teaching merits.
>
> Whilst the studies have become known as contract research, this title is something of a misnomer, because it is only customary to sign contracts with public bodies such as government departments. These contracts usually state the objectives of the study, the reporting procedure, the timing and the cost to be charged. Indeed they appear to be primarily concerned to be able to demonstrate that public funds are not being misused. All the commercial organizations for whom projects are carried out are content simply to have an exchange of letters setting out the objectives of the study, its duration and the costs. . . .
>
> Studies for commercial organizations are not for more than one year at a time but those for public bodies can be for two or three years' duration . . . those studying for a Ph.D. work on real problems in industry or the public sector but no fee is charged and the responsibility for the generation of such studies is with the research supervisor and not with the directors of Lancord.
>
> Many years ago, the staff of the Operational Research Department agreed that no projects would be undertaken which involved any member of the department having to obtain a security clearance, so that no study is carried out which inhibits anyone from discussing his work with a

colleague. However, it is always understood that every precaution will be taken to protect the commercial secrets of the sponsors. Equally, it is acknowledged that there should be complete freedom to publish methodology and techniques. So far, there has never been any objection by sponsors of studies to the publication of papers.

In the same year it was decided that Computer Studies would hive off from the Department of Mathematics—this was a development which had been envisaged for some time and was a natural progression from within the department as the computer specialization became more numerous in staff and student numbers, and sufficiently distinctive in curriculum and research, to become an autonomous unit within the University.

It will be remembered that Sociology was one of the two new developments which had been approved for the 1967–72 quinquennium. In March 1968, however, in the light of a report from the chair committee that a professorial appointment was unlikely to be made, the Development Committee recommended the redistribution of the professorial salary that would thus be released for use in making junior appointments in other departments. At the meeting of the Senate this recommendation was altered to a consideration of establishing the department with staff below professorial level. An appointment was eventually made at senior lecturer level, and by March 1969 Dr. John Wakeford, head-designate of the new department, was requesting the Board of the Senate that he be permitted to accept a modest number of intending major sociology students for the autumn of that year.

No new departments or sections were established during 1970, but in any case the discussion of developments for the 1972–77 quinquennium was once more preoccupying the boards of studies and the Senate.[3.88] The Development Committee, in looking in November 1968 at academic developments for 1969–70, had also considered some of the longer-term questions. For example, the Committee reminded Senate that far more graduate students had already been admitted for 1968–69 than had been intended by the U.G.C. even for the last year of the quinquennium and that "while the growth of graduate members is a matter for satisfaction, it cannot automatically be assumed that matching staff can be provided, since the weighting system might then produce an unduly small increase in undergraduate numbers".[3.89] Furthermore, certain large departments were carrying a heavy weight of teaching, and

---

[3.88] The organizational aspects of the 1972–77 quinquennial application are described and discussed in M. G. Simpson, *Planning University Development* (Paris, 1972), OECD/CERT, Studies in Institutional Management in Higher Education.

[3.89] At the subsequent meeting of the Senate it was noted, however, that concern at graduate student numbers would not be so great if the University (a) had taken as many undergraduates as the U.G.C. wished and (b) could show that its graduate courses were strongly biassed towards the vocational and the practical.

M

it was necessary to consider how far the University should continue to expand within existing departments and how far it wished to propose to the U.G.C. a future diversification. A document of January 1969, sent round to all F.S.S.U. staff, examined some of the underlying problems of the future. The Development Committee saw no difficulty about expansion because the university owned enough land to provide for 15,000 students, residence could be obtained, the next stages of building would be relatively cheap because services and site works were already in existence, and the cellular structure of the colleges would help to prevent social disintegration at larger sizes.[3.90] Furthermore, the Committee advocated fast development partly because "in a number of areas our activity will, in 1971, be at too low a level to be really effective and economic, and in some the range of courses is clearly too limited". This was particularly true of the science departments, for the Committee took the view that the university owed the science departments a doubling or trebling of scientific activity. Nevertheless, even when old and new scientific developments had been increased or begun, and new social science and arts departments started, there would still be a need for expansion in existing arts departments to take up the total number of additional students required.

The Committee also pointed out that the existing departmental structure covered what might elsewhere be called schools

or federations of subjects which in other universities might well be taught in separate departments. Leading examples are Biology and Engineering. Other departments, though named in a way familiar in other universities, are in Lancaster defined with greater breadth: for instance, French Studies. Other departments have a more closely defined field, covered also in other universities: an example is Mathematics, which for some purposes we define more narrowly than elsewhere.

The inclusive "school" is an excellent way of organizing cross-links in a group of cognate subjects. It becomes less effective when it turns out that some subjects need to belong to several schools: arranging co-operation between pairs of separate departments in the triad Economics, Politics, History is less cumbersome than making them into parts of overlapping schools. Our acceptance of a mixed system need not therefore be blamed on muddle-headedness: it may simply reflect the different needs of different subjects—Biology and Engineering feeling it important to assert the unity of areas which are too easily fragmented, while Politics does not

[3.90] It is to be regretted that such sanguine views over the *ease* of expansion no longer obtain: borrowed money has increased in price, some Morecambe residences are in practice not necessarily the best place for students and, even with site works completed, building costs are rising to a level which makes almost any form of residence impracticable. (See also under Chapters 2 and 6.)

want to allow a concept such as "the unity of the social sciences" to interfere with links of equal value, with Philosophy or History.

As the University expands, some of the "school" type departments might expect to grow by occupying parts of the cognate area previously untouched—that is, by internal diversification. Some of the departments which appear more unitary, but which cover a large field, may also wish to grow by internal diversification. . . .

Proposals to add new subject departments must therefore be seen as only part of a larger programme of diversification. The Development Committee considers that diversification, in this wider sense, is not only desirable because it will make growth more convenient; it is also desirable on both educational and research grounds, as a means of multiplying the frontier areas where neighbouring specialisms can profitably trade ideas.

As a corollary of this, the document pointed out that it might be illogical to demand that all three of a student's Part I subjects should come from different departments. The logic of the situation

therefore demands that we should work back from the definition of the Majors (which even though under the umbrella of one department, might require different qualities, as with theoretical and applied physics, or appeal to different interests, as with Russian and Czech) to the allowable Part I combinations and not from the definition of departments: a consequence might be the appearance of several distinct Part I courses in some departments and some such subdivision of the giant course-groups now emerging could certainly be tolerated without loss of economy.

As far as diversification was concerned, there was a problem that suggestions for new developments would come into conflict with the growing national policy of centres of excellence, since the U.G.C. subject committees were liable to find reasons why departments competing with those already in existence should not be established, as had happened recently with a renewed suggestion that German studies be introduced. Yet

it is clear that no great part of diversification can be provided by subjects previously untaught in British universities, nor do we want a forced search for novelty in order to justify growth (no courses in Cosmetology or Morticianship!). What we have to learn in this situation is to fight a case with detailed argument—as we did with Engineering, but notably failed to do with Architecture, at the planning stage for the present quinquennium: showing that what "we" propose is educationally desirable in the circumstances of *this* University, and (though bearing a familiar name) contains elements of novelty and experiment which justify our entry into competition with other universities.

The various committees of the university, as well as departments and individuals, were invited to make suggestions, whether for educational experiment (such as architecture or building science), neglected technologies (ergonomics), fast-growing subjects (decision theory), new area studies (German, Italian), shortage subjects (law), further development of new beginnings (music and drama), or additions to existing strong groups (banking and insurance).

The Development Committee received thirty-six memoranda in response to this invitation; by the time it came to present them to the conference of the Senate in September 1969, further evidence had accumulated that the Government was looking for a continuing slow reduction in real costs per student, that the larger departments were expected to show significantly lower costs than the smaller ones, and that the new universities were the ones on whom the onus rested to make a major contribution to the national requirements for more student places in 1972–77. The Committee anticipated that the expansion needed in 1977–82 would be much greater than in the previous five years and considered therefore that "while we must be careful not to load ourselves with a lot of small, expensive new enterprises, it will be right to provide in the mid-1970's some growing points for possible later expansion". The Committee recommended that the bid for the new quinquennium should be for an increase of students to 6,000 by 1977, which would, in their view, also secure a proper development of the library, the computer and other central services. In a number of cases the Committee thought it would be wise

> to encourage new developments within existing departments (and sharing their services), leaving until later the decision as to whether to establish them as separate units. Such new enterprises are here described as Sections. This device will enable the university to be more adventurous, since it will not commit itself to the administrative and service costs of a full department until there has been an opportunity of assessing the work of a Section.

The Committee wished the U.G.C. to make plain its policy on what proportion of science and technology students it wished Lancaster to have; and suggested sections in materials science, environmental conservation and biochemistry, as well as an engineering design centre, a department of psychology, and developments in architecture and in building science and planning. It did not recommend geography, and considered the likelihood of medicine or veterinary science too remote to make preparations for them: nor, on the advice of the U.G.C., was law to be pushed forward. On the other hand, the vigorous development of the business school was proposed, as well as such new ventures as health services administration, or social work training. It recommended the founding of "courses of training for teachers in higher education, so as to establish Lancaster as the leading centre for such training", but a cautious approach to setting up graduate certificates for intending teachers. The Committee advocated the reinforcement of the accelerated mathematics teaching unit, and as much development in mathematics as student demand allowed. In the language and area studies field, the Committee proposed a Language Services Unit, sections first in German and then in Italian, and a department for a comprehensive study of many aspects of modern Japan. It also noted the need for additional boosts to drama, music and fine art.

The conference of the Senate discussed the document and it was sent to the boards of studies for their consideration, with few changes: law was reinstated, in the form of jurisprudence and international law, the importance of studies in computer-assisted learning was stressed and Japanese was put alongside Chinese, Indian and Arabic studies. One or two other ideas were seen as possible developments within existing departments, such as ethology within philosophy or microbial technology within biological sciences. Industrial relations, environmental conservation, hydrology, and lunar and planetary science were regarded as provisional commitments for 1972–77.

Members of the U.G.C. visited the university on 2 December 1969 and the report of their visit noted:

> [The U.G.C.] at present holds the view (though Government policy is not yet decided) that Lancaster may be asked to grow to 6,000–10,000 students by 1982, which implies a size in the range 5,500–6,500 by 1977, broadly agreeing with our own proposals. In the quinquennium 1972–77 it is expected that there will be a modest increase in the proportion of science and technology students at Lancaster (and therefore a large increase in the absolute number); but it is doubtful if there can be an increase in the proportion of graduate students.
>
> The U.G.C. regards our proposals for development as broadly reasonable (though no final opinion is expressed at this stage): the need for diversification is accepted, e.g. to additional area studies, but the Committee sees great advantage also in the growth of large departments. It is clear that we shall have to meet strong counter-arguments if we propose a professional course in architecture. Members of the Committee showed special interest in (a) courses on Russian, Japan, etc., not based on language: (b) developments in business studies: (c) training courses for teachers in higher education: (d) courses undertaken in co-operation with technical colleges. The U.G.C., while seeing merit in extra-mural work closely integrated with the general work of the university, did not give it any priority.[3.91]

[3.91] University of Lancaster *Reporter*, No. 2, 5 December 1969, page 46.

A document prepared by the Committee of Vice-Chancellors and Principals in the same autumn highlighted some of the issues behind the numbers mentioned above when, in reporting a discussion with the U.G.C. and Mrs. Shirley Williams, the Committee noted that the most significant feature of the talks

> was the tabling of new D.E.S. projections suggesting that the number of school-leavers qualified for entry to higher education in the 1970s would be much higher than contemplated in previously published estimates. . . . If universities were by 1981 to be taking (as in 1963) about 53 per cent of all school-leavers with two or more A levels, and if allowance is made for other entrants and for numbers in Scottish universities, the number of university places in Great Britain in 1981 would be over 450,000. This would represent something like a doubling of student numbers in a decade.
>
> A basic question posed for the government is whether it is to continue with policies based on the assumption that all those qualified and wishing to enter full-time higher education should have the opportunity to do so. If so, the cost implications are substantial. If not, the political and social implications are no less severe.
>
> No conclusions have been reached, but the Committee and the U.G.C. are anxious that the major political decisions should be taken in 1970, so as to permit the universities and the U.G.C. to make effective forward plans and not least to give a rational basis to universities' deliberations and submissions in respect of the next quinquennium. . . .
>
> A good deal of the discussion was in fact in the context of a preliminary examination of the possibilities of achieving some reductions in unit cost in the universities over the 1970s.
>
> Clearly there is a fundamental sense in which it is unrealistic to talk in terms simply of the university contribution to the future without regard to the part to be played by other institutions, including in particular the colleges of education and the polytechnics. In the Committee's view there is still lacking a clear enunciation of the role of the polytechnics as they are now developing; and there seems scope for further thought about possible future development of the colleges of education in directions other than simply the training of teachers. But it is clear that government views as to the extent and character of the future contributions of these institutions are not yet formed.[3.92]

The document then went on to examine the quality of university education and what elements of it (such as the three-fold aim that students be admitted

---

[3.92] Committee of Vice-Chancellors and Principals, "University Development in the 1970's", 5th November 1969. See also their later version of the same document, issued as a pamphlet in April 1970, under the same title.

who are capable of benefitting from a university education, that contact between teacher and taught be close enough to communicate not only facts but also a style of thinking, and that staff should have opportunities to "pursue original work and to advance knowledge as well as to teach") should be safeguarded, while at the same time suggesting and discussing various ways in which the unit costs of students might be reduced. These suggestions for cost-cutting included loans either for all kinds of students, or just for post-graduate students, more restricted admission of overseas students, required employment for a period after graduation for students on grants, greater use of part-time and correspondence courses, a two-year degree course for abler students, a two-year course leading to a different qualification for students not proceeding through the customary three-year course, insertion of a period between school and university, more intensive use of buildings and equipment, more sharing of facilities between institutions, more home-based students, the development of student housing associations and other forms of loan-financed provision for student residence, and a further worsening of student/staff ratios.

The second stage of planning for the next quinquennium was the preparation of a formal submission to the U.G.C. The debate began at the Senate conference of September 1970 and for the following seven months moved to and fro between the boards of studies, the Development Committee and the Senate, each of these bodies having several lengthy discussions and sending reports on to the other bodies. The detail of these debates, in which subjects appeared and disappeared as serious contenders for immediate establishment, and student figures were adjusted and readjusted (especially as between the science and the arts subjects), while the provisional allocation of additional staff followed the student distribution between subjects, is too lengthy for our purposes. Detailed comparison of the two drafts of the preamble to the submission, one dated September 1970 and the other May 1971, is a study of considerable, but too detailed, interest. In moving on to the second premable, however, the intensive study of the future that preceded it should not be forgotten.

The document presenting the second preamble opened by discussing the student numbers of 1970–71, and welcomed

> the U.G.C. suggestion that we should plan to take 5,400 students in 1976–77. If the national situation had allowed, we would have preferred to include more than 1,900 science-based students in this total, since our proportion of science and technology is so much below the national average; and we hope that the possibility of an increase in this sector (which at Lancaster could be achieved at low capital cost) will be kept in mind if the situation changes. . . .

The growth during the quinquennium 1967–72 has enabled us to make considerable progress in eliminating areas of unduly high cost: for instance, administrative costs have fallen from 10 per cent to 7 per cent of total expenditure. Nevertheless, some high-cost activities, undertaken at too small a scale, remain. We intend during the coming quinquennium to correct this, concentrating development . . . on existing departments or on work which grows organically from existing activities and can be mounted with reasonable economy. We have not, however, thought it right to assume any significant worsening of our staff-student ratio, since, although it is difficult to obtain accurate and up-to-date information, we have the impression that the ratio at Lancaster is less favourable than at other similar universities. Members of staff at a university like Lancaster work for long hours. We do not believe that it is possible, either by an increase of effort or by a better organization of work, to achieve further "economies" by a change in the staff-student ratio.

With regard to the balance of studies,[3.93] as between graduate and undergraduate, the university had this to say:

> We appreciate that in many areas of science and the humanities the graduate proportion must be greatly influenced by national policy on studentships, and we have noted the expectation, in the Preliminary Memorandum of General Guidance, that the percentage of "ordinary" graduate students may remain around the 1969–70 level. We must, however, point out that Lancaster is one of the largest centres of graduate business studies in the country. Although the current arrangements for student support are woefully inadequate, potential demand in this area is likely to continue to rise and our own "specialist" approach may, we think, become increasingly important. Much of our demand is for one year Masters' degrees by course work, often taken after a period of experience, and alternative methods of finance are sometimes available. We have, therefore, borne in mind the possibility that the proportion of full-time graduate students at Lancaster will rise above its present level of about 16 per cent. . . .
>
> We think that we should draw attention to the fact that the Masters

---

[3.93] The concept of a "balance of studies" was introduced to correct the situation whereby the increase in the size of a department would be determined solely by pressure of applications for admission to particular degree schemes rather than by what was desirable in terms of subjects complementing and augmenting one another in a planned manner, according to academic criteria. As can be seen throughout this section, however, universities, particularly those who wish to expand their numbers by a given extent over a particular period, have such policy to some extent determined by the number of people who wish to read for a particular degree (which may not, in some arts departments, even necessarily be in an area in which subsequent employment is likely).

degree courses in business studies and in certain science subjects involve highly intensive study for a full calendar year. . . . The load on staff is therefore considerable; and this is reflected in the (apparently favourable) staff-student ratios of certain departments. On the other hand, an essential element of the business courses is the involvement of students in practical projects under the supervision of members of staff; and since this work is normally conducted to yield an income, it makes a contribution to the costs of the university.

As for the balance between the different types of intellectual discipline, the document pointed out that

Lancaster's courses have always, within the limits set by requirements of professional training, attempted to provide for interaction between related subjects and for freedom to broaden the student's experience by entering less related fields. This has meant the provision of a sufficient variety of subjects to achieve relevant interactions: for instance, we need Chemistry as well as Biology, Sociology as well as Politics and Economics, Behaviour in Organizations as well as Operational Research. There are practical reasons why the range needs further small extension: for instance, many language students want to do two languages, which is why we have authorized a German "section" attached to the French Studies department, though without committing ourselves to a major department of German. Similarly, we need Psychology, not only for its own importance, but as a related subject to Education, which is so strongly developed at Lancaster. . . .

In considering the balance of development we have noted certain fields in which there is a rapidly expanding demand for graduates. An example is Accountancy: the department of Financial Control, which is concerned with this subject, is already one of the strongest in the country, and we consider that it should plan for a considerable expansion of undergraduate studies. . . .

We note that there are subjects whose graduates appear to find it difficult to obtain employment. Of course, this does not prove that these subjects ought not to be represented in the University; there may be strong reasons for believing in their cultural importance and educational value. But we do expect that, since there may be a generally increased difficulty in finding employment for graduates, there will be during the coming five years a shift of interest away from subjects believed by students to be vocationally irrelevant or unhelpful. Consequently we have been cautious in our assumptions about the expansion in areas such as Politics and Sociology; and, in the fine structure of our planning, we have encouraged a move towards the more applied and vocational aspects of certain subjects. It should be noted, too, that though we have some established work and some development plans for Fine Art, Music and Drama, we have no intention of establishing professional or major courses[3.94] in any of these subjects; their function is to provide a cultural diversity for students taking other subjects. . . .

The expansion of the coming quinquennium will enable us to bring departments at present too small (in relation to their spread of interests) to a viable size: and we shall thus have a better basis for any further diversification appropriate to the 1980's. The departments which are at present too small include Behaviour in Organizations, Biological Sciences, Chemistry, Computer Studies, Educational Research, Engineering, Environmental Sciences, Financial Control and Physics. We welcome the increased efficiency of teaching and research which will follow their expansion.

The only proposal for an entirely new teaching department was psychology, and the need for adequate funds for equipment was underlined. The School of Education was thought to need provision over and above income from fees and the university wished for "additional activities . . . to support the colleges of education, and we have in mind in particular the need to enliven teaching by a better provision for research. . . . We also intend to continue and extend our interest in research in higher education and in the training of teachers for higher education." In the area of social studies, "we intend to continue a special interest in the applied aspects of Economics and, rather than develop a large centre of sociological theory, we propose to give added attention to problems of the determination of social policy". A further increase could be made in the activities of the department of Computer Studies, particularly with regard to the provision of elementary courses accessible to all members of the university. The university hoped for the development of biochemistry within the department of Biological Sciences, the departments of Chemistry and Physics were to give "further attention to undergraduate and graduate courses designed to give a training of value to industry", building on the experience already gained in mounting bridging courses, while the department of Environmental Sciences was known to undertake

teaching and research over a wide range, from geomorphology to upper atmosphere physics and lunar and planetary studies. It attracts a large number of applications and its interests touch many currently fashionable subjects. While we are alive to the danger of jumping on every passing (and overcrowded) bandwagon, we think that it will be desirable to extend our existing concern with Hydrology: to provide for certain teaching

---

[3.94] Free ninth unit and minor courses were, however, already intended, and a major, at least in music, has since been established.

related to Environmental Conservation [and] to provide for some of the ancillary interests in Environmental Design.

The department of Engineering was to be built up further, and while

the precise form requires further examination, it is desirable that the department should during the quinquennium develop a practical association in design with industrial firms; but it is not anticipated that this will require a significant call on U.G.C. finance.

Concern was expressed that the library should be assisted in its growth as much as possible, for although the university appreciated

that first-rate libraries cannot be provided in every institution of higher education, the position of Lancaster, 55 miles from the nearest large library, has made it essential to give special attention to the development of the University Library. We have spent a higher proportion of income on the Library than most other universities . . . [which] has yielded clear academic advantages, and we propose to continue the same policy, allocating during the coming quinquennium approximately 9 per cent of expenditure.

Future equipment and staff for both the computer and audio-visual aids at adequate levels were included and for the latter

our aim will be to offer incentives for the development of substantial audio-visual material, capable of being used in this university for several years (and thereby reducing teaching loads), and wherever possible capable of sale to other institutions.

Finally, the Careers Office, it was felt, should be allowed a faster expansion than was justified purely by student numbers, and a small sum for the central administration of extra-mural studies was to be included.

While the university was awaiting the outcome of the application, other developments continued as far as the constraints of the remaining finance for the quinquennium and the uncertainty for the future permitted. In particular, the question of the future of Russian and of other east European studies took time and care, both at the Senate and at Board of Studies D. It will be remembered that Russian and Soviet Studies, "concerned with the language, literature, history and thought of Russia and the Soviet Union", had been one of the founding departments. At first its head of department was a senior lecturer, but in October 1966 Professor Sir Cecil Parrott, former British ambassador in Prague, took up his post at the university and assumed the headship of the department. There was at once talk of founding a centre whose special study would be the smaller countries of central and east Europe, and in 1968 an appeal was launched for the founding of a Comenius Centre[3.95] which would remedy the

> Failure to appreciate the differences between political life in Russia and in Central and South East Europe [which] has long distorted Western Studies. After 1948 people assumed that there was no difference between life in, say, Poland, Czechoslovakia, or Yugoslavia, and life in Soviet Russia. But even then there were signs that some of the Communist parties in power in these smaller states, when faced with realities and pressure from below, had begun to question certain formulae in the Russian blueprint. . . . We want to study the national and contemporary history of these countries; their political structure, social affairs, their literature (the key to their thinking) and their culture generally. We wish also to promote cross-fertilization of information and ideas in scientific and technological fields; it will be our aim to bring Central and South East European academics, artists, economists, writers, scientists and educationalists to Britain for this purpose.

The Centre was to provide the necessary teaching and research staff, travel facilities for postgraduates to visit the countries they were studying, short-term visiting fellowships for certain specialists, a comprehensive library, and adequate facilities for language study. Later on, there would be a journal, undergraduate courses, and special exhibitions and films; additionally, the Centre could be a forum for the exchange of ideas between distinguished visitors and the academics of Britain. The appeal was unfortunately not the success that had been hoped for, although some generous gifts of books were received, and funding for some short-term posts was also provided by various donors. It was therefore decided that part of the funds received should be spent on undergraduate Czech courses, and in 1968 a minor course was established, with Part I following soon afterwards.

The distribution of resources between the Comenius Centre and the undergraduate teaching department became, however, rather complex, as did the precise arrangements about Part I. After one lengthy debate at the Senate, Board D held a special meeting in March 1971 when, in regard to Russian and Soviet Studies, members

> stressed the importance of the place of literature as an integral part of a language-based area study and the dependence of scholarly knowledge on an adequate language training.

It was agreed that the degree should be either three or four years long, according to individual student needs, and that, as well as a combined major

---

[3.95] Comenius was a seventeenth century Moravian bishop, a teacher, philosopher and writer who worked and taught in most of the countries of central Europe.

with history, there should be another with French. Unanimous agreement was given to the suggestion that the university put Czech onto a more regular footing, and approval was also given to the setting up of Yugoslav for a limited period of three years. The Senate in May 1971 approved these decisions and teaching in Czech and Yugoslav studies has been proceeding under the umbrella of a newly designated department, Central and South-Eastern European Studies, with Professor Parrott at its head.[3.96] Languages were well served in this year, for German was at last begun, as a section within the French department, while linguistics, under the umbrella of the English department, also became more autonomous and began the development of combined major and single major courses which have since been recognized by the Senate.

In December 1971 the university was notified of its provisional recurrent grant for 1972–73, which did not provide for new developments, the takeover of work previously supported by other bodies, or the loss of local authority income.[3.97] A preliminary survey suggested to the Development Committee that, taking account of the minimum number of twenty lectureships already firmly promised, and of consequent increases in departmental allocations and other expenses, the university would have a deficit of about £150,000 for the year. Exceptional economies were looked for, but even when those had been made, a deficit of £130,000 was still left, which it was feared would severely limit possible development in the second year of the quinquennium and set back expansion plans for the rest of it. The Vice-Chancellor also told the Senate that the building programme for 1973–74, which was about to be announced, "was likely to give rise to little joy", and equipment grants, except for new departments like psychology, or those still building up their departments, such as Engineering or Computer Studies, would be considerably less than in the early years of the university's existence. The assumption had been made, the Vice-Chancellor explained to the Senate, that all additional students for 1972–73 would cost only 85 per cent of the amount required for students already in the university. As before when economy was suggested, it was suggested that appointing committees should appoint as low as possible on salary scales, and members noted dourly that "the fixing of the grant for the provisional year 1972–73 by projections from the previous year bore hardly on a university which had been economical".

[3.96] Russian and Soviet Studies also continued as a separate department.

[3.97] The generous early level of support given to the university by the County Council and other local authorities, in order to give the new university a strong start, were now being cut down or discontinued. The County Council, for example, who had given £50,000 p.a. for ten years cut their donation to £10,000 p.a. (bringing it in line with those made to Manchester, Salford and Liverpool), and in 1972 earmarked this sum for research on behaviour problems of young people, musical activities of benefit to Lancashire, and extra-mural activities based on the Nuffield Theatre Studio.

The university then had to wait in patience for the rest of the quinquennial settlement before being able to proceed any further with new plans. Straws in the wind were duly passed on to the staff. In January the Vice-Chancellor wrote of "cheerful news with which to start 1972: namely that the U.G.C. has approved building starts in 1973–74 which are in line with the programme of expansion to 5,400". It remained to be seen, he went on, "if the recurrent grant matches the increase in physical capacity. But *some* expansion is surely certain: and, even if grants in general are on the mean side, the impact is much less disagreeable during a period of expansion. In particular this will help to maintain promotion prospects for staff." In June 1972 the Finance Officer reported that there had been a supplementary recurrent grant of £158,000 for 1972–73, which brought the total grant for the year up to £2,869,138 and related it to July 1972 prices. The Development Committee noted that

> When the final allocation of recurrent grant for 1972–73 was made as part of the quinquennial settlement, a further supplementary grant would be made related to the expected mid-1972–73 price level. . . . As soon as the Brown index for the period to January 1973 was received, the Government would be ready to consider a claim for supplementation of the grants for the financial years 1973–74 to 1976–77, using the movement of the Brown index over the twelve months January 1972 to January 1973 as representing the movement between July 1972 and July 1973; and similarly in each succeeding year. The Government had said that the extent of supplementation must depend not only on the needs of the University, but also on the country's economic position at the time and on the pressures on public expenditure as a whole. In the next quinquennium, however, unless there were exceptional difficulties,[3.98] they would be ready to supplement the recurrent grant to the extent of at least 50 per cent of the increase in the Brown index in each 12-month period and to give careful consideration each year to a claim for a higher rate of supplementation.

Later in the year a gloomier note was sounded. A memorandum of 7 August from the Vice-Chancellor remarked that it seemed, on making "some calculations based on the rumours now strongly current, that there will be a cut of 5 per cent in planned student numbers and a cut of about 15 per cent in departmental costs per student (equivalent to a change in staff-student ratio from 1:10 to nearly 1:12, and *pro rata* reductions in other departmental expenditure). . . . You will realize, therefore, why we are not anxious to encourage expansionist ideas about expenditure in 1973–74 or later years." Even more sombre was a meeting of the Development Committee at the end of October, when the long delay was fraying people's patience and

---

[3.98] Such exceptional difficulties have, of course, been experienced and cuts in supplementation made accordingly.

The Vice-Chancellor reported that the prospects for the quinquennial settlement were, if anything, getting worse. It was now possible that universities might not receive information about their quinquennial allocations until February. The Government planned to issue a White Paper concerning various aspects of its educational policy.

As though this uncertainty were not enough, the Vice-Chancellor in December reported that as early as the spring of 1973 the U.G.C. would begin discussions with universities about *their 1981 capacity*, since they "were seeking to obtain the Government's approval of future student numbers well in advance (possibly by 1975 for the following quinquennium)".

The long-awaited and much-dreaded settlement, when it finally reached the university on 16 January 1973, was not as bad as had been feared. The recurrent grant was to move upwards from £2·899m for 1972–73 to £4·494m for 1976–77, and the expected growth of full-time students was from 3,000 in 1972–73 to 5,231 in 1976–77.[3.99] Of the students of Lancaster, 768 in 1976–77 were assumed to be postgraduate. The division of fulltime undergraduates was intended to be 2,941 in arts and 1,522 in science. To the Senate the Vice-Chancellor,

made some general remarks about the quinquennial settlement, which was substantially less generous than that for the last quinquennium when a betterment factor of 10 per cent had been available. The funds per student (nationally) had been reduced to 98 per cent of those per student in the last year of the quinquennium. . . .

Lancaster had done fairly well overall, partly because the mix of subjects was relatively favourable. It had suffered only a small reduction in the assumed numbers of students. There was doubt nationally if the undergraduate target for the end of the quinquennium could be met. The university had had its assumed numbers of graduate students only slightly reduced. The figures however were such that it was doubtful whether they would be sufficient to meet the natural increase in graduates. . . . The total grant appeared (when allowance has been made for the changed mix of subjects and for the change in the graduate proportion) to be $4\frac{1}{2}$ per cent less than that which was proposed. However, the university had expected some cut.

There were considerable planning problems in the quinquennium, but

---

[3.99] The submission had asked for £4·138m for 5,400 students but from 1972–73 the figures included provision for minor works, vacation grants (from 1 May 1971 given direct from the U.G.C. as a lump sum to universities according to student numbers, rather than as discretionary awards through local education authorities), and a sum for the effects of inflation between May 1971 and January 1973. It is, therefore, not possible to compare submission and settlement figures without glosses on the meanings of different figures.

especially for next year when the grant would be notably inadequate. This was a result both of unusually high expenditures (arising particularly because Fylde College is coming into being) and of the relatively large increase in staff in 1972–73 which was not matched by an increase in the number of students. In all 13 posts had already been approved for next year and this involved a budgeted deficit.

To the Council, however, the Vice-Chancellor

stressed that Council should appreciate that so far as the quinquennium as a whole is concerned the difficulty is not so much shortage of money. The future is bedevilled more by uncertainty about future student demand. The demand in higher education is fluctuating, not only locally or regionally, but nationally, and it is very difficult to assess the ways in which the demands might develop. Expansion, as far as possible, needs to be concentrated on the building up of existing departments, and holding reserves of money to develop areas very quickly if it appears that the student demands warrant it. . . .

He concluded by saying that care was being taken, when allocating money, to make full allowance for possible promotions. Owing to the increase in staff and the training of new members of staff, the proportion of senior staff is not likely to approach the permitted maximum.

To the Senate he expanded on the theme of meeting the U.G.C. figures and the way in which they were distributed, for, he pointed out,

the university had obligations to the U.G.C. although the committee did not police the way the university applied its grant. However, in making the quinquennial settlement the committee had been severe on the universities which had a high cost per student, so that the university would be well advised not to restrain the size of its intake and allow the cost per student to rise. The university was specifically required not to permit post-graduate students to be substituted for undergraduate, although it would be possible to fall short of meeting the undergraduate target if sufficient applicants of the right standard did not appear. It was difficult to see how the university could reach the target for undergraduates. The annual rate of intake to meet the target would have to be more than doubled towards the end of the quinquennium.[3.100] The Development Committee still desired to

---

[3.100] The Development Committee had pointed out meanwhile that some departments were actually likely to suffer a *fall* in student numbers, at a time when "doubts about Lancaster, which are widespread in the schools" would perhaps affect the applications for 1974, when a massive increase in numbers was needed. At the same time there was nationally a fall in some subjects which had previously been popular; and the "remaining areas of massive excess are medicine, law and English, two of which are not represented at Lancaster".

Aerial view of the site from the north prior to 1961

Aerofilms Ltd.

Executive Committee of the Promotion Council visiting Stanley Park, Blackpool in April 1961. (Mr. V. C. Flatt, Dr. C. R. Claxton and Mr. C. P. A. McCall can be seen standing one behind each other to the left of the photograph)

By courtesy of the West Lancashire Evening Gazette

Lord Derby receiving the 999-year lease of the university site from the Mayor of Lancaster, 25th April, 1963
From left to right: Sir Noel Hall, Sir Alfred Bates, Lord Derby, the Mayor (Councillor Ernest Gardner) and the Vice-Chancellor

By courtesy of the Lancaster Guardian

maintain the principle of a balance of studies but, if it had agreed to present a plan of development showing the originally suggested balance over the whole of the quinquennium, some departments would on present evidence clearly be over-staffed. However, departments with evidence which justified expansion should be encouraged to produce ideas which would command the allocation of posts at present held in reserve. . . .

In reply to a question from Mr. Keat who asked whether the reserve would be used for meeting demands only or whether it would be used for attaining the ideal balance of studies the Vice-Chancellor said that, if the departments of Board A were able to grow, they would have an automatic claim on the reserve. However, if they failed to grow the Development Committee would not necessarily recommend that the areas attracting applications should be reinforced.

Professor Dobbs and Bevington drew attention to the effect that a decline in the number of scientists would have on the attractiveness of the departments.[3.101] Professor Dobbs noted that the reduction in the proposed numbers of students in the sciences should mean a cut of only 1/16th in the staff numbers which had been proposed for 1976–77. The Development Committee, however, had been more severe and had appeared to extrapolate from figures which were available for one year only. Whilst he could not argue for an increase of staff in 1973–74, in the long term building on quality was the only way in which the university could reasonably expand.

It will be seen from this discussion that some not dissimilar problems to those that had arisen from the previous quinquennial settlement were again raising their heads. Moreover, while the student members of the Senate expressed concern about the housing of increased numbers of fellow students, senior members concerned with graduate studies were very concerned that research should not dwindle in importance at the university and that the graduate quotas should be as equitable in their distribution as possible and pay regard to the particular aspirations of Lancaster rather than necessarily to national graduate quotas.

Turning to specific subject areas, nationally the U.G.C. wished to discourage strongly the establishment of any new schools of architecture, were concerned about the "proliferation of small departments and courses in the

---

[3.101] The physical science and engineering departments were acknowledged by the U.G.C. to need extra support staff for costly research already under way, but at the same time were expected to show a bigger fall over the quinquennium in departmental unit costs as, "from the data which have been presented to the Committee it would appear that the room for economies of scale as growth proceeds are . . . more evident at the present juncture in the sciences than in the arts subjects" (letter from the Chairman of the U.G.C., 15 January 1973, paras. 31 and 38 (iv)).

N

less widely used languages", and did not wish to see new schools or departments of education leading to a professional teaching qualification. Although the Ormrod Committee had suggested a one-third increase in the provision of places in law, the Committee wished to discourage, with one exception, the setting up of any new schools of law.[3.102] They expressed themselves desirous, however, of seeing "the expansion of courses for the training of social workers and educational psychologists, since there is a serious national shortage in these fields", and welcomed undergraduate courses combining education with another subject.[3.103]

Within Lancaster itself, no provision had been made for the existing Research Unit in Lunar and Planetary Studies, or for the proposed developments in environmental design and management. The new department of psychology had been provided for, as had additional work in art, drama and music, and Italian "on a modest scale". Business and management studies were to be funded at the level proposed in the university's submission, the "undue pressure" on staff on arts departments was to be relieved with additional secretarial help, and the staff-student ratio in mathematics was to be improved. The careers service could also be strengthened.[3.104]

The Senate, after much debate, decided that in 1973–74 expenditure on staff "should be concentrated on beginning developments that will attract additional undergraduates in later years and on relieving certain pressures". The future of Central and South-Eastern European Studies was confirmed (although no further diversification permitted): provision was to be made for major courses in ecology and biochemistry; an appointment was to be made in classical archaeology in relation to Roman Britain;[3.105] from 1974 there were to be major courses in European Studies, with a full-time director; and in that year Italian Studies would also begin. Furthermore, tentative provision was to be made for teacher training "in case proposals to provide a professional concurrent degree course are approved".

An additional word should be said about Psychology: in the autumn of 1970 the views of five outside assessors were sought about what areas of development in the subject the university should have as first priorities. In November, the referees' views were reported and the matter sent to the Development Committee and the boards of studies; everyone seemed certain that psychology was wanted at Lancaster, but were unclear about what type it should be. Eventually, in May 1971, the Senate accepted a proposal of the Development Committee that the "department of psychology should be broad in its interests, but that central research interests should be sought in

3.102 See, however, page 133 ff.
3.103 Letter from the Chairman of the U.G.C., 15 January 1973, para. 38.
3.104 Ibid., paras. 39–47.
3.105 See Chapter 5, pages 312 to 313.

the areas of human development and learning and of psychology in relation to human biology", and at the same time resolved that a chair appointment be authorized for 1972.[3.106] Three lecturers were added a year later, and the first students admitted to Part I in October 1973.

In discussion, however, of the quinquennial submission and settlement, one recent new development funded from outside the university should not be overlooked. In September 1971 Professor Smart submitted a paper to the Senate in which he explained that he had been

> involved in some negotiations with the Ambassador of the State of Kuwait regarding the possibility of their endowing a Chair of Arabic and Islamic Studies, and of making a suitable grant for books for the library. After a delay of some months in which nothing much has happened, I have recently received a letter to the effect that the Government of Kuwait are looking forward to making budgetary provision for such a Chair.

He thought it possible that the State of Kuwait might go as far as to endow a centre or institute as well as a chair, and asked to be empowered to continue negotiations. This was agreed, and in December 1971 he returned with more definite proposals; a chair in Arabic and Islamic studies should be established at Lancaster, the occupant of which would also have the title of visiting professor at the University of Kuwait, who would bear the cost. The endowment, of £13,500 p.a. from October 1972 for at least seven years, would have added to it an initial £20,000 for books for the library. The professor would also be the director of an Institute of Arabic and Islamic Studies, whose aims would be:

> to strengthen Arabic and Islamic Studies and to promote knowledge of the Arabic and Islamic heritage . . . to bring out the significance of Islamic religion and the Quran, and the contributions of Arabs and Muslims to human knowledge and the heritage of mankind as a whole; and to keep in contact with libraries, research institutes and other places where Arabic and Islamic studies are conducted, in Europe and elsewhere.

The Senate approved the proposal, subject to the person appointed to the chair being "willing to provide undergraduate courses for persons who are not acquainted with the Arabic language", and appointment to the chair, of Professor W. N. Arafat, duly took place. The department and the institute became independent entities from October 1973, when the first students were admitted to a new Part I course.

And what of the future? We have already seen that biochemistry, ecology and Italian studies are promised for 1974, and to these was added mediaeval

---

[3.106] The psychology chair has been filled by Professor Philip Levy, formerly at the University of Birmingham.

studies (to be taught jointly by History, English and French). The eclectic School of Independent Studies[3.107] has already admitted some students, and from 15 December 1973 has had a permanent director, Dr. Frank Oldfield.[3.108] Plans for European Studies are also forging ahead. This idea had been first toyed with in 1971, and a working party set up to discuss broad principles. Substantive proposals reached the Development Committee at the beginning of December 1972, when the Vice-Chancellor reported on the possibility of developing European Studies, "for which there was expected to be a large demand in the teaching and other professions". The Vice-Chancellor then had discussions with the D.E.S. staff inspector with special responsibility for European studies and on 13 December a paper, prepared by Dr. Joseph Shennan, was laid before the Senate. The document explained that

> what follows is an attempt to devise a binary degree scheme which offers a multi-disciplinary non-vocational approach to an understanding of important aspects of Europe so that graduates may be better equipped to make their contribution in the wider world into which Britain is shortly to move.

The planning group's overall concern, he went on, had been "with the coherence of the degree scheme; we wish to avoid any arbitrary joining together of existing courses which might offer only an illusory cohesion", while at the same time it had to be made clear that there were both existing staff and courses which could be incorporated into such a programme. Two schemes were envisaged, both of four years' duration, with a compulsory year in Europe, and a considerable number of integrated courses with consortial teaching were suggested. Scheme A would place the main emphasis on the history, sociology and language and literature of Europe, while Scheme B would concentrate on the contemporary political, economic and sociological aspects of the area. In order to manage such a complex structure, and to give it a clear identity, it was proposed that a special centre be formed. The Senate approved the proposals in principle and passed it to the boards of studies. In February 1973 a further discussion took place, at which it was agreed that an inter-board committee, with Dr. Shennan as its convenor, should meet heads of the main departments likely to become involved, and make proposals about the level of appointment of a director, and about the organizational and teaching arrangements. Detailed discussions about these matters are still continuing and it is hoped to admit the first students to the new Scheme A in the autumn of 1974.

[3.107] See above, pages 112 to 114.

[3.108] Dr. Oldfield came to the university in 1964 as lecturer in Environmental Studies, and left in 1967. After a period as professor of geography at Coleraine he became deputy vice-chancellor of the University of Papua and New Guinea before returning to Lancaster.

Two further new proposals should perhaps detain us briefly, the first being social planning. In June 1971 a document from Dr. John Wakeford came to the Senate explaining that the

> central concern of this Department would be the study of the whole subject of policy-making in the social field in its widest context. Its work might include studies of such things as methods of allocation of wealth and resources, benefits, security to social groups within societies, welfare programmes, developed and under-developed regions, population policy, education priority areas, the work of the Departments of Health, Education, Social Security, Housing, Transport, etc.

He pointed out that basic research into the existing provision of social services in the main had not been and was not being done. Indeed, it was becoming clear, from such research as was being carried out, that

> When it comes to the provision of social services it seems generally expected that professionally accredited social workers are best qualified to do the job. The needs for new services go unresearched, and such provision as there is seems badly distributed. There has been virtually no research on the clients' perspective on the use of various kinds of social workers for various social problems. . . .
> Thus the concern of the department would *not* be directly with the training of social workers, *nor* the establishment of credentials that emulate those provided elsewhere, but the provision at an undergraduate level of a fundamental academic education for those who might later wish to train for particular positions in national and international social services, and at the postgraduate level for those with specialized social science degrees and short courses for those already employed in the field.

The boards of studies were generally in favour of the development and it was agreed that there should be discussions with five or six distinguished and experienced persons to determine what form such a development might take.

This proposal was, however, overtaken by a request from Lancashire County Council in May 1972 that the university provide a vocational degree course for social workers. The Senate formed a small *ad hoc* committee to look into this new suggestion, and after the Vice-Chancellor and Professor Michelina Vaughan (the new head of the department of Sociology) had met representatives of the County Council, the committee drew up a report in October 1973 which recommended

> the provision of such courses. However, we think that it should be made very clear that the university is *not* committing itself to providing a training

facility specifically for Lancashire. We would expect to be regarded as a national centre, though Lancashire and Cumbria (together with other local social service employers, e.g. the Probation service and the Regional Hospital Board) would naturally have some advantage in attracting graduates who have obtained practical experience in their services. . . .

We have particularly in mind the following points:

(a) Many graduates will eventually become administrators and teachers of social work rather than field workers: and many will be concerned with community or group work rather than individual case-work. It is now accepted that the traditional concentration on case-work therefore requires reconsideration.

(b) In particular, we see a need to enable graduates to develop further a constructive interest in problems of social policy; and this implies that there should be a re-examination of contributions to the course from subjects like economics and political science.

(c) The development of social services in rural areas is a neglected subject, to which we could make a contribution in association with Cumbria.

(d) Graduates should be assisted in paying more attention to the implications for the social services of the legal and the broader administrative system. . . .

(e) Graduates should engage in some study of and field work on comparative ethical systems, since some of those with whom they work will have quite different ethical assumptions.

They suggested that the right way to proceed was to develop a degree course in applied social studies, the staff of which would become an additional section within the Sociology department. The boards of studies declared themselves in favour of these proposals but the members of the department, other than its head, were unanimous in their concern at the non-theoretical nature of the courses proposed for a department of sociology. However, the Senate decided to take the matter a stage further and, after a further discussion at a Senate meeting of June 1973, it was decided that the department should be separate and a chair of social administration be authorized.

The other new suggestion, for a department of geography, arose out of the commentary by the Development Committee on the U.G.C. settlement when, while noting that the department of Environmental Sciences was "not keen to develop undergraduate environmental management courses at this stage, considers that this does not fully answer Senate's concern for development of courses in this area on an inter-disciplinary basis", the Committee suggested that the group that had been discussing such courses should continue in being. Further, in the light of the present admissions problems, the Committee asks Senate to consider the establishment of a Department of Geography accessible to non-scientists as well as scientists, and, if it favours the proposal, to authorize a further investigation.

By the September of 1973 these two matters had moved closer together, for the Senate considered proposals from the Development Committee, who themselves had consulted assessors appointed by the U.G.C. They noted that there was evidence of considerable demand by good candidates to read geography, and also that the study of geography had changed considerably in the last ten years, being now less open to the criticisms which caused its original exclusion from Lancaster's curriculum. The Vice-Chancellor reminded the Senate that the Development Committee had been looking at

the possibility of adding new areas to the university's work in environmental sciences in such a way that the new developments would not compete with the department of environmental sciences for applicants for undergraduate study. The majority of the department of environmental sciences was of the view that the activities of the department should be limited strictly to scientific studies of the physical environment. The assessors who had been appointed by the U.G.C. had made a case for a development of socio-economic and human geography.

It was therefore decided that the new department should include both socio-economic and physical geography and that, when an appointment had been made to the chair, detailed discussions would take place between the new department and Environmental Sciences in those areas where there was likely to be an overlap between the two departments. The chair will be filled in 1974 and the department is likely to admit its first students in 1975.

If the short-term future is now clear, what of the long-term? Anyone speculating on Lancaster in 1984 is entering the realm of hazardous conjecture, but some trends can already be seen. The U.G.C. again made a visitation to the university at the end of February 1973 and were clear that the

growth that would be necessary in the universities to meet the student targets set for 1976–77 and 1981–82 fell disproportionately heavily on the new universities. Any falling off in applications in the early years of the quinquennium would impose an even heavier strain on the universities if they were to catch up later. The Committee could only ask them to do their best, and were sure that they would. If at the end of the day there was a shortfall in undergraduate numbers the Committee had no objection to surplus resources being devoted to other worthwhile purposes, for example in the post-experience field. . . .

It had not been possible to give the University the substantial science

expansion which they had requested for the current quinquennium. . . .
Provision had nevertheless been made for some growth in the proportion
of science students at Lancaster, which went entirely counter to the
national trend and involved nearly doubling the number of science students
in absolute terms. The University had also been fortunate in being allowed
to proceed with the development of engineering courses.

For the quinquennium to 1981–82 the Committee had suggested that
the University should consider growing by approximately 50 per cent from
its 1976–77 target; this was faster than the average rate of growth suggested
in the Government's White Paper, to help to allow for a slower rate of
growth in the city centre universities.[3.109]

Areas in which the Committee thought the university might consider
further development included law, accountancy, and biological sciences. Nor
did they see the time ahead as easy: when concern was expressed, for example,
about the shortage of time available for research (exacerbated by worsening
staff-student ratios and extensive committee work) the Committee "could
only suggest that research time had perhaps to be found at the expense of a
wide range of course options, committee work and small group teaching". At
the same time the Chairman of the Committee "congratulated the University
on the success with which they continued to manage their rapid expansion,
making it an excellent example of what a new University could achieve".

These points were taken up by the Vice-Chancellor in his ninth annual
report:

> Size is not everything, and indeed may bring many difficulties; but
> encouragement to expand is perhaps something of a vote of confidence.
> Lancaster, it will be remembered, was the last to be designated of a group
> of six new universities, but the finance provided was expected to make it,
> by 1977, the largest. . . .
>
> The U.G.C.'s proposal for 1981–82 was that we should have 7,250–7,750
> students: on this occasion we actually suggested a reduction to 6,800,
> because we deduced that the larger number would probably contain an
> unacceptably small proportion of scientists and technologists. But, which-
> ever number is finally accepted, it is clear that Lancaster by 1981 is
> expected to have reached a size which in this country has been considered
> "large". . . .
>
> There is room for much argument about the wisdom of rapid growth in
> higher education, and I know that strong and sincere opinions are held on
> both sides. It will, however, be no surprise to any observer of human
> nature that some academics have theoretical doubts about the wisdom of

---

[3.109] Note of the meeting, prepared by the U.G.C., between the University and the
U.G.C. on 28 February 1973.

growth, allied to a practical certainty that their own activities ought to grow or at least get more money. Indeed, one of the beneficial results of growth is that the Vice-Chancellor and the Development Committee can remain fairly sane, since they can occasionally say "Yes" to a few of the innumerable demands from the academic and service departments. The thought of having to deal with so much academic importunity in a period of standstill or contraction, such as we may experience in the 1980's, causes the mind to boggle. I am, however, to be more serious, somewhat disillusioned with the quality of the debate about the virtues and disadvantages of growth. Some excellent universities (for instance, Monash in Australia) have grown much faster than the rate projected for Lancaster: some have a world-wide reputation while staying quite small and static. . . .

I would be happier if we conducted the argument in terms of opportunity. The reason for expanding the British university system is that more young people deserve the opportunity of university education: an opportunity which at present is smaller in Britain than in many other developed countries. The reason for expanding Lancaster faster than other places is simply that we offer the advantage of an expansion which, whatever its problems, is easier than elsewhere.

After describing the situation of the American universities, he concluded by saying:

> The under-privileged in Britain are not quite so conveniently identified as the negroes, Puerto Ricans and Chicanos of America, but they exist. A few find their way to us through such institutions as Ruskin College, Newbattle Abbey and Coleg Harlech. The rest we ignore, or fail to identify because they lack that present-day mark of status, the Good A-level Result. Where is Lancaster's programme to extend opportunities, even to a few, on a basis which remembers need as well as skill in passing examinations? Perhaps we can claim a small beginning, in our discussions intended to provide a special welcome to Open University students wishing to transfer to full-time study; but surely there is far more still to be done.[3.110]

(iv) School of Education

Mention has been made above of Lancaster's School of Education. Although it was not formally constituted until 1967, the Vice-Chancellor had told the Shadow Senate at its first meeting in January 1964

[3.110] University of Lancaster, *Ninth Annual Report presented by the Vice-Chancellor to the Meeting of the University Court*, December 1973, pages 1 to 6.

that he had raised with the Academic Planning Board the question of the nature of the relationship between the University of Lancaster and Teacher Training Colleges in the area, with special reference to the new Church of England Training College [i.e. S. Martin's College], which is due to be opened in Lancaster towards the end of September 1964.

By March the Vice-Chancellor had had further discussions, including with Charlotte Mason College at Ambleside, the scheme at this time being that "appropriately-qualified students . . . should, at the beginning or after a part of the College course, be admitted *by the University* to appropriate degree courses. If such an arrangement is made, the students concerned would obtain a teaching qualification and a degree in a joint course lasting not less than four years." Senate agreed that a scheme leading both to a degree and to a teacher's certificate appeared to raise no fundamental difficulty, and in May the Vice-Chancellor was able to report that a meeting was to be held with six directors of education and nineteen principals of training colleges, colleges of further education and colleges of art, drawn from an area extending from Barrow to Preston and Colne, who would discuss

> possible means of joint consultation and action. Possible fields of common interest included the transfer of students between these other institutions and the University, the running of refresher courses for teachers, and relations between the student bodies.

Negotiations continued for some months with the colleges at Chorley, Poulton-le-Fylde, Ambleside (Charlotte Mason), and Lancaster (S. Martin's), the main issues for decision being how the Certificate of Education and the proposed B.Ed. should fit together, what the relationship of the colleges would be to the university, how they would be funded, and where the university's graduates should go (and on what footing) to do a postgraduate teacher training course. By September 1966 the Vice-Chancellor was able to tell the Senate that the college at Chorley (with 750 students) was likely to wish an association with the university, and that in discussions with all four colleges, a clearer picture was emerging of what it was they were looking for. They did not want to be regarded as junior

> universities, but as specialists in a particular type of training, doing a job different from ours, but worthy of our respect. Much resentment is caused by the tendency of some universities to treat the colleges in a patronizing or paternalistic way. They do not claim to be "equal"; indeed, it is not clear what "equality" could mean. They do claim to be competent at a different job.

The Senate recognized that "the new relationship would involve the University in considerable extra work and responsibility", and that outside help would be needed for certain subjects, such as domestic science, which did not feature in the university's curriculum.

Not long afterwards Professor Alec Ross was appointed to the new chair of Educational Research and was able to take part in the detailed debate that took place over the next few months. It was decided that there should not be a loose federation of colleges affiliated with the university, but that the organization should be integrated with the rest of the university's academic structure as harmoniously as possible. Furthermore Professor Ross felt it important that the director of the school of education (to look after the colleges) should be one and the same person as the head of the department of educational research (to look after the advanced courses and the research programme), to prevent any discord in their aims and objectives. In order that he could be enabled to perform this co-ordinating role, however, it was necessary for him to have substantial administrative backing; and Mr. George Cockburn, the present secretary of the school, has performed this role since 1968.

As a result of the McNair Report,[3.111] the Ministry of Education had set up throughout the country a series of Area Training Organizations, administered through various universities, in an attempt to establish control of numbers of students and content of courses in the colleges of education. The nearest university to Lancaster so designated was Manchester, and in 1967, therefore, the Department of Education and Science transferred from them to Lancaster the validation of courses for colleges coming under the aegis of Lancaster's School of Education, who at the same time assumed responsibility for conducting examinations and awarding degrees.

The School at Lancaster became formally established in 1967.[3.112] Its functions were defined as being:

(a) to improve, co-ordinate, and if necessary (in agreement with the Area Training Organization) to extend the provision for the initial training of teachers and of others intending to engage in educational work, to advance the knowledge and practice of education by research, and generally to encourage the study of education in the region;
(b) to supervise courses of training and to assess the work of students in training and to advise the Secretary of State for Education and Science on the approval of persons as teachers in schools under his regulations;

[3.111] H.M.S.O., *Teachers and Youth Leaders*: Report of the Committee appointed by the power of the Board of Education to consider the supply, recruitment and training of teachers and youth leaders (London, 1944).

[3.112] Its constitution was ratified by the Senate at its meeting on 28 June and 3 July 1967, by the Council on 18 July, and by the D.E.S. in September 1967.

(c) to provide a centre for the educational interests of the area, to provide and co-operate in the provision of conferences and courses of study and to establish relations with the Department of Education and Science, the Local Education Authorities of the Area, and other bodies and persons engaged in educational activities.

The government of the School, subject to the authority of the Council and the Senate, is conducted by two bodies. The first of these is the Delegacy, whose function is to involve organizations outside the university, including representatives of the teachers and the local education authorities, in an advisory and consultative capacity to the school. The second body is the Board of Educational Studies (Board of Studies E) which meets at least once a term, and is responsible to the Senate for the academic work of the School. Reporting to the Board are smaller subject panels for each subject or group of subjects taught in the colleges, who advise the Board on matters concerning the syllabuses and modes of assessment.

The three-year Certificate of Education is taught at all four colleges but with some variation in the subjects being offered and the level at which they are taught. Thus, subjects like education, art and design, and English will inevitably be taught at all four colleges, but philosophy and drama, for example, are taught only at Chorley. The one-year Graduate Certificate in Education is offered by S. Martin's and Poulton-le-Fylde colleges, although the syllabus and assessment methods vary between them. The one-year Bachelor of Education degree course (which follows on from the certificate course or its recognized equivalent) is available at all four establishments, in a wide range of over twenty subjects, but here again the colleges specialize in certain areas which develop naturally from their particular interests and strengths and where their academic and physical resources permit work at honours degree level. The Senate takes a particular interest in the degree courses offered and the arrangements are renewed on a regular basis. Early in 1968 a proposal was made, which was later adopted, that the B.Ed. be extended to include serving teachers, who would be seconded either for a year of full-time study, or on a two-year part-time basis. Provision was also made for those students who needed to be given a guided course of part-time study prior to the B.Ed. course, to bring them up to the necessary standard; and in 1970 it was agreed that a B.Ed. in education alone was permissible. University staff act as chairmen and members of the various boards of examiners in the B.Ed. degree and may act as external examiners for the Certificate.

Teacher training since the Second World War, however, has not been permitted to stand still and the university began to consider the latest in a series of examinations of its structure and working, conducted by Lord James of Rusholme,[3.113] early in 1972, since its findings affected both the role of the colleges and their relationship with the university. The debate that ensued is still not complete, either at Lancaster or nationally, as this work goes to press, but what has happened so far is as follows.

The Senate held a preliminary discussion as early as February 1972 in order to supply responses to certain questions posed by the Committee of Vice-Chancellors and Principals. A fuller document by the Vice-Chancellor and Professor Ross, however, describing some of the main proposals and principal criticisms of the report and discussing the future, came to the March 1972 meeting of the Senate. What at that stage seemed likely to emerge was that a considerable number of colleges would mount the proposed two-year Diploma in Higher Education, would extend their facilities for professional training for new graduates, and would develop degree courses, useful to other professions but directed principally at intending teachers. From a number of different organizational proposals, and in the light of a request from the D.E.S., the Vice-Chancellor and Professor Ross put forward proposals for a closer association with one or more of the colleges of education which were consistent both with the university's charter and with the relevant sections of the James Report. The D.E.S. had specifically suggested St. Martin's College, and the other three colleges were invited by the university to join in the discussions, partly because difficulties were foreseen in an association confined to a single denominational college; any proposed scheme might be applied to Poulton-le-Fylde, although Chorley's position was uncertain and Charlotte Mason too small to participate.

The document emphasized that the colleges, if they came to be associated with the university, would not become

in the formal sense "colleges of the university", because that status would imply that the university took over all the powers of the college Governing Bodies, a change which is considered neither possible nor desirable. ... An associated college would, over a period of about five years, phase out its certificate and B.Ed. work (though retaining, where appropriate, the training of graduates), and would substitute a three-year degree scheme leading to an honours degree of B.A. of the University of Lancaster.

It would be a condition of association:

(a) that college staff should be individually recognized by the university as capable of teaching to honours degree level, no element of the degree scheme being offered until there are sufficient recognized staff to teach it;

[3.113] H.M.S.O., *Teacher Education and Training* (London, 1972): report by a Committee of Inquiry appointed by the Secretary of State for Education and Science under the chairmanship of Lord James of Rusholme.

    (b) as a corollary, that future appointments to college staff should be jointly agreed by the college and the university, being made by a joint appointing committee which must reach an agreed decision;

    (c) that the recruitment of students should be through U.C.C.A., at a level appropriate to a university honours degree.

The boards of studies were consulted and were generally in favour; and the Senate debated the matter twice more, in May and in June. No further mention of the topic was made, however, until February 1972. By this time the Government's White Paper on education[3.114] had been issued, which raised many new issues. Furthermore, S. Martin's College and the university, starting from very different standpoints as regards the religious question, found serious difficulty in reconciling the aims and outlook of a college which had been created within a particular denominational framework with that of a university which specifically forbade any test related to "religious, moral or political belief". A committee was therefore set up to consider the university taking a serious interest in the Diploma in Higher Education. The idea of association with the colleges, as described above, fell away.

In June 1973, however, the Senate, at the same meeting at which it decided in principle to receive proposals for internal Dip. H.E. courses which met certain conditions, also noted that

> a submission had been received from Charlotte Mason College for validation for B.Ed. (ordinary and honours) and for Dip. H.E. (in education and community studies). This request implied that a validating body should be constituted, which should have to run in tandem with Board E from 1974 onwards, although there would be overlapping membership.

An *ad hoc* body was set up to consider the establishment of validation procedures and a paper prepared by Mr. Cockburn, and detailing the committee's proposal, was laid before the Senate of October 1973. After describing the colleges' present offerings the document explained that the White Paper called for colleges of education (a) to raise their minimum standard of entry to two advanced levels, (b) to provide three-year (ordinary) and four-year (honours) B.Ed. degrees, to replace the Certificate in Education, (c) to offer also two-year Dip. H.E. courses and some B.A. courses, and (d) to continue to provide one-year training courses for graduates and one-year (shorter) courses for experienced teachers. It continued:

> The Colleges have stated that they wish to seek validation for these courses through the university. It is of course unlikely that any one College will be able to offer all of these courses in the near future but they are now

---

[3.114] H.M.S.O., Education: *A Framework for Expansion* (London, December 1972), Cmnd. 5174.

developing proposals. . . . The present machinery of the School of Education is not adequate for this purpose (since it is designed to deal solely with courses for intending teachers) and it is suggested that the system outlined below be used in relation to all "new" courses.

The committee envisaged a Board of Studies for Associated Colleges (Board H), on the lines of a trimmed-down Board E and with a similar membership and cross-representation on appropriate university committees. There would be a system of university assessors who would be responsible for specific subjects or areas of study in one or more colleges, including curriculum and assessment, and who would be external examiners for the Dip. H.E. and internal examiners for any degree work undertaken. Proposals on syllabus content and assessment arrangements would be made to the Board by the college academic boards, having first been discussed with the assessor and the college staff. The Board would make recommendations to the Senate for new schemes of study and methods of assessment approved by the Senate. The competence of colleges

> to undertake teaching for specific awards and to operate particular schemes of study would be decided by the Senate (perhaps by committees appointed on the recommendation of the Board). It would be expected that the Senate would require that the University be consulted on staff appointments.

The Delegacy would essentially retain its existing function. These proposals were agreed in outline by the Senate, and no doubt the new arrangement will supersede in due course the existing work of the School of Education: already proposals along the new lines are coming forward from the colleges to the Senate.

Meanwhile, in May 1973 the Senate was asked to consider a proposal that the university validate the courses of Edge Hill College of Education, formerly under the aegis of the University of Liverpool, but because of local government reorganization coming more naturally under Lancaster, and it was agreed that, subject to approval (subsequently received) by the Department of Education and Science, the university should accept responsibility for the validation of their courses from September 1973. Thus the number of colleges for which the university has assumed responsibility now totals five, covering in 1973–74 some 3,700 full-time as well as about three hundred part-time students.

(v) Modes of assessment

It is unfortunate that a disquisition into the evolution of the Lancaster examination system may appear to be one of the more negative aspects of this account of the university, a tale of problems apparently overcome and later re-emerging. In the past decade a number of British universities have felt the need to reform their examination system, in order to make it more fair to candidates, to clarify the system's objectives both for the benefit of the examiners and the examined, and to eliminate flaws that seemed to be inherent in the traditional methods, whilst losing none of the rigour, the public accountability and the professional standards that must remain the hallmarks of any successful examination system. The situation at times is bedevilled by the crusading zeal of some reformers, which can force others into entrenched positions, whatever standpoint each group sets out from: proposed changes may then be blocked because of a keen anxiety about standards which can in some cases exclude any variation in accepted practice. The situation is then yet more aggravated by the long time spans involved, which are necessary in order that all parties concerned, including the institution's external examiners and the students themselves, may be appropriately consulted, that students may be given due warning of any impending change, and that the system finally agreed upon be as proof as possible against misunderstanding, lack of clarity and precise definition, and fraud.[3.115] One only has to see, for example, how many variants the university has made of its Part II regulations—there are over a dozen of them—to see the dimensions of the problem.[3.116]

At first the Senate used to debate every detail of the examination system in full conclave. This, however, was found to be too time-consuming and so an *ad hoc* committee on examination procedures, based principally on representatives of boards of studies, was set up in March 1965, to "investigate and report on the whole process of first-year examinations". In December 1967 this committee was replaced by the standing Committee on Examinations,[3.117] chaired by the Vice-Chancellor or a Pro-Vice-Chancellor and with the Academic Registrar acting as its secretary.

[3.115] The intricacy and time-consuming nature of the necessary procedures was recently forcefully illustrated by the experience of one large arts department, where proposals for fairly radically altered methods of assessment in Part II arose in the staff-student committee and departmental meetings in the spring of 1970, and a departmental working party was set up in the autumn. By the time that the proposals had been considered, and re-considered after amendment, by the department (including the students), the board of studies, the Committee on Examinations, the external examiners and the Senate, two further years had gone by; and it was in the autumn of 1972 that a notice was circulated to students giving details of an assessment method that is to operate fully for the first time in the summer of 1974, i.e. four years and more than a complete generation of undergraduates after the original suggestions!

[3.116] See University of Lancaster, *B.A. Course Handbook*, Section R, available both to staff and students, for detailed current regulations covering both Part I and Part II.

[3.117] The terms of reference of this committee are: "To stimulate an interest in purposes and methods of examination and to examine proposals for particular methods of assessment."

Staff of the new university photographed in the ballroom of the Royal King's Arms Hotel in April 1964

By courtesy of the Lancaster Guardian

Back row (L. to R.) : A. Stephen Jeffreys, Esq., Professor E. H. Lloyd, Professor S. G. Sturmey, Dr. F. Oldfield, Professor C. D. Pigott, D. B. Smith, Esq., Dr. M. G. Simpson, Professor J. C. Bevington, Professor M. M. Willcock, Dr. R. W. H. Small, Professor A. H. Woolrych, Dr. A. Mercer, Professor B. H. P. Rivett, M. D. Forster, Esq., Dr. D. M. Craig

Front row (L. to R.) : Dr. A. W. Phillips, Professor G. Manley, Professor P. A. Reynolds, Lord Derby, Vice-Chancellor A. G. Mackenzie, Esq., Professor E. R. Dobbs, Professor T. E. Lawrenson

Professor Tom Lawrenson lecturing in the Centenary Church, St. Leonardgate,
during 1965–6

By courtesy of the Daily Express

Seminar in progress

John Donat

Let us look first at Part I, held as a qualifying examination at the end of a student's first year,[3.118] as it was conducted in the summer of 1972. All students are required to take three subjects of equal weight in their first year, at least two of which must lead to a possible major subject. In Part II, however, the majority of students are taking a single major, developed from Part I, together with a two-year minor which is usually but not invariably a continuation of another Part I subject, as well as a free ninth unit. This means that when a student comes to take his Part I examinations, he needs a minimum of a majorable mark in one subject, a minorable mark in another, and a pass mark in the third; i.e. he must pass in all three, but at different standards according to the future he has selected for himself. This allows a student a reasonable degree of latitude in experimentation with an unfamiliar subject, whilst ensuring that a certain minimum standard is maintained and that the student is not likely to fail outright in his Part II examinations. If he fails to reach the requisite percentages, and his failure is not condoned because of special circumstances, he is recommended to re-sit in one or more subjects in September. This is intended to ensure that he will not enter Part II without having covered and understood the groundwork provided in Part I. Such a system, however, also has the effect of causing some of the weaker students to spend their summer vacation re-covering old ground rather than commencing the preliminary reading and any required written work for Part II.

Both at the June and September examinations there is a special Part I Board of Examiners, which is a sub-committee of the Senate, made up of heads of relevant departments or their deputies, together with representatives from the Department of Educational Research. The Committee of the Senate, at a special meeting in September, makes a decision on whether a particular student should proceed to Part II, re-sit externally the following summer, or be excluded permanently from the University; and there is a final appeal to the Vice-Chancellor, open to all students.

The question of timing of examinations has proved intransigent. The first prospectus, for 1963–64, advised students that they need not select their Part II choices until after the first examination, "which takes place in the third or fourth term". At a joint meeting in July 1964 between the Academic Planning Board and the Shadow Senate divergences of choice between the natural sciences board, Board A, and the others were evident, in that

Board A wanted terminal examinations in the first year, and no specific incentive to use the long vacation, whilst Boards B, C and D wanted some

---

[3.118] For a time there was a single two-year Part I course in Russian and Soviet Studies: the first-year examination was in Russian and the second-year examinations in the students' other two Part I subjects. From October 1972, however, there was instead a transitional year at the beginning of Part II.

o

form of examination in both April and October . . . and it was agreed . . . that the first year examinations for which Boards B, C and D were responsible should be divided between April and October.

With regard to the form of examinations in the first year, Professor Woolrych said that the Senate . . . had agreed that the test in October proposed by Boards B, C and D could appropriately take a number of different forms. . . . The view had also been taken that only subjects to be continued in the second year should be subject to a test in October.

In the course of further discussion, it was agreed not to attempt to establish uniformity as regards methods of examining at the present stage but to retain the greatest possible freedom and flexibility in this respect, subject to the proviso that the form of examination adopted by one department should not upset the work of another. . . . Members of the Academic Planning Board welcomed the proposal to divide first year examinations between April and October.

However, this decision was modified in November 1964 when the Senate reopened the subject, and

Reference was made . . . to the intention of Board A to introduce a system of continuous assessment of first-year students, which would avoid the need for a sessional examination of any magnitude, and would enable departments to give timely warning to students whose work was unsatisfactory. It was agreed that admission to Part II . . . should depend in all subjects on students' performance in examinations to be held at the beginning of the Summer Term and in re-sit examinations to be held in June, but that Boards B, C and D should consider whether there would be advantages in adopting in the future a system of continuous assessment on the lines proposed by Board A.

The Board A departments wished to accumulate marks throughout the year by several processes, including written and numerical exercises, practical work, and small-scale terminal examinations. The advantages of this scheme they believed to be that the weaker undergraduates could be identified early, marks earlier in the course could be weighted more lightly, revision would be a continuous process rather than a final headlong panic, students could learn from tests and examinations if these were marked and returned to them, and re-sit examinations would become superfluous because members of staff would already know so much about the individual student's abilities and development. The arts departments, meanwhile, were thinking in terms of formal three-hour examinations as their only assessment device. Before the time had come for the examinations to be sat, however, Professor Murray, as chairman of Board D, pointed out that there would be only three weeks between the announcement of the first round of results and the beginning of the re-sit examinations, and in the opinion of his board there was no point in examining students twice on the same work within such a short period: he therefore proposed that for 1965 a system of continuous assessment be substituted for the June re-sit examinations. (It is fortunate that new universities are given the luxury of being able to formulate and re-formulate their examining techniques by only having one year at a time to consider; we find Senate in February 1965 declining, while in the midst of discussions about Part I, to discuss the form or timing of the Part II examinations.)

In the event, two written examinations were given in the Lower Town Hall[3.119] in each subject during the last week of April 1965 and in May an Interim Pass List was issued. In June the performance of all students who had had an F mark somewhere in their assessment, or who lacked an M[3.120] mark, or did not have an aggregate of 120 marks in the three subjects was re-assessed, by a variety of methods,

> in the light of their work in the Summer Term in *all* their subjects, and in certain cases the performance of other students was also re-assessed.[3.121]

On 22 June the Board of Examiners drew up a draft Final Pass List, and in doing so

> paid regard both to [a candidate's] aggregate result and to whether there was evidence that he had achieved a sufficient standard in at least one of his subjects to allow him to proceed to a major course in it.

The list was received by Senate, who considered individually every student whose name was omitted and received reports on each of them from their college tutors, giving evidence of illness and other special features.[3.122] The

---

[3.119] It is an indication of the close liaison with students that marked these early days that twelve students were taken to the Lower Town Hall to inspect it and see whether it was acceptable as an examination hall. They were able to give their assent, it appears, provided the ventilation was improved, the noise reduced, shades put round the light bulbs, vases of flowers put out, and individual desks and accurate clocks provided. Later the Priory Hall was commandeered as well. As of 1973, of course, the accommodation is much more palatial; Part I examinations are held in the Indoor Recreation Centre, while Part II occupy the Great and Minor Halls, and other places around the site.

[3.120] See pages 196 and 199 below for an explanation of F. and M.

[3.121] This and the next quotation are from a report to the Academic Advisory Committee of July 1965.

[3.122] Out of 292 candidates who presented themselves for assessment at Part I, 273 had at the issuance of the Final Pass List satisfied the requirements for admission to Part II, one student was allowed to continue subject to certain special conditions, and 18 had failed but still had the right of appeal to the Vice-Chancellor before being excluded from the university. The Academic Advisory Committee was able to declare itself satisfied with these figures, which represent a success rate of 94 per cent, saying in their report to Council:

> Great care and trouble was taken in the organization and conduct of the examinations at the end of the first year. The Committee was impressed by the study being made

two stages of examination within the ten weeks of the Summer Term did not, however, survive beyond their first trial in 1965, despite the hopes expressed by the Academic Advisory Committee that this system would be given a further trial. As Professor Frank Sibley commented, however, work was not continuing through all three terms, for

> attendance at lectures has increasingly dropped off as the term has pro-
> ceeded until by now one may find at best a handful of students present . . .
> [who] regularly fall into the two groups one would expect: those who mean
> to maintain a major interest in the subject, and those whose status, on the
> April results, is precarious and who therefore need to make their presence
> known. . . . Much of our deliberation this time last year turned on ways
> by which we could make sure that students worked not only in all three
> terms but also in the long vacation. The gosling we have hatched is one
> with precisely opposite characteristics. For many students, Part I is
> effectively over in April (would we really reverse favourable April judg-
> ments in June in any circumstances?),[3.123] the let-down after the tension
> of examinations does not encourage work, the distraction of summer and
> better weather are upon them, and the illusion if not the reality of a
> halcyon calm stretches ahead as far as October.

He therefore recommended that Part I examinations be held in June which, after further debate, they henceforth were, with a re-assessment, including re-sit examinations in September.

Thus the time available for first-year Part I teaching (and, concomitantly, the period available to a student to make up his mind about his choice of major subject(s)) has become twenty-six weeks of term and two short vacations. For Part II the teaching period has stabilized to around fifty weeks, with two long vacations and four short ones, giving a total of twenty-two months between the Part I and Part II examinations (except that part of the Part II examination may be in the second year). Since work that contributes to a student's final degree class is set for both Long Vacations, the positioning of these relative to the ending of Part I, and to the beginning and end of Part II, has always been important in discussions of the use of the nine terms of a Lancaster undergraduate career. The other new English universities have all

---

of the somewhat novel methods employed, with the object of detecting any weaknesses in them and of developing them further in the light of experience gained.

[3.123] A notice sent individually to all students in February 1965 had warned them that "inclusion in the [Interim] List does not guarantee entry into a particular Major or Joint Major course. This is because you may have done relatively badly in your intended Major subject, and the University may wish to suggest transfer to another subject. You must maintain a satisfactory standard in all three subjects during the Summer Term; otherwise your name may be omitted from the Final Pass List".

been restricted to the same length of first degree course, but it is interesting to look at the example of Stirling, which has been able to exploit the Scottish tradition and use four years for its first degree, breaking the time up into eight semesters. The extra year makes possible the use of three semesters for Part I, enabling students more easily to make a radical but well-grounded shift of major subject between the time they enter Stirling and the beginning of Part II, and still leaving close on thirty months for Part II.

The Sub-Committee on Examination Procedures, chaired by Dr. Oldfield, presented a detailed report to the Senate in July 1965, analysing both the Interim and Final Lists, and giving the results of questionnaires that had been circulated to the examiners. They had asked their colleagues what the purpose of Part I assessment was, and the replies which came back included: the diagnosis of ability and an indication of permitted areas of future major study, control of academic standards and of teaching methods, judgment both of individual students' attainments and those of a whole class, and a survey of students' degrees of adjustment to a university environment. What they were not told was that Part I was any kind of apprenticeship for Finals. They found a variation with regard to the use of continuous assessment from near 100 per cent dependence on examinations in some departments to up to 70 per cent dependence on coursework in others.[3.124] Some doubts were expressed about substantial reliance on continuous assessment because of possible unfairness to individuals, in large seminar groups, the need for a variety of types of assessment, the advantage of assessing students at the end of the learning period, the tendency of essays to be mere compilations or written too much in collaboration, the imposition of strain throughout the learning period, a stress on industry to the possible detriment of perception and speed, and the need for examination experience before Finals. In general, however, it seemed that members of staff felt the right balance had been struck between examinations and other forms of assessment.

While they recognized that standardization of structure of assessment would not be acceptable to the departments, the committee were concerned that variations could cause unfairness if students were required to pass on the strength of an aggregate mark, especially if compensation were based only on mathematical considerations. Much debate took place on whether and how far a good mark in one subject could compensate for a weak one elsewhere and many variations of practice were suggested to ensure that students were

---

[3.124] Defined in Regulation 2.1 as "including essays and practical work, undertaken during the session, contributions to discussions in tutorials and seminars, and work carried out under examination conditions at other times of the year".

The use of coursework assessment at Part I now varies between 25 per cent and 60 per cent, except for three departments who rely wholly on examinations and use coursework only as supplementary evidence.

not unduly penalized for experimentation, while also taking seriously the
necessity of coping with three subjects as a unified performance (however
much particular students wished to be specialists from the outset of their
undergraduate career). The latest regulations give a significant amount of
discretion to the Part I Committee of the Senate in the extent to which they
may condone a single anomalously bad mark, or marks which are weak but
not disastrous, and a code of conduct for the negotiations between departments has been ritualized, whilst leaving the responsibility for comparability
of treatment between cases to the chairman of the examiners. To produce
comparable assessments around the critical range of marks, i.e. at the point
where a decision is made about whether an individual student is able to
continue at university and, if he can, in what major and minor subjects, the
committee suggested a range of thresholds, A, B, C and D, corresponding to
the present M, N, Q and F marks, and used since that time.[3.125]

Having reached a clear decision that Part I examinations in June were
preferable to April, the committee then realized that

> in some instances students would have no really sound indication of the
> extent to which their abilities and performance measured up to their
> preferences and aspirations until the very end of the first year,

but confessed themselves unable to do more than recommend departments to
give students "early and well-based indications of progress and performance".
The Committee on Examinations re-considered this point at one of its first
meetings in March 1968, stating that it was a function of the university to
discover at an early stage which students were not doing well, but realizing
also that

> although there is a well developed college tutorial system it is not clear who
> should be responsible for informing students who were not progressing
> well . . . there does not seem to be, in all cases, a sufficiently close link up
> for the feed-back of information about a student's progress between the
> college tutor and the student's three academic departments.

Thus in 1969 an "early warning" system was set up, whereby (in its final
form) students in danger of failing either outright, or in their intended major
subject, or who "for any other reason of academic danger may need
admonition or help", were the subject of reports sent by departments to
college tutors via the central administration, sometimes as a matter of
information and sometimes for the college tutor himself to take action. These
forms, completed in the February of each year, have been found to be of

---

[3.125] M (and A) = 45 per cent and above, N (and B) = 44 to 40 per cent, Q (and
C) = 39 to 35 per cent, and F (and D) = 34 per cent and below. The M and F
categories have since been further refined: see below, page 199.

significant value to college tutors in giving advance warning of possible impending difficulty, as well as a useful guide for both teacher and taught at the mid-point of the year: so much so, that from 1972, similar forms were used for second-year students, and from 1974 also for third-years.

A disagreement between Board A and the others arose about the re-sit examination,[3.126] and the Senate ruled that

> on the recommendation of the Board of Examiners [the Senate] should have the right, in a case of uncertainty about the proper assessment to be given, to permit an undergraduate to re-sit... once in September, following failure in June, this right to rest with the Senate and *not* with the undergraduate.

A year later the Vice-Chancellor, in a paper for the Senate of October 1966 about exclusion of students from the university, noted that while the cases concerned with discipline seemed to be proceeding according to the principles of natural justice, those

> on grounds of academic failure give rise, however, to some concern. It has several times happened that students have brought, on appeal, evidence which ought to have been before Senate at the original determination of the case.... I am very much concerned by the discovery that three students have been admitted to second-year studies, after success in the September examinations, solely because I reversed on appeal a decision of Senate denying an opportunity to re-sit .... It seems to me quite wrong that we should take risks with people's careers in this manner.
>
> Assuming that Part I results are available a clear week before the end of term, I suggest that they should be promulgated in three sections, "Passed", "Allowed to re-sit", and "Called for discussion of failure". Those in the third group would be called in person, with their tutors, before a small committee of Senate, which would have delegated power to pass, to allow a re-sit, or to exclude. The purpose of the interview would be to hear any mitigating circumstances which ought to be taken into consideration, and also to make sure that students who are excluded are given proper and sympathetic advice about alternative careers or courses of study. A similar procedure would be adopted in September.

The outcome of this suggestion was the formation of the Committee of Senior Tutors, inserted procedurally between the Part I Board of Examiners and the Part I Committee of the Senate, which was to be used exclusively for making

---

[3.126] The Board A departments took the view that by the end of June they would have sufficient information from the January and June examination papers they set, continuous assessment from seminars or tutorials, and laboratory course work assessment. They felt, therefore, that students who had failed the whole of Part I in June should be sent down, although they were prepared to re-discuss borderline candidates.

recommendations to the Senate in relation to students who had failed the Part I examination.

Whether a re-sit examination should be a right or a privilege was another topic with almost equal numbers of supporters for either point of view. In 1965, the Senate had agreed that the opportunity to re-sit once in September was not the right of an undergraduate; and neither was the facility of re-sitting once externally. In the autumn of 1966 these strictures were modified by Senate, to an "understanding that a re-sit will normally be allowed and will only be refused in exceptional circumstances"—while also including the useful proposal that a student's choices at Part I should include at least two subjects that could lead to a major subject.[3.127]

In 1968 differences in convention between departments which allowed some departments to use for a second time in September a student's poor continuous assessment, thereby endangering his chance of passing the re-sit examination, led Senate to give departments guidance, later refined into a regulation, that they should regard the September evidence as supplementary and not as mere repetition of the earlier papers, thus

> giving the undergraduate a genuine chance to qualify to proceed to Part II and designed (both in form and content) to examine those areas where during the year the undergraduate has shown weakness; and that, in appropriate cases, departments should set and take into account vacation projects . . . in arriving at the reassessment mark . . . departments should take into account not only the candidate's latest performance in the areas which were re-examined but also his previous performance in those areas which were not re-examined.[3.128]

The granting of a re-sit examination, with the possibility of a subsequent external re-assessment in addition, as a matter of normal allowance but not as a right, remained constant until October 1972 when, in the light of recommendations from an *ad hoc* committee on timing of examinations, the Senate resolved that

> candidates who fail to achieve an overall pass in Part I should have an automatic right to be re-assessed once by examination or in other ways in appropriate subjects the following September

and, at the same time, agreed that the Committee of Senior Tutors should not meet twice as previously, but once only, after the September re-assessments. It remains to be seen whether this re-adjustment within Part I will, as some

---

[3.127] There are certain Part I subjects at Lancaster which, because a department or section is new, or deliberately limited in its development, lead on only to a minor subject, e.g. Czech, or Yugoslav.

[3.128] Examination Regulation A3.4 (ii) and (iv), October 1972.

people fear, affect undergraduates' attitudes to the first round of Part I in June.

Part of the profound change of attitude towards students that has come about within the past decade is shown in the amount of information that students expect to possess about the university's operation in general and their own individual marks in particular. As we have seen, Part I marks were from an early stage disseminated not in pass/fail lists, nor in lists of figures, but in four bands, delineating thresholds of achievement. In 1968 these were refined, so that the pass mark was divided into three categories, M3, M2 and M1, corresponding approximately to third, lower second, and upper second or first class, while the grades denoting failure were divided into F1 and F2, denoting failure and irretrievable failure (with a further refinement of Fc for a condoned failure). An attempt was made in that year to set up a system of scaling, in order to even out the large variation in distribution of grades between different subjects. After trying out a pilot scheme for one year, however, when scaled as well as raw marks were available, it was felt by the majority of departments that whilst a common understanding on the interpretation of grades between subjects was clearly desirable, scaling would not help and would, if anything, rigidify the system.

As an indication of future potential the seven categories already mentioned seemed to departments quite sufficient for their needs. They provide adequate information for the departments concerned, the college tutor, the students themselves, and the grant-awarding local education authorities: they may therefore remain unaltered for the foreseeable future.

If Part I examinations at Lancaster are thought by the reader to be complex in their operation, those for Part II are yet more so. The mediaeval system of the inception of candidates to first degrees after a series of oral disputations with certain masters of arts in the university had been replaced by the introduction of formal written examinations, in Cambridge as early as 1772 (firmly established by 1824), and in Oxford from 1800 onwards.[3.129] Under the pressure of the newly established University of London (which from 1858 set examinations for its external students), the growth of Civil Service examinations, and reform movements within Oxford and Cambridge, written examinations had become normal practice by the mid-nineteenth century. No substantial change took place thereafter until the foundation of the new universities in the 1960's:[3.130] it was an area that even the Robbins Committee in 1963 hesitated to comment upon, merely remarking that

---

[3.129] See H. Rashdall, *The Universities of Europe in the Middle Ages*, Volume III, chapter 5: and Kneale's *Report of the Committee on the Structure of the First and Second Public Examinations* (University of Oxford, March 1965).

[3.130] See H. J. Perkin, *Innovation in the New Universities of the United Kingdom* (OECD, 1969), Part II, chapter 8, pp. 181–191, for his views on new methods of

We have not thought it to be within our terms of reference to enter upon the merits or demerits of the various examination systems of the universities. . . . To inquire whether these systems make possible a just assessment of the ability of candidates would involve intricate research and would raise complex questions beyond our competence to investigate.[3.131]

Most of the British universities have their own royal charters and are granted their own degree-awarding status.[3.132] Gradually the practice of consulting external examiners from other universities has grown up, to guard against the problems found even within the University of Oxford, where the Franks Report noted that

> recent complaints of the lack of uniformity in standards as shown in the results, a lack of uniformity between different Schools and also between different years in the same school, are not without foundation. . . . [The Committee on Undergraduate Studies] should also have the means of making rough comparisons with results and standards in other universities. . . . We also recommend that all boards of examiners in the undergraduate Honour Schools should include one full member who is appointed from outside Oxford. This is now usual; we believe that it should be universal.[3.133]

This is an area where each institution jealously guards its own autonomy, for, as Sir James Mountford has noted, the statistical methods of the General Certificate of Education cannot be applied to the small number of candidates at a particular university, in no subject is the syllabus identical for any two universities, and there is no external agency making known its expectations about a pass rate. For, he says,

> The effectiveness of the maintenance of standards depends upon the collective judgement and traditions of generation after generation of teachers, and upon the care which is taken by older members of staff to guard themselves and their juniors from capricious assessments. This is

---

assessment up to 1968. It is interesting that he is able at that date to be so whole-heartedly optimistic about continuous assessment, which he says "has proved to be a useful and successful innovation, and one which could with profit be adopted by other universities".

[3.131] *Report of the Committee on Higher Education*, Cmnd. 2154, paragraph 574.

[3.132] T. A Owen has discussed in his article, "The Power to Grant Degrees" (*Universities Quarterly*, Vol. 26, no. 3, pp. 271–79, Summer 1972), the less than straightforward legal and constitutional position of various degree-awarding bodies in Britain.

[3.133] *Report of the Commission of Inquiry* (University of Oxford, 1966), Volume I, paragraphs 250 and 252.

not a confidence trick played on students and on the public by an esoteric group of autocrats: it is a skilled art soundly based on exper-ence.[3.134]

Most American universities, by contrast, equate assessment with the grades given by the teacher of a course to each of the students on it. The basis for such grades is the quality of the students' performance of the tasks and exercises set by the teacher. The particular kinds of assessment employed (which include various forms of written examination, essays, oral tests and laboratory work) and the weight each is given in determining the final grade is up to the individual tutor. The grades which a student receives, derived from a much wider and more numerous set of courses than his British counter-part takes, are averaged together at the end of each term to give both an average grade for the term and a cumulative average of all the work done so far. When he graduates, the grades for individual courses, the term averages and the cumulative totals are recorded on a transcript which is made available to the student, to the teaching staff, to other educational institutions and to prospective employers. Students who feel that the grade given them for a course by a member of staff is either unfairly arrived at or inaccurate has recourse to a system of appeals which begins at the departmental level and can proceed as far as the dean of the faculty. The standard of the institution as a whole is attested by a regional accrediting body which covers several states (in a country too large for one body adequately to supervise the system as a whole).

The new British universities have in common with their American counter-parts the system of a degree scheme made up of separately chosen course units, and had from the beginning a will to experiment. Sussex, the first in the field, has an assessment for the B.A. degree which

takes the form of a number of exercises, varying according to the subject between a dissertation written over a period of nine months or an extended essay written over, say, six weeks, and the traditional three-hour unseen paper. During the Autumn and Spring Terms of their final year, all finalists are required to prepare one or two or sometimes more, essays or dissertations for submission as part of the Final examination, but, for the majority of candidates, most of the assessment exercises are written during their final Summer Term.[3.135]

[3.134] Sir James Mountford, *British Universities* (O.U.P. 1966), page 73. A less sanguine view of comparative standards is expressed by R. Cox in "Examinations and higher education; a survey of the literature", *Universities Quarterly*, Vol. 21, No. 3, pp. 292–340, June 1967.
[3.135] University of Sussex, *Guide for applicants*, 1972, page 32.

Similarly, at Essex the Vice-Chancellor took up office saying

> Only systematic research can show how far the British system really measures intellect and originality, and not simply the ability to pass examinations. At this stage we propose no radical change. But we shall vary the circumstances under which a student is assessed: have some short examinations and some long, allow students in certain subjects to make use of text books and reference books, and take into account research projects,[3.136]

while at Stirling the prospectus notes that

> Examinations are not necessarily confined to the essay-type. Other methods such as oral examinations, objective tests, practicals and prescribed tests are used as seem appropriate.[3.137]

Like all prospectus literature, these quotations have a certain enigmatic flavour, which is found also in the Lancaster statement that

> The Part II written examinations in major and combined major subjects and in two-year minor courses include papers on the courses taken in both years of Part II. Course work assessment and (in certain cases) dissertations on project work are taken into account in assessing the class of degree awarded to each candidate and in some cases a unit of assessment is based entirely on such evidence. Part II written examinations are normally held in the Summer Term of the final year, but in certain subjects . . . some formal examinations are also taken at an earlier stage during Part II.[3.138]

In his second year (and first year of Part II) the Lancaster undergraduate will probably encounter final assessment in his free ninth unit,[3.139] which has altered in its status more than once as regards a student's final degree classification. In March 1965 the Senate determined that his mark in this subject "may lead the Examiners to award him a higher or a lower classification but will not be sufficient ground for failing him", while accepting that such courses ''should use some method of continuous assessment within the hours of teaching allotted to the course, thereby avoiding the need for a single formal end-of-course examination". Two months later, however, the Senate decided instead that a final decision on the place of the distant minor

[3.136] A. E. Sloman, *A University in the Making* (1964), page 42.

[3.137] University of Stirling, Prospectus 1972–73, page 16. Experimentation in students assessing each other, although not for the final degree class, is also under way at Stirling. It has been observed that students are harsher in their assessment of their fellows than are members of staff.

[3.138] University of Lancaster, Prospectus 1973–74, pages 29–30.

[3.139] See page 127 above, and 203 to 204 below.

in the degree classification should be deferred until the university had had some experience in teaching and assessing such subjects, and that in the meanwhile they should be classified in the same way as any other course. In July, after chairmen of boards of studies had met together, the March position was reinstated, with the addition of the obligation to inform the student's major department of the percentage classification. So far students had been given no information about the status of the distant minor, but in December 1965 it was agreed they should be warned that a poor performance in the distant minor could affect the class of degree awarded.

A questionnaire sent round to departments offering breadth courses, early in 1969, showed that a variety of methods of assessment were being used, with the main emphasis on essays and practical work, some reliance on seminar performance and written tests, and very little on formal written examinations. At this point, however, various heads of departments were becoming restless about the breadth subject affecting the degree classification at all, but Professor Woolrych, concerned that any proposal should not reduce the incentive to take these courses seriously, suggested that they should be graded as

> Credit, Pass, or Fail; Credit might be equivalent to a II.1 mark or better under the present system. A Fail should have an adverse effect on the final classification, a Pass would be neutral, while a Credit could be taken into favourable consideration when a candidate is otherwise on the borderline between one class and another.[3.140]

The Committee on Examinations considered this suggestion, found it met anxieties about candidates being absent from part of the assessment, and meant there was no need for such students to re-take the breadth subject in the final year. The proposal was therefore adopted although, because of the kind of time-lag mentioned above, it could not even be partially implemented until the Finals of 1970. In 1971 the pass/fail/credit device was predominant, with numerical backing where helpful, but for 1972 two variants were in operation for different specialized categories of student, using either the pass/credit/fail, or a numerical mark.

With the advent of the free ninth unit, however, came the decision to make it of equal weight and standing with the other eight units of assessment and to have it always numerically marked and externally examined. One of the guiding principles of the ninth unit is that as many courses as possible from all those available within the university are to be open to all comers, so that alongside third-year major Politics students taking, say, Conflict Studies may be students who have never touched on that discipline before. Naturally

---

[3.140] Memorandum to Breadth Courses Committee, February 1969.

the university was concerned about finding a way of reasonably assessing the different categories of student likely to take these courses, "whilst recognizing the need to set a reasonable standard", but after enquiring of departments who were opening their courses to free ninth unit students and who had been asked to consult their external examiners, the Committee on Examinations was compelled to agree that, "since there was no simple general solution to the problem, it must be left to individual departments to take any appropriate action to take account of the disparate backgrounds of students taking their free ninth unit courses".[1.141]

Since students are entitled to take any free ninth unit they choose either in their second or their third year, and one chosen from either the second or third year list (subject to conditions imposed by departments), the possible variations in timing of the assessment of these courses can be guessed at. After much debate, it was decided that the principle of students being examined in their free ninth unit in the year in which they studied it should in general be upheld. It has been found that a very substantial majority of students take their free ninth unit in their second year and outside their major subject, so that the system adopted for 1972 is to be continued.

The difference between boards of studies was to show up again in the matter of second-year Final examinations, for as early as May 1964 Senate was appraised of the fact that

> Boards A and B wanted subjects in the second year only to be examined in the second year, whereas Boards C and D proposed that they should be examined in the third year.

Boards C and D at this time were opposed to examinations being held even in the distant minor in the second year, and if assessment was to take place, it should be only "by means of brief terminal tests, or some process of continuous assessment or both". Board A gradually became more separated from Board B in its views, and by March 1966, when the first occasion of Finals was only fourteen months away and discussion became more urgent, was alone in its intention to hold examinations in certain courses during the second year. Although Board C "felt it was undesirable to examine before the end of the third year", because of possible difficulties arising if students taking joint degrees (such as physics and philosophy) were being examined at different times, the discussion of this issue was swept away in another debate about timing of the examinations in minor subjects (which it was eventually agreed should be at the convenience of the department giving the minor course).

And so the matter was left until 1970, when a possible inequity between

---

[3.141] Committee on Examinations, October 1971.

students under different boards gave concern. In the Finals of that year, some Board A students who had not done well in their second-year final assessment papers had been required to re-sit them, although

> If they pass these re-sit examinations they will (it is assumed) continue to study for a classified degree. If a student fails some third-year final papers and is allowed a re-sit, he can aim only for a pass degree.[3.142]

In addition the department of English, early in 1971, proposed to examine in the second year some compulsory language courses. The two problems together brought about an extensive discussion of the problem:

> Before reaching a decision on the proposals of the Department of English, the Committee [on Examinations] proceeded to discuss the general issue of second-year examinations. Professor Sibley spoke in amplification of his memorandum . . . putting the case against [them] . . . except where these were absolutely unavoidable. The Committee noted that the Departments of Classics and History . . . had expressed agreement with Professor Sibley's views. [He] made it clear that his particular objection was to formal examinations in the second year which contributed heavily to the assessment of that unit rather than to relatively light-weight tests; he did not wish to imply that a course should not be assessed entirely in the second year.[3.143]

Other people concerned failed to see the distinction between tests and examinations, and saw possible advantages

> in second-year examinations or examination-like tests: (i) they ensured that students understood their second-year work before proceeding to the third year . . . (ii) they ensured that students did not lose practice in answering a range of questions in a limited time.

The regulation that arose directly out of that debate sums up the present situation, which still displays signs of uneasiness:

> Every new proposal for holding formal examinations in the second year (i.e. in the first year of Part II), other than in free ninth unit courses, shall be carefully considered by the relevant Board of Studies and by the Committee on Examinations, which shall satisfy themselves that a *bona fide* case has been made out and, in scrutinizing such proposals, should pay regard to (a) whether the course in question is likely to be integrated with or related to the student's work in his final year in such a manner

---

[3.142] Agenda for the Committee on Examinations of September 1970.
[3.143] This and the next quotation are taken from the minutes of the Committee on Examinations, February 1971.

as to increase the student's understanding of the course, and (b) the proposed methods, weight and timing of examinations and course work assessment in the course in question, and the likely effect of these on the student's work in his other courses.[3.144]

In what other respects is the Lancaster Part II examination system unlike those of universities founded before 1960? Course work assessment, to which we shall return, is one important feature, but others are: (i) the use of reference material in formal examinations; (ii) the provision of thirty minutes for reading through and selecting questions on certain lengthy text-based examination papers; (iii) the abolition of laboratory work under examination conditions in favour of assessing laboratory note-books as the term progresses; (iv) the increasing use of a *variety* of methods within degree schemes, and (v) the extent of information already noted, which is given to candidates about their performance on particular courses or examinations.

The advantages of these innovations lie in their increased capacity to elicit the best from all candidates, to test a wider variety of material, and to cut down rote learning and the acquisition of techniques acquired simply for the purpose of passing successfully through only one kind of assessment between departments and boards, particularly as regards combined degrees: the problems of what predominance a particular type of assessment ought to have within a total scheme, the anxiety over equivalence of criteria between types of assessment, and the best deployment of the university's external examiners to see whether the system is just and equitable, still remain.

Naturally enough, the performances and characteristics of the candidates under these modified Final examining systems have been the subject of several studies. In 1968 a comparison was made between performance at Advanced Level and at Finals but, as its author said, "nothing remarkable emerges from this Report". The respondents for another study, an investigation on student attitudes to examinations, completed in 1968 under the aegis of the Research Fellow on University Examining Methods (Mr. John Heywood), showed favourable responses to mixed forms of assessment, were rather divided about the value of final examinations at the end of the second year, were quite certain that there should be personal interviews each term about academic performance and regular discussions about written work, and felt that generally continuous assessment had had no effect on final results, but reduced worry, promoted regular work, and placed emphasis on essay-writing rather than wide reading. The scaling of Part I marks was suggested and abandoned again, as we have seen, partly because departments did not like the idea and partly because the definition of the grades was still, even in

---

[3.144] Regulation B 13.1.

1968, too indeterminate and non-standard to be readily accessible to scaling. In an effort to control the use of continuous assessment in the university, an attempt was made in 1969 to create a marking grid, later refined to an experimental record card on which

> The *columns* . . . would represent qualities which the department considers to be appropriate to the provision of a profile of the student's abilities. (This will enable us to compare to what extent the qualities expected of (say) a mathematician are perceived to be different from those expected of an historian.) The *rows* of the cards would refer to elements of assessment made by particular members of staff—class examinations, seminar papers, dissertations, practical work, etc.: the final written examinations could also be included if desired.[3.145]

There was so much opposition to the idea, however, that it was not pursued.

In an attempt to define Part II assessment procedures more precisely and to lessen the variation in procedures between different boards of studies in arriving at a final class of degree, an attempt was then made by Professor Alec Ross to prepare a standard method which could be used by all boards of Examiners for all subjects. Taking as a starting point an array of class marks[3.146] corresponding to the units of assessment, each one was to be fine-graded into good, average or poor of its kind, given a numerical value on a twenty-point scale (a First, for example, could merit 16, 18 or 20 points, and a Third 7, 8, or 9), and a final class determined by totalling the numerical values mentioned above and setting a particular degree class against a particular band of the numerical values. In order to test the consequence of such an arrangement against the existing system, 20 per cent of the marks of the 1971 Finals candidates in certain departments were re-cast in the newly proposed style, but since the approach was found by Senate to be more complex than existing procedures and the hypothetical decisions reached by the coding did not match sufficiently well the degrees awarded at the border-lines, the scheme did not find favour. To meet the needs of the increasingly flexible and complex degree schemes such as consortial courses which were being set up,[3.147] whilst ensuring that external examiners were adequately

---

[3.145] Memorandum by the Vice-Chancellor in amplification of the Marshall Card, from the Committee on Examinations to the Senate, March 1969.

[3.146] The assumption behind this starting point was that the numerical marks for each course had already been negotiated and translated into I, II (i), II (ii), III and Pass, whereas the practice at Lancaster had been (and still is) that a degree class is awarded on the total array of numerical marks.

[3.147] Paper to Committee on Examinations, February 1972:
The more complex degree schemes of the future will mean that combinations are likely to be so varied that it will often be impossible to bring together at one meeting (as happens at present) external examiners representing at least 6 of the 9 units or

consulted, it was acknowledged that a system was needed which would take some account of differences in mark ranges. Another working party to look at assessment was therefore set up (which was also to see whether some kind of profile score could be devised as supplementary information, and to reconsider the previously discarded pass degree). The modifications which this new working party suggested still did not find favour with Senate and the present state of affairs is shown by a Senate minute of March 1972 which agreed that:

> noting the hesitations expressed about the proposed scheme for Part II assessment, no action be taken for one year and that in the meantime no new scheme of study be approved, whether consortial or not, unless the external examiners for all the major or consortial courses involved have certified either that they would be able to attend a joint meeting or that they were satisfied that the final decision should be arrived at in the absence of some of the external examiners involved.

We have already seen how the question of the use of course work assessment (or continuous assessment as it was known until late in 1968) became a contentious issue during the first year of the university's existence in connection with Part I, and what the advantages and disadvantages of it were perceived to be. When Finals were sat for the first time in 1967 this was a feature of the Lancaster system which struck the external examiners very forcibly, and the Academic Advisory Committee in July of that year

> expressed some disquiet about the different ways in which "continuous assessment" was used in the final degree classification of undergraduates (particularly those taking combined major courses).

In fact, great care had been taken to appoint the external examiners well in advance of the need for them so that they could be consulted about systems of assessment being used, and departments had agreed to make arrangements with them concerning the extent of their scrutiny of course work. The difficulty principally arose because some departments used course work only where it could raise examination marks, but others to raise *or* lower them: and because the percentage for which it counted varied so much between subjects. Professor Sibley, who in March 1964 had strongly advocated the use of course work to count for as much as two-thirds of the total weight of marks, for philosophy and for other subjects, naturally came to its defence in the autumn of 1967:

---

internal examiners representing as many as 8 or 9 units. A new procedure is needed which does not rely on the simultaneous attendance of examiners from all departments involved in a scheme of study.

I take it as given and beyond possibility of dispute that the members of a given department, in consultation with external examiner(s) for that department are in a position to decide (a) how best their subject may be taught; (b) the knowledge and skills they seek to impart or develop; (c) the ways appropriate to testing and examining this knowledge and these skills. . . . It is currently emphasized that the universities should be examining their own examining; and in this university we have been encouraged from the outset to experiment, introduce flexibility, and investigate ways of departing where appropriate, from traditional final examination procedures. Our official acceptance of the notion of continuous assessment was an earnest of these intentions.

He also argued that "it would be entirely at variance with the policies of experiment" to require uniformity amongst departments.

Professor Sibley's objection was not only to the notion of uniformity, but perhaps even more to the suggestion that departments provide for the boards of examiners' meetings separate marks for the examination element and for the continuous assessment element, which he saw as

likely to prove at least a red herring; and, at worst, a numerical (and therefore unavoidable) bludgeon—when what is really needed is a verbal discussion of why the candidate is on the borderline. We are trying to classify people, not juggle figures.

A questionnaire sent round to departments in the following spring revealed, predictably, a diverse range of usage. For example, five departments were intending to use course work marks only to raise Part II assessment in 1968, and six in both directions; the maximum percentage accorded to this element varied from 10 per cent to 60 per cent; and attributes stated to be tested by this method, and kinds of work contributing to this element of assessment, are too numerous to list. The Committee on Examinations agreed that it was

desirable that the use of continuous assessment by all departments should follow a common set of principles (though without inhibiting desirable innovation) and that the Committee should prepare, and submit to Senate in due course, proposals for more sophisticated ways of dealing with this problem.[3.148]

The Committee on Examinations continued to investigate the matter, and meanwhile Board C reached a decision, ratified by Senate in December 1968 that of a student's nine final marks (excluding the breadth subject), two could be arrived at without formal written examinations. New approaches were

[3.148] Committee on Examinations, May 1968.

suggested, including a standardized record card,[3.149] as well as proposals designed to clarify and rationalize the use of course work, and to define precisely

> what qualities are being assessed, and to show it is helpful and relevant to provide an assessment of these qualities. We think that it will be agreed— (a) that several different qualities are assessed . . . (b) that the qualities are ill-defined, probably differ from subject to subject, and may not be of proven relevance; (c) that the manner of making and combining the assessments is ill-defined: the process appears to take place in the sub-conscious mind of the examiner, who is supposed to "know" what a First, or a 2.2, looks like.[3.150]

Departmental reactions were, if possible, even more varied than usual when confronted by the new suggestions, and after considering all the objections to them, the Committee on Examinations fell back in November 1969 on the recollection that

> the philosophy behind the proposals was the creation of a clear system which students could understand, where it was known which pieces of course work were taken into consideration in course work assessment and where there was an indication of the manner in which they were included in assessment. There was a danger that the present system was not intelligible or even explicable and that unless we had a clear system there was always the possibility of injustice arising. There was some agreement that although it was desirable that students should be informed of the rules which were applied to their case these rules need not necessarily be the same for each subject. . . .
>
> It was agreed that at this stage the main purpose of the Committee was to make the present system understandable without pressing for uniformity and to consider at a later stage, in the light of further experience, what further rationalization might be desirable.

Mr. Heywood was commissioned to go round departments and find out the differences in usage of course work assessment. He was all too successful for, in June 1970, the Committee expressed concern "at the continued wide variety of ways in which course work assessment marks were determined and used", and therefore recommended to Senate in October that course work assessment should operate both to raise and lower marks, that the boards of examiners were to consult their external examiners and determine what weight course work assessment would have in each unit, that an examination mark and a

---

[3.149] See above, page 207.

[3.150] Memorandum by the Vice-Chancellor for the Committee on Examinations, March 1969.

course work assessment mark should be reported to the relevant board of examiners and "the total settled by the agreed arithmetic process", and that only when the total had been established could boards of examiners "consider other elements which might lead to a mark being adjusted". These proposals were put to departments and boards of studies, and to accommodate the views of those who wished to use course work only to raise marks, a system of continuous assessment which operated both ways, as well as supplementary evidence which operated only to raise marks, was suggested and is enshrined in the university's current regulations.[3.151] The scrutiny of the work that had contributed to the course work assessment was for agreement between the departments and their external examiners. As of 1973, the procedure for departments wishing to experiment is that

> All proposals for variations in the methods of Part II assessment should, after the agreement of relevant external examiners has been obtained, be submitted to the appropriate Board of Studies and should also be reported to the Committee on Examinations: if accepted by the appropriate Board of Studies they should then be submitted to the Senate for approval. . . . Such variations include the number and length of examinations for specific courses, the use of reference material in specific examinations and in examination techniques, and proposals for the admission of marks for dissertations in place of part or the whole of specific units of assessment which would otherwise be derived from performance in formal examinations or other types of evidence.[3.152]

It may be noted in the regulation quoted above that dissertations are included as an accepted element of assessment, although in fact details of their status and provision for them is still unclear. No section of the university has superseded Board C's 1968 ruling that not more than two (excluding the breadth subject) of a student's final marks should be arrived at without examinations, and dissertations and other forms of extended project have gradually entered into more and more degree schemes for certain courses. But, as the Committee on Examinations pointed out in October 1972, there is no generally accepted definition of an undergraduate dissertation, for

> the term "dissertation" was used for work which varied considerably in length and type, that a definition simply in terms of a minimum number of words was inadequate, and that there were other substantial pieces of work at present described by other names (e.g. "projects") which might reason-

---

[3.151] See *Examination Regulations* B2 and II.
[3.152] Regulation B5.

ably be regarded as the equivalent of dissertations. There was also a question as to whether any limitations on the permissible number of Part II dissertations should apply only to cases where the unit of assessment in which the dissertation was offered excluded a final examination.

The Committee concluded that the essence of the problem was to avoid a situation in which a student was so overloaded with very substantial written projects (i.e. dissertations) that his other work suffered, rather than to limit the number of dissertations (however defined) as a matter of principle.

Two more matters connected with examinations should perhaps detain us briefly: the constitution of boards of examiners and, a more recent theme, the desirability of providing academic transcripts analogous to those used in the United States. In early 1966, when a discussion was under way as to whether the minor subject department should automatically be presented at all meetings of boards of examiners,[3.153] it was taken as implicit that "for single major courses the board should consist of all the internal and external examiners of the major department", which by custom was taken to mean all the teaching members of a department.[3.154] In 1970 the regulations were amended to include the stipulation that "names of all internal examiners shall be reported to the Senate before the date at which they commence their duties as examiners", but otherwise remained unchanged, until a controversy arose in one department in 1971. An obligation to examine is laid on members of departments by their contracts; do they also have any kind of right to be examiners? Information on present practices was requested from departments and their views solicited on "the desirability of limiting the number of internal members with a right of attendance", as well as the desirability of having, on the less specialist courses, at least one internal examiner who was not a teacher of the course. The replies that came back from twenty-three departments gave an extremely varied response and the current regulation displays the breadth of the spectrum of views:

> It is recognized that departments have differing views on the composition of Part II Boards of Examiners. Some hold that all members of staff who have taken part in teaching should be full members. . . . Some regard the

---

3.153 It was determined that minor departments should have a right to be represented and given due notice of the times when cases concerning them would be decided, and that if boards of studies wished, they could make the presence of a representative of the minor department obligatory. The custom has, in fact, been that minor departments always do attend.

3.154 The regulation adopted in June 1966 had the following wording: "For single major courses the Board of Examiners shall consist of all internal and external examiners appointed for the examinations in the major subject." External examiners are recommended by departments to boards of studies, and by them to the Senate.

duty of examining as an onerous one which should be undertaken by most or all members of staff in turn, on a rota system. Some consider that there is advantage in as much separation as can be managed between the teaching and examining functions, and would prefer to keep the number of examiners quite small. Some may find advantage in a hybrid system, for example one in which all members of staff who have taken part in Part II teaching assist with assessment, but a more limited group (no doubt varying from year to year on a rota system) will attend and vote at the final Board of Examiners. There are advantages and disadvantages in all these systems, and Senate is not able at this time to rule as to which should be preferred.[3.155]

The notion of academic transcripts had arisen from the last attempt of the working party under Professor Alec Ross to rationalize the examination system, to meet the problem that a degree class and a formal title of a major subject would not be very meaningful in the multi-subject and consortial degree schemes envisaged for the future. The working party saw the need of a profile to supplement the degree class and title, showing a student's range of subjects and his particular strengths and weaknesses, as well as an academic transcript which could be issued to a student when he leaves university, whether he has completed his degree or not. Although Senate approved the suggestion in principle, too many disadvantages were seen, including: the possibility of their becoming something an employer would expect (and not regard just as supplementary evidence), perhaps placing a Lancaster graduate at a disadvantage; that all failure would be revealed in perpetuity; and that other universities and subsequent award-granting bodies might draw the wrong inferences from them. The idea was therefore dropped, although a modified kind of transcript is in future to be made available to those students who go down before completing their degree.[3.156]

Some of the complexity of an examination system which does not rely only on well-worn paths of assessment can perhaps be appreciated by the reader of the foregoing pages; institutions which attempt, as the new universities have, to re-evaluate their procedures and criteria, and experiment with new forms, discover that they have opened a Pandora's box of continual self-enquiry and, at the end of the day, still have not found definitive answers to the basic questions of what a university is trying to evaluate, for whom, and how. The

---

[3.155] Appendix A to the Examination Regulations.

[3.156] The members of the Committee of Vice-Chancellors and Principals (in June 1972) also resisted the development of formal standardized transcripts, on the grounds that they could "militate against efforts to underline the inherent value of three years full time study associated with the concept of a degree", and that universities would probably prefer to retain "the opportunity for comment in confidence on the academic performance of individual students".

Vice-Chancellor, in a paper for the Senate conference of 1972, presented forcefully some salient points:

> It remains unclear what a class in a final honours examination is supposed to measure. High honours are probably quite a good measure of ability to undertake research and teaching in higher education. In so far as a student obtains a higher class by intelligent planning of his time and consistent hard work, the class is indicating qualities relevant for many purposes. But a high class is often obtained despite the existence of faults which will later prove to cancel out the value, to the man and to the world, of high intelligence: and a low class may simply indicate that there has not been time enough to overcome early handicaps. . . .
>
> It is, indeed, obvious that no single indicator of the many dimensions of "quality" can be much use. It can be argued that the classification of honours degrees exists, not to convey information, but to provide the student with a standard (like a four-minute mile) which he can try to beat. . . .
>
> Could we, however, allow students to sort themselves out, by permitting them to opt for an unclassified degree which would be awarded provided their course work had been adequate? It can be argued that some students do not need a classified degree: that they would work more fruitfully free from the special stress of final examinations: that there is no point in treating education as a race which *all* students are required to run.
>
> Such a system could be adapted to provide a greater variety: an unclassified honours degree for those with a record of good and reliable performance in course work, a pass degree for those with an adequate performance at a lower level . . . and a diploma of higher education to those preferring to leave after two years.
>
> The obvious disadvantage is that such an option would attract the drifters. This would have to be dealt with by having some regular, substantial and enforceable requirements of course work. It is argued by some students that they should be allowed to do exactly as they like during the course, and to fail if they wish. This does not seem to me defensible when the greater part of the cost comes from the public purse, and there are not enough places for those wishing to enter higher education.

CHAPTER 4

Organizational Structure

(i) The constitution

There are various constraints on the autonomy of universities, even for those who have their own charter and

> are hereby constituted and henceforth for ever shall be one Body Politic and Corporate with perpetual succession.[4.1]

The first of these, obviously, are the conditions laid down in the individual institution's Charter and Statutes, and the necessity to have any change in them approved by the Lords of the Privy Council. Arising from these are the rights of the Visitor.[4.2] The next constraint is the financial control operated by the U.G.C. and, administered through that agency, by the Secretary of State for Education and Science, on new buildings and academic developments,[4.3] staffing levels, and recurrent expenditure. R. O. Berdahl[4.4] has traced the development of university-state relations up until 1963, but further hearings before the Committee of Public Accounts in 1965 and 1966[4.5] resulted in a report to the House of Commons which elicited, on 26 July 1967, a statement from Mr. Anthony Crosland in which he said:

[4.1] Charter of the University of Lancaster, clause 2.

[4.2] See page 21 in Chapter 1.

[4.3] See the "Preliminary Memorandum of General Guidance on Quinquennial Planning, 1972–77", Appendix II of the *U.G.C. Annual Survey, 1969–70*, Cmnd. 4593.

[4.4] See R. O. Berdahl, *British Universities and the State* (C.U.P. 1959), and also an article by the same author, "University-State Relations Re-examined" in *Sociological Review Monograph No. 7* (1963).

[4.5] See *House of Commons Papers*: 31–1, 108–1, 224–1, 265–1 (1964–65); and 98–1, 158–1 (1966–67).

The Government do not propose to alter the present well-tried and flexible arrangements for financing universities by the capital grants and block recurrent grants made available and distributed on the advice of an independent University Grants Committee. We shall therefore maintain the present system by which block grants are allocated to universities by the University Grants Committee with the consequent freedom of discretion on the part of universities as to how they should be spent. It is no part of the Comptroller and Auditor General's duty to question policy decisions or decisions reached on academic grounds. His function is to comment on the propriety, regularity and efficiency with which moneys voted by Parliament are administered by those to whom they are entrusted.[4.6]

As from 1 January 1968, therefore, the Comptroller and Auditor General has had access to all the books of universities, to have them scrutinized as he sees fit. There are also, as well as the common law of the land, local bye-laws to be taken heed of, as well as more subtle constraints in the way of locally expressed public opinion (particularly through the university's Court), and the opportunities or disadvantages of a particular environment: medicine, agriculture, or textile technology are obvious examples of developments that would be as wholly inapt in some areas as they are well suited to others.

Yet, even having regard to all these limitations on their freedom, British universities still have an enviable liberty in comparison with their counterparts elsewhere. They are free to teach whatsoever they themselves deem to be appropriate material, irrespective of the government in power. They can appoint whomsoever they please, and conduct research into any area which they consider of sufficient interest, subject to having the necessary funds. They can, like public companies with articles of association, solicit funds from private individuals and public bodies and apply them according to their own internally agreed priorities. They are at liberty to examine as they think fit, subject to the consent of their external examiners (themselves members of comparable and sympathetic institutions), and it is their decision whom they admit to degrees and diplomas, and at what level. Even within the limits laid on them in their acceptance of the grants-in-aid and recurrent funds from the public funds, which by 1962 were contributing 88 per cent of universities' total income,[4.7] they are free to allocate these funds at their discretion, within broadly defined limits. Finally, they are able to admit students of their own selection and, again within broad limits, put them into departments in numbers they have themselves determined. Whether universities will continue

---

[4.6] See *Hansard*, Volume 751, Columns 749–754 (1966–67).
[4.7] Appendix 4 to *Report of the Committee on Higher Education* (1963), Table 9.

to enjoy this degree of freedom in the future is an open question, particularly in the light of the most recent White Papers on the subject.[4.8]

Moving from a national to a more local standpoint there are several, apparently conflicting, ways of looking at a university. One participant will see a body of students, being taught in their departments, living in their colleges, and being cared for by the various bodies set up for the purpose. Another will observe a formal organization, starting with the Charter and Statutes, and proceeding through the university committee machinery. Yet another will have a picture of so many feet of main duct or telephone cable, of battalions of waitresses, cleaners, secretaries and technicians, of square footage of flooring and roof space to maintain, of so many car parking spaces, refectory places, or beds. Others may perceive even smaller fragments, while a few will apprehend the whole complex entity. In other chapters we shall be looking through the eyes of the first and last groups: in this one we shall concentrate on the viewpoints of the second and third groups, inasmuch as they look inwards to the mechanisms, first constitutional and secondly managerial, of the university community.

Professor Harold Perkin has described and discussed in detail the government of the new universities.[4.9] As he points out, the U.G.C. in 1964 made it clear that

The members of the Academic Planning Boards had been selected with a view to encouraging such experimentation and we let it be known to the Boards that . . . we were anxious that they should feel free to recommend major departures from the more orthodox pattern of academic development and organization . . . that, for national institutions, there was still too great a tendency to look to local rather than regional or national sources for lay help in the higher levels of university government (e.g. the Court and Council); that some of the higher bodies, particularly the Courts, could be reduced in size and their sphere of influence diminished. . . . While all the new universities intend to follow the orthodox pattern by creating a Court which consists of very large numbers of local representatives—an indication of the importance which they attach to the maintenance of local interest in their universities—they have limited its field of responsibility; and they have gone some way to achieve wider representation of academic staff on matters of academic governance, either through greater provision for non-professorial representation on various bodies, or through the introduction of new bodies such as a General Board consisting of the

[4.8] See: H.M.S.O., *Education: A Framework for Expansion* (Cmnd. 5174, December 1972); and H.M.S.O., *Report from the Expenditure Committee; Further and Higher Education* (December 1972).

[4.9] H. J. Perkin, *Innovation in the New Universities of the United Kingdom* (O.E.C.D., 1969), Chapter 5.

academic staff as a whole, or both. They have also given wardens or their counterparts representation on the Senates. On the whole, however, we should have welcomed in the statutes of the new universities some greater changes in the system of university government. For example, we should like to have seen statutory provision to give junior members of the teaching staff some responsibility for administration of small units (such as correspond to departments in the older civic universities).[4.10]

Professor Perkin expresses disappointment at the limited extent of the organizational innovation he was able to find in the new universities; a disappointment, he felt, hinted at by the U.G.C. in the passage quoted above. However, there are perhaps two considerations which the report and his account do not take into consideration. The first is the weight of the "model" charter and statutes provided by the Privy Council for use by the new universities, based on the form used earlier by the civic universities—comparison may be made, for example, with the charters and statutes of Bristol, Liverpool or Southampton—representing a broad hint of the kind of document which would be acceptable to them. Secondly, British political history is an account of evolution of forms of government, rather than change by revolution: in following the style of gradual change, the new universities were perhaps avoiding the perils that accompany a more revolutionary style, and some of the changes which were achieved may have more far-reaching consequences in the British university system than are realized in 1972. This is particularly so when we look at the growth of student membership of university government.[4.11]

Already the Statutes of the University of Lancaster have been altered, although the Charter remains unchanged and therefore contains historical relics in the way of references to obsolete bodies such as the Executive Council and the Academic Advisory Committee. A Statute Revision Committee was set up in 1967 and after negotiations within the university and submission to the Privy Council, the revised version of the Statutes came into effect on 23 March 1971. Nor is Lancaster alone in this rapid updating of its government: for example, the University of East Anglia has recently set up a Constitution Committee, and Stirling also has a Statute Revision Committee in active operation, while Warwick has been discussing its proposed revisions with the Privy Council. Changes in the Statutes will be discussed as they affect particular issues as we look at the several bodies governing Lancaster.

Taking these bodies in the order in which they appear in the university's Charter, we come first to the Court of the University

---

4.10 U.G.C. *University Development 1957–62* (Cmnd. 2267), paragraphs 296–300.
4.11 See pages 272 to 291 below.

which shall have the right to receive reports on the working of the University, to discuss any matters relating to the University, and to convey its opinions therein to the Council or to the Senate of the University.[4.12]

Other duties of Court include the appointment of future Chancellors, and (on the recommendation of the Council) of future Pro-Chancellors, as well as all Deputy Pro-Chancellors. The Chancellor "shall be entitled to preside" over meetings both of Court and of Council, but in the case of Court, her place is taken by the Deputy Pro-Chancellor, the chairmanship of this body being the one designated function of that office. From 1964 to 1972 this role was filled by Sir Alfred Bates, but at the Court of December 1972 two further Deputy Pro-Chancellors were elected. This made a total of three, and raised the theoretical issue of whether it would not be possible for Court to elect an indefinite number of holders of this post, there being no numerical limit given in the Charter or Statutes.[4.13]

Court is a very large body indeed.[4.14] The chief officers of the university (Chancellor, Pro-Chancellor, Deputy Pro-Chancellors, the Vice-Chancellor and the Pro-Vice-Chancellors) are *ex officio* members, as are all members of the Senate, the Council and the Student Representative Council (bodies to which we shall return). Other *ex officio* members are the Lords Lieutenant and the Sheriffs of Lancashire, Westmorland and Cumberland; the Lord Lieutenant of the Isle of Man; the Anglican bishops of Carlisle, Sodor and Man, Blackburn, and Lancaster; and the Roman Catholic Bishop of Lancaster; the Constable of Lancaster Castle; the Vice-Chancellor of the Duchy of Lancaster, and the Clerk of the Council of the Duchy; members of the House of Commons for certain named constituencies, the mayors and town clerks of the city of Lancaster and the borough of Morecambe and Heysham, the chairman and clerks of the County Councils of Lancashire, Westmorland and Cumberland; and the chairmen and chief education officers of certain named education committees.[4.15] Amongst the appointed members may be mentioned the four nominees of the Privy Council, twenty graduates of the university and fifteen representatives of its assistant staff; persons selected by neighbouring universities and colleges, and by various local government

---

[4.12] Charter of the University of Lancaster, clause 11.

[4.13] Under the revised Statutes, the Deputy Pro-Chancellors are *ex officio* members of the Council. Unless an academic Deputy Pro-Chancellor is elected, therefore, the effect in practice of increasing the number of holders of this office is to increase the proportion of the lay membership of the Council.

[4.14] See Table 4 (page 20) of Appendix 4 to the Robbins Report for some comparative sizes of Court at some civic universities in 1961–62.

[4.15] The membership of the Court (and also of the Council—see page 220 ff below) has been affected by the changes arising out of the Local Government Act 1972. These changes are still under discussion with the Dept. of the Environment at the time of going to press.

bodies, other church representatives, and those appointed by local learned or professional societies and other local associations selected by the university's Council; as well as individuals invited by the Court and the Council. The additional categories created under the revised statutes were the student representatives, the university graduates and assistant staff, and representatives of two regional polytechnics (which had come into existence in the intervening period), as well as an increase in individuals appointed by Court itself and by Council. There is a total possible membership of over four hundred (of whom somewhat more than a quarter are members of the university), but some categories are not filled to their quota, and a certain proportion of members are so under more than one category. Court meets once a year (so far each December), its members having previously received an annual report and statement of accounts. There is also provision for special meetings to be called, to discuss important matters, either by Council or by written request of fifty members of Court. So far no such special meeting has been held, and the annual meetings have usually discussed matters of general educational interest, such as new buildings, new academic developments, finance, and student discipline.

It is important to emphasize that, unlike earlier civic foundations, and although having the same type of membership as their equivalent bodies, Court is not formally designated as the governing body of the university, a role shared at Lancaster by the Council and the Senate. Court is a means of communication with leaders of the local community and the region, a forum for gathering the opinions or channelling the strongly-felt views of representatives of the general public. It fulfils, however, an additional function as the only place where the graduates of the university have a voice (and then only since March 1971): for, despite the expressed wish of the Executive Council in July 1962 that

> recognizing the value of informed graduate opinion, provision should be made for Convocation to act in a general consultative and advisory capacity,

no further mention of it occurs anywhere else in the early discussions of structure, and no body, formal or informal, representative of the graduates of the university has been set up.

Council, by contrast with the Court, is tiny, being by definition of its membership under the Statutes no larger than thirty-one[4.16] persons. Besides the Vice-Chancellor, there are nine other members elected by the Senate (of which no more than six may be professors). The Chancellor, Pro-Chancellor

---

[4.16] Before the Statutes were revised, neither students nor Deputy Pro-Chancellors had seats on Council, which had then a total membership of twenty-five.

and Deputy Pro-Chancellors, who are members *ex officio*, are in practice lay, as are the Mayor of Lancaster and the representatives of the county and the Duchy of Lancaster. The four nominees of the Pro-Chancellor and six elected by Court from its own membership could in theory be either lay or academic, although as of the end of 1972 these two categories are filled, all but one, by non-academic persons. In addition, since the revised statutes came into operation, there are three student members: to provide for the consideration of reserved business there is delegated to a Committee of Council,

> of which in no case students shall be members . . . the power to appoint, promote or dismiss or to determine the powers, duties, remuneration or terms or conditions of office of an officer or class of officer.[4.17]

Council may thus be seen as a partnership between lay and academic and fulfils the requirement of Sir Malcolm Knox of the Academic Planning Board who in November 1962 stated firmly that

> a university ought to be self-governing and that therefore its supreme governing body (the Council) should be so constituted as to be immune so far as possible from political and other non-academic pressures. I believe that at least one half of the Council should be academic, though it is equally essential that some of its members should be drawn from outside the university, though they ought to have either an academic background or else long experience of contact with the affairs of the university. . . . Council should be as small as possible, and that about 20 is the maximum number. As soon as numbers rise above 20, deliberation on important questions of policy becomes impossible. . . . What I want to plead for is more academic representation than the private universities in the U.S.A. have, and some stronger non-academic representation than that which the Scottish University Courts (i.e. in English, Councils), have. . . . The non-professorial members on the St. Andrews University Court are appointed from amongst and by the non-professorial members of the Senate. I think that this is a mistake, and that the non-professorial members of the Council should be appointed by *all* members of the non-professorial staff.

Although Sir Malcolm's last recommendation about election by non-professorial staff to Council was not adopted, at least the situation has remained sufficiently non-rigid for the professorial representation not always to be at the maximum possible. Numbers have been kept small, and there is no observable pressure to increase them. In fact, the figures given by Lord Robbins' committee show most universities have councils of between thirty and fifty

---

[4.17] University of Lancaster, Revised Statute 13 (1).

members,[4.18] and although comparisons with the 1972–73 Calendars of the institutions he cites show several increases in varying amounts, the civic universities have set a pattern of councils of moderate size which Lancaster has been able to trim still further. The Academic Planning Board, in March 1963, saw the Council as

> the governing body of the university, save in such matters as are reserved to the Senate. We have contrived to keep it as small as is practicable because we contemplate it as an effective working body. The Chancellor, Pro-Chancellor and Vice-Chancellor are to be members, *ex-officio*, and in addition we contemplate equal numbers of members of the University academic staff and of outside persons able by their knowledge of and interest in education, and by their out-standing attainments in their own walks of life to contribute effectively to the higher direction of the University.

If we regard the student members as *sui generis*, and the Chancellor as not normally taking part in the routine affairs of the Council this left a ratio in 1973 of seventeen lay members to ten academic members. This may suggest a severe imbalance, but in a small body where the lay attendance is generally low in proportion to the academic, and where the members are able to talk informally and know each other well, at meetings to which other officers of the university are necessarily invited for business relevant to them, consideration of a body's representativeness solely on a numerical basis can be misleading—except perhaps for those occasions on which very contentious issues are being discussed.

The word "supreme" is applied to none of the Lancaster governing bodies, unlike the earlier models of other universities. This was a conscious decision at the time the Charter and Statutes were being drawn up and the parliamentary agents acting for the university had queried the choice of the Council as the governing body rather than the Court. The Vice-Chancellor pointed out that

> the major point about the structure of the governing bodies of the university is copied from the Charter already granted to the University of Sussex, and since we have been under some pressure to go even further and abolish the Court altogether, I think that you need have no fears about the acceptance of the structure proposed. . . . My Academic Planning Board was anxious to avoid the reference to the Council as "supreme" governing body, because there are, in fact, certain powers effectively reserved to the Senate.[41.9]

[4.18] Table 5 (p. 21) of Appendix 4 to the Robbins Report.
[4.19] Letter of the Vice-Chancellor of 12 July 1963 to Messrs. Sherwood & Co.

Previously, decisions had not been divided into discrete categories and distributed between the several bodies of a university's government, as may be seen by the following (characteristic) statement of the customary chain of command

> The Court shall exercise control over the Council by means of Statutes and of resolutions passed at meetings of Court and not otherwise and over the Senate through the Council and not otherwise and over the Boards of the Faculties through the Council and the Senate and not otherwise.

The Lancaster Charter instead provides that there

> shall be a Council of the University (hereinafter called "the Council") which, subject to this Our Charter and the Statutes of the University (including the rights of the Senate of the University defined therein) shall be the Governing Body of the University.
>
> The Council shall have custody and use of the Common Seal of the University, and shall control, manage and administer all the revenue and property of the University.
>
> It shall be the duty of the Council to take into consideration any comments or representations on the affairs of the University made to it by the Court or by the Senate of the University.[4.20]

The Council therefore has the duty to appoint certain key officers of the university; the successors to the first Vice-Chancellor, and also the pro-vice-chancellors, an acting vice-chancellor if such were needed, the university secretary, the librarian, and the college principals (subject to certain types of consultation).[4.21] The appointment, duties, remuneration and conditions of service of the other officers[4.22] of the university are also the responsibility of Council, besides, as we have seen, all the financial dealings of the university. The welfare of all employees and former employees lies in Council's province, as does also certain aspects of the welfare of the students. It usually meets seven times a year, with extraordinary meetings as necessary.

Council's sub-committees illustrate the scope of a selection of its main activities. There is the Finance Committee, charged with the overall supervision and regulation of the university's finances; the Buildings Committee,

---

[4.20] University of Lancaster Charter, clause 12.

[4.21] See Revised Statute 3 (4) to (8). For certain categories, e.g. the vice-chancellor, there is provision for a joint committee of Senate and Council.

[4.22] Officers under the *revised* statutes are defined as meaning "all persons with a contract of service with the University", as well as the Chancellor, the Pro-Chancellor, and the Deputy Pro-Chancellors and "all other holders of unpaid offices in the University". Again, all officers eligible to be members of the F.S.S.U. are, under the revised Statutes, members of the university by virtue of their posts, whereas formerly they were so only "by Ordinance, or by decision of the Council".

which controls the development of the site, and the planning of all buildings, and the general supervision of contract work; and the Assistant Staff Committee which advises on all aspects of the conditions of employment of the assistant staff[4.23] of the University. All these three committees have a lay chairman and, in the case of the first two, certain members selected by Senate and some student representation.

The Academic Promotions Committee, whose name speaks for itself, has in addition to *ex officio* members, an academic membership, appointed by the Senate, who are "either professorial or of a status at which promotion by recommendation of the committee is no longer in question".[4.24] Of these committees, that for assistant staff began as a joint committee of Council and Senate but became in January 1968 a full committee of Council. That for promotions began as a committee of Senate alone, and became a sub-committee of Council as recently as November 1971, when formal procedures for the termination of probationary appointments (and hence any appeals against such terminations) were being negotiated for the first time between the university and the Association of University Teachers: the change thereby making Council, as provided for by the Charter and Statutes, an appeal tribunal,[4.25] until other special bodies had been set up, either regionally or nationally.

Thus in many ways the Lancaster Council may be seen as the natural development of the councils of the civic universities[4.26] in its main functions closely akin to the Councils of other institutions receiving their charters in the mid-sixties, and consistent with a recent pronouncement from the A.U.T. which states of the council that:

> Traditionally, the lay majority has been the guarantee of proper management as well as the expression of local interest. It is right that this majority should persist, though a simple majority is enough. The reasons may have changed somewhat. Effectively the U.G.C. exercises so many detailed controls on funding and spending and the Comptroller and Auditor

---

[4.23] "Assistant Staff" is a broad term and includes all staff not on F.S.S.U. or comparable grades. See also page 251 below.

[4.24] See the *Staff Handbook, 1972–3*, page 92. The Committee is empowered to implement its decisions forthwith, subject to the prior approval of the Chairman of Council, and a subsequent submission to Council of a full report of promotions approved, and other decisions in summary form only. Controversial decisions, of course, e.g. for dismissal or non-confirmation of tenure, are dealt with under special procedures.

[4.25] The ramifications of the Industrial Relations Act, which came into full effect on 1 January 1972, have a bearing on the type of machinery and procedure to be adopted for the future.

[4.26] It is worth reiteration that the custom of having a Council with lay membership comes only from the nineteenth century foundations and has no parallel in the government of Oxford and Cambridge. Nor, indeed, does the Court.

General ensures such a degree of public accountability that the lay majority is now required to strengthen the representations made by the university and to defend its autonomy. In a more complex society lay members can also provide a width of experience and expertise to help develop and protect the university.[4.27]

In other words, the laymen should no longer be members of Council to protect the investment that the local community have made in the university but rather, the centre of control having moved from local to national government, to protect the university against its new masters. Quite a transmogrification, and, interestingly, one endorsed by the Murray Report on the governance of the University of London, which sees lay members as having

> far more important functions, as the last line of defence against undue encroachment on genuine academic freedom of decision by the government machine, and as independent but knowledgeable advisers who are sufficiently detached to be able to scrutinize impartially academic proposals and views on priorities.[4.28]

The debate continues on a national level as to the relative virtues of bicameral or unitary control of internal university government. As long as the Court was the supreme governing body, the unitary (or hierarchical) structure seemed the obvious one. When Court, however, was reduced to an essentially advisory role, then any conflict inherent between the Council and the Senate of a particular institution was bound to show. Lord Robbins' committee categorically stated that it was no part of a Council's function to

> interfere in the business of internal academic organization, still less in matters of syllabuses and curricula. The situation is likely to become intolerable if such attempts are made.[4.29]

The Grimond Report from the University of Birmingham a decade later, however, doubted

> whether the continued division between academic and non-academic matters is valid on grounds of principle or practicability; we doubt whether it is right that the Council should be expected to take decisions on matters which depend basically on academic considerations of which the lay members are kept in ignorance by virtue of their exclusion from academic discussions; we feel there is much to be said for academic members taking

---

4.27 A.U.T.: "Report from the Working Party on the Government of the Universities and the Structure of the Profession," October 1972.

4.28 *Final Report of the Committee of Enquiry into the Governance of the University of London* (1972), paragraph 269.

4.29 H.M.S.O., *Report on Higher Education*, Cmnd. 2154 (1963), paragraph 666.

full responsibility for non-academic as well as academic matters, but with the help and guidance of lay members who can bring experience and expertise from outside the University. . . . These thoughts lead us to consider the possibility of a unicameral Governing Body to combine most of the functions of the existing Council and Senate.[4.30]

Yet, lest the wheel of fashion be thought to be turning heedlessly, two months later, we find the Murray Report on the University of London urging a bicameral system (for a total university staff of 6,500). The argument runs that if a unicameral body were set up which was large, because fully representative, it would have to work through subordinate bodies, and if small enough for decision-making, it would be so unrepresentative as to need a larger body to turn to. The report continues:

It seems to us in fact that the concept of a unitary governmental structure would inevitably be eroded in practice by the sheer size and complexity of the University's responsibilities and administrative needs; and that, whatever the formal constitution might say, the realities of the situation, and the specialization of functions represented by the University as a business institution and by the University as an academic institution, would result in a distribution of real authority not very different from that reflected in the Council/Senate structure which most universities in this country still find serviceable.[4.31]

The mood in the early 1960's, however, was towards two separate bodies with distinct responsibilities. Whether such a separation can be totally accomplished may in the future be put to the test: let us look at two examples. The responsibilities of the Council include provision "for the welfare of the students of the University". Yet the Senate has as one of its functions "The regulation and superintendance of the living conditions and discipline of the students of the University", as well as "The exclusion of any student, permanently or for a stated time, from any part of the University or its precincts, or from attendance at any course or from entry to any examination", and some of these clauses may well be seen to further or hinder a student's welfare. The second example concerns principals of colleges who shall be "generally responsible to the Council and the Senate for maintaining the effective working and good order of that College". Inasmuch as Council has to provide the buildings, premises, furniture and equipment of the university, the principal's responsibility is obviously to Council and, inasmuch as discipline is the affair of the Senate, then it is to that body that he takes disciplinary

---

[4.30] *Consultative Document prepared by the Review Body appointed by the Council of the University of Birmingham* (January 1972), paragraphs 11.13 and 11.14.

[4.31] *Final Report of the Committee of Enquiry into the Governance of the University of London* (1972), paragraphs 275 and 276.

matters. Yet what happens in a case of arson, which may be both damage to fabric and a disciplinary offence, or drug trafficking, where the law relates to the use of particular premises and yet the university also has another disciplinary problem to solve?

The next phase of debate was how large and how professorial the Senate ought to be in its composition. For a university of 3,240 students and 562 F.S.S.U. teaching and administrative staff, the Lancaster Senate of a possible maximum of 72 in 1972–73 is relatively large:[4.32] Warwick in 1970 suggested a maximum of 30,[4.33] and Birmingham in 1972 with over 7,000 students was looking (under the Grimond proposals) for 152, which represented a reduction of forty. Seven of the Lancaster senators in 1972–73, however, were members by virtue of more than one category, reducing its size in practice to 65, and of these nine were students (one *ex officio*, six by virtue of college election, and two student officers by co-optation). Of the remaining 56, one was the vice-chancellor, one the librarian, 29 were professors (of 42 at this rank on the staff, but several were also pro-vice-chancellors, college principals, heads of departments, chairmen of boards or representatives of the colleges or the boards), and the remaining 25 were heads of colleges or departments or chairmen of boards of studies, or elected representatives of those bodies.[4.34]

The size of the Senate will inevitably continue to grow, not as fast as when each professor was automatically a member, but by three with each new college (principal, one other senior member, and one student), two with each new board of study (the chairman and one other), and one with each new department (the head) as well as any corrections that may take place to smooth anomalies, such as an undue number of professors. Bruce R. Williams has pointed out that

In established universities the easiest way to provide for the participation of non-professorial members of the academic staff was to add to the

---

[4.32] Compare Table 9 of the Robbins Report (universities by number of full-time students) with Table 6 of Appendix 4 (membership of senate or academic boards).

[4.33] "Report of the Senate Committee on the Government and Administration of the University of Warwick" (November 1970), Section III (A), paragraphs 2 to 6.

[4.34] By virtue of a provision under the revised statutes, which stipulates that "If at any time the number of members of the Senate who are neither professors nor students falls below three-tenths of the total number of members, the Senate shall co-opt additional members of the University engaged in teaching or research, who shall be neither professors nor students", the proportion of non-professorial staff is safeguarded. Simple arithmetic shows that in 1972–73 the Lancaster Senate was required to have on it twenty-two non-professorial staff, and in fact had twenty-five. The Privy Council was very insistent at the time of the Statutes were revised that there should remain a formula to determine the proportion of non-professorial members of staff. Before the revision of the statutes, informal provision was made for there to be non-voting observers so that, for example, a non-professorial head of department could at least receive the papers of the Senate and be in attendance at its meetings. The 1973–74 Senate is even larger, because further new departments have been created.

membership of senate, often at the cost of making an over-large body still larger. Even some of the new universities, e.g. Lancaster (founded in 1964) and Sussex (founded in 1961), provided for *ex-officio* membership of all professors and a non-professorial membership as a proportion of *ex-officio* members. York (1963) on the other hand, influenced by practice at the London School of Economics, provided for a professorial board (with special responsibility for appointments and promotions) and an elected general academic board of 40, including at least eight professors, while Newcastle upon Tyne, when it separated from Durham in 1963, provided for a senate which is mostly elected by all academic staff and limited to 40 members,

to which he adds a wry footnote:

As a member of the committee responsible for planning the University of Lancaster I bear part of the responsibility for this. At the time, 1962–63, when my own University of Manchester had not changed its constitution, it seemed quite daring to provide for a non-professorial membership at a fixed percentage of what the number of professors might become![4.35]

The Academic Planning Board had thought that "the Colleges can be used as a suitable piece of machinery by which the non-professorial staff would exercise their right to vote some of their number on to the Court and the Senate of the University", and the original statutes followed this in its provision that appointed members of Senate should be "Members of the academic staff, not otherwise members of Senate, appointed by the syndicates of the Colleges in equal numbers from each College" (to a number not exceeding half the number of professors). At a late stage in the revision of the statutes, it was agreed that, in order to preserve the proper representation of non-professorial staff which could increase (but slowly) with the size of the university, while at the same time restoring "a proper symmetry between the academic and social organization of the University", there should be one member of staff elected from each syndicate and one from each board of study (instead of, as previously, two from each syndicate).

The alteration in the *ex officio* membership of the Senate between the original and revised statutes reflects this uneasiness about the role of professors, since the 1964 version has "the vice-chancellor, the professors, the librarian, the principals of colleges if not otherwise members [and] the chairmen of boards of studies if not otherwise members" whereas the 1971 revision has listed "the vice-chancellor, the pro-vice-chancellors, the principals of colleges, the chairmen of boards of studies, the heads of departments,

---

[4.35] Bruce R. Williams, "University Values and University Organization", in *Minerva*, Vol. X, No. 2, April 1972, page 276.

the librarian, [and] the chairman of the Student Representative Council". Of the six colleges, three at present have professors as principals, while of the seven boards of studies, none has a professor as chairman (although the Vice-Chancellor is chairman of one). Depending on the speaker's point of view this absence of professorial dominance in such posts can be argued either as the furthering of the egalitarian process within the university; or as a sign that colleges and boards of studies have no real power but are an outward sham, while the source of authority resides ever more firmly in the departments whose heads, twenty-one of whom are professors, become, it may be argued, more like mediaeval barons[4.36] and ever more contemptuous of the constitutional machinery. Certainly the record of attendance at Senate itself indicates that there is an extent of decision-taking in that body which is felt by members of the university to be significant; of six consecutive ordinary meetings in 1972–73, for example, numbers present fell below seven-eighths of membership on only one occasion (in the middle of the examination period).[4.37]

What, then, are the particular responsibilities of this body? The provision in the Charter spells out clearly what the Senate's distinctive responsibilities and relationship with the Council are to be:

There shall be a Senate of the University (hereinafter called "the Senate") which, subject to this Our Charter and the Statutes of the University, shall be responsible for the academic work of the University, both in teaching and in research, and for the regulation and superintendence of the education, living conditions and discipline of the students of the University.

The Senate may discuss any matters relating to the University, and may convey its opinions thereon to the Council.[4.38]

The Statute which amplifies this statement declares that

the Senate shall have all such powers as are necessary for the discharge of its functions . . . including the following:
(a) The direction, regulation and promotion of the teaching and research of the University.
(b) The conduct of examinations and the appointment of internal and external examiners.
(c) The grant of Degrees, Diplomas, Certificates and other academic distinctions.

[4.36] See, for example, N. Smart, "Red rose and Quaker grey at Lancaster", *Times Higher Education Supplement*, No. 30 (5 May 1972).
[4.37] The high attendance is of course assisted to some extent by the provision for other than co-opted members to be able to send a substitute if they cannot be present themselves.
[4.38] Charter of the University of Lancaster, clause 13.

(d) The regulation and superintendence of the living conditions and discipline of the students of the University.

(e) The exclusion of any student, permanently or for a stated time, from any part of the University or its precincts, or from attendance at any course or from entry to any examination.[4.39]

As for the Council, there is provision for a Committee of the Senate, at which students are not present, for the discussion of reserved business.

The main problem of the Senate has been to keep its great volume of business in a manageable form: it is by no means unknown for meetings to continue for up to five hours, twice a term, and this only with the business rigorously sorted and categorized beforehand, into matters for report, for formal ratification, and for full-scale debate. As its secretary rather despairingly wrote in August 1971:

> The business of the Senate is seldom scanty: each set of papers has dozens of documents in it and demands much time from the reader. The bulk is daunting; no less so is the confusion that arises because the papers are not distributed on one occasion but on several, the last supplementary distribution being made at high speed and imperfectly on the eve of the meeting.

Reports and proposals flow in constantly from all over the university; not only from the sub-committees of the Senate, but from departments, individuals and, to a lesser extent, outside bodies as well. As early as 1966 a small sub-committee, headed by the Vice-Chancellor, reported on the organization of Senate business, noting that

> The purpose of improving the efficiency with which Senate conducts its business is to give Senate every incentive to reduce the time of its meetings and to draw all matters to a firm conclusion.

There were therefore to be statements of motion, brief reports from all sub-committees, a calendar of meetings to co-ordinate business, a more formalized reference numbering of papers, written papers to suggest possible ways of resolving disagreements, a maximum of three hours set for each meeting, and a Nominations and Minor Business Committee, which was to be set up to deal with such matters as "representation on Committees and Working Parties in order to achieve a full spread and balance of members of the University and also decide minor matters which do not warrant the attention of a full meeting of Senate". By the following year, however, the committee structure of the university needed consideration, and the Vice-Chancellor enunciated some general principles with a wider application than Senate alone:

[4.39] Revised Statute 12. The Council does not have to ratify any decision of the Senate taken on the matters defined in the provisions listed above.

As instruments of decision, committees should be as small as possible, and should not be required to decide matters which are of no great importance and could be decided by an individual.

However, committees are on occasion a means of providing a flow of information. . . . This may suggest a larger size than is strictly necessary for the decision function. . . . Committees concerned with controversial problems of allocation or equity should be small, so that members can set on one side their special interests. The larger the committee, the more likely it is that members will act as representatives of an interest rather than as individuals.

The number of man-hours spent on a meeting (and thus its cost) should have some relation to the value of its output. For instance, even if members of staff are valued at their average cost per hour, a meeting of Senate costs at least £450.[4.40] The volume of business probably justifies this cost; perhaps the justification for the time spent by syndicates is less assured. . . .

No Professor should sit on a committee unless there is some reason why the appointment of a more junior member of staff is inappropriate. At present we are preventing our best and most experienced scholars from getting on with work of scholarship.[4.41]

At the same time the Nominations and Minor Business Committee was replaced by a Senate General Purposes Committee.

Yet by December 1968 the plight of the senators would seem to have been desperate, for the business coming to the General Purposes Committee

has consisted of trivialities as easily settled by a pin or computer as by the species *Homo persipiens*. The committee has met but little, deliberated but briefly when it has met. . . . At the same time the business of the Senate is heavy. At its last meeting the Senate's reaction to the impossible demands of a gargantuan agenda was to refer certain items to its committees for preliminary consideration; but some time was wasted which might have been saved had the items been thus referred by some authorized steering committee at the outset.[4.42]

The suggestion was therefore made, and adopted, that there should be a Senate Steering Committee which would "examine on behalf of Senate all proposals, recommendations and requests" and refer items to other committees if they were in need of prior discussion by them, clarify the agenda,

---

[4.40] This at 1967 salary levels, and with Senate at about half its present size.

[4.41] Memorandum by the Vice-Chancellor to the Senate and Council, September 1967. These principles, slightly re-worded, have continued to govern the management of the university's committees since that time.

[4.42] This and the following quotation are from a document for the Senate, written by its secretary, Mr. M. G. de St V. Atkins, in December 1968.

and invite suitable persons to Senate for the discussion of particular items. However,

> It is not intended, nor is the proposal made, that the committee should have the power to refuse to forward to the Senate any motion, proposal, recommendation, etc.: its function would be one of clarifying issues and avoiding duplication—the saving of money and time.

So far this committee, together with such devices as the colour coding of agenda categories, has proved adequate to keep the business of the Senate within bounds: the committee has subsequently had added to it particular responsibility for all matters concerning the university's academic relationships with universities overseas, as well as the operation of the Junior Year Abroad scheme.

The statutory sub-committees of the Senate are the (seven) Boards of Studies and the (six) Syndicates of the Colleges,[4.44] who themselves have their own sub-structure of standing and *ad hoc* committees. The standing committees of the Senate as at December 1972 were: Chairs and Readerships (for consideration of principles about appointments to these posts); Computer Users and Computer Policy Committees; the Development Committee; the Committee for Emergency Investigations (to report on and suggest action following upon acts of disruption within the University); the Examinations Committee;[4.43] the Committee on Intercalations; the Library Committee (to advise on the allocation of the grant, and to provide a forum for the discussion of library matters); the Media Services' Committee; the Committee for the Nuffield Drama Studio and Workshop; the Committee for Research Grants (to be responsible, with the Development Committee, for the overall view of development of research in the university); the Senior Tutors' Committee;[4.43] the Standing Academic Committee;[4.45] and the Undergraduate Admissions Committee.[4.43]

Of these committees, the Standing Academic Committee is the only one given the power under the revised statutes to make decisions without the need for subsequent confirmation by the Senate.[4.46] In addition, the departments each summer form from within themselves—with the addition of their external examiners—Part II examination boards,[4.47] reporting thereafter direct to the Senate.

There are no standing appointing committees, because the composition of

---

4.43 See Chapter 3.
4.44 These are discussed in Chapters 3 and 6 respectively.
4.45 See Chapter 6.
4.46 Statute 13: Delegation of the Powers of the Council and the Senate without requirement of Confirmation.
4.47 See Chapter 3, pages 212 to 213.

these varies according to the level of appointment being made, but a formula has been worked out to cover the appropriate composition of the *ad hoc* committees for the various grades of posts. For a chair, for example, the correct composition is the Vice-Chancellor, a representative of Council, two representatives of Senate (one from an unrelated field), and two or more people from other universities or research establishments, appointed by the Senate. Senior lectureship and lectureship appointing committees have on them the Vice-Chancellor and the head of the department concerned (or their deputies), and one or more persons nominated by the Vice-Chancellor on the advice of the head of the department concerned. Administrative posts on the F.S.S.U. grade have an appointing committee made up in a way comparable to a lectureship committee. The appointing committees, once set up in the correct manner, have the power to select persons to become members of the university, which are then reported to the Senate.

As well as the Standing Academic Committee, there are three other university committees which operate outside the Council or the Senate framework, in the sense that they can meet, make certain decisions, and implement them, without reference to either of the senior bodies of the university. Two of these are the University Tribunal (to which the College Tribunals form an adjunct, as well as being independent entities), and the Committee of Appeals and Equity, which is both the appeal body from the University Tribunal and the appropriate organ for the hearing of other special cases.[4.48] Thus, while the Committee for Emergency Investigations will habitually report to the Senate, the other two disciplinary bodies of the university are not bound to do so. Temporary exclusion of students, for example, on disciplinary grounds does not require confirmation by the Senate, which voluntarily abrogated that responsibility in September 1971, as provided for under the revised statutes.

The other major committee of the university which has this degree of independence is the Committee of Colleges, which, under the revised statutes, has had delegated to it

> without any requirement of confirmation, decisions relating to the membership of Colleges, to the constitution, internal working and good order of the Colleges, and to the constitution and standing orders of the Syndicates of Colleges and Committees thereof.

The committee also deals with recommendations concerning the procedure for the university's ceremonial occasions and candidates for honorary degrees, with the careers office, the student health service, athletics, the counselling service, and advice to the controller of catering on the services he provides.

The plethora of Senate committees that have been laid down is itself a

---

[4.48] See Chapter 6, pages 380, 386, 390 to 392.

recital in miniature of the university's history. For example, there once were committees for medical education, relations with technical colleges, local broadcasting, accommodation in future colleges, honorary degrees, allocation of staff to colleges, allocation of undergraduates to colleges, university dinners, publicity and public lectures, equipment grants, discipline and the law of the land, and control of wireless transmitter, to list but a sample. Although Lancaster is not as sweeping as Sussex, where the entire administrative structure is reviewed annually, the review of committees that takes place each year does eliminate the least necessary and prevents the academic staff from spending their entire time, when not teaching, at meetings of some kind.

We have seen in Chapter 3[4.49] how concerned the Academic Planning Board was to avoid "the dangers that result from divisions between Faculties or Subjects on a narrow departmental basis", and to that end organized boards of studies which were to include all academic members of staff and transcend divisions by faculty and department. We shall now look briefly at the status and role of departments.

Halsey and Trow have commented that the department as such has no place in the formal constitutions of the British universities, but that

> It is not fanciful to see the modern university as a federation of departments each facing outwards towards the research councils for research funds and towards schools and other universities for students and staff while at the same time living together on a campus with faculty boards and the Senate as mechanisms for negotiation and arbitration of their divergent interests.[4.49]

Sir James Mountford has also documented the concern evinced by those founding Keele that the complex course structure they were setting up should be "one of the main instruments for combating the intellectual isolation and departmentalism of university Faculties and disciplines".[4.50] At Sussex Asa Briggs has described how he and his colleagues were able, in adopting an organization by Schools, to avoid the situation where

> New subjects take their place in the map of learning and become sovereign departments, and the map itself is seldom consciously re-drawn. The biological studies, for example, produce exciting new research which rests on cross-boundary thinking, yet in many universities biology, botany and zoology are controlled by independent potentates. . . . When a new subject, like economic history, comes into prominence, it often seeks to command departmental status, thereby shedding its influence with both historians

---

[4.49] A. H. Halsey and Martin Trow, *The British Academics* (1971), pp. 111–112.
[4.50] Sir James Mountford, *Keele: An Historical Critique* (1972), p. 104: see also pp. 4, 63 and 106.

and economists. . . .The Sussex curriculum, based as it is on Schools, which are not super-departments, was deliberately designed to avoid some at least of these dangers.[4.51]

There are those who have been associated with Sussex who will say that for both staff and students such a radical change of organizational structure means a lack of identification with any grouping, particularly since Sussex is not a collegiate university. The Sussex system, however, helped to make innovation at other new universities more readily acceptable.

Lack of self-identification is not the only hindrance to breaking down departmental barriers. A. E. Sloman, in his Reith Lectures of 1963 stated that

Knowledge is undivided. It cannot be fitted neatly into departmental pigeon-holes, and although there are points of intensity which allow subjects to be identified, the allocation of these subjects to isolated and self-sufficient departments has discouraged the development of areas that fall between them. For this reason our schools of study will be the chief academic units. . . . The groupings of departments within schools will, we hope, strengthen the links between them, and the particular groupings of Essex will give it a curriculum which is distinctive. The different schools will themselves overlap, and certain departments will belong to more than one.[4.52]

The range of subjects was limited, and organized into four schools, which between them have links with eleven departments (most of them belonging to two schools, and some to three). Dr. Sloman also described, however, the means by which the first members of staff were selected, the criteria being that

The first professors must clearly be leaders in their field, men of intellectual distinction with the promise of really original work. They must also have the imagination to experiment with new courses and new methods. But we looked for more. These first professors will have to take decisions affecting the whole university, not just in their own field of study, and for several years will bear much of the administrative load.[4.53]

He then goes on to justify big departments which can provide a wide range of experts, carry the heavy costs of complex expensive research equipment, assist the collaboration of eminent colleagues, and help to establish research collections in the university library. The question must have arisen in his listeners' minds as to the balance of influence between the schools he describes and their component departments, and whether the one would not be

---

[4.51] Asa Briggs, "Drawing a New Map of Learning" in D. Daiches, *The Idea of a New University* (1964), pp. 72–73.
[4.52] A. E. Sloman, *A University in the Making* (1964), pp. 27–28; see also pp. 19–26.
[4.53] *Ibid.*, p. 19.

engulfed by the other? Even more fundamentally, one wonders whether the very type of personalities he describes as suitable for founding departments might later wish not to submerge themselves in a school structure?

It is perhaps too soon to tell how the schools of study at Essex have worked out in practice. What is noteworthy is that each of the new universities in their prospectuses make the same claim to be breaking down departmental and/or faculty barriers, not excluding Lancaster, which says of the boards of studies that they "replace the statutory division into faculties". The 1964 version of the Statutes made no mention of departments or their heads, and the full weight of academic decision-making was to be thrown onto the boards of studies. Yet, as at Essex, Lancaster first set about making appointments to chairs, who were also heads of the first departments and, as professors, members of the Shadow Senate which took so many important decisions about curriculum and organization. Other academic staff were interviewed, amongst others, by these heads of departments and took up lectureships in particular departments; from the outset they did not, therefore, identify themselves primarily as members of boards but as members of departments. Similarly, the minutes of the Senate were from the beginning full of references to "departments" and "heads of departments", and no comparable reference was made to chairmen of boards or principals of colleges (the two statutory entities in the university).

We have already seen hinted at, in the works to which I have referred, some of the reasons why there is a strong tendency to choose a departmental structure (self-identification, a grouping for making bids for resources, an association of common academic interests) and no doubt to have altered fundamentally their thinking would, for many members of staff, have been a repudiation of their own academic backgrounds, however much regret was voiced at the Senate conference of 1965[4.54] that departments were so dominant. Yet the implicit assumption that departments were the natural unit may have been one of the reasons why combined majors, for example, have not flourished at Lancaster (in common with other new universities, it should be

---

[4.54] A paper by Mr. John Creed and Mr. Michael Waller which came before the conference noted that

> By starting with departmental units we have assured a "discipline" approach to our courses. . . . At the same time we have claimed the interlocking of courses to be one of our principles. . . . It is the view of the writers of this paper that the institutional guardians of the principle of interlocking courses must be the Boards of Studies. . . . As we are at present constituted, the discretion of a professorial Head of Department is not defined. This is not so very important for the moment, when the University is still not very complex and we are all anxious to make interlocking courses work. But now is the time to consider what kinds of situations might occur in the future. What would happen, for instance, in the case of conflict between a Head of Department and the relevant Board of Studies? In the future institutions may be as important as goodwill.

noted) as the Academic Planning Board had hoped that they would. Yet the departmental boundary is artificial: one only has to listen, for instance, to the discussions of historians and economists, or sociologists and students of politics to realize how very close certain areas of their subjects are; and questions of how, to choose just two examples, material sciences or linguistics should have been dealt with might have looked different in the context of a board or school from the way they were seen in a more departmentally-oriented system.

Practice, however, was not uniform between departments, as is shown by a Senate minute of November 1967 when the Vice-Chancellor proposed that there should be a chairman of each department to whom correspondence should normally be addressed. The Vice-Chancellor suggested that Senate might prefer the term "chairman" to head of department since it emphasized the need, agreed to exist in all large departments, to hold departmental meetings, and it opened up by inference the possibility of appointing a non-professorial chairman.

The position of departments and their heads not unexpectedly came up when the Statutes were being revised. In the prolonged debate on the future membership of the Senate, Professor Woolrych argued in October 1968 that heads of departments should be *ex officio* members for,

> Whether intended by its founding fathers or not, this University has developed a strong departmental structure. We are primarily an academic institution, and the essential decisions about courses both undergraduate and postgraduate, and in some cases about the direction of research, are taken at departmental level. It follows that the most responsible officer should participate in Senate's decisions.

Professor Harold Perkin similarly contended that,

> for a supreme *academic* body, the suggested constitution gives far too much representation to those non-academic organs of the University, the Colleges, and not enough to those academic work-horses, the Departments.

The system proposed at that time, he said, could lead

> to a large Department being represented only by one or two junior members—worthy, no doubt, of their place, but scarcely representative of the academic weight of the subject. Democracy is very well in its place, but democracy in academic matters can all too easily lead to mediocrity, and if nothing else can be said in these democratic days for professors it is still true that they have arrived at their exalted rank and shrinking power by a somewhat stiffer competition than the rest.

Their opinions, shared by others, prevailed, and the revised statutes listed heads of departments as *ex officio* members of the Senate—although underneath Principals of Colleges and Chairmen of Boards of Studies. Departments were also defined for the first time:

(1) There shall be such Departments, containing as members such Officers of the University, as the Senate may from time to time determine; and each Department shall, at least three times in each academic year, arrange a meeting of all these members to discuss its work. . . .

(2) Each Department shall have a Head, to be chosen in a manner to be approved and for a period to be determined by the Senate.[4.55]

Even now, however, there was no formal and binding definition of the function or powers either of a department or its head, and no description of the relationship of a department to any of the other statutory bodies of the university.

Meanwhile the consideration of the period a particular individual should be head of a department was under consideration. The Steering Committee put proposals to the Senate in June 1970, which were considered again in October and ratified by the Council in November, that laid down new principles. In future, when a chair that carried with it the headship of a department,[4.56] or a department with a non-professorial headship, were established, the Development Committee would in each case recommend that the person appointed be head for a limited and stated number of years (usually five). Furthermore, the headship of existing departments was to be reviewed (although not necessarily changed) every five years by the Vice-Chancellor and "such Pro-Vice-Chancellors as are not concerned", by consulting permanent members of staff.

The process of reviewing the existing departments was begun and it must be assumed from the number of changes that were agreed upon that a number of heads of department were glad to lay down their burdens. In one such report of intended changes sent to the Senate in December 1971, however, the Vice-Chancellor noted that "A number of members of departments have raised questions about the possible 'redistribution of the "powers" of heads of department, a rotating chairmanship of departmental meetings etc.' ". In the context of that period it was a question likely to arise in the minds of staff and it is therefore not surprising that at the same meeting the Vice-Chancellor put forward certain proposals about heads of departments to the Senate which, after discussion, agreed that

---

[4.55] University of Lancaster, *Revised Statutes* (1971), No. 16.

[4.56] The Senate in June 1970 defined "head of department" as "the academic director of the department" rather than "the head of administration in a department".

a survey be made of the practice of teaching departments, in order to determine (a) what should be defined as the essential powers of a head of department, (b) what alternative models of departmental organization can be recommended for use, (c) what methods of selection of persons holding responsibility in departments are appropriate.

When replies from the heads of departments (some of whom had consulted their departments) had been received, Professor Philip Reynolds drafted a paper which was put to the Senate for discussion in May 1972, where various comments were made and the document sent back for modification. A re-drafted version was then sent round to all F.S.S.U. staff as well as the various bodies within the university—including, because of the terms of the Industrial Relations Act, the local branch of the A.U.T., which made a number of suggestions, which were debated by the Senate in February 1973. Meanwhile, in October, the Senate declined to take up the suggestion of Councillor Taylor that training in personnel management be offered to those with departmental and similar responsibilities.[4.57]

Professor Reynolds' paper began by explaining that it had "become clear that the minimal provisions of the Revised Statutes needed amplification into a fuller description of the organization of departments, including particularly a definition of the powers, duties and responsibilities of the Head. Not all the comments received in response to the draft could be incorporated, he said, because many of them were mutually contradictory, particularly over the balance between their academic and administrative roles. The contribution made by departments to the furtherance of the purposes of the university, he went on,

> depends not only on the individual qualities of their members, but on the organizational and administrative context within which those members operate. Good leadership and effective administration may well be as important a component of good teaching and research by the Department as a whole as any contribution any particular individual may be able to

---

[4.57] *The Report of the Taylor Enquiry*, Item 11, on staff relationships commented that: Fundamental to all good industrial relations at the workplace are uniform labour practices in the matter of recruitment, and terms and conditions of employment. Uniform practices throughout the University should be adhered to, and only varied in exceptional circumstances. (For example, professors should work within the overall University labour policies, and these should be seen to be impartially applied by all departments. This does not appear to be so at the present time.) . . .

Also, in the matter of probationers, some form of continuous assessment should perhaps be introduced. A probationer should be kept informed of his progress by his head of department throughout his probation, at regular intervals. Professors and those responsible for the management of labour could perhaps benefit from some formal training in this field (Lancaster might well consider sponsoring such a course).

R

make. "Leadership" . . . refers to the capacity which some individuals possess and others do not to stimulate members of a group or organization to optimal performance whether individually or collectively in relation to their purposes.

In the academic context a junior, inexperienced or academically undistinguished member of a Department, is unlikely to possess this capacity, even if he proves to be an effective administrator; but it is not of course the case that the capacity will necessarily be possessed by persons who are senior, experienced or academically distinguished, or all of these.

The ability of a Head of Department to perform his functions is very much affected by the extent to which members of the Department favour his holding of the office. But internal support is not a sufficient condition for appointment. Effective representation of the Department's interests, within and outside the University, require that the head should carry prestige and weight.

These propositions indicate that in most Departments only a small proportion of the members are likely to be able with equivalent success to perform headship functions . . . there should be provision for regular review of headships, and normally for change after one or two terms of office, unless good reason appears for further continuance.

He went on to list the functions and duties of departments, which included the expected items, as well as some which might have been thought to impinge on the functions of the boards of studies, such as academic policy and planning, including new areas for development, staff recruitment policy, changes in courses or course structure, and questions of assessment; or others, such as preparation of estimates and control of departmental expenditure, admission of students, and encouragement and direction of research, which could be redistributed amongst other bodies, such as the boards.

Heads of department he saw as representing the department on the Senate (having a duty to convey its views and represent its interests but not to attend as a delegate), and being responsible to the Senate for the department fulfilling the functions of the university. Appointments Professor Reynolds saw as being made with the help of *ad hoc* departmental committees who would scrutinize applications and assist in drawing up a short list, tenure would be recommended (or otherwise) under procedures agreed with the A.U.T., promotions for academic staff would be recommended by the head after consultation with a senior departmental committee and for assistant staff in consultation with those people that have most dealings with them.

At the discussion of the document, which the Senate accepted as a "general guide", Mr. Russell Keat was concerned that "machinery be established to enable the views of dissidents to be brought to the Senate". Professor

Reynolds is reported as replying that "constitutional proposals could not cover all contingencies and should not normally be made on the supposition that conflict was about to arise", while someone else mentioned the boards of studies as the place where dissident members could report their views. The Senate agreed, however, that a procedure for settling departmental disputes was desirable and after further drafting and referral to the A.U.T., the Senate in September 1973 agreed that where a dispute, other than personal, arises between a head and the teaching and allied members of it,

> the head and a representative of the rest of the department should meet the Steering Committee. Either party may be accompanied by an official of his union or a friend or other appropriate person. If that committee cannot help the parties to resolve the dispute to the satisfaction of both parties, it must propose to the Committee of the Senate whether the Senate should resolve the matter itself or appoint a sub-committee with knowledge of the matter under dispute to investigate further and make recommendations to the Senate.

The prominence which was now being given to departmental matters was also shown by a further resolution in February 1973 that Mr. Atkins should prepare a memorandum which would enable the Senate to determine which officers of the university are members of departments. A sub-committee of the Steering Committee finally made a report on this matter to the Senate in December 1973, and it was agreed that certain members of departments—professors, readers, senior lecturers and lecturers—should be statutory members, as should full-time research staff, and certain part-time staff. A standing committee is to be set up to consider special cases and "adequate arrangements" made to ensure that all other (i.e. non-statutory) members of departments "have a full opportunity to make their views known". Parallel definitions have also been established for the university library.

It will be interesting to see how departments develop in the future at Lancaster, what effect (if any) such inter-disciplinary enterprises such as European Studies or Independent Studies will have on them and whether the development of new disciplines on the boundaries of existing subjects (such as bio-chemistry or geography) affect existing suppositions about their role.

(ii)   The administrative structure

There are not many variants of central[4.58] administrative organization from which universities can choose: most of them, whether they have two or ten

---

[4.58] The assumption is here made that a decentralized administration is fundamentally different and lies outside the ambit of this discussion.

thousand students, use some variant of a hierarchical structure, giving a chain of responsibility upon which others can rely, and incorporating various specialists to take care of particular functions, such as catering or printing. If the hierarchy is fairly long before it broadens out into the specialist officers, then the members of it will probably delegate amongst themselves responsibility for particular functions, while remaining in close touch with each other so that there is a small group of people, e.g. a vice-chancellor, deputy vice-chancellor, and pro-vice-chancellor who will understand in detail what is at issue, be able to talk freely and informally, and who can readily deputize for each other when necessary. If, on the other hand, there is a vice-chancellor and divisions of responsibility or function opening out immediately below him, then more part in the decision-making process can be given to more people, thereby increasing their motivation and commitment to the organization. In practice, of course, much depends on the characteristics of the individuals involved and the success, or otherwise, of their personal interaction with each other, as well as on such external factors as the rate of growth or the physical groupings of parts of the organization.

If vice-chancellors in general tend to be of a temperament that wish to be involved in as much of their universities' organization as possible, then they are likely to want to dispense with line managers and keep in personal touch with their functional staff, whether they be establishment officers, academic registrars and their deputies, catering controllers, or heads of departments. A vice-chancellor in any case tends to be a symbolically pivotal figure whom everyone wishes to consult personally and for whom any substitute is resented as second-best. This is not so much the case at Oxford and Cambridge where the Vice-Chancellor (who is usually also master of a college) until recently held office for only two years, but it is certainly true at the new universities, where the personality of the vice-chancellor is necessarily and inevitably a predominant feature of the image of the institution.[4.59]

A vice-chancellor is, in the first place, on the scene before anyone else; in the case of Mr. Carter, over six months passed before any other officers were appointed to assist him. He was the only officer to be a member of the Executive Council, or the Academic Planning Board and its offspring, the Academic Advisory Committee, which meant he had unique access to the sources of information and decision-making, both locally and nationally through dealings with the U.G.C. By the time the first teaching member of staff took up his appointment in October 1963, Mr. Carter had enjoyed ten months of decision-making: he had shared in the drafting of the interim report of the Academic Planning Board; in conjunction with the Executive

---

[4.59] Christopher Driver comments about Lancaster that "one can be fairly sure that everything at the university, from the constitution to the colours ('Lancaster red and Quaker grey') has a touch of Carter" (*The Exploding University*, 1971, page 179).

Council he had appointed staff; he had helped to choose St. Leonard's House and to select the site development architects; and had prepared a draft petition for the royal charter, as well as the charter and statutes of the university.

If we look at his statutory position, we find it defined in broad terms:

> There shall be a Vice-Chancellor of the University who shall be the chief Academic and Administrative Officer of the University. . . . The Vice-Chancellor shall have a general responsibility to the Council and the Senate for maintaining and promoting the effective working and good order of the university.[4.60]

This gives him the widest scope, there being no statutory boundary either to his responsibility or his power, except inasmuch as he is part of a defined committee structure so that, if the whole of the Council or the Senate are sufficiently united in their views and opposed to his on a particular matter, then he will probably not be able to implement proposals which he personally would wish to endorse—or, at least, not on that occasion.[4.61] On the other hand, as chairman of the Senate and its steering committee, the Academic Promotions Committee, the board of the School of Education, the Committee of Colleges, the Development Committee and the Committee on Examinations, he is in a position to make recommendations and steer discussion as he deems appropriate. As he told the local branch of the A.U.T. in the Michaelmas Term, 1970, he is inevitably in a position of considerable power, because he is the recipient of so much information from so many different kinds of sources and has access to so many areas of influence. All important issues are referred to him sooner or later, this being encouraged by the statement in the administrative handbook that he "is available to any member of the University for business which, by reason of its importance, novelty or confidentiality, cannot properly be initiated elsewhere in the administration"[4.62] and endorsed by the further exhortation in the student handbook that "If you feel you have a problem, or an idea, or a burning sense of injustice, and you do not quite know where to go, please feel free to come and see me about it".[4.63] There is a self-denying ordinance at Lancaster that buildings shall not normally be named after individuals, but the students have paid the Vice-Chancellor the compliment of naming a stretch of water beside the main drive "Lake Carter", an appellation which seems generally to have

---

[4.60] Charter of the University of Lancaster, clause 9 section 1, and Revised Statutes, clause 4.

[4.61] See A. H. Halsey and M. Trow, *The British Academics* (London, 1971), pages 115–116.

[4.62] *Administrative Handbook*, March 1972, page 2.

[4.63] *Lancaster '72*, page 6.

been adopted and which is one small indication of how dominant a figure he is to the student body. Nationally he is a member of the Committee of Vice-Chancellors and Principals whose terms of reference include keeping "all major issues affecting the universities as a whole under regular review so as to be ready in good time to deal with problems as they arise and whenever possible to foresee future problems".[4.64] A seat on this committee puts him in an initially strong tactical position: he is, moreover, constitutionally an *ex officio* member of every committee of the Senate and the Council if he cares to attend, as well as being the final arbiter of appeals in disciplinary cases. Therefore, despite his modest disclaimer, on discussing obedience to statutory decision-making bodies at a time of considerable national publicity for the university, that

> all but one of the decisions that they [i.e. the practitioners of pseudo-serious writing] so generously attributed to the personal dictatorship of the Vice-Chancellor were in fact made by the proper committees, acting in some cases without even knowing my personal views,[4.65]

it would be very difficult to underestimate the extent of his influence at Lancaster.

The Academic Planning Board recommended that "the Secretary of the Court, Council and Senate shall be the Secretary of the University, a title which we prefer to Registrar. The Secretary, under the Vice-Chancellor, will be the head of the administrative and financial staff of the University", and, in the advertisement for that post, further clauses were added that he would be secretary to the principal committees of the three statutory bodies, would be responsible for the administrative staff of the university, and would have (to an as yet undefined extent) responsibility for buildings and capital expenditure. In fact, because of the direction of interests of Mr. Jeffreys, the capital building programme has been a principal concern of his.[4.66]

To assist Mr. Jeffreys at the opening session of the university, there was a Deputy Secretary, a Finance Officer, a Building Development Officer, an Engineer, a Superintendent of Lodgings, and a Catering Officer. The operation of the Secretary's office was thus divided into three main sections:

> (a) an academic and general section; (b) a finance section; and (c) a works and buildings section. The Secretary has a qualified and experienced "lieutenant" in charge of each main section of the office, although he remains responsible (under the Vice-Chancellor) for directing and con-

[4.64] Letter from the Chairman of the Committee of Vice-Chancellors and Principals, September 1966.

[4.65] Charles Carter, "Some reactions to being in the news", *Times Higher Education Supplement*, Number 32, 19 May 1972.

[4.66] See Chapter 2 for an account of the building development.

trolling all facets of the University's administration. . . . In addition to looking after the academic section of the University office the Deputy Secretary assists the University Secretary with the general oversight of all aspects of the University's administration. The academic office will doubtless bear the brunt of the immense amount of committee work inseparable from the administration of a modern and expanding University.[4.67]

Some of the strains of the early years show behind the words of the Vice-Chancellor's report of December 1965 that

> We fight a continuous and reasonably successful battle against over-complex administration and an excess of committees. . . . I think that there is some danger, however, that (by a too easy assumption that administration always follows Parkinson's Laws) we may in future try to hold it below an efficient point.[4.68]

The same note was struck in 1967 when the Vice-Chancellor gave particular thanks to the University Secretary

> and to all the members of the administration, both section heads and the most junior recent recruits. It is customary for academic persons to criticize administrators, and a good university administrator is therefore wise to expect more kicks than ha'pence. But it needs to be said, from time to time, that many members of the administration give service far and beyond any reasonable expectation.[4.69]

There was still a lack of control of resources, however, and the Vice-Chancellor, in commenting upon the tightening financial situation in December 1966, noted that

> We need, I think, a better means of checking extravagance and waste, which are especially irritating in a situation of shortage of money because they show incongruity between our various actions. The Manchester Institute of Science and Technology deals with this by having a separate appointment called "Internal Auditor". We may not yet be large enough for such a post to pay for itself by the waste it prevents.

Despite, however, suggestions being made, in the course of several Council discussions, that outside management consultants might be used, or a con-

---

[4.67] A. S. Jeffreys, "Some Thoughts on University Administration" in the *Lancaster Guardian*, Special Supplement, 1964.

[4.68] First Annual Report to the Meeting of the University Court (December 1965), page 9.

[4.69] Third Annual Report to the Meeting of the University Court (December 1967), page 19.

sortial O and M group set up amongst the northern universities which would fulfil all the requirements of Lancaster, a Council minute of May 1967 recorded a resolution to

> give further consideration to the appointment of an Internal Auditor or Systems Investigator, who would act independently of spending departments, as a watchdog over the efficiency of the University's administrative procedures and would report to the Chairman of the Finance Committee through the Vice-Chancellor.

The proposal was adopted, although the first (and present) incumbent of the post, Mr. James Nicholson, did not come to the university until May 1968. He reports direct to the Vice-Chancellor, while also at times working in conjunction with the University Secretary. He has a roving commission, as he is asked to enquire into and report upon situations in particular areas of the university as they become contentious or particularly complicated. He is able to present an independent assessment of the circumstances as they manifest themselves to him; and thus enable the appropriate committee, or the Vice-Chancellor, to make a decision based on an up-to-date and impartial analysis, whether the primary concern be of finance, logistics, or more delicate and personal considerations. In certain cases a follow-up may also be necessary: and there is a strong likelihood that individuals or departments, made aware of this source of help, will call upon it as other problems emerge. In March 1972 there was also brought in a work study officer, Mr. Robert Birrell.

Mr. Forster had the title of Academic Registrar added to that of Deputy Secretary in November 1966, and became one of four Chief Officers under the Secretary. Only on the academic side was the pattern made more complicated, by having some central, and some departmental, administrators. Most of the latter are based on the science departments, with a few in the arts departments. With some slight modifications, this system of a partially centralized, combined with a partially decentralized administrative structure, continues to the present time. At its best the administrators concerned can respond sensitively and immediately to particular areas of the university, either on the specialist or the diversified basis; at its worst there is overlap, and a breakdown of communication and understanding between the central administration and the outlaying officers.

In September 1970, when the number of pro-vice-chancellors had increased to three, they and the Development Committee considered the development of the administration for a university of a notional future size of 5,000 students, and said that the university's business was "too much dependent on the Vice-Chancellor and too many trivial matters are referred to him for attention". They went on to say that they did not recommend the appointment of a deputy vice-chancellor.

In our view, it is best that the University structure should have a single apex, and that the work of the Vice-Chancellor should be lightened, not by a sharing of responsibility at the top level, but by the taking of more responsibility at lower levels. We do, however, recommend that the Vice-Chancellor should ask each Pro-Vice-Chancellor to specialize in an area of University business.

They were convinced, they said, that

a unitary administration will not do for a University of the size which is now in prospect. This is because we observe early indications of difficulties which will be bound to become more intense. The University Secretary has so many sections responsible to him that he can spend little time in dealing with the problems of any one of them, and has almost no leisure for fundamental thinking about long-range planning, or administrative structure, or the training and mobility of staff. . . .

It would theoretically be possible to retain a unitary administration by introducing an additional layer of officers, so that the University Secretary would be responsible for several chief sectional officers. But we are clear that the prospective size of the University is far below that which would justify such an additional complication. We therefore propose that the administration, under the Vice-Chancellor, should be divided into three offices, one of which would be headed by the University Secretary . . . as with Government, there would be several "departments" but one Civil Service.

The situation which has prevailed since that time has therefore been of a tri-partite division of responsibilities between the University Secretary, the Academic Registrar, and the Secretary for College and Student Affairs, Mr. J. R. Martindale.[4.70] The new system would seem to have been a success for, when the Vice-Chancellor carried out his promised review a year later, only a few marginal changes of function were suggested. As a concomitant of the larger re-organization each of the three pro-vice-chancellors has been particularly associated with each of the three chief officers, so that Professor Keith Morgan is particularly involved with the University Secretary's office, Professor Philip Reynolds with the Academic Registrar's, and Professor Austin Woolrych with that of the Secretary for College and Student Affairs.

Perhaps the main recommendation not implemented was the training and mobility of the staff: with a few notable exceptions, administrative officers have not been sent on training courses or moved from post to post within the university after the general move of 1970. Perhaps this is because the notion of mobility was not incorporated into the system from the outset, as it was at,

---

[4.70] See Appendix (xii).

248 UNIVERSITY OF LANCASTER: QUEST FOR INNOVATION

for example, Warwick, Stirling and East Anglia. In the pioneering days of 1964 and 1965, when all members of the administration were under severe pressure, it must have been difficult to think of a stage at which the management of the place would become so specialized that everyone would not have as much diversity of occupation as he could cope with. Indeed, the qualities that were most highly rated in those early days, of immediate response to emergency, endurance to constant pressure and long hours, and adaptability to many kinds of contingencies, are very different from the quiet precision and attention to detail which are necessary in the periods of consolidation. It is probably not reasonable to look for the fundamentally dissimilar qualities demanded by several different kinds of situation within the same group of people.

During 1971 and 1972, when there was considerable unrest within the university over matters associated with the English department, Councillor Tom Taylor was asked to write a report which was to include recommendations for changes of policy in the structure. In commenting upon the office of Vice-Chancellor, Councillor Taylor described Mr. Carter as

> a man of very great integrity with a remarkable sense of duty and an enormous capacity for work. . . . But any Vice-Chancellor inevitably becomes a target in times of stress. He therefore needs to be assured of strong support at such times, and of assistance in dealing with the increasingly complex problems of a growing university. . . .
>
> It is obvious that much of the time of the administration must be spent on running the very complicated committee system—a formidable task indeed, in a highly democratic organization such as a university, whose members, both senior and junior, are highly articulate. I believe the Vice-Chancellor has need of a full-time deputy, of high academic standing and good ability in administration. . . . The Vice-Chancellor should have the freedom of being relieved of a lot of routine work, and he should have the opportunity of being in a position of advising, thinking, planning future developments and representing the University on regional, national and international bodies.[4.71]

However, as a press release of October 1972 said,

> The suggestion of a Deputy Vice-Chancellor had not found favour with the Senate, although that body (as well as Council) is very conscious of the need to provide relief from his present heavy duties for the Vice-Chancellor. Suggestions to effect this include the reduction of the number of committees he chairs, the extension of the field of activity of the Pro-Vice-Chancellors and of the College Principals and the creation of a small,

---

[4.71] *Report of the Taylor Enquiry*, July 1972, Item 9.

high-powered and easily assembled executive committee which the Vice-Chancellor could consult.

Such an executive committee was, however, seen as pre-empting the administrative role of the Senate Steering Committee, and possibly diverting it from being a consultative, rather than an executive, body. The Senate, in December 1972 therefore approved a further document from the Vice-Chancellor on the role of the pro-vice-chancellors, who are to be of professorial rank and appointed on a five-year basis, and one of whom is to be

> a senior pro-vice-chancellor, on whom additional responsibilities would rest. . . . He would be encouraged to relinquish any responsibility as head of department . . . and would give a considerable amount of time to university business, in association with the Vice-Chancellor when the business is particularly pressing. He will normally act for the Vice-Chancellor in the latter's absence.

The Academic Registrar's office, as the name implies, is concerned with the work of the major committees and bodies of the university which are responsible for formulating policy relating to academic structure and development. The Senate is a major responsibility, and a Deputy Academic Registrar, Mr. M. G. de St V. Atkins, has the servicing of this body as a main function, together with the responsibility for ensuring that decisions of that body are properly actioned, communicated and codified. The co-ordination of the work of the boards of studies is naturally also a part of this office, and is the particular care of Mr. W. G. Fuge. Graduate studies are regarded as sufficiently separate to have their own board of studies and their own officer, Mr. M. G. McDonald, who is responsible for all graduate students from the time they first apply until they get their degree certificate—and, since over a quarter of the postgraduate students at Lancaster are from overseas, these are sent to every point of the globe. Mr. Forster personally services the Development Committee and the Examinations Committee, and his section also deals with the university timetable—no light matter in a university with a degree structure as complex as Lancaster's, where the forbidden combination of Part I subjects is a serious enough matter to merit Senate ratification. He is also responsible for degree-giving and other ceremonial occasions, the various official university publications, and the administration of prizes and scholarships.

Mr. Martindale's office has responsibility for the Committee of Colleges and the liaison between the colleges and the central administration. While not intruding into the province of care for students undertaken by the colleges, a good deal of his time is devoted to the welfare of individual students as well as counselling, the careers advisory service, accommodation and sport. The various university disciplinary bodies are under his care, and since he has been connected with this kind of work since he came to the university, Mr. Martindale has been particularly closely associated with the development of the disciplinary system in all its aspects. His office keeps the central records of each student, and an increasing amount of record-keeping is being done by specially developed computerized methods, the outcome of a fruitful co-operation between Mr. Martindale's staff and the central data processing unit. Finally, the administration of the examinations—which straddle an increasing proportion of the calendar year—is also looked after by Mr. Martindale and his staff.

We shall now consider the work of the University Secretary's office. The work of the building development office is discussed principally in Chapter 2, although the growing maintenance aspect of the office should not be over-looked: this is taken care of by the engineer, Mr. James Cansfield and his staff, in addition to the developmental aspects of their work. The staffing of the engineer's section has been remarkably stable, with very little turnover, and is, on the maintenance side, one of the most consistently trouble-free areas of the university.

One member of the Building Development Office, Mr. Ernest Phillips, has as his primary function the planning and implementation of the minor works programme. Up to 1973 the U.G.C. had given a special grant to the universities for this purpose, according to the needs expressed by each institution in applications received from them; anything extra was found by the university from its recurrent grant. From 1973 onwards, however, it is to be taken wholly from the recurrent grant, at a suggested level of $2\frac{1}{2}$ per cent of the total.[4.72] As the university expands and develops, and as new pieces of legislation (about fire, health and safety) come into force, the original layout and equipping of rooms or sections of buildings are subject to new regulations, or can be adapted to make better provision for administrative or teaching purposes. A year or two after initial completion the occupants of a new building are likely to have suggestions to make for modifications about configuration of rooms, floor finishes, or piped and electrical services. Particularly in a new university, where buildings are constructed on a modular basis to facilitate minor changes of function, there is no reason why any square foot of space should be redundant.

There is no separate post of bursar at Lancaster, and the Finance Officer, Mr. Harold White, is responsible to the University Secretary for the financial administration of the university, which includes day-to-day accounting and preparation of final accounts, costing and budgetary control, and preparation

---

[4.72] This figure, as at the end of 1973, is to be revised downwards because of the national economic situation.

of estimates and forward planning (for both the Finance Committee and the Development Committee). Associated with the finance office is the data processing unit which looks after and controls the input to and output from the university's main computer of all administrative data processing.

The Establishment Office was not one of the original pieces of the university's organization. An Assistant Staff Committee, however, came into being at an early stage. In February 1965 the Senate considered a proposal put forward for a Technical Staffs Committee, which was referred to a small *ad hoc* committee for further deliberation. When they reported back early in March, it was to say that the

> sub-committee did not support the establishment of a separate Technical Staffs Committee . . . since it considered that this would create an unnecessary and undesirable distinction between technical staff and other categories of the university staff, and since it was of the opinion that the salaries, terms and conditions of service of the main categories of assistant staff should be considered by a single body.

It was therefore agreed instead to set up an Assistant Staff Committee, in the first instance as a sub-committee of the Senate, which held its first meeting in June 1965. It was not many months later when a request came from the assistant staff that there should be various consultative groups, divided by type of staff. Although it was not until early in 1968 that the groups were finally established, they proved to be useful in the form set up at that time, and have not been altered since.

Up to 1969 assistant staff had been dealt with by a number of bodies around the university, from departments to the Committee of Colleges, but it became increasingly clear that there was a need for a central co-ordinator, who would cut down the complexity of the existing arrangements and bring into being a consistent and equitable basis for conditions of employment and grading of individuals throughout the university. There was also increasingly a need to have someone to carry on the growing volume of business with the local branches of the trade unions. In July 1969, therefore, a Staff Officer, Mr. James Andrew, was appointed to look after all aspects of assistant staff business.

A year later it was decided that there should be a similar officer who would be responsible for the teaching and other academically related members of the university: previously there had been an office which had handled the paperwork of academic appointments, and Mr. Robert Boumphrey, the finance and legal officer since 1963, looked after the superannuation and record-keeping of such staff. He, therefore, in June 1970 assumed the title of Establishment and Legal Officer, and the two halves of the establishment work were fused together into a single office. A few months later Mr. Andrew was given the title of Deputy Establishment Officer which has meant that each, in principle, can act for the other in his absence.

No machinery parallel to the Assistant Staff Committee has been created on the academic side. The Association of University Teachers has been recognized by the university as the sole bargaining agent in respect of staff on academic and academic-related salary scales, and is from time to time consulted by the Senate about certain general matters, such as departmental organization, or the application of the university rules to senior members, as well as by the Council on matters more directly related to conditions of employment, such as criteria for confirmation of appointment at the end of the probationary period, or an agreed dismissal procedure. A Joint Consultative Group was set up in 1969 to consider the particular problems of F.S.S.U. administrative staff, but this has not proved a very effective or much consulted body, perhaps because in the main administrators have either used the A.U.T. or have entered into individual negotiations with the university.

The reader should not assume that the administrative structure at Lancaster is in any way regarded as immutable. The Vice-Chancellor, in August 1973, wrote to all members of the F.S.S.U. administrative staff in the light of negotiations that

> have been in progress for some time about national scales for administrative staff. We hope that these are near their conclusion: and we are anxious that, when an agreement is reached, we should be able to propose placings on the new scales as quickly as possible. . . . We also want to take a forward look, and consider how the responsibilities of administrative posts will change as the university expands, and what regrading may be required.

A firm of management consultants was therefore invited to carry out during the autumn of 1973 a brief survey using the techniques of questionnaire and interview of the administrative structure at Lancaster, and this is to be continued, on an internal basis, during the early months of 1974.

Despite all the care that has been taken over the university's constitution, its committee structure and its administrative organization, it is very hard to be confident that one has got the mix just right—that decisions are being made at the correct levels, with the maximum efficiency combined with an appropriate degree of consultation, or that the various parts of the structure are inter-acting satisfactorily with each other. There is one general problem which recurs, and that is, ironically, the difficulty of the various parts of the university being able to communicate satisfactorily with each other. Such a problem may seem improbable in the setting of such carefully constructed constitutional and committee structures and so great a degree of democracy, but Lancaster is not alone in facing this problem. At Oxford Lord Franks' Commission had noted that

To maintain the morale of a university, the most important element in its success is that the staff should be informed about, and assent to, the main decisions of policy, and should have the means of making its voice felt in these, and in lesser matters, where it cares sufficiently to do so.[4.73]

Nor have more recent institutions fared better, for Roger Young, reporting on Stirling in 1973, itemized the communications as follows:

there is too much tendency to secrecy and confidentiality about things which need not be kept confidential; policy-decisions have not been effectively announced in the past; too many people seem to find it difficult to get access to information that is relevant to their lives on the campus; many do not even know how to set about trying to get access to such information; there is, in general, a feeling that easy, two-way communication between ordinary members of the University and the University authorities is not available; this has bred distrust and some alienation.[4.74]

Nor was concern about communication at Lancaster something which came only when numbers grew large, for as early as the Senate conference of March 1965 it was agreed that

the administration should consider means of improving the flow of information both between itself and individual members of staff, and between the various bodies and committees in the University.

The same theme appeared much later in the Taylor Report when Councillor Taylor recommended that there be an official university newspaper,

because I feel there is a pressing and immediate need to find a really effective method of disseminating factual information very quickly if "wrong impressions" and "bad feelings" are to be avoided, and if we are to eliminate that crippling sense of frustration occasioned either by ignorance or by quite irrational fears of "what is going on in University House".[4.75]

Mr. Michael Kirkwood, in a paper for the Senate of October 1972, followed this up with suggestions about how to make colleges more effective in the communication chain, so that vertical flows of information could be rapid and effective and lateral communication could be encouraged. Certain steps have been taken. In 1969 the *Reporter*, to give an outline account of the proceedings

[4.73] University of Oxford, *Report of Commission of Inquiry*, Volume I (Oxford 1966), paras. 440ff.
[4.74] *Report on the Policies and Running of Stirling University* (the Roger Young Enquiry), October 1973, page 21.
[4.75] University of Lancaster, *Report of the Taylor Enquiry* (July 1972), item 3.

of the Senate and certain other committees, was launched. In January 1974 an Information Officer, Mr. Roger Grinyer, took up his appointment, and he is expected to launch a university newspaper during the course of 1974, as well as seeking other ways of improving internal communication. It will be interesting to see how much he can achieve, given the perennial difficulty of conveying information quickly, lucidly and intelligibly.

The early history of catering is a far from harmonious story, and gives an illustration of the kind of severe management problems institutions can find themselves in. It will be remembered that the university began its existence in St. Leonard's House. In a town devoid of cheap, large-scale catering outlets, it was essential that the four hundred and more people who suddenly appeared should have facilities provided for them by the university, but equally it was not possible to do so on a collegiate basis because everything was small-scale, and because the division of students into collegiate groupings could only be a matter of nomenclature at a time when the university was occupying temporary accommodation and the colleges as physical entities did not exist. Another, even more fundamental decision, however, was that a fixed proportion of a student's grant should not be deducted for his accommodation and food, which meant that from the beginning there was no assured income upon which the university could base its costings.

A university catering officer was appointed and a refectory opened in St. Leonard's House in October 1964. At this stage there was a captive clientele, for the only alternative was the rather spartan restaurants of the town, self-catering not then being a possibility in the lodgings that all students occupied. A sub-committee of the Senate to discuss refectory business was set up in February 1965, but at first did no more than discuss the times of meals.

The first rumblings of discontent, however, were expressed in a letter of March 1965 from Stanley Henig, the chairman of the senior common room, who wrote to remonstrate about the curtailment of refectory services in the vacations:

> It is an open secret that the reason for certain recent changes in hours of opening etc., has been that the refectory has been running at a loss. A fundamental question which therefore ought to be discussed, and as soon as possible, is the extent to which normal commercial criteria should apply and the extent to which the refectory can be regarded as a service.

He asked for the widening of the terms of reference of the sub-committee including discussion of meal services when the university

> begins to move to Bailrigg. There is wide-spread concern that the decision to have separate dining rooms for each college will mean that each meal centre will be the same.

There was even a high table at lunchtimes in these far-off days, as evidenced by a plea from the professor of mathematics that more than two waitresses be provided for it since "at the moment these two literally run to and from the kitchen with dishes in their hands". One local newspaper, alert for problems, thereupon printed an item headed "Professors may lose their bread and butter", in reference to the possible withdrawal of the free rolls and butter that were provided to compensate for the staff meal costing 4/- rather than the student price of 3/6.

In March 1966, a new Refectory Committee was set up as a joint sub-committee of the Council and the Senate, to have "responsibility for the general control and policy of catering services and for the oversight of the work of the Catering Officer and his staff", a body of which Miss Gordon, the headmistress of the Lancaster Girls' Grammar School, was chairman.

Catering as an integral part of college life, which might have been presumed to be an important feature of a collegiate university, was not given a very positive send-off, for at the policy-making Senate conference of March 1966, in a discussion of college organization, there is only a neutral comment recorded that

> Space for dining accommodation and corresponding kitchen facilities influences the economic size of a college; provision of a number of restaurants, etc., of different types and sizes (not necessarily commercial restaurants) would give freedom to have smaller colleges (e.g. with 200 students).
>
> Young people object to institutional life, and students might prefer to prepare their own meals,

and the constitutions of the first two colleges make no reference to dining together (except for occasional feasts) as a vital feature of the collegiate system—a fact which is worth bearing in mind both in any discussion of the history of the colleges and of catering. The same lack of interest about collegiate dining facilities is shown in the minutes of the first meeting of the Refectory Committee in May 1966 when some items which were deferred related to "the pattern of liaison between Colleges and Catering Department", and "Will there be any formal dining in the evenings?". Similarly, at the next meeting later in the same month, the response to a proposal by the Catering Officer that there be a central catering building, where "stores of all kinds could be kept and where the basic preparation of food could be completed, as a distribution centre for the different college kitchens", was merely that the idea "should be explained to the College Management Committees to ensure that there is no misunderstanding about the nature and purpose of the Central Catering Building". Yet again, in June, Dr. David Dew-Hughes reported on behalf of Bowland College Management Committee that "there

s

would be no formal dining on the Oxford and Cambridge 'hall' pattern next year".

These internal, structural questions were not, however, the only problems facing the committee, as Miss Gordon noted in her report to the Council meeting of July 1966 when she commented that

> Two difficult problems had recently emerged, first the recruitment of staff, particularly part-time staff for Bailrigg catering services, and, secondly, the question of the transport of staff to and from Bailrigg. Sir Fred Longworth said that the problem of travelling expenses or increased wages for staff was one which, from his experience, would have to be tackled sooner or later.

The third academic year saw the opening of arts teaching accommodation at Bailrigg and, with it, the first of the refectories in Bowland College. Thereafter two separate establishments, three miles apart, had to be run in parallel, until St. Leonard's House was finally closed down in 1972. It was now that the problem of recruitment for the more remote Bailrigg site became so difficult and it was in order to widen the catchment area of possible staff recruitment that the Catering Officer suggested the payment of travelling expenses, which met strong opposition from a Mr. S. H. Whitaker who argued that

> If such a step were taken, it would be extremely difficult to prevent its extension to all staff. Once paid, travelling expenses would become a right and eventually claims would be made also for payment for time spent on travelling.
>
> During subsequent discussion, it was pointed out . . . that there might well be a large reservoir of suitable part-time workers on the Hala Carr Estate barely more than a mile away, that the eventual solution to the problem might have to consist of providing special transport, that the problem might be eased by a re-allocation of working hours and the introduction of a five-day working week, and that any extra staff costs would have to be passed on in order to balance the estimates of the catering services.

Nor was there a satisfactory response to a series of advertisements, for although there was a batch of thirty applications from kitchen staff living in Galgate, little more than a mile away, most of the applications were withdrawn when the shift system and evening work were explained. Furthermore, part-time staff stood to lose as much as 12/6 a week out of £4 on travelling costs. Thus Miss Gordon reported to the Council meeting of October 1966 that

> two meetings had been almost exclusively concerned with the problem presented by the transport expenses of the part-time catering staff. The

Committee had resisted suggestions that transport allowances should be paid or transport provided as it was considered that this might become a dangerous precedent and make it difficult to resist similar claims from other categories of staff.

Worse was immediately to follow. Only 28 replies were received in response to 398 circulars distributed around the Hala Carr estate inviting women "to register as willing to be considered for catering work at Bailrigg should their services be required". The financial position of the refectory services made a suggestion that a vehicle to carry part-time workers to and from Lancaster wholly impracticable, for deficits were rising steeply: over a three-month period during the Long Vacation there had been a loss of £1,800, and a further deficit was expected from the Bowland refectory. The Refectory Committee minute of November 1966 continues:

> A long discussion followed on the reasons for the losses. It was pointed out that many students missed meals completely, partly because of the noise, congested conditions and long queues at peak hours. . . . Some members expressed disquiet that students should jeopardize their health by missing meals. The Finance Officer said that as a University Refectory was fully utilized for only 30 out of 52 weeks in a year some loss was probably inevitable unless all students were charged for all meals, as at Durham, or unless the Refectories could be used during the vacations for conferences, etc., which would not be possible until other accommodation was available at Bowland College in two years time.

Although the refectories' profit picked up once term was under way, the increase in trade was not sufficient to offset the vacation losses. There were also complaints about, and constant readjustments of, the opening and closing hours of the various outlets—this being the Senate's particular anxiety, especially about the arrangements made for vacations.

A further movement away from centralized catering to self-catering of some kind was mirrored in the debate about commercially sponsored residences early in 1967.[4.76] In a document of the Vice-Chancellor's for the Senate and the Council, entitled "The shape of future colleges", he argued that

> The accommodation provided must be in "flatlets", where students can cook some of their own meals and do most of their own cleaning, so that higher rents may be offset by lower living costs. . . .
>
> Mr. Haydn Smith's plans are based on standard units, capable of being combined so as to give room for seven or ten students on each floor of a

---

[4.76] See Chapter 2 for a discussion of these residences.

three-storey building, these students having single or double rooms of good size, and sharing a substantial and properly equipped kitchen-dining room. . . .

It is a consequence of this scheme that the College dining hall, in Furness and later colleges, would become even smaller (in relation to the total membership of the college) than that in the early colleges. This reduction in size is inevitable in any case, for the U.G.C. has discovered that substantial numbers of students will, at any one meal, use snack bars or other means of feeding instead of getting a set meal. The provision already planned or made, in Bowland, Lonsdale, Cartmel and County colleges, is considerably in excess of the likely demands on it; and that required in later colleges, with provision for students to cook their own meals, would be much smaller. . . .

Consequently, I suggest that we should drop the idea of a hall in which the college meets for meals, substituting periodical formal dinners for the *whole* college at one sitting, in the Central Hall. If only 200 places are required for each college, I suggest that this would be much more pleasantly provided in a series of smaller restaurants, each offering its own speciality: for instance, a Salad Bowl, a Fish Restaurant, an Indian or Chinese style restaurant, a Quick Service bar. This would also make it much easier to provide for club and society dinners.

The site development architect, Mr. Gabriel Epstein, was a strong supporter of such a view, as can be seen from the letter written to the principal of Lonsdale College in March 1966:

Right from the start we were concerned that the colleges, while providing what is needed for their members, should not be too self-sufficient, and in our very first discussions with the U.G.C., they warned us against this happening, saying that it would detract from the life of the university as a whole. Now ever since college syndicates have been formed, I have felt, but I may of course be wrong, that the danger described by the U.G.C. might be a reasonable one. As a planner, I am naturally interested in the liveliness of the university as a whole, and because of this I am concerned that not too much of this should be drained off the pedestrian spine and into the "hinterland". It may be considered that the dining rooms are not an important social element of the colleges, particularly since they cannot hold all the members of the college at one sitting. I should therefore much prefer a system of restaurants along the spine, and as I was saying the other day, I feel that these might well be relatively small places, serving virtually a single menu each. This would provide variety in catering in atmosphere, and in price levels, and would ensure some competition between them.

Mr. Bernard Thorpe, the university's adviser on shops, had also, he reported,

> advocated restaurants because "the operation of dining halls is certainly
> restricted to serving meals at set times of the day. While perhaps this is
> preferable at midday, if you want to encourage university life to extend
> late into the evening, there must obviously be provision for meals to be
> taken at widely different times between say 4.00 p.m. and 10.00 p.m. and
> meals of different qualities, styles and prices. A restaurant can handle
> this, but a dining hall cannot. There is also an essential difference in
> atmosphere which I suggest could be important".

The Vice-Chancellor amplified this statement to the Senate of February
1967 when he pointed out that

> The college dining hall as an institution was already threatened by the
> results of an enquiry by the U.G.C., which indicated that it was not neces-
> sary to have dining halls that provided for more than 40 per cent of the
> membership of a college at one sitting. It looked very much as if the dining
> hall would not find a place in the new colleges.

The varied reactions to the proposal for commercially sponsored residences
and their implications for catering are interesting. But, more locally, each
college syndicate had a different view to present. Bowland, for example,
welcomed a diversity of restaurants, while being concerned that a consequence
might be cheap and uninteresting meals in the Bowland refectory. County
supported the idea of a large central banqueting hall. Furness agreed that they
were in favour of having only small specialized restaurants—but a month
later, asked for three outlets of their own (as well as a private dining room) for
60, 90 and 110 people respectively! Lonsdale, in the meanwhile, was
particularly concerned about the level of facilities provided in the vacations.
In other words, there was a piecemeal reaction amongst the academic staff
which meant that decisive action had to come from elsewhere.

At the Senate conference in March, Professor Willcock, the principal of
Bowland College, spoke of "intense difficulties of communication" with the
Catering Officer, for "the methods of making contact with him were almost
bound to cause a negative reaction on his part. It was without doubt the
greatest difficulty in College organization that the College had no say in how
the kitchen was run." This attitude was reflected again in the general discussion on the catering department when

> The point was made that at present the Colleges had no effective control
> over the catering services and that the Refectory Committee's policies and
> decisions too often conflicted with the wishes of Senate and of the
> Colleges. Professor Dobbs reported that the "shadow" Syndicate of the

County College had been considering how to promote college life. One of its aims would be to try to ensure that a high proportion of its members took lunch in the College dining hall. This would involve experimenting with systems other than cash for paying for lunches. He considered that the Colleges should have a reasonable amount of autonomy in the running of their dining halls and given scope for experiment to try to make their own catering services pay.

It was suggested in discussion that, with the increase in the number of colleges, each college should be given more effective control over the catering services provided in its building, and also that, with effect from the beginning of the next academic session, the Refectory Committee should be replaced by an arrangement under which a separate refectory committee would be established for each college refectory. . . .

The Vice-Chancellor undertook to propose to the Council that, from October 1967 (when the Lonsdale College building was available), the present Refectory Committee's responsibility for college refectories should be transferred to the relevant College management Committees.

In the event, it was decided not to equip the Central Hall for banquets, but since then it has so far proved possible to accommodate formal university dinners in such places as Cartmel Lecture Theatre.

By May 1967 the catering deficit for the year was being estimated at £5,000, and the Finance Committee was taking a hand in the matter—to the dismay of the members of the Refectory Committee, who felt that they were being slighted, and the views of the colleges were not being taken into due consideration. A paper written by the University Secretary for the Finance Committee of May 1967 summed up the dichotomy of interests competing in the area of university catering when he said that it was essential that such services be

efficiently managed and they should be expected, with the aid of agreed subsidies, to pay their way

while also endorsing the view that it was

of the highest importance that the University's catering services be planned and operated in such a way that they are properly adequate for and consonant with the many and varied needs of a University institution. Catering services can and should make a very important contribution to the quality of corporate life of the University.

The contribution they were not making can be seen in the strongly worded memorandum of one student representative who wrote, also in May 1967, that

At 6.00 this evening nearly every table was piled high with dirty crockery, customers were still streaming in and one main dish was already off the menu.

I well appreciate that due to difficulties of staffing it may not be possible for the refectory management to provide a service which would match that of the Café Royal but this is no excuse for allowing the refectory to assume the appearance of a pigsty as it usually does at peak hours. The problems of clearing the refectory might well be of a complexity that would baffle the ordinary mortals among us. But the fact that a university competent to tackle advanced problems of industrial organization through its Systems Engineering and Operational Research departments, is yet utterly incapable of clearing the dirty crockery off its refectory tables is nothing less than a crying shame.

The Finance Committee decided to recommend to the Council that a new Catering Services Policy Committee be set up to decide on policy for all catering services.

Council at the end of May decided that the matter should properly go to the college syndicates for their consideration, but while reports were awaited events overtook deliberation, and in October 1967 the new policy committee was established, and the Refectory Committee laid down.

The deficit for the year ended 31 July 1967 was £5,500, with a further deficit incurred during the Long Vacation of £2,940. Meanwhile, St. Leonard's House was becoming more and more uneconomic in its operation, and there were problems connected with the transfer of staff between St. Leonard's House and Bailrigg. Just at the beginning of the new academic year, moreover, the Catering Officer resigned at very short notice, and a temporary arrangement was made with a commercial catering firm. A circular put around the university, dated 5 October 1967, noted that negotiations were in train with a firm of professional caterers

> who will act as consultants and will offer certain managerial services and advice. . . . It is not proposed that the existing catering arrangements should be altered, but only that the necessary ancillary buying and costing services and financial controls should be provided. . . . In view of the emergency and of the need to start the term with a first class catering service, the consultants have been asked to provide their services from noon tomorrow.

No more than a month later, however, pressure was coming from the Joint Colleges Refectory Committee to have another catering officer appointed as soon as possible. It was generally agreed that the experiment with the catering firm, which had in any case been entered into on a temporary basis, was not a success, either in financial or managerial terms. Mr. Michael Argles in particular spoke of the need to appoint

> A full-time University Catering Officer, with specified powers and duties, who should be a man of ability and imagination, with status and power to act. In no other way can the confidence of the Refectory Staff be renewed or catering at this University be properly considered and organized.
>
> The present system of control and responsibility does not work, I myself am involved, as a complete amateur, in technicalities and details in which I have little or no competence,

as well as in endless discussions with the commercial catering firm or the university's own catering staff, to the detriment of his primary duties.

The Catering Policy Committee papers of 27 November 1967 give a record of the U.G.C.'s view of catering at Lancaster. When the duties of a catering controller were analysed, it was found that two important functions, the co-ordination of the various catering outlets and the arrangement of special functions (such as degree congregation entertaining) required a central catering office. If this were to be set up, it could carry other duties, such as purchasing, financial control, staff recruitment and training, and forward planning. The U.G.C., on looking closely at Lancaster, had found that there was no economic case to be made out for a central food preparation unit because it was not economic on a scale as small as a university. The catering manager would therefore not stand in a relationship to the colleges as wholesaler of prepared food to retail establishments, but would need actual managerial control of the kitchens and refectories: a manager of adequate quality, who would receive a salary commensurate with his merit, would not be satisfied to act as adviser to kitchens he did not control.

This policy was accepted by the university, but the implementation of it was not to be so easy, particularly as the deficit continued to increase. A memorandum of February 1967 for the Finance Committee covering the first six months of the 1967–68 financial year showed a deficit of £5,287, almost double the figure for the same period a year before and portending a deficit for the whole year of up to £10,000, in addition to the charges already made by the commercial catering firm. It was suggested by the Finance Committee that prices be raised forthwith, but the Catering Policy Committee decided to leave such a change until the new catering manager who had been appointed took up his post on 1 April.[4.77] At the same time that the deficit was growing, demand was falling off and complaints about choice and standard were increasing.

[4.77] For a time Cartmel College had its own catering manager, but his role, although introducing a further dimension of complexity at the time, is not so central that it needs to be narrated here.

In addition, the students were becoming involved on behalf of the refectory staff: a manifesto circulated in May 1968 called students' attention to the fact that refectories had been closed "during normal meal hours, and that on many occasions the serving bays have been understaffed . . . as a direct result of a large number of resignations by general assistants, in reaction to poor wages and the low standards of working conditions". A Federation meeting at the beginning of June suggested that a travel allowance, to cover the cost of their journeys, be given to all refectory staff, as well as a "full review of working conditions to ensure that present grievances do not result in more resignations and consideration be given to the matter of paid lunch breaks". Nor were the academic staff any more satisfied: a document by Mr. Argles on catering policy of June 1968 speaks of "over-provision of service points, falling demand, rising raw material costs, changing eating patterns, demand for better food, and steeply rising deficits".

In this climate of an increasing lack of control, with a mounting deficit and a large-scale desertion by the students of the central facilities, a working party on catering, chaired by Professor Simpson and including the Internal Auditor, was set up. Working from their analysis of the situation the Vice-Chancellor drew up a policy document, designed to bring resident students back into the refectories, which went to the Catering Policy Committee in June 1968:

> The provision of meals and snacks at a large and growing number of different eating places is wholly uneconomic. The reason for this is that the demand is very much below the designed capacity. Only about 30 per cent of students take even one main meal in a refectory. The turnover is only about 20–25 per cent of that for which the catering facilities were designed. . . .
>
> The catering services are running this year at a deficit of £8,000–£10,000. Next year and in 1969 the situation will be much worse, for there will be even more eating-places, and also a considerable increase of facilities for students to cook their own meals. Each kitchen and each refectory or snack-bar needs a certain basic staff, however small the demand. The result of having kitchens operating far below capacity is that the staff cost per main meal served becomes very high. . . .
>
> There is no solution by way of the university subsidizing meals, or meeting the loss in vacations. If we regularly go beyond the existing concealed subsidy of providing the kitchen premises free of charge, the University Grants Committee will simply refuse to provide an amount of grant equivalent to any cash subsidy which appears in our estimates; for we are expected to run our catering services so that, over the years, they break even.
>
> The Catering Policy Committee considers that there are only two

possible solutions: to cut the number of separate eating-places and kitchens until those that remain are operating nearer to capacity: or to follow the practice of almost all other universities, and require residents to pay for a certain proportion of meals in the refectory. The first of these solutions ... strikes at the root of the College system, and is clearly likely to be unacceptable to members of Cartmel and County Colleges. The second solution involves charging all residents (and all others wishing to buy a "season ticket") for 50 or more main meals per term, at about five shillings each. The price to "casual users" would then be rather higher than this....

It is understood that the *Lonsdale* Syndicate has accepted what is broadly the second solution, and it is assumed that they would also accept rationalization between the colleges (e.g. only one refectory open) at weekends and in vacations. It is also understood that the *Cartmel* Syndicate, while not necessarily accepting all the arguments presented to the Catering Policy Committee, accepted the second solution. The *Bowland* Syndicate has not yet formed a view.

The tickets were to be compulsory for first years and on offer to everyone else. These proposals were extensively discussed for the last month of the summer term in college syndicates and junior common rooms, as well as by the S.R.C., and a report made to the Finance Committee at the beginning of July that

a strong student view emerges which is opposed to any form of compulsory contract for any group of students: and an equally strong collegiate view opposed to any form of rationalization which involves closing a college kitchen. The students argue that, given a voluntary system of termly "season tickets" offering a uniform price advantage, and given improvements in the quality of food, the demand will be and will remain adequate to support economic working of both the Bowland/Lonsdale and Cartmel kitchens. . . . If a voluntary system is tried, and fails, it will naturally be difficult to introduce compulsion in the middle of the year or in any subsequent year: much the best time to introduce a new system is at the *beginning* of student residence in October of this year.

In the event, compulsion was not used for, as a Council minute of July 1968 records

Council received and approved a statement, to be issued to all students, describing proposals to offer, with effect from October 1968, substantial discounts (which would increase as the year progressed) to students who purchased a minimum number of refectory meals tickets in advance.

Yet even now the worst point had not yet been reached. At the end of August the Internal Auditor, echoing comments made by the Finance Officer some months before, found a very low level of hygiene in the food stores; and in September Mr. Michael Argles, as chairman of the Joint Colleges Refectory Committee, had to write to the catering manager about the quality of food, the standard of supervision, and the quality of public and staff relations. Meanwhile the students were submitting detailed memoranda about a number of topics, from the siting of menu boards and tray racks to the improvement of traffic flow, and it was only a very short way into the Michaelmas Term 1968 before there were complaints about the unimaginativeness of the food being served, and the inflexibility and general inconvenience of the ticket contract system in Bowland and Lonsdale as against Cartmel (where there was a greater variety of different prices of ticket available).

The deficit on the year's trading for 1967–68 had come to £12,812 and the preliminary estimate made by the Finance Officer in December 1968 for the 1968–69 year was of an anticipated loss of almost £26,000. He therefore recommended that there be introduced an inclusive residential charge on all succeeding generations of students, or the closure of a number of outlets and the severe cutting back of the facilities offered by others. The Catering Policy Committee, at the end of February 1968, came down against

a system of control which is divided between the colleges. It therefore asks the secretary of the university to investigate how, without injustice to the present managers of catering or their staff, the university can rapidly move towards a centralized system under a single controller responsible to the Council through the secretary.

College catering accounts would henceforward merge into a single university refectory account, and the catering staff of colleges would become part of the catering staff of the university.

Council at the end of March was informed that

the Finance Committee approved the recommendation of the Catering Policy Committee that responsibility for catering be removed from the colleges and that a centralized system of catering be instituted under a single controller responsible to the Council through the Secretary of the University.... The Secretary added that Miss Cowell, the senior catering advisor to the Department of Education and Science had visited the university on the 18, 19 and 20 March and had made a thorough inspection, visiting every kitchen and serving point. She was in general agreement with the proposals of the Catering Policy Committee and recommended the appointment of a controller.

Although the catering deficit at the end of the 1968–69 financial year reached a total of £16,637, the situation was about to be transformed by the appearance of Mr. René Diserens, who came to Lancaster with experience of organizing catering at the London School of Economics at the beginning of June 1969. He was horrified at what he discovered at Lancaster, particularly at the misuse and lack of training of what intelligent and well-motivated staff there were available. To assist him in ascertaining the needs and opinions of users, the Catering Policy Committee was reconstituted as the Catering Advisory Committee, and, as a further piece of rationalization, the system of meal tickets, which had dwindled away during the year, was dropped.[4.78] The policy committee, at its final meeting, agreed that the new controller should be advised

> that the university would expect the maintenance of some sort of catering services throughout the year, and also must for the present maintain a service at St. Leonard's House, even if it be unprofitable;
> that the catering service should as far as financially possible take account of the collegiate structure of the university;
> that the university had allowed to students a substantial degree of self-catering in the colleges; that the catering services should be organized so that as much variety as possible was provided.

From the outset he was given full responsibility for the financial and managerial control of the University's catering services, including collegiate catering, conference catering and special functions and was able to deploy the catering staff as "a single force".

Within a fortnight of his arrival, Mr. Diserens had surveyed the whole range of facilities currently on offer. One far-reaching decision made during the summer was not to open the new refectory in County College or two of the three new restaurants in Furness. Only the Assistant Staff House was to be opened and one take-away fish and chip shop. The bars of the new colleges were to be opened, however, and half of all the bars' profits were to go into the central catering fund. The other outlets were to be kept open for the time being, including St. Leonard's House.

Of course there were to be difficulties. Standards (and morale) had been falling for too long for people to do other than expect to encounter problems, and students had become accustomed, in the face of poor service, dull food and rising prices, to cater for themselves to a much greater extent than had been anticipated in the early days. Lost customers were regained slowly, while at the same time a cost-efficient service was being created: in November 1969, for example, the Internal Auditor found himself able to point out that the new controller of catering was not "sitting down bemoaning his fate", the university was not drifting into further difficulties, and a more effective and

---

[4.78] It should be noted that both the university catering manager and the Cartmel college manager left during 1969.

attractive service was in the process of being created. Certainly as early as February 1970 the Council noticed that the trading figures for August to December 1969 "showed very encouraging results"; and the deficit for the 1969–70 year was only £5,876 (reduced still further to £3,572 when £2,304 of bar profits was included), in spite of a continuing fall in users of the main meal services. Income from conferences and other functions was also helping to improve the situation.

A paper prepared by Mr. Diserens in May 1970 had given the tenor of the new approach, when

> faced with a history of catering deficits, I had to formulate policies for the immediate and long term future. This meant reviewing customer level and demand, number and type of outlets, provision of space and equipment and the urgent need to rationalize catering trading until the deficit was eroded.

In short, budgetary control was replacing guesswork and close daily supervision was being substituted for the imprecise logistical arrangements that had occurred so far, so that stores, purchases, sales and accounts, brought under central control, enabled the service and profits of the system to be considered as an entity.

The academic year 1970–71 therefore opened in a spirit of greater optimism. The Assistant Staff House was opened, as well as a fish and chip shop at the south end of the site, while an unremunerative coffee bar was closed down and the St. Leonard's House services greatly contracted. After considerable debate it was also agreed that the catering department should take 5 per cent of the turnover of the nine licensed bars around the university, instead of 50 per cent of their profit (except for one new college that was exempted because of capital expenditure being incurred), but it was conceded that all the food sold in bars was to be provided by the controller of catering.

By November, Mr. Diserens was able to report to the Committee of Colleges that usage of the refectories was up by 20 per cent over the previous autumn, with at least half the students using a coffee bar and having a main meal in the refectory each day: but with a catering capacity already (on U.G.C. norms) existing for almost four thousand people, it was difficult to recommend the opening of any more colleges' facilities. The extent to which the effort to provide individualized catering for each college had disappeared can be seen in a comment of the time to the effect that "as bars were almost the only distinctive feature of colleges it was desirable that each new college should have a bar". Indeed, since the requirement for them appeared to be insatiable, there seemed no financial difficulty in setting up further bars as more colleges opened.

Yet familiar difficulties still intruded themselves. In March 1971, for example, the college principals again raised the question of transport to and from Bailrigg for cleaning and catering staff. The Building Development Officer had noted some months before that departments were setting up coffee and tea facilities of their own, and the question arose again in respect of the suggested provision of common room facilities for Gillow House—the decision made being that special areas known as common rooms should not be provided other than on a collegiate basis. There was no resistance, however, to further cookers being provided for students' self-catering, provided that colleges could afford them. Such extended self-catering put a heavy strain on kitchen areas not intended to cope with anything more elaborate than the preparation of light snacks, as the public health inspector found when he came round in April on a tour of inspection and discovered inadequate hygienic standards.

Mr. Diserens from early on carried out a policy of making himself accessible to students from colleges and the S.R.C., arranged special meetings or *ad hoc* bodies to give him further information about the consumers' eye-view of the catering services, and tried to ensure that student complaints were not submerged but brought to his attention. This altered approach gradually brought about improved communication with members of the university and the tide of opinion slowly moved from expecting a poor quality of food and service to an expectation of higher standards, which in its turn produced higher turnover. Yet, as the Internal Auditor pointed out in March 1971, while Mr. Diserens was taking care that a less costly catering service "should not be detrimental so far as the quality and range of foods his department is prepared to offer", nevertheless

> if we are not to incur substantial deficits and at the same time provide a very comprehensive range for long spells during every day of the week it is inevitable that we will have a sort of "institutional catering".

This approach was echoed in a minute of the Catering Advisory Committee held the previous month at which the University Secretary reported on a meeting with the U.G.C.

> concerning heavy losses being made by universities on catering services. The Comptroller and Auditor General was disturbed at the magnitude of these losses—more than half a million pounds in 1969–70 and estimated at some £630,000 in the current year—and informed universities that the Treasury would not continue to tolerate such losses.

In the spring of 1971 a project group from the university's own M.A. in Business Analysis carried out a survey of catering needs and demands, including self-catering. Apart from some useful statistics, their report gives an illustration of attitudes. Refectories, for instance, "by their size and design, by the manner in which food is served, by the collection of cutlery and the total atmosphere under which food is eaten, have led to the message that it doesn't matter about you, that eating is functional and that alone". The J.C.R.s, however, in which snacks are served, provided surroundings in which "People felt able to talk freely, to function individually and to relax. Reasons given were the 'atmosphere', the lower ceilings, the variation and scattering of seats and the 'people'."

Amongst the self-caterers

> There was little complaint at the number of people using the kitchens; a code of behaviour is developed and the whole system operates as part of a social unit. The inconvenience is tolerated for its advantages in freedom from restraint and individuality compared with the institutionalized act of going and eating in the refectories. . . .
>
> The food is not radically different from that served in the refectories, nor is it higher in quality necessarily, but it looks different, you know what is in it, you can have as much as you want and do what you want.

Most of the self-caterers recognized the expense of getting their ingredients from the shops on the site and the cost of the time involved, but neither of these factors weighed as heavily as those described above.

The vindication of Mr. Diserens' management came at the end of the 1970–71 financial year when he was able to show a total revenue of £154,382 compared with the previous year's £128,526, an increase in turnover of 20 per cent which, when the 5 per cent turnover from the bars was included, produced a minute deficit of £141. This percentage of bar turnover, however, was being jealously watched by the colleges, and in June the Committee of Colleges and the Finance Committee agreed that

> Colleges should no longer pay 5 per cent of bar takings to the Catering account. The Catering Controller said that he was of the opinion that licensed trading should logically come under the same control as catering, that this was one of the more profitable aspects of catering and that colleges had agreed to make the contributions to the Catering Account in order to retain control of the bars. This income enabled him to aim at a "breakeven" account while at the same time providing some uneconomical services. . . .
>
> The question of the provision of bars for conference was considered and it was agreed that discussions with colleges should be undertaken with a view to the Controller of Catering becoming responsible for the service of drinks at an agreed price per head, before, during and after a function.

The income from conference bar takings was not, however, sufficient to make up the loss of revenue from their customary usage, in spite of some price increases which were made in order to keep up with inflation. At the October meeting of the Finance Committee, therefore,

> the Controller of Catering drew the attention of the committee to a suggestion of the U.G.C. that income from shops . . . could properly be used to help balance catering trading accounts,

and an agreed portion of the shops' rent income was made over to the credit of the catering account. At the same time the students took over the coffee bar in Alexandra Square and have been running it ever since.

During 1971–72 the catering situation went from strength to strength, with the usage of the refectories continuing to increase, although at a slower rate of growth, and the conference and special functions trade also expanding rapidly. A decision was taken in the spring of 1972, with the ready consent of the colleges, that this mode of operation be continued for a further ten years. It was agreed that Mr. Diserens would be responsible to the Finance Committee

> primarily to provide a comprehensive catering service without loss: but the Finance Committee may, at the request of the Committee of Colleges, direct him to provide particular loss-making services.

The Catering Advisory Committee was laid down, and the Committee of Colleges took over its functions and was to make proposals to Mr. Diserens for the conduct of catering services on the understanding "that he would adopt such proposals unless he could show that they would lead to an increase of deficit, damage goodwill, or do harm to labour relations". During the year, St. Leonard's House finally closed and the Assistant Staff House came fully under Mr. Diserens' control. There was a triumphant conclusion to the year, for, on a turnover of £192,019[4.79] and with the revenue from the shops added in, the catering account showed a profit of £4,824.

With a new quinquennium about to start, and the catering services becoming profitable, there was during the year some pressure for the opening of other colleges outlets that had so far been kept in mothballs. The existing services, it was felt, were all clustered in the centre of the University, in the first colleges to be opened, and now the County College, at the northern end of the site, and Furness College at the southern end, wished to make use of the refectory space built into their accommodation. When Miss Cowell came up in the summer of 1972 however, she found that the existing outlets were adequate, on a numerical basis and with the existing pattern of demand, for the 1972–77 quinquennium. Her view was that any further outlets would lessen the demand for those already existing and prevent them reaching their

---

[4.79] Approximately a quarter of this was attributable to the refectories, a quarter to conferences, 15 per cent to the coffee bars, 12 per cent to special functions and the remaining quarter to various common rooms and other small-scale operations.

full capacity, and on this basis there was no justification for the investment of U.G.C. money in further catering equipment at Lancaster. The County College catering equipment has since been sold.

The sagacity of her warning was revealed all too soon, for after a promising beginning to 1972–73, rising costs and wages and the fact of there being a smaller increase in student population than had been expected brought losses where previously there had been gains: so that by halfway through the Michaelmas Term of 1972 anxiety over the catering situation for the whole financial year had again raised its head, and at the end of the financial year here was a small deficit of £1,717.

As we have already seen, the development of the conference trade at Lancaster helped to ameliorate the catering situation. After a tentative beginning in 1968–69, the volume has increased each year until, in 1971–72, the total turnover from conferences and special functions (including both the catering and college accounts) was £87,367.

Lancaster, of course, is one of numerous higher education centres which uses conferences to augment income and increase the level of usage of its costly buildings.[4.80] In 1972–3 there are available 1,702 beds and 740 refectory places,[4.81] and the conference officer, Mr. Malcolm Ellacott, has had as his target the utilization of an average of 400 of these places during the conference season. The season is normally regarded as being the four weeks of the Easter vacation and the twelve weeks of the summer, although the former is complicated by the large number of students who stay up for revision, and there is also a certain limited amount of trade at Christmas.

The conferences are extremely varied in type, ranging from charitable, professional or learned organizations to large manufacturers, and in size may be anything between a couple of dozen and several hundred. A number may run concurrently, housed in separate colleges, and, wherever possible, they are allocated a special refectory designated as their own (while some catering provision is also set aside for students who are still in residence).

The volume of business has been growing steadily as news of Lancaster's amenities is spread by word of mouth. At first the local hoteliers of Morecambe and Blackpool were concerned that the university might detract from their business, but the peak of the conferences comes in July when the hotels are not in a position to accommodate them.[4.82] Some of the conference groups return on a regular annual or bienniel basis and these provide a core

[4.80] See *The Times* supplement on conferences (13 February 1973), p. IV.
[4.81] The number of refectory places is low because of the extent of students' self-catering.
[4.82] In order to avoid ruffling local feelings, the university has declined to join in the consortium of universities involved in the conference trade which has been organized by the British Tourist Authority.

T

around which others will group themselves: bookings may extend up to three years ahead at any given time.

Lancaster has obvious attractions, being a compact site which is quiet, well provided with car parks, common rooms, bars and lecture halls with all modern facilities, and with easy access to the Lake District and other famous beauty spots. It can provide almost any level of service which is required, and puts on, for the larger affairs, special dinners or exhibitions, or dances in the Great Hall. The income from these functions helps in a number of ways. For the university, it has the effect of increasing the utilization of buildings which would otherwise lie fallow for twenty weeks or more of each year, brings in work for the assistant catering staff, most of whom would otherwise not be needed in the vacations, and helps the central catering account. For the colleges, it brings in sorely-needed revenue, which they may spend as they see fit (subject, naturally, to the rules of the university), thus increasing the autonomy that they feel so strongly about. For the students it holds down rent levels and keeps their term-time meals at a lower price level than they would otherwise be. Therefore, although conferences represent a good deal of work, both within the central administration and within the colleges, they make a significant contribution to the general welfare of the university, and one which it is hoped can be further extended in the future.[4.83]

(iii)   Student representation

Probably the most notable single change in the constitutional structure of the university has been the development of student representation at every level of committee. This feature was not envisaged at the foundation of the new universities: Graeme Moodie, Professor of Politics at the University of York since 1963, notes that one governmental problem not foreseen at York was

> the impatient and at times obsessive demands of students for participation, "democracy" or transformation.[4.84]

Sir Eric Ashby and Dr. Mary Anderson, who have given a valuable account of the historical development of student representation, confirm that student pressure for representation did not build up until the mid-sixties and that it was, if anything, the masters as much as the scholars who took the initiative.[4.85]

[4.83] For a detailed discussion of Lancaster's conference trade, see J. Andelin and M. Macfarlane, *Vacation Use of the University of Lancaster* (University of Birmingham, 1972, unpublished thesis).

[4.84] Graeme C. Moodie, "University Government", in *Contemporary Problems in Higher Education*, edited by H. J. Butcher and E. Rudd (McGraw-Hill, 1972).

[4.85] See E. Ashby and M. Anderson, *The Rise of the Student Estate in Britain* (Macmillan, 1970), especially pages 74–75, 103–108.

They note that in the early years of the twentieth century only at the Queen's University of Belfast was provision made for a (graduate) student to sit on the executive governing body, although students had already taken their seats on the Courts of some universities.[4.86]

Innovative Keele did not in 1949 attempt any experimentation in this area and Lord Robbins' Committee spoke merely of the desirability of social intercourse between staff and students. The charters and statutes bestowed upon universities in the 1960's distributed membership of governing bodies amongst the senior members of their universities, Lancaster being no exception to this, and it was not until the Charter and Statutes of Coleraine (1970) that provision to permit student membership was embedded in a university's original instrument of government. Lancaster's Academic Planning Board makes no reference to this topic in its report to the U.G.C. of 1963, and the Court, Council and Senate counted no students amongst their original numbers.

The subject of student involvement seems to divide into three distinct stages: first, the areas, such as general welfare, where the student was presumed to have personal interest and relevant and common knowledge; secondly areas, such as academic curricula or the examination system where he was still presumed to have personal interest, but little or no competence; and thirdly areas, such as staff appointments, where he was considered to have a peripheral personal interest (that is, he wanted to be taught seventeenth century French history, rather than a choice between two relatively young and inexperienced lecturers both specializing in studies of Louis XIV), but no competence whatsoever. The first ground was conceded easily, the second caused more heart-searching but had developed by the end of the decade to wide-spread representation on central decision-making bodies, while the third (which we shall not long pause over) recrudesces from time to time as it did for example, at Sussex over a controversial appointment in the field of international relations.[4.87]

Thus A. E. Sloman in 1964, in trying to foresee the Essex structure, stated that

> I must mention one other important part of this structure of government, the student himself. All student activities will be directed by a *students' council*, with its president, vice-president, and other officers. This will organize such matters as debates, societies, sports and athletics, will allocate funds, and represent student opinion directly and informally to the Vice-Chancellor, and formally to the senate. The students will also be

[4.86] *Ibid.*, pages 52–54. See also E. Ashby, *Masters and Scholars* (OUP, 1970), pages 25–34.
[4.87] See *The Times Higher Education Supplement*, Numbers 15 (21 January 1972) and 18 (11 February 1972).

represented on the university court. All this is what happens, I believe, in many universities. But we should like to give students more say in university policy, particularly as regards student life, than is provided by the students' council, and we want to co-ordinate better the different efforts made to provide student facilities. We propose, therefore, to set up a *student affairs committee* of the senate, headed by a dean of students, having members drawn both from the students and from the student advisers I referred to in an earlier lecture. The student affairs committee will be responsible through the senate for all aspects of student welfare: the residential and study accommodation, provision for clubs and societies, physical education and student health.[4.88]

Similarly at Sussex, in the same year, Maurice Hutt, in speaking enthusiastically of the participation of junior members in the running of Falmer House (which provided social and cultural amenities for both junior and senior members of the university) commented that

Of course, participation in the work of these and other university committees is the lot of relatively few of the student body. But it is nevertheless important that there is thus, on the part of undergraduates generally, a sort of vicarious involvement with the running of those aspects of the University which concern them most closely.... And in no one area is it more important to reduce the possibilities of mutual misunderstandings than that of discipline, for it is here in particular that the generations meet and differ.[4.89]

Two years later, at York, Lord James mirrored a very similar situation when he wrote

More difficult was the evolution of a Students' Representative Council, and the student body spent a good deal of time and effort in devising a constitution, once they had set up a "caretaker" committee. Some matters that to some universities seem a matter for the staff rather than the students were left to the students themselves, such as whether to wear gowns. Some students have said that they would have preferred more of these things to be settled by "authority" before they arrived, but my own view is that the course we took was right. It is certainly clear that from the start a staff-student committee should be set up, and student representatives on relevant committees, e.g. the Catering Committee, should be appointed as soon as possible.[4.90]

[4.88] A. E. Sloman, *A University in the Making* (London, 1964), pages 84–85.
[4.89] M. Hutt, "Undergraduates and their Problems", in D. Daiches, *The Idea of a New University* (Deutsch, 1964), pages 50 and following.
[4.90] Lord James of Rusholme, "The University of York", in Murray G. Ross, *New Universities in the Modern World* (Macmillan, 1966), page 47.

When in 1968 Sussex decided to co-opt annually seven students as full members of their Senate, except for certain items selected by the chairman, Professor Perkin remarked that "The success of the move will certainly be closely watched by the other universities".[4.91] Such watchfulness, however, was not necessary in the Lancaster of 1964, where students were not even being given the choice of whether or not to wear gowns.[4.92]

Is there a place for students in university government, useful both to them and to the senior members of the university? The Hart Committee at the University of Oxford,[4.93] looking at this question in 1968–69, rejected any assumption that a "university either is or should be a microcosm of society at large", or that, because students had a vote, this entitled them to "share in the government of a university in all its aspects", but supported the view that "those who have the authority to decide academic matters which are of vital concern to any generation of students, such as the syllabus and methods of teaching and examination or assessment, should be under an obligation to explain the exercise of their authority to students and to modify their practice in the face of cogent criticism". There should, they recommended, be regular channels of communication, for while students cannot "bring to problems of the long-term allocation of the University's resources the skill and experience which that work requires", nevertheless

> at the best they will have many constructive and interesting ideas to contribute to the solution of immediate academic problems; at the worst their proposals will reveal sources of discontent before they become aggravated or show where more discussion and explanation of current arrangements are needed. There is little need to demonstrate at length the fact that Junior Members have a unique experience of the present working of some of the policies which the University has chosen to adopt, and can provide, by their criticism, a constant and necessary stimulus for its improvement.[4.94]

Meanwhile the Committee of Vice-Chancellors and Principals and the National Union of Students were preparing their joint statement to the effect

---

[4.91] H. J. Perkin, *Innovation in the New Universities of the United Kingdom* (O.E.C.D., 1969), page 201.

[4.92] The wearing of gowns was a topic which exercised the Senate at a number of its meetings. As early as March 1965, for example,

> Reference was made to an apparent falling off of the observance by undergraduates that they must wear gowns at all lectures. It was agreed after discussion that, so long as this regulation remained, members of the academic staff should take all necessary steps to enforce it.

This was a losing battle, however, and in May 1967 the Senate approved an S.R.C. proposal that the wearing of gowns be ended.

[4.93] *Report of the Committee on Relations with Junior Members* (Supplement Number 7 to the University of Oxford *Gazette*, volume xcix, May 1969).

[4.94] *Ibid.*, paragraphs 29, 31 and 136.

that there should be "effective student presence on all relevant committees" concerning (a) student welfare, where students sought varying degrees of participation, and (b) curriculum, organization and planning, where students' views should be properly taken into account, but not (c) decisions about individual members of staff or students, where student presence was deemed to be inappropriate.[4.95]

The first mention of student representation at Lancaster comes in March 1965 at a Senate conference in Borrowdale, when it was decided

> to consider, at a future meeting, the constitution of a joint staff-student committee, to replace the present informal arrangements.

At the same meeting, the Senators agreed that

> Syndicates of the Colleges are to be asked whether there should be student representation on the Syndicates,

and noted that

> A suggestion was made that there should be student representation on the University Court.

At the end of the academic year a report from the Staff/Student Committee noted, under a minute headed "Communication of Information to Students", that

> Whilst it was explained that every attempt was made to ensure that all decisions on matters of importance to the student body were communicated as quickly as possible to the student representatives, it was agreed that the Vice-Chancellor should raise on Senate the possibility of student *observers* attending certain parts of Senate meetings, and as *observers* at certain other Committee meetings where appropriate.

And the Senate subsequently expressed itself as being willing to admit student observers, "in order that they might express the students' point of view to Senate and listen to its deliberations on these matters". The Refectory Committee meanwhile agreed to a membership of four students, students having previously expressed their "regret" at not being consulted over refectory hours of opening; while Lonsdale Syndicate agreed that the matter of student representation be left in abeyance for the time being. This syndicate had already, however, in December 1964 agreed that there should be a joint planning committee with Bowland, "to co-operate with the Building Development Officer in the planning of the permanent college buildings", on which

---

[4.95] "Joint Statement from the Committee of Vice-Chancellors and Principals and the National Union of Students," 7 October 1968.

there were to be the two J.C.R. presidents and two other students. Although Bowland Syndicate, by September 1965, had not yet "fully approved" this constitution, the committee nonetheless went into operation with student representation. Thus, at completion of the university's first academic year, students were full members of the Joint Athletics Committee, the Joint College Planning Committee, and the Joint College Refectory Committee as well as having the Staff/Student Committee.

During the summer, however, it was found necessary to increase lodgings charges[4.96] and in the turmoil that followed (the students alleging, amongst other things, that they had not been properly consulted), the officers of the Students' Council were invited to join two meetings of the Senate, on 6 and 8 October 1965. In the course of the discussion Mr. J. C. Green

> said that the students considered that communications between the Senate and the Students Council had not been altogether satisfactory and that the views and interests of students were not sufficiently taken into account when decisions were taken on matters which concerned them. He mentioned that the Junior Common Room was shortly to vote on a motion that there should be a student representative on Senate who would attend such parts of meetings of Senate as were concerned with student welfare, so that decisions would be taken in the full knowledge of students' views. (The Vice-Chancellor pointed out that such representation was not possible under the present University Statutes.)

The students' main proposals were that "representatives of the students should be allowed to take a full part . . . in future negotiations on lodgings charges and on other matters relating to lodgings" and that revision of the regulations governing occupation of flats "should be made in consultation with the student representative". The Vice-Chancellor, in reply,

> stressed that the University could not enter into negotiations on these matters under duress. . . . However, he reminded the student officers that . . . the University was willing to discuss lodgings matters with a properly constituted body of representatives of students and was also willing that such representatives should be involved in future discussions and negotiations with landladies on lodgings charges and other related matters.

The students, however, were beginning to exert pressure for direct representation on the existing decision-making bodies, in preference to being consulted via bodies created especially for them. Thus, we find at the Staff/Student Committee meeting of 18 October 1965,

---

[4.96] See Chapter 6, pages 369 to 371, for a full account of this episode.

In answer to further requests from members of the Students' Council for representation on occasions when matters affecting the student body were being discussed, the Principal of Bowland College reported that consideration was at present being given by Bowland College Syndicate to a proposal that there should be student representation on the Syndicate. The Vice-Chancellor reported that he would consider the proposals . . . that Senate agendas (possibly in a restricted form) should be made available to the Students' Council, and that after seeing these agendas members . . . should be allowed to seek representation at meetings of Senate on those occasions when specific matters of student interest were being discussed. (In making this proposal members of the Students' Council accepted Senate's right to refuse on occasions requests for student representation.)

Opinion amongst the staff seems to have been fairly evenly divided, for the Senate, at a meeting of 13 November 1965, "rejected on a vote, by a narrow majority" a proposal to send a copy of (all but the strictly confidential) Senate agenda "so that the Students' Council might be in a position to ask to be heard by Senate on any matter which concerned the students", while approving an alternative proposal that the University Secretary "should inform the Students' Council by letter, before each meeting of Senate, of those items arising on the agenda which might be of concern to the students", and agreeing that "Senate should be willing to consider the attendance of student representatives . . . for the discussion of specific items of interest to students, though it should reserve the right to refuse a request for the attendance of student representatives".

Meanwhile Council, acting on the initiative of the Vice-Chancellor, had agreed on 19 October that "the student body be invited to nominate six students to be members of the Court of the University". This was promptly followed up, for by the next meeting of Council on 21 December it was reported that the Chairman of Council had already approved the nomination of six students in order that they "could attend the Annual Meeting of the Court on 4 December"—their first appearance on a statutory body. Furthermore, Bowland Syndicate on 13 October, had considered a proposal by Professor Sturmey that a recommendation be made to Senate that there should be student representation on the syndicate, for

> Whilst at this stage he did not wish the Syndicate to discuss in detail either the number of student representatives to sit on the Syndicate nor how these members should be nominated he . . . believed that only with student representation could the Syndicate claim to be fully representative of all members of the College.

After discussion the proposal was agreed, and approved in principle by the Senate on 13 November.

Bowland and Lonsdale Colleges were deliberately keeping in approximate step with each other as they each struggled to formulate a college constitution which they hoped would endure for some years to come. On 8 December 1965 both syndicates met with very similar agenda items on student representation. Bowland had set up a working party on this topic at its November syndicate meeting, which reported in December that its members

> had thought it necessary to exclude student representatives from meetings of the Syndicate when such items as reports from Senate, matters relating to examinations, etc., were being discussed and therefore had proposed that a "College Management Committee" be established on which there would be student representation.

Some concern was expressed, however, about the lack of definition of the duties of the proposed committee, while others were "unhappy that no specific proposals were made in the report that there should be full student representation at meetings of the Syndicate", and so a final decision was delayed.

Lonsdale had had an informal meeting of senior members on 25 November, at which Professor Tom Lawrenson reported that he had embodied, in proposals for student government, some student representation on Syndicate, with reciprocal Syndicate representation on the College Students' Council. Then had followed a very familiar cry: "the difficulties arising from student representation on the Syndicate were discussed. Some members felt that if student members were included the function of the Syndicate, as an instrument of expression of the non-professorial staff, would be impaired." This anxiety came to the fore at the full meeting of the syndicate on 8 December at which

> The majority of members agreed with Dr. Small's suggestions that if student representatives were invited to attend Syndicate meetings they would play a rather passive role and that the Syndicate would cease to act as a forum at which members of the teaching staff could raise and discuss freely any issue pertaining to the conduct of the University. It was therefore agreed to recommend that some of the functions of the Syndicate should be delegated to a College Management Committee consisting of sixteen members and the Principal, of which eight members would be students. It was proposed that this committee would deal with all matters directly concerning students, e.g. the organization of activities within the College, and general questions of discipline. The Syndicate would, therefore, confine itself to questions relating to the conduct of the University as a whole, and, in particular, could deal more fully with problems arising from tutorial duties.

By 12 January 1966 the names of eight junior members of the college were before the syndicate and were approved as members of the new management committee. Once the mechanism had been established, it appears to have been easily assimilated by the college and although Bowland took until the late spring to complete its deliberations by the end of the academic year it too had arrangements equivalent to those set up by Lonsdale.

In February 1966 the U.G.C. made a quinquennial visit to the university and asked to meet student representatives. Good impressions seem to have been created, for in the subsequent report to the university it was said that

> The Committee had the clear impression that the students enjoyed ease of communication with the University authorities. They had spoken of co-operation and consultation with their seniors and had said that they had plenty of opportunities for putting their points of view and that often indeed they got a considered reply. Things might get more difficult as the University grew bigger but at present there was clearly a sound basis of staff/student relationships and the students were generally content.

In March "the student officers reported [at a meeting of the Staff/Student Committee] that following a recent informal meeting at Knowsley with Lord Derby, the Pro-Chancellor had agreed to place before the next meeting of the Council a request that representatives of the students be allowed to attend such parts of meetings of the Council when matters pertaining to the students were under discussion". He was as good as his word, and Council thereupon resolved that "matters which were of direct concern to the student body should be discussed by Council immediately after it had received the reports [from various bodies] . . . and that the Council should allow two student representatives from each college to attend part of its meeting so that they might have an opportunity to express the students' viewpoint on these matters". As Eric Ashby has pointed out, students were pushing at a door that was already ajar.[4.97] It was, therefore, in keeping with the prevailing temper of that time that when the Cartmel shadow syndicate[4.98] was becoming established early in 1966, the Student Council was invited to nominate twenty students who would be prepared to discuss the college's future activities, of whom five were invited to attend meetings on the planning, decoration and furnishing of the college and "to attend such parts of meetings of the 'shadow' Syndicate as were of direct concern to the students". The students accepted this invitation and "urged the importance of having a substantial junior membership of the 'shadow' college at as early a date as possible . . . in order

---

[4.97] Ashby and Anderson, *op. cit.*, page 97.

[4.98] A shadow syndicate is a nucleus of existing members of the university, and potential members of a new college, who meet to plan its building and constitutional development before it opens.

that work could begin on the design of a college scarf and tie and the drafting of a Junior Common Room Constitution"—modest demands indeed! Similarly, when a Bookshop Committee was set up in March 1966 Senate decided at the initial discussion of it to include "some student representatives to be nominated by the Student Council".

The same steady progression continued during the 1966–67 academic year. In December 1966, for example, the Library Committee recommended to the Senate that its membership "should be increased to include two student representatives—one undergraduate and one graduate student, both appointed by the Student Council. It was agreed that the student representatives should normally be sent all agenda papers for meetings of the Library Committee, but might be requested to leave should any confidential matters arise." Senate acceded to this request, as it did to another in May 1967 when it agreed that "copies of the non-restricted section of the Senate Minutes should be supplied to the Student Representative Council". On the Buildings Committee minutes, however, it was decided that, "having regard to the complexity and technicality of the minutes, it would be preferable for a progress report on building matters to be made available to students, possibly through the medium of 'Scan' twice a term".

Students were not consulted, however, about the selection of persons invited to receive honorary degrees and, on ascertaining their names and disliking the university's choice, in April 1967 a small group wrote a letter, also released to the student press, to the Vice-Chancellor stating, amongst other objections, that

> Our final objection to the selection of candidates is a more general one. Many universities are at last acknowledging the adult status of the student. . . . The award of honorary doctorates of the University of Lancaster is a matter which reflects on ourselves as students at that university. Yet, our elected representatives were never consulted before the decision was made as to the disposition of these awards. Of course, we do not ask, Sir, for the right to decide for ourselves, as merely one segment (if the major one) of the University, to whom these degrees should be given. Such would be tantamount to impertinence. But all we do claim is that representatives of the student body have a right to be consulted on matters of such import as this. We hope, Sir, that you will bear this principle in mind on future occasions.

In his reply the Vice-Chancellor expressed his regret that the students concerned "should have been so foolish as to release this letter to the student press before sending it to me and discussing the contents with me", but agreed that he thought "it would indeed be useful if the Honorary Degrees Committee of Senate were to have discussions with the Students' Council on future occasions, if only to prevent misconceptions arising". The Senate, however, was not so convinced but finally resolved that in future

> students should be allowed an opportunity to suggest persons or classes of persons who might be considered for the conferment of honorary degrees, but that the final selection of names should rest with Senate.

The Vice-Chancellor further undertook to discuss this suggestion with the S.R.C., as well as to write to and meet the students who had questioned the original decision, and after a statement in *Scan* drafted by Professor Lawrenson, the matter was allowed to rest.

In September 1967 there was a thorough analysis of the university's committee structure, in the course of which the Vice-Chancellor noted that arrangements for representation on the Senate and the Council were extra-statutory concessions; and that in any case (as was anticipated by the Academic Planning Board) the constitution of Senate would require review.

He therefore recommended the establishment of a Statute Revision Committee, whose membership was to include (on a seven-person body) one person appointed by the Student Council. The Senate also agreed that the students should attend the proposed Committee of Colleges for items of special concern to students (including honorary degrees) and, in addition, that two students should become full members on each of the Audio-Visual Aids Committee, the Library Committee, and the Committee for Publicity and Public Lectures. Furthermore, the Buildings Committee was invited to add to its membership "two student representatives, to be present for those parts of the meeting at which all the professional advisers are present (but not for the private meetings which appoint professional advisers)", which it did by the end of the calendar year; and the new Committee on Examinations was to be "reminded that it will need to consult student opinion".

The Staff/Student Committee had discussed its own future in March 1967 and the Vice-Chancellor echoed the feeling of that meeting in September when he commented that

> This committee is anomalous: most of its functions ought to belong to the Colleges or to consultation with students at Senate meetings: but its existence is appreciated by students, as a means of informal discussion of ideas. . . . I suggest that the present Staff/Student Committee should be laid down, and replaced by a regular informal meeting between the Vice-Chancellor and Secretary, with such other administrative officers as may be relevant on a particular occasion, and the Student Council.

Although Senate agreed with this proposal, few such relatively large-scale meetings ever took place. Meetings between the Vice-Chancellor and the student S.R.C. officers, however, continued on an informal but regular basis.

It was true that the students had less need of a committee of their own to make their views heard. They were, for example, becoming an increasingly integral part of the college syndicates. Bowland, in March 1967, had agreed on a vote that

> subject to the proviso as stated in the Constitution that the Principal or the Vice-Principal and one other senior member of the College have the right to ask the student representatives to withdraw from meetings of the Syndicate . . . voting rights should be conferred on the student members of the Management Committee when present at meetings of the Syndicate.

The newer colleges overtook the longer established ones in this matter, for in November 1967 Senate approved a resolution from Cartmel that "the Syndicate of the College be allowed to have six members of the junior common room as full members",[4.99] and another from County that "the Syndicate of the College be allowed to admit a number of undergraduate and graduate students (six in all in 1967–68) to membership of the Syndicate", except that the college recognized, *inter alia*, that the junior members could be asked to withdraw if matters which were confidential to senior members arose. Lonsdale, lagging behind the other colleges, came up a month later with a proposal that two representatives of the J.C.R. "be permitted to attend, speak and vote at meetings of the Syndicate of Lonsdale College, subject to the condition that they should be required to be absent for the discussion of certain matters, to be designated from time to time by the Principal".[4.100]

Meanwhile, students were taking their seats on more university committees. In October 1967, for example, the new Breadth Courses Committee provided for "two representatives of the Student Representative Council . . . who would not, however, be involved in the consideration of individual exemptions [from following the existing rules on breadth courses]", in November the Computer Committee was to have as members "two postgraduate students appointed by the Students' Representative Council who shall be active users of the computer and shall be selected from different departments", and in May 1968, the reconstituted Bookshop Committee had on it two undergraduates and one graduate student.

The summer of 1968, it will be recalled, was the period of the most

---

[4.99] In fact, Cartmel had overlooked the fact that the Statutes laid down that membership of syndicates was a matter for Senate's approval, and had had students sitting as members since December 1966.

[4.100] The number of junior members of the college syndicates continues to increase and in the 1972–3 session varied between under ten and over twenty at different syndicates. It is the writer's personal experience that with a larger number (and proportion) of students, they speak more as individuals and less as mandated representatives of their J.C.R. On the other hand, if they proportionately and vocally dominate the meeting, senior members may thereby be dissuaded from attending.

turbulent student activism internationally that had ever been experienced: at the same time the University of Lancaster was deeply involved with its statute revisions, one of the main considerations being the kind of student representation which it would be reasonable to have at different levels of the university. Considering how far-reaching the proposals were to be, it was not out of keeping with their tenor that when some third-year economics students absented themselves from a class test at the beginning of the Michaelmas Term 1968, the university felt able to declare, in a press statement, that it believed

> the students' actions were intended to draw attention to a desire to discuss certain matters relating to courses and examinations. In desiring discussion of such subjects, students are knocking on an open door: ample opportunities exist, in the Economics Department, in the Committee on Examinations, and by attendance of students at Senate itself.

A document of September 1968 issued by the Statute Revision Committee discussed the problem in these terms:

> We believe that it is not in dispute that students should be informed and consulted about a wide range of subjects, affecting not only their physical welfare but also the education which the University is offering to them. We do not, however, see this as a "right" deriving in a legalistic way from the definition of students as "members of the University", but rather as a matter of common sense, likely to yield an understanding and co-operation which will improve the effectiveness of the University in advancing knowledge, wisdom and understanding. . . . It would be possible to inform and consult students through a system of consultative committees without decision-making power. . . . Such committees would be a further complication in an already complex committee structure, and there might sometimes arise a doubt as to whether the views expressed in them had been fully and fairly represented to the decision-making body. . . . We think that the experience at Lancaster of the presence of students at Senate and Council, and their membership of many important committees, shows that there is an advantage in understanding and mutual trust to be obtained from first-hand contact, which would be hard to obtain through reporting links with a consultative body. Sometimes the ideas of junior members of the University are better than those of senior members. . . . We believe, therefore, that the most effective way of informing and consulting students (and of getting the advantage of their ideas) is to make them actual members of decision-making bodies. But we all agree that there are limits to the application of this principle: we must define these limits, and state the scale of student participation which we think appropriate.

We consider, first, that though it may be proper to bring students into consultation about certain principles of the examination system, the actual conduct of examinations should be clearly and wholly independent of those being examined. It is for the senior members of the University, in consultation with the external examiners, to set a standard; and this standard then has necessary implications for the content of courses, though we see advantage in the consultation of students about teaching methods. Second, though the greater part of the disciplinary system is operated with student participation, there are certain ultimate disciplinary powers which ought to remain with senior members—namely, the powers of suspension or removal from the University, grave penalties which seem to us to require greater independence and continuity of judgement than can reasonably be expected of student representatives. Third, we think it necessary to reserve to senior members the power of admission, which is exercised with the assistance of confidential reports which ought not to be shown to fellow-students. . . .

Fourth, we would not think it right to involve students in the appointment of individual members of the academic or assistant staff, or in their subsequent promotion, confirmation in office or dismissal. We have considered whether to propose, as a further exclusion, research policy, on the grounds that this is no business of students; but events in the United States convince us that this is not a separation which can properly be made, since teaching and research are to some degree in competition for the same resources. Decisions about specific research proposals are in practice made by heads and senior members of departments: more general questions of policy, if they arise, can, we think, properly be discussed in the presence of student representatives. . . .

We see no reason why students should not be full members of the Council of the University. We note that there has long been student representation on the Governing Body of the Queen's University, Belfast: and that the Statutes of the University of Bradford have been interpreted so as to allow such representation. . . .

Both academic work and discipline are responsibilities of the Senate under the Charter. This rules out full student membership of Senate for all purposes, if our list of excluded topics is to be maintained. We therefore suggest a device used by the University of Sussex, by which a Senate, of senior members only, meets to deal with the excluded topics, but delegates other functions to a body (here called the Board of the Senate) in which students are included. In the draft, we have proposed that such delegation should not require subsequent confirmation of decisions by Senate, and we see no great objection to this, since the members of Senate will be a large majority of the Board of the Senate. If, however, the Privy Council considers that confirmation is necessary as an expression of the responsibility of Senate under the Charter, we see no difficulty in following the Sussex practice, by which Senate has a short formal meeting to ratify the decisions reached by the joint body.

The committee therefore proposed that there be three students on the Council and five on the Senate; the Senate already had the power to add them to the other university bodies.

These numbers, plus the addition of the members of the Student Representative Council (about twenty-five in all) proposed as members of the Court, were suggested by the student representative on the Committee, Mr. R. J. Walker; and were also in line with a precedent Mr. Walker quoted, of proposals made earlier that year at L.S.E., where the Committee on the Machinery of Government had made recommendations for full membership by students "on almost all bodies in its machinery of government", while recognizing, members said, that the committee

> has adopted a bold and unprecedented line different from that of any other university or higher education institution in the United Kingdom. It has done so in the belief that such involvement of School members in common tasks will encourage habits and attitudes reinforcing the unity of the School, will contribute to the pooling of experience and views on which policies and decisions can be more firmly made, will contribute to the dissemination within the School of accurate information about its purposes and working, and will assist in making staff, Governors and administrators on the one hand and students on the other less mutually mysterious.[4.101]

Not everyone consulted about the statute revision, however, felt student representation to be an unalloyed benefit. Professor Dainton commented in May 1968 that

> much of the initiation of policy will be bound to reside in the committees and sub-committees of Senate. . . . I have always recommended here [i.e. Nottingham] that their representation should be on departmental boards and on the relevant committees. In short, I think that their influence is likely to be greatest at the point at which the issues are really debated in detail.[4.102]

I suspect that students who have already been brought into the affairs

---

[4.101] *First Report of the Committee on the Machinery of Government of the School,* chaired by Lord Bridges (London School of Economics and Political Science, February 1968), Section K, page 23.

[4.102] A point echoed by Ashby and Anderson, *op. cit.,* pages 138–142; except that they take the line that the decisions are so "dispersed and diluted that no one, whether student or vice-chancellor, can get his hands on it" (i.e. the power to make binding decisions).

The Vice-Chancellor, Mr. C. F. Carter

John Donat

H.M. the Queen talking to students at The County College, 17th October, 1969

By courtesy of the Lancaster Guardian

The oak tree in County College courtyard

John Donat

Posters along the North Spine

John Donat

of the university in this way may have a clearer realization of the realities of the situation. It was interesting to me when, a few days ago in discussion with students, the question of possible membership of Council and Senate came up here, to hear the view expressed by one and forcibly reiterated by another, "from what we hear of both those bodies, we don't think we would like to be on"!

In the event (to anticipate strict chronology by a few months), the Privy Council was sent the proposed revisions in March 1969: there was then a delay until early in 1970, largely due to the Privy Council's receiving at that time a number of proposed revised statutes from other institutions which included some form of student representation. Naturally, as the Vice-Chancellor pointed out to the Statute Revision Committee, "the Privy Council does not want to approve one particular system without full consultation with the Government and the U.G.C.". During this lull, the Vice-Chancellor was appraised of a more radical suggestion, put forward by the University of Newcastle-upon-Tyne, which made students full members of Senate itself, "but with the understanding that certain reserved matters would be dealt with by other bodies . . . the proposal to make students full members of Senate has the advantage of preventing the emergence of a belief that the senior members of Senate decide a lot of things, without consultation with students, in their separate meeting".[4.103]

The reply from the Privy Council stated that Their Lordships would require to be satisfied that "there is adequate provision to ensure the student representatives are genuinely representative of the student body", and that the student representatives would not participate in the reserved areas of business as defined in the Joint Statement from the Committee of Vice-Chancellors and the N.U.S.[4.104] From this interchange and other discussions emerged the concept of a Senate which would discuss and make decisions on all categories of business except for the reserved areas, these being sent to a Committee of the Senate which would consist of senior members only. The same device was suggested for the Council, and adopted for both committees in the revised Statutes.[4.105] It was not immediately obvious how student representatives should be selected from within a collegiate university which yet had a central Student Representative Council. Mr. Walker had reported in December 1968 that "the suggestion that the colleges should be the constituencies for the election of student representatives . . . was unlikely to

---

[4.103] Letter of the Vice-Chancellor to the Privy Council, 30 January 1970.
[4.104] The reserved areas were defined as "decisions on appointments, promotions and other matters affecting the personal position of members of staff, the admissions of individuals and their academic assessment".
[4.105] See Revised Statutes 10 to 13.

U

gain the assent of the student body". Early versions of the revisions therefore suggested that the students be chosen on the basis of one student per college, the chairman of the S.R.C. and three or more students elected by that Council. Their Lordships, however, considered "the proposal for there to be a minimum of 10 student members on the Senate excessive" and the eventual student membership was the chairman of the S.R.C. *ex officio* and "One student elected by and from the students of each College, in an election by secret ballot in which all students of that College shall be eligible to be candidates and to vote".[4.106] (These provisions were linked to an official and statutory recognition of the S.R.C. which was incorporated into the new statutes.)

In the meanwhile, however, students were admitted, with full voting rights, to a Board of the Senate, whose decisions were subsequently formally ratified by Senate itself, an arrangement which lasted from October 1968 until the Revised Statutes came into operation in March 1971.

The Statute Revision Committee had contemplated the possibility of students becoming members of boards of studies, but had agreed to leave consideration of this until later. In fact, an initiative came from a small group of staff on Board of Studies D—the voting was very close—in December 1970. The Board of the Senate received the report from Board D in January 1971 and, at the same meeting, another from the Development Committee to the effect that it had "agreed by a majority that it would support the extension of student representatives to all other boards of studies, excluding the Board of Graduate Studies". The Academic Registrar had also sought the views of most departments on this matter, and found only five wholeheartedly in favour, seven which were opposed, and the remaining seven expressing varying degrees of indifference or scepticism. The views of the other boards of studies were next solicited and found two in favour and two which rejected, with large majorities, the suggestion that they should have students on their boards. The Senators, however, decided in March 1971 that all boards should be uniform in this matter, and that for a trial period of one year each of them should have "as members one student elected by and from the students of each departmental consultative committee in the board in such a manner as each consultative committee shall decide". Since 1971 students, selected on the basis described, have become a regular feature of all the boards of studies, which by now all members of staff probably take for granted; and very technical and boring must some of the business seem to the students at these meetings, for names of new representatives do not come forward with much readiness at the beginning of each academic year.

4.106 Revised Statute 11 (I), Class II. It is possible, however, for the Senate to use its co-options under Class III to augment the student numbers; a further two had a seat on the Senate by this means in 1972-3, making a total of nine.

We have already looked at Professor Dainton's suggestion that the most effective kind of student representation was at departmental level. At Lancaster departments were given no statutory recognition; under the revised version they still have no statutory powers. As they are not formally organized (in the statutory sense), each of them developed individual styles. One early report is from the Board D departments, of which three (Classics, English and Russian) had, by November 1968, consultative staff-student panels, while the fourth (French) already had student members of the full departmental meeting, with full voting rights except for the obvious reserved items. A year later, still in connection with the statute revision, the Vice-Chancellor asked the Board of the Senate for "advice on how and when to make a check about the arrangements for staff/student consultation at departmental level" and, with the endorsement of the S.R.C., asked departments for reports on their existing arrangements. In a memorandum dated Christmas Eve, 1969, he noted several different patterns, being: (a) a forum of all students (or of all Part II students); (b) an elected committee or committees; (c) elected committee *and* forum (or meetings with students of particular years); (d) an elected committee at which any other student could attend; (e) sectional syndicates and forum; or (f) student membership of a departmental committee. He had found one of these types of arrangements existing in all but two departments which had students (one having received no nominations and the other being very new).

Two more years passed and the Steering Committee in December 1971 advised the Senate that, "as the statutes provide that the method of departmental consultation between members of the departments and students taking courses in the department shall be approved by the Senate . . . it is requesting departments to provide a full report on the method of consultation used and will in due course consider the reports received and advise on the canons to be used in determining whether the form of consultation is suitable". The replies received by March 1972 indicated that a large majority of departments had set up staff/student consultative committees, which customarily met at least once a term, and which had varied means of reporting back to a main departmental meeting. Two departments (for special reasons obtaining at that time) had no formal machinery in operation, and five departments had students either as full members of departmental meetings or present for substantial portions of them; although in all cases the reserved areas were safeguarded. Senate felt able to approve these forms of consultation, merely adding a rider that "in those departments in which students do not attend the departmental meeting the staff/student consultative groups should be scheduled to meet five times a year, or three times if provision is made for extraordinary meetings to be called at the request of a small number of students".

There has been no significant change in the formal arrangements since this appraisal of March 1972, and students have seats on all committees except those dealing with the personal affairs of staff (Academic Promotions, Assistant Staff and appointing committees), or with the admission of students. For most of these committees, and the Senate and Council in particular, students attend regularly and participate fully. Lest anyone be deluded into thinking student representation a dead issue, however, and the statement of the Committee of the Vice-Chancellors and Principals[4.107] the last word on the subject, one has only to look at the events at Lancaster in the last year to see how fallacious this is. Students in the department of Politics asked during the academic year 1972–73 for "50–50 representation", i.e. that there be an equal number of students to staff at departmental meetings. The matter was not resolved and during the end of the 1973 Michaelmas Term and the 1974 Lent Term became a matter for a boycott by students in the Politics Department. Mass meetings were held and the boycott spread. The whole matter has been referred to a special working party of the Senate; in the meanwhile part of a statement issued by the S.R.C. Administrative Committee in *Scan* of 4 Feb. 1974 shows some of the reasons why it is a safe assumption that the university has not heard the last of student representation:

One way the mass of students can support their reps in their attempts to improve student departmental representation is to make every effort to attend the meetings which they call, involve yourselves in the discussions and the actions aimed at achieving the aims of the present campaign, so that representation isn't just a meaningless word to people. The current fight to improve representation has revealed many areas of fundamental disagreement, issues which so obviously go deeper than a mere dispute over numbers and which directly involve students' relation to their own education.

All departments should realize that the basic issues arising out of the present dispute in the Politics Department are not confined to Fylde College. Irrespective of whether it's 50–50 or just one, whether you go on strike, decide to withdraw your reps from committees until a satisfactory agreement's been reached, sit in, etc., the arguments are essentially the same: we want to share in the decisions about our education, they effectively say no. That's why students in every department, if they believe in the principle that they are entitled to be properly represented, should support the Politics students, and indeed every other department demanding better representation. This doesn't mean it's necessary to

---

4.107 *Student Participation in University Government*, October 1971, lists in tabular form the extent of student representation of Councils and Senates and of the other University committees by topic, e.g. examinations, discipline, library, finance.

demand 50–50 in every department: it's up to the majority of students at mass meetings in each one to decide on the precise formulation of their demands. The demands students in your department make deserve the support of all other students, because it's the same issue really: this applies no less to the fight of the Politics students.

No department can win if it isolates itself from the campaign in the University generally.

CHAPTER 5

The University and the Region

As we have seen in Chapter 1, the proposal that a university be founded at Lancaster came in the first instance from within the county of Lancashire, and without their initiative it would have gone elsewhere. Why did the people who made this effort wish a university to be established in this area? If one poses such a question, one will of course receive a variety of answers, but amongst them is the often expressed hope that the university will bring a number of benefits to the region in which it is placed, including opportunities for employment, stimulus to the local economy and, perhaps less specifically expressed, but as keenly looked for, expectations of enlarged educational and cultural opportunities for those living in the environs of the university. Yet, on the other hand, no person or body in the region ever drew up a list of desiderata to be looked for from the university; nor indeed would it have been appropriate to address such a document to an independent corporate institution such as a university. What impact the university has had, therefore, has come about partly as a simple result of its mere existence (including the importation of a number of people into the area, some for thirty weeks and some for the entire year); partly as the result of official policy from within the university outwards towards the community or from local government authorities inwards towards the university; and partly as the outcome of the initiative and goodwill of members of the university and the region who have striven to prevent the university becoming an isolated community. If the further question is then asked, does it matter if the university does remain apart from the community, there are a number of refutations to such a suggestion. Reference may be made, for example, to the first chapter of Dr. Joyce Long's study of the relationships between the universities and the general public,[5.1] for a conspectus of the literature on the subject. Derman Christopherson also makes a relevant comment when he remarks that

> In this country as in many others there is a tendency for too much of the artistic, cultural and intellectual life to centre on the capital. The universities are not by themselves large enough magnets to draw away the largest artistic and musical events, but as centres of interest and action in the cities of which they form part they can do a good deal to maintain a reasonably lively and forward-looking programme of artistic events. . . . The universities, as they become more involved in social problems and perplexities in general, naturally turn their attention to those that present themselves on their own doorsteps. There can be few universities that are not involved in research, and in some cases in the practical application of the results of research, on whatever are the urgent problems of their locality—problems of poverty, problems of housing and the social services, in some cases problems arising from the presence of racial or cultural minorities, problems of the pollution of the environment and what can be done to prevent or remedy it. In matters of this kind members of universities, student members as well as their seniors, may find themselves in the position of acting as the conscience of the community, and no doubt bringing upon themselves some of the discomforts which are the consequences of an active conscience.[5.2]

To isolate and examine the impact of a university on a region is, however, more difficult. Two recent publications, from Exeter and Stirling, look at the economic effect of a university on its surrounding area.[5.3] Dr. Brownrigg's study of Stirling has the closest relevance to Lancaster in that he is looking at a new source of employment and income at the time of its first introduction to the region: he concludes by estimating that

> by 1976, in its mid-growth stage, the University of Stirling will add, at constant 1969–70 prices, between £3·9 millions and £4·9 millions to the income level of the local economy. It will add, in both direct and indirect employment terms, between 2,600 and 3,400 jobs to the local labour market. As a result of immigration to study and employment at the University and elsewhere, it will add between 7,200 and 8,200 persons to the local population.

[5.1] Joyce Long, *Universities and the General Public*, Educational Review Occasional Publications No. 3 (Birmingham, 1968).

[5.2] Derman Christopherson, *The University at Work* (S.C.M., 1973), pages 51–2; see also pages 49 and 50.

[5.3] F. M. M. Lewes and Ann Kirkness, *Exeter—University and City: a study of the economic and social interactions caused by University growth* (University of Exeter, 1973), and M. Brownrigg, "The Economic Impact of a New University" in *Scottish Journal of Political Economy*, Vol. XX, No. 2, June 1973, pp. 123–39.

Nearer to home, studies were made in 1967 of aspects of the Lancaster economy and the effects that the university was having on the region.[5.4] The data relate, however, mainly to 1964–66, when the university was newly established and no further studies have been undertaken since that time. One comment of Miss Fulcher's, however, is of continuing relevance and should be quoted:

> The analysis given in this paper suggests that an apparent injection of £1,060 thousand in the year 1964–65 and £2,180 thousand in the year 1965–66 into the economy of the Lancaster sub-region is unlikely to lead to an increase in local income equal to this even if account is taken of the multiplier effects of such expenditure. The small local impact can be accounted for by a number of factors. Firstly because a large part of the apparent injection never enters the sub-region; for example, university gross expenditure upon wages and salaries, as 25 per cent of this is siphoned off in one form or other [such as taxation]. Secondly because this study has concentrated upon the Lancaster sub-region: a small area with an employed population of some 44 thousand in 1965. In such a unit it is inevitable that a large part of local requirements must be supplied from outside that sub-region either directly or indirectly, and a low local multiplier must therefore result. . . . The university is also still in the early stages of its development and it is arguable that performance in the early years is not a good guide to the future, especially as the university has moved from a central Lancaster location to one at Bailrigg.[5.5]

The task of evaluating the university of Lancaster's economic impact on the region is not made easier by other complicating factors, such as the running down of some local industry (the Waring and Gillow furniture factory, opened by Robert Gillow in 1695, and closed in the early 1960's, and the silk mill at Galgate which ended operations in 1970, are two examples that spring to mind), the fact of there having been a declining population in Lancaster during the 1950's, and its importance as an agricultural market town, which makes an estimation of the income flowing in and out of the Lancaster

[5.4] M. N. Fulcher, J. Rhodes, J. Taylor, "The Economy of the Lancaster Sub-region"; J. Taylor, "Six Study Papers on the North West"; and M. N. Fulcher, "University Development in the Lancaster Sub-region" (unpublished reports, Department of Economics, University of Lancaster, 1966 and 1967).

[5.5] Fulcher, op. cit., page 56. Miss Fulcher's definition of the Lancaster sub-region includes Lancaster and Morecambe municipal boroughs, Carnforth urban district and Lancaster and Lunesdale rural districts. The term "region" as used by the writer is applied much more loosely to an area of north Lancashire, Westmorland and part of Cumberland, and the western section of the West Riding of Yorkshire within about a thirty-mile radius of Lancaster. (The terminology used throughout pre-dates the 1974 local government re-organization.)

sub-region a more difficult calculation than it is for other, more self-contained places. Other new employers of labour have come into Lancaster during the early 1960's, including the regional Headquarters of the National Blood Transfusion Centre, the Spastics Training Centre, the new service stations on the M6 motorway, and the Heysham nuclear power station which is under construction by C.E.G.B. Even in its relation with neighbouring sub-regions, Lancaster's position is not a simple one. Up to 1972, it was part of a narrow strip of the north-west region which was not itself receiving financial assistance from the Department of Trade and Industry but was surrounded by development areas and intermediate areas that, by virtue of receiving Government assistance themselves, were to a certain inevitable extent drawing new industry away from Lancaster. In March 1972, however, those parts of the North-West which had not previously been designated as assisted areas were classified as intermediate areas. The main benefits to incoming firms are financial assistance towards the cost of new buildings, and of modifications to those already existing, as well as training grants when additional employment is created. The effects of this alteration in status for the future will be difficult to distinguish from the effects of the continued expansion of the university.

All that can be done, therefore, is to look at the gross sums of money that the university is spending which can be shown as coming into the area and the immediate employment that it has created—while being very conscious that all one is pointing towards are the immediate consequences of such additional finance and not how this income affects the community at large, as it spreads beyond the first pocket into which it is put. Estimated figures will relate to the 1972–73 academic year.

To begin with, there are three thousand or so students who come into the area for thirty (and often more) weeks each year, almost all of them with tax-free grants and other supplementation amounting to between £400 to £500 each to spend on rent, food, clothes, books, cinemas and other heads of expenditure. Although it is very difficult to ascertain what proportion of this sum comes to the immediate locality,[5.6] even if it is only £100 and above per head, that yields an immediate input of at least £300,000 per annum. Furthermore, there were, in 1972–73, 562 academic or equivalent staff on salaries ranging from just over £1,000 to over £6,000 (gross): a salary bill of well over a million pounds, much of which may pass directly into the locality (in payment for housing, food and other goods and services).

Besides these newcomers to the community, however, there are just over seven hundred assistant staff at the university, of whom almost a fifth are part-time.[5.7] Unlike the students and academic staff, these people are drawn

---

[5.6] See below, page 120, for further comment on this point.

[5.7] The university's total labour force of close on 1,300 people may be compared with the North Lancashire and South Westmorland Hospital Board with approximately

in the main from the locality, and their salaries, of around £1,400 gross per head on average for those who are full time, contribute directly to the community in and around Lancaster. There will also be some consequent increase in staff and turnover in various public services which will have some effect on the immediate locality—the Post Office, and the gas, electricity and water boards are obvious examples—and local building firms have been used for certain parts of the development of the university site. Rates are paid each year; £125,743 went to the city, for example, in 1972–73. Supplies of one kind and another are also purchased locally: again, precise figures are hard to ascertain, but catering supplies of over £56,000, printing and stationery amounting to some £13,000 and a laundry bill of about £8,000 are instances of the kind of expenditure by the university in the immediate area. Adding all these items together seems to suggest a minimum figure of some two million pounds or more being spent in or around Lancaster each year. S. Martin's college of education, which also opened in 1964, should not be forgotten in this context. In the 1971–72 academic year there were 772 students, 89 academic and equivalent staff and 130 assistant staff, whose monetary contribution can be approximately pro-rated from the information given above about the university.

Other features of Lancaster's economy will also be likely to change over a period of years. A recent article in the *Financial Times* noted that, according to sources in the Town Hall, with the increased university population (and the conference trade that is growing up there and at S. Martin's College), the new patterns of demand being set up are reflected in the increasing sophistication of the shops and catering trades and a much wider range of goods on sale.[5.8] Already one can detect more demand for boutiques and other specialist clothing shops, and at least one of the city's bookshops has greatly enlarged its stock and premises, as well as increasing its staff from two to ten in less than a decade.

The effect on such matters as houses is again difficult to ascertain. One estate agent has given it as his opinion that there has been an increased demand both for the older stone houses of character and for the better quality executive residence, both within Lancaster itself and in the outlying villages of up to ten or fifteen miles away. He also notes, amongst the younger staff, an almost insatiable appetite for farm cottages and isolated barns which can be converted and modernized for their families. Once again, however, the rapid rise in the prices of property over the whole country and the market

---

2,100 employees, Lansil with 2,100, Storey Brothers with 2,000 and Nairn Williamson with 1,000. The Deputy Establishment Officer estimated, in November 1971, that 95 per cent of the assistant staff are recruited locally: one formidable and increasing shortage is of secretarial staff.

[5.8] James Nicholson, "The University Fosters Growth", in the *Financial Times*, 19 May 1972.

for weekend or retirement houses and cottages in and near the Lake District from, for example, businessmen from Manchester or Leeds, has blurred the effect of the coming of the university.[5.9]

One traditional contribution of the universities to the community is in the field of extra-mural studies. Dr. Long noted in 1968 that all the established universities except Reading had extra-mural departments: she discusses the attitude of the new universities and notes that none of them had set up an extra-mural department by 1965, although several of them, including Lancaster, were expressing an active interest in such a development.[5.10] Since then Sussex has set up a Centre for Continuing Education on a modest scale, but none of the others has yet followed suit.

The first documented discussion of such activity at Lancaster occurred very early, at a meeting of the Academic Planning Board in February 1963 when it was agreed that extra-mural studies should be left for the future but, when they did come, should be incorporated as part of the work of the university as a whole. At the first meeting of the Shadow Senate in January 1964, the Vice-Chancellor echoed and amplified these comments when he said that the University

> must obviously recognize its responsibilities in this field, but he doubted the wisdom of creating an orthodox department of Extra-Mural Studies along traditional lines. . . . It was agreed to give the matter further consideration at a subsequent meeting, having regard to the responsibilities of the Universities of Liverpool and Newcastle upon Tyne in the area.

Liverpool shortly afterwards invited Lancaster to send an observer to meetings of their Board of Extension Studies until "such time as Lancaster establishes independent extra-mural courses"; an arrangement which still stands. Leeds followed suit, and a representative, Professor Woolrych, was duly appointed; while the University Secretary agreed to be a point of contact for adult education purposes for any enquiries from either of these institutions. But, while the university felt able to send delegates to other bodies to show an interest—including, later in 1964, Dr. David Craig as the university's observer on the Universities Council for Adult Education—when the Committee of Vice-Chancellors and Principals wrote in August 1964 to ask about the future financing of extra-mural departments, the Senate agreed that it had no views to put forward.

[5.9] An interesting and detailed study of the university's and S. Martin's impact on housing forms part of Christine M. Booth's "A Study of the Socio-Economic Impact of the University on the City of Lancaster" (unpublished Cert. Ed. dissertation (1973), St. John's College, York). See also Brenda Coles, "The Residential Patterns of Staff and Students at S. Martin's College and the University of Lancaster" (unpublished Cert. Ed. dissertation (1973), S. Martin's College, Lancaster).

[5.10] Joyce R. Long, op. cit., pages 33 to 38.

No further discussion of this subject took place until a Senate meeting of June 1965, when, on a proposal from the Vice-Chancellor, it was agreed to "approve in principle the establishment of a joint committee of the University and the Workers Educational Association to consider means of stimulating adult education in the area". In November Dr. Craig reported back to the Senate on discussions held, proposing that

> the University should assume responsibility for providing adult education facilities in a large area of the North West, including certain areas where such facilities were at present provided by the Universities of Leeds, Liverpool and Newcastle upon Tyne. It was envisaged that a number of appointments to the academic staff of the University would be made subject to the condition that the appointees would undertake some extra-mural teaching to adult classes organized by a responsible organization. The salaries of such staff would be financed partly from the University's ordinary recurrent U.G.C. grants and partly from funds provided by the Department of Education and Science.

Senate members in January 1966 discussed two memoranda, one from Dr. Craig advocating general education courses "in the spirit of the Robbins Committee's ideal that unnecessary barriers inside the educational system should be done away with, or at least lowered, where this can be done without endangering principles of control or standards". The other, from Professor Phillip Reynolds, and supported by the Development Committee, argued that "a major part of the University's responsibility in this area should consist of the provision of refresher courses and specialist short courses designed to bring and keep qualified persons in a wide range of occupations up to date in the field of knowledge in which they are practising". The Senate did not, on this occasion, attempt to resolve the deadlock of these differing aims, but agreed instead that the Vice-Chancellor should enter into preliminary discussions with the existing W.E.A. and extra-mural organizations that already had responsibility for the adult education in which Lancaster University might have an interest. It was also agreed that the next quinquennial estimate should include provision for the salary of an organizer of extra-mural work, and this was echoed again at a meeting in March, in reference to the University of Sussex, where it was envisaged that there would be no director of extra-mural studies, but rather an administrative assistant who would deal with external relations and that some university posts which would be created would carry some explicit extra-mural duties.[5.11] At the Senate conference later the same month the Vice-Chancellor presented a paper in which he stated that the university, wishing as a matter of policy to strengthen

---

[5.11] In spite of this disclaimer, the University of Sussex's Centre for Continuing Education has both a director and an assistant director, and five full-time staff tutors.

its links with its neighbourhood, nevertheless found itself in an area whose extra-mural concerns were being cared for by the universities of Liverpool, Leeds and Newcastle. After discussion with these other universities, he therefore suggested forming a new extra-mural area which might encompass the northernmost section of Lancashire, Westmorland, and parts of Cumberland and the West Riding of Yorkshire. He proposed that there should be a widely representative committee, including members of the university, the local education authorities, and the W.E.A., and that the work to be done should be defined as widely as possible. Administrative responsibility would lie with a Secretary for Community Relations; and, despite the precedents set elsewhere, he believed it to be undesirable to build up a considerable staff of full-time tutors and preferred to see "a defined part of the time of certain ordinary members of university staff set free for extra-mural work", an idea welcomed by the U.G.C. in the report of their visit to the university at that time. Senate endorsed these suggestions and by July the Vice-Chancellor was able to report that the universities of Leeds, Liverpool and Newcastle-upon-Tyne had agreed that Lancaster should accept responsibility for the newly defined area—but clarification had still to be obtained from the Department of Education and Science of the extent of the financial support which would be forthcoming to support the university's efforts in this sphere. Accordingly a request for this development was included in the quinquennial submission to the U.G.C. as "organizing staff for a committee for community courses and activities". One of the economies agreed by the Senate in December 1966, however, when the grant for 1967–68 was £200,000 less than had been hoped, was the postponement *sine die* of any development of extra-mural work.

No further discussion took place until the following autumn when it was raised again in the context of the university having been invited to send representatives to a conference organized by the Universities' Council for Adult Education, specifically to discuss new universities and extra-mural work. It was agreed that Dr. Craig should represent the university at the conference, and the Development Committee was requested to take extra-mural studies into consideration when considering the apportionment of the recurrent grant for 1968–69. At the subsequent discussion, at the end of November 1967, it was agreed that there could probably be provision before the end of the quinquennium (perhaps in 1970) for the appointment of an organizer in extra-mural work.

The next recorded initiative came from Board of Studies D who, in November 1969, passed a proposal to the Board of the Senate that a scheme of extra-mural studies under the aegis of the University be implemented as soon as possible. The Senate minute records that "the Development Committee regretted that university funds did not allow of such a development being undertaken in the present quinquennium" but that it was proposed to seek the guidance of the U.G.C. for the next quinquennium. Dr. Craig, who attended the Senate's discussion of this matter, reiterated his earlier advocacy of the appointment of members of staff with both internal and extra-mural teaching duties, and the Vice-Chancellor suggested that the Department of Education and Science, which three years before had been unwilling to increase its support for extra-mural teaching in north Lancashire and its environs, might again be approached. When he reported back to the Senate in March 1970, however, it was to say that the D.E.S. had told him that "it was not prepared to create a new responsible body for adult education until the Russell Committee had reported, which would be in about two years' time". Other bodies and persons were continuing to look hopefully towards the University of Lancaster for help in this direction, however, for in January 1971 the Vice-Chancellor himself requested the Board of the Senate to "redefine its attitude to extra-mural studies in order that appropriate replies might be made to external enquiries", and commented further that "to await the report of the Russell Committee on adult education was to assume that the only kind of extra-mural studies which the university could undertake would be of the traditional kind". The Senate therefore decided to appoint a committee *ad hoc* on extra-mural studies, to examine the possibility of developing extra-mural studies at an early date, to examine relationships between the university and the Open University and to consider whether to try and ensure that if a local broadcasting station were set up it would include some provision for this type of activity. While this new committee was in its early stages of discussion, however, the quinquennial submission for 1972–77 was in the course of preparation and it is interesting to see that, in essence, the university was taking a consistent line, in regarding "work in this area as best done by ordinary members of the university, any extra costs so far as possible being recouped by charges", except for a small sum for the central administration involved.

The committee *ad hoc* met during the spring and early summer of 1971 and considered various approaches to extra-mural work in the way of several small-scale ventures rather than the establishment of a traditional school of extra-mural studies. By June they were in a position to put specific proposals before the Senate, the first being that, as from 1972, part-time courses might be established which would lead to a completed Part I level over a period of two years: at that point the student could either obtain a suitable sub-degree level academic award or be eligible to enter the university to complete Part II. The next proposal was that some experimental work in extra-mural studies be undertaken, with the co-operation and free participation of certain members of the university, to gauge and estimate the demand for adult education: further discussion of this proposal was deferred. Thirdly, it was suggested that a tutor-organizer be part of the quinquennial submission, which the committee saw as possibly leading to the appointment of academic staff with both internal and external duties. This was agreed to, and the Senate also noted that reference should be made to the difficult situation in which the university found itself, of having no finances and no possibility of having any until the Russell Committee had reported. The views of the boards of studies were sought and duly received, but at the November meeting of the Senate sufficient difficulties had been seen that the extent of the opposition, coupled with some hesitation expressed by the Development Committee, caused the Senate to agree to defer any more discussion of these possibilities until the quinquennial settlement was received from the U.G.C. The Vice-Chancellor was, however, able to report that the University of Liverpool was prepared, if the U.G.C. gave Lancaster the funds to provide administrative services for extra-mural studies, to transfer to Lancaster part of the grant for such services that it had received from the D.E.S. This was little comfort, however, when the quinquennial settlement came from the U.G.C. in January 1973, for the letter from Mr. Kenneth Berrill merely noted that "universities will wish to review their role in the field of adult education in the light of the report of the Russell Committee when it is available". When the report was published a few weeks later, it anticipated that the universities would receive increased revenue for their increased participation in this area of education, as well as being expected to contribute from their own funds;[5.12] but, at the time of writing, the report has not been debated in Parliament nor any policy statement made on it by the Secretary of State for Education. Yet the report served to endorse the approach Lancaster had been tentatively adopting when it noted that

[We] follow the thinking behind the decision of certain newer universities to eschew the traditional extra-mural department and to seek ways fo integrating the extra-mural work more closely with their day-to-day teaching and research.[5.13]

The *ad hoc* committee on extra-mural studies fell into desuetude, but various individuals continued to attempt to keep interest alive amongst the members of the university, and others maintained their links with the Institute of Extension Studies at the University of Liverpool, fitting in teaching commitments in the Lancaster area in addition to their full-time teaching load at the university. The Taylor Report reinforced the continuing efforts of such individuals when, in dealing with internal and external personal relationships, Councillor Taylor emphasized that

---

[5.12] H.M.S.O., *Adult Education: A Plan for Development* (1973), paras. 213–223.
[5.13] *Ibid.*, paras. 212 and 217.

the University must never neglect its personal relationships with the surrounding community and, although much has already been done in this field (especially in the early days of the University) much more remains to be done.

   To this end I strongly recommend the creation of an extra-mural centre in the city following an enquiry into the kind of ways in which the University can best serve the wider educational and cultural needs of the city and district.[5.14]

It was in the spirit of these comments that the University Secretary in October 1972 put before the Development Committee some draft proposals for continuing education in North Lancashire. Amongst other possibilities mooted was again an expression of need for a co-ordinator of community educational services (with the salary possibly being shared between university and local authority funds); that certain mature students be allowed to attend such of the university courses as would suit their individual requirements; that short-term secondments from industry be arranged; that as far as possible the resources of the university be married with the special welfare problems of the community; that the university might organize the training of teachers in the field of adult education; that university/community clubs be set up; that university staff be encouraged to go and teach in adult education centres, not just their primary subject, but also whatever areas of practical interest they had; and that the university should act as a centre for cultural activities in the fullest co-operation with similar ventures in the local community. These proposals on continuing education,[5.15] although received favourably by the Development Committee, were not at that time passed on to the Senate. At the end of May 1973, the *ad hoc* committee on extra-mural studies was re-established, but the proposals it revived are thwarted by the national economic situation of late 1973.

   Although attempts to set up some kind of extra-mural studies have not been immediately successful, there are nevertheless other ways to forge links between university and host community. It was concern for such bonds that caused the Vice-Chancellor to write to the mayor of Lancaster, Mr. Christopher Preston, as early as December 1963, asking

   whether we could not take some steps to make relations between the University and the town still closer, during the coming period of rapid development. We have benefited greatly by the help which we have

---

[5.14] University of Lancaster, *Report of the Taylor Enquiry* (May–July 1972), item 10.
[5.15] The term "continuing education" or "éducation permanente" is felt to convey more adequately the concept of an educational system which makes provision for education from birth to grave. See, for example, its use in the report of the international nference on mass higher education held at Lancaster in September 1972, in *Higher ucation*, Vol. 2, No. 2 (May 1973).

Pedestrians on the North Spine

John Donat

Sitting on the steps in Alexandra Square

John Donat

Parents and graduands outside the Great Hall, June 1973

John Donat

already received, but there is always a danger of a failure of understanding when dreams start to be turned into realities.

We might perhaps jointly found, I hope before the end of your Mayoralty, a "Town and Gown Club" which would meet, say for a monthly lunch, and discuss (or hear speakers about) questions relating to the development or work of the University, of the College of Education, and of the City and neighbourhood. Such a club might be formed by the nomination of equal numbers by the Mayor and the Vice-Chancellor (or the Vice-Chancellor jointly with the Principal of the College of Education); it might have a limited membership, so that election would be regarded as something of an honour, but it could spread its influence by allowing members to bring guests.

Mr. Preston responded warmly to this idea—and indeed has been a mainspring of the Club ever since—and a preliminary discussion of aims and organization took place in April. By November the outline of the club had stabilized, and it had been agreed that there should be some thirty members (raised to fifty in 1966), representing equally on the one side the city and on the other the university and S. Martin's College, with provision built in for the rotation of members and for the mayor of the city "for the time being" having automatic membership. The club was intended

> to remain a private affair, with no special publicity and it should increasingly turn its attention to practical questions arising out of the impact of the University on the Town and the Town on the University. . . . Among the matters which it was thought should be considered were the development of drama in Lancaster, the relevance of the City's redevelopment plans, and the ways of encouraging use of the Bailrigg facilities by the general public.

By July 1966 the Vice-Chancellor was able to report that the club had discussed such matters "as lodgings, student life, academic developments, the City of Lancaster plan, relations with Morecambe, the possibility of a Civic Theatre; on the last, it initiated the discussions, now proceeding, for the improvement and wider use of the Grand Theatre". A note of doubt is struck, however, for the Vice-Chancellor comments that he hopes that people will agree that "despite the obvious limitations of this venture, it is worth while to continue it".

It is perhaps inevitable that an organization of this kind becomes moribund as a university grows rapidly in size to the extent that only a comparatively small number of staff are known personally to each other, and as people's commitments mount up, particularly during term-time, to the point where, for most of them, the relationship of town and gown may seem somewhat unreal. Whatever the causes, the Vice-Chancellor found it necessary in November 1969 to write to members, suggesting a reorganization: a membership of eighty and invited guests, meetings to be held at the university[5.16] three times a year, in the early evening, when after a light supper, a paper would be read on some topic of specific interest to Town and Gown alike, followed by free and informal discussion. This format for the club's meetings has persisted to the present time, and topics covered during recent meetings have been as diverse as the present-day problems of a county chief constable with particular reference to militant minority groups, the rise and fall of the shrievalty, the architecture of the local theatre and the design of the new power station at Heysham.

One particularly useful and practical suggestion which arose out of the club's deliberations was the concept of Enterprise Lancaster.[5.17] This was first bruited at a special meeting of the club specifically arranged in April 1967 to discuss the question of attracting to Lancaster industrial developments which would be related to the university. The scheme that was put forward to the Senate in July spoke of attracting small enterprises (of up to twenty workers at their initiation), science-based and managed by scientists, by offering them certain services and advantages. The types of industry to be attracted were not laid down in advance, but the city would be able to lease factory space, help in finding housing, and assist with public services, while the university could offer appropriate scientific, financial and technical expertise, as well as social and cultural links; the good road and rail communications, adequate labour supply and superb countryside would help to reinforce the contributions of city and university. To weld these facilities together into a coherent scheme, which would be custom-designed for each incoming firm, the city and the university proposed to finance jointly the post of industrial co-ordinator. Senate approved the scheme without demur and in August 1968 Mr. Richard Kelsall took up the post of co-ordinator, with an office in the Town Hall but a pattern of activity which frequently brings him to the University.

Lancaster, as a city centre of employment, depends heavily on firms which are engaged in the manufacture of textiles, plastics and coated fabrics: there is a dearth of firms in such areas as engineering, or electronics. The unemployment figures for the Lancaster sub-region were from 1964 to 1970 not only above the national figure but also above that for the north-west region; and particular peaks of unemployment occurred both in 1962–63 when Waring and Gillow were taken over by G.U.S. and their factory in Lancaster

[5.16] Originally some meetings were held in the town but, for a number of reasons, the venue has now been shifted to the university.
[5.17] I am indebted to Mr. Richard Kelsall and Miss Christine Booth for permission to use parts of the material laid out below.

closed down and again in 1966–67 after redundancies resulting from the merger of James Williamson and Michael Nairn of Kirkcaldy. A total loss of three thousand male jobs in the Lancaster sub-region occurred between 1962 and 1971.

Particular efforts were made to attract more general industry and, in particular, labour intensive forms which would help the unemployment problem in the recession of 1968–72. The decision of the well-known Yorkshire firm of Hornsea Pottery to open a manufacturing plant in Lancaster which has used a local architect and a local builder and which will eventually provide employment for three hundred local people and attract over 350,000 visitors each year, was naturally welcomed by the city. The small, science-based firms which can benefit from proximity to a university with expertise in the business sciences perhaps marks, however, the particular attraction that Lancaster has to offer over other industrial sites.

John F. Millard Ltd., who package medical and surgical products under sterile conditions, with the aid of the latest micro-biological techniques, is one enterprise which has settled in Lancaster; and another is Lancaster Synthesis Limited, who manufacture high purity chemicals for use by research and educational institutions. Yet another firm that has come in which could be seen as fulfilling what the *Financial Times* described as the city's search for "a natural process of growth which will inject new vitality into the city and at the same time improve the quality of life"[5.18] is the Medical and Technical Publishing Company Limited (together with the associated International Research Communication System Limited) which publishes mainly scientific and technical textbooks and journals, and research reports in the medical sciences.

A particular aid to the enterprise and these businesses has been the availability of St. Leonard's House after it had been vacated by the University. The Department of Adult Studies[5.19] is based there, but, now that the university has given up most of the building, there are still units of almost 4,000 square feet on each floor which have been turned by the City into what are known as flatted factory units for new small firms to use as "seed-beds" until they are established. The building, which is owned by the city, is rented out at very nominal rates per square foot with the hope that by the time the firms have outgrown the accommodation there they will be in a better position to take up larger accommodation at commercial rates nearby. This idea has been so successful that Enterprise Lancaster is now seeking further accommodation of the same seed-bed type, and the Department of Trade and Industry (Small Firms Division) is interested in giving support to this idea.

[5.18] *Financial Times*, 19 May 1972.
[5.19] The Department of Adult Studies is part of the College of Art, and is financed by the local education authority.

To encourage the owners or managers of the smaller firms to discuss their problems and find out ways of sharing their knowledge, experience and facilities a local Small Firms Club was set up; co-operative purchase schemes to obtain better discounts and the possibility of a commonly owned service company are the kinds of areas where two small firms, even if dissimilar in function, are stronger than one. The strongly independent spirit of small firms has always to be respected and fostered, while at the same time they are given as much help as possible to obtain the savings and economies of scale of larger concerns.

Alongside this club is the Advisory Panel for Local Organizations, which was set up by the university in 1972 with the object of "raising the level of employment and prosperity in the Lancaster area by offering advice and counsel to the organizations within it". It had been noticed that many small organizations felt hesitant about approaching the university because they did not know whom to contact, there being a general feeling that the university was unapproachable and not interested in problem definition and solution at a relatively low level. Except in exceptional cases where a relatively larger-scale exercise is called for, no fee is charged, partly because these consultations give departments the benefit of being involved in real-life situations. Mr. John Halstead, the administrator of the School of Management and Organizational Sciences, agreed to be the point of contact for the scheme, and a leaflet was widely circulated which offered "personal discussions with suitable experts from the wide range of Departments at the University". Already, in its first year of operation, over fifty contacts have been made through this advisory service, which suggests that it is meeting a definite need in the community.

Enterprise Lancaster can, therefore, be seen as essentially different from other industrial developments by virtue of its being a partnership between city and university. Despite some setbacks, such as the voluntary liquidation of one small firm that came up and the withdrawal of another specialist scientific glass-ware firm because there was not as large a volume of local business as had been anticipated, there has been growing recognition in the city and the locality of the benefits the organization has already brought and will in the future bring to the locality.

A university is in a position, moreover, to help even more directly, by its primary activities of teaching and research, the community around it. There have been, for example, series of management courses for senior officers of the County Council under the course directorship of Mr. Brian Blake, of the Public Authorities Courses Unit, but drawing also on the knowledge and experience of the departments within the School of Management and Organizational Studies. The work is not completely philanthropic because an appropriate fee is charged, but there has up to now been an element of subsidy from the university and, furthermore, the motivation behind the initial setting up of the course was Mr. Blake's wish, endorsed by the university, to meet the social need of enabling local government to operate more effectively than it perhaps always has in the past.

Several of the business departments run masters' degree courses which contain, as an integral part of the training, some practical work with industry or local government which, as with the Advisory Panel, is mutually beneficial: to the students, who learn in a real situation, and to the firms and enterprises who have the benefit of free consultation; thus a student from the Department of Systems Engineering, for example, might look at the total paper flow of an organization. Sometimes even undergraduates can be involved in such projects (although with the requirement of a larger degree of staff supervision), as with the triple major in Economics, Mathematics and Operational Research: work done has included such investigations as the emergency performance of the ambulance service, or delivery delays of a local firm. More often, members of staff will be approached to do research into larger-scale projects: an example of this is reported in a study of May 1973 by J. C. Wilkinson entitled "Public Transport for the Elderly" (a study into the feasibility of establishing a regular minibus service for the benefit of the senior citizens of Lancaster).

So far we have been looking at teaching and research which benefit the community while, because they relate closely to the primary objectives of the university or can charge fees, do not carry any direct extra costs to the institution. However, it will be recalled that in the early days some two and a quarter million pounds were donated to the university, much of it out of local pockets. The Vice-Chancellor noted at the 1970 conference at Windermere that it looked as though no more funds would be forthcoming from industry and commerce, but that the appeal fund

> received over £20,000 per year from local authorities, and this sum might be increased in the next quinquennium. The University hoped to persuade the county councils and the county borough councils at present subscribing to general funds to subscribe to the appeal fund instead. A means of persuading them might be by strengthening their interest in the University, if it could be done. He suggested that the University might do so by arranging to set aside annually a sum of between £5,000 and £10,000 which could be used to support projects of research undertaken in the University at the request of or for the benefit of local authorities or the local community.

The Vice-Chancellor pursued the matter at the next meeting of the Board of the Senate in October when it was agreed that the Senate would recommend to the Finance Committee and the Council that £10,000 of appeal money received from local authorities in 1971–72, and not less than £5,000 for each of the years 1972–73 and 1973–74 be set aside to form a Local Authorities'

(Small Projects) Research Fund.[5.20] An invitation was to be sent to all local authorities which had contributed to the appeal or to general funds "to submit ideas for projects of research which might be undertaken by the university to the practical benefit of their citizens". The university's Council welcomed the idea and when the local authorities were asked for suggestions, over a hundred and thirty proposals were received, which were then reduced to a short list of fifty, including such subject areas as physical planning (e.g. land use), systems (e.g. organization of a fire service), planning and amenity (e.g. under-utilization of water resources for recreational purposes), marketing, administration and labour relations, as well as biological, chemical and physical topics. The seven topics finally chosen were the control of odours from processing of animal by-products (a cause of the strongest resentment, as any connoisseur of the local *Lancaster Guardian* will know), certain problems of the economy of the Lake District, the establishment of an inter-departmental environmental improvement team (a systems engineering project), the planning of the nursing services in Westmorland,[5.21] a plan for open-plan offices and a study of their effect on behaviour (a project which is still continuing), the investigation of the future of Morecambe (which is still under active investigation by Mr. C. S. Riley of the Department of Marketing), and the preparation of an operational and planning model of Preston docks, taking into account associated waterways and land transport links.

A university is, however, a considerable power-house of educational and cultural opportunity of all sorts: so much so that it may even be in danger of swamping other ventures in the region, for it is noteworthy that both the Lancaster Film Society and the Lancaster Music and Arts Club ceased their activities within a few years of the university's advent. From 1964 to 1971 there was a series of inaugural lectures to which the general public were invited to come, and from time to time there have been certain public lectures given by such distinguished people as, for example, Dr. F. S. Dainton, Professor Hugh Trevor-Roper, Sir Tyrone Guthrie, Mr. Cecil King and Dr. Walter Perry. More recently, a series of Wednesday lunchtime lectures, organized by Mr. Michael Argles, has been arranged and some of these, which vary in topic through the whole spectrum of interests of members of the university, may be of interest to a wider public; as, for instance, a talk on the exploration of the moon, given by Dr. Gilbert Fielder, proved to be.

The city looked to the university for leadership in the field of music and the university responded with a series of international subscription concerts,

---

[5.20] The initial total sum of £20,000 set aside for this project was subsequently raised to £30,000.

[5.21] See: C. Gregory and A. Hindle "Community Nursing in Westmorland", December 1972 (prepared under the auspices of the Unit for Operational Research in the Health Services, University of Lancaster).

which got off to a strong start under the directorship of Mr. John Manduell[5.22] in the autumn of 1969, with the help of financial assistance from the B.B.C. (as well as other forms of very useful co-operation, including, for example, six concerts relayed or recorded for Radio 3 during the one season 1972–3), the Universities' Arts Trust and the Arts Council of Great Britain. As the brochure of the first season noted "these concerts collectively represent the most ambitious and far-ranging series of musical events ever planned in Lancaster" and from the beginning they have been a draw to people from a very wide area, as well as attracting the attention of the national press. A great strength has been the existence of a resident quartet and a resident pianist who can play in their own right (as quartet, solo pianist or ensemble) or augment other groups from outside. A report from the present director, Dr. Denis McCaldin, to the Council in May 1973 commented that

> In the past four years music has come to occupy a significant place in the life of Lancaster University and the surrounding region. A succession of distinguished artists have visited the campus. . . . Implicit in the creation of the Department of Music in 1971 was the hope that these artists would make an increasingly valuable contribution to our academic studies, not only through their concert appearances but also in seminars and master-classes. Central to this development was the role of the Lancaster Ensemble (Jan Čap and the Sartori String Quartet) whose appointment carried a dual responsibility for its members as performing artists in residence and as teachers. . . . External relations with the surrounding community have also been good; a valuable proportion of our audiences continue to travel considerable distances to attend our concerts.

In reply to a question from a member of the Council when the report was presented, Dr. McCaldin said that there had been requests for concerts from schools "and the Lancaster Ensemble had undertaken some work in educational and other institutions in the area. Informal talks were taking place with the management of the Duke's Playhouse for activities outside school hours and he hoped there would be developments within the next five years, both on and off the campus, for children".

Mention of the Duke's Playhouse leads us on to consideration of theatrical activities. When the university came to Lancaster there were two centres of theatrical activity; the mobile Century Theatre which brought professional theatre to Lancaster for a few weeks each year and the productions of various amateur societies (and in particular the Lancaster Footlights Club, LADOS (an operatic society) and the Red Rose Club), which were staged in the Grand Theatre, an eighteenth-century building which had been extensively rebuilt

[5.22] Now principal of the Royal Northern College of Music, Manchester.

in the early twentieth century after much of it had been destroyed by fire and
which was owned by the Footlights Club. There were proposals in 1965 to
modernize and extend this building (which had been described as a "complicated, haphazard, cellular growth of extreme working inconvenience") by the
City Council, to whom the Footlights Club was to sell the theatre, which
would then have been leased to a trust. The university associated itself with
these suggestions, the City Architect, Mr. Allan Heppenstall, drew up plans
and City's Finance Committee gave its blessing in principle to the scheme,
but it foundered because the conditions which the Footlights wished to impose
were unacceptable to the City. The Senate, when it was advised by the
Vice-Chancellor of what had happened, agreed that he should again raise with
the City the possibility of establishing a city theatre. Some months went by
and then, in September 1968, the City Architect's department produced plans
for the alteration of and additions to St. Anne's Church in Moor Lane, built
in 1796, but now being used as a furniture repository. The University
Secretary therefore put a document to the next meeting of the Council,
stating that

> It is important for the well-being of both University and City that a
> professional theatre/cinema be established in Lancaster. Since the popula-
> tion of the University (even at, say, 3,000) will fall well below a number
> capable of sustaining a professional company for its exclusive benefit, it is
> reasonable (indeed necessary) to think in terms of sharing both cost and
> advantages with the City. . . . By promoting these services in the context
> of the wider local population, self-interest and social service coincide. A
> firmly-established area of co-operation in the heart of the City will serve
> as a valuable link between University and City.

The estimated total costs for both the alterations to the existing church and
the new extension block (of two storeys, to the north and east of the existing
building) was £65,000. The Town Clerk was hoping to receive £20,000 from
the Arts Council, £7,500 from the National Film Theatre Trust, and £20,000
from the City, and it was hoped that the university might be able to contribute
a capital sum of £10,000 on the understanding that the management, control
and administration of the Civic Theatre was to be vested in a Board of
Trustees on which the university would be adequately represented. The
proposal was unanimously agreed by the university's Council who referred to
the project as "fraught with tremendous possibilities for the cultural health of
the area", and there was a good deal of support locally: a public meeting at
this time attracted an unprecedented number of people and a local supporters'
club was there and then set up. Severe difficulties emerged during 1969 over
the representation of the various bodies concerned in the governing body of
the theatre, and by the time these problems were resolved to the satisfaction of

the parties concerned (including the university), the effect of various improvements and inflation had between them raised the cost to £108,000. However, the various bodies who were contributing raised the amount of the capital sums they were putting into the scheme; and the university made a further contribution of £3,000 in addition to the £10,000 already promised.[5.23]

The Duke's Playhouse, as it was named, was officially opened in November 1971 by Lord Eccles, and in 1972 severed its ties with the Century Theatre, becoming the base for an independent theatrical company. A theatre audience takes time to grow, but Mr. Peter Oyston, the artistic director since 1969, is confident that he can build up a vital and exciting theatre but not "to educate them, to improve their lives, we're not cultural missionaries. We're just theatre and all that theatre means—excitement, humanity, reality, pathos, all these things."[5.24] The theatre, which the Town Clerk told the writer would not have been feasible without the coming of the university and S. Martin's College (with the potential audience they brought in their wake), continues to look to the university for mutual support and co-operation.

Meanwhile, of course, the university has also been putting on a number of productions in the Nuffield Theatre Studio,[5.25] some of them mounted by the student Theatre Group, others by Orbit (a travelling theatre sponsored by the Arts Council) and the rest by touring companies. The studio opened its doors in March 1969 with the Bailrigg Fair, a multi-media production which included some scenes from Jonson's *Bartholomew Fair*; and since then films, opera, and dance, as well as plays, have been on offer. In the 1972–73 season, for example, there was an Orbit production of Molière's *Imaginary Invalid*, a performance of Wycherley's *The Country Wife* which grew out of the work of a new minor course in Theatre Studies, and a production which grew out of a consortium of interests in the departments of music, theatre studies and visual arts, of Handel's *Acis and Galatea*; as well as visiting companies.

The other arts are by no means neglected. A grant from the Northern Arts and Sciences Foundation for the establishment of a fellowship in the arts (known as the Granada Fellowships) for a period of five years at a maximum of £2,500 per annum was announced by the Vice-Chancellor to the Council in November 1966. This was "to secure the services of a practitioner in one of the arts (including music) to promote and inspire artistic activity in the university and to assist with the development of artistic activity in the

[5.23] On the city side, a notable speech in October 1970 by the late Alderman Douglas Clift, who later became the chairman of the Century Theatre Management Committee and the subsequent Duke's Playhouse Board of Directors, persuaded the City Council to raise its contribution by an extra £15,000 and to under-write such costs as were not covered by other bodies. The Pilgrim Trust was also able to give £5,000.
[5.24] *Lancaster Guardian*, 5 November 1971.
[5.25] See Chapter 2, pages 79 to 81, for an account of the building of the Studio, the constraints put on its use, and the way in which these were modified.

neighbourhood". The funds were expended in different areas: on a poet (Mr. Adrian Mitchell), a painter (Mr. Jeff Hoare), a composer (Mr. Anthony Gilbert) and a sculptress (Mrs. Ann Hirsch-Henecka).

During 1970, Professor Basil Ward, an architect who, having retired in the area, was giving a course in the history of Western architecture, and Mr. Geoffrey Beard, later a senior lecturer in fine arts, laid proposals before the Development Committee for a Centre for the Study of the Visual Arts to be established, and in June the Vice-Chancellor submitted the draft of an appeal which he proposed to send out to various potential benefactors. The function of the proposed Centre was described as stemming from "a rapidly growing awareness of the influences of the total environment upon the community".

By the Senate conference of September 1970 (at Windermere) the Vice-Chancellor was able to report that the "Development Committee regarded the University's commitment to the proposed Centre . . . as a firm one. Substantial donations in support of this development had been promised or were in prospect, and it was therefore essential to inform prospective donors what our intentions are." At first a separate building and a director at professorial level were envisaged, but by the time an advertisement had been drafted the duties of the post had become so wide that no one applied whose interests could embrace all those the appointing committee were looking for. After an open meeting and other deliberations two senior lectureships in the visual arts were advertised. Mr. Geoffrey Beard (who looks after the Centre for Visual Arts and has special responsibility for the general and extra-mural interests of visual arts) and Mr. Ewart Johns (who is head of the department—as it has recently been named—of Art and the Environment) were appointed. A pamphlet issued in 1972 spoke of the Centre for Visual Arts as being

> an experiment in the broadening of university education, and for a well-structured programme of undergraduate and post-graduate studies. It will sponsor conferences, seminars and other activities for people interested in the visual arts, from Britain and overseas. Courses will be provided in the practice, appreciation and understanding of art, architecture and environmental conditions in all forms (including historical and contemporary expressions). The Centre will arrange and display exhibitions . . . and acquire works of art.
>
> It will be possible by such methods . . . to have a wide and stimulating effect on corporate life there and in the surrounding region.

In at least one area, the university has been able to cooperate with, and enlarge, an activity which was already flourishing. Lancaster was one of a series of Roman garrison forts from the late first to late fourth century A.D., and had an extensive civil settlement associated with it. Chance finds were the only evidence of the Lancaster fort until 1927 when Professors Newstead and

Droop came from the University of Liverpool to study the area to the north-west of the castle and priory. In the 1950's and again in 1965 Professor Sir Ian Richmond carried out explorations of the same area, assisted by local archaeologists who continued to make small-scale excavations after his death. At first the staff of the university, and in particular Dr. David Shotter, joined in as interested individuals, but the need for both a larger-scale organization and more finance became increasingly evident. In early 1971, therefore, a proposal was put to the boards of studies on behalf of a group of people in the university who felt archaeology would be a desirable area of growth, which pointed out that the

> North of England is rich in remains of all periods, particularly of the Roman occupation. In recent years, whilst a great deal of attention has been paid to the extreme north (particularly Cumberland and Hadrian's Wall) and south (particularly Ribchester and Wilderspool) of the region, the middle section (South Westmorland and North Lancashire) has been largely neglected. This, of course, is an area eminently suitable for the involvement of this University. . . .
>
> The most interesting [site] is that of the Roman Fort at Watercrook, and there appears to be a good possibility that the University could acquire the right to dig it over a period of years.

They therefore requested that an additional post in Romano-British archaeology (under the wing of the department of classics) be established, and that finance for equipment be provided. The boards of studies were in the main in favour of this development, and Senate, at its meeting of June 1971, agreed that the proposals should be implemented. Later in the same year the Lancaster Archaeological Society was founded, with Dr. Shotter as its first chairman, and the excavations carried out in 1972 and 1973 under the auspices of the University of Manchester and of the society attracted a good deal of attention in Lancaster and further afield. The appointment of the archaeologist to the university staff has now occurred, and the incumbent, Dr. Timothy Potter, will initiate the first excavation at the Watercrook site at Kendal—which has been leased to the university—at Easter 1974, with annual digs thereafter. Meanwhile a field survey, carried out by members of the department of environmental sciences, has been able to pinpoint the lines of masonry beneath ground level by means of proton magnetometer and resistivity survey techniques. The university is therefore likely to be able, in the next few years, in conjunction with interested local individuals, museums, and antiquarian societies, to draw a far more definitive map of a section of the north-west in Roman Britain than has ever been possible before.

Additional strength has been given to developments such as this by the establishment of the Centre for North-West Regional Studies, which came into full operation from January 1974. The idea has been in the mind of the Reader in Regional History, Dr. John Marshall, for some years, and found its way onto paper as early as October 1969 when he argued for "regionally-oriented study in the university, economic, historical, sociological or archaeological" in a spirit of "cross-disciplinary cooperation of a kind originally envisaged in the university's approach to teaching and education". A working party on regional studies set up by Board of Studies C held a meeting in July 1970 which uncovered the very large amount of current or projected regional research already going on in various departments. In Biological Sciences, for example, work was going on in association with the Forestry Commission, with the Lancashire Naturalists' Trust and with the local Nature conservancy centre, and the department was engaged in a detailed survey of hill farming. The History department was already involved with the social history of local communities, and the department of environmental sciences was carrying out climatic studies of the area, as well as work on coastal erosion. The department of economics was giving advice to farmers and to local industries in the area, while the department of English was interested in folk sources and the literature of the region. There was, however, a great lack in that there was no co-ordinating body which could keep a record of activities, put researchers in touch with others, serve as a clearing house for information on projects and publications, hold seminars and conferences, and generally publicize and encourage study of regional problems and topics in the north-west.

An informal panel therefore requested in November 1970 that a centre for regional studies be established and, although this request was then turned down by the Development Committee, a small sum of money was set aside to launch the *Regional Bulletin*, whose stated functions were to include reports of regional research in progress, suggestions of further ties which could be created between the university and the community, and information about regionally-related work in the university and the colleges of education and to act as a vehicle for ideas for future work.

The *Bulletin* and such events as a colloquium on the Morecambe Bay barrage scheme (held in June 1972) were useful, but Dr. Marshall and the Panel still insisted that there was a need for a fully-developed Centre which had a physical entity and administrative and library support. A further document was therefore put to the Development Committee in November 1972 who, when the quinquennial settlement had been received by the university in January 1973 made a provisional allocation of funds and passed the proposal forward to the Senate. A further document prepared for the Senate drew attention to centres with a similar function that had been set up at the universities of Durham (in 1972) and East Anglia (in 1967), and stressed the interdisciplinary nature of the proposal and the involvement it would entail between different kinds of educational institution in the region. The Senate in February approved the proposal in principle and a constitution for the centre was agreed with the Senate in June; already various research projects—such as a socio-economic history of the County Council from 1889, the beginning of an oral history of the region (particularly as regards dying industry), and preparations for the promised visit of the British Association in 1976—are in train.

Nor should we overlook the resources of the Centre for Physical Education (or the Indoor Recreation Centre as it is more familiarly known) whose director, Mr. Joe Medhurst, has always taken a very outward-looking stance ever since he came to the university in 1967. He believes that such facilities as a university can often afford should be made as widely available to the public as possible, particularly during the vacations. In an article in the *Regional Bulletin* of 1971[5.26] he noted that twenty thousand visitors had made use of the Centre since its opening and went on to say that

> Each year all secondary schools in the division are invited to make regular use of the facilities during the mornings as part of the school physical education programme, and during the current year Greaves County Secondary School, Skerton County Secondary School and Our Lady's High School use the Centre on four mornings a week at no charge.
>
> Every consideration is given to accommodating local sports and other organizations for special events. For example, Lancaster town badminton matches have frequently been held in the Sports Hall during the past three winters, and occasional events such as visits by Scout associations, a county squash match, judo and karate courses, keep-fit rallies, and local basketball matches have been accommodated at various times. . . .
>
> It is also pleasing to see student-run clubs reciprocating with local clubs in the use of facilities, and, in particular, members of local judo and karate clubs who now look upon the University Centre as their second home. . . .
>
> For a few weeks in the year, and especially during the Christmas and Easter vacations and in September, the Centre is used more by the public than by members of the University, and is very much a community sports centre on the lines of those local authority centres now established throughout the country. . . .
>
> Clubs are permitted to use the soccer pitches whenever possible, although grass by its very nature can only withstand a limited amount of hard wear each week.

This policy has continued, and in a report to the Senate of September 1973 Mr. Medhurst justified the continuation of this policy by pointing out that

---

[5.26] *Regional Bulletin, op. cit.* No. 1, May 1971, pages 11 to 14.

implicit in the Sports Council's ten-year "Sport for All" campaign was the need to open up all the sports facilities to the community that already exist in the higher education establishments of the country, particularly in an area such as Lancaster, where the university's centre is the only purpose-built indoor sports facility in the area.

The reader will by this point be able to see that the university as an institution is actively pursuing a policy of involvement with the community which will develop as it becomes larger and older, and which will increasingly make an impact on the local community. Nor should the contribution of individual members of staff be forgotten, since they are becoming more and more sought after, for example, as committee members for various local bodies or as local councillors, at city and at county level.[5.27]

It may well be asked at this stage what part the students take? Student politicians in recent years have emphasized the need to help the community; what in practice do they achieve at Lancaster? The answer is, of course, that what lies in their power to accomplish is limited because their funds are limited (personally, to an extreme extent, and as a body, less so but with constraints on how their available finance may be spent), their time scarce, and their stay at the university usually amounting to no more than ninety weeks spread over three years. Many individual students are eager to help where they can, and housepainting, house repairs or gardening for old age pensioners, visiting in the mental hospitals of the city and teaching immigrant children the English language are the kinds of scheme which are picked up each year. Additionally, as at many other universities, the students usually hold a rag week (known in Lancaster as Charities Week) in the Lent Term when by a combination of cajolery, amiable blackmail and entertainment they raise an amount of between £2,000 and £3,000 to distribute amongst local charities; the Royal Lancaster Infirmary, the Lancaster Spastics Training Centre, and the North West Cancer Research Fund have all been recipients of funds from these rags in recent years.

There is not very much day-to-day communication between the bulk of students and the city. The Bailrigg site is almost three miles from the city's centre and beyond the walking habits of the large majority of students, especially since the route takes them along the busy and noisy A6 trunk road. A recent survey,[5.28] covering a small sample of just over two hundred resident students, whose objective was to discover, amongst other information, what use students made of Lancaster and Morecambe, showed that it was the unusual student who went to Lancaster more than twice a week—many

---

[5.27] See: University of Lancaster, *Ninth Annual Report by the Vice-Chancellor* (December 1973), page 13, for further details of their involvement.

[5.28] I am grateful to the Hon. Robert Peel for permission to use the unpublished material given in this summary.

going less often than this—while for Morecambe the figures were even lower, with an average of three visits per academic year. Shopping and visits to the cinema, the theatre and the local pubs were the main reasons for such visits as did take place, although the amount spent by each student when he reached the town varied hugely; the average amount was £29 per head spread over half the academic year, but the variation was so great that not too much should be inferred from that figure. A small minority—4 per cent of the men and 9 per cent of the women—went to the city for community reasons, such as going to church or taking part in one of the social welfare groups of the city. Two-thirds of the sample would go to Lancaster more often if the distance was not so great and/or the cost of transport was not so high, although the frequency with which students go into the town is not affected by whether or not they own a car. Some of the replies reflect a regret, which many students express, that the university has been sited so far away from the town—but, of course, irrespective of the U.G.C. reasons which governed the decisions on siting the new universities in the early 1960's, there would be possible disadvantages of higher building costs and less economical use of space, and a dispersal of facilities with the concomitant anonymity of students, that tend to be overlooked by students who see Bailrigg as claustrophobic.

When, in May 1961, the *Lancaster Guardian* reported[5.29] the choice of Bailrigg as the proposed university site, this choice was said to be "hailed with delight in Lancaster". The Mayor of Lancaster, Councillor P. J. Oliver, commented that "the news will be received with joy by the people not only of the city but of a wide area surrounding", the Town Clerk spoke of it as "the best thing that has happened to Lancaster since the foundation of the firm of Jas. Williamson and Son", Ald. Ernest Gardner, the president of the Trades Council, said that he believed "this is the biggest single step ever taken to make this city really great" while the *Lancaster Guardian* itself noted that "Equally as pleased were ordinary residents of the city and the university was a talking point throughout Lancaster this week". A letter from the mayor in the same paper a fortnight later[5.30] in calling the city to support the appeal for financial support being launched by Lord Derby, said that he believed that the citizens of Lancaster were "completely united in their desire to see such a project come to fruition".[5.31] In November, when the news came that Lancaster had been chosen by the Government for a new university, the mayor (by now Coun. Mrs. M. J. Lovett-Horn) was reported[5.32] as saying "It's wonderful. It's absolutely marvellous. We have been waiting with

---

5.29 *Lancaster Guardian*, 5 May 1961.
5.30 *Ibid.*, 19 May 1961.
5.31 See Chapter 1, pages 12 to 17 for a full account of this period.
5.32 *Lancaster Guardian*, 24 November 1961.

bated breath for a long time. Now the news has come. It will be an exciting renaissance for the city," while the Town Clerk commented that

> This is most heartening news for Lancaster generally. Everyone has been hopeful of this result and now I think there will be real jubilation. The establishment of a university here is bound to have the deepest and the most fundamental repercussions on the whole of city life. Educationally and culturally, it will have a most marked effect.
>
> Naturally it will bring increased trade and prosperity to the city but I think the educational and cultural effects will be the most important. We now look to building up Lancaster as a sound educational centre. We have the College of Further Education and the College of Art both with fine reputations, some excellent schools and the university will put the seal on the lot.

The financial generosity of the city, the county and the wider region deserves the warmest acknowledgement. The County Council has been the university's largest single benefactor, for not only did the Council give the university the County College but for ten years (1962–72) also contributed an annual grant of £50,000 to the general revenue account. Lancaster City Council showed its munificence by giving the university £15,000 each year—until 1973, when a decision was made to substitute £1,000 instead.[5.33] Other county and borough councils have made grants—Westmorland, Barrow-in-Furness, Blackburn, Blackpool and Preston, for example, were early generous contributors and various local county, county borough, borough, urban district and rural district councils have given extremely valuable help to the appeal funds.[5.34] These sums, together with those contributed by industry, have enabled the university[5.35] to make faster advances with its capital building programme than would otherwise have been possible, to be more imaginative in its range of facilities and, in particular, to provide more residential accommodation for students than would have been possible without such funds.

Relations with the community, however, have not always been serene. As one local councillor remarked to the writer, it was perhaps unfortunate that a major change in the appearance of the majority of students coincided almost exactly with the opening of the new universities: a small point, no doubt, but indicative of the gulf that some people feel to have grown up between universities and the general public. Perhaps expectations were pitched too high,

---

[5.33] See *The Lancaster Guardian* for 23 February, 1973.

[5.34] Full details of the sums received are listed in the annual accounts of the university, which are published each December.

[5.35] See Appendix (ix) for details of how sums of money donated to the Appeal Fund have been expended.

both in terms of financial benefit to the local community and of the cultural and educational benefits to be derived. At first the university was so pre-occupied with setting up a curriculum, organizing a building programme and finding out how to look after and teach its students in the most effective and efficient way, while also allowing the staff to keep up as far as possible with their own programmes of research, that all the available finance and, even more importantly, all the available time, was expended on internal university operation. Again, the neighbouring town of Morecambe had special problems, being a famous holiday resort looking nevertheless for an extra fillip to its finances. When the university came, and great emphasis was laid on the suitability of Lancaster because of the abundant accommodation at More-cambe, hopes were raised that a not inconsiderable proportion of the seven thousand beds available there could be used from October to June each year by university students. In fact, the maximum number of students in digs (as opposed to flats, which students have always found for themselves and which are of a fundamentally different kind of accommodation to the boarding houses traditional to Morecambe) was probably somewhat over one thousand in 1967: and the number has subsequently fallen much lower, although it may well rise again before the beginning of the next quinquennium. A further worry arose when the university began to take in conference trade, when it seemed for a while that the university would be detracting from Morecambe's own conference trade.[5.36] Nor did the disciplinary problems[5.37] of this and other universities in the late 1960's do other than to create a rift between university and community.[5.38] In this Lancaster is by no means on her own, as the writer has discovered in discussion with others of the new universities; and as was made clear in a speech given by Professor Pat Rivett, with experience of two new universities, who commented that there has been a long history of stormy relations existing between any university and the community, but that there seemed to be an increasing sensitivity to all student activities, which results in the least harmful escapades receiving the maximum amount of publicity and moral censure.

In his analysis of the causes for this sensitivity, which existed between universities and the towns in which they were placed, Professor Rivett mentioned the fact that most new universities had been situated where they were as a result of local initiative. Immediately after the success of this initiative and the creation of the university, other people from outside the

---

[5.36] See Chapter 4, pages 271 to 272.
[5.37] See Chapter 6, pages 366 to 394.
[5.38] A Morecambe *Visitor* editorial, for example, of 3 May 1972 spoke of the university authorities being "blackmailed" by their students and concluded by saying that "If the authorities do not act firmly their supporters will begin to question their capability of maintaining order at Bailrigg".

2B

town or region concerned had come in to organize and run the university.
Apart from secretarial and assistant staff, the university was largely
staffed by strangers and a feeling arose both amongst the people coming
in to run the university and amongst local people into whose environment
the university came, that the new staff saw themselves as colonizers bringing culture and education to an hitherto underprivileged area. . . .

Yet another cause of strain and sensitivity between town and university
stemmed from the basic function of the university which was to nurture
the spread of enquiry and questioning. Such activities were not always
welcomed and did not make a university a comfortable neighbour.

Often too, the establishment of a university resulted in many young
people moving into what was frequently an older area. By and large, new
universities had been put into what were almost retirement zones with the
inevitable strain between young and old. . . . Professor Rivett stressed that
on the whole that strain which did exist was between the middle aged
section of the community which was already in residence and the
incoming young. . . .

As a result of all these facts, misconceptions existed among the general
public about the place of a university within the community, and it was
often considered to be a strange and rather unnatural accretion to
local life.[5.39]

Various attempts have been made to set up an arrangement whereby
relations with the general public may be made as amicable as possible, and
an agreed procedure was set up at an early stage for dealing with press relationships so that publicity going out from the university should be as positive
and informative as possible. In June 1965 a Publicity Committee was set up
with this specific aim in mind, but apart from occasional rather tentative
proposals about such suggestions as an internal press council to establish
what was reasonable as content for the student newspapers (since their
news items were so frequently picked up by the national and local press), it
was ineffective, and such publicity as emanated from the university came from
the Secretary's office. In 1969 an external relations office was set up, which was
to deal with degree ceremonies and visitors as well as press relationships, but
after a couple of years this was disbanded. The Taylor Report advocated the
early appointment of an information officer, for although Councillor Taylor
believed that public relations "at the level of University policy and strategy
are best handled by those senior administrative officers who are deeply
immersed in the higher direction of the University's affairs", nevertheless

---

[5.39] Taken from a summary of a speech by Professor Pat Rivett to the Town and
Gown Club, 3 February 1970.

at another (and important) level there is a great deal to be done in publicizing the work and achievements of academic departments, the many facets of student life, the life and work of the colleges, not to mention the University's musical, theatrical, artistic and athletic activities, etc., etc. All this can only be handled effectively by a trained professional who has the ability to present material in an acceptable form to the mass media.[5.40]

The post was created, after some initial hesitation within the university about what the functions of it might be, and with the coming of Mr. Grinyer in January 1974, there will be a clear channel of communication between the university and the community.

With the passage of time, however, the situation may well ease itself; and indeed, in the opinion of a number of observers, relations between the university and the community at Lancaster have in the main been better than at some of the other new universities. One key figure in the relationship is always the mayor of the time who, as a member of the Council, has been the main link with Lancaster. Certainly the university was much encouraged by the recent offer of the National Westminster Bank to second one of its managers for a five-year period to the university while continuing to pay his salary: he is to give especial attention to activities "which will enhance co-operation between the University and the surrounding community in fields of interest beneficial to both". The material and intellectual benefits to the community will become more readily apparent; the inevitable irritations, given goodwill on both sides, will not loom so large as they did at first; and joint ventures of a kind (such as Enterprise Lancaster) which are already developing, will become more numerous and should engender good-will. The *Financial T mes* in May 1972 anticipated that "The personality of the university will continue to imprint itself on the fabric of the town. Cultural activity will go on expanding and the transformation of Lancaster from a quiet country town to a more vibrant university town"[5.41] will continue, while a *Lancashire Evening Post* editorial in October 1973 commented that "it is no bad thing to measure the success of a university by its service to the community around it, and by this yardstick Lancaster University can be proud of its achievements. . . . Economically, socially, culturally, and environmentally it has done for North Lancashire every bit as much as realists might have hoped. And it still only has 3,000 students."[5.42]

[5.40] *Report of the Taylor Enquiry*, May to July 1972, Item 4. See also Chapter 4, pages 252 to 254.
[5.41] *The Financial Times*, 19 May 1972.
[5.42] *Lancashire Evening Post*, 2 October 1973.

CHAPTER 6

The Student Body

(i) The collegiate ideal

Let us imagine that mythical creature, the typical student, whom we shall call T.S., and who came up to Lancaster in October 1972 as a first-year undergraduate. He was one of over eight hundred students admitted through the U.C.C.A. scheme, but one of over a thousand newcomers that year. He quickly found that there were twice as many men as women amongst the new students, but on the other hand, coming from Yorkshire, he found himself one of a very large contingent (42 per cent) from northern England.

He had been told that as a first-year student he would be given a room in college and, having no particular views on the desirability of one college over any other, allowed himself to be put into one at random. He came up before the beginning of Full Term for Introductory Week and spent a bewildering few days going to lectures given by departments about the subjects they had on offer, attending the Indoor Recreation Centre to sign up for three first-year subjects; and going back to the same place the next day for the Societies' Bazaar, at which he was offered a baffling selection of extra-curricular activities, from a Community Welfare Group to a Math Society, as well as hardier pursuits, including canoeing, hiking and speleology. He went to a number of parties, at which there seemed always to be an inexhaustible supply of beer, and met his college tutor, his college principal and—a particularly important figure for the first few weeks—his college bursar. He learnt routes to the Library, the Great Hall, the Chaplaincy Centre and other landmarks, as well as the names and locations of all the snack bars.

Term began and he was left to grapple by himself with the timetables of his different departments. From having too much information there now seemed far too little, and most people seemed too busy or disinclined to repeat what he had heard before and passed over in a blur. He had booklists to work through, but found that other enterprising individuals had already taken the key books out of the library; and what was left of his grant after paying his rent to the college did not seem to amount to very many books if he was going to purchase any meals at all.

The lectures seemed unexpectedly general and in seminars, which sometimes consisted of as many as ten students, he always seemed to get left out or to express himself inadequately. He trailed off to his college tutor who was as affable as ever but who left him with the distinct impression that he was being told to grow up; and the third years who had been up in Introductory Week and attendant upon his every question seemed not to have any time for him now. Various other first-years seemed to be as miserable as he was and a few faces disappeared permanently. It seemed always to be raining and although he could get round the site without going into the open, the covered walkways themselves formed wind tunnels which made him shiver miserably. And life in his residence block seemed bleak, with the kitchens rapidly getting filthy and a high level of noise that seemed to go on unceasingly day and night.

During the Lent Term, however, T.S. began to feel that he knew the place a little better, and when he went into his junior common room or college bar, there were a number of people to nod to and sit with. There were some concerts too, which were free for students, and some dance groups which hitherto had been only names to him, actually turned up in the Great Hall for his delectation. His essays began to come back: he was assured that he was getting very reasonable marks in at least two of his subjects and would not be one of those for whom a mid-term report in the Lent Term would go in from the department to mysterious University House and thence to his college tutor. Furthermore, there were some lectures and seminars to which he now looked forward, because they related to the reading he was doing and enhanced it. He did not go home every weekend as he had the previous term, when the student running the bus booking service had regarded him as one of his most regular customers, but went instead on a long hike around the Lake District and other local climbing spots, as well as to several good parties. His circle of acquaintances seemed to be widening very rapidly and, after the irritation of so many people coming in and out of his room one evening had subsided, he realized that although he would have to sit up until the small hours if he was to be adequately prepared for his first seminar the next day, at least he had passed the stage when everyone else seemed to be sharing all the "in" jokes except him and he had no idea which girl would be prepared to go to the next dance with him. There was a demo about grants in the last fortnight of term, and although the S.R.C. officers seemed to be very dissatisfied with the turnout in comparison with those of heroic and legendary marches in previous years, T.S. enjoyed himself well enough marching along the A.6 in bright sunshine to the Town Hall, where students from the local technical college joined the university contingent, speeches were made, and everyone straggled back to Bailrigg, feeling mightily pleased with themselves because they had turned out and the rest had not. And after all, T.S. reflected, even if his photograph did appear in the local newspaper, his parents were safely on the other side of the Pennines and probably would not hear of it.

He went home for Easter in a state of some euphoria, unallayed by his parents' complaints about shoulder-length hair and patched jeans, and at the beginning of the Summer Term took on the editorship of his college newsheet, which meant a share in an office. He had a rude shock, however, when he was presented with even more reading lists and more essays, and was told that a seminar paper he gave in his intended major subject was not up to scratch. He cut lectures for some days and worked frantically in the library, refusing to sun himself on the steps in Alexandra Square with his friends, on the grounds that the Part I exams were coming up and this miserable university, where a man was expected to bring no less than three subjects up to Part I level—an impracticable idea, it seemed to him, and no better than school—meant that he had to devote himself exclusively to work. Nor did his mood improve when he was told that he had to register for next year's courses and decide what his major department was to be even before the examinations had begun. When he went along to the registering departments he understood anew, as he deliberated between his three possibilities for a major and a minor subject and tried to select a free ninth unit from an apparently endless list, the saying current amongst students that anyone who could understand the course structure at Lancaster deserved a degree on that basis alone. He oscillated unhappily between on the one hand feeling that he was at university under false pretences and should be out on a building site, and on the other hand that university courses were a load of rubbish and no one on the staff knew how to construct a syllabus or would stop driving him to an early grave between overwork and lack of guidance. In desperation he went to see the student counsellor who at least seemed prepared to listen and take him seriously, although he wondered whether anyone had noticed him going into her office and would think he was going crazy.

He wondered whether he might be ill for the exams, but found himself in the middle of June going into the Indoor Recreation Centre at the time appointed, with his seat number card and his fountain pen clutched in a sweaty hand. The sight of some familiar textbooks waiting on his desk calmed him down, but although the first paper was reasonable, he found the questions long and wished that he knew some of the texts rather better so that he could find the pertinent quotations more easily.

He had all kinds of grandiose schemes for projects when exams were over, but soon realized that he was too exhausted to do more than lie in the sun and deplore the lack of a swimming pool. Since, unlike previous years, Part I results were not to be out before the end of term he was forced to plan for the next year in the apparent expectation of coming back. He went to his intended major department and received an even more formidable book and essay list for the vacation than he had become accustomed to during the year, but at least a friend told him that there was definitely a place for him in a certain very desirable flat in Lancaster. He returned home rather apprehensively, trying to reassure himself that since he had not been summoned at the end of term by his major department, he could not be in serious difficulties, and was immensely relieved when a letter arrived a week later telling him that he had passed all three subjects at the level necessary to proceed to Part II without a re-sit examination in early September. T.S. realized with relief that he could go on his long vacation job and his hitch-hiking holiday across Europe, and felt October to be a very long way distant.

T.S., of course, was fortunate, because although he encountered several of the incipient problems of student life, he did not succumb to them, and the agencies that are provided at Lancaster were sufficient to see him through his various stages of first-year development. A fundamental precept of the Lancaster plan for the care of students was that the university should be collegiate. The Robbins Report had warmly endorsed[6.1] the collegiate principle, saying

> The promotion of social intercourse between teachers and students is desirable. When we turn to living accommodation for students we enter the realm of necessity. In 1961–62 . . . 28 per cent of students in the universities . . . were living in accommodation associated with the institution they were attending.
>
> The proportion of university students provided with residence has remained roughly constant since before the war. The proportion of those living at home had fallen by over a half (from 42 per cent to 20 per cent) and is still about 1 per cent lower each year than the year before. The proportion in lodgings has therefore risen sharply (from 33 per cent to 52 per cent), and there is every sign that in most places the limit of available lodgings has now been reached. Indeed, if we consider the nature of some of the lodgings in which circumstances oblige students to live, the distances that they are forced to travel to their work, the lack of privacy—there are cases where three students share one study-bedroom—and the

---

[6.1] *Report on Higher Education*, Cmnd. 2154 (1963), paragraph 585ff. See also H.M.S.O., *Halls of Residence* (1957), chaired by Prof. W. R. Niblett.

absence of any kind of supervision, it can be said that the limit has already been passed. . . .

The expansion we are recommending will make a very great increase in housing provided by universities imperative. We think that, both on educational grounds and on grounds of necessity, provision should be made for a number equivalent to two-thirds of the additional students who will come into the universities to live in accommodation of one kind or another, provided by the university.[6.2]

When considerations of cost were being deliberated by the committee, they declared that

it is not unreasonable to expect that the nation should be prepared to spend a higher proportion of it [i.e. the increase in national income] on services such as higher education. One may buy less of services such as bus travel if one's income rises, but surely not less education.[6.3]

The U.G.C. development report for 1957–62 echoed these sentiments, saying

the variations range from the University of Keele with 97 per cent of its students in residence to Birmingham University with only 10 per cent in residence. . . .

We found—and we welcomed—during our visitations the widespread conviction in all the universities of the role that university residence can play in university education. A great deal of thought is being given to the planning of such residence, and experiments are being made with different types of accommodation—the orthodox hall of residence, groups of study-bedroom and common-room blocks around centralized refectory facilities or the university refectory, the conversion of large houses or hotels and the provision of student flats.[6.4]

It was therefore in keeping with the tenor of the period that the Lancaster Academic Planning Board in March 1963 recommended

that all members of the University, teachers and taught, shall, on appointment or admission, become members of units which at the moment we call "Colleges". These Colleges will be groups not to exceed six hundred under-graduates in number with an appropriate proportion of post-graduates and teaching staff. The staff members of each College will provide such advice and tutorial assistance as may be appropriate to members of their College and others. Each College will be mixed by

[6.2] *Ibid.*, paragraphs 587–9.
[6.3] *Ibid.*, paragraph 635.
[6.4] U.G.C., *University Development 1957–62*, Cmnd. 2267 (1964), paragraphs 72–3.

academic subjects both among under-graduates, post-graduates and teachers. They will be mixed by sex and they will also be mixed because each will contain a percentage (in the early days at least) of those who live "out". . . . What is proposed is not the college system as it exists in Oxford or Cambridge, because we do not propose anything approaching the autonomy in matters of policy and finance which such colleges have customarily enjoyed. Our system goes considerably further than the hall of residence system because it covers all undergraduates whether in residence or not and seeks to provide a supplementary, but we believe to be useful, focal point for all members of the academic staff in addition to that provided by their specialist and departmental affiliations.

Two colleges, Bowland and Lonsdale, came into existence (at least in name) in 1964, Cartmel and County two years later, and Furness and Fylde in 1968. The twinned colleges of Pendle and Grizedale are in the process of being built, and Rossendale has already had a planning committee in existence for over three years. Inhabitants of the north of England will at once observe that the names of the colleges, except County, have been adopted from areas around the university—Lonsdale, Furness and Cartmel to the immediate north and north-west, Bowland and Pendle to the east, Fylde to the south, Grizedale on the edge of the Lake District, and Rossendale to the south, picking up the historical associations of the region. Indeed, in two of the colleges, Cartmel and Furness, the names of the villages within the district have been used to designate the separate blocks within the college: thus we have, for example, Bigland, Flookburgh and Lindale within Cartmel, and Kirkby, Ireleth, Lowick and Pennington within Furness.

The County College is an exception, being so named in recognition of the very generous gift from the County Council of this building. It is distinctive in being smaller than the others and not having any arts teaching accommodation housed within it because, as Mr. Roger Booth, the County Architect, has noted

> the patrons, meaning the County Fathers, suddenly revealed a distinctly "unilateral" personality. They did not want their gift confused with any teaching space at all. Teaching was the Government's affair, and their money was not the Government's but came directly from the people of Lancashire.[6.5]

Although Kent and York of the new universities are also collegiate, a comparison of constitutions shows that Lancaster has integrated the colleges more fully with the governmental and organizational structure of the university than have the others:

[6.5] Article in the County *College Gazette* (date unknown).

There shall be colleges of the University, which shall be established by the Council on the recommendation of the Senate, each with such name and style as the Council shall determine. For each College there shall be a Syndicate which shall be a Committee of the Senate. . . .

The Principal of a College shall be a chairman of the Syndicate of that College, and he shall be responsible to the Council and the Senate for maintaining the effective working and good order of that College.

Amongst the *ex officio* membership of the Senate, moreover, there are all the principals of colleges, while amongst the elected and appointed members are elected members from the syndicates.

Yet the question constantly recurs: what is the place of a college in a modern university? Sir Noel Hall, the Chairman of the Academic Planning Board, saw them as units which were small enough to enable students to get to know each other within groups of a manageable size. At present the colleges have, as was originally set out in early planning documents, an average of five hundred students each, of whom just over half are resident (in the case of The County College, three-quarters), there being in 1972–73, 1,782 beds for 3,054 students. Sir Noel Hall has told the author that the colleges were a very deliberate part of the early design. They were not intended to be merely halls of residence with wardens acting as clerks, but were to give all students a place to which they could belong; including those living out of residence. The college would form a constituency within which people would know others and be known, and from which student representatives could be elected to convey the grassroots information and opinion to the larger central student bodies. By using this device, Lancaster could, whatever its ultimate size, avoid the kind of problem that can occur in larger universities, such as London, where student elections become a farce because the electorate are very unlikely to know the candidates. In short, the intention was to draw the best out of the Oxford and Cambridge collegiate tradition and impart it to the new universities.

Yet there are fundamental difficulties about making an attempt of this sort. Even the most traditionally organized of the universities have encountered within the last decade a change of mood amongst students and a repudiation of previously accepted customs such as, for example, communal dining in a hall. Furthermore, the Lancaster colleges have no teaching function and take no part in the admissions procedure as do, for example, the colleges at Durham. Dr. Clive Church has documented fully these changes, nationally and locally, and has concluded that the collegiate ideal involves a basic clash of values

with academic interests over the centre of gravity in the University, but although many staff and students are in practice moving away from acceptance of the former, in true British fashion they have refused to face up to this. They therefore continue to think themselves supporters of the collegiate system, even though they actually act on different premises. . . . Instead the latent lack of acceptance of the collegiate ethos combined with other pressures and events . . . undermines the colleges, despite the practical requirement for a form of collegiate organization within the modern university.[6.6]

The colleges have been at the centre of a continuing debate since the founding of the university, and it is worth tracing some of the steps in the discussion. In a discussion between the Academic Planning Board and the Chief Educa- tion Officer of Lancashire, as early as June 1962, Mr. Lord

referred to criticism about the lack of tutorial and pastoral care for students in the average provincial University. . . . He referred also to the difficulties facing students who were living in lodgings many miles from their University, particularly those in the industrial areas, and he hoped that great importance would be attached to halls of residence at Lancaster.

Professor B. R. Williams, on the other hand, voiced the opinion, in an undated paper of about the same period, that

There is space for residence though there is not likely to be adequate finance to create a residential university. I do not think that we should be greatly worried about this. The "virtues of residence" are frequently over-rated. Much that is claimed for residence derives from an idealized, or an out-of-date, ideal of life at Oxford and Cambridge. Residence is said to give a convenient place of living, a valuable contact between staff and students, and membership of a relatively small group which extends opportunities to develop mind and character in a satisfactory way. In fact there are three distinct parts to this problem, that of physical residence, that of contact between student and teacher, and that of group organization. . . .

Contact between student and teacher mainly arises at a place determined by the organization of teaching. In Science, in all universities and colleges, this place of contact is in the Science buildings. In other subjects, outside Oxford and Cambridge, the place of contact is in the teaching departments, and not in the place of residence. This is so even in the completely residential university at Keele.

It follows I think that we should look carefully at the nature of "the

---

[6.6] Clive H. Church, "The Colleges and their Place in the Development of the University of Lancaster: an Interpretation" (1973), unpublished MS. See also his forthcoming article in the *Higher Education Review*.

teaching departments" in modern universities to see how they could be changed to ensure satisfactory staff-student relationships.

The Board, however, came down on the side of a system of what they called interchangeably houses or colleges

> in which resident and non-resident under-graduates and academic staff would be brought, on a corporate basis, into close association. . . .
>
> The "House" (each for say 400 students and with staff ratio of 1/10) would be the basic unit for the provision and organization of facilities for dining, private study, tutorship, recreation, leisure etc., for all students (resident and non-resident) belonging to the "House".
>
> All members of staff would be assigned to a "House" with dining and other rights . . . and would provide tutorial and other supervision and counselling for undergraduate members of the "House". . . . The Head of each "House" would be a senior member of the academic staff particularly suited for this position of responsibility which would need to carry special considerations including appropriate residential accommodation close to or associated with the "House".
>
> The "Head" (who would be of Senate-membership status) would take part in the distribution of under-graduates between "Houses" after their admission to the university. He would also expect to take part in making academic appointments where membership of his house was an integral part of the vacancy to be filled. The day to day administration of the house would be in the hands of a Domestic Bursar or Warden, with appropriate staff, who would be responsible to the Head of the house, the Heads of houses together with the Vice-Chancellor in the Chair constituting a Management Committee for all matters relating to residence, student life and livelihood, reporting direct to the Council.

The Board made the collegiate concept one of the cornerstones of their submission to the U.G.C. in March 1963, as we have seen, and had it accepted in principle. The Vice-Chancellor, however, sounded a warning note in November 1963, just after the publication of the Robbins report, when he indicated to the Executive Council

> that it was not the normal policy of the University Grants Committee to grant-aid the provision of Halls of Residence in the early years of a University so long as lodgings were available in sufficient numbers. He suggested however, that in view of the proposals for a rapid increase in University development, a case for special consideration might be put to the University Grants Committee to test whether they would be prepared to finance one or perhaps two residential colleges at Lancaster, although

if a choice had to be made the emphasis would always need to be placed on teaching accommodation,

whereupon there was placed on record the strong and unanimous desire of the Executive Council that

the University should have residential accommodation available on a College basis at the earliest possible time and that the Vice-Chancellor be authorized to press this matter to the utmost with the University Grants Committee.

He accordingly sent the U.G.C. a letter in which he drew their attention to the proposed building programme which

includes three Colleges, each being for 250 residents, 250 or more non-residents, and associated staff members. Since there will be no provision for refectories, and (at this stage) no provision for student or staff social activities outside the Colleges, we assume that at least one-third of the cost of these Colleges will be met by your Committee. My Executive Council wishes me also to draw to your attention the fact that the Robbins Committee, while stressing the importance of student accommodation, has by its report considerably weakened our ability to provide it; for the response of the business community to an appeal for a large sum of money is now to urge upon us reliance on the Government's declared generosity.

To the Shadow Senate and the Academic Planning Board, however, his pessimism remained unallayed, as may be seen from a document drawn up by him and the University Secretary of December 1963 in which they explained that,

As far as we can tell, it will be a long time before we can claim to have exhausted the supply of lodgings in the area. This fact reduces our ability to get support for traditional residence as an element in a "crash programme". . . .

But if we build 8 colleges in the next 10 years, and if a quarter of their cost is met by the U.G.C. (which is probably too hopeful), we shall still be left to find nearly £3 million. We do not think that this sum will be found. . . . Nor do we want to swallow up all our "free capital" in student residence; there are many other important areas where we shall need the freedom given by extra funds.

If we start on an over-ambitious college programme and fail to complete it, the result will be to create a distinction between resident "haves" and non-resident "have-nots". We therefore think that *priority* should be given to proper accommodation for non-resident students, and that the extension of residence should be determined by the amount of money available. It must be remembered that "residence" here means "bed and breakfast": for we propose that all (or nearly all) students should take an evening meal as well as lunch at the university, so that they will, in fact, be resident for most of their waking hours. We therefore suggest as a first step the building of "College Clubs", capable of later conversion into colleges of the normal kind. Each College Club would have about 160 "Study Bedrooms" of the normal size, but initially these would be furnished as studies shared by 3 non-resident students (with desks, clothes lockers and bookshelves),

and he then went on to describe the other facilities which would be needed. The Shadow Senate was content with this strategem, while suggesting that "teaching accommodation for non-laboratory subjects might profitably be associated with such study centres. This attachment would bring a closer relationship between at least some members of staff and the student body."

The growing pessimism was found to be justified early in 1964 when the amount of capital available to the new universities for building appeared to be both uncertain and diminishing, although the Vice-Chancellor was able to tell the Shadow Senate in March 1964 that

he had heard from Sir John Wolfenden to the effect that the University Grants Committee were very sympathetic towards the idea of non-residential "study and social centres" and agreed that they would be ready in principle to recommend non-recurrent grants for non-residential student accommodation provided in such buildings. They felt unable, however, to accept for grant purposes the residential accommodation which might be provided for the College principals or for resident supervisory or domestic staff, except in the case of a resident porter or janitor.

The Shadow Senate of May 1964 was asked to go through the process of allocating staff and students to the colleges, finding suitable names, and deciding on a method of appointment of a principal. It was in a document for this meeting that the Vice-Chancellor suggested that six professors be put into each college and "the other members of the staff of each department into the other College. This gives a suitable spread of subjects, whilst also giving Assistant Lecturers a chance to blow off steam in a body where their head of department does not sit".

There was also a proposal, which was not adopted, that students should be allocated to colleges by region, which it was hoped would establish connections with a manageable number of schools. The hope at this time was that the principals would be resident, once there were college buildings, and so interim principals were elected. By the time the colleges were built, however, members of staff had already bought houses in Lancaster and the neighbourhood and were reluctant to uproot themselves and their families and come into residence. Furthermore, the Vice-Chancellor had in a paper of December 1965 to the Senate, pointed out that only with the extravagant use of appeal money could we provide staff flats of a size and comfort to suit a resident principal and his family; it gradually became accepted that some relatively junior members of staff might need to be used as college principals. It has been possible so far to have at least one officer of each college in residence, unmarried members of staff or those who are still relative new-comers to the university being the most frequent occupants of the rent-free accommodation that accompanies this degree of college involvement.

Naturally the colleges featured prominently in the appeal literature that was sent out and of the £2¼ million that came in to the university, almost £1 million was spent on collegiate accommodation, including the staff flats.[6.7] By the summer of 1964 Lancaster had heard that non-recurrent capital funds were available to build the first college—on the non-residential basis described above, in the first instance. The Vice-Chancellor told the first meeting of the Council in December 1964 that

> The theory of the "study" development is that it is better to provide tolerable working conditions quickly for a lot of students than to provide full residence for a few and nothing for the rest. It was also conceivably a method of getting more money out of the Government, by persuading them to provide residence in two stages (first, the building of studies for non-resident students: second, their conversion to study-bedrooms). U.G.C. finance has become so tight, however, that no advantage of this kind seems likely to occur. Nevertheless, it still seems right to begin with an experiment with studies for non-resident students.

Somewhat earlier, in July, the Vice-Chancellor had told the Shadow Senate that

> The teaching accommodation in the first two Colleges was planned in units of 16 teaching rooms. Each College would contain 36 staff rooms but the plan provided for a certain amount of elasticity, and other rooms could be diverted to use as staff rooms if this should prove necessary.

This raised, in the mind of at least one head of an arts department, the question of the long-term plans for the arts departments. Professor Woolrych argued strongly for centralizing non-laboratory departments in one building. He told the Senate that he felt some of the staff had not been sure earlier in the year as to whether the proposed housing of arts teaching accommodation within the colleges was a temporary economy measure or intended as a perma-nent solution, for

---

[6.7] See Appendix (ix) for a list of the expenditure of the Appeal money.

I understand that there will be enough teaching accommodation in our first two colleges to house even our biggest non-laboratory departments for years to come. Even so I hope that departments will not be located in colleges permanently. Although it is much better (in my view) to have a department concentrated in a college than not to have it concentrated at all, department and college will have no functional connection with each other, since each department's staff and students will be distributed among all the colleges. . . .

I hope we have postponed rather than abandoned the planning of a single building, or closely-grouped complex of buildings, to house the humanities and social sciences. The proposals which were still in the air at the end of last year to house them under the same roof as the library made excellent sense, and helped to reconcile me to foregoing a departmental library. . . . But the strongest case for grouping the non-laboratory departments together is that it will greatly facilitate the close consultation and co-operation between them which our degree schemes, more than most, will demand. If our business is the interlocking of subjects, are we wise to start by physically separating them?

The Senate as a body would appear to have had no very strong views on the matter (although individual members of staff, such as Professor Tom Lawrenson strongly advocated dispersed departments), for the minute of the meeting simply records that

In the course of general discussion, the Vice-Chancellor said that he had assumed that majority opinion would favour the system adopted at York, where arts departments were housed in the colleges but each department was centralized in one place. . . . The Vice-Chancellor went on to refer to the possibility, which he said he would explore, of housing a considerable concentration of arts departments in the tower of the third College[6.8] and of building some of the later colleges without teaching accommodation. He added that a separate arts building would probably lead to a less efficient use of accommodation. Such a building would tend to be under-used in the evenings whilst the colleges, which under the system at present proposed would be able to use certain teaching rooms for evening activities, would have to have special rooms for these purposes if teaching departments were concentrated outside the colleges.

An idea of the ethos of the first college may be obtained from the following vignette of Bowland College written by Professor Willcock in 1972:

[6.8] Early plans for Cartmel College included a small tower.

In the very earliest days, back in 1964, the University was of course in the warehouse building in St. Leonard's Gate in the town; and colleges were very hypothetical entities indeed. Nevertheless, two colleges were formed, and all staff and students were allocated to one or the other. Even before the first students came, there had been meetings of the Syndicate of what at first was called College A: . . .

In July 1964, they chose the name Bowland;[6.9] and in October had a serious debate on how to pronounce it. (Specialist advice was given that the pronunciation to rhyme with "bow" as in "bow and arrow" was philologically more correct than the pronunciation with the short "o" sometimes found in the locality itself.) Also in October the first Principal (Professor Bevington) was appointed, and the first Dean (Dr. Mercer).

In October came the students—to a strange and difficult existence. . . . But nevertheless there was interest in being present at the creation of something new and important. Students were not on Syndicate for the first year, so that their activities are less recorded in my papers. I remember hearing however of an early escapade in the town, taken more seriously by the police than it would have been at a more ancient seat of learning; and an incipient and precocious rent strike at the start of the second year. . . . In October we moved to the Bowland College building on the Bailrigg site. For two years, the College housed Arts teaching Departments, and provided day studies for non-resident students; but (apart from the flats) there were no residents. During the first year, Bowland was the University of Bailrigg; in the second Lonsdale shared that burden.

Lonsdale followed a similar pattern to Bowland, being formally created by the Council in January 1965, and having as its first principal Professor Tom Lawrenson. For the first year a Joint Colleges Planning Committee sat to determine the future constitutions and physical layout of the colleges when they moved to their new buildings at Bailrigg, but thereafter, with the addition of the third college, Cartmel, in December 1965, it was decided that each college should have a planning committee of its own.

The government of the colleges was to be conducted by syndicates who, by a decision of the Senate in September 1964, were at first intended to be responsible for the nomination of the principal and the appointment of other college officers and college staff; to "make proposals to the Buildings Committee for the planning or improvement of the structure of the College", to make provision for the governance of the college, and to "exercise a general care over the students of the College, to plan for the College an active intellectual, cultural and social life, and to initiate measures and to receive and decide

---

[6.9] Later the college bar was called, by a neat use of a local name, the Trough of Bowland, and an appropriately painted sign hung outside it.

2c

upon proposals for the general well-being of members of the College". All teaching members of the university are automatically members of syndicates and, by virtue of being asked to act as college tutors (which is at the discretion of the college syndicates), so are F.S.S.U. administrative staff and various other special categories of staff.

The bulk of the undergraduates, to judge by the issues of *Carolynne* and *John O'Gauntlet* of the first two years, accepted the collegiate principle without debate. They were so involved with reacting to their immediate environment at St. Leonard's House that theoretical discussion of the virtues of one kind of organization over another were part of the thinking of only a few of the more politically minded students who began, in the first twelve months, making moves towards having a central students' union.[6.10]

Anxiety about the progress of the collegiate system was expressed by the non-professorial staff at the time of the preparation in December 1965 for the U.G.C. visitation, in which it was said that

> If our own collegiate system is ever to become viable, then it must be expressed in college buildings with a strong core of residence. Since, having started sooner and faster than most other new universities, we are at present working in makeshift conditions, our system strikes many undergraduates (who are not given in any case to viewing matters *sub specie aeternitatis*) as meaningless, and there is increasing pressure for a completely separate union structure of student government. . . . We feel that this would create a gulf between staff and students, and every month of delay in the building of the colleges makes the problem more acute and will render it more difficult of solution in the years to come.

And, as regards study rooms,

> The academic policy of the university, aiming to provide a wide *choice* of subjects . . . and subject *combinations* which cross the normal faculty barriers, will inevitably extend the time-table into the evenings, and that is the desire of all. The number of reading places planned in the Library will be reasonably adequate only if we are able to supplement them with study-work-rooms and study-bedrooms as programmed. We feel further that students who live seven miles away and who have access to the University through one of the worst bottle-necks in the North of England, namely Skerton Bridge, must have a base, for working and living, which

---

[6.10] See below, pages 357 to 366. In case readers wonder what provision is made at Lancaster for graduate students it should be explained that in January 1966 the syndicate of Bowland College in the face of "strong opposition" from the college's J.C.R. president, suggested that the college should have a Middle Common Room. Although the Senate agreed that each college could decide for itself whether to create this facility, none of them have done so.

they can occupy in between lectures and tutorials: the work facilities in many of our lodgings render this imperative, as does the fact that within our system of lodgings landladies do not provide the evening meals, which will be provided in the Colleges. We want our undergraduates, in short, to *live* in the university.[6.11]

The Vice-Chancellor therefore suggested that, while not losing the essential ingredients of collegiate life, there should be a radically different pattern of residence, based on a social centre, a block of bed-sitting rooms and quiet rooms of varying sizes. Professor Dobbs is recorded as having expressed concern at such a concept, "which he considered would tend to destroy collegiate life at Lancaster", while the Vice-Chancellor foresaw a time when the university might be forced to provide this type of accommodation or none at all.

The U.G.C., in the report following their visit, pronounced themselves satisfied with the college system, for there had been "emphasis on the College as a unit, with the syndicate as the forum for discussion and consultation. No doubt as the colleges moved into their buildings each was likely to develop a characteristic flavour of its own; already in some respects the Colleges were moving in rather different directions. . . . The Principals and Deans had given a very interesting account of the College pattern and the function of the syndicates and the difficulties which were likely to arise, as the Colleges multiplied, in allocating staff appropriately."

In March 1966 Professor Woolrych again questioned the value of putting arts teaching accommodation in the colleges, saying that

I think of the colleges as places where undergraduates go to study on their own, as well as to eat, relax and enjoy the corporate social life of a limited community. This sense of identity will not be made easier if a college's corridors swarm once an hour with undergraduates who do not belong to the college, but are going to and from classes taken by members of staff who for the most part are themselves non-members of the colleges.

The Vice-Chancellor, however, felt that the Senate should declare whether the separation of teaching and living accommodation was desirable on academic grounds, and the Syndicates whether "the removal of teaching rooms usable by student societies in the evenings would be a serious loss to the Colleges".

The second Senate conference took place later that month, and not surprisingly the colleges were one of the main topics for discussion. Coming towards the end of the second year of the university's existence, six months

---

[6.11] Reference should also be made, by students of the subject of colleges, to "The Development of Lonsdale College—A Basic Statement of Intent", which came to Lonsdale Syndicate in June 1966 and to the Senate the following month.

before arts staff and students were to move from St. Leonardgate to Bailrigg but two and a half years before any students were able to come into residence, the conference was a useful barometer of current opinion. Dr. G. J. Paxman saw colleges as a focus of communal life, a means of improving staff/student relationships, and a framework for the promotion of student welfare. He felt that

> for colleges to obtain maximum effectiveness, it would be necessary for them to acquire some character or individuality. Colleges should be encouraged to experiment. This would give rise to differences in many aspects of college life.

Professor Willcock wished to emphasize the community concept of the whole site, and to remind the Senate that the architect wished the colleges to be

> part of a larger unity, the small-town atmosphere of the site. The life of the students is to be free, and not determined by the fixed patterns of College life; activity should flourish throughout the university.
>
> Coming from a place [i.e. Cambridge] where the colleges are too powerful, and the university too weak, I am completely won over to this conception. We have to strike a balance, in the normal life of the students, between the community life of the college and the wider world outside. If we strike the right balance, we can get the best of both worlds—the advantages of college membership without its restrictions.

Turning to more practical matters, he reported that

> Good modern theory on student accommodation encourages the de-velopment of small social groups living together with some sort of cooking facilities. Figures that I have seen suggest that the optimum size for the small social group is between 10 and 14, with a preference for the smaller number. . . .
>
> The question of allocation of sleeping accommodation in a mixed college has not, so far as I know, been decided. Even whether the four-strong work-study rooms in October will be single-sex has not been discussed. The architect has been careful to plan the buildings so that this decision remains open, and there are various lockable doors at intervals in case we wish to lock them. . . .
>
> There are three possible arrangements for mixed student accommoda-tion; what is called the hotel method, whereby rooms are allotted as they come, irrespective of any sex difference; secondly, dividing the sexes in different parts of the same building; thirdly, if you happen to have two buildings, putting one sex in one, and the other in the other.

This is a matter which affects the whole university, and one on which the Senate's views would be most useful. It is presumably true that the colleges cannot act completely differently on a matter like this.

Dr. Paxman had referred to the development of agreement for "according colleges a maximum degree of autonomy outside strictly academic matters", while Professor Willcock saw a problem of

allowing the colleges to exist as in any way separate organizations within a university that would like to run itself efficiently. Everything in the way of administration which the college takes over lessens the economy of the efforts of the University administration. . . .

The college has a College office. What will it be used for? We must define the functions of College and University. A college is concerned for the welfare of its students, and that is its reason for corporately existing. The university is concerned with the academic side, selection of students, planning of courses, organization of teaching. The university authority will have in due course to let the College take over some aspects of student welfare which are now handled centrally. The sort of things which I personally expect the college to take over in due course include—and this may shock the University Secretary—the arranging that students shall register with a medical practitioner; and the keeping of records of the individual students' doctors; holding each student's U.C.C.A. form.

Yet even though there were problems within the college system, Professor Willcock nevertheless "expressed his whole-hearted belief in the tutorial system", and the mood of the Senators was to take the suggestions made to them even a step further by proposing, for example, that colleges might take over admissions. There was also a suggestion that "a small college might be provided for graduate or mature students", although some of the staff present were in favour of these categories of students being spread over the colleges. The Senate agreed that college syndicates should discuss both the distribution of students within residences and the question of the relationship of college tutors to students. Apparently problems of lack of communication in this area were already beginning to make themselves felt, for the minutes of the Staff/Student Committee of June 1966 record that

The University Secretary read to the meeting a letter from Mr. P. Smart, secretary of Lonsdale College, expressing the concern felt by a number of first year students at apparent lack of contact between tutors and tutees.

This concern amongst students was confirmed by the student representatives, who indicated that some students were unaware of the identity of their tutors.

From the discussion it appeared that greater effort was required from both tutors and tutees to implement the system in the manner originally envisaged, and it was agreed that an attempt would have to be made to remedy the situation.

A copy of the letter, together with a note of the committee's views, was therefore sent to senior tutors. No report came back but it is interesting to note that in March 1967 at the same committee,

> consideration was given to the channels of communication by which teaching departments and college tutors were able to receive information that students living in flats were unable, through illness or other cause, to attend the university.
>
> The Superintendent of Lodgings detailed the existing procedure, which was operating satisfactorily, but he emphasized that a little difficulty was being experienced because some students omitted to notify his office when they changed flats.
>
> The discussion then turned to the care of students living in flats who might be taken ill. A suggestion was put forward that sick rooms should be provided on University premises for students suffering from illness who were unable to fend for themselves, and particularly so for those suffering from infectious diseases.

The role of the college tutor varies in practice between one college and another, and even within a college, for the one constant feature of the system seems to be that this is essentially an interaction of individuals for which one cannot legislate. Formal arrangements vary quite a lot. In Furness, for example, each student has two tutors, either of whom he can go to see, and one of whom will be from a department whose discipline is close to his major subject and another from a distant discipline. In Cartmel, on the other hand, there are informal groups of tutors, who may or may not join together for purposes of entertaining their tutees, and in general a student will be assigned to a tutor whose discipline is close to his own. In the County College, however, under-graduates are assigned not to a single tutor, but to a group of tutors with a convener who is responsible for keeping up-to-date information on all the students assigned to his group, and who is the first point of contact for anyone from outside the college who needs information about a particular student.[6.12] Certainly no formal statement of a college tutor's duties exists, although the senior tutor of each college invariably draws up a code of conduct for the tutors of that college.

The question of medical facilities for students was beginning to make itself

[6.12] See J. Heywood, "A Case Study of an Innovation in a New University: The Development of the Group Tutorial System in the County College of the University of Lancaster", August 1970, for further details.

felt, as is evidenced by the fact of the Vice-Chancellor personally consulting Sir George Godber (Chief Medical Officer of the Ministry of Health) whose advice, given in March 1967, was that

(a) All normal medical needs of students should be carried out by the National Health Service. He recommends the appointment of a suitable group practice in the neighbourhood for this purpose; alternatively, it might be possible to appoint a general practitioner to serve each college.

(b) The special needs of students are, he thinks, much more limited than is sometimes suggested, being confined to a few psychiatric problems and some special age-group problems such as drug-taking. He considers that for a considerable time to come it will suffice to have some part-time assistance from a member of staff of Lancaster Moor Hospital.

Hitherto, students had registered individually with general practitioners, although the university had also appointed a part-time Medical Officer, Dr. R. M. Moffitt. In April 1967, therefore, the Vice-Chancellor reported that he had discussed the matter with Dr. Moffitt:

The suggestion had been made that the colleges should have separate doctors but the Medical Officer was opposed to this and thought that a centralized medical centre with full facilities and centralized medical records was essential. The Medical Officer had had discussions with the local medical committee and it appeared that there would be no difficulty in arranging for a group practice to serve the University. This was done at other universities and also at S. Martin's College.

The Senate agreed that in principle all medical services and records should be centralized, and that the University Secretary should investigate the possibility of a group practice taking over the university medical service from October 1967.

To move forward in time for a moment, these proposals were, in the main, adopted. Bailrigg House was adapted as a medical centre and equipped with nine beds. Dr. Moffitt's group practice was selected by the university and four doctors (including one female) from it make themselves available to students and staff at specified times during the week. There are two resident nursing sisters, and a psychiatrist and a physiotherapist come up to the university each week during term. Most of the expenses of this unit are paid for by the local Executive Council, with an agreed contribution coming from the university. There is no compulsion, however, for students to register with this particular practice rather than any other.

There can be no doubt that this centre plays a most valuable role in university life. Students are able to retreat there away from the clamour and tension of the rest of the campus and, in surroundings which are architecturally very different, surrounded by pleasant gardens and an open landscape, can be cared for by people who are not involved in the academic milieu. The Royal Lancaster Infirmary is sometimes prepared to discharge students earlier because they know they can be so well looked after at the Centre; and there are several students each year who take their Part I or their Final examinations in this more tranquil setting, under appropriate supervision.

Meanwhile, to return again to February 1967, the Vice-Chancellor was introducing the Senate to the idea of loan-financed residences for future colleges, which in turn raised again the question of the location of arts teaching accommodation. An *ad hoc* committee, with the ponderous title of Teaching Accommodation in Future Colleges, was set up and in March gave an interim report, recommending that non-laboratory departments should continue to be housed in collegiate premises. The informal Senate conference later in the month chose to consider the "dichotomy of control" (to quote Professor Willcock again) that was causing difficulties in the relationships of the colleges to the university. There were problems with the kitchens[6.13] and with the Building Development Office, inasmuch as colleges were not sufficiently consulted about "what was done—whether in the choice of furniture or the selection of trees to adorn the College courts, or the supervision of the decoration in College Rooms", as well as with the Finance Office. The Finance Officer "at present considered that it might be simpler all round if the Colleges tried to run their own financial affairs; but that if they used his staff, they should pay for this work. Professor Willcock considered this reasonable and suggested that the best solution would be for there to be a particular clerk in the Finance Office who would undertake the accounting for the Colleges".[6.14]

Professor Bevington concluded with a suggestion, which has to some extent been adopted, that the college tutor should belong to the same major department as the undergraduate, since he "did not fully agree with Professor Willcock's distinction between the University's responsibility for academic matters and the Colleges' responsibility for welfare".

There were, of course, other problems. Professor Willcock had noted in an early report to Bowland Syndicate that the same small group of people were undertaking all the extra college tasks. There were also those who doubted the value of time spent on college syndicate meetings, as is evidenced by certain

---

6.13 See Chapter 4, page 259 ff

6.14 For a while this system was implemented exactly as described here, but latterly college finances have again come under the direct care of the Finance Officer himself.

remarks of Mr. M. G. de St V. Atkins in September 1967 who voiced an opinion that

> When a syndicate is half as large again as senate, it becomes very question-able whether more than the briefest formal meeting to endorse decisions taken on its behalf can be justified. And something more than cost is involved. Even in universities which make no pretence to having a col-legiate structure, scholarship is being stifled by the administrative and legislative obligations which fall necessarily or are assumed chivalrously or officiously by teachers. The additional burden of administering colleges should be made as light as possible. . . .
>
> It has been agreed by the "shadow" syndicate [of the County College], and I hope that the syndicate will confirm, that a small executive committee should carry out the policy decisions of the syndicate. I am not persuaded, for reasons implicit in what has been said above, that there is any decision that does not itself modify or make policy. . . . I should, therefore, submit that we are being realistic instead of simply pietistic if we decided that policy as well as day-to-day decisions were to be made by this small committee and that the syndicate simply elected the committee to govern it and ratified its decisions when they had been made.

The division of members of the university in 1964 between Bowland and Lonsdale colleges had had perforce to be arbitrary, but for subsequent colleges the method was rather different. The planning committee of Cartmel, the third college, was set up relatively late, in December 1965, but its early organization was a paradigm for the others which followed:

(i) A small "shadow" Syndicate with a Chairman should be formed for Cartmel College.

(ii) All members of the Syndicates of Bowland College and of Lonsdale College should be asked whether
(a) they wish to become a member of Cartmel College,
(b) they are prepared to become a member of Cartmel College, if asked,
(c) they would object to being transferred to Cartmel College.
Six members of the "shadow" Syndicate will then be selected *by lot* from among those in category (a). These six will be empowered to select a further six members from among those in categories (a) and (b), with a view to achieving a "balanced" membership (i.e. balanced in terms of spread of subjects, spread of seniority, sex, etc.).

(iii) The twelve members of the "shadow" Syndicate will then elect a Chairman, who will continue to act until the time comes for the election of a Principal.

In this way the college would develop its own ethos, since the original core of people had a right of invitation to others—Cartmel quite consciously elected to present a rather left-wing image, as demonstrated by its choice of officers, its decision somewhat later not to have a senior common room, and by the number of students which it proposed at different stages to have on its syndicate, a number often in advance of most of the other colleges.

Furness produced an innovation in its system of government, by deciding to create a College Council "which in the exercise of power delegated by the Syndicate shall be the governing body of the college" on day-to-day matters, leaving the syndicate (which has no student members) free to discuss university business and to make recommendations thereon to the Senate. Supporters of the Furness system say that the business of its syndicate meetings bears much more relation to the concerns of the university at large than that of the other colleges who, it is felt, fritter away their time on domesticities. Even here, however, there is still a problem of dwindling attendances by senior members of the university. Sometimes, as in the case of Fylde, the kinds of experimentation which were suggested had to go through several submissions to the Senate before being accepted and in the meanwhile the college had no mechanism by which to regulate itself. A standard temporary form of constitution for future new colleges was therefore drawn up in November 1970 and, after scrutiny by the Committee of Colleges, was approved by the Board of the Senate.

The practical administration of Furness and County had now to be organized for the Buildings Committee and the Council needed to know as a matter of urgency what each of the colleges' intentions were. Until shadow syndicates were set up for them, therefore, it was agreed that the syndicates of Bowland and Lonsdale respectively would "be responsible for advising on the planning" of the other two new colleges. After many trials and tribulations, more relevant to a chapter on building, the residences opened in the autumn of 1968 and, in Cartmel at least, memories are cherished by members of staff of being called out almost as the students were arriving to haul upstairs bedsteads and mattresses, and to put rooms in order. The Vice-Chancellor was able to speak in his annual report of December 1968 of having had during the year "the satisfaction of seeing the building programme reach the stage at which the architects' overall concept has become a working reality. . . . The first parts of our residential accommodation, in Bowland and Cartmel Colleges, are occupied, and further large additions to residence will be made during the coming year. . . . We now have some 530 students in residence".

During 1968–69, however, some of the disadvantages of the residential buildings revealed themselves; particularly over-intensive use of those kitchens which had been designed only for the preparation of snacks, the poor standard of sound insulation in modern buildings built to U.G.C. norms, lack of privacy, and other aspects of communal living which distressed some of the residents so much that they published, in June 1969, the notorious Black Issue of *Carolynne*. Called "Decay of a Community", it made allegations of use and sale of drugs, intimidation and threats of violence, prostitution, organized theft, and a high degree of noise and squalor. The consequent investigating committee set up under the chairmanship of Professor Lawrenson had some general recommendations to make which illuminate some of the difficulties which had appeared, sometimes as the ironical obverse of the best features of Lancaster:

> We have hard evidence that the atmosphere of communal living in residence is *not* conducive to serious study and constitutes an abiding affront to a sensitive and civilized conscience. We do not consider that the state of communal living in certain sections of our residence ought ever to be tolerated in a university, and we assure the Senate that it would not be tolerated in a large block of flats in an urban context.

> We therefore recommend that immediate steps be taken by all Colleges to ensure that a much greater proportion of senior members *with supervisory and disciplinary duties* lives in the Colleges. Their duties would clearly be to ensure that the College regulations are observed. They should specifically be instructed not to "snoop", but to investigate any breach of regulation which comes to their attention. . . . We very strongly advise that these should be treated as *posts* and not elective offices. . . .

> Colleges have been compelled this last year to admit far more first-year students, relatively to second- and third-years, than is good for a residential community. The balance of years should be rectified, as much as possible and with all speed. Final-year students should be "mixed in" if possible, and not segregated. . . .

> We submit that the Colleges were meant to be places of study. It should be understood once and for all that this cannot be achieved architecturally, and especially in terms of sound insulation, within the building standards that we are permitted. It can only be achieved by self-imposed discipline or other-imposed discipline. We are quite satisfied that in considerable areas of residence self-discipline has not been achieved by the students themselves.

There followed a proposed regulation about the control of noise and the report continued:

> The sexual behaviour of certain students has undoubtedly caused very grievous offence to others. We have hard evidence on this. We recommend that the Vice-Chancellor, acting on behalf of Senate during the vacation, should introduce with immediate effect a common regulation that all male

visits to women's study bedrooms, and all women's visits to men's study bedrooms, are not permitted between the hours of midnight and 11 a.m. We vehemently reject a common opinion which has it that because it is difficult to enforce a regulation, you should not have it. The regulation is there to be wielded when an infringement is forced upon the attention. . . .

We recommend that the units housing one sex in the Colleges should *immediately* be made larger, thus ensuring greater privacy. We also believe that students who persistently behave with conspicuous promiscuity should be excluded from residence.

In general the Senate conference of September 1969 endorsed these comments although there was intense opposition to the proposed regulations from most of the colleges; there was also some discussion about the need of a professional counselling service. Although it did not prove possible to put common regulations into effect forthwith, colleges re-examined their own codes of conduct, to bring them into line with new university rules that were being discussed at the same time.

Furness College Council had suggested as early as March 1969 that the Committee of Colleges should examine the question of collegiate planning and the need for existing colleges to be still more involved in planning for future colleges. Finally, in February 1970, two college principals (Mr. John Creed and Dr. Brian Duke) wrote the first of a series of papers on colleges in a university of 6,000 students. They asserted that a function of the college was

> to provide a social and residential frame-work for both senior and junior members of the University. Beyond this, however, there has been a certain vagueness. . . . It has generally been agreed that academic functions cannot in the main be Collegiate at least as far as curricular activities are concerned. There has consequently been a tendency for Colleges to be concerned with matters of management in their broadest sense, and with matters of staff-student relations. There has also been a growing feeling in some quarters that certain non-academic functions require organization on a University-wide scale, simply for reasons of economy (the obvious example is catering). There have been a number of areas in which it is generally agreed that Colleges should themselves organize and arrange matters but that there should be some common principle underlying their procedures. This has been particularly true of residence arrangements and disciplinary matters and in each of these cases there is a great deal of room for discussion about the extent to which there should be generally applicable principles.

They would have wished to see more "intellectual cross-fertilization coming from the College system" by means of debating or literary societies so that the colleges should "primarily be communities of scholars". The tutorial function they saw as the colleges' most successful function so far, "though this is not to say that the success is in any way complete". As to disciplinary functions, they saw this as

> a Collegiate responsibility if the community is to have any real independence. While there must be University rules and University offences, and in consequence University courts, the Colleges should retain control over all cases of offences within the College which do not involve a penalty of exclusion from the University.

With residential arrangements and finance they sought independence combined with a certain necessary degree of parity of treatment. They defended the role of college syndicates, saying that

> we believe that there are tremendous merits in the system we have whereby the governing power of the College rests finally with a body on which the academic staff members of the College are in the majority. We do not believe that a single autocratic warden would be a desirable substitute.

Finally, they endorsed the idea of having teaching departments housed in colleges while "emphatically rejecting" any suggestion "that membership of a College should be determined by the fact of a person teaching in it".

The principal of Furness College, Professor Philip Reynolds, declared that he had been looking for a "different kind of analysis, one which discussed the kinds of structures that were appropriate to the different functions of a university" and for the Senate conference of September 1970, in a paper called "Colleges in a University of 6,000—and beyond", said that

> Past human experience suggests that it is difficult for communities above some size to sustain a many-faceted corporate life. What that size may be is difficult to determine, but it is almost certainly smaller than 6,000.
>
> It would then follow that the University must be broken down into smaller units, and this means creating microcosms of itself, not creating sub-bodies to each of which some of its functions are variously delegated. The University then would exist in its microcosms and in its own minimally essential co-ordinating role. . . .
>
> The Colleges, which, as I interpreted the Charter and Statutes, were envisaged as such microcosms, have not so functioned because as Colleges they have performed no academic role. Increasingly they have come to be seen as social and welfare institutions, and under the pressures of cost-effectiveness (catering), external relations (University discipline), and student aspirations for self-direction, they have steadily lost capacity to function effectively even in these regards.

He therefore proposed that each college should house at least five departments, of widely differing disciplines, with not more than ten members of a
department in any one college. The staff who had teaching rooms in the
colleges would be their senior members, and would act as college tutors to
students of the same subject areas, with an associated senior member of the
college to act in a strictly pastoral capacity where that was needed. He also
recommended that the government of the Colleges should also be changed to
follow the Furness pattern:

> The effects of these changes on Departments it is not my task to examine;
> but I would think each group of say 8–10 members of staff in a College
> should have a secretary in the college, and I incline to Clive Church's
> suggestion that each Board of Studies should have a building containing
> "cores" of major departments in the Board, including, say the head of
> department or chairman, a departmental secretary and/or administrative
> officer, departmental records, perhaps research units, and so on. . . .
>
> In these circumstances it would seem to me that the Colleges could and
> should handle the part-academic, part-welfare functions in which both
> University and Colleges now tend wastefully to become involved, and that
> the Secretary of each College should be a full-time officer like the present
> Academic Registrar, with a multiplicity of functions at the College level.

Amongst other suggestions, Professor Reynolds proposed that the Academic
Promotions Committee should take some account of what college principals
had to say, that colleges should be represented on all appointing committees
and that first-year seminars and tutorial teaching might be organized on a
collegiate basis (an idea which did not find much support at the time, but
which has recurred in people's minds more than once since then).

Dr. Brian Duke, however, did not accept the premise that interest in the
colleges amongst senior members was dying out, for in County

> Over 50 per cent of the senior members of Syndicate, for example, hold
> office or serve on a College committee. Five out of six of the college officers
> were appointed after contested elections and the last year has seen a trend
> towards more contested elections. Syndicate meetings are not attended by
> anything like the number one would hope, but neither are Boards of Studies.

He pointed out that in a large university the informal groupings arising from
shared interests or departmental activities rely too much on chance[6.15]
whereas the college

[6.15] In this connection it is interesting that a number of students have told the
writer that friendships do not arise, in their experience, because of shared seminars.
This is the experience of staff, also, who cannot expect that information conveyed to
one member of a seminar group will be conveyed to the others by word of mouth.

is not, of course, itself a face to face group, but it can very easily and efficiently facilitate a many faceted set of such groups. It is small enough to attract real loyalty and is ideal for the workings of a participatory democracy. To be successful it needs to span most of, if not all of, the disciplines (members do change courses—they may not want to change Colleges as a result), it needs to have a real life of its own—autonomy in as many respects as possible. . . .

To fulfil these objectives many people believe that the Colleges should have more academic involvement. In this respect the details of an experiment which The County College is attempting this October may be of interest. Each incoming first-year student has been assigned to a College academic advisor and they will meet before any other official meetings. The tutorial groups will meet later on the same day. Most senior members of Syndicate serve as academic advisor for one single or joint major course. They will be able to discuss the nature of courses and the problems of registration.

The outcome of these weighty documents and a long discussion was not clear-cut. It was agreed to recommend to the Senate for further consideration the suggestions that colleges be represented on appointing committees, that they participate in the work of the Academic Promotions Committee, that individual members of departments be allowed to have a room in their college rather than their department, that colleges be free to promote inter-disciplinary academic discussion on courses, that students have an academic adviser close to his major subject and another "pastoral" tutor, that colleges could deviate from the pattern of all having the same cross-section of academic disciplines, and that each syndicate be invited to say what the desirable maximum size of any department housed within it might be. The proposal about college representation on appointing committees did not pass the Senate—although applicants for posts were to "be made aware of the importance of the colleges in the university"—but the comments of college principals could be placed alongside other evidence for the Academic Promotions Committee. A few individuals preferred to have rooms in their colleges, but the practice was unusual and died out again. Colleges continue to be free, as they always have been, to promote intellectual activities, but this expression of hope is related to the problem that the colleges do not provide a social life for senior members of the university: one of the great debates is whether any form of reorganization could bring about an improvement of this dearth or whether the university should cut its losses and set up a staff club. The colleges have each evolved their own modifications of the tutorial system and, to generalize over the university, there has been a tendency to assign students to tutors within the general area of their academic studies.

A more specialized suggestion was that of the planning committee of College 9[6.16] who suggested that the college make special provision for graduate students, but the Senate conference appeared not to be in a mood for such innovation, for while

> there need be no objection in principle to a college being planned for a particular "life-style" . . . the planning committee should be asked to define precisely the "life-style" which they sought and its relationship to the membership of the college. It was agreed that, in any event, it would not be acceptable for such a college to absorb more than half of the University's graduate students.

Meanwhile other pressures on the structure of colleges were making themselves felt. A report of April 1970, commissioned by the Buildings Committee, took the view that too few of the academic staff were prepared to be involved in the colleges particularly now that the pioneering days were past; that non-resident and graduate students were contributing to a decline in college identification that was already taking place; and that future colleges, if devoid of arts teaching and catering accommodation, would become mere dormitory blocks. Furthermore, the study-rooms for non-resident students, the lynch-pin of the first colleges, were under fire for, as the Vice-Chancellor explained in an open letter of October 1970,[6.17]

> a very difficult problem has arisen over studies for non-resident students. These were originally provided by the U.G.C. as an experiment; but it has now become evident that, despite the success of the experiment, the U.G.C. will no longer pay for accommodation which it is not building in other universities, and which involves an excess over its "norms". (The U.G.C. adds together study places and library reading places; and the present large extension to the library has consequently undermined our case for studies.) After discussing the alternatives (all disagreeable) the Board of the Senate, at its conference in September, suggested (a) that in new colleges we should provide a reading room for non-residents . . . (b) that so far as possible non-resident graduate students should be provided for in departments; (c) that new colleges should be built so that studies can be added later if funds are available.[6.18]

[6.16] Later amalgamated with the planning committee of College 10 to become the postulated Rossendale College of 950 students.

[6.17] Letter from the Vice-Chancellor to members of the University: No. 2, October 1970, entitled "About money and buildings".

[6.18] The study rooms in colleges already built have in part been given over to arts teaching accommodation so that later colleges can have some study accommodation. Not all students wish to avail themselves of such rooms.

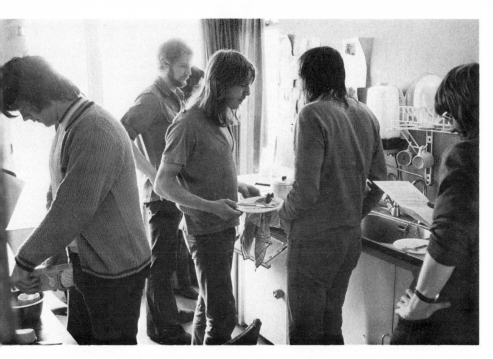

The evening meal: a kitchen of a commercially sponsored residence in Cartmel College

John Donat

Student Leaders in Bowland Bar

John Donat

Final examinations in the Great Hall

John Donat

The problem regarding arts teaching buildings was still unresolved, however:

> Senate was earlier minded to detach some of these from Colleges, so that large departments (or groups of related departments) could stay together without overwhelming a host college. . . . Unfortunately there is no time to engage in a leisurely discussion of this matter. . . . However, the immediate decisions are not as difficult as they appear. Fylde College site would be under-used if we did not include teaching there. The case for a separate building for the Business School departments rests on the special needs of courses for business men, and on the desirability of bringing together departments which will have to work jointly to achieve development in one of the U.G.C.'s priority areas. If these two developments are agreed, the area of doubt is whether (as earlier suggested) we build an English building which also includes studies for County College: or whether a building on that site should simply be regarded as a college building containing several parts of departments.

In October he referred to extra teaching rooms being put in Fylde College, to the first stage of the business school building, and to the possibility of "a teaching building beyond the 'Learning Aids Building', forming a quadrangle with the Theatre Studio and Cartmel and County Colleges. It is *not* intended to build teaching into any of the colleges to be built in the next quinquennium."

When a special meeting of the Committee of Colleges was held in April 1971, however, to consider plans for future colleges (and in particular of the twinned colleges of Pendle and Grizedale),

> Criticisms were made of the smallness of the site, of the totally enclosed nature and size of the courts, and of the height of the buildings. All these features were thought to be conducive to noise, oppressiveness and a lack of privacy. . . .
>
> Two new features of the proposed Colleges were thought to be particularly undesirable, namely the magnitude of the reduction in floor area per room to 90 square feet, and the absence of teaching accommodation. Both of these factors imply a higher student population density than in most existing Colleges. Most members of the Committee thought it would be an answer to the criticisms which had been levelled at the plans to incorporate teaching rooms into these future Colleges rather than concentrate them in the Teaching Building. It was therefore agreed to recommend to the Senate that the Teaching Building should not be built and that teaching areas should be introduced into Pendle and Grizedale Colleges.

Although the Senate Steering Committee referred this back on the grounds that building plans were too far advanced to make such a change, it is the case

2D

that an arts teaching building is not at present part of the current building programme, and the planning committee of Rossendale has made provision in its schedule of accommodation for the incorporation of arts teaching space if this is deemed appropriate when final plans for the college are being drawn up. The final resolution of the problem of arts teaching accommodation has still not been reached, although a memorandum of the Vice-Chancellor's on future development, dated March 1973, speaks of both "arts and science buildings" to cater for a student body of 7,750 by 1982.[6.19]

During 1972 there was a dispute in the English department which received widespread national publicity, and in the subsequent investigation by Councillor Tom Taylor one facet he scrutinized closely was the colleges, on which he commented:

> I am obliged to say that I sense a fair amount of disappointment with the collegiate system in its present form, not only as regards disciplinary matters, but because (as is often alleged) the colleges are not fostering (as they were intended to) a virile community life for both staff and students. I consider that this matter is of such cardinal importance to the well-being of the University that it deserves separate and really thorough investigation by a small working party. . . . If colleges engendered a greater sense of "belonging" then much of the frustration felt by students and staff would be eradicated.

A joint committee of the Council and Senate was set up, which received comments from syndicates, junior common rooms, departments and individual members of the university on "how they see the role of the college both now and in the future and their views on how any desired end can be achieved". Whether, as the committee recommended, there will be close definite links between particular colleges with particular departments has not reached a point of final decision.

The views of senior members of the university about the colleges are difficult to ascertain. A lot of them are concerned principally with their subject discipline and regard any other activity as a worrying and unnecessary diversion. Some would like to see the colleges disappear at once, although only a minority express themselves as forcefully as the writer of a recent paper whose concluding paragraph read as follows:

The sum of disbelief
In short
(a) the prescription by which the colleges have been created is imprecise and structurally inadequate;

6.19 Some student members of the university have advocated a central student union building: see *Scan* for 26 February 1973.

(b) no clear evidence is available of advantages that they confer and which alone would justify the high expenditure of public money on them;

(c) they are unlikely to be able to work because of a want of purpose, a want of adequate financial and organizational mechanisms and a want of persons to run them and of the means of attracting such persons;

(d) the privy council ought to be asked to change the charter so that the university is not required to spend public money unnecessarily.[6.20]

Others continue to see virtue in their existence, at least as far as the students are concerned:

Many [students] feel some sense of attachment to the college where they live, and are aware of differences in appearance, life-style, and organization between the colleges: in other words, some rudimentary sense of college identity is gradually coming into existence. No one should suppose that such a sense can be created quickly, and it is likely to take deep root only when the university is much larger than it is now: it may be that the colleges are only just beginning to function effectively as residential units within the larger unit of the university. Students who come here from elsewhere are impressed with the degree of concern for the individual which this university displays, and its humane attitude to students. Obviously this is not simply a consequence of the collegiate system, but many students believe the system plays a very important part. This virtue, in my opinion, is worth a great deal and is not lightly to be discarded.[6.21]

A further complication is the status of the college fee, a sum of £20 per head payable by local education authorities as part of the undergraduate grant to students at collegiate universities. Lancaster has been eligible to receive this additional income since October 1968 when the first residences opened. The advantages that arise from this fee to the students are precisely those kinds of intangible benefits that are most difficult to quantify, but they include the provision of a type of administrative care (both from college officers and domestic bursars) and social environment beyond that available in a conventional hall of residence. As the 1972–77 quinquennium came into view the Committee of Colleges held anxious discussions about what would happen if the U.G.C. decided, because of pressure from the local education authorities, to swallow it up in the block grant. It is of interest that it was considered of sufficient value for the members of the Development Committee in July 1971 to advocate that it should be continued at the existing level, even at the price of making a small reduction in the standards of provision for

6.20 M. G. de St V. Atkins, "A Worm's Eye View", March 1973.
6.21 Dr. J. Anthony Tuck, "The Colleges—a Defence of the Status Quo", April 1973.

teaching departments. Concern, however, was expressed at "the lack of incentive for colleges to exercise economy and the lack of criteria against which to judge whether college income was being used appropriately and efficiently", and the Committee of Colleges was duly warned of this concern. In fact, the university is now assured of the income arising from this fee for the present quinquennium, but no one knows what will happen thereafter.[6.22]

An important hardening of the national heart, however, was demonstrated by the Government documents which appeared towards the end of 1972— *Education: Framework for Expansion* and *Report from the Expenditure Committee*,[6.23] both of which looked to a growth in the number of students living at home as a means of relieving problems of residence. The Expenditure Committee commented that

> We trust that it is now recognized both in the universities and the local authority sector that the cost of purpose-built [residential] accommodation . . . is out of all proportion to the need, and indeed that such halls of residence can be provided only at the expense of alternative ways of accommodating a greater number of students more economically.

> Whereas formerly U.G.C. paid the full cost of residential accommodation in universities, since 1970 they have adopted the practice of contributing a subsidy of 25 per cent of the overall cost of buildings, professional fees and furniture . . . and placing on universities the onus of financing the remainder through borrowing. . . .

> We consider that U.G.C. were right in deciding to introduce loan financing for the provision of residential accommodation, though we sympathize with the difficulties experienced by universities in borrowing on the open market at commercial rates of interest and at the same time charging rents which fell within the limits approved by U.G.C. and which students could afford to pay out of their maintenance grants.

The committee then goes on to recommend student housing associations and an increase in the number of home-based students, especially as the Secretary of State for Education and Science had commented that

> In considering the future shape and pattern of higher education we shall have to look very carefully at the question of student residence. . . . Students naturally want to be independent of their parents and to have the experience of living and working in new surroundings. Nevertheless, it is open to question whether the general public, which has to foot the bill, would accept that all, or almost all, students have a right to accommodation

---

[6.22] As from October 1974, the fee is to be £26 p.a.
[6.23] Cmnd. 5174, and 48–1 of December 1972, respectively.

in a distant university even though there is one offering similar courses within travelling distance of their houses.

Nevertheless, they did not entirely endorse the view that institutions of higher education (including universities)

> ought to recruit their students solely on a regional basis; we recognize that they have now established their claim to serve national as well as local needs, and that some can offer courses of unique value which ought not to be restricted to students from the immediately surrounding area. We do not accept, however, at a time when, as Lord Annan put it, the choice may lie between "higher education at home or no higher education at all"

that the "virtually complete freedom" of students to go where they choose "without any restraint" should continue, and therefore recommended that there should be encouragement, on a voluntary basis, to attend local universities—while giving a warning that if this did not succeed, stronger measures might be taken.[6.24]

It is in this context that the note of a meeting between the U.G.C. and the University of 28 February 1973 can be seen, when

> One of the major preoccupations of those the Committee had met during the day was student residence. The Committee shared the concern that had been expressed and had the present loan-financed residence scheme under review. The Committee remained, convinced, however, that the system of loan finance was the only means of obtaining the necessary beds from the resources made available by the Government. Lancaster was in any case in an extremely fortunate position in relation to the great majority of universities; over 55 per cent of its students were currently in residence, there was a substantial block of debt-free residence which could help to spread the burden of servicing loans, there was an untapped pool of lodgings still available[6.25] and no local pressure on lodgings from other institutions. The University was still able to charge a rent lower than the notional rent element in the student grants.

At present most students can go into residence for two of their three years if they need to, but by the end of the 1972–77 quinquennium, even with the additional five hundred beds which will be available in Pendle and Grizedale Colleges, there will only be 2,200 beds for 5,400 students. There is simul-

---

[6.24] *Report from Expenditure Committee*, 48-1, paragraphs 86–98.
[6.25] Morecambe in 1961, for example, was able to produce evidence which showed that the town had a reservoir of 7,000 beds available; probably the maximum used by the university has been just over one thousannd.

taneously dissatisfaction expressed amongst students with the level of rents,[6.26] anxiety about the number who can be accommodated on the site rather than spending relatively long periods each day on travel (which has an inhibiting effect on full participation in university activities), and dismay about the method of distribution of the equalization charges which arise from the commercially sponsored residences amongst the colleges.[6.27] Meanwhile, with the reduction of U.G.C. norms over the last few years, study bedrooms at Lancaster are being planned on a basis of 90 square feet for each student, which represents a 25 per cent decrease in floor area compared with the accommodation provided in the first colleges.

The university therefore finds itself in the kind of unresolvable situation which it reached over the twinned colleges of Pendle and Grizedale. On the one hand there is a requirement for more residential accommodation in a collegiate university which has been asked by the U.G.C. to take a large increase in student numbers, and on the other governmental discouragement for more custom-built residences and the difficulty of finding finance, especially at a time of particularly rapid escalation of building costs. The Vice-Chancellor had foreseen in January 1972 that, with the rate of inflation and the high cost of loan finance, the building of the residential areas of these colleges was problematical, and would raise student rents (under the equalization scheme) to a perhaps unacceptable level. He therefore circulated the university's student officers to solicit their views on whether the residential areas should be deferred, while recognizing that if a postponement did take place, "more students will be seeking flats in the neighbourhood, and there will probably therefore be some increase in the rents paid by non-resident students". The reply he received was somewhat muted, but seemed on the whole to be in favour of proceeding with this additional residential accommodation. Even when the problem of funds had been solved the university still had to cut out some of the special fittings and furniture which were reconciling the colleges' planning committees to the reduced floor area: cuts which elicited the following protest from one student member:[6.28]

> It was anticipated in the planning of Pendle and Grizedale that the present system of standard rents (i.e. single room with CH and WB same all over campus) would continue. The excessive smallness (90 square feet) of the new rooms was to be offset by the superior finish, etc.

6.26 A proportion of the students at Lancaster have been on a rent strike, not as a move against the university, so much as an expression of national solidarity with the N.U.S.' campaign for higher grants.

6.27 It was decided in 1968 that the loan charges for the colleges with commercially sponsored residence should be shared equally between all the colleges and not shouldered just by the colleges which included this type of accommodation.

6.28 Mr. Dick Harris in *Scan*, 21 May 1973.

The general increase in rents consequent upon paying for the loans necessary to build Pendle and Grizedale has already been agreed with the student body and is limited by another agreement with the student body that rents will not rise proportionately faster than grants. This places an effective limit on how much we can borrow for building these colleges.

In response to the unexpected increase in costs, about £180,000 has been saved by trimming the buildings in various ways,

of which cuts amounting to £30,000 included the omission of fitted drawers under the beds, a cheaper standard of furniture, and a less adaptable system of lighting. Mr. Harris continued:

Unfortunately, the new colleges will have no source of uncommitted funds—whereas other colleges have roof flats which were provided free as a kind of endowment, the new colleges will have no roof flats. . . .

It is evident to me that the quality of the new rooms as they are now proposed is such that to charge the same rent for them as is charged for the larger and better rooms in, say, Bowland will cause dissent—to say the least. Indeed, there was doubt in my mind about the possibility of applying the standard rents even before the cuts were made. . . .

Now, dear brethren, which is it to be? Can the campus tolerate a general increase in rent to cover borrowing that £30,000 (say about £4,000 a year between total 1974 residents) or can you find another way to prevent the new members having to live with the (perfectly ghastly) drawbacks described above?

There is no clear answer to such a question.

(ii) A federal student union

The provision of as many centralized facilities as there are at Lancaster can be seen as part of the reason for the erosion of the colleges' position in the university. Another, even stronger, centripetal force which revealed itself during the first year of the university's existence was the movement amongst certain student leaders towards setting up a central student union.

The original constitution for student government followed in essence the plan of the Academic Planning Board that student affairs should run on a collegiate basis, and vested authority in a body known as the University J.C.R. (which was a meeting of the whole student body) and in the two college junior common rooms of Bowland and Lonsdale, with provision for further separate bodies to be set up as the colleges increased in number. The "government, control and administration" of the University J.C.R. was deputed to a committee called the Student Council which was "the supreme governing body of the University J.C.R., and responsible for its actions to that body".[6.29] Douglas Chivers, in the 1966–67 Student Handbook, wrote as follows:

> In view of the fact that the Colleges have so far not existed as physical entities the S.R.C. has assumed an overwhelming importance in student administration and decision-making at the expense of the College councils, a tendency which seems likely to continue for some time to come, but as the developments at Bailrigg proceed, the Colleges will gradually become the principal governing units and the role of the S.R.C. will diminish in importance. . . .
>
> The Student Council holds a weekly formal meeting which is often long and heated. The Minutes of these meetings may be inspected at any time by members of the J.C.R.

The Student Council had responsibility for allocating finance to student organizations which were organized centrally, such as sport, and big social events such as large dances. The sum of money to be shared around was not inconsiderable—by the third year of the university's existence, for example, it already amounted to £13,000. The council also set up various sub-committees to look after particular areas of student interest, such as lodgings, Charities Week, or the university bookshop.

In June 1965, however, Messrs. John Kind (the treasurer of Lonsdale College) and D. C. S. Shearn (a graduate student in the Department of Operational Research), presented a report, having had a discussion with the Vice-Chancellor, on the future of the Student Council, which began by looking at the university as they saw it developing in the short term:

> When a student joins the University he/she is immediately attached to a college, and this will be *one* of the centres of activity. At the same time, however, some of the students' activities must be organized on a University basis, e.g. sports clubs, orchestra, debating society, theatre group, will assist on a University scale, although at the same time they may be duplicated in colleges.

6.29 The organization of the University J.C.R. and the Student Council (the S.R.C.) continued to be altered in detail during 1964–65 by the Staff/Student Committee. Unfortunately no minutes survive of the University J.C.R. prior to December 1965, but the informality of the formulation of procedure at this stage of development, amongst just over three hundred students, can be gauged by the following Student Council minute of 22 October 1964: "The Chairman altered their designation to that of President, and the Vice-Chairman to that of Vice-President. The formation of various sub-committees was discussed. It was decided that it was necessary to appoint a Dance Chairman." Nor were minutes very full, as is evidenced by the following of 3 February 1965: "All present except Miss Wood. Suggestions dealt with. Claims dealt with. Mr. Catello left half hour before the end without proper reason."

This will provide University representation in sports, etc., and will enable societies which might not flourish in a college of 500 people, e.g. an orchestra, to run effectively in a University of 6,000. Collegiate societies will enable those who are not good enough to represent the University to take an active part in social activities. In this way many more people will participate than in a conventional University.

It seemed to them that a possible organization might be seen as follows:[6.30]

The exact relationship between the University organizations will be left, in large measure, to the students. To co-ordinate the activities of the University societies some central organization and representation is required. To this end we will have to have a Students Union which will be similar to other University unions but with no union building. Student activities will take place in lecture rooms and other University premises but permanent space will be allocated to union administrative offices.

In effect the present Student Council is attempting to carry out the function of the union executive, but its present structure does not lend itself to such a role. There is no effective leadership because there are two presidents, and with further collegiate expansion the situation would become chaotic. At the same time the undesirable situation would exist whereby the college President would be concerned more with University than college matters. We, therefore, consider it desirable to have a Union which is largely independent of the colleges. . . .

At the head of the Union there will be the President, Vice-President, Secretary and Treasurer together with the two main sections of the Union, the athletic Union and the Social Committee. The President, Vice-President, Secretary and Treasurer would be elected by the student body as a whole *without* college considerations. We do not think that it would be a good thing if the President of the Union was also a President of a college. . . .

We now have to consider the relationship between the union and the colleges. At the highest level, the Union Council and presidents of the colleges will sit as one body, the "Student Council", the Chairman of which will be the President of the Union. . . .

Our proposals are of a long term nature but require early implementation. We hope that this report will be considered by the University J.C.R. at a very early stage next session.

Professor Lawrenson, the principal of Lonsdale College, thought long and deeply over their suggestions and in August 1965 prepared an open letter in

---

[6.30] The conditional future tense should be understood for the simple future tense in several of the following paragraphs.

reply. He dealt with the practical difficulty of having two or more presidents by saying that he had always assumed that from amongst them would emerge a senior president who would take the chair. He then continued

> The point that some Junior Member activities must be organized on a university, rather than college, basis, is of course taken, though it must be immediately stated that in no instance are they different in nature from college activities: they differ only in level and quality. The analogy of Halls of Residence in other universities is true only to a limited extent. . . . Once our colleges are built they will be infinitely more important than the provincial Hall of Residence, for they will be the main expression of the corporate nature of the university—in which, I repeat, everybody is seen to be a student, and the dividing line is by seniority, not by "teachers" and "taught". Aside from the Departments and Boards, and below the Senate, there is nothing *but* the Colleges, and this is the specific intention of the Academic Planning Board.
>
> Your proposals, in so far as they postulate a non-collegiate "Union", run counter to these ideas. Agreed, there has to be a supra-collegiate body for the purposes you mention. This is not in question. What I think you have not produced is a valid reason why such a body should not *arise out of* the colleges. . . . My chief objection to the *word* "union" lies in the obvious damage to "staff"- "student" relationships that it has already wrought up and down the country. Masses of linguistically (and historically) naïve under-graduates imagine it to be largely a Trades Union, from which it is but a short step to the assumption that the "students" are labour and the "staff" capital. If you are looking for a real "prole" in the university, you will find him not among the undergraduates but in the new Assistant Lecturer with two or more children, a house to buy, and a private library to build.
>
> Heresies of this sort have met and joined with what was in fact a neo-Germanic impulse at the formation of our provincial universities (especially the earlier ones), in an unholy alliance to preserve the distance between senior and junior members; the don who imagines that his advancement depends entirely upon the research that he can do and the number of papers that he can publish is delighted with the "unions": they keep the undergraduates away from him. A fugitive junior membership thus finds itself in complete agreement with an abdicatory professoriate, and all the brave tutorial and advisory schemes and joint common rooms never quite cope with this basic schism.
>
> I have already, and gladly, conceded the necessity for a supra-collegiate body, not only for the reasons you mention but also for the ones you don't: those matters which are of genuine sectional interest to the junior member-

ship of a university as opposed to its total membership: lodgings, for example, grants and that rumbling gastronomic *basso continuo* against which all our affairs seem to be conducted: food. You must have a body which can take care of these, as it were trade-unionesque, affairs, and to effect authoritative liaison with the N.U.S. What I now most sincerely urge you and your colleagues to do is to give your best consideration to a top body which arises organically from the colleges, because within the context in which we are speaking, I repeat that *there is nothing but the colleges*. I feel that the body you propose would be, in time, schismatic and *in vacuo*, devoid of real roots among its constituents in a collegiate university of, say, 6,000.

He then went on to propose a particular structure which made the Student Council the apex of the rest of the student body and not a separate entity or divorced from the J.C.R.s,[6.31] and coupled it with a proposal for a degree of reciprocity between the syndicates and the junior common rooms. As to the method of electing the president of the Student Council, he agreed that

The easiest way would be for the Senior President to be elected from among the Presidents, by themselves, acting as an electoral college. This would obviate one weakness of your proposals, in which you have two sets of elections for the same *sorts of thing*: College and "Union". But if you feel (as you well may) that the total electorate is not being sufficiently consulted in the most important position of the lot . . . we should still bend our best efforts towards avoiding two separate elections,

and he then went on to discuss how the "senior" president might be selected.

The students, however, were not pleased with this suggestion and, in a paper dated 18 October, written by John Kind and entitled "The Views of the Student Council on Professor Lawrenson's Open Letter", argued that (a) in a student body of, say, 6,000, the Council president could emerge from a vote of, say, 250 votes from half his college electorate to be president of the whole student body, (b) a college president who was also a council president would be likely to neglect his college responsibilities, and (c) he would show preference to the college who had elected him. The document went on to say that the Union Council and the College Councils should be autonomous units who would each run their own affairs but who would "come together to discuss matters of the higher importance, for example finance".

It is difficult to gauge the views of the general student body over this matter. The two student publications, *John O'Gauntlet* and *Carolynne*, both gave space to the proposals but, apart from an anxiety about whether the student-

---

[6.31] Which, indeed, with emendations and after a great deal more discussion, is essentially what we now have.

proposed scheme would be workable in the division of powers and functions between the college organization and the central union, merely noted that it was "the unanimous proposition of the college presidents" (all two of them!) that such a division of responsibility was necessary, and asked rhetorically "When must the new plans be implemented?" The Staff/Student Committee of the time had as its student representatives only members of the Student Council, and therefore do not give an indication of what the main body of undergraduate thought on the matter was. A special meeting of the Staff/ Student Committee was held on 25 October to discuss the union proposals, but it is tantalizing to have only the official minute of that meeting and a brief holograph minute of a meeting of Student Council at which "Mr. Kind expressed the wish that Professors Lawrenson and Bevington should not be made too angry and that in all discussions, extreme tact would be necessary".

Even if tempers were not lost, however, serious misunderstandings arose. A memorandum of Professor Lawrenson's, dated 1 June 1966, takes up the story again:

> After considerable discussion, the staff-student committee finally reached agreement, the essential compromise being in the following clause:
> (i) that elections for all College Presidents and for all College Vice-Presidents, Secretaries and Treasurers will take place together.
> (ii) that approximately one term later elections for membership of the Union Council will take place.
>> Only those junior members of the university currently holding office as a College President will be eligible to stand for the position of President of the Union Council. Voting at this election will be by all junior members of the University,

and a similar procedure was to be adopted for the other officers. A working party of staff and students was set up with the purpose of implementing the proposals so far accepted, but instead re-cast them and placed an essentially new document, incorporating John Kind's original proposals, before the J.C.R., which approved it.

The Senate minute of 1 June made a note of "a serious difference of opinion between the senior and the junior members of the working party" and looked at the new student proposals which visualized a

> Student Representative Council (S.R.C.) which would be the main student policy making body and would be responsible for the entire range of student activity which did not lie within the terms of reference of the various College Junior Common Rooms. . . .
> The membership of the S.R.C. would include: Four officers—Chairman,

Deputy Chairman, Secretary and Treasurer—who would be elected directly by all junior members of the University *without consideration of college*,

as well as representatives of the colleges' J.C.R.s and other officers.

It was perhaps predictable that the outcome of the meeting was yet another working party who were able to come to the Senate of 28 September, bringing with them a draft constitution which was the direct fore-runner of the one still in force, inasmuch as there was now talk of a "federation" of junior common rooms comprised of all the student members of the university, and no further word of separate Union and College Councils. Nevertheless, despite the closer integration of the centralized and collegiate elements of student government Professor Dobbs expressed the view that the proposed constitution was inconsistent with the description of the University as a "collegiate university", and also that it was less democratic than was desirable, in that it placed too much power in the hands of the officers of the Student Representative Council, while other members of the Senate also had misgivings.

Another lengthy discussion took place at the Senate Meeting of 12 October, at which the anxieties of the Bowland and Lonsdale syndicates were voiced that the "proposed constitution would weaken the colleges by creating too strong a student government outside the Colleges", and that funds for student activities should not be in the bailiwick of the S.R.C. but should be allocated by a partnership of colleges and the central student union. Mr. John Kind, who in company with other students was then called in to the meeting, "argued that it was inevitable at present that most student activities should be organized on a University basis; it followed . . . that only a small proportion of the funds (at most £1 per capita) was required to finance student activities within each college". The Senate at this point decided that junior and senior members of the colleges should discuss together what should be done. Meanwhile the University J.C.R., who had last been consulted in mid-May, had a long debate on 27 October at which Mr. Kind stated

that the constitution was an attempt to balance all possible interests. It was difficult to project oneself into the future but he stressed that the proposed constitution was only intended to operate for a maximum period of two years. . . . Mr. Christopher then asked why the senior members of the University were playing such a large part in the formulation of the constitution. The chairman (Mr. John Stafford) pointed out that the present J.C.R. constitution states that approval of Senate in such matters must be obtained. Miss Elizabeth Waite spoke in favour of the senior members having some sway, saying that in most cases they would be identified with the University for a longer period than the students. . . .

During the ensuing discussion it became evident that the meeting was strongly in favour of general Union meetings for certain purposes.

The colleges, when consulted, expressed concern about the part the proposed organization would play as a counterweight to their own function, partly as regards the manner of distribution of funds and their use and also concerning the chairmanship of the annual meeting at which they were shared out: the other main point of debate was whether the Administrative Committee, which was to have important executive powers, should have as its secretary and treasurer students elected from the whole body (which would strengthen the central union) or from within the S.R.C. (which would strengthen the colleges). The Staff/Student Committee had another long debate, the Senate a further discussion in mid-November, the University J.C.R. two meetings on two successive weeks (the first marked by filibustering and boredom, according to *John O'Gauntlet*, and the second by low attendance), and the Senate, at a meeting a few days before Christmas was at last told that

> the committee appointed to examine the Constitution of the University of Lancaster Students' Federation, although it was not satisfied with the latest draft which was still subject to further consideration, had decided that it would be unreasonable to hold up elections under the new Constitution and had authorized the Student Council to proceed with them on the clear understanding that various details, including future electoral procedure, would be further discussed.

The details continued to be negotiated between the Student Council and a Pro-Vice-Chancellor, Professor Reynolds, but the essential provisions of the new constitution have remained since 1967: there was a constitutional conference in 1968, but its findings were not debated or voted upon by Federation. There is then the Federation of Junior Common Rooms,[6.32] which has taken over the function of the University J.C.R. and is comprised of all the student members of the university, which meets several times a term "to determine the opinion of the students of the University of Lancaster on important issues". This body can be summoned by the chairman of the S.R.C., the Senate or the Vice-Chancellor, or by sixty of its members. Although Federation has the right to be consulted on important issues, the S.R.C., which is made up mostly of college delegates who can impose a veto by walking out and making a meeting inquorate, does not have to implement

---

[6.32] The student constitution states that "The Federation shall be composed of College J.C.R.s who shall be solely responsible for their own internal government" and while its objects are "the furtherance and advancement of the purposes of the University by the promotion of social and educational relationships among students of the University", nothing in it "shall affect the rights of the College J.C.R.s to pursue, in relation to their own members, these or any other objects".

the decisions of the Federation meetings. On the other hand Federation can, if it becomes too dissatisfied with the way its elected officers are discharging their obligations to the student body, recall them and force re-elections (as has been known to happen).

This conflict between the wish to keep the larger, more democratic body (Federation) supreme or the smaller, perhaps better-informed body (S.R.C.) dominant means that there is a constant see-saw in the policy of these bodies. Mr. Matthew Plesch, one-time chairman of the Constitutional Committee, has described the conflict as being "fought between the radical left and the moderate left (there being no political right at the time, in Federation meetings. The radical left was the Communist Party and all to the left plus sympathizers; the moderate left being such as the "Liberals and Radicals", the "Labour Club" members and such like) in terms of "democracy" versus "bureaucracy". This was because the radical left wanted power (quite naturally) and found that although it could control a Federation meeting, by derision, overcheer, chanting, brow-beating the chairman, and sheer pre-paredness, it could not pull in enough votes at the polls to control the S.R.C."[6.33] There is always a continuing danger that small determined groups will continue to call for special Federation meetings until the measures that they want are voted through.

The Student Representative Council is defined as "the supreme governing and policy-making body of the Federation, but its authority shall be subject to the Constitutions of the Federation and the College J.C.R.s", and this partnership is evinced in its membership, for some officers are elected by the whole student body but there are also three representatives from each of the college J.C.R.s.[6.34] Non-member students can attend any of the S.R.C. meetings. When the annual distribution of the student fees is made between central and college purposes, there is an annual conference, at which there are equal numbers from the S.R.C. and the colleges, with an independent chairman chosen by the conference itself. The general administration of Federation

---

[6.33] See also Matthew Plesch's article, "Money, Power and Responsibility in Federation" in *Lancaster Comment*, No. 28 (1 March 1973), pages 11 to 14.

[6.34] In practice the J.C.R.s, whose executives often bear a close and increasing resemblance to the S.R.C. Administrative Committee structure, tend to elect their college officers onto the S.R.C. and they in turn often become S.R.C. officers. The view has been expressed to the author by several students with experience of both J.C.R. and S.C.R. administration that the university avoids having as student officers the professional student politician, because the Lancaster student officers tend to emerge in the first instance from the college structure. If this is true—and the evidence seems to point that way—then the colleges are enabling student officers to emerge from groups where their qualities can be personally known, rather than as a result of good publicity or attractiveness to some small pressure group. It has also been said that this absence of the "professional" student politician has assisted Lancaster in being one of the student enterprises in the country with the least financial peculation or incompetence.

affairs is given to a small executive committee, the Administrative Committee, consisting of the six elected officers of the S.R.C.[6.35]

Thus, a student can raise business at the J.C.R. meeting of his own college, or can put pressure on his J.C.R. representatives to have matters raised at the S.R.C. level, or can get together with a sufficient number of his fellow students to have a special Federation meeting called. In practice, of course, the student body is reluctant to attend meetings. Meetings of both the J.C.R.s and Federation are constantly in danger of being inquorate, and elections for an S.R.C. chairman (and the leader of the whole student body) which raise a vote from a third or more of the student body are considered a rarity indeed.

Probably the single most important change is the increasing professionalism of student affairs, and the increasingly important role of the S.R.C. The Administrative Committee has grown by three members and taken on an increasing amount of work. There was, for a period, an administrative officer to look after this and other central student committees and to control the finance, an experiment which may be repeated. There is now also a full-time salaried social manager, whose responsibilities include arranging the well-established Friday night dances and entertainment, as well as such special events as the graduation ball. Above all, there is a sabbatical S.R.C. president, so that a student elected to this office postpones continuation of his studies for a year. Mr. Jerry Drew, chairman in 1972–73 and again in 1974, feels that this has been useful and that provided a student of the right personality is elected, who is "reasonably dedicated and hard-working", then

> there will be undoubted advantages, issues will be studied in depth and there will be no academic distraction. If, on the other hand, the opposite type is elected, then you will have to risk not gaining substantial advantages, and also having your Chairman cut off. Providing that the Chairman has friends, etc., he is no more, no less likely to get cut off from the student body than any other student president. But the potential will always be there.

(iii) Discipline and unrest

When thinking about disciplinary procedures, the reader should forget at once the university system of even a decade ago, when there was a plethora of regulations governing behaviour, from the wearing of gowns to the entertainment of male students by their women friends. Nor would any student now tolerate, or member of staff expect, the once-observed practice of serving

---

6.35 Information about Federation meetings and those of the Administrative Committee just described is given in *Scan*, the weekly news bulletin produced by the S.R.C. and distributed free around the university at the beginning of each week.

Operating a football machine

John Donat

Weight lifting in the Indoor Recreation Centre

John Donat

At work in the University Library

John Donat

Reconstitution in the Nuffield Theatre Studio of a French Baroque stage setting

Hotel de Bourgogne

afternoon tea with the door of the study bedroom standing ajar so that a College Officer could look in at any time, or of applying for a special pass if coming into a residence after 10.30 p.m. The reasons for such a change lie beyond the scope of this work; but the lowering of age of majority to eighteen, which came about as a consequence of the Latey Report of 1968, meant the final end of staff being regarded as *in loco parentis* to students, and made manifest what students had been clamouring for, i.e. the recognition of themselves as independent adults, responsible for all their actions and liable under the law of the land for whatever offences they committed.

There is, of course, provision made in the Charter for the university "to prescribe rules for the discipline of the students of the University", and the powers of the Senate include

The regulation and superintendence of the living conditions and discipline of the students of the university

as well as

The exclusion of any student, permanently or for a stated time, from any part of the University or its precincts, or from attendance at any course or from entry to any examination.

Beyond this bare framework, it was up to the university to create its own disciplinary structure.

There was one area, however, when the first students came up in 1964 that had to be adequately regulated, as a matter of some urgency, and that was the relationship between the university and its landladies. It is therefore not surprising that the first draft documents on discipline, dated April 1964, should be entitled "For the Guidance of Householders Offering Accommodation to Students" and "Notes for Students Living in Approved Lodgings", and deal with what provision was to be made for students in the way of food and facilities and what the householders could expect in terms of quietness, punctuality and conduct of their visitors, as well as offering a mechanism for dealing with any friction that arose between the two sides.

In May 1964 a small sub-committee on student accommodation was asked to consider general university regulations, in order to deal on the one hand with such academic matters as unsatisfactory progress or examination performance, and on the other with disciplinary cases arising out of landladies' complaints and such obvious areas of difficulty as gambling, indebtedness, or damage to university property.[6.36] Academic discipline was seen as

---

[6.36] There was a proposal, quickly discarded, that college tutors should be called "regents", after the Scottish system. The main disciplinary officer in each college was at first known as the senior tutor, but very soon this was altered to the present title of dean.

2E

pertaining to boards of studies, while the original proposal for non-academic discipline was that it should be looked after by a separate standing committee of Senate. On a suggestion made by Professor Reynolds and agreed by the Shadow Senate of 8 July 1964, however, it was deemed in the first instance to be the concern of the colleges, each of which was to have its own disciplinary committee. Meanwhile, separate library regulations were drawn up and although these were submitted for approval to the Senate, they remained a separate code, self-administered by the Library.

At the September 1964 meeting of the Senate, detailed proposals were discussed and agreed, with small variants in the regulations made as between graduate and undergraduate students. The principles governing this code of conduct were to be that there should be as few regulations as possible, that they should be "liberal", and that their language should not suggest that students were either delinquents or children; while a general regulation was enunciated that "In the interests of the University's academic and social life and of its good standing, students are required at all times to behave responsibly and considerately and to observe the University, Library and Lodgings regulations currently in force". Already students were being included in the disciplinary structure, for provision was made to set up in 1965 student disciplinary bodies to consider infringements of the non-academic regulations referred to them by college deans. Money from fines was to be at the disposal of colleges, with the stated intention that it was probably to be used for the relief of needy students.

So far so good, and the only matter not clarified was the standing of the student newspapers, *John O'Gauntlet* and *Carolynne*, which came into existence within a term of the first students coming up.[6.37] The editor of *Carolynne* had asked whether or not material for the magazine should be submitted to the university for approval before publication, and the Vice-Chancellor had seen the editors of both publications. In March 1965 he reported that neither paper wished to be the official voice of the student body, while both "profess themselves to be conscious of their responsibility to maintain the University's good name". The Senate therefore decided that both editorial groups should be regarded as student societies, although not thereby given the right to apply for student council funds, and both were in future to bear on the title page a statement that they were independent.

A sign, perhaps, of a new spirit abroad was that by May 1965 students were beginning to press for permission to take flats rather than lodgings; and it was decided on the recommendation of both existing college syndicates, to allow

---

[6.37] See M. E. McClintock, "Whither Student Journalism?" in *Lancaster Comment*, 18 January 1973, for an account of the rise and decline of student journalism at Lancaster.

students who were either over 21 or in their third year to do so.[6.38] The part that the press, both outside the university and within it, was to play in any difficult situations that arose was quickly revealed, however. In early June 1965 both the *Lancaster Guardian* and the Morecambe *Visitor* were carrying reports of statements by Mr. Paul Stafford, the secretary of Bowland J.C.R., about rumours of rent increases. A minute of the Council of October 1965 gives the background:

> The Vice-Chancellor said that, when the University had reached agreement with the Association representing the landladies of Morecambe on the lodgings charge for the first session, a condition of this agreement had been that the charge should be reviewed before the start of the 1965–66 session. During the Summer Term 1965 discussions had taken place with the landladies' representatives regarding the level of the lodgings charge. ... Agreement had finally been reached with the landladies' representatives on an increase in the weekly lodgings charge from £3.10.0 to £4.0.0.
>
> The proposed increase had been discussed with student officers at a meeting of the Staff-Student Committee held on 14 June 1965 and also with the Students' Lodgings Committee, before it was announced to students on 29 June. However, a number of students who had returned home before the end of the Summer Term had not been aware of the increase, and there was also some feeling among students that the increase had not been properly discussed with them.

In the first week of the new Michaelmas Term, therefore, an indignation meeting was held and a joint statement issued by *Carolynne* and *John O'Gauntlet* which declared that students were being held to ransom by the landladies, and asked for a "mass *refusal* to pay lodgings fees until the matter has been discussed with *our* representatives" followed by a "series of demands". Finally, the manifesto declared,

> Last term two hundred and sixty students signed a petition opposing any increase in lodgings fees. The increase is now upon us and the need for those students to stick by their earlier declaration is vital. But the opposition of second year undergraduates is not enough—they *must* have the support of a majority of first year students if the undergraduate body as

---

[6.38] The safeguards were still quite stringent, however. The Senate/Student Committee on Lodgings was to specify (in January and February 1966) that only single undergraduates in their second or third years (as well as graduates, married undergraduates and those aged over 21) were eligible, that they had to find their own flats but, when found, they were to be inspected and approved by the Superintendent of Lodgings, parental consent in writing was necessary for students under 21, the college tutor and the college dean had to be informed, and college disciplinary committees had the power "to revoke an undergraduate's right to live in unsupervised accommodation".

a whole is to have enough power to force new negotiations on the authorities concerned.

At a meeting of the Senate on 6 October, for part of which the students were in attendance, the Vice-Chancellor noted that "unfortunate statements emanating from student sources which had appeared in the local press had made the negotiations with landladies more difficult"—and by now the national press had taken up the story. The Senate therefore issued two statements, the first about the joint statement of the student newspapers, which in part read as follows:

> The Senate considers that the issuing of the recent broadsheet, with the number of falsities which it contains and the general atmosphere of cheap sensationalism which surrounds it, is an action which is calculated to bring the University into disrepute. . . .
>
> The Senate requires that each of the student newspapers shall publish a statement in its next issue from the Secretary of the University on the facts of the recent increase in lodgings charges and related matters and shall publish it on its front page without editorial comment. No issue may be published until that statement is ready.

The second concerned the immediate problem of rents, which were already due:

> Students are required to pay forthwith the lodgings charge as notified at the end of last term, which has been agreed with the landladies. . . . The Senate emphasizes that, once this present dispute has been settled and all students have paid their fees, the University is willing to discuss lodgings matters with a properly constituted body of representatives of students.

The student body, however, was not satisfied and a meeting of the University J.C.R. on 7 October passed, almost unanimously, a motion which stated that students would withhold their rents for two weeks while information was collected on

> (1) inadequate lodgings standards in Lancaster and Morecambe; (2) lodgings rates, standards and systems in other Universities; (3) analysis of costs to landladies. After this has been collected it can be presented to the Senate, and proposals from the Lodgings Committee[6.39] and students can be discussed at the student meeting in 13 days time. The resolutions passed at the meeting concerning lodgings can then be presented to Senate together with the information collected. If the students are not satisfied with the result of this, more militant action will be taken.

[6.39] The Lodgings Committee had been set up as a sub-committee of the University J.C.R. in June 1965.

The Senate therefore had to be called together again, on 8 October, when students were again in attendance for part of the meeting. The Vice-Chancellor agreed that the "course of events in June had been unfortunate in a number of respects", including the short period in which negotiations with the landladies had had to be completed, the publicity given by the local press, and preoccupation with the first set of Part I examinations. The chief cry was still that students be represented in future negotiations on lodgings and, on being satisfied that they would be so included the "student representatives agreed to report these assurances to the student body . . . and to use their best endeavours to help a peaceful settlement of the dispute about the lodgings charge". The students also questioned the degree of control that the Senate wished to have in future over the student press and the Vice-Chancellor emphasized that there was no intention to censor these papers, but the Senate would "look at future issues of the papers after publication with particular care to ensure that they did not do harm to the interests and good name of the University. It was agreed that students should give consideration to the possibility of the Student Council in some way exercising surveillance over the student papers". The student presidents, however, backed up by the view of the Staff/Student Committee, were firm in their view that the student publications were independent "and could not be controlled by the Student Council, which did not in any case wish to exercise a supervisory function".

The Senate also set up a special Senate/Student Committee on Lodgings, whose purpose was to discuss future pricing and disciplinary policy for both lodgings and flats. There were, however, no further major difficulties in connection with lodgings.

It should not be forgotten that the college syndicates were meanwhile drawing up separate disciplinary codes. All such sets of rules came to the Senate for approval, and while they differed in their particulars, the overall scheme was similar from one college to another and, in miniature, close to the machinery established by the university—except that there was usually a junior disciplinary body (on which staff were not to sit) and a senior disciplinary body which was a mixture of junior and senior members.[6.40]

The Senate had decided in June 1965 that it should itself exercise the power of excluding students because of academic failure and not delegate this power.[6.41] In February 1966, however, arising out of a situation where no less than five cases needed immediate consideration, it was decided to establish a

---

[6.40] Reference may be had to the individual colleges' handbooks and "The Rules of the University of Lancaster" (1972 edition) for an account of the colleges' bodies and their relationship to the central university disciplinary machinery.

[6.41] For serious breaches of non-academic regulations, a committee consisting of two college principals and the pro-vice-chancellor were authorized to take action as they saw fit.

Standing Academic Committee which would "consider and act upon cases of unsatisfactory academic performance, breaches of academic regulations, and individual cases of academic difficulty, and where necessary to make recommendations to Senate". Cases could be referred to it by the Senate or a head of department, students would be required to wear academic dress and would be accompanied by their college tutors.

It was in the middle of the university's third year that a certain mood of rebelliousness appeared amongst sections of the student body—in the space of three months there was a large-scale flour bomb fight in the Market Square of Lancaster at the end of the Charities' Week parade, drugs were found in some students' digs, and there was a fuss (again involving the student press) over the university's choice of honorary graduands.[6.42] A Council minute of 22 March noted, amongst other items,

> that Senate had rescinded its regulation that gowns should be worn at undergraduate lectures. Sir Stanley Bell expressed some concern at the tendency towards increased student indiscipline in British universities . . . the Vice-Chancellor referred to recent developments which had led the Senate to issue the statement on drugs, a copy of which was attached to the report. Whilst there was no evidence that any students of the University had taken drugs other than Indian Hemp or had set up a channel of supply to other students, there was a danger that those using the less dangerous illegal drugs would place themselves in a position in which they might be pressed or tempted to experiment with more dangerous drugs.
>
> The Vice-Chancellor reported that the celebration of Charities' Week had become deplorably like that of "rags" in other universities. Lancaster was too small a town to absorb such disturbances. In addition the magazine produced for the occasion, *Bacchus*, had been in exceedingly bad taste, even for a publication of that kind.

The statement on drugs referred to had been approved by the Senate the week before, and pointed out that students

> are subject to the law of the land, and are not protected from the normal penalties of breaking the law. In addition, students have obligations to protect the good name of the university and to prevent harm to their fellow-students. It is for the colleges to consider whether these obligations justify the imposition of penalties additional to those imposed for the breaking of the law. Senate has, however, decided that if any student is proved to have acted deliberately in pressing the sale of illegal drugs of any

---

[6.42] It is of interest that, browsing through newspaper cuttings of the period, this seems to be the first year that several other universities had experienced trouble with drugs. 1967 was also the first year of trouble at L.S.E.

kind to his fellow-students, or by his own initiative has set up a channel of supply to other students, that student will be permanently excluded from the university.

The protest about honorary degrees centred around lack of consultation and the apparent association of the people selected with financial and military interests. The former was part of a longer-term problem,[6.43] and the latter, after the Vice-Chancellor had made clear that publication in the student press should not have preceded consultation with him, was dealt with by a clear statement that it was university policy

> to award honorary degrees for distinction in scholarship or in service to the community or both. In no case is any candidate considered in relation to any financial contribution, past or prospective, to the University.[6.44]

A quieter reform in that spring was a reconsideration of the function of the Standing Academic Committee. The chairman, Professor Reynolds, wished to emphasize—a view endorsed by the Senate of May 1967—that

> cases should be referred to it only if Heads of Departments wish for academic reasons to recommend the expulsion of a student from the University. It is for the Committee to decide whether to approve this recommendation, or to take other action. . . . The Committee should not be used as a bogey-man to assist Departments to frighten students into working properly.

The spring seems to be a heady time for universities. It was in May 1968 that Lancaster's name really made its way into the national press about a student matter, called variously the "mixed bedrooms affair" or the "first Craig affair". What began it was a Cartmel syndicate meeting of 1 May 1968 which, when giving final consideration to the residence regulations of the new college to be opened in the autumn, considered proposals:

> (i) that double rooms in Cartmel College shall be occupied by members of opposite sexes only if they are married.
> (ii) that the regulations should be amended so that residential corridors in Cartmel College can be allocated to a single sex only.

The first of the two proposals was carried; the second defeated. For an account of what happened next, let us look at the report the Vice-Chancellor was later to give to the Council of the affair:

> When Cartmel College discussed the arrangement of its accommodation, it is understood that Dr. Craig proposed that there should be complete freedom even if this meant an unmarried couple sleeping in the same room. This proposal was heavily defeated, and the Syndicate of the

---

[6.43] See Chapter 4 (iii), pp. 272 to 291, on student representation.
[6.44] Note by the Vice-Chancellor, published in *Scan*, 12 June 1967.

College (which includes students) decided that all accommodation for first-year students should segregate men and women, that students of later years wishing to live in segregated sections should have priority in the allocation of the remaining rooms, but that any accommodation left over should be allocated on a hotel principle, without regard to sex. This is the proposal referred to as "mixed corridors", and subsequently vetoed by Senate.

The next incident in the story is that a student member of the Syndicate, not realizing that its proceedings (being subject to ratification by Senate) were still confidential, revealed them to the independent student newspaper *Carolynne*. He admitted his action freely, has offered sincere apologies and has resigned from the Syndicate. Information about a possible leak in *Carolynne* reached the Cartmel College authorities, and warnings against publication were given, but were apparently too late. *Carolynne's* editor is newly appointed, and is not in effective control; responsibility for the subsequent actions is thought to rest on a member of their editorial staff, who appears to recognize no responsibility to the University and believes in an absolute journalistic right to publish confidential information if it comes his way. The man concerned has been called before a discipline committee of Lonsdale College.[6.45] Having written up the story for publication, but before its actual appearance in *Carolynne*, the same man or his associates proceeded to sell it to the Manchester offices of the popular daily and Sunday press. It has been admitted by one of the papers that a regular arrangement for the payment of fees to students for titbits of university information exists, and it is believed that the fees may be substantial. None of the newspapers sent a reporter to see me or the University Secretary at this stage, but reporters called on Dr. Craig, who gave an exposition of his views on sexual experiment before marriage. (He believes in extra-marital, but not promiscuous, relations.) Mrs. Craig was also interviewed.

Stories, obviously harmful to the interests of the University, appeared in the northern editions of the popular newspapers on Saturday, 11 May, the most damaging being in the *Daily Express*. There being little chance of getting daily papers to print any satisfactory disclaimer of an obviously juicy story, I thought it right at this stage to concentrate on getting a corrective note to the local press; and this was sent on 11 May. On 12 May much worse stories appeared in the Sunday press;

and the B.B.C. also interviewed some students (outside university premises). By 13 May the Further Education sub-committee of the County Education

---

6.45 See *Carolynne* No. 32 (9 May 1968) for the journal's original story and No. 33 (6 June 1968) for further extended articles on the subject.

Committee had voted to defer consideration of their annual grant of
£50,000.[6.46] It was against this background that the next Senate meeting took
place on 15 May and "after considerable discussion", it was agreed

> 1. That arrangements for student residence must have regard to the
> proper interests of parents and of the wider community, along with the
> wishes of men and of women students. No arrangements would be made
> which might in any way be interpreted as an invitation to sexual licence.
> Consequently rooms for men and women would be arranged in separate
> blocks, floors or sections of buildings, to an extent which ensured that
> proper privacy from the other sex could be obtained.
> 2. That accordingly the proposals of Cartmel College for mixed corridors
> should be rejected and that the syndicate of the college should be asked
> to submit to a future meeting of Senate revised proposals.

The Vice-Chancellor was authorized to issue a press release stating the
university's policy and "completely dissociating the Senate from the opinions
stated to have been expressed by Dr. Craig"; and also to meet the Student
Council, as well as suspending Dr. Craig from his position as Dean of Cartmel
College, pending the meeting of the Council on 22 May. The Council, after
discussion around a question put by the Bishop of Blackburn, "to consider
whether it is proper for a person holding a college office to make statements
to the press on matters of public morality which are at variance with the
policy of the University", issued its own press statement, saying that

> The Council of the University of Lancaster notes with approval the firm
> support given by the Senate to accepted standards of public morality. It
> has conveyed its thanks to the officers of the Student Representative
> Council for their constructive approach to problems arising from recent
> press publicity about the confidential proceedings of a college meeting and
> the views of a member of staff. The Council have set up a sub-committee[6.47]
> to consider the matter further. As is proper during an investigation, Dr.
> Craig must remain suspended from the office of Dean, though not of
> course of Senior Lecturer.

Two special meetings of Cartmel syndicate were held. The first was on 21
May, the day before the Council meeting, at which Dr. Craig offered his
resignation as dean of the college "on the ground that my recent statements
to the Press on a controversial point of College residence have contributed
to a situation in which University finances are in jeopardy and in which

---

[6.46] This grant was subsequently restored to the university, as were others cancelled
at the height of the crisis.
[6.47] The sub-committee consisted of Lord Derby, the Vice-Chancellor, Sir Alfred
Bates, Sir Noel Hall, Councillor Taylor and the Bishop of Blackburn.

unfortunate misapprehensions have arisen regarding the climate of behaviour at the University", but the motion for accepting the resignation, moved by the principal, was (narrowly) voted down, and the resignation withdrawn. The second meeting, on 28 May, was attended by the Vice-Chancellor, who "recommended that the Syndicate should accept Dr. Craig's generous offer of resignation, making it very clear that this acceptance carried no stigma". A statement published in *Scan* around the university on 3 June 1968 noted that

> Dr. David Craig having a second time offered his resignation as Dean of Cartmel College, the Syndicate of the College has thought it right to accept it. In doing so, the College acknowledges that the resignation will clear the way for a fundamental discussion within the University about ways of ensuring freedom of speech and discussion, about the limits of the public expression of views which the acceptance of certain offices may entail, and about the problems of relations with the Press, which recent events have brought to our attention.[6.48]

A meeting of Cartmel J.C.R. passed unanimously a resolution noting the resignation with regret and expressing its appreciation for the excellent work Dr. Craig had done for the college, but in general everyone was extremely relieved that the episode was over—for feelings had run high, particularly at Cartmel syndicate and on the Senate and Council. In late June and early July the Senate considered two proposals arising from the affair. The first concerned the appointment of college officers, on which the Senate agreed in principle that such an officer "will on all occasions uphold the standing of his office, and accept a limitation of his freedom to express his views in public where these views conflict" with the demands of his office; and in future college officers were to receive letters of appointment from the University Secretary which would incorporate such a definition of their obligations. As regards the editorial staff of *Carolynne*, it was decided not to take disciplinary action against the particular student whose decision it had been to publish, but instead draw up for future use a regulation, applying equally to junior and senior members of the university, stating that

> It is a serious offence for a member of the University to communicate to another person, whether inside or outside the university, information about business of the university, defined as confidential. . . .
>
> If such disclosure is made in a newspaper or periodical conducted wholly or in part by members of the university, an editor and/or members of the editorial board of the newspaper or periodical will be regarded as having

---

[6.48] *Scan* on 16 May noted "with deep misgiving that matters, while known to the editorial board of *Carolynne* to be of a confidential and damaging nature, were nevertheless published openly in that magazine and that this action has resulted in grave repercussions on the student interest in this University".

committed the offence, as well as the writer of the material which makes the disclosure.

If 1968, the year of international student uprisings, passed with only one incident at Lancaster, 1969 was more chequered. On 28 January 1969, the university experienced its first sit-in of the main administration building when students, concerned about events at the London School of Economics, demonstrated in Alexandra Square and afterwards occupied (peacefully) the Senate Room on the top floor of University House. A motion was passed by a meeting of Federation two days later regretting "the introduction of violence into student political affairs in this University. Moreover, while continuing to deplore violence, this Federation deplores the calculated employment of provocative tactics of such a nature that violence is a likely result".

Senate began in February to express anxiety about criminal actions "which for sufficient reason cannot or should not be brought to the attention of the police" but which the Vice-Chancellor proposed should be punishable by the university. He pointed out that

> this was a difficult issue. The general policy was that students who committed criminal offences should be dealt with by the police and the courts. There might be occasions, however, on which the presence of the police at the university would be considered undesirable or likely to be misunderstood. . . . It was not proposed that a criminal offence should of itself be punishable both by the courts and the university, though it was possible to conceive of certain extreme cases in which this would be almost unavoidable.

The debate appears to have shown up some weaknesses in the existing disciplinary code, for a committee was set up to examine "with all deliberate speed and in consultation with a representative of the university's solicitors, the general adequacy of the disciplinary system in the university and its relation to the law of the land". There was also, now that the colleges were providing residence, sometimes conflict over responsibility for cases involving students of more than one college, or of students from one college misbehaving in another.[6.49] Noise late at night, or disturbances in the bars were obvious examples of nuisances that caused this sort of difficulty.

The working party on law and the university met several times, basing their discussions on a memorandum prepared by Professor W. A. Murray on

---

[6.49] There was protracted discussion of an inter-college code both within syndicates and on the university bodies, of varying degrees of elaboration but one too detailed to describe here. The *eventual* solution was that "Where a complaint is made against members of two or more Colleges or involves an alleged offence by a member of one College on the premises of another, the investigators of the Colleges shall consult together in deciding how to proceed" ("Rules of the University of Lancaster", 7.3.4., 1972).

"Legal Aspects of the University". This preliminary attempt to create a definitive code was intended to include maintenance of order at political meetings and a definition of who was responsible "as guardians of the peace in public areas of the University" before the beginning of the next academic year. By the time it was available to the Senate, however, in late June, events had overtaken it. On 25 June *Carolynne* published confidential information about first-year examination results, as well as the Black Issue, which contained a number of serious allegations about student behaviour, including prostitution, organized theft, intimidation and drug-taking "to expose what was going on in the hope that it could be put right".[6.50] A sub-committee of the Senate was at once set up to conduct a preliminary enquiry and came to the conclusion that many of the statements in *Carolynne* were unjustified, but also that a substantial number merited further scrutiny. Meanwhile the students' council had recommended that *Carolynne* be denied all facilities in the university.[6.51] A committee of enquiry with disciplinary powers was accordingly set up by the Senate on 1 July, chaired by Professor Tom Lawrenson and including Professor Philip Andrews and the University Secretary. This committee met intensively[6.52] in what was by then the beginning of the Long Vacation, interviewing students who were thought to be involved, as well as the student journalists concerned, and student officers. Members of staff, particularly college officers, were also seen. The Vice-Chancellor, acting on behalf of the Senate in the Long Vacation, and having regard to the statement that "the conditions in parts of the residences of this University are scandalous, squalid and disgraceful", sought to introduce regulations governing the observance of residence rules, visiting hours in study bedrooms between different sexes, and the abolition of loud noise and music between certain hours. He did so reluctantly, he said, because the new rules had not been discussed with either the junior or the senior members of the Senate, but he had a statutory responsibility to maintain the good order of the university and wished everyone coming into residence the next term to have seen and assented to the regulations before the beginning of it, or to have had the chance not to take up a place in residence if they did not wish to agree to them. The student chairman, Mr. Steve Westacott, was disturbed that more consultation had not taken place, and that so much of the discussion had taken place at the Senate (where students did not sit) instead of at the Board of the Senate (where they did), for "there can be little doubt that all is

---

[6.50] *Carolynne*, No. 43, 24 and 25 June 1969. The matter was at once taken up by the national press.

[6.51] This ban on accommodation and other forms of help continued until the final demise of *Carolynne*, two and a half years later.

[6.52] The committee met for a total of 35 hours and took the testimony of 40 witnesses, producing nearly 250 closely-typed pages of oral evidence from which they drew their summary for the Senate. See pages 345 to 347 above for an account of their findings.

not well in residences of this University, but it is imperative that those who are involved in communal living should decide how they wish to conduct their affairs". In short, a discussion about living conditions had turned back into a political discussion about student representation; and furthermore, some senior members of the university were not ready to accept such specific regulations or to enforce them. After some exchange of correspondence between the Vice-Chancellor, the colleges and "such student officers as are here in vacation. . . . I have suggested that what is needed is a general prohibition of action which unreasonably offends or disturbs other members of the university; a clear and easy means by which occasions of offence or disturbance can be brought to the notice of disciplinary authorities and an assurance of such consequent action as is proper in each case: and perhaps an arrangement by which residents in a particular area of a college, who want to be undisturbed, can make supplementary regulations applying to that area".[6.53] No further attempt was made to set up specific rules of conduct on a university-wide basis, but the colleges continued to evolve their own codes of conduct; for, as the Senate conference at the end of September 1969 noted, an advantage of a local system of rules was that many issues could be dealt with without making students feel inhibited about talking to senior members of the university because of feelings of disloyalty to their fellow students. The Vice-Chancellor presented to the conference a paper entitled "Of rules, their making and enforcement", in which he propounded the principles (a) of rules being equally applicable to both senior and junior members of the university, without distinction, (b) of "delegates" who would have responsibility for defined geographical or functional areas of the university, both to prevent offences and to decide on action if any occurred, (c) of a choice, in appropriate cases, between using the university system of rules, or those of the public courts of law, (d) that there should be no double jeopardy and (e) that the administration of justice should be seen to be fair and the processes of discipline clearly stated and uniform.

A triumvirate consisting of the Vice-Chancellor, Professor Murray and Mr. Steve Westacott put forward to the Senate conference specific proposals for such delegates and the idea was accepted in principle, as was another suggestion that a Committee on Discipline[6.54] should be set up to carry out a general

[6.53] "Letter to students expecting to return to the University next year" from the Vice-Chancellor, August 1969. Special "quiet blocks" have been designated in the colleges since that time, but noise, in modern buildings, continues to be a problem.

[6.54] The Committee was later known as the Committee on Rules and continued its work until 1972. The quotations concerning the setting up of this body are taken from minutes of both the Board of the Senate and the Council, and the information about aediles was published also in the newly-instituted *Reporter*, which began publication in October 1969.

One other incident marked the autumn. The Queen visited the university on 17 October and, as she was passing through Alexandra Square, a mock investiture of a

review of the rules of the university "and to draft a simple, just and intelligible code of regulations for the domestic and public life of the University", as well as "such questions as the relationship between University regulations and the law of the land, and the means of ensuring that procedure for investigating complaints, for judging alleged offences and for appeals conformed to principles of natural justice whilst avoiding undue formality or delay". In the meantime, the Board of the Senate had agreed that the

> Vice-Chancellor should, with the concurrence of the Board, nominate a group of persons, to be called Aediles, who would share the Vice-Chancellor's statutory responsibility for the good order of the University.

The student body, meanwhile, was becoming concerned about discipline. A federation meeting on 20 November 1969 asked that there be 50 per cent student membership of all disciplinary committees, including committees of appeal.

At the next meeting of the Board of the Senate the Vice-Chancellor had cause to report on paint being sprayed in a lecture theatre, masked students having interrupted a politics lecture, and a discussion on the Vietnam war (organized by American students) being interrupted by masked invaders. This last incident had been referred to a college disciplinary committee, but because proposals for dealing with inter-college disciplinary matters were under consideration by the Committee on Rules and had not been ratified by the Senate, none of the people summoned appeared. There was an obvious need for some interim disciplinary machinery and the Board of the Senate therefore instituted, in December 1969, both an interim University Tribunal and a Committee of Appeals and Equity to hear appeals from the Tribunal.

By January 1970 the Committee on Rules had prepared the first draft of a unified code, drawing together rules relating to lodgings, colleges, departments, the library, and vehicles, and instituting clear procedures whereby every member of the university would know what the hierarchy of domestic tribunals and the correct method of using each one was to be. To secure the agreement of as much of the university as possible, the first and second drafts were sent to all college syndicates and junior common rooms, as well as to other university officers, before being put before the Board of the Senate in May 1970. The new code could not be considered in isolation, however, for while various bodies in the University were looking at it, other issues were being raised.

One was a backwash from the University of Warwick, about whether there

---

toad as Archduke of Lancaster (a reference to the Queen in Lancashire often being referred to as Duke of Lancaster) was being held. It caused a stir at the time, and press and television coverage was given to it, but it was no more than a piece of mischief by a single individual.

were held files of secret information about students, particularly concerning political or moral issues. Lancaster was not directly affected but the Vice-Chancellor considered it wise to issue a press statement which stated firmly that

> The Charter forbids the University to put a member at a disadvantage by reason of sex, race, colour, or political, moral or religious belief. Although the wording of the section refers to "tests" relating to admission, graduation, the holding of office or other advantages or privileges in the University, I am sure that it would be generally agreed that a broader interpretation is desirable: the University should not in any way use chance knowledge of qualities and beliefs which have no direct relevance to the pursuit of the purposes of the University, to disadvantage one of its members.
>
> Accordingly, we do not keep, and will not keep, any set of secret files on students or staff: and we do not initiate, nor shall we initiate, enquiries about irrelevant qualities or beliefs. . . .
>
> It is to the credit of our many generous financial backers that no one has ever asked that we should change a policy as a condition of continued support. A very small number of individual donors, knowing our policies, have indicated that they do not wish to continue to help us: such decisions are natural and inevitable. If anyone in future tries to use financial pressure to persuade us to alter a policy, I shall have to explain that the duty of a University is to follow the purposes set out in the Charter, at the sole discretion of the responsible bodies thereby created. This is what university autonomy is about: it is a freedom and protection which distinguishes us from institutions in the public sector.

The students nevertheless felt it necessary to hold an emergency meeting of Federation at which they passed a number of motions about files at Warwick and Lancaster, including the following:

> Federation deplores the keeping of files of a non-academic nature recently brought to light at Warwick and the Vice-Chancellor of Warwick for acting upon information concerning the political activities of students and prospective students communicated to him by self-interested parties using this academically irrelevant material in a prejudicial manner. . . .
>
> Federation welcomes the Vice-Chancellor's assurances that no secret files are kept and urges its members, past and present, staff and student, to look at any documents pertaining to themselves kept by the departments or administration should they require to see them.[6.55]

[6.55] *Scan* Special, 26 February 1970. An analysis of the situation about files at Warwick is contained in the *Report of the Right Hon. The Viscount Radcliffe, G.B.E., as to procedures followed in the University [of Warwick] with regard to receiving and retaining of information about political activities of the staff and of students,* 14 April 1970.

The Board of the Senate, at its next meeting in March 1970, took the opportunity of having a full discussion on information about students held centrally, and it was agreed that

> Any student may, by appointment, have his central record file extracted in his presence and be given a full list of its contents. . . . A student may ask for any completed record [of confidential records which must not be shown to the student except with the agreement of the originator] to be removed from the file and destroyed (whether or not he has seen it). The administration will agree to this unless it is thought that the student's welfare will be prejudiced by the loss of the record, in which case the matter will be referred to the Vice-Chancellor to discuss with the student. At the conclusion of this discussion the student's wishes must be accepted, unless the University has legal grounds for retaining the record; but the student will be asked to sign a dated statement showing that he has asked for the destruction of the record.
>
> Records about irrelevant political, religious and moral issues will not be kept in student files.

Despite a salvo from the Socialist Society, the question was essentially defused as far as Lancaster was concerned; and it was left to departmental staff-student committees and college syndicates to discuss what should be done about information on students held in those places, and to the Senate to review whether it was necessary to have a comparable system of access to staff records. Only a tiny minority of students have availed themselves of the opportunity to know about the contents of their files, numbering tens rather than hundreds, over the past three years.

Yet at the very same meeting of the Council, 18 March 1970, that the Vice-Chancellor was expounding on dispelling the "unnecessary mystery about records", and noting that "universities had to conduct their relations with industry very carefully and avoid any undesirable involvement or interference of industry in the relationship between universities and their students", he had also to meet anxieties expressed by a lay member of the Council about a student who had been fined by the city magistrates on a charge of malicious wounding. The Council member wished to know why additional action had not been taken against the student by the university; and the Council, with two dissentient voices, placed on record its grave concern at the case and asked that, "in future, the Council should be fully informed as soon as possible of all details in cases where the good name of the University was at stake". The Vice-Chancellor explained that the Pro-Chancellor, Lord Derby, had in mind "a system by which students who appear before the courts would automatically be reported to a committee of *Council*, under his chairmanship, which would have power to suspend or expel. Such a system would be contrary to the Statutes, under which Senate has the whole responsibility for discipline."[6.56] An exchange of correspondence took place during April between the Pro-Chancellor and the Vice-Chancellor, in the course of which the latter stated that

> The responsibility for the discipline of students rests entirely on Senate, which alone has the power to suspend or to expel. It is, in my view, entirely wrong for Council to discuss the case of an individual student, without notice, and on the evidence of an emotional rendering of an inaccurate (or, at least, untested) newspaper report. . . . Our students do not stand to the university in the relationship of servant to master; they are members of a corporate body which must deal with them in accordance with its rules and the principles of natural justice—which include the principle that a man should not be convicted twice for the same offence.

Lord Derby replied

> I quite see your point of view but, at the same time, one cannot get away from the fact that anything that affects the good name of the University must affect the Council, and whereas I am completely with you that the question of discipline does not become a Council affair one cannot deny that it does become a Council affair when there is any likelihood of any funds being lost or the appeal damaged in any way.
>
> I think members of the Council are feeling more and more that the Council is merely a rubber stamp, and I must admit that I, too, feel that things are pointing that way.

The Vice-Chancellor sent this and further correspondence to the Board of the Senate, saying that he regarded it as "essential in the light of this correspondence, that Senate should conclude its discussions on the system of discipline forthwith, so that no uncertainty exists either about the rules or about the system for administering justice".

The memorandum containing the correspondence was leaked to the student press and both *Spark* (published by the Socialist Society) and *Impulse* (published by the Liberal and Radical Association) published, on 23 April, extracts from the correspondence as well as comments upon it. On 30 April, *John O'Gauntlet* published the complete correspondence as well as an editorial which included the following:

> We can see the nature of some of the people chosen as lay members of Council. We can see their opinions and their demands for more power to put these opinions into action—an irresponsible demand directly contravening the statutes of the University. . . .

[6.56] Memorandum from the Vice-Chancellor to the Board of the Senate, 6 April 1970; from which the following two quotations are also taken.

2F

The man who does emerge with distinction from this whole disgraceful affair is the Vice-Chancellor. Though many would wish for a differing form of University hierarchy, we are fortunate in having a man with the nature and ability of Carter. The bumbling autocrats of Liverpool, Manchester or Warwick would have accorded with Lord Derby only too readily.

There were now no less than three issues tangled with each other: (a) whether someone at a university could be put in a position of "double jeopardy" by being punished twice for the same offence, (b) what should be done about the continued disclosure of confidential information; and (c) whether Senate had the whole statutory responsibility for discipline.[6.57] It was against this background that the Board of the Senate came to discuss the new disciplinary code on 6 May.

The preamble of the new code stated the principles on which future rules were to be based:

> The main purpose of rules is to remind members of the community of the ways in which they should exercise self-discipline for the benefit of all. In those exceptional cases in which, because of a failure of self-discipline, rules have to be enforced, justice requires that defined procedures be followed. . . .
>
> In certain cases, and subject to safeguards, the University or a College may wish to use its system of justice to enforce a law of the land; for it is sometimes better that a community should deal with the lesser misdemeanours of its members, rather than require the intervention of the police and the public courts of law. But the law of the land is not sufficient to regulate a university community; there must in addition be other rules to protect the members of the University in pursuit of the objects of the University, and to ensure that individuals do not by their actions unreasonably lessen the freedom and convenience of others.[6.58]

There were to be two categories of rules: general, applying to all members of the university; and sectional, applying to particular kinds of people (such as members of a college), or relating to a particular place (such as safety rules in a laboratory). Furthermore, the rules were to apply to all members of the university whether students or academic staff,[6.59] since the committee regarded it

---

[6.57] At one stage there was a suggested provision for a member of Council to have a seat on the Committee for Appeals and Equity, but this was not adopted.

[6.58] The Rules of the University of Lancaster, Section 1.1. Quotations are taken from the final 1972 edition of the rules where they follow the tenor of the original, or except where otherwise stated.

[6.59] Provision was also made that, by agreement with the Joint Consultative Groups for assistant staff, certain categories of rule would be applied to the assistant staff. So far only rules covering car parking have been so applied.

as a matter of principle that every member of the University should be willing to be treated equally—except perhaps, that the obligations of senior members should be regarded as more onerous than those of junior. . . . We note that only one objection has been received.[6.60]

Various matters were referred back to the Committee on Rules, especially points concerning confidentiality, and the membership, method of appointment and obligation to service on the various disciplinary bodies.

Two days later the Council held a special meeting about the disclosure of the confidential correspondence between the Vice-Chancellor and Lord Derby, which led on to a more fundamental discussion of the respective roles of the Senate and the Council, particularly with regard to discipline. Sir Noel Hall expressed the view

> that the Council's statutory responsibility in regard to the revenue and finances of the University entitled it to request information on a wide range of matters in order that it could properly discharge its responsibilities, and that the Council had a right to satisfy itself that the Senate had properly discharged its responsibilities where this might be in doubt. . . . However, the statutory responsibility of the Senate for the discipline of students of the University was clear, and it would be quite wrong for the Council to be involved in the University's disciplinary machinery for students.

Meanwhile, out in Alexandra Square a noisy demonstration was going on, and the Council agreed to receive a deputation of sixteen students who asked that Lord Derby resign as Pro-Chancellor (and that he also address the student demonstration!), and that the composition of the Council be changed to exclude anyone with "investments in South Africa or in the war industry in Indo-China", and to include "students and working class representatives". The Vice-Chancellor explained the statutory position on changes in composition on changes in composition of the Council and made it clear that Lord Derby did not wish to resign as Pro-Chancellor and neither did the university wish him to. The deputation withdrew, but shortly afterwards an uninvited group of demonstrators made their way in to the Senate Room and, after some verbal exchanges, the meeting was brought to a close. A further meeting of the Senate took place the next day and discussed the whole episode, after which the Vice-Chancellor issued a statement around the university in which he commented that

---

[6.60] The Vice-Chancellor suggested that a copy of the rules be sent to all senior members, asking for their assent to them, and that Council later consider what action should be taken by any who did not assent. This was not done, and the application of the rules to senior members became a live issue again during discussion of them in 1972 and 1973.

Some members of the University, on Friday, behaved to the Council as though they wanted to illustrate and confirm all the worst things which are said about students. This is understandable, if the purpose is to develop a political confrontation, regardless of the issue on which it is based and of the harm done to students everywhere in the process. It is neither understandable nor excusable, for those who genuinely desire to propose changes in the structure of the university. For you cannot cause change by shouting at people, but only by convincing them that you have a reasonable case. . . . I would like to remind students that proposals were made many months ago for regulating the appearance of the police on the campus,[6.61] and for ensuring that any official request for police aid should require careful consideration by two University Wardens acting together.[6.62] We cannot stop private individuals referring things to the police if they wish, nor can we stop the police acting on their own initiative. These proposals would, however, have given us a useful protection. They have not been carried out because there were student objections to the idea of University Wardens, and we have been waiting for counter-proposals from the S.R.C. It would be appreciated if these proposals could be produced.

A number of students were fined, some by summary proceedings and others by the University Tribunal (against a background of student disapproval that any of their number be members of the tribunal); and at the next meeting of the Board of the Senate in June, proposals were put forward by the Vice-Chancellor and the chairman of the Student Representative Council for the appointment of six investigators, three being senior members of the university and three junior, who would be available to look into

> any alleged offence which had taken place or was taking place in an area of the university not covered by the investigatory functions of the Deans of Colleges . . . if a senior member was first summoned to undertake such an investigation, it should be his duty as soon as possible to associate with himself a junior investigator, and vice versa.

While respecting the rights of private individuals to call the police in emergencies

> proposals to bring the police into the university to control disorder or to deal with actual or alleged or expected offences under the law of the land should be made to the vice-chancellor or to *two* of the investigators (one senior and one junior) acting together.

6.61 Plain clothes policemen had appeared at the university during the demonstration.
6.62 The term "warden" had at this stage been adopted in place of "aedile".

The details of what happened next are not clearly revealed by the documents of the period,[6.63] and the intervention of the Long Vacation made an already complicated situation even more so. The Board of the Senate duly proceeded to appoint the three senior investigators. The chairman of the S.R.C., Mr. Robert Bond, had put forward names of some junior investigators, subject to ratification. The S.R.C. at the beginning of term, ratified them, "subject to S.R.C. discussion on the whole issue of investigators". At another meeting a few days later the appointment of junior investigators was condemned, their withdrawal demanded and a request for a working party made. A meeting of Federation about the same time also "condemned" the action of the university regarding investigators, and the meeting of the Board of the Senate on 21 October agreed that the Vice-Chancellor and two other senators should meet the S.R.C. "to discuss outstanding differences". The Vice-Chancellor, in a memorandum of 28 October entitled "On the Proposition that Ladders are better than Snakes", tried to take the discussion back to first principles by pointing out that (a) complaints were sometimes made that a member of the university had broken a rule; (b) automatic proceedings before a disciplinary tribunal on the receipt of a complaint would be wrong "because many of the complaints are ill-supported by evidence, and a few are malicious"; (c) therefore an investigation was needed to see whether a charge should be laid; (d) there existed college machinery, normally with student participation, for such an investigation, but (e) deans of colleges already had enough to do and there were complications if members of several colleges were involved; and therefore (f) "it was suggested that we should have a university investigatory system, similar to and parallel to the college system". He went on:

> Having laboriously climbed up this ladder, it appears that a number of snakes lay in the way. These were probably the consequence of trying to do too many things at the same time. For the present, I think that it will be best if I refrain from calling on the senior and junior investigators so far appointed or nominated, and go back for the time being to the use of the college system, dealing with any matters which arise by asking the Principals of the Colleges, in turn, if they will arrange for the services of appropriate persons to investigate each complaint. I hope that the S.R.C. will then be willing to discuss precise terms of reference for those who investigate non-collegiate matters, and if possible to allow this to be an area in which junior and senior members take an equal share of responsibility.

[6.63] Reference should be made to the minutes of S.R.C. and of Federation, as well as *Scan* for the Michaelmas Term, 1970, for a partial account of some student views about investigators. Unfortunately the documentation is not complete and the full range of attitudes therefore not revealed.

The Federation meeting the next day, however, voted against the appointment of any student to the Senate working party, and the new S.R.C. chairman, Mr. William Corr, resigned because

> Loath though I am to agree with the V.C. rather than with an articulate section of the people by whom I was elected, I cannot but realize that a deliberate campaign is being fostered, misrepresenting the issues in the "Investigators" saga, with the intention of goading the majority of students into taking part in wholly pointless militant action against an "opponent" who has proven himself to be fairly amenable to discussion in the past. . . .
>
> Nevertheless, I remain opposed in principle to the whole concept of "junior investigators" unless their powers and functions are so clearly defined as to place them completely above suspicion.

More delays occurred, but early in 1971 meetings were supposed to be held between, on the one side, the Vice-Chancellor, Dr. John Garner and Dr. Brian Duke and on the other Messrs Hogan Burke, Bill Corr and Matt Plesch. Meanwhile the other pieces of new machinery were coming into operation, such as the University Tribunal and the Committee of Appeals and Equity. There was some difficulty in finding members for these committees, and in at least one case the procedures of the Committee for Appeals and Equity were challenged. There was sufficient unsureness about the way in which the rules were being administered, moreover, for the Board of the Senate to decide in March 1971 to revive the Committee on Rules, and further painstaking and involved meetings were held.

A meeting was called in June to discuss investigators, but none of the junior members of the committee came to the meeting. Other students who were rounded up at very short notice to come and talk later claimed at a subsequent Federation meeting that nothing they had said could be any part of the university policy on investigators. A stalemate on this idea had therefore been reached and, with the advent of yet another Long Vacation, the idea that student investigators would emerge from the Student Representative Council or from Federation became increasingly remote, especially since some of the J.C.R.s set their faces against such a system.

At the end of the summer term, however, University House (including the telephone exchange) and the adjoining computer building were occupied by students who were acting, as a consequence of a decision by Federation, in support of a group of women day cleaners who were campaigning for free transport from Lancaster and Garstang to the university. Examination results were held up, and first year students sent home before they had heard whether they had passed their qualifying examinations or not. A small Senate sub-committee which was set up to advise the Vice-Chancellor on what might be done was divided in its views, but after a day of consultation it was decided to take out an injunction against the students "for possession of property" against the "wrongful occupants" of the buildings, so that they became trespassers and could legally be arrested if they remained within the building. The students left a few hours later. The Council at its next meeting at the end of the month received an account of the action taken, and authorized the Vice-Chancellor "in the event of the wrongful or illegal occupation of any part of the University premises, to take on Council's behalf any action which might be necessary or appropriate in law to secure a rapid end to the occupation".

The injunction was, of course, the first time that the university had taken such stringent action against its junior members and, looking back, it may be seen as the end of an age of innocence for the university. Certainly in July the Vice-Chancellor felt it necessary to send out a very firmly worded memorandum to all members of staff, the Student Representative Council, and the Council, making it clear that

> There must be no question about the right of (peaceful) *demonstration* in favour of any cause, however unpopular it may be with those in authority, unless such demonstration is prohibited by the general law of the land: and no rule of the university should prohibit a demonstration which would otherwise be legal.

However, there had also been disruption, which he defined as

> an organized obstruction of the purposes of the university, other than by a strike of employees. A "sit-in" in an area otherwise unused, which allows people to get on with their work, is a *demonstration*: a "sit-in" which prevents the continuance of normal work is disruption, as would be the interruption of lectures, the sabotage of examinations, the denial of free speech to visiting speakers, and so on.

This could not be tolerated. He went on:

> Some members of the university regard disruption as a permissible means of coercing the university to follow a particular line. This is because they accept as their first duty the changing of an established order of which the university is seen as a part, rather than as an independent critic. They want to transform the university to make it part of a new political order; and they therefore regard the promise to obey the Charter as of no effect, disloyalty in this respect being nullified by the acceptance of a higher loyalty. . . . I am in no doubt that it is our duty to disregard their views, and to attend to the purposes for which the university was established, to its obligations in law, and to the views of the majority of its members. That means that disruption must be prevented, or, if it occurs, must be defeated. . . .

I am in no doubt that the university's own legal system, in its present form, *is* ineffective in discouraging disruptive action. There is no advance warning of a significant penalty. It will therefore be supposed that the offences which can readily be proved (for instance, presence in an occupied building during a sit-in) will carry only a minor penalty, since they can be committed by people who are no more than bystanders; and that the offences which might be taken seriously, for instance complicity in the original organization of the disruption, will be impossible to prove. I shall be putting proposals to the next meeting of Senate to strengthen our defences at this point.

At the first Senate meeting of the new academic year, in September, the Vice-Chancellor placed before it a paper on possible action to be taken on the occurrence of disruption for, he reported,

> after the brief disruption last term it had been brought to the university's notice that, although an injunction in a similar case might be granted, it was the duty of a chartered body with powers of discipline to arrange, as far as it could, that that discipline was maintained. There was a gap in the rules of the university which, although they could be used effectively against a student or member of staff who conspired to obstruct, could not be used with certainty against persons who might assist an obstruction by their presence. It was therefore suggested that the Senate should be able to declare that continued presence which assisted an obstruction should itself be an offence.

Concern was expressed that there should first be more discussion within the university, and also that any such procedure should be both effective and simple. A small sub-committee, including Professor Malcolm Willcock, Miss Amy Wootten and Mr. Andy McLaughlin, therefore agreed to meet the Vice-Chancellor to draw up a further document, which was in turn tabled at the November meeting, having in the meantime been before syndicates and junior common rooms, as well as the Committee of Colleges. The proposals recognized "the right of staff and students to engage in peaceful demonstrations" but not to "obstruct or impede the work of another group". Members of the university with a grievance "are required to use the proper constitutional means of rectifying it". A new committee, for Emergency Investigations, was established, consisting of a pro-vice-chancellor, one member of the Committee of the Senate, one member of the assistant staff and two students (there being a panel of several within each category to call upon) who would come together (with at least one hour's notice being given) if a disruptive act "is a serious possibility, or if such an act has occurred" and would be asked to report on the cause of or occasion of or excuse for the threatened or actual occurrence, and to suggest any necessary action to provide reliable facts to those concerned or to remove any real grievance. The Committee may publish a report. Any proposal from the Committee which requires action from other Committees of the University shall be considered by those Committees without delay.

If a disruptive act was already occurring or about to do so, and the Committee already called, then the Vice-Chancellor could call a special meeting of Senate, giving three hours' notice. The Senate would decide whether the act was minor, "in the sense of being readily able to be stopped, or having trivial consequences, or having consequences which can be offset without significant harm to the work of life of the university", or grave. In the latter case the Senate would decide on appropriate action and penalties, notice of which would be posted up around the university. Anyone, senior or junior, who failed to comply with the prescribed action would be brought before the University Tribunal and, in addition, an officer of the university "may, in a case of exceptional gravity, be subject to the procedure (agreed with the A.U.T.) by which he may be suspended from office and a proposal be made to Council for his dismissal".[6.64]

The effect of the establishment of this new committee together with some hostility towards university investigators, caused the Committee on Rules to change direction somewhat, as may be seen by this memorandum of February 1972 sent to the Committee of Colleges:

The Committee on Rules is about to report to Senate, after several exhausting meetings, and hopes thereafter to be excused from service for about twenty years. It is making two proposals of great significance to the Colleges, and the Committee of Colleges may wish to indicate whether it supports them.

The first is to extend the jurisdiction of College tribunals so that the demands on the University Tribunal become much smaller. The proposed wording is:

A College Tribunal has jurisdiction in the case of an alleged breach of a Rule of that College, or of a University Rule within the College, or of a University Rule in relation to a member of the College. Where a complaint is made against members of two or more Colleges or involves an alleged offence by a member of one College on the premises of another, the investigators of the Colleges shall consult together in deciding how to proceed. Investigators may refer a case to the University Tribunal or (by agreement) to the Tribunal of any College, the alternative jurisdiction of another College Tribunal notwithstanding.

[6.64] See "The Rules of the University of Lancaster," Section 7.8. (1972).

In other words—now that we have explicit appointments of College investigators they can arrange between them where to refer a case. The University Tribunal would be mainly used for (a) grave cases, normally involving members of several Colleges; (b) appeals against Library and Parking fines. The proposal is a return to an earlier position, and considerably extends the power of the Colleges in disciplinary matters.

The second proposal is to abolish University Investigators, and simply give the Secretary for Student and College Affairs, when a complaint comes to him, power to call on members of a panel consisting of all College investigators.

The revised code of rules was sent round syndicates and junior common rooms and was approved by the Senate on 22 March, with thanks being offered to the members of the Committee on Rules "for their impressive and devoted labours". This Committee was laid down, although in its place sprang up another *ad hoc* body, the Committee on the Enforcement of Rules which has been building up a pragmatic case law based on the precedents established by particular disciplinary cases.

In fact the rule on disruption had already been used before the whole code's revision was complete. At the end of January 1972 there was strong feeling within the student body about the situation in Northern Ireland (and in particular certain deaths in Londonderry on Sunday, 30 January). The Irish Solidarity Campaign, chaired by Mr. Mick Murray (at that time the Chairman of S.R.C.), voted on the evening of 31 January to occupy the Senate Room as a protest against the deaths and broke down three doors of University House in doing so. A meeting of the Senate was called for the next day and a compromise was reached with the student body whereby the Federation meeting was to be held in the Faraday Lecture Theatre, the Town and Gown Club was to be able to meet in the Senate Room as previously arranged and the students were permitted to re-occupy the Senate Room until the evening of 2 February.[6.65] Furthermore the student body agreed to meet the cost of the damage to the doors of University House. This was done, and the Vice-Chancellor told the Council that he believed it to be "the majority view of academic staff that, on this particular occasion, it was proper to deal with the matter by agreement, and without any disciplinary action. I do not in fact feel very strongly about the settlement in this particular case, which was a minor incident which did not significantly obstruct the work of the University"—although he was concerned at the acceptance by some members of Senate of sit-ins as being an almost normal means of agitation, and wished to reject absolutely such a viewpoint. However, a petition, which had been

---

[6.65] Thereafter a number of students held a torchlight procession, with banners, to Dalton Square in Lancaster.

signed by ninety-one members of the academic, administrative and assistant staff, asked the Council to

> examine the apparent failure of Senate to carry out its responsibility under the statutes to make satisfactory arrangements for student discipline. It appears that disruptions of the University's activities and damage to its property (the responsibility of Council) may take place with impunity.

Given this division of opinion over such a relatively small incident, it is not surprising that when there was a boycott of classes and a further occupation of University House in March 1972 over the proposed dismissal of Dr. David Craig, there was even more determination amongst some members of the Senate to apply the rules with stringency. This episode, however, did not alter the fundamental levels of the disciplinary code, and is also still too recent (and the wounds these events caused too raw) to relate in full. In summary form, however, what happened was the following. Dr. Craig and Professor Murray, who had both been members of the department of English since 1964, and who were already involved in considerable debate over the proper way in which to examine Part II courses, in the spring of 1971 disagreed about the contents of a Part II examination paper in twentieth-century literature. Later that summer Dr. Craig was told that he would no longer be teaching this course; he appealed to a sub-committee of the Council, which decided that the instructions had been within the head of the department's jurisdiction, and he later requested the A.U.T. to take up the matter on his behalf. Early in 1972 two temporary lecturers in the same department, who said they had been given verbal promises (though by a person with no authority to give such promises) of permanent posts, were instead considered alongside other candidates for posts in the department, and were not offered them. At the same time another lecturer, also in the field of modern literature, had his probation extended by a further year. The students of the department had been restive since the autumn of 1971; during the last week of the Lent Term 1972 many of them boycotted classes and a number of students in other departments followed suit. Dr. Craig went round the departments addressing students about the Free University which he and others wished to create, and the charges against him, which constituted grounds for proposing his dismissal, arose out of the speeches he had made to the students. There was considerable national publicity and students occupied University House for one day. Dr. Craig's case was heard by the Committee of the Council on 2 May 1972 and an agreed settlement, negotiated by the lawyers of the two sides and agreed by the Council, was reached, whereby the motion for dismissal was adjourned *sine die*, and Dr. Craig was to continue as a senior lecturer but outside the English department.

The Pro-Chancellor, Lord Greenwood, at the same period asked Councillor

Taylor "to consider the underlying causes of and predisposing conditions for recent disputes and disruption in the University, and to recommend any changes of policy which he might consider desirable". His report was published in July 1973, and sections of it are referred to elsewhere in this work.

Since that time the University has been quiet: the only issue of any importance for student politicians of the university was the rent strike in the spring of 1973, but this had no consequences for the disciplinary code, and was principally dealt with by individual colleges and the Council.

(iv) Student Welfare

A student at Lancaster has a choice of agencies on hand to give him assistance when he needs it, although unlike some universities, such as Sussex, they are deliberately not welded together as a single service but create informal links of their own.[6.66] As we have already seen, the colleges provide, in addition to a social setting, a system of personal tutors to listen to a student's difficulties, whether academic or personal, advise him how best to approach whichever piece of the university's services he may need, and act as his counsel for advice if he is summoned before any of the disciplinary bodies of the university (or possibly even before a local magistrate's court). Obviously he can turn to his departments, particularly that for his major subject, in which the head and the members of staff who teach him will feel a responsibility towards him. There is the Medical Centre to nurse students who are ill or in need of special care. Perhaps mention should be made of the Chaplaincy Centre, which is similar to the Medical Centre inasmuch as its funding comes principally from without the university.[6.67]

The chaplains work far more as a team than is suggested by their denominational roles, and meet regularly, hold joint activities, and encourage as much sharing and trust as possible between students from different backgrounds. Students come in casually for snacks and coffee and can sit around in the central lounge, talk to each other or to the chaplains, or work in the small library. During term-time (and increasingly during the vacations) the Centre has a fairly high level of activity going on for most of the twenty-four hours of each day, making the place a valuable point of informal, casual contact. Special mention should be made of Father John Turner, the Roman Catholic chaplain for the first eight years of the university, who was particularly successful in establishing the trust and mutual respect that prevails

---

[6.66] An attempt was made during 1972–73 to set up a Personal Welfare Sub-Committee of the Committee of Colleges, which would have co-ordinated the different forms of welfare and advisory activity among students, but the suggestion came to nothing.

[6.67] See Chapter 2 for a description of the Chaplaincy Centre *qua* building.

between the Centre and the university, so that the chaplains can play their part very much in harmony with the university and its policies and yet maintain their own separate and distinctive ethos. The present Roman Catholic priest, Father Brian Noble, is a Lancaster man, and the Anglican chaplain, the Reverend Paul Warren, came from a curacy at Lancaster Priory in 1970.

A careers advisory service was one of the earliest of the service agencies set up for students. A sub-committee of the Senate in December 1965 recommended that a careers office be opened from the beginning of the Summer Term 1966 at St. Leonardgate, and that Miss Jean Owtram[6.68] be the first careers adviser. Particular emphasis was laid on her gathering information about

> the most effective ways of establishing contact with students and potential employers, and how best to achieve a two-way traffic of information between students and employers to ensure that information about the "career interests", qualifications and propensities of individual students and the specific needs of particular employers . . . is made fully available to both parties.

The student use of the service built up gradually and by September 1970 Mrs. Argles and her assistant were expecting to help about three-quarters of each year's finalists, and were finding that "staff and facilities have been strained to their limits at peak periods of activity". Nevertheless, they were able to take a fairly sanguine view of career prospects for Lancaster graduates for, although the "employment market for graduates . . . is not expanding so rapidly that a casual approach is likely to be successful in the more competitive and attractive fields", the extent of the problem was merely that "late starters are finding it more and more difficult to get appointments in the areas of their first choice".

Twelve months later, however, their annual report gloomily analysed a year

> during which the whole picture of graduate employment has changed, and it seems unlikely at present that the old pattern will ever return. The Cassandra-like warnings which have been sounded in all University Appointments Boards' reports lately . . . have been unfortunately proved correct, and the difficulties met with by all but the most outstanding candidates for employment this year have been far greater than usual.

The result of this changed situation, of course, was an increased workload for the Careers Office as students were forced to consider second, third and fourth alternatives and as those who were unable to find employment con-

---

[6.68] Later, Mrs. Jean Argles.

tinued discussions with the Careers Office for months after graduation. The option of registering as soon as students came up in their first year had always been open, but now students were strongly advised to register well before their third year, and are also encouraged to look at their choice of Part II courses with the implications of their career structure in mind as well as their academic interests. Lord Robbins' committee foresaw in 1963 that as more people with types of training that had been relatively scarce in the past became available, graduates could not expect that there would "be an infinite extension of demand in particular occupations",[6.69] and it has therefore become necessary for those with degrees to look at untraditional career fields, with concurrent extra help needed from those advising them. In addition, the careers officers are willing to help students who go down from Lancaster without completing their degrees, both by providing information and in giving advice on what might be suitable—a valuable aid for someone who at that stage is likely to think him or herself as a complete failure. In these circumstances it was particularly fortunate that an active Careers Advisory Committee was established, under the energetic and concerned chairmanship of Professor Peter Nailor.

The importance of the service and its need for continuing enlargement was brought out in a document of January 1973 to the university's Finance Committee, which spoke of its being student-orientated:

> this was required by Senate in the original mandate. The needs of students, not of employers, therefore must come first. As employers find it easier to fill their graduate vacancies, students find it harder to get jobs. This also includes post-graduate students, whose prospects have been affected by the slowdown in the growth of higher education. As a result, the first demand made by students on Advisers is *time* . . . fewer students now complete their plans before leaving University (this is a national, not a local, phenomenon). There is therefore a new problem of overlap: the Careers Service works with at least two years' "output" concurrently—the immediately past and the present Final Years—and could advantageously do far more work with pre-final students. . . .
>
> Students need time to analyse (with help) their aims and abilities (especially non-academic skills), the wider field of employment which most now need to consider, the adjustment to reaching the end of their educational programme, and the need to make the first wholly personal decision on their own futures. If each of the two Careers Advisers continue to interview five "new" students for five days in each week, without interruptions (i.e. 5 to 6 hours continuous interviewing minimum daily), and attend only to routine correspondence during the remainder of the day,

---

[6.69] *Report on Higher Education*, Cmnd. 2154 (1963), paragraph 193.

this will still take up about a term and a half before every Finalist can be seen. This would not include any time for work with postgraduates, "drop-outs", second-year students, and others previously seen;

or for liaison with academic staff, employers, useful external agencies and all the other necessary background work. Furthermore,

Much work is not with the "top" students but with the less self-sufficient, who need more personal (i.e. labour-intensive) help over a longer period. Ideally, these students should be followed up individually to ensure that they know that help is available when it is needed, but in fact there is little time to do this adequately and regularly for those still at the University, let alone those who have left.

It was decided, therefore, that from October 1973 onwards there would be three careers advisers, to carry the increased load that a nationally more complex situation confronting university graduates has placed on the service. In this connection it is interesting that one of the two items of central expenditure per student that the U.G.C. specifically excepted from a decrease for the national 1972–77 quinquennial settlement was the provision of careers advice, where they felt that expenditure should be increased by 5 per cent per student.

The suggestion for a central counselling service first arose out of the recommendations of the Lawrenson investigating committee to the Senate conference of September 1969, when in the course of discussion of its findings it was suggested that a professional student counselling service and more psychiatric facilities might be needed. The idea did not emerge again, however, until January 1971 when, in connection with the committee *ad hoc* on student progress,[6.70] the Board of the Senate approved a recommendation that

the Committee of Colleges should explore by consultation with the colleges, the Student Representative Council, the medical centre, the career advisers and such persons and bodies outside the university as may be thought appropriate the need for, and the financing of, a central counselling unit.

In short, the principle of such a facility was not an integral part of the original plans but arose mainly in response to particular difficulties which revealed themselves at a time when the Vice-Chancellor felt it necessary to tell his staff that

[6.70] Set up by the Board of the Senate on 21 October 1970 to consider matters arising from the Wakeford report on withdrawal of first-year undergraduates, there having been an apparently unduly high number who did so in the 1968–69 academic year.

There is also no doubt that the Lancaster image is not as good as it was. This is partly the inevitable result of no longer being an interesting infant: but conversations with many people around the country convince me that members of staff must take very seriously indeed the effect on our reputation of the allegations about drug-taking and extreme permissiveness. . . . There were in fact things seriously wrong with our community last year. One consequence was an extraordinarily high rate of withdrawal and of first-year academic failure: another has been a higher rate of withdrawal of potential new students, which may have had a serious effect on the science departments.[6.71]

Fylde College now took a lead. Its syndicate in October 1970 considered a paper which suggested that

> much of the tutorial load on senior members is produced by a very few junior members with serious emotional, rather than academic or financial problems. "Emotional" covers a range of problems from severe psychiatric cases (which of course have to be referred to the medical centre) to instances where students have difficulty in adjusting to the university environment, in establishing a self-identity or have a low motivation to a university career. Another basic source of student distress is difficulty or problems in personal relationships. It is probable that there have been many occurrences of student problems in these areas which have not come to the notice of tutors. . . .
>
> Senior members lack the necessary experience, skill and training to cope successfully with all the student problems of this nature with which they may be faced. Students, of course, realize this and prefer usually to do without the amateurish help of someone who is an academic and who is involved in the authority structure of the university. There is, we believe, need throughout the University for a student counselling service, independent of the administrative and academic structure, to which students can seek advice on problems which cannot be conveniently labelled "accommodation"," careers", "medical" or "academic". We would regard this as supplementary to the college tutorial system and not as a substitute for it. . . . What we propose is the *immediate* appointment of a part-time student counsellor to Fylde College.

By the time, therefore, that the Committee of Colleges had the matter under discussion at its meetings in January 1971, there was simultaneously a university-wide move towards appointing a full-time student counsellor and

---

[6.71] Letter from the Vice-Chancellor to members of the F.S.S.U. staff and the Council, September 1969.

a single college's proposal to go ahead at once on a part-time appointment—which Fylde College did, Mrs. Greta James taking up the post in May 1971.

One student in particular, Paul Howard, who was both academic affairs vice-chairman of the S.R.C. and a member of the Committee of Colleges, espoused this cause. He prepared two reports, one being a comparative study with other universities where—as in so many areas—practices were found to vary widely, and another arguing for the provision of a counselling service at Lancaster. The Vice-Chancellor, at the February 1971 meeting of the Committee of Colleges, which received his reports, commented that, according to advice he had received from the U.S.A., the university should "be careful in jumping to the conclusion that the provision of such services would automatically lead to a better situation. The position in American universities or colleges, where such services are freely available, suggests a decline in the interest of members of the academic staff in the welfare of students." Certainly the onus was seen to rest on the colleges, both for the necessary finance and for the organizational functions of the service.

The months went by, however, without a decision having been made and at the end of October a gloomy article by Paul Howard entitled "Death of Student Counselling" was published in *Lancaster Comment*,[6.72] setting out the arguments for such a service again, demonstrating that it would not interfere or overlap with existing advisory services, whether in colleges, departments or as a centrally based agency, and decrying the lack of progress due, Mr. Howard felt, not only to its competing claims with other candidates for funds and the attitude of some staff that students should stand on their own feet, but because it had been lost in a welter of university sub-committees and student inquoracy. However, he should not have worried. At a meeting of the Committee of Colleges in January 1972 Fylde College was able to report that, in the light of its experience to date, it was in favour of the extension of student counselling throughout the university, as Fylde was

at the moment very satisfied with the progress of counselling. People are becoming more willing to approach the counsellor direct, instead of being referred by tutors; tutors have received help in dealing with problems of their students.

Four of the other five colleges had reported in favour of the introduction of counselling and two of them would have been prepared, without further discussion, to help with the cost of the service. A report by Dr. Paxman and Mr. Howard noted that the other bodies who provided student welfare services within the university saw this addition as a useful adjunct to their own provision. A decision on whether the service was needed at once was more difficult because

---

[6.72] *Lancaster Comment*, 28 October 1971, pages 1–3.

2G

we cannot find any form of critical evidence to show whether a professional counselling service at Lancaster would be worthwhile. Existing services elsewhere are well used and in their annual reports give impressive figures for numbers of cases dealt with etc. Their relevance to the Lancaster situation of such figures is not obvious because of the point already made that no two universities have the same social and administrative structure.

A firm decision, however, was clearly necessary, and the Committee reported to the Senate its agreement "to recommend to the Finance Committee that it should authorize expenditure by the Colleges to establish a student counselling service . . . to be in operation at the beginning of the next academic year". The idea received the particular approbation of Councillor Taylor in his report of July 1972 in which he welcomed it "as a wise move to provide additional help in this field. After the first Counsellor has been appointed and his activities examined, then perhaps this appointment could be extended".[6.73]

By the time his report came to be discussed by the Council and the Senate, Mrs. James was in post as the full-time university counsellor (and Fylde had again filled their part-time post). She is physically located in close proximity to the Careers Advisory Service, so that students do not feel self-conscious if they are observed walking in that direction. Students can ring up for an appointment at any time or, if the matter is urgent, she tries to fit them in almost at once. The principle has been established that consultations are always confidential, and no information about them is passed on to any other agency without the student's permission.[6.74] The main difficulty of the service so far has been not to keep students waiting unduly long for initial interview and to keep up with the necessary level of paperwork.[6.75]

In company with several other universities (Essex being the first to set the example), the Lancaster students decided to back up the other welfare services with their own Nightline, which has been in operation since October 1971. Every night of term, from 10.00 p.m. to 8.00 a.m., a widely advertised telephone service with an easily memorable number is manned by two volunteer students, usually one male and one female. Essentially this service is to cater for those students who, in spite of all the services already available, nevertheless remain alone: "They may dislike communicating with any form

---

6.73 Report of the Taylor Enquiry (1972), item 7.

6.74 The leaflet of information about the service circulated around the university in October 1972 states, however, that "There is when appropriate, co-operation between the Counselling Service, the University Health Service, the Careers Advisory Service and, of course, college tutors."

6.75 As from January 1974 there are to be two student counsellors.

of authority, not want to ask for help, not know how to put their feelings into words or, quite simply, may feel they do not have a specific problem."[6.76]

Nightline (or the "Friendly Night Owls", as they call themselves) is a service similar to the Samaritans in that it is a confidential telephone service staffed by lay volunteers, but is unlike in that it does not see its primary function as suicide prevention but tries to cater for a very wide range of student problems. The volunteers are prepared to lend a sympathetic ear to those in trouble and know how to arrange for their help to be supplemented by the other services. The freedom of the caller is respected: for example, although the Nightline students are prepared to go to the room of anyone to talk, this would never be forced on a caller. So also is the confidentiality of the service, for information is not revealed to anyone outside the organization without the caller's express permission, and using the service therefore carries no stigma.

Seventy-six students volunteered to help with Nightline during its first year of existence, and fifty-two were used to man the telephone, having first been given some general preparation by way, for example, of explanation of telephone techniques and guidance on types of depression. The university has supplied the necessary telephone extensions and the S.R.C. the accommodation and the small fund needed for furnishings and advertisement. During 1971–72 there were 126 calls received, of which only twelve were obviously hoax calls. Academic problems were the most frequent, as might be expected, but others ranged from anything between the difficulties of sleeping in a noisy block to those with a history of attempted suicide.

Nightline, therefore, can offer a distinctive service in that students who seem to slip through the nets of all the existing services will come:

> Some will not go to the Medical service, for example, if they do not perceive their case as medical. And, too, there is the feeling that, along with the doctor's almost impossible task of giving people with problems sufficient time to talk about them, there is an apparent tendency to treat human problems as something best dealt with by a drug, an anti-depressant of some sort. Similarly, there is some evidence to support the idea that students do not go to their tutors or lecturers, because they perceive them as in some way tied up with the establishment. Academics have got *through* the system. They are "successful". Students who are experiencing problems may be justified in feeling that academics do not really understand what sort of world their students come from, or the issues they have to face. The values embodied in learning from books, academic grades and

---

[6.76] David and Jennifer Thompson, "Nightline—A Student Self-Help Organization", 1973, on which I have drawn heavily for this description, and the quotation below.

examinations, may be of far less significance for present-day students than for those in the past. New values are replacing the old. A compulsive drive towards individual achievement is becoming less acceptable to young people in general, who seem to be much more attracted by the values of self-realization.

Appendices and Statistics

Appendix (i)

NEW POST-WAR UNIVERSITY FOUNDATIONS

Name of institution	Founding of promotion cttee. or equivalent	Government announcement	Royal charter	First student intake: (a) date and (b) number	
				(a) (Oct. except where otherwise stated)	(b) (Graduate and undergraduate) number
University of Keele (formerly Univ. Coll. of N. Staffordshire)	1946	1947	1949 (as College) 1962 (as Univ.)	1950 1962	151 853
University of Sussex	1956	Feb. 1958	1961	1961	52
University of East Anglia	c. 1959	Apr. 1960	1964	1963	113
University of York	c. 1956	Apr. 1960	1963	1963	214
University of Essex	1960	May 1961	1965	1964	122
University of Kent at Canterbury	1960	May 1961	1965	1965	458
University of Warwick	c. 1958	May 1961	1965	1965	436
University of Lancaster	1961	Nov. 1961	1964	1964	330
University of Stirling	1946–1964	July 1964	1967	1967	165
The New University of Ulster (at Coleraine)	Lockwood Report, 1965	Feb. 1965	—	1968	445
Open University	White Paper, 1966	Feb. 1969	1969	Jan. 1971	24,344

Appendix (ii)

OUTLINE CHRONOLOGY

14 April 1961	First meeting of the Executive Committee of the Council for the Promotion of a University in North-West Lancashire.
2 May 1961	Decision taken by Executive Committee to put forward Lancaster rather than Blackpool to the U.G.C.
12 May 1961	Submission by Promotion Council to the U.G.C.
14 June 1961	Visitation by U.G.C. to Lancaster.
23 November 1961	Announcement by the Government that a new university was to be founded in Lancaster.
31 January 1962	Promotion Council dissolved, and in its place two bodies set up, i.e. the Executive Council for the Establishment of a University at Lancaster and the Academic Planning Board.
1 April 1962	Bailrigg taken out of Lancaster Rural District and included in the City's boundary.
7 June 1962	Executive Council incorporated as a company, limited by guarantee and not having any share capital.
11 June 1962	Announcement made that H.M. The Queen to be the Visitor, H.R.H. Princess Alexandra the Chancellor, and the Earl of Derby the Pro-Chancellor.
20 July 1962	The Directors of the Executive Council met together for the first time, and the Common Seal was adopted.
4 December 1962	Professor C. F. Carter met the Executive Council and the following day an announcement was made that he was to be Vice-Chancellor.
January 1963	The lease of the Bailrigg site received by the Executive Council, for 999 years, at £1 a year.
2 July 1963	The choice of site development architects, Messrs. Bridgewater, Shepheard and Epstein, announced. Announcement made that the former Waring and Gillow premises were to be leased to the University for temporary accommodation.

11–12 January 1964	First meeting of Shadow Senate.
14 September 1964	The grant of the Royal Charter came into operation (this being the day upon which the Great Seal was affixed by order of the Privy Council).
18 September 1964	First meeting of formally constituted Senate.
6 October 1964	The first student intake, of 294 undergraduate and 36 graduate students, admitted to Lancaster, at St. Leonard's House.
18 November 1964	Princess Alexandra installed as Chancellor of the University, and some honorary degrees conferred.
23 November 1964	The University appeal was publicly launched.
26 November 1964	Site work began at Bailrigg.
5 December 1964	The first meeting of the Court.
15 December 1964	The Executive Council's authority ceased, and the University Council met for the first time.
19 January 1965	The gift of £500,000 by the County for the founding of a college was announced (subsequently named The County College). The establishment of Bowland and Lonsdale Colleges was confirmed by Council.
18 May 1965	The purchase of Hazelrigg Farm was announced to Council.
October 1965	The first science undergraduates were admitted. The blazon of University Arms was approved.
4 December 1965	The first congregation for the conferment of (one-year) higher degrees was held in the Ashton Hall, Lancaster.
21 December 1965	Cartmel College was established by Council.
October 1966	First teaching and administrative buildings opened at Bailrigg.
July 1967	First B.A. degrees awarded.
1 August 1968	Furness College came into being.
October 1968	Student residences opened, and natural science departments moved up to Bailrigg.
1 August 1969	Fylde College came into being.
11 October 1970	Academic Advisory Committee dissolved.
January 1972	Lord Greenwood of Rossendale became Pro-Chancellor, the Earl of Derby having retired from this post in April 1971.

Appendix (iii)

INITIAL MEMBERS OF STAFF, 1964–65

(first heads of departments in italics)

C. D. Pigott, Professor of Biology, B.A., Ph.D. (Cambridge); formerly lecturer in botany at the University of Cambridge: together with a lecturer (Dr. T. A. Mansfield) and an assistant lecturer (Mr. C. Adams).

J. C. Bevington, Professor of Chemistry, B.A., Ph.D. (Cambridge), D.Sc. (Birmingham), F.R.I.C.; formerly Reader in Chemistry at Birmingham; together with a senior lecturer (Mr. R. W. H. Small), a lecturer (Dr., now Professor, K. J. Morgan) and a research associate (Mr. M. Johnson). He was a Pro-Vice-Chancellor from 1969 to 1973 and first principal of Bowland College until 1967.

M. M. Willcock, Professor of Classics, B.A. (Cambridge); formerly Senior Tutor at Sidney Sussex College; appointment commenced in October 1965, together with two lecturers (Mr. J. L. Creed and Mr. G. T. Fowler, later a member of Parliament and Minister). He succeeded Professor Bevington as principal of Bowland College.

S. G. Sturmey, Professor of Economics, B.Econ. (Adelaide), Ph.D. (Manchester); formerly Reader in political economy at University College, London; together with one senior lecturer (Dr. A. B. Cramp) and two assistant lecturers (Mr. P. R. Herrington and Mr. D. W. Pearce). He resigned in July 1967 to take up a United Nations post with UNCTAD in Geneva, and was succeeded by Professor P. W. S. Andrews, who died in March 1971. (He was succeeded as head of department until 1973 by Professor A. I. McBean, M.A. (Glasgow), B.Phil. (Oxford), when the headship passed to Professor H. Townsend, B.Sc., London.)

W. A. Murray, Professor of English, M.A. (Glasgow); formerly Professor of English at the University of Khartoum; together with two lecturers (Dr D. M. Craig and Miss B. A. Woolrich).

G. Manley, Professor of Environmental Studies, B.A. (Cambridge), D.Sc. (Manchester); formerly Professor of Geography, Bedford College, London; together with a lecturer (Dr. F. Oldfield) and an assistant lecturer (Dr. Ada W. Phillips). He retired in April 1968 as Emeritus Professor and was succeeded as head of department by Professor A. Hunter.

T. E. Lawrenson, Professor of French Studies, B.A., Ph.D., Dip.Ed. (Manchester); formerly lecturer in French, University of Aberdeen; together with a senior lecturer (Dr., now Professor, H. W. Wardman), two assistant lecturers (Mr. D. A. Steel and Mr. A. E. Pilkington), and a lectrice (Mrs. F. Steel). He was the first principal of Lonsdale College until June 1967 and has been Public Orator since 1964. Dr. Steel succeeded Professor Lawrenson as head of department in 1972.

A. H. Woolrych, Professor of History, B.A., B.Litt. (Oxon.), F.R.Hist.S.; formerly senior lecturer in modern history at Leeds; together with one lecturer (Dr. K. Ball), one assistant lecturer (Mr. D. A. Hamer) and one temporary assistant lecturer (Mr. M. H. Merriman). He has been a Pro-Vice-Chancellor since 1972.

F. H. Lawson, Professor of Law, D.C.L. (Oxon.), Hon.LL.D. (Glasgow), F.B.A.: Emeritus Professor, University of Oxford, and Fellow of Brasenose College.

E. H. Lloyd, Professor of Mathematics, B.Sc., Ph.D., D.I.C. (London); formerly Assistant Director of the Mathematics Department Imperial College, London; together with a senior lecturer (Dr. R. Henstock), a lecturer (Mr. G. J. Tee) and an assistant lecturer (Mr. P. L. Walker). He has been principal of Lonsdale College since 1967; and was succeeded in August 1971 as head of department, first by Dr. A. Talbot and secondly by Dr. E. Tagg.

B. H. P. Rivett, Professor of Operational Research, B.Sc., M.Sc. (London); formerly Manager of Operational Research in Europe for A. Anderson & Co.; together with a Reader (Dr., now Professor, M. G. Simpson), a senior lecturer (Dr., now Professor, A. Mercer) and a project officer (Mr. H. D. Dunn). He resigned in 1967 to become Professor of Operational Research at the University of Sussex, and was succeeded by Professor Simpson.

F. N. Sibley, Professor of Philosophy, B.A. (Oxford); formerly chairman of Philosophy Department, Cornell University; together with a lecturer (Mr. J. W. Roxbee Cox, now principal of Fylde College).

E. R. Dobbs, Professor of Physics, B.Sc., Ph.D. (London), F.Inst.P.; formerly Fellow in Physics of the University of Cambridge; together with one senior lecturer (Dr., now Professor, W. M. Fairbairn), one lecturer (Dr. P. M. Lee), one research associate (Dr. A. G. Betjemann), and one visiting research associate (Mr. J. M. Perz). He resigned in 1973 to take up the Hildred Carlile Chair of Physics in the University of London at Bedford College, and has been succeeded as head of department by Professor Fairbairn.

P. A. Reynolds, Professor of Politics, B.A. (Oxon.), F.R.Hist.S.; formerly Professor of International Politics, University College of Wales, Aberystwyth; together with two lecturers (Mr. S. Henig, later M.P. for Lancaster, and Mr. R. J. Price). He has been a Pro-Vice-Chancellor since 1964 and was chairman of the Shadow Syndicate and subsequently principal of Furness College from 1967 to 1970. Professor P. Nailor, M.A., Oxford, became head of department in 1973.

D. M. Waller, Lecturer in Russian, B.A. (Manchester), M.A. (Oxford), who resigned in 1971.

J. Heywood, F.R.A.S., M.C.P., and *W. T. Koc,* M.A. (Oxford), Lecturers in Higher Education: Mr. Heywood is now a Professor at Trinity College, Dublin.

Appendix (iv)

ARMS OF THE UNIVERSITY

The blazon of the arms is as follows.

ARMS: Or a Fess wavy Argent charged with two barrulets wavy Azure between in chief two Roses Gules barbed and seeded and in base an Open Book proper bound and clasped on a Chief Gules a Lion passant Or.

CREST: On a Wreath of the Colours in front of two Quill Pens in Saltire points downward Azure feathered Or a Herdwick Ram's Head caboshed proper.

SUPPORTERS: On the Dexter side a Bull Gules armed unguled and collared and pendent from the collar a Parnassus Flower Or and on the Sinister side a Dragon Gules collared and pendent from the Collar a Fleurs de Lis Or.

When the arms were designed it was decided to allude to the counties of Cumberland and Westmorland and the county of Lancaster north of the Ribble, as well as to the city and the duchy of Lancaster. The Fess wavy Argent charged with two barrulets wavy Azure in the arms alludes to the river Lune; the two Roses in chief come from the arms of the council of the administrative county of Lancaster, the Open Book in base is a symbol of learning and the Lion passant Or on the Chief comes from the arms of the duchy. The two Quill Pens in Saltire in the crest refer to the learned activities of the university and the Herdwick Ram's Head caboshed comes from the arms of the county of Westmorland. In the supporters the Bull is taken from the Dexter supporter of the arms of the council of the county of Cumberland (and is itself a representative of the Dacre Bull at Naworth), and the Parnassus Flower is also taken from the arms of the council. The Dragon represents the ancient Kingdom of Cumbria which extended over much of the area mentioned, and the Fleurs de Lis is taken from the arms of the city of Lancaster.

Appendix (v)

PERSONS ADMITTED TO HONORARY DEGREES

18 November 1964

DOCTOR OF LAWS
*Field Marshal Lord Slim
The Right Honourable Harold Wilson
Sir Noel Hall
County Alderman Sir Alfred Bates
*County Alderman Mrs. K. M. Fletcher

19 July 1967

DOCTOR OF LETTERS
His Grace the Lord Archbishop of York
   (The Most Reverend and Right Honourable Dr. Frederick Donald
   Coggan)
The Right Honourable the Lord Morris of Grasmere

DOCTOR OF SCIENCE
Professor Russell Lincoln Ackoff
*Professor Dame Kathleen Lonsdale

DOCTOR OF LAWS
*The Right Honourable the Earl Peel
Sir Donald Stokes

15 July 1968

DOCTOR OF LAWS
Professor Ota Sik
   (Director of the Institute of Economics of the Czechoslovak Academy
   of Science)

DOCTOR OF SCIENCE
Professor Harry Godwin, F.R.S.
   (Professor of Botany, University of Cambridge)
Professor Sir Nevill Mott, F.R.S.
   (Cavendish Professor of Experimental Physics, University of Cambridge)
Professor Ronald George Wreyford Norrish, F.R.S.
   (Former Professor of Physical Chemistry, University of Cambridge)

4 July 1970

DOCTOR OF LETTERS

Sir Arthur Bliss
James Cameron, Esq.
Gabriel Epstein, Esq.
Professor W. J. M. Mackenzie
The Right Honourable George Woodcock
Professor R. C. Zechner

8 July 1972

DOCTOR OF LAWS

The Right Honourable The Earl of Derby

DOCTOR OF LETTERS

M. Jean-Louis Barrault, Officer of the Legion of Honour
The Right Reverend Trevor Huddleston, Suffragan Bishop of Stepney
Mr. Peter Ustinov

DOCTOR OF SCIENCE

* Professor Cornelius Lanczos
* Deceased.

Appendix (vi)

INAUGURAL LECTURES, 1965–71

27 January 1965	Professor G. Manley "This North-Western Environment"	Environmental Studies
10 February 1965	Professor P. A. Reynolds "The Shape of World Politics"	Politics
12 March 1965	Professor S. G. Sturmey "The Skills of Economists"	Economics
12 May 1965	Professor B. H. P. Rivett "The Concepts of Operational Research"	Operational Research
26 May 1965	Professor W. A. Murray "Why was Duncan's Blood Golden?"	English
16 June 1965	Professor T. E. Lawrenson "The Place of the Theatre in the Modern Humanities"	French Studies
1 November 1965	Professor E. R. Dobbs "Quanta and Quarks"	Physics
10 November 1965	Professor A. H. Woolrych "Puritanism, Democracy and the English Revolution"	History
24 November 1965	Professor E. H. Lloyd "The Relevance of Mathematics"	Mathematics
23 February 1966	Professor F. N. Sibley "Philosophy and the Arts"	Philosophy
18 May 1966	Professor M. M. Willcock "The Poet of the Iliad"	Classics
1 March 1967	Professor G. M. Jenkins "Systems and their Optimization"	Systems Engineering
12 January 1966	Professor C. D. Pigott (No title)	Biological Sciences
25 January 1967	Professor R. J. Lawrence "Marketing, Better or Worse"	Marketing
26 April 1967	Professor A. B. Clegg "The Chemistry of Sub-Atomic Particles"	Nuclear Physics
8 November 1967	Professor W. T. W. Potts "Fish, with a Pinch of Salt"	Biological Sciences
13 December 1967	Professor A. I. MacBean "Economics and the World Food Problem"	Economics

17 January 1968	Professor Sir Cecil Parrott "Slavs or Slaves?"	Russian and Soviet Studies
14 February 1968	Professor N. Smart "The Principles and Meaning of the Study of Religion"	Religious Studies
20 March 1968	Professor A. M. Ross "Teaching and the Organization of Learning"	Educational Research
8 May 1968	Professor H. J. Perkin "The History of the Future"	Social History
30 October 1968	Professor M. G. Simpson "A Cooks' Tour"	Operational Research
19 February 1969	Professor J. R. Perrin "Financial Control: the Next Twenty Years"	Wolfson Professor of Financial Control
5 March 1969	Professor A. Mercer "Operational Marketing Research"	Operational Research
7 May 1969	Professor K. J. Morgan "Science or Art? A Personal View of Organic Chemistry"	Chemistry
3 December 1969	Professor P. B. Checkland "Systems and Science, Industry and Innovation"	Systems Engineering
11 February 1970	Professor S. Shimmin "Behaviour in Organizations: Problems and Perspective"	Behaviour in Organizations
11 March 1970	Professor B. Higman "The Organization of Intelligence"	Computer Studies
13 May 1970	Professor P. Nailor "Medes and Persians"	Politics
14 October 1970	Professor M. J. French "The Engineering Animal"	Engineering
18 November 1970	Professor A. Talbot "Approximation Theory or A Miss is Better Than a Mile"	Mathematics
21 April 1971	Professor W. M. Fairbairn "Demons, Chinamen and Mr. Mark"	Theoretical Physics
12 May 1971	Professor C. W. Clenshaw "Mathematics by Numbers"	Mathematics

Appendix (vii)

THE UNIVERSITY OF LANCASTER'S BUILDING PROGRAMME, 1964–74

Name of building (listed by architect)	Completion dates of phases	Cost (£)[1] as stated in the 1973–4 building programme	Usable area (sq. ft.)
Messrs. Shepheard and Epstein (London) (G. Epstein, P. Shepheard et al.)			
University House	August 1966	176,462	21,300
Bowland College and residence	College September 1966 Residence September 1968	989,984	109,800
Lonsdale College, residence and Assistant Staff House	College September 1967 Residence September 1969	738,436	91,000
Great Hall complex (including the Nuffield Theatre Studio and the Jack Hylton Music Rooms)	Fine Arts September 1968 Great Hall September 1969	371,734	34,400
Furness College	College September 1970	431,198	47,200
Grizedale College and residence } Pendle College and residence	September 1974	988,243	85,000
Pavilion	December 1967	28,733	2,100
Boiler house	August 1966 and phases to December 1971	283,786	—
Shops and banks	With Bowland residence and Furness College	See under Bowland and Furness	See under Bowland and Furness
Site works (including pedestrian spine) and landscaping	From 1966 onwards	1,042,481	—
Recreation Fields	From 1967 onwards	74,539	—
Messrs. Tom Mellor and Partners (Lytham St. Anne's and Milnthorpe) (T. Mellor, J. Ashworth, K. Hunt)			
Library and Bookshop	September 1966, July 1969, January 1971	548,649	57,200

Name of building	Completion dates of phases	Cost (£)[1] as stated in the 1973–4 building programme	Usable area (sq. ft.)
Physics and Chemistry	September 1967, September 1968, July 1970	1,136,586	95,100
Computer Building	December 1966, September 1967	69,958	5,800
Indoor Recreation Centre	December 1967, February 1971, July 1973	158,469	23,700
Environmental Sciences and Biological Sciences	September 1969, December 1970	948,177	71,800
Learning Aids Building	June 1969	60,547	5,700
Gillow House	August 1974, May 1975	832,101	55,500
Taylor Young and Partners (Manchester) (Haydn W. Smith)			
Cartmel College and residence	September 1968, March 1970	779,486	101,700
Central workshop and Service Station	July 1969	68,771	10,800
Furness College residence and Fylde College Phase 1 residence	September 1969, September 1970	372,541	63,820
Fylde College and residence Phase 2	March 1971, December 1973	595,115	64,400
Engineering	September 1972	513,350	54,700
Cassidy and Ashton Partnership (Preston) (G. W. G. Cassidy)			
Chaplaincy Centre	March 1970	124,000	14,500
Lancashire County Council (Preston) (Roger Booth, County Architect)			
County College	September 1969	529,000	62,400
C. B. Pearson & Son (Lancaster)			
Conversion to St. Leonard's House	1964 and 1966	230,061	—

[1] Not included are telephones (£79,000); minor works; conversions at St. Leonard's House and Bailrigg, and subsequent re-conversions; the playgroup/crèche (£24,000); or various miscellaneous items.

Appendix (viii)

SELECTED FINANCIAL INFORMATION 1964-73[1]

	Year ending 31 July 1965 £	Year ending 31 July 1966 £	Year ending 31 July 1967 £	Year ending 31 July 1968 £	Year ending 31 July 1969 £	Year ending 31 July 1970 £	Year ending 31 July 1971 £	Year ending 31 July 1972 £	Year ending 31 July 1973 £
Turnover for year (general revenue account, excluding College revenue accounts)	355,641	633,430	984,732	1,480,653	1,882,386	2,308,913	2,911,142	3,233,844	3,854,773
Expenditure:									
Salaries of teaching and comparable staff	110,196	222,012	343,686	440,138	573,702	819,771	1,086,444	1,265,056	1,538,561
Salaries of assistant staff	17,849	36,599	63,707	91,241	112,939	157,226	196,835	219,977	277,492
Library (including salaries and books)	28,544	53,575	65,231	82,186	127,397	147,669	191,654	210,671	217,869
Student facilities and amenities[2]	8,819	12,812	32,454	47,695	50,474	50,097	59,864	72,018	92,575
Income:									
Recurrent grant	196,025	359,975	657,176	993,422	1,152,222	1,324,386	1,661,758	2,072,528	2,869,138
Other Parliamentary Grants[3]	26,794	52,017	26,549	47,036	133,085	208,673	355,122	461,302	238,918
Grants for special researches	24,428	37,837	61,482	108,896	136,968	166,858	189,963	209,679	267,269
Students' fees	23,815	55,109	84,094	127,661	179,509	231,888	257,969	245,172	252,353
Donations	17,000	17,000	17,000	20,826	34,986	33,677	38,098	27,130	52,916
Grants from local Authorities[4]	97,718	97,927	95,121	96,510	95,343	89,193	78,901	77,301	31,556
Assets:									
Land, buildings and equipment (cumulative)	844,084	2,153,026	4,399,395	7,368,985	10,405,175	12,581,175	13,930,485	15,304,686	16,231,197

[1] For complete information, see *University of Lancaster, Accounts* (1964-73), published each December.

[2] Includes careers and counselling, catering loss and subsidy, accommodation office, students' health service, and physical education and grounds,

[3] Includes salary supplementation, rates, and other ear-marked grants (except those from the research councils).

Appendix (ix)

THE USES OF THE APPEAL FUND, 1964–71

(1) Residential and other accommodation for students   £   £

   *(a) The County College (a residential College for over 300
students)   529,000

   (b) Lonsdale Annexe, providing residential accommodation
for an additional 129 students   163,166
                                                         692,166

(2) Cultural and welfare facilities

   †(a) The Nuffield Theatre Studio and Workshop, primarily
for experiments in ancient and modern drama (including
£27,000 for necessary equipment)   107,162

   †(b) The Jack Hylton Music Rooms   60,043

   †(c) The Fine Arts Studios, for creative work in painting,
sculpture and pottery   32,134

   *(d) The Chaplaincy Centre, providing two chapels, rooms
for the Jewish Community, 2 flats for resident chaplains,
common rooms, etc.   147,000

   (e) Contribution towards the Duke's Playhouse   13,000

   (f) Contribution towards the support of a resident quintet   3,810
                                                         363,149

(3) *Contributions towards establishment of Professorships,
Fellowships, and Departments, including Marketing and
Systems Engineering   343,822

(4) Supplementing "shortfalls" in annual Treasury grants to
provide urgently-needed additional facilities and amenities   £   £

   (a) Telephone exchange   4,000

   (b) Biological Sciences Field Station   3,196

   (c) Landscaping   4,962

   (d) Lonsdale College   163,260

   (e) Engineering project laboratory   35,000

   (f) Additional car parks   6,831

   (g) Additional equipment for the computer   5,600
                                                         222,849

(5) Recreational facilities (indoor and outdoor)

   *(a) Indoor Recreation Centre (phases I and II), consisting
of a large and a small sports hall, four squash courts,
weight-training room and a sauna bath   141,557

   (b) Recreation fields (phase I), providing 2 soccer pitches,
2 rugger pitches, 2 all-weather playing areas, 1 cricket
pitch   35,246

(c) Pavilion	5,111	
*(d) Miscellaneous sports facilities	6,930	
		188,844

(6) To provide various revenue-earning commercial facilities on the Bailrigg site

(a) Coffee bar at the east end of Alexandra Square	2,000	
(b) University bookshop and associated coffee bar	24,600	
‡(c) Banking and shopping facilities in Alexandra Square	83,583	
(d) Garages and workshops for staff and students	9,014	
(e) Petrol service station	8,498	
		127,695

(7) Providing 56 flats at Bailrigg for members of staff in Bowland, Lonsdale, Cartmel, Furness and Fylde Colleges — 155,212

(8) Special Researches

*(a) Earmarked donations	90,557	
(b) Local Authorities Research Fund	30,000	
		120,557

(9) Supplementing various Treasury grants for specific projects to provide better or larger facilities — 68,277

(10) *Prizes, Studentships and Scholarships — 61,669

(11) †The creation of a fund for the purchase of works of art and for the general improvement of the environment by landscaping, creation of gardens, planting, etc. — 41,500

(12) Purchase of additional land at Hazelrigg (152 acres) for long-term University developments — 37,462

(13) †Miscellaneous minor expenditures — 31,100

(14) *Turner and Newall Travel Fund (used to help with the expenses of academic staff when away from Lancaster at academic conferences or engaged in research) — 30,000

	2,484,302
Reserved for other developments in the immediate future	94,689
TOTAL	2,578,991

* Earmarked donations.
† Part of the cost met from earmarked donations.
‡ Includes expenditure met from rents received in advance from the banks (put in to effect reconciliation with the building programme).

Appendix (x)

UNIVERSITY OF LANCASTER: STUDENT NUMBERS, 1964-1973

	1964-5	1965-6	1966-7	1967-8	1968-9	1969-70	1970-1	1971-2	1972-3	1973-4
Undergraduates in Lancaster				1,200	1,618	1,949	2,291	2,330	2,352	2,432
in France				29	34	51	62	43	39	40
occasional				4	12	4	5	8	13	24
Junior Year						65	82	66	64	90
Sub-total	294	700	1,039	1,233	1,664	2,069	2,440	2,447	2,468	2,586
Graduates in Lancaster					272	338	419	517	561	591
elsewhere					38	25	32	26	25	18
Sub-total	34	69	152	186	310	363	451	543	586	609
Total full-time Students	328	769	1,191	1,419	1,974	2,432	2,891	2,990	3,054	3,195
Part-time graduate students				36	57	64	113	150	156	221
Staff registered for higher degrees				12	20	23	24	28	20	36

Appendix (x)—continued

		1964–5	1965–6	1966–7	1967–8	1968–9	1969–70	1970–1	1971–2	1972–3	1973–4
Diploma students									120	10	10
Total full-time and part-time students		338	776	1,225	1,443	2,051	2,519	3,029	3,188	3,240	3,462
Total full-time students at Lancaster						1,902	2,356	2,798	2,941	3,000	3,147
Admissions to first year		294	423	365	496	808	749	848	804	813	901
Undergraduates men		174	425	667	791	1,065	1,319	1,586	1,594	1,598	
women		120	275	372	442	599	750	854	853	870	
Graduate students men		31	65	146	177	277	327	401	481		
women		3	4	6	9	33	36	50	62		
Proportion of women full-time students	%	37	36	32	32	32	32	31	31		
Full-time teaching staff		41	84	130	160	188	250	292	308	348	377

Appendix (xi)

ACADEMIC DEVELOPMENTS, 1964–1975

	Year of origin (customarily October)
Accounting and Finance (formerly called Financial Control)	1968
Arabic and Islamic Studies	1973
Art and the Environment (formerly Visual Arts)	1973
Behaviour in Organizations	1969
Biochemistry	1974
Biological Sciences (formerly called Biology)	1964
Central and South-Eastern European Studies (see under Russian and Soviet Studies)	1971
Chemistry	1964
Classics (including Archaeology from 1973)	1965
Computer Studies	1969
Ecology	1974
Economics	1964
Educational Research (formerly Higher Education)	1967
Engineering	1969
English (and Linguistics)	1964
Environmental Sciences (formerly called Environmental Studies)	1964
European Studies	1974
French Studies	1964
Geography	1975
German Studies	1971
History	1964
History of Science	1966
Independent Studies	1973
Italian Studies	1974
Marketing	1965
Mathematics	1964
Mediaeval Studies	1974
Music	1968
Operational Research	1964
Philosophy	1964
Physics	1964
Politics	1964
Psychology	1972

Appendix (xi)—*continued*

	Year of origin (customarily October)
Religious Studies	1967
Russian and Soviet Studies (formerly called Russian)	1964
Social Administration	1974
Sociology	1969
Systems Engineering	1965
Theatre Studies	1972

Appendix (xii)

CENTRAL ADMINISTRATIVE STRUCTURE AS AT NOVEMBER 1973

CHANCELLOR
PRO-CHANCELLOR ———— DEPUTY PRO-CHANCELLORS
VICE-CHANCELLOR
  ├─PRO-VICE-
     CHANCELLORS — with particular responsibility for
        (1) Academic affairs
        (2) Administrative function
        (3) Student & College affairs

  ├─ACADEMIC
    ├──Heads of departments
    ├──Directors of academic
        operations, e.g. Music
                 Nuffield Theatre Studio
    ├──College principals Independent Studies   Report
    └──Librarian   European Studies   via the
                 Language Services Unit Senate
                 Indoor Recreation Centre
                 Visual Arts Centre
                 North-West Regional Studies Centre

  ├─ADMINISTRATION—CHIEF OFFICERS
  ├── *University Secretary*
     ├──Building Development Officer
     ├──Controller of Catering
     ├──Establishment and Legal Officer
     ├──Finance Officer and data processing
     ├──Administrative Services Officer
     └──Work Study Officer
  ├── *Academic Registrar*
     ├──Deputy Academic Registrar (Senate, degree congregations, etc.)
     └──Senior administrative assistants { 1. Graduate studies / 2. Boards of studies, timetable, etc.}
  ├── *Secretary for Student and College Affairs* (functions include responsibility for athletics, examinations and discipline)
     ├──Undergraduate Admissions Officer
     ├──Undergraduate record office
     ├──Accommodation and Conference Officer
     ├──Careers Officers
     └──(Medical Centre)
  └─OFFICERS REPORTING DIRECT
    ├──Systems Investigator
    ├──Press and Information Officer
    ├──Administrator of the School of Management and Organizational Sciences
    ├──Student Representative Council
    └──Secretaries of committees of which Vice-Chancellor is chairman

Appendix (xiii)   BACHELOR OF ARTS DEGREES, 1967-1968

Major Course	1967 HONOURS I	II(i)	II(ii)	III	Pass	Aegrotat	Fail	Total	1968 HONOURS I	II(i)	II(ii)	III	Pass	Aegrotat	Fail	Total
Biological Sciences									3	10	11	5				29
Chemistry + Physics									4	8	11	5	3			31
Classics										1	2	1				4
Classics (combined major)																
Classical + Mediaeval Studies																
Classics + Religious Studies																
Computer Studies									2	4	32	5	1			44
Economics + Financial Control		9	16	13	2		1	41								
Economics + Mathematics																
Economics + Maths + Operational Research																
Economics + Politics	1	3		1	1			6		2	7	2				11
Engineering																
English		3	27	8	1	1		40		13	25	10	2	1	1	52
English + French Studies			1	2				3		2	4					6
English + Philosophy			2	2				4				3				3
Environmental Sciences		2	4	2	2			10		3	8	4	2		1	18
Financial Control																
French Studies		10	22	5	1			38		7	13	1		1	1	23
Greek + Philosophy				1				1			1					1
History	1	11	32	10	1			55	14		25		1			40
History + Philosophy		11		3				14		5	6	1				12
History + Politics		1	1					1		1	1					2
Latin + English				1				1		3	5					8
Latin + French Studies								7	1	2	3	5	3			14
Mathematics	1				2											
Mathematics + Operational Research																
Mathematics + Philosophy										1						1
Modern History + Economics		3						5	1	2	6					8
Philosophy + Religious Studies	3	9		6	1			19	1	2	3	3	1			10
Physics																
Applied Physics									3	3			1			7
Physics									3	2	7	4			1	17
Theoretical Physics									1		2	1				4
Physics of the Environment																
Physics + Philosophy	1	1	7	6			1	16	5	7		3	1			16
Politics																
Politics + History + Philosophy										1						
Politics + Philosophy	1		1	1	1			3		2	1	1				4
Politics + Religious Studies											1	1				1
Religious Studies																
Religious Studies + Sociology																
Russian and Soviet Studies																
Sociology																
							2	366	16	91	184	55	16	1	2	366

Major Course	1969 HONOURS								1970 HONOURS							
	I	II(i)	II(ii)	III	Pass	Aegrotat	Fail	Total	I	II(i)	II(ii)	III	Pass	Aegrotat	Fail	Total
Biological Sciences	1	5	13	1	1		1	22		5	12	4				21
Chemistry	4	8	9	9	3		3	36	2	4	7	5	3			21
Chemistry + Physics									1		3					4
Classics		4	2					6								
Classics (combined major)																
Classical + Mediaeval Studies																
Classics + Religious Studies																
Computer Studies																
Economics																
Economics + Financial Control	1	5	17	3	3			29		11	24	5	3		2	45
Economics + Mathematics									1	1	2					4
Economics + Maths + Operational Research																
Economics + Politics	2	2		1	1			6	1	1	2					4
Engineering		1	6	3				10								
English	1	11	17	5				34	2	27	35	6	1		1	72
English + French Studies		1						1			2					2
English + Philosophy	1	1	1					2		1	1	1				3
Environmental Sciences	1	2	8	6	1			18		4	7	3				14
Financial Control																
French Studies		10	10	2	1			23		10	8	4	1		1	24
Greek + Philosophy																
History	1	10	26	1		1	1	40		28	28	1				57
History + Philosophy										1						1
History + Politics		5	6	1	1			13		10	14	2				26
Latin + English											2					2
Latin + French Studies											2					2
Mathematics	2	4		9				15	2	4	10	2			3	21
Mathematics + Operational Research										2	2					4
Mathematics + Philosophy																
Modern History + Economics		1		2				3								
Philosophy	1	5		2				8		3	3	1	1			8
Philosophy + Religious Studies										1	2					3
Physics																
Applied Physics		2	2	1				5		3	3	4	1			11
Physics	4	2	10	5				21	2	3	4	4				13
Theoretical Physics																
Physics of the Environment		1	3	1	1			6				1				1
Physics + Philosophy											2					2
Politics		2		1				3		9	22	1	1		3	36
Politics + History + Philosophy		6	7	5	1			19								
Politics + Philosophy									1		2					3
Politics + Religious Studies									1	1	2					4
Religious Studies	2	2						4	1	4	3		1			9
Religious Studies + Sociology																
Russian and Soviet Studies																
Sociology									1	3	1					5
TOTAL	14	85	147	58	13	1	6	324	13	132	202	47	16	1	11	422

BACHELOR OF ARTS DEGREES, 1971–1972

Major Course	1971 HONOURS I	II(i)	II(ii)	III	1971 Pass	Aegrotat	Fail	Total	1972 HONOURS I	II(i)	II(ii)	III	1972 Pass	Aegrotat	Fail	Total
Biological Sciences	3	5	18	7	1			34	1	14	22	4	1		2	44
Chemistry	6	9	19	6	3		1	44	3	5	10	10	4		2	34
Chemistry + Physics	1	4	1	2	1			9	1		1					2
Classics										1						1
Classics (combined major)																
Classical + Mediaeval Studies																
Classics + Religious Studies			1					1								
Computer Studies	2	5	3	3	3			16	2	7	12	10	1		4	36
Economics + Financial Control	2	17	34	18		3		74	3	16	35	8	4		2	68
Economics + Mathematics Control											2					2
Economics + Maths + Operational Research										1	1	1				3
Economics + Politics	1							6	1							1
Engineering					1			6			6	1				7
English	1	30	48	10	9		3	101	2	25	45	13	7		2	94
English + French Studies	1		1					2			2	1	1	1		5
English + Philosophy		4						4			2	1	1			4
Environmental Sciences	3		10	4	2			19	2	5	8	3			2	20
Financial Control	1							1		3	4	5	1			13
French Studies	1	21	24	2	1			49	2	15	36	3	1	1	1	59
Greek + Philosophy			1					1	1							1
History	3	37	53	6		1	1	101	7	37	34	3		1	1	83
History + Philosophy		9	9	1				19			1	1				2
History + Politics		1	1					2		5	5	1				11
Latin + English										1	2	1				4
Latin + French Studies										2						2
Mathematics	1	10	8	2	4			25	3		6	3	5			17
Mathematics + Operational Research																
Mathematics + Philosophy										1	2					3
Modern History + Economics	2	2	11	5	3		1	24		1	1					2
Philosophy										4	5	2				11
Philosophy + Religious Studies			1					1	1		1		1			2
Physics																
Applied Physics	2	3	3	1				9	2	1	2	1	3			9
Physics	2	4	7	3	1			17	1	5	5	5	2		1	18
Theoretical Physics				3				3		2		1				3
Physics of the Environment										1	2	1				4
Physics + Philosophy											1	1				2
Politics	3	23	45	6	2			79	3	28	20	2	2		1	56
Politics + History + Philosophy	1							1								
Politics + Philosophy		4						4				1				1
Politics + Religious Studies																
Religious Studies		10	7	3	2			22		8	16				1	25
Religious Studies + Sociology					2				2							2
Russian and Soviet Studies	1	5	3	1				10		2	3	1			1	7
Sociology		5	3	1	1			10	2	10	10	1		2	1	26

_1973_

Major Course	HONOURS				Pass	Aegrotat	Fail	Total
	I	II(i)	II(ii)	III				
Biological Sciences	4	13	24	6	1			48
Chemistry	2	8	8	14	3		2	37
Chemistry + Physics		1		1	1			3
Classics				1				1
Classics (combined major)	1	3	2					6
Classical + Mediaeval Studies		1						1
Classics + Religious Studies								
Computer Studies	3	7	16	6	3			35
Economics	2	15	20	7	2		3	49
Economics + Financial Control		2	1	2				5
Economics + Mathematics			1					1
Economics + Maths + Operational Research								
Economics + Politics		1	2					3
Engineering		2	6					8
English		32	50	11	4		3	100
English + French Studies		1						1
English + Philosophy		2	1					3
Environmental Sciences	2	8	15	7	3		1	36
Financial Control		2	11	2	1			16
French Studies		16	25	1	1			43
Greek + Philosophy						1		1
History	2	37	33	3	3			78
History + Philosophy		1						1
History + Politics		5	8	2				15
Latin + English								
Latin + French Studies		2	2					4
Mathematics	2	3	4	3	3			15
Mathematics + Operational Research								
Mathematics + Philosophy	2		3	1				6
Modern History + Economics		1						1
Philosophy		7	3	1	2			13
Philosophy + Religious Studies				1			1	2
Physics								
Applied Physics		4	3	3				10
Physics		3	6	6	7		1	23
Theoretical Physics	2	4	4		1			11
Physics of the Environment		1		1				2
Physics + Philosophy	1		1					2
Politics	1	17	31	4	2		4	59
Politics + History + Philosophy								
Politics + Philosophy			1					1
Politics + Religious Studies		1						1
Religious Studies	1	8	3		1		1	14
Religious Studies + Sociology		1						1
Russian and Soviet Studies		1	4	1	1		1	8
Sociology	5	21	24	2	1			53
TOTAL	30	233	320	87	40	1	17	728

Appendix (xiv)

STUDENT WASTAGE, 1964–73[1]

	Admitted		Finalists								Total	Loss (over 3 years)	Loss as % of entry
	Pt I	Pt II	1967	1968	1969	1970	1971	1972	1973	1974			
1964	294		262	2							264	30	10·2
1965	423			362	21						383	40	9·4
1966	365				296	39	1		1		337	28	7·7
1967	493	1			1	368	69	4	1		443	51	10·3
1968	808	4				4	604	88	3		699	113	13·9
1969	752	6					6	563	85 re-sits 3 finalist 1 re-entry 1973 finish in 1975, 1		658	97	12·8

	Admitted	Finalists				Total	Loss (over 3 years)	Loss as % of entry
1970	848	8	re-sits 11 finalists 89 finish in 1975 3	613	8	725	131	15·4
1971	804	10	re-sit 1 600	8				
1972		19	finalist 17					

Successful candidates	262	364	318	411	680	663	711	
Fail	2	2	5	11	12	21	17	
Allowed re-sit	3	5	2	6	4	11	15	
Other reasons for repeat	—	—	1	3	—	—	2	
Total finalists	267	371	326	431	696	695	745	722 (estimate)

[1] The figures quoted should be compared with national figures. The U.G.C. in its publication *Enquiry into Student Progress* (1968), showed for example, that the figure for Great Britain for 1965-6 (all reasons, all periods of study) was 13·3%, with a range from Cambridge's 3·4% to Loughborough's 34% (Table 57, p.70).

Appendix (xv)

CHOICE OF FREE NINTH UNITS, 1972–3 and 1973–4

Major course	Number registered for major		Number registered for F.N.U. in major department		Total number of F.N.U.s taken in department	
	1972–3	1973–4	1972–3	1973–4	1972–3	1973–4
Biological Sciences	50	59			19	15
Chemistry	32	40			11	8
Economics	68	52	3	25	4	30
English	78	97	13	6	41	30
Env. Sciences	44	43			10	5
French Studies	39	44	1	9	6	14
History	72	81	13	9	33	22
Mathematics	19	23		1	2	1
Philosophy	26	15	1	2	28	12
Physics	32	41				
Politics	61	50	10	6	39	24
Rel. Studies	28	36	2	9	15	21
Russian	8	6	1	3	22	19
Computer Studies	28	26			5	9
Fin. Control	9	5				
Engineering	33	27				
Sociology	48	33	6	2	28	16
Acc. & Finance	9	25			2	
Chem/Phys.	1					
Econ/Poli.	4		1 (Econ)			
Linguistics		4				4
Classics						65
English/French	2	6	1 (Fren)			
English/Phil.	2	6				

Major Course	Number registered for major		Number registered for F.N.U. in major department		Total number of F.N.U.s taken in department	
	1972–3	1973–4	1972–3	1973–4	1972–3	1973–4
E.S./Phys.	4	2				
History/Phil.	1					
History/Poli.	9	11	1 (Hist)	1 (Hist)		
Latin/Engl.	1		1 (Clas)			
Latin/French	2	1	2 (Clas)			
Math/Phil.	1	2	1 (Phil)			
Hist/Econ.	3	4		1 (Econ)		
Phil/Phys.	1	2				
Phil/R.St.	2	2				
Poli/Hist/Phil.		1				
Poli/Phil.	2	2		1 (Poli)		
Grk/R.St		1				
Econ/F.Cl.	3	9				
Econ/Math	1	2		2		
R.St/Socl.	4	1		1 (R.St)		
Math/Op.R.	3	3				
Latin/Greek	5	3	3 (Clas)			
Poli/Socl.	4	2				
Czech/Ling	1					
Math/E.S.	1					
Ec/M/OR	3					
Fr.St/Russ.		3				
Latin		2				
Poli/R.St.		1				
Engl/Ling.		3		1 (Engl)		
Fren/Ling.		1				
Phil/Socl.		1				
Fren/Germ		2				
Czech						3

2J*

Appendix (xv) continued

FREE NINTH UNITS TAKEN WHICH ARE UNATTACHED TO MAJOR COURSES

Major Course	Total number of F.N.U.s taken in department	
	1972–3	*1973–4*
Behaviour in Organizations	15	14
C.S.E.E.		5
Classics	58	
Czech Studies	10	
Elementary Maths	1	1
German		2
History of Architecture		
Hist. of Science	35	25
Ind. Studies	31	10
Italian	15	28
Law	85	84
Mathematical Methods	1	1
D. M. Craig's Courses	36	57
Music	22	21
Operational Research	6	2
Visual Arts		57
Yugoslav Studies	6	1

Appendix (xvi)

CHANGES OF MAJOR SUBJECT AT END OF PART I, SUMMERS 1972 and 1973

Subject	No. stating as intended major 1972	1973	Loss 1972	1973	Gain 1972	1973	Total taking Part II 1972	1973
Biological Sciences	58	59	9	8	2	7	51	58
Chemistry	49	51	18	14	5	3	36	40
Classics and	6	2	5	0	0	1	1	3
Latin and Greek					6		6	
Economics	70	55	34	24	21	24	57	55
English	84	78	23	20	43	40	104	98
Env. Sciences	42	41	11	9	10	12	41	44
French Studies	47	50	15	17	9	13	41	46
History	52	50	18	14	47	47	81	83
Mathematics	35	25	20	7	3	5	18	23
Philosophy	10	5	6	4	10	9	14	10
Physics (App.)	13		6		4		11	
Physics (Phys.)	32	54	19	18	14	5	27	41
Physics (Theoretical)	2		0		14		16	
Politics	32	34	17	14	48	26	63	46
Rel. Studies	20	18	12	4	6	23	14	37
Russian (3rd year)	3	2	0	1	0	2	3	3
Russian (4th year)	17	12	4	8	0	0	13	4
Computer Studies	38	26	12	4	15	3	41	25
Financial Control and Acc. Fin.	20	18	10	4	6	16	16	30
Engineering	20	24	9	5	3	8	14	27
Sociology	24	29	8	14	35	18	51	33
Chem./Physics	9	2	5	2	0	0	4	0
Econ./Maths/O.R.	13	1	11	1	1	0	3	0

Appendix (xvi)—continued

Subject	No. stating as intended major		Loss		Gain		Total taking Part II	
	1972	1973	1972	1973	1972	1973	1972	1973
Econ./Politics	12	3	9	1	6	0	9	2
English/French	16	19	13	15	0	1	3	5
English/Phil.	22	20	21	15	1	2	2	7
Env. Sciences/Phys.	11	6	10	3	1	1	2	4
Greek/Phil.	1		1		0		0	0
History/Phil.	8	2	8	2	0	0	0	0
History/Politics	41	28	31	21	6	3	16	10
Latin/English	2	1	1	1	0	0	1	0
Latin/French	4	2	1	1	0	0	1	1
Maths/Phil.	2	4	1	4	0	2	1	2
Mod. History/Econ.	7	14	5	11	1	1	3	4
Phil./Phys.	3	4	1	3	0	1	2	2
Phil./Rel. Studies	4	5	4	2	2	0	2	3
Pol./Hist./Phil.	5	8	5	7	0	0	0	1
Pol./Phil.	8	5	6	5	0	2	2	2
Class + Med. Studies	1	1	1	1	1	0	2	0
Econ. + Fin. Control	8	32	5	27	2	4	5	9
Econ. + Maths	2	2	1	1	0	1	1	2
Rel. Studies + Socl.	2	8	0	6	1	0	3	2
Maths + O.R.	—	4	—	3	6	2	6	3
History + Russian		1		1		0		0
French + Russian		3		3		2		2
Latin		2		1		1		2
Pol. + Rel. Th.		2		1		0		1
Engl. + Ling.		3		2		2		3

N.B.   The figures under "loss" include people who withdrew, returned to Part I and other causes.

Select Bibliography

I. BOOKS

Abbott, Joan. (1971).
Student Life in a Class Society. Pergamon

Aitken, Robert. (1966).
Administration of a University. University of London Press

Armytage, W. H. G. (1955).
Civic Universities; aspects of a British tradition. Ernest Benn

Ashby, Eric. (1970).
Masters and Scholars: Reflections on the Rights and Responsibilities of Students.
Oxford University Press

Ashby, Eric and Anderson, Mary. (1970).
The Rise of the Student Estate in Britain. Macmillan

Axelrod, Joseph *et al.* (1969).
Search for Relevance: the campus in crisis. Jossey-Bass, Inc.

Bacon, F. (1605).
The Advancement of Learning

Beloff, Michael. (1968).
The Plateglass Universities. Secker & Warburg

Berdahl, R. O. (1959).
British Universities and the State. University of California Press and Cambridge
University Press

Bettenson, E. M. (1971).
The University of Newcastle-upon-Tyne: A Historical Introduction 1834–1971.
University of Newcastle-upon-Tyne

Birks, Tony. (1972).
Building the New Universities. (Photographs by Michael Holford.)
David & Charles

Blaine, G. B. and McArthur, C. C. (1971).
Emotional Problems of the Student. Butterworth

Bligh, Donald A. (1972).
What's the Use of Lectures?. Penguin

Brosan, G., Carter, C., Layard, R., Venables, P. and Williams, G. (1971).
Patterns and Policies in Higher Education. Penguin Education Special

Burkhardt, G. Norman.
The Functions and Methods of Universities: A Personal and Mainly Retrospective View.
Clayton Memorial Lecture & Presidents' Address

Butcher, H. J. and Rudd, E. (Editors). (1972).
Contemporary Problems in Higher Education. McGraw-Hill

Butterfield, H. (1962).
The Universities and Education Today (Lindsay Memorial Lectures, 1961).
Routledge & Kegan Paul

CAFD. (April 1972).
*The Craig Affair: The background to the case of Dr David Craig and others,
University of Lancaster.* Council for Academic Freedom & Democracy

Caine, Sir Sydney. (1969).
British Universities: Purpose and Prospects. Bodley Head

Christopherson, Derman. (1973).
The University at Work. SCM Press

Cockburn, Alexander & Blackburn, Robin. (1969).
Student Power: Problems, Diagnosis, Action. Penguin Special.

Cullingworth, J. B. (1963).
Housing in Transition; a case study in the City of Lancaster, 1958–62. Heinemann

Daiches, D. (Editor). (1964).
The Idea of a New University: An experiment in Sussex. Andre Deutsch

Dressel, Paul L. and associates. (1971).
Institutional Research in the University: A Handbook. Jossey-Bass Inc.

Driver, Christopher. (1971).
The Exploding University. Hodder & Stoughton

Dundonald, James. (1962).
Letters to a Vice-Chancellor. Edward Arnold

Fielden, John & Lockwood, G. (1973).
Planning and Management in Universities: A Study of British Universities. Chatto &
Windus for Sussex University Press

Gallie, W. B. (1960).
A New University: A. D. Lindsay and the Keele Experiment. Chatto & Windus

y Gasset, José Ortega. (1930).
Mission of the University. Kegan Paul, Trench, Trubner & Company, 1946. (First
published in Spain in 1930)

Gunn, Alexander. (1970).
*The Privileged Adolescent: An outline of the physical and mental problems of the student
society.* Medical & Technical Publishing Company

Halsey, A. H., and Trow, Martin. (1971).
The British Academics. Faber

Hodgkinson, H. and Meeth, L. R. (Editors). (1971).
Power and Authority: Transformation of Campus Government. Jossey-Bass Inc.

James, Lord, of Rusholme. (1966).
The Start of a New University. Manchester Statistical Society

Kerr, Clark. (1963).
The Uses of the University; The Godkin Lectures at Harvard University, 1963.
Harvard University Press

Laub, Julian Martin. (1972).
The College and Community Development: A socio-economic Analysis for Urban and Regional Growth. Praeger Publishers, N.Y.

Lawrenson, T. E. (1957).
Hall of Residence: Saint Anselm Hall in the University of Manchester, 1907–1957.
Manchester University Press

Long, Joyce R. (1968).
Universities and the General Public. Educational Review Occasional Publication No. 3.
University of Birmigham

Malleson, Nicholas. (1965).
A Handbook on British Student Health Services. Pitman Medical Publishing Company.

Michener, James A. (1971).
Kent State: What Happened and Why. Random House Inc. Published in England by
Martin Secker & Warburg

Moberley, Sir Walter. (1949).
The Crisis in the University. SCM Press

Mountford, Sir James. (1966).
British Universities. Oxford University Press

Mountford, Sir James. (1972).
Keele: An Historical Critique. Routledge & Kegan Paul

Newman, John Henry, Cardinal. (1852)
The Idea of a University.

Newsome, Audrey et al. (1973),
Student Counselling in Practice. University of London Press.

Niblett, W. R. (1962).
The Expanding University. Faber

Niblett, W. R. (Editor). (1969).
Higher Education: Demand and Response. Tavistock Press

Open University. (1972).
The Early Development of the Open University: Report of the Vice-Chancellor, January
1969 – December 1970

Oxford, University of. (March 1965).
Report of the Committee on the Structure of the First and Second Public Examinations
(chairman: W. C. Kneale). Supplement No. 3 to the University Gazette (No. 3229)

Oxford, University of. (1966).
Report of Commission of Inquiry (chairman: Lord Franks). Volumes I and II.
Clarendon Press

Oxford, University of. (May 1969).
Report of the Committee on Relations with Junior Members (chairman: H. L. A. Hart).
Supplement No. 7 to the University Gazette, vol. xcix, (No. 3393)

Perkin, H. J. (1969).
Innovation in Higher Education: New Universities in the United Kingdom. (A
Report for the Organization for Economic Cooperation and Development.) OECD

Rashdall, Hastings. (1895).
The Universities of Europe in the Middle Ages. Oxford University Press, 1895. New edition, edited by F. M. Powicke and A. B. Emden, 1936, 3 vols.

Robbins, Lord. (1966).
The University in the Modern World and other papers on higher education. Macmillan

Rooke, Margaret Anne. (1971).
Anarchy and Apathy: Student Unrest 1968–1970. Hamish Hamilton

Ross, Murray G. (Editor) (1966).
New Universities in the Modern World. Macmillan

Ryle, Anthony. (1969).
Student Casualties. Allen Lane, Penguin Press

Scott, John H. MacCallum. (1973).
Dons and Students: British Universities Today. Plume Press

Simpson, M. G. (1972).
Planning University Development. OECD

Sloman, Albert E. (1964).
A University in the Making: The Reith Lectures, 1963. BBC Publications

Snow, Sir Charles P. (1963).
The Two Cultures: and A Second Look. (An expanded version of The Two Cultures and the Scientific Revolution. I, Rede Lecture, 1959; II, The Two Cultures: A Second Look. Cambridge University Press

Thompson, E. P. (1970).
Warwick University Limited: Industry, Management and the Universities. Penguin Education Special

Vice-Chancellors and Principals, Committee of, and the National Union of Students.
Joint Statements. 7 October 1968

Vice-Chancellors and Principals, Committee of, and the Association of University Teachers. (Spring 1969)
Assessment of Undergraduate Performance. Background paper to Universities' Conferences.

Vice-Chancellors and Principals, Committee of. (October 1971)
Student Participation in University Government.

Vice-Chancellors and Principals, Committee of. (February 1972)
Report of an Enquiry into the Use of Academic Staff Time

Yamamoto, K. (Editor). (1968).
The College Student and his Culture: An Analysis. Houghton Mifflin Company

II. HER MAJESTY'S STATIONERY OFFICE

University Development 1947 to 1952, published July 1953; (Chairman: Sir Arthur Trueman), Cmd., 8875

U.G.C.: Report of the Sub-Committee on Halls of Residence; (Chairman: W. R. Niblett), 1957

University Development 1952–1957, published September 1958; (Chairman: Sir Keith Murray), Cmnd., 534

University Teaching Methods: Interim report of the Committee. The Use of Vacations by Students; (Chairman: Sir Edward Hale), April 1963

Committee on Higher Education. Report of the committee appointed by the Prime Minister under the chairmanship of Lord Robbins, 1961–63, published September 23rd, 1963; Cmnd. 2154

Appendix 1. (Robbins); The Demand for Places in Higher Education. Cmnd., 2154–I

Appendix 2(A). (Robbins); Students and their Education. Cmnd. 2154–II

Appendix 2(B). (Robbins); Students and their Education. Cmnd. 2154–II–I

Appendix 3. (Robbins); Teachers in Higher Education. Cmnd. 2154–III

Appendix 4. (Robbins); Administrative, Financial and Economic Aspects of Higher Education. Cmnd. 2154–IV

Appendix 5. (Robbins); Higher Education in Other Countries. Cmnd. 2154–V

Evidence (Robbins): Part I. Written and oral evidence received by the committee.
Volumes:

A. Cmnd. 2154–VI	B. Cmnd. 2154–VII
C. Cmnd. 2154–VIII	D. Cmnd. 2154–IX
E. Cmnd. 2154–X	F. Cmnd. 2154–XI

Evidence (Robbins): Part 2. Documentary evidence submitted to the committee. Cmnd. 2154–XII

University Development 1957–1962, published February 1964; (Chairman: Sir Keith Murray), Cmnd. 2267

Report of the Study Group on the Government of Colleges of Education; (Chairman: T. R. Weaver), D.E.S., 1966

University Development, 1962–67. (Chairman: Sir J. Wolfenden), November 1968. Cmnd. 3820

The Open University. Report of the Planning Committee to the Secretary of State for Education and Science; (Chairman: Sir P. Venables), 1969

Report from the Select Committee on Education and Science, Session 1968–69. Student Relations, Volume I, July 1969; 449–1

U.G.C., Annual Survey, Academic Year 1969–70, presented to Parliament in February 1971, Cmnd. 4593

U.G.C., Annual Survey, Academic Year 1970–71, presented to Parliament in February 1972, Cmnd. 4893

James, Lord of Rusholme. *Teacher Education and Training* (Report by a Committee of Inquiry appointed by the Secretary of State for Education and Science, under the Chairmanship of Lord James of Rusholme), 1972

Report from the Expenditure Committee, Volume I, Further and Higher Education, 8 December 1972, 48–I

Education: A Framework for Expansion, December 1972, Cmnd. 5174

Adult Education: A Plan for Development (Report by a Committee of Inquiry appointed by the Secretary of State for Education and Science under the chairmanship of Sir Lionel Russell), 1973

III. REPORTS ETC. (Published and unpublished)

Andeline, J. & MacFarlane, M.
Vacation Use of the University of Lancaster. M.Sc./Dip. in Op. Res. for the Dept. of Engineering Production, University of Birmingham. (1971–72)

Association of University Teachers.
The Remuneration of University Teachers, 1970–71. London. (August 1971)

Birmingham, University of.
Consultative Document prepared by the Review Body appointed by the Council of the University of Birmingham. (Chairman: J. Grimond). University of Birmingham. (1972)

Birmingham, University of.
Report of the Review Body appointed by the Council of the University of Birmingham.
(Chairman: J. Grimond). University of Birmingham. (1972)

Blin-Stoyle, R. J.
A Report on Undergraduate Teaching Methods and Costs. University of Sussex.
(March 1971)

Booth, C.
A Study of the Socio-Economic Impact of the University on the City of Lancaster.
Dissertation for Certificate of Education at St. John's College, York. (1973)

Capstick, M.
Some Aspects of the Economic Effects of Tourism in the Westmorland Lake District.
University of Lancaster. (1972)

Coles, B.
The Residential Patterns of Staff and Students at S. Martin's College and the
University of Lancaster. Dissertation for Certificate of Education, S. Martin's College,
Lancaster. (1973)

Fulcher, Margaret N.
Aspects of University Development in the Lancaster Sub-region. Dept. of Economics,
University of Lancaster. (December 1967)

Fulcher, M. N., Rhodes, J. & Taylor, J.
The Economy of the Lancaster Sub-region. Dept. of Economics, University of
Lancaster. (July 1966)

Lancaster, University of.
Report of the Taylor Enquiry. University of Lancaster. (8 May–5 July 1972)

Lewes, F. M. M. & Kirkness, Anne.
Exeter—University and City. University of Exeter. (1973)

London, University of.
Final Report of the Committee of Enquiry into the Governance of the University of
London. (Chairman: Lord Murray of Newhaven). University of London. (1972)

Manchester Statistical Society.
"Can we get Higher Education cheaper?". C. F. Carter. (December 1965)

Taylor, J.
Six Study Papers on the North West. Dept. of Economics, University of Lancaster.
(January 1966)

Times Higher Education Supplement.
No. 1, 15 October 1971 (continuing; published weekly).

Warwick, University of.
Report of the Rt. Hon. The Viscount Radcliffe, G.B.E., as to procedures followed in
the University with regard to receiving and retaining of information about political
activities of the staff and of students. (April 1970)

Young, R.
Report on the Policies and Planning of Stirling University from 1966–1973 made to the
University Court on 22 October 1973

IV. ARTICLES

The Architects' Journal
Volume 156, No. 29, 19 July 1972, pp. 114–166. *"Prospect of Lancaster"*, *"Morecambe,
a suitable case for treatment"*, *"Lakeland, is this the bliss of solitude?"*

Daedalus
Volume 97, No. 1 (of the Proc. of the American Academy of Arts and Sciences), Winter 1968. *Students and Politics*

Higher Education
Volume 2, No. 2, May 1973. Special Issue: *Mass Higher Education*

Lancaster Guardian
Special Supplements *The University of Lancaster*. April 1964; 18 December 1964; 26 March 1965; 25 June 1965; 3 June 1966

The Listener
Volume LXXIX, No. 2032, 7 March 1968, pp. 291–93. David Martin, *"Trouble in the University"*

The Listener
Volume LXXV, No. 1936, 5 May 1966, pp. 645–47. Stuart McClure, *"The University of Lancaster"* (Britain's new universities—VIII)

The Listener
Volume LXXVII, No. 1975, 2 February 1967, pp. 157–58. Stuart McClure, *"Whither Britain's new universities?"*

The Listener
Volume LXXX, No. 2064, 17 October 1968. University number: *Student Revolt and its Consequences*

The Listener
Volume LXXXI, No. 2085, 13 March 1969, pp. 329–31. Christopher Ricks, *"Student Thought"*

The Listener
Volume LXXX, No. 2049, 4 July 1968, pp. 1ff. John Sparrow, Donald Davie, Richard Gilbert, *"Studentismus"*

The Listener
Volume LXXXVIII, No. 2275, 2 November 1972, pp. 597–600. Noel Annan (first Dimbleby Lecture), *"What are universities for, anyway?"*

Minerva
Volume X, No. 2, April 1972, pp. 259–79. Bruce R. Williams, *"University Values and University Organization"*

New Statesman
15 December 1972, Volume 84, No. 2178, pp. 892 and 894 Michael Irwin, *"A Framework for Contraction"*

Nova
November 1966, *"Married to a degree: Lancaster"*

Oxford Magazine
New Series, Volume 3, No. 22, 6 June 1963, pp. 348–49. Charles F. Carter, *"The University of Lancaster"*

Progress
Summer 1963, pp. 194–98. C. F. Carter, *"On Founding a University"*

Scottish Journal of Political Economy
Volume XX, No. 2, June 1973, pp. 123–39. M. Brownrigg, *"The Economic Impact of a New University"*

Sociological Review Monographs
No. 7, October 1963. (ed.) Paul Halmos, *Sociological Studies in British University Education* University of Keele

Universities Quarterly
Volume 21, No. 3, June 1967, pp. 269–372. Special Issue: *Examining in Universities*

Universities Quarterly
Volume 24, No. 2, Spring 1970, pp. 123–36. R. G. Jobling, *"The location and siting of a new university"*

V. PUBLICATIONS OF THE UNIVERSITY OF LANCASTER

Administrative Handbooks
Administrative Handbook   December 1970
Administrative Handbook   August 1972

Annual Reports (Presented by the Vice-Chancellor to the Meeting of the University Court)
First Annual Report   4 December 1965
Second Annual Report   7 December 1966
Third Annual Report   9 December 1967
Fourth Annual Report   7 December 1968
Fifth Annual Report   6 December 1969
Sixth Annual Report   12 December 1970
Seventh Annual Report   11 December 1971
Eighth Annual Report   9 December 1972
Ninth Annual Report   15 December 1973

Building
The first seven year plan (1964–71)
Four years of building at Bailrigg (1964–68)
Progress and Prospects (1964–71)

Carolynne
From No. 1   October 1964
to No. 58   December 1971 (discontinued)

Charter and Statutes   27 July 1964
Charter and Revised Statutes   23 March 1971

Continuum
Nos. 1–15   (Undated, continuing)

Furst (Furness College)   Issued at irregular intervals
                                            during term

Higher Education Bulletins
No. 1   December 1968
No. 2   March 1969
No. 3   June 1969
No. 4   December 1969
No. 5   May 1970
No. 6   December 1970
New Series
Vol. 1, No. 1   May 1972
Vol. 1, No. 2   November 1972
Vol. 1, No. 3   February 1973
Vol. 2, No. 1   Summer 1973

John O'Gauntlet
No. 1 to   December 1964 to
No. 92   December 1972 (discontinued)

Lancaster Comment
No. 1   October 1970
to No. 37   January 1974 (continuing)

Lancaster University Reporter
From No. 1   31 October 1969
to No. 35   28 June 1974 (discontinued)

Pendragon (County College)
From No. 1   6 May 1968
to No. 152   January 1974 (continuing)

Publications by Members of Staff
Publications by members of staff   1963–1971
Publications by members of staff   1972
(with additions and amendments covering earlier years)

Reports of the Librarian
                                                      1964–1965
                                                      1965–1966
                                                      1966–1967
                                                      1968–1969
                                                      1969–1970
                                                      1970–1971
                                                      1971–1972
                                                      1972–1973

Scan
No. 1   January 1969 (continuing:
                                                          published weekly)

Staff Handbook
Staff Handbook   1967–1968
                                                      1968–1969
                                                      1969–1970
                                                      1970–1971
                                                      1971–1972
                                                      1972–1973
                                                      1973–1974

Staff Newsletters
Vol. 1, No. 1   June 1968
Vol. 1, No. 2   October/November 1968
Vol. 1, No. 3   June 1969

Student Guides (produced by John O'Gauntlet)
                                                      1965
                                                      1966
                                                      1967
                                                      1968
                                                      1969
                                                      1973

Student Handbooks (produced by S.R.C.)
No. 1   1966–1967
No. 2   1967–1968
No. 3   1968–1969
No. 4   1969–1970
No. 5   1970
No. 6   1971
No. 7   1972

Lancaster Student Guide   1973

The County College Gazette
1. No. I
2. No. II
3. No. III
4. No. IV
5. No. V (1973)

University Accounts

                                                1964–1965
                                                1965–1966, 1966–67
                                                1967–1968
                                                1968–1969
                                                1969–1970
                                                1970–1971
                                                1971–1972
                                                1972–1973

University Graduate Studies Prospectus

                                                1968–1969
                                                1969–1970
                                                1970–1971
                                                1971–1972
                                                1972–1973
                                                1973–1974

University Prospectus

                                                1963–1964
                                                1964–1965
                                                1965–1966
                                                1966–1967
                                                1967–1968
                                                1968–1969
                                                1969–1970
                                                1970–1971
                                                1971–1972
                                                1972–1973
                                                1973–1974
                                                1974–1975

Index

(Bold numbering indicates main entry)

Morgan, K. J., 408, 415: as pro-vice-chancellor, 247

Morris, Lord of Grasmere, 25

M.6 motorway, 20, 47

Mountford, Sir James, xvi, 200, 234

Murray, Sir Keith, 15

Murray, M. A., 362

Murray, W. A., 36, 192, 393–4, 408, 414: building programme, 79f, 81, 82; discipline, 377–8, 379

Music, Department of, 139, 141, 155–6, 162f, 168, 176; accommodation for, 82; Sartori Quartet, 309

musical activities, 308–9

Nailor, P., 396, 409, 415

Nairn, Michael (of Kirkcaldy), 305

National Farmers' Union (N.F.U.) 9, 16, 17

National Union of Students (N.U.S.), 356, 361: on student representation, 275–6, 287

National Union of Teachers (N.U.T.), 9

National Westminster Bank, 88, 321

Nelson, A. V., 88

Newbattle Abbey, 183

Newcastle-upon-Tyne, University of, 147, 228, 287, 297–9

New Planet City, 96

Newth, D. R., 25

Nicholson, J., xvii, 245–6, 263ff

Nightline, 400–2

Noble, B., 395

noise, problem of, 58–9, 73, 345, 351, 377–9

non-resident students, provision for, 66, 74, 328, 331–2, 333, 335, 336, 350

North Staffordshire, University College of, see Keele

North-West Regional Studies, Centre for, 313–5; Panel of, 314

Norwich, see East Anglia, University of

Notice of Planning Consent, 20

Nuffield Theatre Studio, 58, 63, 79–81, 155, 311: Nuffield Foundation, help of, 80; Nuffield Theatre Club, 81

"occasional" students, 94

Oldfield, F., 178, 195, 408

Oliver, Coun. P. J., 317

Open University, 183, 300

Operational Research, Department of, 134, 135, 139, 157, 158–9

Orbit, 311

Owtram, Jean, see Argles, Jean

Oxford, University of, 22, 116, 132, 150–1, 199–200, 224, 242, 256, 326, 329: Franks Report on, 200, 252–3; Hart Committee at, 275

Oyston, P., 311

Parliamentary Agents, 29–30, 222

Parrott, Sir Cecil, 169–71, 415

Parrott, K., 155

Part I, 100, 108, 132, 137, 153, 161, 191, 198, 324: aggregate examination mark for, 195–6; assessment of, 191–9, 206; change of major subject at end of, 108, 114–5; grades for, 196, 199; time available for teaching of, 194ff; timing of Part I examinations, 191ff

Part II, 100f, 109–11, 114, 132: assessment of, 199–212; examination regulations, 190; time available for teaching of, 194–5

Paxman, G. J., 338–9, 399–400

Peel, 2nd Earl (Arthur William Ashton), 11, 412

Peel, Hon. Robert, 316

Pendle College, 87–9, 327, 351, 355–7

Perkin, H. J., 108, 199–200, 217–8, 237, 415

Phillips, A. W., 408

Phillips, E., 250

Philosophy, Department of, 134, 137, 150–2, 161

Physics, Department of, 147, 168, 175: building for, 57, 63, 69, 70; founding subject, 134

Piggott, C. D., 408, 414

planning permission, 16–17, 20

playing fields, 16, 47, 64–5: boathouse, 64; discussion re Salt Ayre, 64

Plesch, M., 365, 388

Plymouth, 11

Politics, Department of, 134, 137, 157,

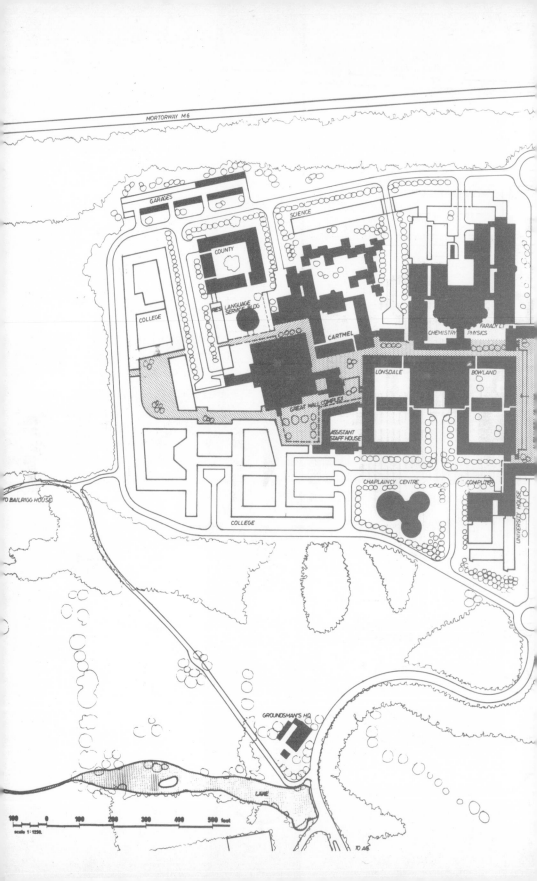

MOTORWAY M6

GARAGES

SCIENCE

COUNTY

COLLEGE

RES

LANGUAGE
SERVICE BLDG

CARTMEL

CHEMISTRY PHYSICS FARADAY L

LONSDALE BOWLAND

GREAT HALL COMPLEX

ASSISTANT
STAFF HOUSE

TO BAILRIGG HOUSE

CHAPLAINCY CENTRE

COMPUTER

UNIVERSITY HOUSE

COLLEGE

GROUNDSMAN'S HQ

LANE

TO A6

100   0   100   200   300   400   500 feet
scale 1:1250